D1599489

Mind as Motion

This cartoon pokes fun at automatic drum machines and the "techno" music popular in the 1980s. However, the image also illustrates several central themes of the dynamical approach to cognition: the importance of timing, the naturalness of periodicity, the intimate, real-time bond between perception and motor control, as well as between the body and events in the environment. It also illustrates the delight humans find in communal entrainment of all kinds, from singalongs to ballroom dancing to military parades. Drawing by W. Miller. © 1984 The New Yorker Magazine, Inc.

Mind as Motion

Explorations in the Dynamics of Cognition

edited by Robert F. Port and Timothy van Gelder

A Bradford Book
The MIT Press
Cambridge, Massachusetts
London, England

© 1995 Massachusetts Institute of Technology
All rights reserved. No part of this book may be reproduced in any form by any electronic or mechanical means (including photocopying, recording, or information storage and retrieval) without permission in writing from the publisher.

This book was set in Palatino by Asco Trade Typesetting Ltd., Hong Kong and was printed and bound in the United States of America.

Library of Congress Cataloging-in-Publication Data

Mind as motion : explorations in the dynamics of cognition / edited by
  Robert F. Port and Timothy van Gelder.
     p.   cm.
  Includes bibliographical references and index.
  ISBN 0-262-16150-8
  1. Cognition. 2. Cognition—Research—Methodology. 3. Cognitive
science. 4. Artificial intelligence. I. Port, Robert F. II. Van
Gelder, Timothy.
  BF311.M553   1995
  153—dc20
                                          94-23127
                                            CIP

Contents

Preface

Contemporary cognitive science is in a state of flux. For three decades or more the field has been dominated by an artificial intelligence (AI)–based computational paradigm which models cognition as the sequential manipulation of discrete symbolic structures. Recently, however, this paradigm has taken on a decidedly weary cast; progress has slowed, and limitations and anomalies mount up. Now, more than at any time since the 1950s, researchers throughout cognitive science are actively investigating alternative frameworks within which to develop models and descriptions. Of these alternatives, arguably the most general, widespread, and powerful is the dynamical approach.

Right across cognitive science, researchers are applying the concepts and tools of dynamics to the study of cognitive processes. The strategy itself is not new; the use of dynamics was prominent in the "cybernetics" period (1945–1960), and there have been active dynamical research programs ever since. Recent years, however, have seen two important developments. First, for various reasons, including the relative decline in authority of the computational paradigm, there has been a dramatic increase in the amount of dynamical research. Second, there has been the realization in some quarters that dynamics provides not just a set of mathematical tools but a deeply different perspective on the overall nature of cognitive systems. Dynamicists from diverse areas of cognitive science share more than a mathematical language; they have a common worldview.

Mind as Motion presents a representative sampling of contemporary dynamical research. It envisions the dynamical approach as a fully fledged research program standing as an alternative to the computational approach. Accordingly, this book has a number of aims. One is to help introduce dynamical work to a wider audience than the research efforts might have reached individually. A second aim is to articulate and clarify the dynamical approach itself, both in its conceptual foundations and as a set of specific methods for investigating cognitive phenomena. Third, and most important, this book is intended as a contribution to progress in cognitive science. It is an investigation into the nature of cognitive systems.

Mind as Motion has been designed to render contemporary, state-of-the-art dynamical research accessible to a general audience in cognitive science, including readers who might have no particular background in dynamics. Consequently, the book provides a conceptual and historical overview of the dynamical approach to cognition (chapter 1), a tutorial introduction to dynamics for cognitive scientists (chapter 2), and a glossary covering the most frequently used terms. Additionally, each chapter finishes with a Guide to Further Reading which usually lists introductory or background material as well as further research in the same area.

Dynamics tends to be difficult. Most cognitive scientists have relatively little training in the mathematics of dynamics (calculus, differential equations, dynamical systems theory, etc.) compared with their background in the discrete mathematics of computer science (logic, complexity theory, programming, etc.). Consequently, some of the chapters can be quite formidable, and readers new to the dynamic approach may have difficulty appreciating the arguments and why they are interesting. To help deal with this problem, we have provided each chapter with a brief introduction which surveys the main moves and helps locate the chapter's particular contribution in the wider landscapes of the dynamical approach and of cognitive science. We are of course very much aware that a few paragraphs cannot do justice to the depth and complexity of the ideas presented in the chapters themselves; we hope only that they serve adequately as guides and incentives.

The chapters in this book span a great deal of contemporary cognitive science. We have been particularly concerned to demonstrate that it would be mistaken to suppose that dynamics is naturally suited for "peripheral" or "lower" aspects of cognition, while "central" or "higher" aspects are best handled with computational models. On the one hand, many of the chapters are targeted at aspects of cognition that have traditionally been regarded as the home turf of computational modeling. Thus, for example, language receives more attention in this volume than any other broad cognitive phenomenon; the chapters by Saltzman; Browman and Goldstein; Elman; Petitot; Pollack; van Geert; and Port, Cummins, and McAuley all focus on one aspect or another of our ability to speak and understand. Similarly, Townsend and Busemeyer demonstrate that dynamics applies to another aspect of cognition that is traditionally regarded as "central," namely decision-making.

On the other hand, the dynamical approach aims to break down the dichotomy itself. The distinction between higher or central and lower or peripheral cognitive processes is a contemporary remnant of the traditional philosophical view that mind is somehow fundamentally distinct in nature from the material world (the body and the external physical world). From this point of view, cognitive science studies the inner, abstract, disembodied processes of pure thought, while other sciences such as mechanics study the behavior of the body and physical environment. This dichotomy also usually regards cognitive processes as complex and difficult to study, whereas the body is relatively unproblematic, a simple machine.

The dynamical approach rejects this dichotomy in most of its guises. Cognitive processes span the brain, the body, and the environment; to understand cognition is to understand the interplay of all three. Inner reasoning processes are no more essentially cognitive than the skillful execution of coordinated movement or the nature of the environment in which cognition takes place. The interaction between "inner" processes and "outer" world is not peripheral to cognition, it is the very stuff of which cognition is made. Consequently, *Mind as Motion* is even-handed in its treatment of the inner, the bodily, and the environmental. Certain chapters focus on phenomena that primarily take place internally (e.g., Townsend and Busemeyer; Elman; Petitot; Grossberg; Metzger), others focus primarily on phenomena in the environment (e.g., Bingham), while the majority focus either on bodily processes or span these various domains (e.g., Beer; Turvey and Carello; Thelen; van Geert; Saltzman; Browman and Goldstein; Port, Cummins, and McAuley; Reidbord and Redington).

It must be stressed that the dynamical approach is *not* some wholly new way of doing research that is separate from all existing research paradigms in cognitive science and hopes to displace them. Rather, to see that there is a dynamical approach is to see a way of redrawing one's conceptual map of cognitive science in accordance with the deepest similarities between various forms of existing research. Thus, most chapters in this book also belong to some other school of thought. For example, neural networks are dynamical systems which constitute an excellent medium for dynamical modeling, and many chapters in *Mind as Motion* also count as connectionist or neural network research (e.g., Beer; Elman; Pollack; Port, Cummins, and McAuley; Grossberg). Other chapters represent research of the kind that has been taking place under the banner of ecological psychology (e.g., Bingham; Turvey and Carello), while others fall into the mainstream of developmental psychology (e.g., Thelen; van Geert) or cognitive psychology (e.g., Townsend and Busemeyer; Metzger). One form of dynamical research into cognition that is notably absent from *Mind as Motion* is neuroscientific investigation. It is now so uncontroversial that the behaviors of the internal building blocks of cognitive processes—synapses, neurons, and assemblies of neurons—are best described in dynamical terms that, under our space constraints, it seemed reasonable to cover other aspects of cognition instead.

The origins of *Mind as Motion* lie in a conference held at Indiana University in November 1991. This informal 3-day gathering brought together a selection of researchers from diverse branches of cognitive science to discuss their work under the general heading "Dynamic Representation in Cognition." Despite their many differences, it was apparent to all involved that dynamics provides a general framework for a powerful and exciting research paradigm in cognitive science. An edited book was planned in order to build on the momentum of the conference and to articulate this alternative vision of how cognitive science might be done. The book grew in size and scope to the point where a good number of the major figures in the area are included.

Nevertheless, the book makes no pretense to being exhaustive in this regard. Many significant lines of current research that would fit the purposes of this book very well are represented only in citations or in the Guides to Further Reading. Surely others have been missed altogether.

The broad perspective on cognitive science advanced by *Mind as Motion* has grown directly out of the exceptionally active and fertile dynamics research environment at Indiana University. For feedback, ideas, and encouragement we are particularly grateful to the Dynamoes, an informal interdisciplinary group of faculty members interested in dynamical research; these include Geoffrey Bingham, David Jones, Richard McFall, William Timberlake, Linda Smith, Esther Thelen, James Townsend, Margaret Intons-Peterson, and Richard Shiffrin. We are also grateful to Indiana University for various kinds of support of this group's activities. Among the students, former students, and postdoctoral fellows who have also contributed to the dynamics environment are John Merrill, Sven Anderson, Jungyul Suh, and Devin McAuley. Numerous people helped with the book in various ways, including Diane Kewley-Port, Joe Stampfli, Devin McAuley, Louise McNally, Mike Gasser, Gregory Rawlins, Charles Watson, Scott Kelso, Gary Kidd, Brian Garrett, and Gregor Schöner. Special mention must be made of the efforts of Fred Cummins and Alec Norton, who are not only contributors to the volume but also assisted in numerous other ways as well. We are grateful to Karen Loffland, Linda Harl, and Mike Mackenzie for secretarial assistance, and to Trish Zapata for graphics. Harold Hawkins and the Office of Naval Research supported both the original conference and the production of this volume through grants to Robert Port (N0001491-J-1261, N0001493, and N0001492-J-1029). Timothy van Gelder was supported in 1993–1995 by a Queen Elizabeth II Research Fellowship from the Australian Research Council. The editors shared the work of preparing this book equally; for purposes of publication, names are listed alphabetically. Finally, and perhaps most important, the editors are grateful to all the contributors for their patience and willingness to deal with our seemingly endless requests for revisions.

Mind as Motion

1 It's About Time: An Overview of the Dynamical Approach to Cognition

Timothy van Gelder and Robert F. Port

How do we do what we do? How do we play tennis, have conversations, go shopping? At a finer grain, how do we recognize familiar objects such as bouncing balls, words, smiles, faces, jokes? Carry out actions such as returning a serve, pronouncing a word, selecting a book off the shelf? Cognitive scientists are interested in explaining how these kinds of extraordinarily sophisticated behaviors come about. They aim to describe *cognition*: the underlying mechanisms, states, and processes.

For decades, cognitive science has been dominated by one broad approach. That approach takes cognition to be the operation of a special mental *computer*, located in the brain. Sensory organs deliver up to the mental computer representations of the state of its environment. The system computes a specification of an appropriate action. The body carries this action out.

According to this approach, when I return a serve in tennis, what happens is roughly as follows. Light from the approaching ball strikes my retina and my brain's visual mechanisms quickly compute what is being seen (a ball) and its direction and rate of approach. This information is fed to a planning system which holds representations of my current goals (win the game, return the serve, etc.) and other background knowledge (court conditions, weaknesses of the other player, etc.). The planning system then infers what I must do: hit the ball deep into my opponent's backhand. This command is issued to the motor system. My arms and legs move as required.

In its most familiar and successful applications, the computational approach makes a series of further assumptions. Representations are static structures of discrete symbols. Cognitive operations are transformations from one static symbol structure to the next. These transformations are discrete, effectively instantaneous, and sequential. The mental computer is broken down into a number of modules responsible for different symbol-processing tasks. A module takes symbolic representations as inputs and computes symbolic representations as outputs. At the periphery of the system are input and output transducers: systems which transform sensory stimulation into input representations, and output representations into physical movements. The whole system, and each of its modules, operates cyclically: input, internal symbol manipulation, output.

The computational approach provides a very powerful framework for developing theories and models of cognitive processes. The classic work of pioneers such as Newell, Simon, and Minsky was carried out within it. Literally thousands of models conforming to the above picture have been produced. Any given model may diverge from it in one respect or another, but all retain most of its deepest assumptions. The computational approach is nothing less than a research paradigm in Kuhn's classic sense. It defines a range of questions and the form of answers to those questions (i.e., computational models). It provides an array of exemplars—classic pieces of research which define how cognition is to be thought about and what counts as a successful model. Philosophical tomes have been devoted to its articulation and defense. Unfortunately, it has a major problem: Natural cognitive systems, such as people, aren't computers.

This need not be very surprising. The history of science is full of episodes in which good theories were developed within bad frameworks. The Ptolemaic earth-centered conception of the solar system spawned a succession of increasingly sophisticated theories of planetary motion, theories with remarkably good descriptive and predictive capabilities. Yet we now know that the whole framework was structurally misconceived, and that any theory developed within it would always contain anomalies and reach explanatory impasses. Mainstream cognitive science is in a similar situation. Many impressive models of cognitive processes have been developed within the computational framework, yet none of these models are wholly successful even in their own terms, and they completely sidestep numerous critical issues. Just as in the long run astronomy could only make progress by displacing the earth from the center of the universe, so cognitive science has to displace the inner computer from the center of cognitive performance.

The heart of the problem is *time. Cognitive processes and their context unfold continuously and simultaneously in real time.* Computational models specify a discrete sequence of static internal states in arbitrary "step" time (t_1, t_2, etc.). Imposing the latter onto the former is like wearing shoes on your hands. You can do it, but gloves fit a whole lot better.

This deep problem manifests itself in a host of difficulties confronting particular computational models throughout cognitive science. To give just one example, consider how you might come to a difficult decision. You have a range of options, and consider first one, then another. There is hesitation, vacillation, anxiety. Eventually you come to prefer one choice, but the attraction of the others remains. Now, how are decision-making processes conceptualized in the computational worldview? The system begins with symbolic representations of a range of choices and their possible outcomes, with associated likelihoods and values. In a sequence of symbol manipulations, the system calculates the overall expected value for each choice, and determines the choice with the highest expected value. The system adopts that choice. End of decision. There are many variations on this basic "expected utility" structure. Different models propose different rules for calculating the choice

Timothy van Gelder and Robert F. Port

the system adopts. But none of these models accounts perfectly for all the data on the choices that humans actually make. Like Ptolemaic theories of the planets, they become increasingly complex in attempting to account for residual anomalies, but for every anomaly dealt with another crops up elsewhere. Further, they say nothing at all about the temporal course of deliberation: how long it takes to reach a decision, how the decision one reaches depends on deliberation time, how a choice can appear more attractive at one time, less attractive at another, etc. They are intrinsically incapable of such predictions, because *they leave time out of the picture*, replacing it only with ersatz "time": a bare, abstract sequence of symbolic states.

What is the alternative to the computational approach? In recent years, many people have touted *connectionism*—the modeling of cognitive processes using networks of neural units—as a candidate. But such proposals often underestimate the depth and pervasiveness of computationalist assumptions. Much standard connectionist work (e.g., modeling with layered backprop networks) is just a variation on computationalism, substituting activation patterns for symbols. This kind of connectionism took some steps in the right direction, but mostly failed to take the needed leap *out* of the computational mindset and *into* time (see section 1.3, Relation to Connectionism, for elaboration).

The alternative must be an approach to the study of cognition which *begins* from the assumption that cognitive processes happen in time. *Real* time. Conveniently, there already is a mathematical framework for describing how processes in natural systems unfold in real time. It is *dynamics*. It just happens to be the single most widely used, most powerful, most successful, most thoroughly developed and understood descriptive framework in all of natural science. It is used to explain and predict phenomena as diverse as subatomic motions and solar systems, neurons and 747s, fluid flow and ecosystems. Why not use it to describe cognitive processes as well?

The alternative, then, is the *dynamical* approach. Its core is the application of the mathematical tools of dynamics to the study of cognition. Dynamics provides for the dynamical approach what computer science provides for the computational approach: a vast resource of powerful concepts and modeling tools. But the dynamical approach is more than just powerful tools; like the computational approach, it is a worldview. The cognitive system is not a computer, it is a dynamical system. It is not the brain, inner and encapsulated; rather, it is the whole system comprised of nervous system, body, and environment. The cognitive system is not a discrete sequential manipulator of static representational structures; rather, it is a structure of mutually and simultaneously influencing *change*. Its processes do not take place in the arbitrary, discrete time of computer steps; rather, they unfold in the *real* time of ongoing change in the environment, the body, and the nervous system. The cognitive system does not interact with other aspects of the world by passing messages or commands; rather, it continuously coevolves with them.

The dynamical approach is not a new idea: dynamical theories have been a continuous undercurrent in cognitive science since the field began (see section 1.4). It is not just a vision of the way things *might* be done; it's the way a great deal of groundbreaking research *has already* been carried out, and the amount of dynamical research undertaken grows every month. Much of the more recent work carried out under the connectionist banner is thoroughly dynamical; the same is true of such diverse areas as neural modeling, cognitive neuroscience, situated robotics, motor control, and ecological psychology. Dynamical models are increasingly prominent in cognitive psychology, developmental psychology, and even some areas of linguistics. In short, the dynamical approach is not just some new kid on the block; rather, to see that there is a dynamical approach is to see a new way of conceptually reorganizing cognitive science as it is currently practiced.

This introductory chapter provides a general overview of the dynamical approach: its essential commitments, its strengths, its relationship to other approaches, its history. It attempts to present the dynamical approach as a unified, coherent, plausible research paradigm. It should be noted, however, that dynamicists are a highly diverse group, and no single characterization would describe all dynamicists perfectly. Consequently, our strategy in this chapter is to characterize a kind of *standard* dynamicist position, one which can serve as a useful point of reference in understanding dynamical research.

The chapter is generally pitched in a quite abstract terms. Space limitations prevent us from going into particular examples in much detail. We urge readers who are hungry for concrete illustrations to turn to any of the 15 chapters of this book which present examples of actual dynamical research in cognitive science. It is essential for the reader to understand that *detailed demonstrations of all major points made in this overview are contained in chapters of the book.*

Before proceeding we wish to stress that our primary concern is only to understand *natural* cognitive systems—evolved biological systems such as humans and other animals. While the book is generally critical of the mainstream computational approach to the study of cognitive systems, it has no objections at all to investigations into the nature of computation itself, and into the potential abilities of computational systems such as take place in many branches of artificial intelligence (AI). While we think it *unlikely* that it will be possible to reproduce the kind of intelligent capacities that are exhibited by natural cognitive systems without also reproducing their basic noncomputational architecture, we take no stand on whether it is possible to program computers to exhibit these, or other, intelligent capacities.

1.1 WHAT IS THE DYNAMICAL APPROACH?

The heart of the dynamical approach can be succinctly expressed in the form of a very broad empirical hypothesis about the nature of cognition. For decades, the philosophy of cognitive science has been dominated by the

Timothy van Gelder and Robert F. Port

computational hypothesis, that cognitive systems are a special kind of computer. This hypothesis has been articulated in a number of ways, but perhaps the most famous statement is Newell and Simon's *Physical Symbol System Hypothesis*, the claim that physical symbol systems (computers) are necessary and sufficient for intelligent behavior (Newell and Simon, 1976). According to this hypothesis, natural cognitive systems are intelligent by virtue of being physical symbol systems of the right kind. At this same level of generality, dynamicists can be seen as embracing the *Dynamical Hypothesis:* Natural cognitive systems are dynamical systems, and are best understood from the perspective of dynamics. Like its computational counterpart, the Dynamical Hypothesis forms a general framework within which detailed theories of particular aspects of cognition can be constructed. It can be empirically vindicated or refuted, but not by direct tests. We will only know if the Dynamical Hypothesis is true if, in the long run, the best theories of cognitive processes are expressed in dynamical terms.

The following sections explore the various components of the Dynamical Hypothesis in more detail.

Natural Cognitive Systems Are Dynamical Systems

What Are Dynamical Systems?   The notion of dynamical systems occurs in a wide range of mathematical and scientific contexts, and as a result the term has come to be used in many different ways. In this section our aim is simply to characterize dynamical systems in the way that is most useful for understanding the dynamical approach to cognition.

Roughly speaking, we take dynamical systems to be systems with numerical states that evolve over time according to some rule. Clarity is critical at this stage, however, so this characterization needs elaboration and refinement.

To begin with, a *system* is a set of changing aspects of the world. The overall *state* of the system at a given time is just the way these aspects happen to be at that time. The *behavior* of the system is the change over time in its overall state. The totality of overall states the system might be in makes up its *state set*, commonly referred to as its *state space*. Thus the behavior of the system can be thought of as a sequence of points in its state space.

Not just any set of aspects of the world constitutes a system. A system is distinguished by the fact that its aspects somehow belong together. This really has two sides. First, the aspects must interact with each other; the way any one of them changes must depend on the way the others are. Second, if there is some *further* aspect of the world that interacts in this sense with anything in the set, then clearly it too is really part of the same system. In short, for a set of aspects to qualify as a system, they must be interactive and self contained: change in any aspect must depend on, and only on, other aspects in the set.

For example, the solar system differs from, say, the set containing just the color of my car and the position of my pencil, in that the position of any one planet makes a difference to where the other planets will be. Moreover, to a first approximation at least, the future positions of the planets are affected *only* by the positions, masses, etc., of the sun and other planets; there is nothing else we need take into account. By contrast, the position of my pencil is affected by a variety of other factors; in fact, it is unlikely that there is *any* identifiable system to which the position of my pencil (in all the vicissitudes of its everyday use) belongs.

Dynamical systems are special kinds of systems. To see *what* kind, we first need another notion, that of *state-determined* systems (Ashby, 1952). A system is state-determined only when its current state always determines a unique future behavior. Three features of such systems are worth noting. First, in such systems, the future behavior cannot depend in any way on whatever states the system might have been in *before* the current state. In other words, past history is irrelevant (or at least, past history only makes a difference insofar as it has left an effect on the current state). Second, the fact that the current state determines future behavior implies the existence of some *rule of evolution* describing the behavior of the system as a function of its current state. For systems we wish to understand, we always hope that this rule can be specified in some reasonably succinct and useful fashion. One source of constant inspiration, of course, has been Newton's formulation of the laws governing the solar system. Third, the fact that future behaviors are uniquely determined means that state space sequences can never fork. Thus, if we observe some system that proceeds in different ways at different times from the same state, we know we do not have a state-determined system.

The core notion of a state-determined system, then, is that of a self-contained, interactive set of aspects of the world such that the future states of the system are always uniquely determined, according to some rule, by the current state. Before proceeding, we should note an important extension of this idea, for cases in which changing factors external to the system do in fact affect how the system behaves. Suppose we have a set S of aspects $\{s_1, \ldots, s_m\}$ whose change depends on some further aspect s_n of the world, but change in s_n does not in turn depend on the state of S, but on other things entirely. Then, strictly speaking, neither S nor $S + s_n$ form systems, since neither set is self contained. Yet we can *treat* S as a state-determined system by thinking of the influence of s_n as built into its rule of evolution. Then the current state of the system *in conjunction with the rule* can be thought of as uniquely determining future behaviors, while the rule changes as a function of time. For example, suppose scientists discovered that the force of gravity has actually been fluctuating over time, though not in a way that depends on the positions and motions of the sun and planets. Then the solar system still forms a state-determined system, but one in which the rules of planetary motion must build in a gravitational constant that is changing over time. Technically, factors that affect, but are not in turn affected by, the evolution of a system are known as *parameters*. If a parameter changes over time, its changing effect can be taken into account in the rule of evolution, but then the rule itself is a function of time and the system is known as *nonhomogeneous*.

Now, according to some (e.g., Giunti, chapter 18), *dynamical systems* are really just *state-determined systems*. This identification is certainly valuable for some purposes. In fact, it is really this very inclusive category of systems (or at least, its abstract mathematical counterpart) that is studied by that branch of mathematics known as *dynamical systems theory*. Nevertheless, if our aim is to characterize the dynamical approach to cognition—and in particular, to contrast it with the computational approach—it turns out that a narrower definition is more useful. This narrower definition focuses on specifically *numerical* systems.

The word "dynamical" is derived from the Greek *dynamikos*, meaning "forceful" or "powerful." A system that is dynamical in this sense is one in which changes are a function of the *forces* operating within it. Whenever forces apply, we have accelerations or decelerations; i.e., there is change in the *rate* at which the states are changing at any given moment. The standard mathematical tools for describing rates of change are *differential equations*. These can be thought of as specifying the way a system is changing at any moment as a function of its state at that moment.[1] For example, the differential equation

$$\ddot{x} = -\frac{k}{m}x$$

describes the way (in ideal circumstances) a heavy object on the end of a spring will bounce back and forth by telling us the instantaneous acceleration ($\ddot{x}$) of the object as a function of its position (x); k and m are constants (parameters) for the spring tension and mass, respectively.

State-determined systems governed by differential equations are paradigm examples of dynamical systems in the current sense, but the latter category also includes other systems which are similar in important ways.

Whenever a system can be described by differential equations, it has n aspects or features (position, mass, etc.) evolving simultaneously and continuously in real time. Each of these features at a given point in time can be *measured* as corresponding to some real number. Consequently we can think of the overall state of the system as corresponding to an ordered set of n real numbers, and the state space of the system as isomorphic to a space of real numbers whose n dimensions are magnitudes corresponding (via measurement) to the changing aspects of the system. Sometimes this numerical space is also known as the system's state space, but for clarity we will refer to it as the system's *phase space*[2] (figure 1.1). The evolution of the system over time corresponds to a sequence of points, or trajectory, in its phase space. These sequences can often be described mathematically as functions of an independent variable, time. These functions are *solutions* to the differential equations which describe the behavior of the system.

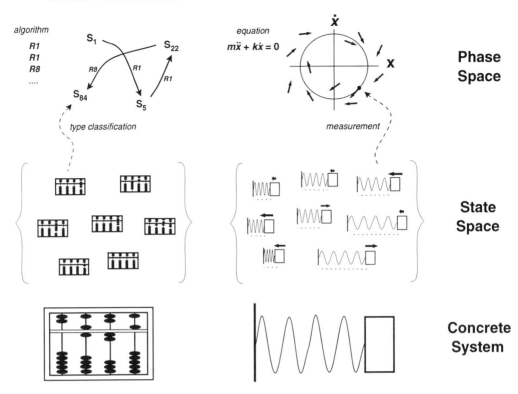

COMPUTATIONAL

DYNAMICAL

Phase Space

State Space

Concrete System

Figure 1.1   Mass-springs and computers are two different kinds of concrete state-determined system. (Our figure depicts an abacus; strictly speaking, the abacus would have to be automated to count as a computer.) Such systems are always in a particular state at a given point in time. This state is only one of many states that it *could* be in. The total set of possible states is commonly known as the system's *state space*. Corresponding to the state space is a set of abstract elements that is also commonly known as the system's state space, but which for clarity we refer to as its *phase space*. Possible states of the system are mapped onto elements of the phase space by some form of classification. In the computational case, tokens of symbols in the concrete system are classified into types, allowing the total state of the system to be classified as instantiating a particular configuration of symbol types. In the dynamical case, aspects of the system are measured (i.e., some yardstick is used to assign a number to each aspect), thereby allowing an ordered set of numbers to be assigned to the total state. Sequences of elements in the phase space can be specified by means of rules such as algorithms (in the computational case) and differential equations (in the dynamical case). A phase space and a rule are key elements of abstract state-determined systems. A concrete system realizes an abstract system when its states can be systematically classified such that the sequences of actual states it passes through mirror the phase space sequences determined by the rule. Typically, when cognitive scientists provide a model of some aspect of cognition, they provide an abstract state-determined system, such that the cognitive system is supposed to realize that abstract system or one relevantly like it.

Timothy van Gelder and Robert F. Port

Now, phase-space trajectories can be specified in a variety of ways. Differential equations constitute one particularly compact way of describing the shape of all possible trajectories in a given system. This kind of specification is useful for some purposes but not for others. A common alternative is to specify trajectories by means of a discrete mapping of any given point in the phase space onto another point. For example, perhaps the most-studied family of dynamical systems is the one whose rule is the "logistic equation" or "quadratic map" (Devaney, 1986)[3]:

$$F_\mu(x) = \mu x(1 - x)$$

For any particular value of the parameter μ, this equation determines a particular mapping of every point x in the phase space onto another point $F_\mu(x)$. A mapping like this can be regarded as giving us the state of a system at a subsequent point in time $(t + 1)$ if we know the state of the system at any given time (t). When the rule is written so as to bring this out, it is known as a *difference equation*, taking the general form

$$x(t + 1) = F(x(t))$$

If we take any given point in the phase space and apply ("iterate") the mapping many times, we obtain a phase-space trajectory.

Mathematicians and scientists often describe dynamical systems by means of discrete mappings rather than differential equations. In many cases these mappings are closely related to particular differential equations describing essentially the same behavior. This is not always the case, however. Consequently, a more liberal definition of *dynamical system* is: any state-determined system with a numerical phase space and a rule of evolution (including differential equations and discrete maps) specifying trajectories in this space.

These systems, while only a subset of state-determined systems in general, are the locus of dynamical research in cognitive science. They find their most relevant contrast with *computational* systems. These systems have states that are configurations of symbols,[4] and their rules of evolution specify transformations of one configuration of symbols into another. Whereas the phase space of a dynamical system is a *numerical* space, the phase space of a computational system is a space of configurations of *symbol types*, and trajectories are sequences of such configurations.

Why is it that dynamical systems (in our sense) are the ones chosen for study by dynamicists in cognitive science? Here we briefly return to the traditional idea that dynamics is a matter of forces, and therefore essentially involves rates of change. In order to talk about rates of change, we must be able to talk about *amounts* of change in *amounts* of time. Consequently, the phase space must be such as to allow us to say *how far* the state is changing, and the *time* in which states change must involve real *durations*, as opposed to a mere linear ordering of temporal points.

Now, these notions make real sense in the context of dynamical systems as defined here. Numerical phase spaces can have a metric that determines distances between points. Further, if the phase space is rich enough (e.g., dense) then between any two points in the phase space we can find other points, and so we can talk of the state of the system at any time between any two other times. Thus the notion of time in which the system operates is also one to which a substantial notion of "length" can be applied; in other words, it comes to possess some of the same key mathematical properties as *real* time. Note that neither of these properties is true of computational systems such as Turing machines; there, there is no natural notion of distance between any two total states of the system, and "time" (t_1, t_2, etc.) is nothing more than order. Consequently it is impossible to talk of how fast the state of the system is changing, and as a matter of fact, nobody ever tries; the issue is in a deep way irrelevant.

The importance of being able to talk about rates of change is that all actual processes in the real world (including cognitive processes) do in fact unfold at certain rates in real time. Further, for many such systems (including cognitive systems) *timing* is essential: they wouldn't be able to function properly unless they got the fine details of the timing right. Therefore, in order to provide adequate scientific descriptions of the behavior of such systems, we need to understand them as systems in which the notion of rates of change makes sense (see Cognition and Time, below). Dynamicists in cognitive science propose dynamical models in the current sense because they are such systems. It may well be that there are other, less well-known mathematical frameworks within which one could model change in real time without using specifically numerical systems. As things stand, however, dynamical systems in cognitive science are in fact state-determined numerical systems.

A wide variety of fascinating questions can be raised about the relations between dynamical and computational systems. For example, what is the relationship between an ordinary digital computer and the underlying electrical dynamical system that in some sense makes it up? Or, what is the relation between a dynamical system and a computational simulation or emulation of it? Even more abstractly, how "powerful" is the class of dynamical systems, in comparison with computational systems? However, we must be very careful not to allow the fact that *there are* many such relationships, some of them quite intimate, to blind us to an important philosophical, and ultimately practical, truth: dynamical and computational systems are fundamentally different *kinds* of systems, and hence the dynamical and computational approaches to cognition are fundamentally different in their deepest foundations.

Natural Cognitive Systems as Dynamical Systems Describing natural phenomena as the behavior of some dynamical system lies at the very heart of modern science. Ever since Newton, scientists have been discovering more and more aspects of the natural world that constitute dynamical systems of one kind or another. Dynamicists in cognitive science are claiming that yet another naturally occurring phenomenon, *cognition*, is the behavior of an appropriate kind of dynamical system. They are thus making exactly the same kind of claim for cognitive systems as scientists have been making for so many other aspects of the natural world. In the Dynamical Hypothesis, this is expressed as the idea that natural cognitive systems *are* dynamical systems.

Demonstrating that some aspect of the world constitutes a dynamical system requires picking out a relevant set of quantities, and ways of measuring them, such that the resulting phase-space trajectories conform to some specifiable rule. These trajectories must correspond to the behaviors of theoretical interest. So, if we are interested in *cognitive* systems, then the behaviors of interest are their *cognitive performances* (perceiving, remembering, conversing, etc.), and it is *these* behaviors, at their characteristic time scales, that must unfold in a way described by the rule of evolution. Consequently, the claim that cognitive systems are dynamical systems is certainly not trivial. Not everything is a dynamical system, and taking some novel phenomenon and showing that it *is* the behavior of a dynamical system is always a significant scientific achievement. If the Dynamical Hypothesis is in fact true, we will only know this as a result of much patient scientific work.[5]

Natural cognitive systems are enormously subtle and complex entities in constant interaction with their environments. It is the central conjecture of the Dynamical Hypothesis that these systems constitute single, unified dynamical systems. This conjecture provides a general theoretical orientation for dynamicists in cognitive science, but it has not been (and in fact may never be) demonstrated in detail, for nobody has specified the relevant magnitudes, phase space, and rules of evolution for the entire system. Like scientists confronting the physical universe as a whole, dynamicists in cognitive science strive to isolate particular aspects of the complex, interactive totality that are relatively self-contained and can be described mathematically. Thus, in practice, the Dynamical Hypothesis reduces to a series of more specific assertions, to the effect that particular aspects of cognition are the behavior of distinct, more localized systems. For example, Turvey and Carello (see chapter 13) focus on our ability to perceive the shape of an object such as a hammer simply by wielding it. They show how to think of the wielding itself as a dynamical system, and of perception of shape as attunement to key parameters of this system. The Dynamical Hypothesis, that entire cognitive systems constitute dynamical systems, is thus comparable to the Laplacean hypothesis that the entire physical world is a single dynamical system.

Many cognitive processes are thought to be distinguished from other kinds of processes in the natural world by the fact that they appear to depend crucially on *knowledge* which must somehow be stored and utilized. At the heart of the computational approach is the idea that this knowledge must be *represented*, and that cognitive processes must therefore be operations on these representations. Further, the most powerful known medium of representation is symbolic, and hence cognitive processes must manipulate symbols, i.e., must be computational in nature.

In view of this rather compelling line of thought, it is natural to ask: How can dynamicists, whose models do *not* centrally invoke the notion of representation, hope to provide theories of paradigmatically *cognitive* processes? If cognition depends on *knowledge*, how can there be a dynamical approach to *cognition*? The answer is that, while dynamical models are not *based* on transformations of representational structures, they allow plenty of room for representation. A wide variety of aspects of dynamical models can be regarded as having a representational status: these include states, attractors, trajectories, bifurcations, and parameter settings. So dynamical systems can store knowledge and have this stored knowledge influence their behavior. The crucial difference between computational models and dynamical models is that in the former, the rules that govern how the system behaves are defined over the entities that have representational status, whereas in dynamical models, the rules are defined over numerical states.[6] That is, dynamical systems can be representational without having their rules of evolution defined over representations. For example, in simple connectionist associative memories such as that described in Hopfield (1982), representations of stored items are point attractors in the phase space of the system. Recalling or recognizing an item is a matter of settling into its attractor, a process that is governed by purely numerical dynamical rules.

The Nature of Cognitive Systems   The claim that cognitive systems are computers, and the competing claim that natural cognitive systems are dynamical systems, each forms the technical core of a highly distinctive vision of the nature of cognitive systems.

For the computationalist, the cognitive system is the brain, which is a kind of control unit located inside a body which in turn is located in an external environment. The cognitive system interacts with the outside world *via* its more direct interaction with the body. Interaction with the environment is handled by sensory and motor *transducers*, whose function is to translate between the *physical* events in the body and the environment, on the one hand, and the *symbolic* states, which are the medium of cognitive processing. Thus the sense organs convert physical stimulation into elementary symbolic representations of events in the body and in the environment, and the motor system converts symbolic representations of actions into movements of the muscles. Cognitive episodes take place in a cyclic and sequential fashion; *first* there is sensory input to the cognitive system, *then* the cognitive system algorithmically manipulates symbols, coming up with an output which *then* causes movement of the body; the whole cycle then begins again. Internally, the cognitive system has a modular, hierarchical construction; at the highest level, there are modules corresponding to vision, language, planning, etc., and each of these modules breaks down into simpler modules for more elementary tasks. Each module replicates in basic structure the cognitive system as a whole; thus, the modules take symbolic representations as inputs, algorithmically manipulate those representations, and deliver a symbolic specification as output. Note that because the cognitive system traffics only in symbolic representations, the body and the physical environment can be dropped from consideration; it is possible to study the cognitive system as an autonomous,

Timothy van Gelder and Robert F. Port

bodiless, and worldless system whose function is to transform input representations into output representations.

Now, the dynamical vision differs from this picture at almost every point. As we have seen, dynamical systems are complexes of parts or aspects which are all evolving in a continuous, simultaneous, and mutually determining fashion. If cognitive systems are dynamical systems, then they must likewise be complexes of interacting change. Since the nervous system, body, and environment are all continuously evolving and simultaneously influencing one another, the cognitive system cannot be simply the encapsulated brain; rather, it is a single unified system embracing all three. The cognitive system does not interact with the body and the external world by means of periodic symbolic inputs and outputs; rather, inner and outer processes are *coupled*, so that both sets of processes are continually influencing each other. Cognitive processing is not cyclic and sequential, for all aspects of the cognitive system are undergoing change all the time. There is a *sense* in which the system is modular, since for theoretical purposes the total system can be broken down into smaller dynamical subsystems responsible for distinct cognitive phenomena. Standardly these smaller systems are coupled, and hence coevolving, with others, but significant insight can be obtained by "freezing" this interaction and studying their independent dynamics. Of course, cognitive performances do exhibit many kinds of sequential character. Speaking a sentence, for example, is behavior that has a highly distinctive sequential structure. However, in the dynamical conception, any such sequential character is something that emerges over time as the overall trajectory of change in an entire system (or relevant subsystem) whose rules of evolution specify not sequential change but rather simultaneous, mutual coevolution.

Natural Cognitive Systems Are Best Understood Using Dynamics

In science, as in home repair, the most rapid progress is made when you have the right tools for the job. Science is in the business of describing and explaining the natural world, and has a very wide range of conceptual and methodological tools at its disposal. Computer science provides one very powerful collection of tools, and these are optimally suited for understanding complex systems of a particular kind, namely *computational* systems. If *cognitive* systems are computational systems, then they will be best understood by bringing these tools to bear. If the Dynamical Hypothesis is right, however, then the most suitable conceptual tools will be those of *dynamics*. So, whereas in the previous sections we described *what it is* for natural cognitive systems to *be* dynamical systems, in the following discussion we describe what is involved in applying dynamics in *understanding* such systems.

What Is Dynamics? Dynamics is a very broad field overlapping both pure and applied mathematics. For current purposes, it can be broken down into two broad subdivisions. *Dynamical modeling* is describing natural phenomena *as* the behavior of a dynamical system in the sense outlined in the previous discussion. It involves finding a way of isolating the relevant system, a way of measuring the states of the system, and a mathematical rule, such that the phenomena of interest unfold in exactly the way described by the rule. Obviously, effective dynamical modeling involves considerable exploration of both the real system being studied, and the mathematical properties of the governing equations.

Dynamical systems theory is the general study of dynamical systems. As a branch of pure mathematics, it is not directly concerned with the empirical description of natural phenomena, but rather with abstract mathematical structures. Dynamical systems theory is particularly concerned with complex systems for which the *solutions* of the defining equations (i.e., functions that specify trajectories as a function of time) are difficult or impossible to write down. It offers a wide variety of powerful concepts and tools for describing the general properties of such systems. Perhaps the most distinctive feature of dynamical systems theory is that it provides a *geometric* form of understanding: behaviors are thought of in terms of locations, paths, and landscapes in the phase space of the system.[7]

Some natural phenomena can be described as the evolution of a dynamical system governed by particularly straightforward equations. For such systems, the traditional techniques of dynamical modeling are sufficient for most explanatory purposes. Other phenomena, however, can only be described as the behavior of systems governed by nonlinear equations for which solutions may be unavailable. Dynamical systems theory is essential for the study of such systems. With the rapid development in the twentieth century of the mathematics of dynamical systems theory, an enormous range of natural systems have been opened up to scientific description. There is no sharp division between dynamical modeling and dynamical systems theory, and gaining a full understanding of most natural systems requires relying on both bodies of knowledge.

Understanding Cognitive Phenomena Dynamically   Dynamics is a large and diverse set of concepts and methods, and consequently there are many different ways that cognitive phenomena can be understood dynamically. Yet they all occupy a broadly dynamical perspective, with certain key elements.

At the heart of the dynamical perspective is *time*. Dynamicists always focus on the details of how behavior unfolds in real time; their aim is to describe and explain the temporal course of this behavior. The beginning point and the endpoint of cognitive processing are usually of only secondary interest, if indeed they matter at all. This is in stark contrast with the computationalist orientation, in which the primary focus is on input-output relations, i.e., on what output the system delivers for any given input.

A second key element of the dynamical perspective is an emphasis on *total state*. Dynamicists assume that all aspects of a system are changing simultane-

Timothy van Gelder and Robert F. Port

ously, and so think about the behavior of the system as a matter of how the total state of a system is changing from one time to the next. Computationalists, by contrast, tend to suppose that most aspects of a system (e.g., the symbols stored in memory) do *not* change from one moment to the next. Change is assumed to be a local affair, a matter of replacement of one symbol by another.

Because dynamicists focus on how a system changes from one total state to another, it is natural for them to think of that change as a matter of movements in the *space* of all possible total states of the system; and since the phase spaces of their systems are numerical, natural notions of *distance* apply. Thus, dynamicists conceptualize cognitive processes in *geometric* terms. The distinctive character of some cognitive process as it unfolds over time is a matter of how the total states the system passes through are spatially located with respect to one another and the dynamical landscape of the system.

Quantitative Modeling   Precise, quantitative modeling of some aspect of cognitive performance is always the ultimate goal of dynamical theorizing in cognitive science. Such research always requires two basic components: data and model. The data take the form of a time series: a series of measurements of the phenomenon to be understood, taken as that phenomenon unfolds over time. The model is a set of equations and associated phase space. The modeling process is a matter of distilling out the phenomenon to be understood, obtaining the time-series data, developing a model, and *interpreting* that model as capturing the data (i.e., setting up correspondences between the numerical sequences contained in the model and those in the data). When carried out successfully, the modeling process yields not only precise *descriptions* of the existing data but also *predictions* which can be used in evaluating the model.

For an excellent example of quantitative dynamical modeling, recall the process of reaching a decision described briefly in the introductory paragraphs. We saw that traditional computational (expected-utility theory) approaches to decision-making have had some measure of success in accounting for what decisions are actually reached, but say nothing at all about any of the temporal aspects of the deliberation process. For Busemeyer and Townsend (Busemeyer and Townsend, 1993; see also chapter 4), by contrast, describing these temporal aspects is a central goal. Their model of decision-making is a dynamical system with variables corresponding to quantities such as values of consequences and choice preferences. The model describes the multiple simultaneous *changes* that go on in an individual decision-maker in the process of coming to a decision. It turns out that this model not only recapitulates the known data on *outcomes* as well as or better than traditional computational models; it also explains a range of temporal phenomena such as the dependence of preference on deliberation time, and makes precise predictions which can be experimentally tested.

Qualitative Modeling   Human cognitive performance is extraordinarily diverse, subtle, complex, and interactive. Every human behaves in a somewhat different way, and is embedded in a rich, constantly changing environment. For these kinds of reasons (among others), science has been slow in coming to be able to apply to cognition the kinds of explanatory techniques that have worked so successfully elsewhere. Even now, only a relatively small number of cognitive phenomena have been demonstrated to be amenable to precise, quantitative dynamical modeling. Fortunately, however, there are other ways in which dynamics can be used to shed light on cognitive phenomena. Both the data time series and the mathematical model that dynamical modeling requires can be very difficult to obtain. Even without an elaborate data time series, one can study a mathematical model which exhibits behavior that is at least *qualitatively* similar to the phenomena being studied. Alternatively, in the absence of a precise mathematical model, the language of dynamics can be used to develop qualitative dynamical descriptions of phenomena that may have been recorded in a precise data time series (see Dynamical Description, below).

Cognitive scientists can often develop a sophisticated understanding of an area of cognitive functioning independently of having any elaborate data time series in hand. The problem is then to understand what kind of system might be capable of exhibiting that kind of cognitive performance. It can be addressed by specifying a mathematical dynamical model and comparing its behavior with the known empirical facts. If the dynamical model and the observed phenomena agree sufficiently in broad qualitative outline, then insight into the nature of the system has been gained.

Elman's investigations into language processing are a good example of qualitative dynamical modeling (Elman, 1991; see also chapter 8). In broad outline, at least, the distinctive complexity of sentences of natural language is well understood, and psycholinguistics has uncovered a wide range of information on human abilities to process sentences. For example, it is a widely known fact that most people have trouble processing sentences that have three or more subsidiary clauses embedded centrally within them. In an attempt to understand the internal mechanisms responsible for language use, Elman investigates the properties of a particular class of connectionist dynamical systems. When analyzed using dynamical concepts, these models turn out to be in broad agreement with a variety of general constraints in the data, such as the center-embedding limitation. This kind of agreement demonstrates that it is possible to think of aspects of our linguistic subsystems in dynamical terms, and to find there a basis for some of the regularities. This model does not make precise temporal predictions about the changing values of observable variables, but it does make testable *qualitative* predictions about human performance.

Often, the system one wants to understand can be observed to exhibit any of a variety of highly distinctive *dynamical* properties: asymptotic approach to a fixed point, the presence or disappearance of maxima or minima, catastrophic jumps caused by small changes in control variables, oscillations, chaotic behavior, hysteresis, resistance to perturbation, and so on. Such properties can be observed even without knowing the specific equations which in fact govern the evolution of the system. They are, however, a particularly rich source of constraints for the process of qualitative dynamical modeling, for they narrow down considerably the classes of equations that can exhibit qualitatively similar behavior.

Dynamical Description   In another kind of situation, we may or may not have good time-series data available for modeling, but the complexity of the phenomena is such that laying down the equations of a formal model adequate to the data is currently not feasible. However, even here dynamics may hold the key to advances in understanding, because it provides a general conceptual apparatus for understanding the way systems—including, in particular, nonlinear systems—change over time. In this kind of scenario it is *dynamical systems theory* which turns out to be particularly useful.

For example, Thelen (see chapter 3) is concerned with understanding the development, over periods of months and even years, of basic motor skills such as reaching out for an object. At this stage, no satisfactory mathematical model of this developmental process is available. Indeed, it is still a major problem to write down equations describing just the basic movements themselves! Nevertheless, adopting a dynamical perspective can make possible descriptions which cumulatively amount to a whole new way of understanding how motor skills can emerge and change, and how the long-term developmental process is interdependent with the actual exercise of the developing skills themselves. From this perspective, particular actions are conceptualized as attractors in a space of possible bodily movements, and development of bodily skills is the emergence, and change in nature, of these attractors over time under the influence of factors such as bodily growth and the practice of the action itself. Adopting this general perspective entails significant changes in research methods. For example, Thelen pays close attention to the exact shape of individual gestures at particular intervals in the developmental process, and focuses on the specific changes that occur in each individual subject rather than the gross changes that are inferred by averaging over many subjects. It is only in the fine details of an individual subject's movements and their change over time that the real shape of the dynamics of development is revealed.

1.2   WHY DYNAMICS?

Why should we believe the Dynamical Hypothesis? Ultimately, as mentioned above, the proof of the pudding will be in the eating. The Dynamical Hypothesis is correct only if sustained empirical investigation shows that the most powerful models of cognitive processes take dynamical form. Although there are already dynamical models—including many described in this book

—which are currently the best available in their particular area, the jury is still out on the general issue. Even if the day of final reckoning is a long way off, however, we can still ask whether the dynamical approach is *likely* to be the more correct, and if so, why.

The dynamical approach certainly begins with a huge head start. Dynamics provides a vast resource of extremely powerful concepts and tools. Their usefulness in offering the best scientific explanations of phenomena throughout the natural world has been proved again and again. It would hardly be a surprise if dynamics turned out to be the framework within which the most powerful descriptions of cognitive processes were also forthcoming. The conceptual resources of the computational approach, on the other hand, are known to describe only one category of things in the physical universe: manmade digital computers. Even this success is hardly remarkable: digital computers were designed and constructed by us in accordance with the computational blueprint. It is a bold and highly controversial speculation that these same resources might also be applicable to natural cognitive systems, which are evolved biological systems in constant causal interaction with a messy environment.

This argument for the dynamical approach is certainly attractive, but it is not grounded in any way in the specific nature of cognitive systems. What we really want to know is: What general things do we *already know* about the nature of *cognitive* systems that suggest that dynamics will be the framework within which the most powerful models are developed?

We know, at least, these very basic facts: that cognitive processes always unfold in real time; that their behaviors are pervaded by *both* continuities and discretenesses; that they are composed of multiple subsystems which are simultaneously active and interacting; that their distinctive kinds of structure and complexity are not present from the very first moment, but emerge over time; that cognitive processes operate over many time scales, and events at different time scales interact; and that they are embedded in a real body and environment. The dynamical approach provides a natural framework for the description and explanation of phenomena with these broad properties. The computational approach, by contrast, either ignores them entirely or handles them only in clumsy, ad hoc ways.[8]

Cognition and Time

The argument presented here is simple. Cognitive processes always unfold in real time. Now, computational models specify only a postulated *sequence* of states that a system passes through. Dynamical models, by contrast, specify in detail not only *what* states the system passes through, but also how those states unfold in real time. This enables dynamical models to explain a wider range of data for any cognitive functions, and to explain cognitive functions whose dependence on real time is essential (e.g., temporal pattern processing).

Timothy van Gelder and Robert F. Port

When we say that cognitive processes unfold in real time, we are really saying two distinct things. First, real time is a continuous quantity best measured by real numbers, and for every point in time there is a state of the cognitive system. For an example of a process unfolding in real time, consider the movement of your arm as it swings beside you. At every one of an infinite number of instants in time from the beginning to the end of the motion, there is a position which your arm occupies. No matter how finely time is sampled, it makes sense to ask what position your arm occupies at every sampled point. The same is true of cognitive processes. As you recognize a face, or reason through a problem, or throw a ball, various aspects of your total cognitive system are undergoing change in real time, and no matter how finely time is sampled, there is a state of the cognitive system at each point. This is really just an obvious and elementary consequence of the fact that cognitive processes are ultimately physical processes taking place in real biological hardware.

The second thing we mean by saying that cognitive processes unfold in real time is that—as a consequence of the first point—*timing* always matters. A host of questions about the way the processes happen *in* time make perfect sense: questions about rates, durations, periods, synchrony, and so forth. Because cognitive processes happen in time, they cannot take too little time or too much time. The system must spend an appropriate amount of time in the vicinity of any given state. The timing of any particular operation must respect the rate at which other cognitive, bodily, and environmental processes are taking place. There are numerous subtleties involved in correct timing, and they are all real issues when we consider real cognitive processing.

Since cognitive processes unfold in real time, any framework for the description of cognitive processes that hopes to be fully adequate to the nature of the phenomena must be able to describe not merely *what* processes occur but *how* those processes unfold in time. Now, dynamical models based on differential equations are the preeminent mathematical framework science uses to describe how things happen in time. Such models specify how change in state variables at any instant depends on the current values of those variables themselves and on other parameters. Solutions to the governing equations tell you the state that the system will be in at any point in time, as long as the starting state and the amount of elapsed time are known. The use of differential equations presupposes that the variables change smoothly and continuously, and that time itself is a real-valued quantity. It is, in short, of the *essence* of dynamical models of this kind to describe how processes unfold, moment by moment, in real time.

Computational models, by contrast, specify only a bare sequence of states that the cognitive system goes through, and tell us nothing about the timing of those states over and above their mere order. Consider, for example, that paradigm of computational systems, the Turing machine.[9] Every Turing machine passes through a series of discrete symbolic states, one after another.

We talk about the state of the machine at time 1, time 2, and so forth. However, these "times" are not points in real time; they are merely indices which help us keep track of the order that states fall into as the machine carries out its sequence of computational steps. We use the integers to index states because they have a very familiar order and there are always as many of them as we need. However, we mustn't be misled into supposing that we are talking about *amounts* of time or *durations* here. Any other ordered set (e.g., people who ran the Boston Marathon, in the order they finished) would, in theory, do just as well for indexing the states of a Turing machine, though in practice they would be very difficult to use. To see that the integer "times" in the Turing machine are not real times, consider the following questions: What state was the machine in at time 1.5? How long was the machine in state 1? How long did it take for the machine to change from state 1 to state 2? *None of these questions are appropriate*, though they would be if we were talking about real amounts of time.

Now, let us suppose we have a particular Turing machine which adds numbers, and we propose this machine as a model of the cognitive processes going on in real people when they add numbers in their heads. The model specifies a sequence of symbol manipulations, passing from one discrete state to another; we suppose that a person passes through essentially the same sequence of discrete states. Note, however, that the Turing machine model is inherently incapable of telling us anything at all about the *timing* of these states and the transitions from one state to another. The model just tells us "first this state, then that state ..."; it makes no stand on how long the person will be in the first state, how fast the transition to the second state is, and so forth; it cannot even tell us what state the person will be in halfway between the time it enters the first state and the time it enters the second state, for questions such as these make no sense in the model.

Of course, even as far as computational models go, Turing machines do not make good models of cognitive processes. But the same basic points hold true for all standard computational models. LISP programs, production systems, generative grammars, and so forth, are all intrinsically incapable of describing the fine temporal structure of the way cognitive processes unfold, because all they specify—indeed, all they *can* specify—is *which* states the system will go through, and in what order. To see this, just try picking up any mainstream computational model of a cognitive process—of parsing, or planning, for example—and try to find any place where the model makes any commitment at all about such elementary temporal issues as how much time each symbolic manipulation takes. One quickly discovers that computational models simply aren't in that business; they're not dealing with time. "Time" in a computational model is not real time, it is mere order.

Computationalists do sometimes attempt to extract from their models implications for the timing of the target cognitive processes. The standard and most appropriate way to do this is to assume that each computational step takes a certain chunk of real time (say, 10 ms).[10] By adding assumptions of

Timothy van Gelder and Robert F. Port

this kind we can begin to make some temporal predictions, such as that a particular computational process will take a certain amount of time, and that a particular step will take place some number of milliseconds after some other event. Yet the additional temporal assumptions are completely ad hoc; the theorist is free to choose the step time, for example, in any way that renders the model more consistent with the psychological data.[11] In the long run, it is futile to attempt to weld temporal considerations onto an essentially atemporal kind of model. If one professes to be concerned with temporal issues, one may as well adopt a modeling framework which builds temporal issues in from the very beginning—i.e., take up the dynamical approach.

One refuge for the computationalist from these arguments is to insist that certain physical systems are such that they can be described at an abstract level where temporal issues can be safely ignored, and that the most tractable descriptions of these systems must in fact take place at that level. This claim is clearly true of ordinary desktop digital computers; we standardly describe their behavior in algorithmic terms in which the precise details of timing are completely irrelevant, and these algorithmic descriptions are the most tractable given our high-level theoretical purposes. The computationalist *conjecture* is that cognitive systems will be like computers in this regard; high-level cognitive processes can, and indeed can *only* be tractably described in computational terms which ignore fine-grained temporal issues. Note, however, that this response concedes that computational models are inherently incapable of being fully adequate to the nature of the cognitive processes themselves, since these processes always do unfold in real time. Further, this response concedes that *if there were* a tractable dynamical model of some cognitive process, it would be inherently superior, since it describes aspects of the processes which are out of reach of the computational model. Finally, computationalists have not as yet done enough to convince us that the only tractable models of these high-level processes will be computational ones. Dynamicists, at least, are still working on the assumption that it *will* someday be possible to produce fully adequate models of cognitive processes.

Computationalists sometimes point out that dynamical models of cognitive processes are themselves typically "run" or simulated on digital computers. Does this not establish that computational models are not inherently limited in the way these arguments seem to suggest? Our answer, of course, is no, and the reason is simple: a computational simulation of a dynamical model of some cognitive process is not itself a model of that cognitive process in anything like the manner of standard computational models in cognitive science. Thus, the cognitive system is not being hypothesized to pass through a sequence of symbol structures of the kind that evolve in the computational simulation, any more than a weather pattern is thought to pass through a sequence of discrete symbolic states just because we can simulate a dynamical model of the weather. Rather, all the computational simulation delivers is a sequence of symbolic *descriptions* of points in the dynamical model (and thereby, indirectly, of states of the cognitive system). What we have in such situations is a dynamical model plus an atemporal computational approximation to it.[12]

Continuity in State

Natural cognitive systems sometimes change state in continuous ways; sometimes, on the other hand, they change state in ways that can appear discrete. Dynamics provides a framework within which continuity *and* discreteness can be accounted for, even within the same model. The computational approach, by contrast, can only model a system as changing state from one discrete state to another. Consequently, the dynamical approach is inherently more flexible—and hence more powerful—than the computational approach.

This argument must be carefully distinguished from the previous one. There, the focus was continuity in *time*; the claim was that models must be able to specify the state of the system at every point in time. Here, the focus is continuity in *state*; the claim is that models must be capable of describing change from one state to another arbitrarily close to it, *as well as* sudden change from one state to another discretely distinct from it.

Standard computational systems only change from one discrete state to another.[13] Think again of a Turing machine. Its possible (total) states are configurations of symbols on the tape, the condition of the head, and the position of the head. Every state transition is a matter of adding or deleting a symbol, changing the head condition, and changing its position. The possibilities, however, are all discrete; the system always jumps directly from one state to another without passing through any in-between. There simply *are no* states in between; they are just not defined for the system. The situation is like scoring points in basketball: the ball either goes through the hoop or it doesn't. In basketball, you can't have fractions of points.

When a computational system is used as a model for a natural cognitive process, the natural cognitive system is hypothesized to go through the same state transitions as the model. So a computational model can only attribute discrete states, and discrete state transitions, to the cognitive system.

Now, quite often, state transitions in natural cognitive systems can be thought of as discrete. For example, in trying to understand how people carry out long division in their heads, the internal processes can be thought of as passing through a number of discrete states corresponding to stages in carrying out the division. However, there are innumerable kinds of tasks that cognitive systems face which appear to demand a continuum of states in any system that can carry them out. For example, most real problems of sensorimotor coordination deal with a world in which objects and events can come in virtually any shape, size, position, orientation, and motion. A system which can flexibly deal with such a world must be able to occupy states that are equally rich and subtly distinct. Similarly, everyday words as simple as *truck* seem to know no limit in the fineness of contextual shading they can take on. Any system that can understand *Billy drove the truck* must be able to accom-

Timothy van Gelder and Robert F. Port

modate this spectrum of senses. Only a system that can occupy a continuum of states with respect to word meanings stands a real chance of success.

Many dynamical systems, in the core sense that we have adopted in this chapter, change in continuous phase spaces, and so the dynamical approach is inherently well-suited to describing how cognitive systems might change in continuous ways (see, e.g., Port, Cummins, and McAuley, this volume, chapter 12). However,—and this is the key point—it can also describe discrete transitions in a number of ways. The dynamical approach is therefore more flexible—and hence, again, more powerful—than the computational approach, which can only attribute discrete states to a system.

The dynamical approach can accommodate discrete state transitions in two ways. First, the concepts and tools of dynamics can be used to describe the behavior of systems with only discrete states. A dynamical model of an ecosystem, for example, assumes that its populations always come in discrete amounts; you can have 10 or 11 rabbits, but not 10.5 rabbits. However, perhaps the most interesting respect in which dynamics can handle discreteness is in being able to describe how a continuous system can undergo changes that look discrete from a distance. This is more interesting because cognitive systems appear to be thoroughly pervaded by *both* continuity and discreteness; the ideal model would be one which could account for both together. One kind of discrete change in a continuous system is a *catastrophe*: a sudden, dramatic change in the state of a system when a small change in the parameters of the equations defining the system lead to a qualitative change—a bifurcation—in the "dynamics" or structure of forces operating in that system (Zeeman, 1977; see also Petitot, chapter 9).[14] Thus, high-level, apparently discrete changes of state can be accounted for within a dynamical framework in which continuity and discreteness coexist; indeed, the former is the precondition and explanation for the emergence of the latter.

Multiple Simultaneous Interactions

Consider again the process of returning a serve in tennis. The ball is approaching; you are perceiving its approach, are aware of the other player's movements, are considering the best strategy for the return, and are shifting into position to play the stroke. *All this is happening at the same time.* As you move into place, your perspective on the approaching ball is changing, and hence so is activity on your retina and in your visual system. It is your evolving sense of how to play the point that is affecting your movement. The path of the approaching ball affects which strategy would be best and hence how you move. *Everything is simultaneously affecting everything else.*

Consider natural cognitive systems from another direction entirely. Neurons are complex systems with hundreds, perhaps thousands of synaptic connections. There is some kind of activity in every one of these, all the time. From all this activity, the cell body manages to put together a firing rate. Each cell forms part of a network of neurons, all of which are active (to a greater or lesser degree) all the time, and the activity in each is directly affecting hundreds, perhaps thousands of others, and indirectly affecting countless more. The networks form into maps, the maps into systems, and systems into the central nervous system (CNS), but at every level we have the same principle, that there is constant activity in all components at once, and components are simultaneously affecting one another. No part of the nervous system is ever completely inactive. As neurophysiologist Karl Lashley (1960) put it, "Every bit of evidence available indicates a dynamic, constantly active system, or, rather, a composite of many interacting systems ..." (p. 526).

Clearly, any fully adequate approach to the study of cognitive systems must be one that can handle multiple, simultaneous interactive activity. Yet doing this is the essence of dynamics. Dynamical systems *are* just the simultaneous, mutually influencing activity of multiple parts or aspects. The dynamical approach is therefore inherently well-suited to describe cognitive systems.

A classic example of a dynamical model in this sense is McClelland and Rumelhart's "interactive activation network" (McClelland and Rumelhart, 1981). This model was designed to account for how a letter embedded in the context of a five-letter word of English could be recognized faster than the same letter embedded within a nonword string of letters and even better than the single letter presented by itself. This "word superiority effect" suggested that somehow the whole word was being recognized at the same time as the individual letters that make up the word. Thus, it implied a mechanism where recognition of the word and the letters takes place simultaneously and in such a way that each process influences the other. McClelland and Rumelhart proposed separate cliques of nodes in their network that mutually influence one another by means of coupled difference equations. The output activation of some nodes served as an excitatory or inhibitory input to certain other nodes. This model turned out to capture the word superiority effect and a number of other related effects as well.

Almost all computational approaches attempt to superimpose on this multiple, simultaneous, interactive behavior a sequential, step-by-step structure. They thereby appear to assume that nothing of interest is going on in any component other than the one responsible for carrying out the next stage in the algorithm. It is true, as computationalists will point out, that a computational model can—in principle—run in parallel, though it is devilishly difficult to write such a code. The "blackboard model" of the Hearsay-II speech recognition system (Erman, Hayes-Roth, Lesser, et al. 1980) represents one attempt at approaching parallelism by working within the constraints of serial computationalism. The "blackboard," however, was just a huge, static data structure on which various independent analysis modules might asynchronously post messages, thereby making partial analyses of each module available for other modules to interpret. This is a step in the right direction, but it is a far cry from simultaneous interactive activation. Each module in Hearsay-II can do no more than say "Here is what I have found so far, as stated in terms of my own vocabulary," rather than "Here is exactly how your activity should change on the basis of what has happened in my part of the system,"—the kind of interaction that components governed by coupled equations have with one another. Other methods of parallelism more sophisticated than this may certainly be postulated in principle, but apparently await further technological developments.

Multiple Time Scales

Cognitive processes always take place at many time scales. Changes in the state of neurons can take just a few milliseconds, visual or auditory recognition half a second or less, coordinated movement a few seconds, conversation and story understanding minutes or even hours, and the emergence of sophisticated capacities can take months and years. Further, these time scales are interrelated; processes at one time scale affect processes at another. For example, Esther Thelen (see chapter 3) has shown how actually engaging in coordinated movement promotes the development of coordination, and yet development itself shapes the movements that are possible; it is in this interactive process, moreover, that we find the emergence of concepts such as *space* and *force*. At finer scales, what we see (at the hundreds-of-milliseconds time scale) affects how we move (at the seconds scale) and vice versa.

The dynamical approach provides ways of handling this variety and interdependence of time scales. For example, the equations governing a dynamical system typically include two kinds of variables: state variables and parameters. The way the system changes state depends on both, but only the state variables take on new values; the parameters are standardly fixed. However, it is possible to think of the parameters as not fixed but rather changing as well, though over a considerably longer time scale than the state variables. Thus we can have a single system with both a "fast" dynamics of state variables on a short time scale and a "slow" dynamics of parameters on a long time scale, such that the slow dynamics helps shape the fast dynamics. It is even possible to link the equations such that the fast dynamics shapes the slow dynamics; in such a case, we have true interdependence of time scales.

Note that it is other features of the dynamical approach, such as continuity in space and time, and multiple simultaneous interactive aspects, which make possible its account of the interdependence of time scales. The computational approach, by contrast, has no natural methods of handling this pervasive structural feature of natural cognitive systems.

Self-Organization and the Emergence of Structure

Cognitive systems are highly structured, in both their behavior and their internal spatial and temporal organization. One kind of challenge for cognitive science is to *describe* that structure. Another kind of challenge is to explain *how it got to be there*. Since the computational framework takes inspiration from the organization of formal systems like logic and mathematics, the traditional framework characteristically tackles only the problem of describing the structure that exists. Models in this framework typically postulate some initial set of a priori structures from which more complex structures may be derived by application of rules. The question of *emergence*—of where the initial elements or structures come from—always remains a problem, usually ignored.

A major advantage of the dynamical approach is that dynamical systems are known to be able to create structure both in space and in time. By structure, we mean something nonrandom in form that endures or recurs in time. Thus an archetypal physical object, such as a chair, is invariant in form over time, while a transient event, like a wave breaking on a beach, may recur with temporal regularity. The words in human languages tend to be constructed out of units of speech sound that are reused in different sequences (e.g., *gnat, tan, ant,* etc.), much like the printed letters with which we write words down. But where do *any* such structures come from if they are not either assumed or somehow fashioned from preexisting primitive parts? This is the question of "morphogenesis," the creation of forms. It has counterparts in many branches of science, including cosmology. Why are matter and energy not uniformly distributed in the universe? Study of the physics of relatively homogeneous physical systems, like the ocean, the atmosphere, or a tank of fluid, can begin to provide answers. Some form of energy input is required plus some appropriate dynamical laws. Under these circumstances most systems will tend to generate regular structure of some sort under a broad range of conditions.

The atmosphere exhibits not only its all-too-familiar chaotic properties, but it can also display many kinds of highly regular spatiotemporal structures that can be modeled by the use of differential equations. For example, over the Great Plains in the summer, one sometimes observes long "streets" of parallel clouds with smooth edges like the waves of sand found in shallow water along a beach or in the corduroy ridges on a well-traveled dirt road. How are these parallel ridges created? Not with any form of rake or plow. These patterns all depend on some degree of homogeneity of medium and a consistently applied influx of energy. In other conditions (involving higher energy levels), a fluid medium may, in small regions, structure itself into a highly regular tornado or whirlpool. Although these "objects" are very simple structures, it is still astonishing that any medium so unstructured and so linear in its behavior could somehow constrain itself over vast distances in such a way that regular structures in space and time are produced. The ability of one part of a system to "enslave" other parts, i.e., restrict the degrees of freedom of other, distant parts, is now understood, at least for fairly simple systems (Haken, 1988, 1991; Kelso, Ding, and Schöner, 1992; Thom, 1975).

The demonstration that structure can come into existence without either a specific plan or an independent builder raises the possibility that many structures in physical bodies as well as in cognition might occur without any externally imposed shaping forces. Perhaps cognitive structures, like embryological structures, the weather and many other examples, simply *organize themselves* (Kugler and Turvey, 1987; Thelen and Smith, 1994). Dynamical models are now known to account for many spatial and temporal structures in a very direct way (Madore and Freeman, 1987; Murray, 1989). They enable us to understand how such apparently unlikely structures could come to exist and retain their morphology for some extended period of time. We assume that cognition is a particular structure in space and time—one that supports intelligent interaction with the world. So our job is to discover how such a structure could turn out to be a stable state of the brain in the context of the body and environment. The answer to this question depends both on structure that comes from the genes and on structure that is imposed by the world. No theoretical distinction need be drawn between learning and evolution—they are both, by hypothesis, examples of adaptation toward stable, cognitively effective states of a brain (or an artificial system). The primary difference is that they operate on different time scales.

In both computer science and in cognitive science, the role of adaptation as a source of appropriate structure is under serious development (Forrest, 1991; Holland, 1975; Kauffman, 1993). Most of these methods depend on differential or difference equations for optimization. Thus, a final reason to adopt the dynamical perspective is the possibility of eventually accounting for how the structures that support intelligent behavior could have come about. Detailed models for specific instances of structure creation present many questions and will continue to be developed. But the possibility of such accounts developing from dynamical models can no longer be denied.

Embeddedness

If we follow common usage and use the term *cognitive system* to refer primarily to the internal mechanisms that underwrite sophisticated performance, then cognitive systems are essentially embedded, both in a nervous system and, in a different sense, in a body and environment. Any adequate account of cognitive functioning must be able to describe and explain this embeddedness. Now, the behavior of the nervous system, of bodies (limbs, muscles, bone, blood), and of the immediate physical environment, are all best described in dynamical terms. An advantage of the dynamical conception of cognition is that, by describing cognitive processing in fundamentally similar terms, it minimizes difficulties in accounting for embeddedness.

The embeddedness of cognitive systems has two rather different aspects. The first is the relation of the cognitive system to its neural substrate. The cognitive system somehow *is* the CNS, but what are the architectural and processing principles, and level relationships, that allow us to understand how the one can be the other? The other aspect is the relation of the cognitive system to its essential surrounds—the rest of the body, and the physical environment. How do internal cognitive mechanisms "interact" with the body and the environment?

A computational perspective gives a very different kind of understanding of the behavior of a complex system than a dynamical perspective. Given that the behavior of the nervous system, the body, and the environment are best described in dynamical terms, adopting the computational perspective for internal cognitive mechanisms transforms the *issue* of embedding into a *problem*: how can two kinds of systems, which are described in fundamentally different terms, be related? That is, describing cognition in computational terms automatically creates a theoretical gap between cognitive systems and their surrounds, a gap which must then somehow be bridged.

In the case of the embeddedness of the cognitive system in a nervous system, the problem is to account for how a system that is fundamentally dynamical at one level can simultaneously be a computational system considered at another level. The challenge for the computationalist is to show how such a dynamical system configures itself into a classical computational system. It is a challenge because the two kinds of system are so deeply different. Of course, it is not *impossible* to meet a challenge of this kind; standard digital computers are systems that are continuous dynamical systems at one level and discrete computational systems at another, and we can explain how one realizes the other. However, this provides little reason to believe that a similar cross-level, cross-kind explanation will be feasible in the case of natural cognitive systems, since computers were constructed precisely so that the low-level dynamics would be severely, artificially constrained in exactly the right way. Finding the components of a computational cognitive architecture in the actual dynamical neural hardware of real brains is a challenge of an altogether different order. It is a challenge that computationalists have not even begun to meet.

The embeddedness of the cognitive system within a body and an environment is equally a problem for the computational approach. Again, the problem arises because we are trying to describe the relationship between systems described in fundamentally different terms. The crux of the problem here is time. Most of what organisms deal with happens essentially in time. Most of the critical features of the environment which must be perceived—including events of "high-level" cognitive significance, such as linguistic communication—unfold over time, and so produce changes in the body over time. In action, the movement of the body, and its effects on the environment, happen in time. This poses a real problem for models of cognitive processes which are, in a deep way, atemporal. For the most part, computational approaches have dealt with this problem by simply avoiding it. They have assumed that cognition constitutes an autonomous domain that can be studied entirely independently of embeddedness. The problem of how an atemporal cognitive system interacts with a temporal world is shunted off to supposedly noncognitive transduction systems (i.e., somebody else's problem). When computationalists do face up to problems of embeddedness, the interaction of the cognitive system with the body and world is usually handled in ad hoc, biologically implausible ways. Thus inputs are immediately "detemporalized" by transformation into static structures, as when speech signals are transcribed into a spatial buffer. Outputs are handled by periodic intervention in the environment, with the hope that these interventions will keep nudging things in the right direction. Both methods require the addition to the model of some independent timing device or clock, yet natural cognitive systems don't have clocks in anything like the required sense (Glass and Mackey, 1988; Winfree, 1980). The diurnal clocks observed in many animals, including humans, do not help address the problem of rapid regular sampling that would appear to be required to recognize speech (or a bird song or any other distinctive pattern that is complex in time) using a buffered representation in which time is translated into a labeled spatial axis.

The dynamical approach to cognition handles the embeddedness problem by refusing to create it. The same basic mathematical and conceptual tools are used to describe cognitive processes on the one hand and the nervous system and the body and environment on the other. Though accounting for the embeddedness of cognitive systems is still by no means trivial, at least the dynamical approach to cognition does not face the problem of attempting to overcome the differences between two very different general frameworks. Thus the dynamics of central cognitive processes are nothing more than aggregate dynamics of low-level neural processes, redescribed in higher-level, lower-dimensional terms (see Relation to Neural Processes, below). Dynamical systems theory provides a framework for understanding these level relationships and the emergence of macroscopic order and complexity from microscopic behavior. Similarly, a dynamical account of cognitive processes is directly compatible with dynamical descriptions of the body and the environment, since the dynamical account never steps outside time in the first place. It describes cognitive processes as essentially unfolding over time, and can therefore describe them as occurring in the very same time frame as the movement of the body itself and physical events that occur in the environment.

That cognitive processes must, for this general reason, ultimately be understood dynamically can be appreciated by observing what happens when researchers attempt to build serious models at the interface between internal cognitive mechanisms and the body and environment. Thus Port et al. (see chapter 12) aim to describe how it is possible to handle auditory patterns, with all their complexities of sequence, rhythm, and rate, without biologically implausible artificialities such as static input buffers or a rapid time-sampling system. They find that the inner, cognitive processes themselves must unfold over time with the auditory sequence, and that their qualitative properties (like invariance of perception despite change in rate of presentation) are best described in dynamical terms. In other words, attempting to describe how a cognitive system might perceive its essentially temporal environment drives dynamical conceptualizations inward, into the cognitive system itself. Similarly, researchers interested in the production of speech (see Saltzman, chapter 6; Browman and Goldstein, chapter 7) find that to understand the control of muscle, jaw, etc., we need models of cognitive mechanisms underlying motor control that unfold dynamically in time. That is, attempts to describe how a cognitive system might control essentially temporal bodily movements also drives dynamics inward into the cognitive system. In short, whenever confronted with the problem of explaining how a natural cognitive system might interact with another system that is essentially temporal, one finds that the relevant aspect of the cognitive system itself must be given a dynamical account. It then becomes a problem how this dynamical component of the cognitive system interacts with even more "central" processes. The situation repeats itself, and dynamics is driven further inward. The natural outcome of this progression is a picture of cognitive processing in its entirety, from peripheral input systems to peripheral output systems and everything in between, as all unfolding dynamically in real time: *mind as motion*.

1.3 RELATION TO OTHER APPROACHES

A careful study of the relation of the dynamical conception of cognition to the various other research enterprises in cognitive science would require a book of its own. Here we just make some brief comments on the relation of the dynamical approach to what are currently the two most prominent alternative approaches, mainstream computationalism and connectionism. In addition, we discuss how the dynamical approach relates to the modeling of neural processes and to chaos theory.

Relation to the Computational Approach

Much has already been said about the relation between the computational and dynamical approaches. In this section we add some clarifying remarks on the nature of the empirical competition between the two approaches.

Earlier we characterized cognition in the broadest possible terms as all the processes that are causally implicated in our sophisticated behaviors. Now, it has always been the computationalist position that *some* of these processes are computational in nature and many others are not. For these other processes, traditional dynamical modes of explanation would presumably be quite appropriate. For example, our engaging in an ordinary conversation depends not only on thought processes which enable us to decide what to say next but also on correct movements of lips, tongue, and jaw. Only the former processes would be a matter of internal symbol manipulation; the muscular movements would be dynamical processes best described by differential equations of some sort. In other words, computationalists have always been ready to accept a form of *peaceful coexistence* with alternative forms of explanation targeted at a different selection of the processes underlying sophisticated performance. As we mentioned in section 1.2, the computationalist position is that the processes that must be computational in nature are distinguished by their dependence on "knowledge"; this knowledge must be represented somehow, and the best candidate is symbolically; hence the processes must be computational (symbol manipulation). In fact, from this perspective these knowledge-dependent, symbolic processes are the only *genuinely* cognitive ones; all other processes are peripheral, or implementational, or otherwise ancillary to real cognition.

Now, it has never been entirely clear exactly where the boundary between the two domains actually lies. The conflict between the computational and dynamical approaches can thus be seen as a kind of boundary dispute. The most extreme form of the computationalist hypothesis places the boundary in such a way as to include *all* processes underlying our sophisticated behaviors in the computational domain. Probably nobody has ever maintained such a position, but during the heyday of AI and computational cognitive science in the 1960s and 1970s many more processes were thought to have computational explanations than anyone now supposes. Similarly, the dynamical hypothesis draws the boundary to include *all* processes within the dynamical domain. According to this ambitious doctrine the domain of the computational approach is empty, and dynamical accounts will *eliminate* their computational competitors across all aspects of cognition. It remains to be seen to what extent this is true, but dynamicists in cognitive science are busily attempting to extend the boundary as far as possible, tackling phenomena that were previously assumed to lie squarely within the computational purview.

There is another sense in which computationalists have always been prepared to concede that cognitive systems are dynamical systems. They have accepted that all cognitive processes, including those centrally located in the computational domain, are *implemented* as dynamical processes at a lower level. The situation is exactly analogous to that of a digital desktop computer. The best high-level descriptions of these physical systems are cast in terms of the algorithmic manipulation of symbols. Now, each such manipulation is simply a dynamical process at the level of the electrical circuitry, and there is a sense in which the whole computer is a massively complex dynamical system that is amenable (in principle at least) to a dynamical description. However, any such description would be hopelessly intractable, and would fail to shed any light on the operation of the system *as computing*. Likewise, human thought processes are based ultimately on the firing of neurons and myriad other low-level processes that are best modeled in dynamical terms; nevertheless, the computationalist claims that only high-level computational models will provide tractable, revealing descriptions at the level at which these processes can be seen as *cognitive* performances.

It may even turn out to be the case that there is a high-level computational account of some cognitive phenomenon, *and* a lower-level dynamical account that is *also* theoretically tractable and illuminating. If they are both targeted on essentially the same phenomenon, and there is some precise, systematic mapping between their states and processes, then the computational account would not be eliminated but simply implemented. A relationship of this kind has been recently been advocated for certain psycholinguistic phenomena by Smolensky, Legendre, and Miyata (1992). An alternative possibility is that a high-level, computational description of some phenomenon turns out to be an *approximation*, framed in discrete, sequential, symbol-manipulating terms, of a process whose most powerful and accurate description is in dynamical terms. In such a case only certain of the states and processes in the computational model would stand in a kind of rough correspondence with features of the dynamical model.

Relation to Connectionism

For the purposes of this discussion, we take connectionism to be that rather broad and diverse research program which investigates cognitive processes using artificial neural network models. Defined this way, connectionism is perfectly compatible with the dynamical approach. Indeed, neural networks, which are themselves typically continuous nonlinear dynamical systems, constitute an excellent medium for dynamical modeling.

Thus the two approaches overlap, but only partially. On the one hand, despite the fact that all connectionist networks are dynamical systems, many connectionists have not been utilizing dynamical concepts and tools to any significant degree. At one extreme, connectionists have used their networks to directly implement computational architectures (e.g., Touretzky, 1990). More commonly, they have molded their networks to conform to a broadly computational outlook. In standard feedforward backpropagation networks, for example, processing is seen as the sequential transformation, from one layer to the next, of static representations. Such networks are little more than sophisticated devices for mapping static inputs into static outputs. No dynamics or temporal considerations are deployed in understanding the behavior of the network or the nature of the cognitive task itself. For example, in the famous NETtalk network (Rosenberg and Sejnowski, 1987) the text to be "pronounced" is sequentially fed in via a spatial input buffer and the output is a phonemic specification; all the network does is sequentially transform static input representations into static output representations. To the extent that the difficult temporal problems of speech production are solved at all, these solutions are entirely external to the network. Research of this kind is really more computational than dynamical in basic orientation.

On the other hand, many dynamicists are not connectionists. This is obvious enough on the surface; their intellectual background, focus, and methods are very different (see, e.g., Turvey and Carello, chapter 13; Reidbord and Redington, chapter 17). But what, more precisely, is it that distinguishes the two kinds of dynamicist? If we compare the various contributions to this book, some features of a distinctively connectionist approach emerge. Most obviously, connectionists deploy network dynamical models; they can thus immediately be contrasted with dynamicists whose main contribution is dynamical description (see discussion in section 1.1). Even among those that offer formal dynamical models, there are contrasts between connectionists and others, though the distinction is more one of degree and emphasis.

One kind of contrast is in the nature of the formal model deployed. Connectionists standardly operate with relatively high-dimensional systems that can be broken down into component systems, each of which is just a parametric variation on a common theme (i.e., the artificial neural units). Thus, for example, the connectionist systems used by Randy Beer in his studies of simple autonomous agents are defined by the following general differential equation:

$$\tau_i \dot{y}_i = -y_i + \sum_{j=1}^{N} w_{ji} \sigma(y_j - \theta_j) + I_i(t) \qquad i = 1, 2, \ldots, N$$

In this equation each y_i designates the activation level of i-th of the N individual neural units, and w_{ji} the weight which connects the i-th unit to the j-th unit.[15] This equation is thus really a schema, and if we were to write all the equations out fully, we would have one each for $\dot{y}_1$, $\dot{y}_2$, etc. All these equations take the same form, which is to say that each of the component subsystems (the neural units) are just variations on a common type.

Now, the models deployed by nonconnectionist dynamicists typically cannot be broken down in this way; they are not made up of individual subsystems that have essentially the same dynamical form. For example, the model system deployed by Turvey and Carello (chapter 13) to describe coordination patterns among human oscillating limbs

$$\dot{\phi} = \Delta\omega - a\sin(\phi) - 2y\sin(2\phi) + \sqrt{Q}\xi t$$

has only one state variable (ϕ, the phase difference between the limbs). (See Norton [chapter 2] for plenty of other examples of dynamical systems—including multivariable systems—that cannot be broken down in his way.)

Another kind of contrast is the connectionist tendency to focus on learning and adaptation rather than on mathematical proofs to demonstrate critical properties. Much effort in connectionist modeling is devoted to finding ways to modify parameter settings (e.g., the connection weights) for networks of various architectures so as to exhibit a certain desired behavior, using techniques like backpropagation and genetic algorithms. Nonconnectionists, by contrast, rely on equations using many fewer parameters, with their parameter settings often determined by hand, and typically concentrate proportionately more attention on the fine detail of the dynamics of the resulting system.

In section 1.1 we claimed that connectionism should not be thought of as constituting an alternative to the computational research paradigm in cognitive science. The reason is that there is a much deeper fault line running between the computational approach and the dynamical approach. In our opinion, connectionists have often been attempting, unwittingly and unsuccessfully, to straddle this line: to use dynamical machinery to implement ideas about the nature of cognitive processes which owe more to computationalism. From the perspective of a genuinely dynamical conception of cognition, classic PDP-style connectionism (as contained in, for example, the well-known volumes Rumelhart and McClelland, 1986, and McClelland and Rumelhart, 1986) is little more than an ill-fated attempt to find a halfway house between the two worldviews. This diagnosis is borne out by recent developments. Since its heyday in the mid- to late-1980s, this style of connectionist work has been gradually disappearing, either collapsing back in the computational direction (hybrid networks, and straightforward implementations of computational mechanisms), or becoming increasingly dynamic (e.g., the shift to recurrent networks analyzed with dynamical systems techniques). Connectionist researchers who take the latter path are, of course, welcome participants in the dynamical approach.

Relation to Neural Processes

All cognitive scientists agree that cognition depends critically on neural processes; indeed, it is customary to simply *identify* internal cognitive processing with the activity of the CNS. Neuroscientists are making rapid progress investigating these neural processes. Moreover, the predominant mathematical framework among neuroscientists for the detailed description of neural processes is dynamics, at levels ranging from subcellular chemical transactions to the activity of single neurons and the behavior of whole neural assemblies. The CNS can therefore be considered a single dynamical system with a vast number of state variables. This makes it tempting to suggest that dynamical theories of cognition must be high-level accounts of the very same phenomena that neuroscientists study in fine detail.

This would only be partially true, however. Not all dynamicists in cognitive science are aiming to describe internal neural processes, even at a high level. A central element of the dynamical perspective (see The Nature of Cognitive Systems, above) is that cognitive processes span the nervous system, the body, and the environment; hence cognition cannot be thought of as wholly contained *within* the nervous system. Thus, in modeling cognition, dynamicists select aspects from a spectrum ranging from purely environmental processes (e.g., Bingham, chapter 14) at one extreme to purely intracranial processes (e.g., Petitot, chapter 9) at the other; in between are bodily movements (e.g., Saltzman, chapter 6) and processes which straddle the division between the intracranial and the body or environment (e.g., Turvey and Carello, chapter 13). To select some local aspect of the total cognitive system on which to focus is not to deny the importance or interest of other aspects; choices about which aspect to study are made on the basis of factors such as background, available tools, and hunches about where the most real progress is likely to be made.

Clearly, the idea that the dynamical approach to cognition is just the high-level study of the same processes studied by the neuroscientists is applicable only to those dynamicists whose focus is on processes that are completely or largely within the CNS. Other dynamicists are equally studying *cognition*, but by focusing on other aspects of the large system in which cognitive performance is realized.

What is involved in studying processes *at a higher level*? This simple phrase covers a number of different shifts in focus. Most obviously, dynamical cognitive scientists are attempting to describe systems and behaviors that are *aggregates* of vast numbers of systems and behaviors as described at the neural level. Whereas the neuroscientist may be attempting to describe the dynamics of a single neuron, the dynamicist is interested in the dynamics of whole subsystems of the nervous system, comprised of millions, perhaps billions of neurons. Second, the dynamicist obviously does not study this aggregate system by means of a mathematical model with billions of dimensions. Rather, the aim is to provide a *low-dimensional* model that provides a scientifically tractable description of the same qualitative dynamics as is exhibited by the high-dimensional system. Thus, studying systems at a higher level corresponds to studying them in terms of lower-dimensional mathematical models. Third, dynamical cognitive scientists often attempt to describe the neural processes at a larger *time scale* (see Multiple Time Scales, above). The cognitive time scale is typically assumed to lie between roughly a fifth of a second (the duration of an eyeblink) on up to hours and years. It happens to be approximately the range of time scales over which people have awareness of some of their own states and about which they can talk in natural languages. Neuroscientists, by contrast, typically study processes that occur on a scale of fractions of a second.

Relation to Chaos Theory

Chaos theory is a branch of dynamical systems theory concerned with systems that exhibit chaotic behavior, which for current purposes can be loosely identified with sensitivity to initial conditions (see Norton, chapter 2, for further discussion). Sometimes, especially in popular discussions, the term *chaos theory* is even used to refer to dynamical systems theory in general, though this blurs important distinctions. Chaos theory has been one of the most rapidly developing branches of nonlinear dynamical systems theory, and developments in both pure mathematics and computer simulation have revealed the chaotic nature of a wide variety of physical systems. Chaos theory has even come to provide inspiration and metaphors for many outside the mathematical sciences. It is therefore natural to ask what connection there might be between chaos theory and the dynamical approach to cognition.

The answer is simply that there is *no* essential connection between the two. Rather, chaos theory is just one more conceptual resource offered by dynamical systems theory, a resource that might be usefully applied in the study of cognition, but only if warranted by the data. None of the contributors to this volume have deployed chaos theory in any substantial sense. In this early stage in the development of the dynamical approach, researchers are still exploring how to apply simpler, more manageable models and concepts. The very features that make a system chaotic constitute obvious difficulties for anyone wanting to use that system as a model of cognitive processes.

On the other hand, there are reasons to believe that chaos theory will play some role in a fully developed dynamical account of cognition. Generically, the kinds of systems that dynamicists tend to deploy in modeling cognitive processes (typically continuous and nonlinear) are the home of chaotic processes. Not surprisingly, certain classes of neural networks have been mathematically demonstrated to exhibit chaotic behavior. Of more interest, perhaps, chaos has been empirically observed in brain processes (Basar, 1990; Basar and Bullock, 1989). In one well-known research program, chaotic behavior has been an integral part of a model of the neural processes underlying olfaction (Skarda and Freeman, 1987) (though here the role of chaos was to provide a kind of optimal background or "ready" state rather than the processes of scent recognition themselves). There have been fascinating initial explorations of the idea that highly distinctive kinds of complexity in cognitive performance, such as the productivity of linguistic capacities, might be grounded in chaotic or near-chaos behavior (see, e.g., Pollack, chapter 10). Accounting for such indications of chaos as already exist, and the further uncovering of any role that chaotic notions might play in the heart of cognitive processes, are clearly significant open challenges for the dynamical approach.

1.4   A HISTORICAL SKETCH

The origins of the contemporary dynamical approach to cognition can be traced at least as far back as the 1940s and 1950s, and in particular to that extraordinary flux of ideas loosely gathered around what came to be known as *cybernetics* (Wiener, 1948). At that time the new disciplines of computation theory and information theory were being combined with elements of electrical engineering, control theory, logic, neural network theory, and neurophysiology to open up whole new ways of thinking about systems that can behave in adaptive, purposeful, or other mindlike ways (McCulloch, 1965; Shannon and Weaver, 1949; von Neumann, 1958). There was a pervasive sense at the time that somewhere in this tangled maze of ideas was the path to a rigorous new scientific understanding of both biological and mental phenomena. The problem for those wanting to understand cognition was to identify this path, and follow it beyond toy examples to a deep understanding of natural cognitive systems. What were the really crucial theoretical resources, and how might they be forged into a paradigm for the study of cognition?

Dynamics was an important resource in this period. It was the basis of control theory and the study of feedback mechanisms, and was critical to the theory of analog computation. It figured centrally in neuroscience and in the study of neural networks. The idea that dynamics might form the general framework for a unified science of cognition was the basis of one of the most important books of the period, Ashby's *Design for a Brain* (Ashby, 1952). Interestingly, it was so obvious to Ashby that cognitive systems should be studied from a dynamical perspective that he hardly even bothered to explicitly assert it. Unfortunately, the book was mainly foundational and programmatic; it was short on explicit demonstrations of the utility of this framework in psychological modeling or AI.

During this period two other important strands from the web of cybernetic ideas were under intensive development. One was the theory of neural networks and its use in constructing "brain models" (abstract models of how neural mechanisms might exhibit cognitive functions) (Rosenblatt, 1962). The other was the theory of symbolic computation as manifested in the creation and dominance of LISP as a programming language for AI and for models of psychological processes. Potted histories of the subsequent relationship between these two approaches have become part of the folklore of cognitive science, and the details have been traced in other places (e.g., Dreyfus, 1992). For current purposes, it suffices to say that, although they were initially seen as natural partners, and although research of both types was sometimes even conducted by the same researchers, beginning in the late 1950s, neural network research and computationalism separated into distinct and competing research paradigms. The computational approach scored some early successes and managed to grab the spotlight, appropriating to itself the vivid phrase "artificial intelligence" and the lion's share of research funding. In this way computer science came to provide the theoretical core of mainstream cognitive science for a generation. Neural network research, nevertheless, did continue throughout this period, and much of it was strongly dynamical in flavor. Of particular note here is the work of Stephen Grossberg and colleagues, in which dynamical ideas were being applied in a neural network context to a wide range of aspects of cognitive functioning (see Grossberg, chapter 15).

By the early 1980s mainstream computational AI and cognitive science had begun to lose steam, and a new generation of cognitive scientists began casting around for other frameworks within which to tackle some of the issues that caused problems for the computational approach. As is well known, this is when neural network research burgeoned in popularity and came to be known as *connectionism* (Hinton and Anderson, 1981; Rumelhart and McClelland, 1986; McClelland and Rumelhart, 1986; Quinlan, 1991). Since connectionist networks are dynamical systems, it was inevitable that dynamical tools would become important for understanding their behavior and thereby the nature of cognitive functions. The recent rapid emergence of the dynamical approach is thus due, in large measure, to this reemergence of connectionism and its development in a dynamical direction.

Apart from cybernetics and neural network research, at least three other research programs deserve mention as antecedents to the contemporary dynamical approach. One is derived from the physical sciences via biology, another from pure mathematics, and the third from experimental psychology. The first began with the question: Can the basic principles of description and explanation applied with such success in the physical sciences to simple closed systems be somehow extended or developed to yield an understanding of complex, open systems? In particular, can general mathematical laws be deployed in understanding the kinds of behaviors exhibited by *biological* systems? One natural target was the biological phenomenon of coordinated movement, since it involves regular, mathematically describable motion. Yet the study of coordinated movement cannot avoid eventually invoking notions such as intention, information, and perception, and so must overlap with psychology. At this nexus arose a distinctive program of research into human motor and perceptual skills which relied on resources proposed by physicists and mathematicians such as Pattee, Prigogine, Rosen, and Haken, and was inspired by Bernstein's insights into motor control (Bernstein, 1967). This program is exemplified in the work of Turvey, Kugler, and Kelso (Kelso and Kay, 1987; Kugler and Turvey, 1987).

Dynamics is, in the first instance, a branch of mathematics. Applications of dynamics in various areas of science have often flowed directly from developments in pure mathematics. A particularly dramatic example of this phenomenon has been applications derived from the development, principally by René Thom, of catastrophe theory. This theory is an extension of dynamics, in combination with topology, to describe situations in which there arise discontinuities, i.e., sudden, dramatic changes in the state of a system.[16] Discontinuities are common in the physical, biological, cognitive, and social domains, and are the basis for the formation of temporal *structures*, and so the development of catastrophe theory led directly to new attempts to describe and explain phenomena that had been beyond the scope of existing mathematical methods. Of particular relevance here is application of catastrophe theory to the investigation of language and cognition. Initial proposals by Thom and Zeeman (Thom, 1975; Thom, 1983; Zeeman, 1977) have been taken up and developed by Wildgen (1982) and Petitot (1985a, b) among others. This work has involved some radical and ambitious rethinking of problems of perception and the nature of language.

A third major source of inspiration for dynamical modeling came from Gibson's work in the psychology of perception (Gibson, 1979). Gibson asserted that it was a mistake to devote too much attention to models of internal mechanisms when the structure of stimulus information remained so poorly understood. Since both the world and our bodies move about, it seemed likely to Gibson that the structuring of stimulus energy (such as light) by dynamical environmental events would play a crucial role in the achievement of successful real-time interaction with the environment. The resulting focus on discovery of the sources of high-level information in the stimulus turns out to dovetail nicely with continuous-time theories of dynamic perception and dynamic action. The inheritors of Gibson's baton have had many successes at specifying the dynamic information that underlies perceptual and motor achievement (e.g., see Turvey and Carello, chapter, 13; Bingham, chapter 14). The work of the ecological psychologists has been a key influence in encouraging researchers to adopt a dynamical perspective in various other areas of cognitive science.

These five lines of research have recently been joined by other dynamics-based investigations into a wide variety of aspects of cognition. What explains this recent surge in activity? Partly, of course, it is the spreading influence of the research programs just described. But another important factor has been the rapid development in mathematics of nonlinear dynamical systems theory in the 1970s and 1980s, providing contemporary scientists with a much more extensive and powerful repertoire of conceptual and analytical tools than were available to Ashby or McCulloch, for example. At a more prosaic level, the continuing exponential growth in computing resources available to scientists has provided cognitive scientists with the computational muscle required to explore complex dynamical systems. In recent years a number of new software packages have made dynamical modeling feasible even for researchers whose primary training is not in mathematics or computer science.

Finally, of course, there is the nature of cognition itself. If the dynamical conception of cognition is largely correct, then a partial explanation of why researchers are, increasingly, applying dynamical tools may lie simply in the fact that cognitive systems are the kind of systems that call out for a dynamical treatment.

ACKNOWLEDGMENTS

This research was supported by a Queen Elizabeth II Research Fellowship from the Australian Research Council to the first author, and the Office of Naval Research grants N0001491-J-1261, N0001493, and N0001492-J-1029 to the second author. Critical feedback from John Haugeland, Esther Thelen, and James Townsend was especially useful in its preparation.

NOTES

1. Technically, a differential equation is any equation involving a function and one or more of its derivatives. For more details on differential equations, and the mass-spring equation in particular, see Norton, chapter 2.

2. The notion of phase, like that of dynamical system itself, differs from one context to another. In some contexts, a phase space is taken to be one in which one of the dimensions is a time derivative such as velocity. In other contexts, phase is taken to refer to position in a periodic pattern, as when we talk of the phase of an oscillating signal. Our notion of phase here is a generalization of this latter sense. Since the rule governing a state-determined system determines a unique sequence of points for any given point, every point in the space can be understood as occupying a position (or "phase") in the total pattern (or "dynamic") fixed by the rule. Our use thus accords with the common description of diagrams that sketch the overall behavior of a dynamical system as *phase portraits* (see, e.g., Abraham and Shaw, 1982).

3. For an example of the use of forms of the logistic equation, as a difference equation, in cognitive modeling, see van Geert, chapter 11.

4. In fact, the total state of a computational system is more than just a configuration of symbols. A Turing machine, for example, has at any time a configuration of symbols on its tape, but it is also in a certain head state, and the head occupies a certain position; these must also be counted as components of the total state of the system.

5. In particular, one could not demonstrate that cognitive systems are dynamical systems merely by showing that any given natural cognitive system is governed by some dynamical rule or other. Certainly, all people and animals obey the laws of classical mechanics; drop any one from a high place, and it will accelerate at a rate determined by the force of gravitational attraction. However, this does not show that *cognitive* systems are dynamical systems; it merely illustrates the fact that heavy objects belong to dynamical systems.

6. A more radical possibility is that dynamical systems can behave in a way that depends on knowledge without actually *representing* that knowledge by means of any particular, identifiable aspect of the system.

7. For a more detailed introduction to dynamics, see Norton, chapter 2.

8. Of course, a range of general and quite powerful arguments have been put forward as demonstrating that cognitive systems must be computational in nature (see, e.g., Fodor, 1975; Newell and Simon, 1976; Pylyshyn, 1984). Dynamicists remain unconvinced by these arguments, but we do not have space here to cover the arguments and the dynamicists' responses to them.

9. Turing machines are a particularly simple kind of computer, consisting of one long tape marked with squares that can contain symbols, and a "head" (a central processing unit) which moves from square to square making changes to the symbols. They are very often used in discussions of foundational issues in cognitive science because they are widely known and, despite their simplicity, can (in principle) perform computations just as complex as any other computational system. For a very accessible introduction to Turing machines, see Haugeland (1985).

10. One *inappropriate* way to extract temporal considerations from a computational model is to rely on the timing of operations that follow from the model's being *implemented* in real physical hardware. This is inappropriate because the particular details of a model's hardware implementation are irrelevant to the nature of the model, and the choice of a particular implementation is theoretically completely arbitrary.

11. Ironically, these kinds of assumptions have often been the basis for attacks on the plausibility of computational models. If you assume that each computational step must take some certain minimum amount of time, it is not difficult to convince yourself that the typical computational model has no hope of completing its operations within a psychologically realistic amount of time.

12. Precisely because discrete models are only an approximation of an underlying continuous one, there are hard limits on how well the continuous function can be modeled. Thus, it is well known to communications engineers that one must have at least two discrete samples for each event of interest in the signal (often called Nyquist's theorem). The cognitive corollary of this is that to model dynamical cognitive events that last on the order of a half-second and longer, one must discretely compute the trajectory at least four times a second. Anything less may result in artifactual characterization of the events. Since the time scale of cognitive events is relatively slow compared to modern computers, this limit on discrete modeling of cognition would not itself serve as a limiting constraint on real-time modeling of human cognitive processes.

Timothy van Gelder and Robert F. Port

13. This is true for computational systems when they are considered at the level at which we understand them as computational. The same object (e.g., a desktop computer) can be seen as undergoing continuous state changes when understood at some different level, e.g., the level of electric circuits.

14. Note that when continuous systems bifurcate there can be *genuinely* discrete changes in the attractor landscape of the system.

15. For a more detailed explanation of this equation, see Beer, chapter 5.

16. Note that this informal notion of *discontinuity* should not be confused with the precise mathematical notion. It is a central feature of catastrophe theory that systems that are continuous in the strict mathematical sense can exhibit discontinuities—dramatic, sharp changes—in the more informal sense.

REFERENCES

Ashby, R. (1952). *Design for a brain*. London: Chapman & Hall.

Basar, E. (Ed.). (1990). *Chaos in brain function*. Berlin: Springer-Verlag.

Basar, E., and Bullock, T. H. (Ed.). (1989). *Brain dynamics: progress and perspectives*. Berlin: Springer-Verlag.

Bernstein, N. A. (1967). *The control and regulation of movement*. London: Pergamon.

Busemeyer, J. R., and Townsend, J. T. (1993). Decision field theory: a dynamic-cognitive approach to decision making in an uncertain environment. *Psychological Review, 100*, 432–459.

Devaney, R. L. (1986). *An introduction to chaotic dynamical systems*. Menlo Park, CA: Benjamin/ Cummings.

Dreyfus, H. L. (1992). *What computers still can't do: a critique of artificial reason*. Cambridge, MA: MIT Press.

Elman, J. L. (1991). Distributed representations, simple recurrent networks, and grammatical structure. *Machine Learning, 7*, 195–225.

Erman, L. D., Hayes-Roth, F., Lesser, V. R., et al. (1980). The HEARSAY-II speech understanding system: integrating knowledge to resolve uncertainty. *Computing Surveys, 12*, 213–253.

Fodor, J. A. (1975). *The language of thought*. Cambridge, MA: Harvard University Press.

Forrest, S. (Ed.). (1991). *Emergent computation: self-organizing, collective, and cooperative phenomena in natural and artificial computing networks*. Cambridge, MA: MIT Press.

Gibson, J. J. (1979). *The ecological approach to visual perception*. Boston: Houghton-Mifflin.

Glass, L., and Mackey, M. (1988). *From clocks to chaos: the rhythms of life*. Princeton NJ: Princeton University Press.

Haken, H. (1988). *Information and self-organization: a macroscopic approach to complex systems*. Berlin: Springer-Verlag.

Haken, H. (1991). *Synergetics, computers and cognition*. Berlin: Springer-Verlag.

Haken, H., Kelso, J. A. S., and Bunz, H. (1985). A theoretical model of phase transitions in human hand movements. *Biological Cybernetics, 51*, 347–356.

Haugeland, J. (1985). *Artificial intelligence: the very idea*. Cambridge, MA: MIT Press.

Hinton, G. E., and Anderson, J. A. (Ed.). (1981). *Parallel models of associative memory*. Hillsdale, NJ: Erlbaum.

Holland, J. H. (1975). *Adaptation in natural and artificial systems*. Ann Arbor: University of Michigan Press.

Hopfield, J. (1982). Neural networks and physical systems with emergent collective computational abilities. *Proceedings of the National Academy of Sciences of the United States of America, 79*, 2554–2558.

Kauffman, S. A. (1993). *The origins of order: self-organization and selection in evolution*. New York: Oxford University Press.

Kelso, J. A., and Kay, B. A. (1987). Information and control: a macroscopic analysis of perception-action coupling. In H. Heuer and A. F. Sanders (Eds.), *Perspectives on perception and action*. Hillsdale, NJ: Erlbaum.

Kelso, J. A. S., Ding, M., and Schöner, G. (1992). Dynamic pattern formation: a primer. In J. E. Mittenthal and A. B. Baskin (Eds.), *Principles of organization in organisms*. Reading, MA: Addison-Wesley.

Kugler, P. N., and Turvey, M. T. (1987). *Information, natural law, and the self-assembly of rhythmic movement*. Hillsdale, NJ: Erlbaum.

Lashley, K. S. (1960). The problem of serial order in behavior. In F. A. Beach, D. O. Hebb, C. T. Morgan, et al. (Eds.), *The neuropsychology of Lashley*. New York: McGraw-Hill.

Madore, B. F., and Freeman, W. L. (1987). Self-organizing structures. *American Scientist, 75*, 253–259.

McClelland, J. L., and Rumelhart, D. E. (1981). An interactive-activation model of context effects in letter perception: Part 1, an account of basic findings. *Psychological Review, 88*, 375–407.

McClelland, J. L., and Rumelhart, D. E. (Eds.). (1986). *Parallel distributed processing: explorations in the microstructure of cognition*, Vol. 2: *Psychological and biological models*. Cambridge, MA: MIT Press.

McCulloch, W. S. (1965). *Embodiments of mind*. Cambridge, MA: MIT Press.

Murray, J. D. (1989). *Mathematical biology*. Berlin: Springer-Verlag.

Newell, A., and Simon, H. (1976). Computer science as empirical enquiry: symbols and search. *Communications of the Association for Computing Machinery, 19*, 113–126.

Petitot, J. (1985a). *Les catastrophes de la parole*. Paris: Maloine.

Petitot, J. (1985b). *Morphogenèse du sens*. Paris: Presses Universitaires de France.

Pylyshyn, Z. W. (1984). *Computation and cognition: toward a foundation for cognitive science*. Cambridge, MA: Bradford/MIT Press.

Quinlan, P. (1991). *Connectionism and psychology*. Chicago: University of Chicago Press.

Rosenberg, C. R., and Sejnowski, T. J. (1987). Parallel networks that learn to pronounce English text. *Complex Systems, 1*, 145–168.

Rosenblatt, F. (1962). *Principles of neurodynamics: perceptrons and the theory of brain mechanisms*. New York: Spartan Books.

Rumelhart, D. E., and McClelland, J. L. (Eds.). (1986). *Parallel Distributed Processing: explorations in the microstructure of cognition*, Vol 1: *Foundations*. Cambridge, MA: MIT Press.

Shannon, C. E., and Weaver, W. (1949). *The mathematical theory of communication*. Urbana: University of Illinois Press.

Skarda, C. A., and Freeman, W. J. (1987). How brains make chaos to make sense of the world. *Behavior and Brain Sciences, 10*, 161–195.

Smolensky, P., Legendre, G., and Miyata, Y. (1992). *Principles for an integrated connectionist/ symbolic theory of higher cognition*. (No. CU-CS-600-92.) Computer Science Department, University of Colorado, Boulder.

Thelen, E., and Smith, L. B. (1994). *A dynamic systems approach to the development of cognition and action*. Cambridge, MA: MIT Press.

Thom, R. (1975). *Structural stability and morphogenesis* (Fowler, D. H., Trans.). Reading, MA: Benjamin.

Thom, R. (1983). *Mathematical models of morphogenesis*. Chichester, England: Ellis Horwood.

Touretzky, D. S. (1990). BoltzCONS: dynamic symbol structures in a connectionist network. *Artificial Intelligence, 46*, 5–46.

Von Neumann, J. (1958). *The computer and the brain*. New Haven: Yale University Press.

Wiener, N. (1948). *Cybernetics: or control and communication in the animal and the machine*. New York: Wiley.

Wildgen, W. (1982). *Catastrophe theoretic semantics: an elaboration and extension of René Thom's theory*. Amsterdam: Benjamins.

Winfree, A. T. (1980). *The geometry of biological time*. New York: Springer-Verlag.

Zeeman, C. (1977). *Catastrophe theory: selected papers 1972–1977*. Redwood City, CA: Addison-Wesley.

2 Dynamics: An Introduction

Alec Norton

The word *dynamics* simply refers to the way a system changes or "behaves" as time passes. In the scientific literature, the use of this word may merely indicate that the author wishes to consider some system as evolving, rather than static. Or the author may refer to an attempt to formulate a more precise (either quantitative or qualitative) relation between an increasing time parameter and specific measurable elements of the system. Here, a large body of mathematics called *dynamical systems* becomes relevant. This chapter introduces the reader to certain basics of mathematical dynamical systems that will be useful in understanding the various modeling problems treated in the rest of this book.

We begin with a little background. For more details, the reader is referred to the survey article (Hirsch, 1984). Terms that appear in *italic* type, if not defined where they appear, are defined in the Glossary at the end of the book.

First, a *system* is some collection of related parts that we perceive as a single entity. For example, the following are familiar systems: the solar system, the capitalist system, the decimal system, the nervous system, the telephone system. Hirsch notes:

A *dynamical* system is one which changes in time; what changes is the *state* of the system. The capitalist system is dynamical (according to Marx), while the decimal system is (we hope) not dynamical. A mathematical dynamical system consists of the space of [all possible] states of the system together with a rule called the *dynamic* for determining the state which corresponds at a given future time to a given present state. Determining such rules for various natural systems is a central problem of science. Once the dynamic is given, it is the task of mathematical dynamical systems theory to investigate the patterns of how states change in the long run. (Hirsch, 1984, p. 3).

Mathematical analysis requires that the state of a system be described by some clearly defined set of variables that may change as a function of time. A state is then identified with a choice of value for each of these variables. The collection of all possible (or relevant) values of these variables is called the *state space* (or sometimes *phase space*).

The most important dynamical system in scientific history is the solar system. The sun, planets, and moon are the parts of the system, the states are their possible configurations (and velocities), and the basic problem is to find the dynamic by which one can predict future events like eclipses. Historically this has been done by constructing various geometric or mathematical models for the system, e.g., those of Ptolemy, Copernicus, Brahe, Kepler.

After Galileo, Newton, and Leibnitz, the concepts of instant, velocity, and acceleration permitted the cosmos to be modeled by means of simple mathematical laws in the form of *differential equations*. From these, the visible behavior of the planets could be mathematically deduced with the help of the techniques of calculus. In the 18th and early 19th centuries, Euler, Laplace, Lagrange, the Bernoullis, and others developed "Newtonian" mechanics and the mathematics of differential equations (see section 2.1), used with great success to model an ever-increasing number of different physical systems.

The technique of formulating physical laws by means of differential equations (whose solutions then give the behavior of the system for all time) was so powerful that it was tempting to think of the entire universe as a giant mechanism ruled by a collection of differential equations based on a small number of simple laws. Since the solutions of a differential equation depend on the starting values assigned to the variables, it would then simply be a matter of specifying the *initial conditions*, e.g., the positions and velocities of all the particles in the universe, to then be able to predict with certainty all future behavior of every particle.

Today we know that *sensitivity to initial conditions* makes this impossible in principle, and, even for very small systems with only a few variables, there is another (related) serious difficulty inherent in this program: most differential equations cannot be solved exactly by means of mathematical formulas. For example, to this day the motion of three (or more) point masses in space acting under the influence of their mutual gravitational attraction is understood only in special cases, even though it is a simple matter to write down the differential equations governing such motion.

This profound difficulty remained unapproachable until in 1881 Henri Poincaré published the first of a series of papers inventing the point of view of what we now call dynamical systems theory: the *qualitative* study of differential equations. Rather than seeking a formula for each solution as a function of time, he proposed to study the collection of all solutions, thought of as curves or *trajectories* in state space, for all time and all initial conditions at once. This was a more geometric approach to the subject in that it appealed to intuitions about space, motion, and proximity to interpret these systems. This work also motivated his invention of a new discipline now called algebraic topology. Poincaré emphasized the importance of new themes from this point of view: *stability*, *periodic trajectories*, *recurrence*, and *generic behavior*.

One of the prime motivating questions was (and still is): Is the solar system stable? That is, will two of the planets ever collide, or will one ever escape from or fall into the sun? If we alter the mass of one of the planets or change its position slightly, will that lead to a drastic change in the trajectories? Or, can we be sure that, except for tidal friction and solar evolution, the solar system will continue as it is without catastrophe, even if small outside perturbations occur?

These are qualitative questions because we are not asking for specific values of position or velocity, but rather for general global features of the system over long time periods. This viewpoint requires thinking of the space of all possible states of the system as a geometric space in which the solution trajectories lie (as described below), and then using topological or geometric reasoning to help understand such qualitative features.

After Poincaré, the twentieth century saw this viewpoint expand and develop via pioneering work of Birkhoff (1930s), Kolmogorov (1950s), Smale, Arnol'd, and Moser (1960s), and others. The advent of computers and graphics has assisted experimental exploration, permitted approximate computation of solutions in many cases, and dramatized such phenomena as chaos. Nowadays dynamical systems has expanded far beyond its origins in celestial mechanics to illuminate many areas in physics, engineering, and chemistry, as well as biological and medical systems, population biology, economics, and so forth.

In the case of complex systems like the brain or the economy, the number of different relevant variables is very large. Moreover, firms may enter or leave a market, cells may grow or die; therefore the variables themselves are difficult to firmly specify. Yet the state of mathematical art dictates that any tractable mathematical model should not have too many variables, and that the variables it does have must be very clearly defined. As a result, conceptually understandable models are sure to be greatly simplified in comparison with the real systems. The goal is then to look for simplified models that are nevertheless useful. With this caveat firmly in mind, we now proceed to discuss some of the mathematics of dynamical systems theory.

In the following discussion, we assume only that the reader's background includes some calculus (so that the concept of derivative is familiar), and an acquaintance with matrices. Some references for further reading appear in section 2.4. (For a refresher on matrix algebra, see Hirsch and Smale, 1974.)

2.1 INTRODUCTORY CONCEPTS

In formulating the mathematical framework of dynamical systems, we may wish to consider time as progressing continuously (*continuous time*), or in evenly spaced discrete jumps (*discrete time*). This dichotomy corresponds to the differences between *differential equations* and *difference equations*; *flows* and *diffeomorphisms*. (These terms are defined below.)

We begin with the continuous time case, and proceed to discuss discrete time.

Differential Equations in Several Variables

In this section, we remind the reader of the basic terminology of differential equations. The real variable t will denote time (measured in unspecified units), and we use letters $x, y, z, \ldots$ to denote functions of time: $x = x(t)$, etc. These functions will be the (state) variables of the system under study. If we run out of letters, it is customary to use subscripts, as $x_1(t)$, $x_2(t)$, ..., $x_n(t)$ in the case of n variables, where n is some (possibly very large) positive integer. We denote by R^n the space of all n-tuples $(x_1, \ldots, x_n)$ of real numbers, representing n-dimensional Euclidean space.

The derivative (instantaneous rate of change) of x at time t is denoted $\dot{x}(t)$ (or sometimes $x'(t)$ or $(dx/dt)(t)$). [Note that $\dot{x}$ is the name of the function whose value at time t is $\dot{x}(t)$.]

The derivative $\dot{x}$ of x is a function that itself usually has a derivative, denoted $\ddot{x}$, the *second derivative* of x. This can continue indefinitely with the third derivative $\dddot{x}$, fourth derivative, etc. (though frequently only the first and second derivatives appear).

A *differential equation* in one variable (or one dimension) is simply an equation involving a function x and one or more of its derivatives. (Note that we are speaking exclusively of *ordinary* differential equations—equations in which all of the derivatives are with respect to a single variable (in this case time t). *Partial* differential equations involve partial derivatives of functions of more than one variable, and are not discussed in this chapter.)

Example 1   A simple frictionless mass-and-spring system is often modeled by the equation

$m\ddot{x} + kx = 0$.

Here x is a function of time representing the linear displacement of a mass, and m and k are constants, *mass* and the *spring constant* (or stiffness), respectively. To be clear, we emphasize that this means that for each time t, the number $m\ddot{x}(t) + kx(t)$ is zero. This is satisfied by sinusoidal oscillations in time.

Given this equation, the problem is to find a function $x(t)$ that satisfies this equation. Such a function is called a *solution* of the equation. In fact there will be very many such solutions, in this case one corresponding to each choice of the initial conditions $x(0)$ and $\dot{x}(0)$. The general solution (see Hirsch and Smale, 1974, or any beginning text on ordinary differential equations) is

$x(t) = x(0)\cos((\sqrt{k/m})t) + (\sqrt{m/k})\dot{x}(0)\sin((\sqrt{k/m})t)$.

Typically a system has more than one state variable, in which case its evolution will be modeled by a *system* (or collection) of differential equations, as in

Example 2

$\dot{x} = x + z$

$\dot{y} = 2x + y - z$

$\dot{z} = 3y + 4z$.

Here one seeks three functions $x(t)$, $y(t)$, and $z(t)$, satisfying all three of these equations. This is a *linear* system of equations because it can be written as a single vector equation in the following matrix form: $\dot{X} = AX$, where

$$X = \begin{bmatrix} x \\ y \\ z \end{bmatrix}, \qquad \dot{X} = \begin{bmatrix} \dot{x} \\ \dot{y} \\ \dot{z} \end{bmatrix}, \qquad A = \begin{bmatrix} 1 & 0 & 1 \\ 2 & 1 & -1 \\ 0 & 3 & 4 \end{bmatrix},$$

and we are using ordinary matrix multiplication.

We say this is a *three-dimensional system* because it is expressed in terms of three state variables x, y, z (and hence a solution $(x(t), y(t), z(t))$ defines a curve in *three-dimensional* Euclidean space).

The virtue of a linear equation is that it is relatively easy to solve by standard methods. In a strong sense, linear equations are completely understood.

Of course, often systems of equations are not linear, like

Example 3

$$\ddot{x} = \dot{x} - y^3$$

$$\ddot{y} = -\dot{y} + x^3.$$

If a system is not linear, all bets are off: typically nonlinear equations cannot be solved explicitly. Nonlinear equations are important because (1) most systems are modeled by nonlinear, rather than linear, equations, and (2) solutions can have complicated and interesting behaviors, requiring various qualitative techniques of dynamical systems to analyze. (See examples 10 and 16.)

Vector Fields, Trajectories, and Flows

The matrix notation is very important because it provides us with a way of viewing any system as a *first-order system* involving perhaps more variables (first-order meaning that only the first derivatives of the variables are involved).

Example 4   The system in example 3 can be written as a first-order system by introducing new variables. Let $u = \dot{x}$, $v = \dot{y}$. Then our new state variables are x, u, y, v, and the system in example 3 is equivalent to the four-dimensional first-order system

$$\dot{x} = u$$

$$\dot{u} = u - y^3$$

$$\dot{y} = v$$

$$\dot{v} = -v + x^3.$$

From now on, we suppose that any given system of differential equations has already been put into this first-order vector form. In general, we then write it as

$$\dot{X} = F(X), \tag{1}$$

where $X = (x_1, \ldots, x_n)$ and F is a function from R^n to R^n. Note that for a *linear* system $\dot{X} = AX$, the function F is simply the *linear* function $F(X) = AX$. Within this framework, any differential equation can be specified simply by specifying the function F, called a *vector field*. In coordinates, we can express the value of F as

$$F(x_1, \ldots, x_n) = (F_1(x_1, \ldots, x_n), \ldots, F_n(x_1, \ldots, x_n)),$$

where the functions $F_1, F_2 \ldots, F_n$ are real-valued functions of n variables and are called the *component functions* of the vector field F. Thus, in example 4, we have

$$F(x, u, y, v) = (u, u - y^3, v, -v + x^3)$$

and the component functions are $F_1(x, u, y, v) = u, F_2(x, u, y, v) = u - y^3$, $F_3(x, u, y, v) = v, F_4(x, u, y, v) = -v + x^3$.

An *initial condition* for equation (1) is simply a choice of initial values

$$x_1(0), x_2(0), \ldots, x_n(0)$$

for each of the state variables. Equivalently, this is a choice of an initial vector $X(0)$, which then determines a unique solution of equation (1).

Geometrically, you should think of a vector field on R^n as the assignment of a vector (direction and magnitude) at each point of R^n. Also, $X(t)$ is to be interpreted, for each t, as the coordinates of a point in R^n, so that the function X represents a *trajectory*, or curve, through space. The point $X(t)$ moves around continuously as t increases, tracing out its trajectory.

With this scheme, $\dot{X}(t)$ represents the velocity vector of the trajectory of X at the point $X(t)$, i.e., a vector tangent to the trajectory at that point, whose magnitude is given by the instantaneous speed of the point $X(t)$ along the trajectory. Therefore equation (1) has a simple geometric interpretation: given the vector field F, solutions of equation (1) are simply trajectories that are everywhere tangent to F, and which have speed at each point equal to the magnitude of F. In terms of states, the system of equation (1) simply tells us how the rate of change $\dot{X}$ of the state variable X at time t depends on its position $X(t)$ at that time (figure 2.1).

We have now arrived at our new view of differential equations: by converting them into a system of equations in the form of equation (1), we think of the problem in the following geometric way: given a vector field F, find the solution trajectories that pass through the field in the proper way.

Note that starting at two different points in space will produce two different solution trajectories (figure 2.2), unless the two points happen to lie on a single trajectory to begin with. Typically any given starting point determines a complete trajectory going forward and backward infinitely far in time. Moreover no two trajectories can cross. These are consequences of the so-called fundamental existence and uniqueness theorems for differential equations (see, e.g., Hirsch and Smale, 1974), and are true, for example, for any smooth and bounded vector field.

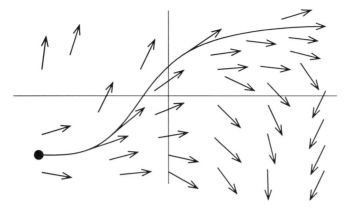

Figure 2.1 A vector field on R^2 along with a single solution trajectory.

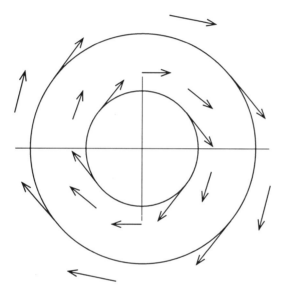

Figure 2.2 Two trajectories for the vector field $F(x, y) = (y, -x)$. These trajectories are periodic cycles.

The object of interest in dynamics, then, is the whole pattern of all the trajectories in the state space R^n. Each trajectory corresponds to a different solution of the equations (corresponding to different initial conditions). We now want to know various properties of this collection of trajectories and how to interpret them in terms of the behavior of the system being modeled. The picture of all the trajectories in the state space (also called the *phase space*) is called the *phase portrait*.

In dynamical systems one denotes the full solution of equation (1) by the *flow* $\phi(t, x)$. This is just a fancy notation for the position of a point x after it has followed its solution trajectory for a time t. For fixed x, $\phi(t, x)$, thought of as a function of t, is then simply a solution trajectory. For fixed t, $\phi(t, x)$,

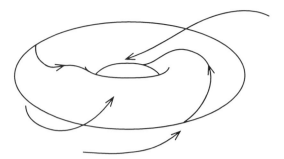

Figure 2.3 A toroidal manifold is shown along with the phase portraits of solutions on and approaching the manifold (in this case, a two-dimensional surface configured in three-dimensional space).

thought of as a function of x, is a transformation of the state space that moves each point along its own trajectory by the time t. The flow $\phi(t, x)$ of a vector field $\mathbf{F}$, then, is in effect the complete solution of equation (1); it gives all of the solutions for all possible initial conditions.

Sometimes only a certain collection of solution trajectories is relevant, all of which happen to lie on some surface inside the full state space (or higher-dimensional analog of a surface, called a *manifold*). By restricting attention to such a manifold, one sometimes speaks of a vector field *defined on the manifold* (figure 2.3). (See Guillemin and Pollack, 1974, for a treatment of the subject of manifolds.)

Discrete Time Dynamics

Consider the simple differential equation in one variable

$$\dot{x} = g(x). \tag{2}$$

The derivative $\dot{x} = dx/dt$ can be approximated by the difference quotient $\Delta x/\Delta t$, where $\Delta t = t_1 - t_0$ is a small difference between two time values, and $\Delta x = x(t_1) - x(t_0)$ is the corresponding difference in the values of the function x.

Hence equation (2) can be approximated by

$$\Delta x = g(x)\Delta t,$$

or, more explicitly,

$$x(t_1) - x(t_0) = g(x(t_0))(t_1 - t_0). \tag{3}$$

Often we are interested in a discrete sequence of evenly spaced times, say $t = 0, 1, 2, 3, \ldots$ It is more common to use one of the letters i, j, k, l, m, n when denoting integers. With this change our equation becomes

$$x(k + 1) - x(k) = g(x(k)),$$

a so-called *difference equation*. We can simplify a little bit by writing $f(x) = g(x) + x$, so that equation (3) becomes

Alec Norton

$$x(k+1) = f(x(k)) \qquad (k = 0, 1, 2, 3, \ldots) \qquad (4)$$

for some function $f \colon R \to R$.

From equation (4), note that $x(k) = f(x(k-1))$, so that

$$x(k+1) = f(f(x(k-1))) \equiv f^2(x(k-1)),$$

where the notation $f^2(x)$ means $f(f(x))$, and in general $f^k(x)$ means $f(f(\ldots f(x) \ldots))$ (k times).

Continuing, we get

$$x(k+1) = f^{k+1}(x(0)) \qquad (k = 0, 1, 2, \ldots)$$

or, more simply,

$$x(k) = f^k(x(0)) \qquad (k = 1, 2, \ldots). \qquad (5)$$

Equation (5) represents the most typical way of viewing a discrete dynamical system: it is one given by *iterating* a function f, starting from various initial values. Moreover x can be a real number or more commonly a point in R^n, in which case f is a function from R^n to R^n.

One should be careful to distinguish this function f from the vector field **F** described just previously, although the concepts are analogous since both describe a change that depends on the current state. One thinks of a vector field as a velocity vector at each point whose coordinates are the values of the coordinate functions of the vector field. In contrast, for a discrete dynamical system, the vector $f(x)$ is thought of as the new location of the point x after one iterate (unit of time).)

Iteration of the function f, starting with the initial value x_0, produces the (*forward*) *orbit* of x_0: the sequence

$$x_0, x_1, x_2, x_3, \ldots,$$

where $x_i = f^i(x_0)$ for $i = 0, 1, 2, \ldots$.

This is to be compared with the orbit of a vector field, which is a continuous trajectory or curve through the state space.

Exercise   Let $f \colon R \to R$ be defined by $f(x) = 2x$. The reader is encouraged to investigate what happens to various points under iteration by f.

Time-One Maps, Poincaré Sections, and Diffeomorphisms

The finite difference approximation discussed above is only one way to arrive at a discrete dynamical system from a differential equation. More commonly, one considers the *time-one map of a flow*, or the *induced map on a Poincaré section*.

Given the flow $\phi(t, x)$ for a vector field F on R^n, one can define a function $f \colon R^n \to R^n$ by the rule

$$f(x) = \phi(1, x).$$

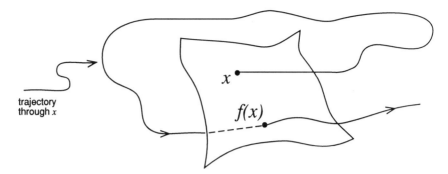

Figure 2.4 A Poincaré section for a vector field, showing a trajectory through x and its next intersection with the cross-section, at $f(x)$. A display of repeated iteration of the function can be very revealing about the dynamic behavior of the trajectories of the vector field.

This function is called the time-one map of the flow; its action is simply to move every point of the state space R^n along its solution trajectory by one unit of time. (Similarly we could just as well define the time-T map.)

Because of the standard properties of the flow of a nice-enough vector field, the time-one map will be a *diffeomorphism*, i.e. a differentiable mapping f of R^n that has a differentiable inverse (denoted f^{-1}). By means of f^{-1} one can move backward in time to obtain the *backward orbit* of x_0,

$$x_0, x_{-1}, x_{-2}, \ldots,$$

where $x_{-k} = (f^{-1})^k(x_0) \equiv f^{-k}(x_0)$. One can also speak of the *full orbit*

$$\ldots, x_{-2}, x_{-1}, x_0, x_1, \ldots.$$

Another very useful technique for passing from a flow to a diffeomorphism is to consider a Poincaré section, or cross section, of the vector field. This is a surface (of dimension one less than the dimension of the state space) that is nowhere parallel to the vector field. Starting at some point on this surface, if one follows the solution trajectory through that point, one will immediately leave the surface, travel around in state space, and then perhaps return to strike the surface once more (figure 2.4). Wherever this happens, one can define a *first-return mapping* which takes the initial point on the Poincaré section and sends it to the next intersection point of the trajectory with the section. (The trajectory may never again intersect the cross section, in which case the first-return map is not defined at that point.)

Orbits of the first-return map correspond closely with the trajectories of the flow, and one can often study the latter simply by investigating the former. The great merit of passing from a flow to a first-return map for some cross section is that one thereby reduces by one the number of dimensions of the problem, and this often makes a big difference in our ability to visualize the dynamics. In practice real three-dimensional systems of differential equations are often studied by taking a cross section and looking at the first-return map. Duffing's equation is interpreted this way in example 16 below.

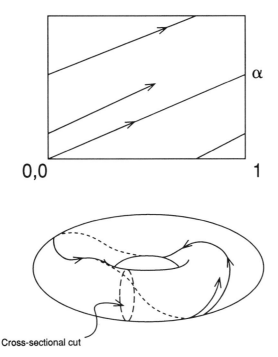

Cross-sectional cut

Figure 2.5 The top panel shows the torus opened up into a plane. Thus the left and right edges represent the same sectional cut through the torus, and the top and bottom edges similarly represent the same ring around the torus. A portion of an irrational trajectory is also shown. The bottom panel shows the usual view of the torus embedded in R^3.

Example 5 Consider the vector field on the torus given by irrational rotation, as follows. We represent the torus as the unit square in the plane with the opposite sides identified (glued together). On it define a constant vector field with the time-one map $F(x, y) = (1, \alpha)$, where α is some irrational number between 0 and 1. The solution trajectories are then lines parallel to the vector $(1, \alpha)$ through every point on the torus (figure 2.5). (When a trajectory reaches the right-hand edge, it reappears at the corresponding point on the left, and similarly for top and bottom.)

We can take as our Poincaré section the vertical circle indicated by the dotted line. The reader should convince himself or herself that the first return map in this case is the irrational rotation of the circle $f(x) = x + \alpha \pmod 1$. See example 13 below for this notation.

Endomorphisms

Not all diffeomorphisms arise as time-one mappings of flows. Given a random diffeomorphism, one can still iterate it and thereby produce a dynamical system. In fact it is not necessary that the function be invertible: any function $f: R^n \to R^n$ can be iterated and so the forward orbits are always defined (but perhaps not the backward orbits). A possibly noninvertible function from a space to itself is called an *endomorphism* (as opposed, e.g., to a function from one space to another). Any such thing can be iterated and thought of as a dynamical system, and in fact some very simple examples can produce very interesting dynamics.

Example 6 The subject of much current research is the study of the dynamics of functions on the unit interval $[0, 1]$ like $f_a(x) = ax(1 - x)$, where a is some positive parameter, each different value of which yields a different function. The problem here is to understand the dynamics of the functions f_a for different values of a, and how the dynamics changes or *bifurcates* as the parameter (hence the function) is changed.

For values of a between 0 and 1, the reader can discover that every point in $[0, 1]$ simply tends to 0 under iteration. As a increases past 1, 0 becomes a repelling fixed point and a new attracting fixed point appears. The system has undergone a *bifurcation*. Further increase in the value of a leads to successive bifurcations in which the attracting fixed point splits into two attracting points of period two, each of which later splits into pairs of period-four points, etc. At the end of this so-called period doubling cascade, the map becomes chaotic. The interested reader should see Devaney (1986) for more on this topic.

Attractors and Bifurcations

There is no general agreement on the precise definition of an attractor, but the basic idea is straightforward. Here is one version.

Let F be a vector field on R^n, with flow ϕ. A closed set $A \subset R^n$ is an *attractor* for this flow if (1) all initial conditions sufficiently close to A have trajectories that tend to A as time progresses, (2) all trajectories that start in A remain there, and (3) A contains no smaller closed subsets with properties (1) and (2).

More precisely, let $d(x, A)$ denote the distance between a point x and the set A. Condition (1) means there exists $\varepsilon > 0$ such that $d(x, A) < \varepsilon$ implies $d(\phi_t(x), A) \to 0$ as $t \to +\infty$.

Condition (3) follows if A contains a dense orbit, that is, a trajectory that visits every region of A infinitely often. Sometimes this stronger condition is used instead of (3).

A similar definition can be made for diffeomorphisms (i.e., for the discrete case).

Attractors are important because they represent the long-term states of systems. If we imagine that most real systems have already been evolving for some time before we observe them, then we would expect that attractors represent the behaviors we actually observe in nature, at least for systems that have settled into their long-term behaviors.

Often, as in a marble rolling around in a bowl, the attractor is simply the fixed point corresponding to the resting position at the bottom [attracting fixed point, or sink: examples 8, 11(ii)]. Other times the attractor is a periodic orbit representing a steady-state oscillating behavior [attracting periodic orbit: example 9 $(a < 0)$].

One of the insights afforded us by dynamical systems theory is that these are not the only regular long-term behaviors for systems: there are also *strange* or *chaotic attractors*. In this case the attractor contains within it expanding directions that force nearby trajectories to rapidly diverge from one another as time progresses (examples 15, 16). Often such attractors have a fractal geometric structure, with irregularity repeated at arbitrarily small scales.

A point of fundamental interest is to understand how an attractor changes as the dynamical system (vector field, differential equation, diffeomorphism) itself is changed. The system may contain various parameters that can take on different values and lead to different dynamical behaviors. As the parameters change gradually, it is of great importance to know how the attractors change.

Often, a small change in the parameters will lead to a correspondingly small change in the shape of the attractor, but no change in its qualitative features. Other times, a parameter value is reached at which a sudden change in the qualitative type of the attractor occurs. When this happens, we say the system has undergone a *bifurcation*.

The study of bifurcations is a large subject, but we can say a few words here about the simplest cases of bifurcation of an attracting fixed point (see Guckenheimer and Holmes, 1983, for more information).

Consider the following equations:

$$\dot{x} = a - x^2 \qquad \text{(saddle-node)}, \tag{i}$$

$$\dot{x} = y + x(a - x^2 - y^2) \tag{ii}$$

$$\dot{y} = -x + y(a - x^2 - y^2) \qquad \text{(Hopf)}.$$

Next to the name of each of two standard bifurcations is an equation or set of equations that exhibit that bifurcation as the parameter a passes through the value zero. The following sequence of diagrams illustrates what happens as a system undergoes a saddle-node bifurcation in one dimension (figure 2.6).

The case of the Hopf bifurcation is described further in example 9 below.

One point of importance here is that a "generic" (i.e., typical) system of equations

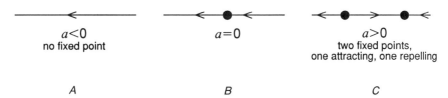

$a<0$	$a=0$	$a>0$
no fixed point		two fixed points, one attracting, one repelling
A	B	C

Figure 2.6 With respect to equation (i) above, with $a < 0$ there is no fixed point, as shown in A; with $a = 0$ there is a saddle as in B; and with $a > 0$, there are two fixed points, one stable and one unstable, as shown in C.

$$\dot{X} = F_\mu(X),$$

depending on one real parameter μ, will, at a bifurcation value for a fixed point, undergo one of these bifurcations (Guckenheimer and Holmes, 1983). That is, along some one- or two-dimensional subset of the state space containing the equilibrium, the qualitative behavior of the system will look like one of these. Therefore understanding the bifurcations (i) and (ii) means understanding all at once the way attracting fixed points bifurcate for generic systems of even very large dimension.

There are other standard types of bifurcations that can occur when further constraints are imposed on the systems being considered. Any specific family of systems might have a nonstandard bifurcation, but then a small pertubation of the family may produce a standard one. Furthermore, systems that depend on two or more parameters will generally undergo more complicated types of bifurcations (as studied in the field of bifurcation theory).

2.2 STABILITY AND CHAOS

To introduce some further concepts, including *stability* and *chaos*, we devote the remainder of this chapter to a series of basic illustrative examples.

Example 7 Here we return to consider the frictionless mass-and-spring system of example 1 (figure 2.7),

$$m\ddot{x} + kx = 0.$$

For simplicity we take $m = k = 1$. Letting $\dot{x} = u$, we obtain the two-dimensional first-order system

$$\dot{x} = u$$

$$\dot{u} = -x.$$

Here, the vector field is simply $F(x, u) = (u, -x)$, and the solution is

$$x(t) = x_0 \cos(t) + u_0 \sin(t)$$

for the initial conditions $x(0) = x_0$, $u(0) = u_0$ (see Hirsch and Smale, 1974, to learn how to solve such equations). The phase portrait in the phase plane (i.e.,

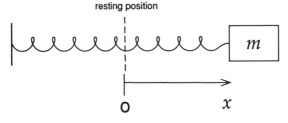

Figure 2.7 A simple, frictionless oscillator with a mass (m) at position x and with resting position 0.

Alec Norton

state space R^2) then consists of concentric circles centered at the origin (figure 2.8).

An initial condition corresponds to some starting point in the plane, and then the state (x, u) of the system evolves according to $(x_0 \cos(t) + u_0 \sin(t), -x_0 \sin(t) + u_0 \cos(t))$: i.e., it follows the circular trajectories in a clockwise direction. (It is easier to see this in the case $u_0 = 0$, when the solution is of the form $(x_0 \cos(t), -x_0 \sin(t))$.)

For the physical system, this corresponds to the mass oscillating back and forth periodically about its equilibrium position at the origin. Since x represents position (distance from rest position) and u velocity, we see that the speed of the mass is greatest as it is passing through its equilibrium position, and the speed is zero when the spring is stretched or compressed the most.

The origin $(0, 0)$ corresponds to the state in which the mass is sitting at rest at its equilibrium position. This is called a *fixed point* of the flow, or a *zero* of the vector field. A system starting out at a fixed point will remain there forever.

An important question about a fixed point is: Is it stable? There are two notions of stability of fixed points, as follows. A fixed point is *Lyapunov-stable* if points near the fixed point continue to remain nearby forever. The fixed point is *asymptotically* stable if nearby points actually tend toward the fixed point as time progresses.

For our mass-and-spring example, the origin is Lyapunov-stable but not asymptotically stable: points near the origin follow circular trajectories that remain nearby but do not tend to the origin in the limit as $t \to \infty$.

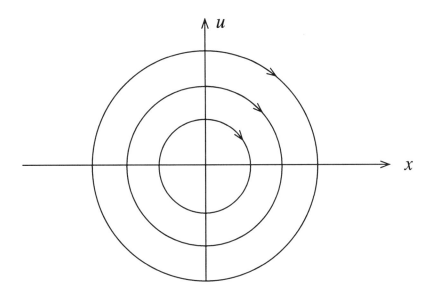

Figure 2.8 With no friction, the oscillator will sweep out concentric circles in the phase plane. The diameter of the circle depends on the initial state. Larger circles mean wider excursions along x as well as larger peak velocities along $\dot{x}$.

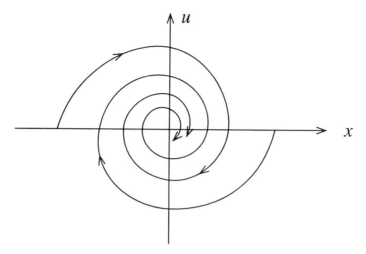

Figure 2.9 The phase portrait of a mass-and-spring system with a friction term. Amplitude of x and $\dot{x}$ approach zero over time.

Example 8 Since the drag force of sliding friction is roughly proportional to velocity, adding friction to the mass-and-spring system of the previous example is typically modeled by adding a first-derivative term to the equation, as in

$$\ddot{x} + \dot{x} + x = 0.$$

In terms of our variables x, u,

$$\dot{x} = u$$

$$\dot{u} = -x - u.$$

The solution trajectories of this system turn out to spiral down toward the origin (figure 2.9). Since the vector field is $\mathbf{F}(x, u) = (u, -x - u)$, $(0, 0)$ is again a fixed point. By inspecting the phase portrait, it is clear that this fixed point is both Lyapunov-stable and asymptotically stable. We also say it is an *attracting fixed point*, because all nearby points tend in toward the origin as time proceeds. (An attracting fixed point is the simplest version of an *attractor*.) This makes physical sense because we expect friction to cause the oscillations to die down toward the resting position.

Example 9 Let a be a real parameter, and consider the system

$$\dot{x} = y + (a - x^2 - y^2)x$$

$$\dot{y} = -x + (a - x^2 - y^2)y.$$

For $a < 0$ we have a single attracting fixed point at the origin. Observe what happens when a is gradually increased. When it reaches $a = 0$, we still barely have a single attracting fixed point toward which every trajectory tends. When $a > 0$, the origin becomes a *repelling* fixed point—i.e., a fixed

Alec Norton

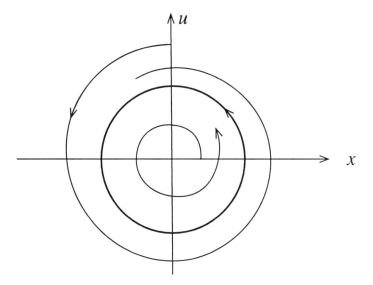

Figure 2.10 Phase portrait for $a > 0$. Note the attracting periodic orbit shown with the thicker line. The origin is a repelling fixed point.

point toward which trajectories tend as time runs backward to $-\infty$. Springing out from the origin is a new attractor: an *attracting cycle* (or attracting periodic orbit). All trajectories, except for the fixed point at the origin, tend toward this new cycle. This phemomenon is a simple example of a *Hopf bifurcation*, in which, as a parameter changes across some critical value (in this case 0), an attracting fixed point gives birth to an attracting cycle and itself becomes repelling (figure 2.10).

Example 10 A simple frictionless pendulum, as shown in figure 2.11, can be described by the variables x and u, where x is the angle of deviation from the vertical, and $u = \dot{x}$ is the angular velocity (figure 2.11).

Newton's laws lead to the equations of motion

$$\dot{x} = u$$

$$\dot{y} = -c \sin x,$$

where c is a constant proportional to the length of the pendulum.

Fixed points appear whenever the vector $(u, -c \sin x)$ is zero; i.e., $u = 0$ and $x = k\pi$, and k is any integer. The phase portrait is shown in figure 2.12.

Here the origin is Lyapunov-stable, while the point $p = (\pi, 0)$ is an unstable equilibrium called a *saddle point*. Two trajectories tend asymptotically toward p in forward time, two in backward time, and other trajectories come near but then veer away. This point corresponds to the pendulum at rest pointed straight up, delicately balanced. Any small perturbation will tend to push it onto one of the nearby trajectories—either one cycling around a rest point (oscillating behavior), or one moving off toward infinity to the right or left (the pendulum rotates continuously around in one direction).

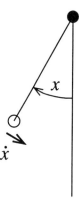

Figure 2.11 A simple pendulum has variables x, position, and $\dot{x}$, velocity. Part of its phase portrait, without friction, resembles figure 2.8, but is expanded in figure 2.12.

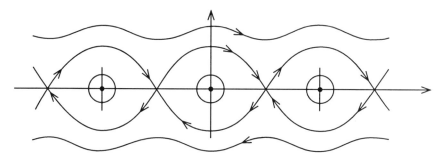

Figure 2.12 The phase portrait of a frictionless pendulum. The three dots represent the same critical point (at the bottom). The sinusoids are the separatrices leading to the unstable saddle points when the pendulum remains straight up. The wavy lines at top and bottom are trajectories that spin around over the top of the pendulum in opposite directions.

Example 11 We now turn to similar considerations for some discrete-time dynamical systems, beginning with three simple functions of one variable:

(i) $f(x) = 2x$. This simple diffeomorphism has a single fixed point (zero) which is *repelling*, meaning that nearby points move away under iteration (or: nearby points tend to zero under backward iteration, i.e. application of the inverse f^{-1}). All other points tend to infinity under iteration. Figure 2.13*A* shows behavior beginning at $\pm 1/2$.

(ii) $g(x) = f^{-1}(x) = (1/2)x$. Here the origin is an attracting fixed point, and all points on R tend to 0 under iteration.

(iii) $h(x) = e^x - 1$. Here, points to the left of the origin tend, under interation, to 0, while points to the right tend away. Since 0 is then neither an attracting nor a repelling fixed point, it is called a *neutral* fixed point.

Note that $|f'(0)| > 1$, $|g'(0)| < 1$, and $|h'(0)| = 1$. This is no accident: If x_0 is a fixed point for f, and $|f'(x_0)| > 1$, then x_0 is repelling; if less than 1, x_0 is attracting; if equal to 1, the fixed point may be either repelling, attracting, or neutral.

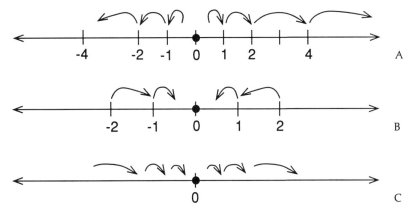

Figure 2.13 *A, B,* and *C* illustrate iteration of the functions $f(x) = 2x$, $g(x) = (1/2)x$, and $h(x) = e^x - 1$, respectively.

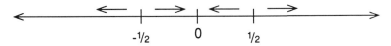

Figure 2.14 Illustration of example 12. Beginning near $-1/2$ or $+1/2$, points either converge toward 0 or tend to infinity.

Exercise Find an example of a function $f : R \to R$ such that 0 is a repelling fixed point, but $|f'(0)| = 1$.

Example 12 Let $f(x) = x^3 - (3/4)x$ (figure 2.14). This function has three fixed points: $x = 0, 1/2, -1/2$. The reader should check that 0 is attracting and $1/2, -1/2$ are repelling.

Example 13 The circle can be represented by the unit interval $[0, 1]$ with the endpoints identified; since 0 and 1 are then two representatives for the same point, we omit 1 and take the notation $[0, 1)$ as representing all magnitudes from 0 to 1, but excluding 1 itself.

We think of the numbers in $[0, 1)$, then, as representing angles on the circle (where a full turn is taken to have angle 1 instead of 2π to simplify notation). Addition in $[0, 1)$ is then just the addition of angles on the circle: $(1/2) + (3/4) (\text{mod } 1) = 5/4 (\text{mod } 1) = 1/4 (\text{mod } 1)$. Here "mod 1" tells us to add or subtract an integer so that the result lies in $[0, 1)$.

Consider the rotation $R_a(x) = x + a (\text{mod } 1)$ for various rotation angles a.

(i) $a = 1/3$. Here R_a has no fixed points, but every point of the circle is a *periodic point* of period 3: after three iterations of R_a, each point return to itself (figure 2.15).

In general, we say a point x_0 is a *periodic point of period k for a map f* if $f^k(x_0) = x_0$, and if k is the least positive integer with this property. A periodic

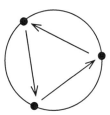

Figure 2.15 A graphic representation of a periodic point with period 3. Successive rotations of multiples of 1/3 lead only between the three angles shown.

point of period 1 is a fixed point. An attracting periodic point for f of period k is one which is an attracting *fixed* point for the iterate f^k. Similar definitions hold for repelling and neutral periodic points. In the case of the rotation by 1/3, every point is a neutral periodic point of period 3.

(ii) $a = 2/5$. Check that each point of the circle $[0, 1)$ is a periodic point of period 5.

(iii) $a = 1/\sqrt{2}$. In this case R_a has no periodic points of any period, because the angle of rotation is irrational. Instead of repeating after a finite number of steps, the forward orbit of each point fills in the whole circle more and more densely. We say that the map is *transitive*, because it has a dense orbit (and in fact every orbit is dense).

Example 14 Let $f: [0, 1) \rightarrow [0, 1)$ be the *angle doubling map of the circle,* defined by $f(x) = 2x \, (\mathrm{mod}\, 1)$. This map exhibits the basic features of "chaos," namely, *sensitive dependence on initial conditions, transitivity,* and *dense periodic points.*

Sensitive dependence on initial conditions means that any two nearby starting points rapidly diverge from each other as iteration continues. That is, if x and y are two nearby points on the circle, then the distance between $f^k(x)$ and $f^k(y)$ grows (exponentially fast) with k. The reason is that one can see from the definition of f that the distance between any two nearby points simply doubles with every iterate—until the distance between them is more than 1/4. See below for more on this concept.

Dense periodic points: Any small interval on the circle contains a periodic point (of some period) for f. To see this, the reader can verify that if $x = p/(2^k - 1)$ for any integer p, that $f^k(x) = x \, (\mathrm{mod}\, 1)$.

In particular, there are infinitely many periodic points for f (though only finitely many for any given period).

Transitivity: This simply means there is a dense orbit. This is not hard to prove, but we will not do so here. (See Devaney, 1986.)

Example 15 The *solenoid map* is a three-dimensional diffeomorphism defined on the "solid torus" $S = S^1 \times D^2$, where S^1 denotes the unit circle and $D^2 = \{(x, y) \in R^2: x^2 + y^2 \leqslant 1\}$ is the unit disk in the plane (figure 2.16).

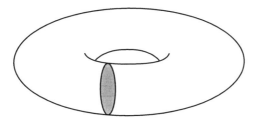

Figure 2.16 This solenoid map is defined on a solid torus, as opposed to the two-dimensional manifold of figure 2.5.

Figure 2.17 A single iteration of the mapping in example 15 generates a longer, narrower solid torus that wraps around twice inside the first one.

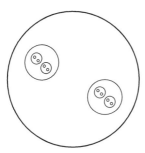

Figure 2.18 Repeated iteration of the mapping in example 15 embeds additional tori within each previous torus. This display is a cross-sectional cut through three iterations.

The mapping $f: S \rightarrow S$ is defined by

$$f(\theta, x, y) = (2\theta, (1/4)x + (1/2)\cos\theta, (1/4)y + (1/2)\sin\theta).$$

The action of f is to stretch the solid torus out, wrap it around twice, and place it inside the original solid torus (figure 2.17).

Then f^2 takes the original solid torus to a very thin one wrapped four times around the original, etc. The resulting attractor, obtained as the intersection of all these thinner and thinner tubes, is called a *solenoid* (figure 2.18).

Every point of the original solid torus tends toward this solenoid; points on the solenoid itself experience a stretching apart very similar to that of the angle-doubling map of the circle. In fact, f restricted to the solenoid exhibits all the chaotic properties of the angle-doubling map, so it is called a *chaotic attractor*. (See Devaney, 1986.)

Example 16   *Duffing's equation.* We can illustrate a few more ideas with the equation

$$\ddot{x} + \delta \dot{x} - x + x^3 = \gamma \cos(\omega t),$$

used to model the forced vibration of a stiff metal beam suspended vertically between two fixed magnets on either side (see Guckenheimer and Holmes, 1983; Vector Fields, Trajectories, and Flows, above). Here δ is a small positive constant, γ represents the magnitude of the periodic forcing term, and ω represents the frequency of forcing. Though there is no general solution expressible in terms of elementary formulas, we can still study the system as follows.

Writing this as a first-order system, we get (changing x to u):

$$\dot{u} = v$$

$$\dot{v} = u - u^3 - \delta v + \gamma \cos(\omega t).$$

Note that the vector field is time-dependent, so this is a *nonautonomous* system. To deal with this, we convert the time variable into a third-space variable as follows:

$$\dot{u} = u$$

$$\dot{v} = u - u^3 - \delta v + \gamma \cos(\omega \theta).$$

$$\dot{\theta} = 1.$$

Here u and v are as before and θ is a new angular variable which increases at constant rate from zero to $2\pi/\omega$ and then repeats. (This is permitted because of the periodicity of cosine.) Therefore we can think of θ as moving around a circle of length $2\pi/\omega$.

The state space is then $R^2 \times S^1$: the space of all triples (u, v, θ), where u and v are real numbers and θ represents an angle. In this case a convenient cross-section is the two-dimensional set $\Sigma = \{(u, v, \theta): \theta = 0\}$, where we can take u and v to be coordinates for Σ.

The first-return map $f : \Sigma \to \Sigma$ of the flow to this cross-section is then simply the time-$2\pi/\omega$ map of the flow for the three-dimensional system above, restricted to Σ. This is easy to present graphically by plotting the orbits of various points with a computer: start at any point $(u, v, 0)$, and plot the u and v coordinates of the trajectory after times in multiples of $2\pi/\omega$. Here is the picture one obtains for the values $\omega = 1$, $\delta = 0.2$, $\gamma = 0.3$ (figure 2.19).

The result is apparently a chaotic attractor (viewing it only in cross-section). That is, nearby initial conditions tend closer to this set as time progresses, but within the set, nearby orbits diverge from one another. See Guckenheimer and Holmes (1983) for a more complete discussion of this situation.

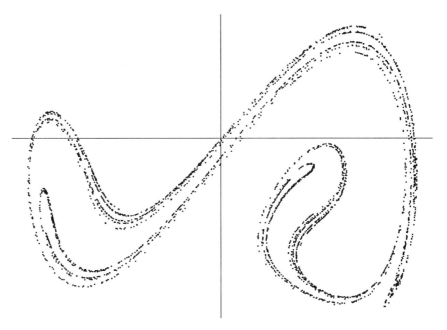

Figure 2.19   The Poincaré section (first-return map) of Duffing's equation is shown after 1000 iterations. This chaotic attractor shows how points will converge to this complex shape under iteration, yet within this general pattern nearby points diverge from one another.

2.3   CONCLUSIONS

We have made a general survey of what dynamical systems are and how they are analyzed by mathematicians. It should be clear that one way this research has progressed is by relaxing the search for specific solutions for specific initial conditions. The sensitive properties of dynamical systems force us to do so, since very small differences in initial conditions may be magnified over a short time to dramatically different states.

Instead, a wide range of methods have been developed during the 20th century for describing and evaluating the qualitative properties of dynamic models. These qualitative and topological properties turn out to offer many insights into the behavior of actual complex systems.

REFERENCES

Devaney, R. L. (1986). *An introduction to chaotic dynamical systems*. Menlo Park, CA: Benjamin/ Cummings.

Guckenheimer, J., and Holmes, P. (1983). *Nonlinear oscillations, dynamical systems, and bifurcations of vector fields*. New York: Springer Verlag.

Guillemin, V., and Pollack, A. (1974). *Differential topology*. Englewood Cliffs, NJ: Prentice Hall.

Hirsch, M. W. (1984). The dynamical systems approach to differential equations. *Bulletin of the American Mathematical Society (New Series)*, 11, 1–64.

Hirsch, M. W., and Smale, S. (1974). *Differential equations, dynamical systems, and linear algebra.* New York: Academic Press.

Guide to Further Reading

This has been a very elementary introduction to some basic ideas of mathematical dynamical systems. For the reader wishing to learn more, the visual introduction to dynamics by Abraham and Shaw (1982) is especially accessible. For a general mathematical background, read Hirsch (1984). This article begins with an excellent historical discussion of dynamical systems, requiring no technical background, followed by some general discussion at a higher technical level than this chapter. The last section of the article discusses so-called monotone flows, important in population dynamics. Also excellent reading is the little paperback by Steven Smale (1980), a collection of articles and essays by one of the founders of the modern era of dynamical systems. It contains a reprint of his important 1967 mathematical survey article "Differentiable Dynamical Systems," along with nontechnical discussions, reminiscences, and essays on economics and catastrophe theory. For a basic textbook on dynamics, try Devaney (1986), which has been an influential introduction to discrete dynamical systems. Much of the book can be read with only a background in calculus, and it provides a valuable overview of many of the key ideas of modern dynamical systems. Hirsch and Smale jointly authored a popular text (1974) which gives a thorough introduction to the basic concepts, with many examples and applications. Only an exposure to the calculus of several variables is required; the reader need have no prior familiarity with linear algebra or differential equations. For a text with a more applied flavor, there is Guckenheimer and Holmes (1983), which concentrates on continuous time dynamics. Many standard examples of nonlinear differential equations are discussed and analyzed, and there is some treatment of bifurcation theory. This is an excellent general reference for those who have already been exposed to a first course in differential equations, such as Hirsch and Smale. Also excellent is the result and detailed survey by Robinson (1995). For those wishing to learn more about manifolds, look to Guillemin and Pollack (1974) as a standard and accessible mathematics text. Prerequisites include linear algebra and a year of analysis past calculus. An excellent and more advanced treatment is Hirsch (1976).

Abraham, R., and Shaw, C. (1982). *Dynamics—a visual introduction*, Vols. 1–4. Santa Cruz, CA: Ariel Press.

Devaney, R. L. (1986). *An introduction to chaotic dynamical systems.* Menlo Park, CA: Benjamin/Cummings.

Guckenheimer, J., and Holmes, P. (1983). *Nonlinear oscillations, dynamical systems, and bifurcations of vector fields.* New York: Springer Verlag.

Guillemin, V., and Pollack, A. (1974). *Differential topology.* Englewood Cliffs, NJ: Prentice-Hall.

Hirsch, M. W. (1984). The dynamical systems approach to differential equations. *Bulletin of the American Mathematical Society (New Series)*, 11, 1–64.

Hirsch, M. W., and Smale, S. (1974). *Differential equations, dynamical systems, and linear algebra.* New York: Academic Press.

Hirsch, M. W. (1976). *Differential topology.* New York: Springer Verlag.

Robinson, C. (1995). *Dynamical systems.* Boca Raton, FL: CRC Press.

Smale, S. (1980). *The mathematics of time.* New York: Springer Verlag.

3 Time-Scale Dynamics and the Development of an Embodied Cognition

Esther Thelen

EDITORS' INTRODUCTION

Cognition is in many ways an emergent phenomenon. Mature cognitive systems are the result of a long and always ongoing process of self-organization and adaptation, and if we really want to fully understand the nature of the mature system we must see it in this context. One of the strengths of the dynamical approach to cognition is its ability to describe the emergence of complex structures and processes. Consequently, the first of the applications-oriented chapters in this book is a sweeping view of cognitive development from a dynamical perspective.

As a developmental psychologist, Esther Thelen's immediate concern is with questions such as: How do infants acquire such seemingly simple skills as reaching out and grasping an object? She finds that dynamics provides the best framework within which to formulate specific answers, but it also provides much more. Thelen argues that taking up the dynamical perspective leads to dramatic reconceptualization of the general nature of cognitive development, and indeed of the product of development, mind itself.

Laying the foundation for these ambitious claims are highly detailed developmental studies. In this chapter Thelen describes two sets of studies, one of reaching and grasping, and another of coordinated kicking. Both are cases of infants acquiring control over the forceful interactions of their bodies with their environments. Dynamics provides a powerful vocabulary for describing these developmental processes. Changes in behavior come to be understood in terms of attractors, stability, potential wells, parameter adjustment, and so forth. Taking over this vocabulary facilitates a whole new way of seeing how sophisticated capacities emerge. New abilities take shape in a process of gradual adjustment of the dynamics governing the range of movements currently available; this adjustment is effected by exploratory activity itself. Since infants can begin this process of adjustment from very different starting points, it is highly unlikely that there is any predetermined, genetically coded program for development. It is rather a self-organizing process in which solutions emerge to problems defined by the particular constraints of the infant's immediate situation.

How does this connect with the nature of cognition and mind? Thelen adopts the Piagetian perspective that "thought grows from action and that activity is the engine of change." At the same time, however, she rejects Piaget's conception of the end-state of cognitive development as an objective mind reasoning about the world by means of abstract logical structures. This "objectivist" conception of mind has recently been challenged by philosophers and cognitive scientists who insist that mind is fundamentally embodied, and, in particular, that the bodily experience of force is essential to thought and language. Consequently, to understand how infants come to be able to control the forceful interactions of their bodies with their environment is to gain insight into the nature of cognitive processes as they emerge. A dynamical perspective on development, according to which change occurs at many time scales, and change at one scale shapes and is shaped by change at others, thus provides a general framework within which to understand the origin and nature of embodied cognition, and in this sense, to help resolve the problem of the relation of mind to body.

3.1 INTRODUCTION

As this book attests, the concepts and tools of dynamical systems offer powerful and perhaps revolutionary ways of understanding human cognition. For nearly half a century, the dominant metaphor for understanding mind, brain, and behavior has been that of information processing, a metaphor based on serial computation. Dynamics has the potential, I believe, to supplant this accepted view with new principles that are more biologically plausible and yet apply across many levels of mental phenomena.

The implications of adopting a noncomputational view of mind are profound and widespread. Such a view challenges long-held and cherished constructs such as symbolic representation, the modularity of knowledge, and the distinction between knowledge and performance. But dynamics also holds great promise for understanding some of the most recalcitrant issues in the mind sciences. These may include such problems as the origins of novelty in brain and behavior, the sources of individual differences, the nature of category formation, and the fluid and context-sensitive aspects of human behavior (see Smith and Thelen, 1993; Thelen and Smith, 1994).

One of the most persistent issues in the brain-mind sciences is that of mind-body dualism. What is the relation between the abstract and reflective mind and the qualities of the flesh and of the world in which mind sits? How can these two levels coexist in the same individual? Is there a connection between the domains of biology and physics and those of mind and cognition? Such questions have plagued philosophers and psychologists for millennia, and still do. As Searle (1992) wrote, "... there really has been only one major topic of discussion in the philosophy of mind for the past fifty years or so, and that is the mind-body problem" (p. 29).

I suggest here that a dynamical systems analysis can offer insights into this "major topic of discussion." I argue that understanding transactions between body and mind should begin with a developmental analysis based on dynamics, the study of processes that are continuous in time. In particular, if we can show continuities *in time* between the physical and the mental—that they share the same dynamics—we can bridge the gulf between the traditional duality of levels, body and mind. To understand continuities in time, we must look toward development, growth, and change within an individual's life span. Toward this goal, I will argue, as have other developmental psychologists before me, that the mundane physical events of infancy are indeed the very foundations of thinking, the uniquely human way of adapting to the world. But I want to go further. I will also claim that the way in which infants acquire seemingly simple body skills supports a particular view of human cognition, thinking grounded in and inseparable from bodily action. That thought is thus *embodied*—containing within it the very essence of our bodily experience—flows directly from considering minds' origins and from the assumption that the time scales of processes at different levels are tightly interwoven. There can be no discontinuities in processes that occur over time. What infants do in everyday life, what they perceive, how they act, and what they remember are joined seamlessly to how they think. Since a major developmental task of infancy is gaining control of the body, cognition is thus embodied as its origins deal with actions of the body in the world. Thus, since the processes of perceiving and acting and the processes of thinking continue to share the same time-scale dynamics, they cannot be separated in levels. Mind and body are united at the beginning of life and nowhere along life's path do their processes split asunder.

3.2 MODELS AND METAPHORS

My line of reasoning depends on taking seriously the evocative title of this book, *Mind as Motion*. What the editors had in mind, I believe, was to portray mental activity not as a structure of static representations, but as flow through time. An apt metaphor in this case is a mountain stream flowing over a rocky bed. Both the global course of the stream and its local whirls and eddies emerge from the architecture of the streambed and the force of the water flow, but are in no way programmed by those constraints. The pattern of a whirlpool may be quite stable as long as the water pressure and streambed do not change. Or a new pattern may form in response to a stray rock entering the bed or after a heavy rain. The eddy itself is not symbolically represented anywhere, yet it contains within it both its past history—the melting of the snow on the mountain and the configuration of the bed upstream—and its immediate constraints.

Under particular laboratory conditions, the behavior of water flow and turbulence can be mathematically captured by systems of nonlinear dynamical equations. Indeed the science of dynamical systems is preeminently a mathematical science, born from just such problems of understanding complex and time-based processes as patterns of flow. But whether or not our particular mountain stream can, in practice, be mathematically described by us does not alter the fundamental truth of its existence, that *pattern lives in flow and lives only in flow.*

Because mathematical modeling has also been a dominant tradition in the cognitive sciences, there is a seductive danger of appropriating the mathematics of dynamical systems with insufficient consideration of their fundamental truths. Fitting dynamical equations to behavioral data and simulating behavior with dynamical models are critical steps in our understanding. But to adopt mathematical dynamics without acknowledging the radical implications of a truly dynamical cognition reduces dynamics to just another model du jour, or at worst, a redescription of the prevailing structural and computational state of affairs. Along with the mathematical language of dynamics, must come, I believe, the fundamental assumption that pattern only emerges in process, and thus a rejection of symbols, structures, and stages as "things" that live in the head. I will also argue here that a dynamical approach erases the traditional boundaries of mental life. There can be no description of a purely "inner life": every mental and behavioral act is always emergent in context, just as are the eddies in the stream. Perception, action, and cognition form a single process, with no distinction between what people really "know" and what they perform. There are no distinctions between acting, learning, and developing; processes of change all live within a single, nested time scale.

3.3 SOME BACKGROUND ON THE DEVELOPMENT OF BODY AND MIND

I think the best way to put some life into these abstractions is to explain the conventional wisdom about the relation of the simple motor skills of infancy and the emergence of thought. Until quite recently motor skill development was seen as a necessary, but psychologically uninteresting part of infant development. Textbooks routinely published (most still do) illustrations and explanations of the stagelike emergence of the major "motor milestones" such as rolling over, sitting up, crawling, and walking. The message these texts delivered was the amazing orderliness and universal character of the unfolding skills. This view of development came directly from the work of Arnold Gesell and Myrtle McGraw in the 1930s and 1940s, who described these stages in great detail (see, e.g., McGraw, 1940; Gesell and Ames, 1940). More important was their developmental account: the ordered progression of the emergence of skills reflected the maturation of the brain. They believed that motor coordination and control was a product of autonomous brain development, which happened as infants got older. Although some contemporary developmentalists still invoke maturation as a developmental mechanism, there is no evidence that the brain autonomously matures from codes in the genes, and like an independent executive, causes the body to obey.

Unwittingly perhaps, these early pioneers fostered a profoundly dualistic view. They envisioned motor development as thoroughly biological and encapsulated. Although infants' skills reflected changes in the brain, such skills were not part of mind in any way. In fact, Gesell himself disdained mentalistic descriptions and preferred to stick exclusively with observables in posture and movement. What has come through in the textbooks, and in the minds of many developmentalists, is that the biological side of human existence lives in the first few chapters, and having dispensed with our biological side, we can now move on to more interesting chapters.

3.4 THE PIAGETIAN LEGACY

It was the seminal developmental theorist Jean Piaget who made developmentalists consider another approach: that thought grows from action and that activity is the engine of change. Piaget believed that infancy—the sensorimotor period, he called it—formed the foundation of cognition through building the mental structures in which higher thought was embedded. Piaget (1952) described his own infants with brilliance and understanding, surely the best developmental descriptions ever written. In his words, even the baby's simple acts—sucking and batting, looking and smiling—took on profound meaning. According to Piaget, mental life was truly constructed through the combination and change of these simple acts.

Where I and many other contemporary developmentalists differ from Piaget is not in his account of the seamless connections between action and thought, but in the very nature of mind that is the product of this developmental process. Piaget believed that human cognition was a biological adaptation designed to know the truths about the world by logical structures. He wanted to understand how people acquired and perfected these logical structures during development. Piaget made several assumptions that may be challenged by a dynamic cognition—first, that there are logical relations in the world to be discovered, and second, that people symbolically represent these relations in mind through a series of propositional structures.

Readers may recall that in the typical Piagetian developmental sequence of understanding, say, objects or space, young infants are prisoners of their immediate perceptions and they cannot escape the boundaries of their bodies. They do not understand, for example, that an object still exists when it is hidden from sight, or that the window stays in the same place when they rotate their bodies. According to Piaget, therefore, infants and children must shed their subjective, context-grounded, illogical, and embodied solutions for the ideal abstractions of formal logic. That is, real cognition means rising above the here-and-now of bodily existence, of perception and action in the world, to a level of pure symbol manipulation, as development proceeds inexorably toward real cognition. Thus, although Piaget broke from the maturationists and gave experience a preeminent role as a developmental mechanism, he retained their fundamental dualism.

3.5 ALTERNATIVES TO MIND-BODY DUALISM

Although rarely recognized or acknowledged, some form of mind-body dualism is a continuing assumption behind, and the consequence of much contemporary cognitive science. Cognitive models that seek to represent an objective and knowable world with formal systems of symbols, logic, and computation have been termed *objectivist* (Johnson, 1987; Lakoff, 1987), *materialist* (Searle, 1992), and *cognitivist* (Varela, Thompson, and Rosch, 1993). These critics point out that two kinds of profound dualism result from assuming that the world is understood through propositional logic or computational structures or that mind is at core rational, encapsulated, abstract, and a priori. The first is the denial of the relevance of the physical body in all its instantiations through movement, feeling, and emotion. The second is the separation of intelligent behavior from the subjective self, from consciousness, imagination, and from commonsense understanding. In both cases, these critics argue, cognitivist models are divorced from major and essential aspects of human experience.

There is a new, but growing, challenge to rational and propositional views of mind. These thinkers reject the assumption that minds work like digital computers. They suggest that knowing—categorizing the world, acting in it, giving the world meaning, and reflecting upon our acts—is at core non-propositional, fluid, messy, imaginative, personal, emergent, constructive, contextual, and metaphorical. They consider that knowledge and consciousness are not above experience, but directly grounded in it; the terms used are *embodied* (Johnson, 1987; Lakoff, 1987; see also Talmy, 1988), *enactive* (Varela, Thompson, and Rosch, 1993), and embedded in the *background* (Searle, 1992). There is no separation of mind from body because there is no sense in which the mental is abstracted from the material. All is process, all is emergent. Consciousness, imagination, beliefs, and desires are coequal with reasoning and language, and all are as much part and parcel of human neural activity as is movement or perception.

3.6 EMBODIED COGNITION

One promising path to reconciliation of persistent dualism is through a psychology of embodied cognition. According to Johnson (1987), humans make sense of the world not through abstract, propositional logic (although they can use logic to describe the world) but in a profound and fundamental way, based on real, bodily experience. At the very core of meaning—the way we categorize, remember, talk about, and act in the world—are our experiences as physical beings within a physical world. For example, we encounter *containment* continually in our daily lives. As Johnson (1987) writes:

We are intimately aware of our bodies as three-dimensional containers into which we put certain things (food, water, air) and out of which other things emerge (food and water wastes, air, blood, etc.). From the beginning, we experience constant physical containment in our surroundings (those things that envelope us). We move in and out of rooms, clothes, vehicles, and numerous kinds of bounded spaces. We manipulate objects, placing them in containers (cups, boxes, cans, bags, etc.) In each of these cases there are repeatable spatial and temporal organizations. In other words, there are typical schemata for physical containment. (p. 21)

These ideas of containment, Johnson maintains, come to pervade not only our actions but our thought and our language. For instance, he believes that prepositions such as *in, out, over, near, under,* and so on have meaning only because we have this pervasive, embodied notion of containment—we have experienced it in daily life. The extensions of containment go beyond logic into metaphor and imagery, so that understanding of the term *leave out* in the sentence, "I don't want to leave any relevant data out of my argument" (p. 35) goes beyond the physical relationship to a more metaphorical one, based nonetheless on the primal physical understanding.

Embodiment may be at the core of our understanding of literature as well. For example, Turner (1991) suggests that our recognition of the symmetries in poetic structure and metaphor has its origins in the symmetries and polarities of the body, and that we learn these relationships because we have lived with them in embodied form. "We have a felt, schematic, embodied understanding of bilateral symmetry, and we employ this schematic understanding constantly, moment to moment, in every aspect of our existence, to make sense of our world and to interact with it" (p. 70). The highest levels of human art are part of these interactions.

Along with symmetry and containment, the idea of *force* embodiment is particularly relevant to my developmental account here (Johnson, 1987; Talmy, 1988). Physical force is something that we deal with at every instance that we move. In order to move through space, we must control our muscle forces. And all our causal relations with our environments require some sort of forceful interaction as we act on objects or they act upon us. Because forceful interactions pervade our daily experience, they also come to infuse meaning. In language, force is the root meaning of verbs expressing compulsion, blockage, counterforce, diversion, enablement, attraction, and so on. Although these verbs may be used in abstract ways, "I am attracted to the ideas of John Dewey," the meaning is of a forceful pull toward them. Likewise, the common verbs such as *could, must, can, might,* and so on are understood because our experience has included forceful necessity, overcoming barriers, impulsion, and other acts of force on the environment. Language, in Johnson's and Talmy's views, taps into prelinguistic meaning, rather than giving meaning. Experience gives meaning.

3.7 DEVELOPMENTAL DYNAMICS AND EMBODIED COGNITION

Can we move from these philosophical issues of the nature of mind to consideration of the processes and mechanisms by which real people acquire an embodied cognition in their real minds and brains? Here is where I believe that the solution will lie in dynamical conceptualizations, and especially by looking at the origins of cognition from a dynamical perspective. But my claim is even stronger: that the developmental data are compelling in support of these new anticomputational views. What is required is to reject both Piaget's objectivist vision of the end-state of development as looking like a Swiss logician, and the maturationist conviction that there is an executive in the brain or a code in the genes that directs the course of development. Instead, I consider development to be a continuous, contingent, emergent, embedded, nonlinear process that is captured by general principles of dynamical theory.

In particular, I will show in the remainder of the chapter how a dynamical view of development supports *force* embodiment, a particular aspect of a nonobjectivist cognition. To do this, I begin with a summary of a dynamical systems approach to the development of action and cognition emphasizing the notion of embedded time scales. Next I describe several experimental studies that show that understanding and controlling body forces is a foundational task of infancy. Finally, I offer a more abstract account of how the simple motor tasks of infancy can become embedded in the dynamics of higher cognition.

3.8   A DYNAMICAL SYSTEMS APPROACH TO DEVELOPMENT

A dynamical systems approach to development offers an alternative to both the maturationist and Piagetian accounts I described earlier (readers are referred to the following for extended explications: Smith and Thelen, 1993; Thelen, 1989; Thelen, Kelso, and Fogel, 1987; Thelen and Smith, 1994; Thelen and Ulrich, 1991). A fundamental assumption in a dynamical approach to development is that behavior and cognition, and their changes during ontogeny, are not represented anywhere in the system beforehand either as dedicated structures or symbols in the brain or as codes in the genes. Rather, thought and behavior are "softly assembled" as dynamical patterns of activity that arise as a function of the intended task at hand and an individual's "intrinsic dynamics" or the preferred states of the system given its current architecture and previous history of activity. Behaving organisms are systems with high dimensionality: they are composed of many, heterogeneous subsystems—neural, physiological, mechanical, and so on—with a nearly infinite number of possible combinations of elements. In dynamical terms, we can see actions and mental life as manifestations of self-organization of these multiple contributing elements. That is, the behavior represents a reduction of the degrees of freedom of the contributing subsystems into a pattern that has form over time. Using my mountain stream example, the flow pattern of the water may be complex, but the pattern is an enormous reduction of the system's potential complexity arising from the configuration of the stream bottom, the individual water molecules, rate of flow, temperature, wind, and so on, all of which contribute to, but do not program the pattern. Similarly, behavior, although complex, has "sucked in," so to speak, the complexity of the subsystems that support it.

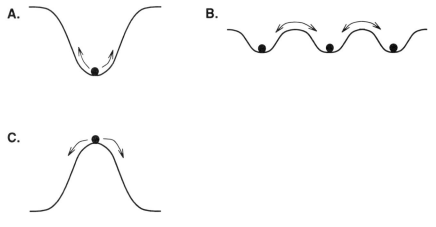

Figure 3.1 Potential well depiction of relative stability of states in a dynamical system. (*A*) Attractor. (*B*) Shallow attractors showing multistable states. (*C*) Repellor.

Some of the resulting self-organized patterns of action and thought are very stable because of the intrinsically preferred states of the system and the particular situation at hand. Such patterns of thought and action may be thought of as strong attractors in the behavior space. They attract nearby trajectories, and performance is consistent and not easily perturbed. In the conventional depiction, the potential well is narrow and deep (figure 3.1A). Other patterns are unstable, they are easily perturbed by small changes in the conditions, and performance within the same subject is highly variable and not dependable. Their potential wells are shallow and the system easily shifts between multiple patterns (figure 3.1B). Portions of the space may actually act as repellors, representing coordinative patterns that rarely appear and are highly unstable when they do (figure 3.1C).

Development, then, can be envisioned as a changing landscape of preferred, but not obligatory, behavioral states with varying degrees of stability and instability, rather than as a prescribed series of structurally invariant stages leading to progressive improvement. Although some behavioral preferences are so stable that they take on the qualities of a developmental stage, the stability is a function of the organism-in-context, not a set of prior instructions. In other words, development looks stagelike only because in the immediate assembly of the activity within a context, certain patterns are strongly preferred. Stages are not obligatory prescriptions; rather, they are descriptions of probabilities of certain states.

Developmental change, in turn, can occur only as current preferred patterns are modified by changes in the cooperating elements or the conditions that assemble the pattern of activity. According to general dynamical principles, change cannot occur if the system is rigidly stable—if the attractor is too strong. As system parameters change, however, the coordination of the participating elements may dissolve, resulting in the system searching for a new pattern of stability. Thus, new forms of behavior—the first step or the

Time-Scale Dynamics and the Development of an Embodied Cognition

first word or the ability to remember the location of the window—can be seen as the product of the confluence of components within a specific problem context rather than the revelation of innate abilities or the inevitable march of determined stages. Dynamical systems shift or bifurcate into new attractors through the destabilization of existing stable forms. Development is likewise a series of both gains and losses as old ways of solving problems are replaced by more functional forms.

This series of evolving and dissolving attractors can be depicted as a landscape of potential wells over time (figure 3.2). In the landscape, time is represented as flowing from back to front. Each horizontal curve represents a state space at a particular point in time: a stability landscape, or the probability that a particular pattern will emerge in a given situation. These are depicted as potential wells, as in figure 3.1. Deep wells represent highly probable behavioral outcomes, while flat portions of the curves indicate the system will hardly ever take on that configuration. As the organism grows, perceives, acts, remembers, and encounters new situations, the old stabilities may be modified or lost completely to new forms as dynamic bifurcations or phase shifts. In addition, the landscape may develop areas of multiple stabilities, representing the more differentiated and adaptive abilities that come with age. These are shown as wide attractors depicting a general category of actions, and containing multiple small basins standing for multiple, task-specific solutions. Note again that the landscape does not prescribe or predetermine a class of behaviors; it is rather a representation of the probabilities of certain actions given particular supporting contexts.

3.9   EMBEDDED TIME SCALES

In this approach, the continuity of time scales is of critical importance. Development, which happens over weeks, months, and years, is part and parcel of the same dynamics as real-time activity, the time scale of seconds and minutes. Mental states and the actions they engender are fluid, flexible, task-specific, and stochastic (not inevitable); they arise only in the confluence of the organism's intrinsic dynamics and the task. Development has no independent dynamics, but development happens because the organism is continually acting and thinking in the environment, and these activities themselves change the organism. *Thus, how individuals solve problems in the real-time scale directly affects the solutions that evolve in ontogenetic time.* Development begins with the local dynamics; it is the local dynamics that shape the long-time landscape.

To put this notion somewhat more formally, let us consider the transition from spontaneous movements of limbs to intentional actions, as I describe more concretely below. From birth, and long before infants can sit, crawl, walk, or reach for objects, they are continually waving their arms and kicking their legs. Moving limbs have many springlike characteristics, and indeed, early spontaneous movements in infants may be modeled by a simple,

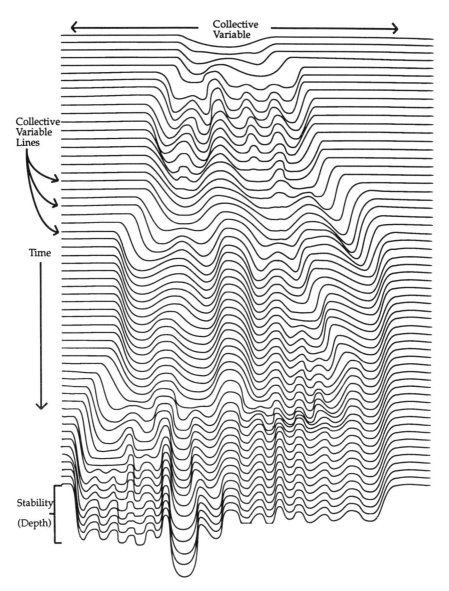

Figure 3.2 An ontogenetic landscape; development is depicted as a series of evolving and dissolving attractors. Time moves from back to front. Each horizontal line portrays the probability at any point in time that the system (as indexed by a collective variable) will be in various attractor states. Deep and steep attractors are very stable. Note that the attractor states must flatten out—the system must lose stability—before a new landscape furrow develops. As time progresses the landscape develops multiple stable behavioral attractors. (From Muchisky, M., Gershkoff-Stowe, L., Cole, E., et al., in press.)

Time-Scale Dynamics and the Development of an Embodied Cognition

damped mass-spring with a regular forcing function (Thelen, Corbetta, Kamm, et al., 1993; Thelen, Kelso, and Fogel, 1987), represented by equation (1),

$$mx + kx + Sx = F(t) \tag{1}$$

where x is the displacement of the spring and its derivatives, m is mass, k is the frictional or damping coefficient, S is stiffness, and $F(t)$ is the time-dependent energy burst provided by muscle contraction. In this equation of motion describing the ongoing state of the limb system, the coefficients m, k, and S are all *parameters* of the system, and $F(t)$ can also be "parameterized," or take on many values. At any point in time, the mass and the frictional coefficient are constant, as these are determined by the child's anatomy and the elastic and viscous properties of the muscles. However, for each instance of movement, two contributions to the spring can be modulated: the stiffness, determined by the ratio of contraction of agonist and antagonist muscles, and the timing and amplitude of the energy delivered to the limb through the forcing function. In early infancy the settings of these parameters are likely not intentional, but are rather a function of the infant's generalized state of excitement or arousal. That is, excited infants generate more stiff and more vigorous movements, with consequent higher amplitudes and velocities. During normal everyday activities, therefore, infants experience a wide range of spring parameters as they move in and out of a range of energy states, from highly aroused to deep sleep.

Of course, flailing arms and legs are not very useful. In order to achieve intended goals—to put an attractive toy into the mouth or to locomote toward the family pet—infants must adjust their limb spring parameters very specifically to achieve a requisite level of stiffness and they must impart bursts of muscle energy at just the right level and time. They *learn* to do this, I believe, from experiencing the many different values of the spring parameters generated by their spontaneous movements and movements produced in the presence of a goal. That is, the process involves *exploring* the range of parameter values in the state space and *selecting* those values that match the affordances of the environment and the goals of the child. Thus particular spring-parameter values emerge as attractors in the landscape for certain classes of actions, as might be depicted in figure 3.2.[1]

Thus, the first way that the local dynamics evolve into developmental dynamics is through the system continually learning as it acts, each action providing information on the local landscape, and the cumulative effect cascading into the developmental landscape. But there is a second way in which the time scales of action are seamlessly woven with the time scales of development. In equation (1), I characterized mass and damping as constants, which they are over the course of a single activity. Over longer time scales, however, both parameters change dramatically as infants gain weight and as the composition of their limb tissues changes. Most important for our dynamical account is that these changes, too, are a function of the local dynamics. Just as adults can change their body architecture through athletic training, so too do infants directly modify their structures through movement and weightbearing. Activity changes the biochemistry and the anatomy of muscles and bones—it makes them larger, stronger, more dense, more efficient, and so on. These changes occur over a more prolonged time scale than do changes in behavior, but they are part and parcel of the same dynamic. Thus, equation (1) both captures a self-organizing system in real time and is embedded in a larger dynamic specifying a relation between activity and parameters like mass and stiffness.

The spring dynamic may also account for phase shifts or discontinuities, that is, the appearance or disappearance of novel forms. For instance, when newborn infants are held upright, supported under the arms, and with their feet on a table, they typically perform steplike movements. These leg movements may be described by the spring equation. But over the next few months, these stepping movements disappear. In earlier studies, Fisher and I showed that newborn step disappearance was likely a result of the leg mass increasing at a faster rate than muscle strength (Thelen and Fisher, 1983). Babies' legs get too fat for their muscles to lift up! In terms of equation (1), m is increasing faster than F. The effect would be to decrease the displacement and velocity to a point where the energy cannot overcome the mass, and no movement is possible: a behavioral shift. (This shift has been simulated experimentally by adding progressively heavier weights to infants' legs; Thelen, Fisher, Ridley-Johnson, et al., 1982.) Conversely, as infants gain relatively more strength than mass in the latter part of the first year, they shift back to being able to lift their legs in the upright position, and even to support their weight.

The point of this example is to illustrate the impossibility of drawing distinctions between the time scales of change. Although change occurs in the fractions of a second of a human action, in the days and weeks of learning, and in the months or years of what we call development, all are embedded in the same, interrelated dynamics. This notion of the continuity and embeddedness of time scales is made especially transparent in the example of limbs-as-springs with tunable parameters. But I hope to show that the example goes beyond biomechanics in two ways. First, I maintain that the developmental processes by which infants learn to tune their limb springs—exploration and selection—are the same for all behavioral development, including the development of higher cognitive processes. And second, that "limb tuning" itself, as a preeminent activity during infancy, lays a substantive foundation for all mental activities.

3.10 DEVELOPMENTAL ORIGINS OF EMBODIED COGNITION

In section 3.1, I claimed that a major developmental task of infancy was gaining control of the body. This becomes evident to any person who has observed an infant even for a short time. Babies spend much of their waking hours doing things with their bodies—poking, banging, bouncing, crawling, waving, kicking, crying, babbling. These activities often look playful and sometimes look rather disconnected from any particular intentional goal. I will give some examples of studies of such movements. What the dynamical approach suggests is that, because of the seamless continuities between time scales and levels, these common and indeed unremarkable movements may be laying the foundation of an embodied cognition. As infants explore and learn how to control the forceful interactions of their bodies within their environment, they learn about forces in the specific and local context of those activities. As the force dynamics, in turn, pervade many and varied activities, a more abstracted sense of force emerges and indeed becomes inherent in the dynamics of all mental activity.

3.11   LEARNING ABOUT FORCES IN INFANCY

In this section I present several examples of infants exploring and learning how to control the forceful interactions of their bodies with their environments. The situations are those in which infants have certain desires and goals and need to solve force-environment problems in order to get what they want. In each case, this involves multiple processes—some motivation to do the task, the ability to perceive the task and the layout of the environment, and the ability to control the limbs and body sufficiently to seek a match between their motivation and the particular demands of the task. The examples are young infants learning new skills—in this case how to reach and grasp an object and how to best kick their legs in order to get a overhead mobile to move.

Reaching

We reach and grasp objects so many hundreds of times during the day that it seems to be the most commonplace of acts. Reaching, in reality, requires extraordinary coordination and control. To reach for your morning coffee, you must first translate the three-dimensional position of the cup, transduced through your visual system into a set of coordinates that allow you to move your arm—in a sense converting head-eye coordinates into shoulder-hand coordinates. This is so you can plan on where you want your hand to end up. But that is just the beginning of your problems. Moving your hand is not like controlling a video game with a joystick, where the input is directly related to the output. The anatomy of your arm and the construction of muscles makes the system highly nonlinear—muscles stretch in different ways depending on what you are doing—and it is nearly impossible to get your shoulder and elbow working together to get your hand to do something in a perfectly straight line (try rapidly drawing a long, perfectly straight line on a blackboard!). If you move your arm forward rapidly, you need to hold your trunk steady, or it will follow along. Also, a rapid movement creates its own internal perturbations—forces generated at the shoulder knock the elbow off course. As adults, we have compensated for these non-linearities so thoroughly that we do not even know they are there.

The neural, mechanical, and computational interface needed for human arm trajectory formation poses a major, and yet unsolved problem engaging engineers, neuroscientists, robotics specialists, and computer scientists. If the control problem has got them stymied at MIT, how in the world does a 2-month old or a 10-month old infant do it? One way might be to build in solutions beforehand. This would be the same as putting the solutions in the hardware design—circuits and chips that have the computations figured out and wait for the baby to turn them on. This leads us to the baby-in-the-head problem. Who designed the chips? Did they get in the head through natural selection, so that people with better reach programs grabbed more food and thus were at a reproductive advantage?

Studying the problem of the origins of reaching from a dynamical systems perspective begins with constructing an attractor landscape, as illustrated in figure 3.2. That is, we want to know, across time, and for a particular situation, which patterns of behavior are stable and when they change. We need to know when systems shift into new forms and when they stay the same. This, in turn, will allow us to discover what parameters actually engender the change. Of the many subsystems that contribute to the final behavior, which are critical in the emergence of a stable reach attractor? To learn this about reaching, my colleagues and I tracked the development of reaching in four infants week by week from the time they were 3 weeks old, barely able to lift even their heads, until they were 1 year old and grabbing things, feeding themselves Cheerios, and playing pat-a-cake. Because, according to our dynamical principles, new forms of behavior must be discovered from the current inherent dynamics, we recorded not just infants' reaching behavior but their ongoing, spontaneous, nonreaching movements as well. Thus, we were able to observe how new forms arose from the dynamics of the existing modes.

The most dramatic transition in reaching were the infants' first successful attempts to touch objects held out for them (Thelen et al., 1993). In our study, two infants reached first at 12 and 15 weeks of age, and the other two, at 20 and 21 weeks. We discovered several important things about this transition to first reaches. First, that infants fashioned reaching from their ongoing movement dynamics. Second, that because individual infants had individually different spontaneous prereaching movements, they had to solve different problems to get the toys they wanted. Third, that all of the infants had to solve problems of adjusting their limb forces to the task. To illustrate this, I contrast in this chapter just two of the four infants, Gabriel and Hannah, before, during, and after their reaching transition. Figure 3.3 is a photograph of Gabriel in the experimental setup.

These two infants had dramatic differences in their overall movement energy. Gabriel was a very active infant. When we placed him in an infant seat, his posture was stiff, his head thrust forward, and he flapped his arms in

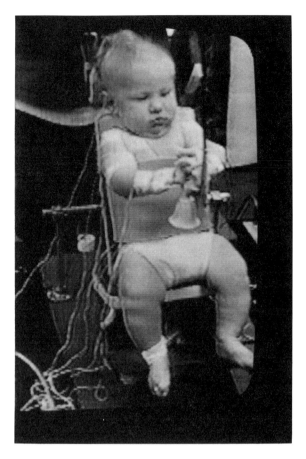

Figure 3.3 Gabriel in the experimental setup, with movement sensors and electromyographic electrodes tracking three-dimensional displacements of his arms and muscle activity.

seeming avid anticipation of the toy, almost seeming to fly out of the chair. Gabriel's movements were characterized by wide excursions, high velocities, and repetitive cycling. Hannah, on the other hand, was more of a looker than a doer. She was alert and engaged, and she assessed the situation carefully before moving. Her posture was relaxed, and her movements were smooth and deliberate.

Gabriel's prereaching movements fit well the model of limb as oscillating spring. Figure 3.4 illustrates Gabriel's spontaneous flapping movements in the week before he reached. I have plotted two examples of the excursions of his hands over the 14 seconds of motion, recording on a *phase plane*, which plots two dimensions of the movement, displacement and velocity, against each other. Although this is a small sample of behavior, it resembles the periodic dynamical behavior of a *limit cycle*, depicted as a closed orbit to which nearby trajectories are attracted. In a damped system such as a limb, oscillations are maintained by a periodic infusion of energy, provided in this case by bursts of muscle contraction in Gabriel's shoulder muscles. These phase portraits are

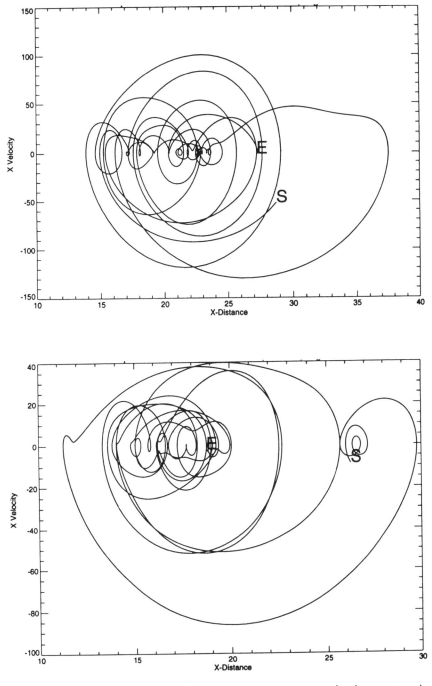

Figure 3.4 Two examples of Gabriel's spontaneous arm movements when he was 14 weeks old (the week before the onset of reaching) depicted on a phase plane: direction in the x-axis (movement from left to right; origin is to the infant's left.) vs. velocity. Each hand trajectory is about 14 seconds of movement.

Time-Scale Dynamics and the Development of an Embodied Cognition

remarkable in their similarity to portraits generated by a forced mass-spring. (Formal characterization of the attractor dimension is not possible because normal infants never produce the long series of movements and thus, the volume of data needed for such analyses.)

In contrast, I have no such recordings of Hannah's spontaneous arm movements. Before she learned to reach, she kept her arms close to her body and made mostly small movements of her hands. In terms of equation (1), she did not provide sufficient force or stiffness to overcome the mass of her arm. Her arms did not enter a limit cycle attractor because the energy parameters were too low.

It should be apparent that in order to make the transition from their preferred spontaneous upper limb movements to limb movements in the service of reaching out and getting a toy, Gabriel and Hannah faced different spring problems. By 3 to 4 months of age, both infants seemed to have a pretty good idea that they wanted the toy and they also seemed to "know" where it was located in space. However, both of their problems were force-related —in Gabriel's case how to get his energetic, off-the-wall movements under control so he could get his hand in the vicinity of the toy. Hannah, in contrast, had to add energy—she needed to stiffen her muscles and extend her arm.

When we observed the actual first-reach dynamics, this is what we saw. Gabriel's first reaches emerged right out of his flaps. He swatted at the toy by going right from the flap to a reaching movement. His movements were stiff, and largely generated from the shoulder. Hannah, in contrast, had slow, well-coordinated movements initiated from a dead stop. She generated low velocities and low forces. Figures 3.5 and 3.6 illustrate these differences by presenting exemplar movements just before and during their very first reaches. In each figure, the top panels show hand pathways as projected onto a two-dimensional plane (like a movie screen in front of the infant). The second set of panels gives the corresponding three-dimensional speeds of the movements, and the third row of panels, the actual calculated torques acting at the shoulder (for details of the model used to calculate torques, see Schneider, Zernicke, Ulrich, et al., 1990; Thelen, Corbetta, Kamm, et al., 1993).

Hannah (see figure 3.5) solved her reaching problem by moving slowly and deliberately, and her resulting movements are rather smooth, direct, and mature-looking. Her hand takes a relatively direct course to the object; she generates low velocities and corresponding low forces at the shoulder. Although Gabriel (see figure 3.6) attempted to slow down his movements as he approached the toy, he still seemed to be captured by his exuberant spring dynamics. Note that his hand pathway has large loops and diversions on the way to the target, and his movements are fast compared with Hannah's. His movements generated high inertial torques and his muscles also produced large forces. The continuity of Gabriel's reach with the spring dynamics of his arms is especially clear when the reaches are viewed in the context of ongoing movements in the phase plane: figure 3.7 gives two examples. The actual

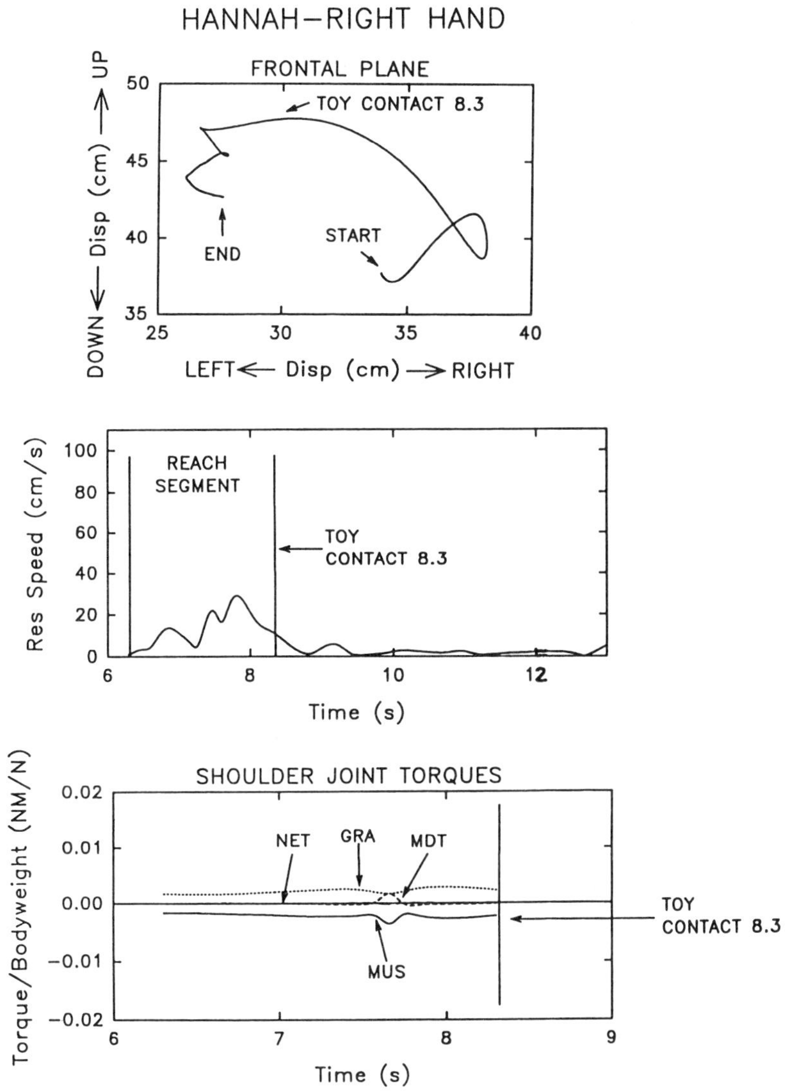

HANNAH—RIGHT HAND

Figure 3.5 Hannah's first goal-directed reaches at age 22 weeks. (*Top*) Hand trajectory projected onto the frontal plane. (*Middle*) Resultant three-dimensional hand speed during the reach segment. (*Bottom*) Active and passive torques acting on the shoulder joint during the reach. Positive torques act to extend the joint; negative torques act to flex the joint. NET, sum of all torques rotating the shoulder joint; GRA, torques due to the pull of gravity; MDT, torques rotating the shoulder that result from the movement of other, mechanically linked segments of the arm; MUS, torques rotating the shoulder arising from muscle contraction and tissue deformation. (From Thelen, E., Corbetta, D., Kamm, K., et al., 1993.)

Time-Scale Dynamics and the Development of an Embodied Cognition

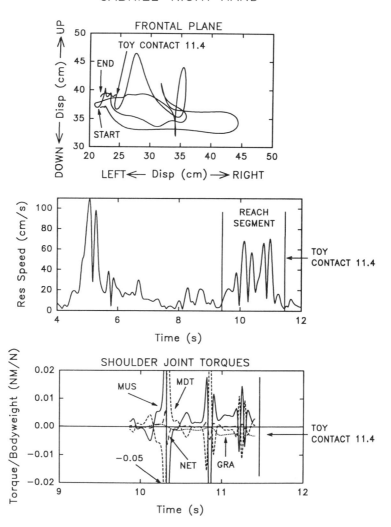

Figure 3.6 Gabriel's first goal-directed reaches at age 15 weeks. (*Top*) Hand trajectory projected onto the frontal plane. (*Middle*) Resultant three-dimensional hand speed during the reach segment. (*Bottom*) Active and passive torques acting on the shoulder joint during the reach. Positive torques act to extend the joint; negative torques act to flex the joint. NET, sum of all torques rotating the shoulder joint; GRA, torques due to the pull of gravity; MDT, torques rotating the shoulder that result from the movement of other, mechanically linked segments of the arm; MUS, torques rotating the shoulder arising from muscle contraction and tissue deformation. (From Thelen, E., Corbetta, D., Kamm, K., et al., 1993).

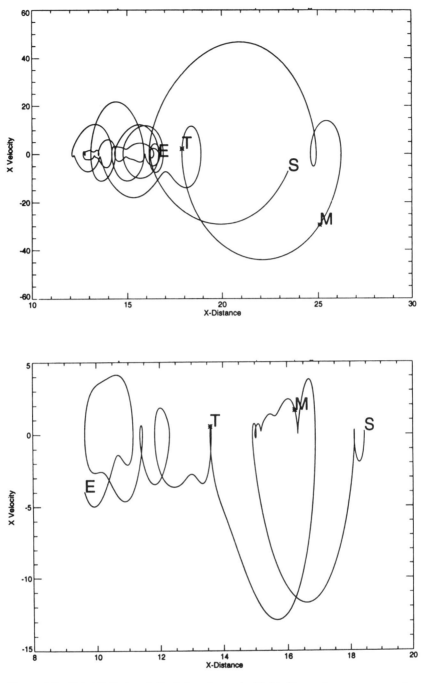

Figure 3.7 Gabriel's first goal-directed reaches embedded in his spontaneous movements, as depicted on the phase plane. S, start of movement; M, start of reach; T, end of reach; E, end of movement.

reach itself (the portion of the trajectory between the letters M and T) have the same characteristic dynamics as the spontaneous movements that preceded and followed it.

The infants (and the two others we studied) generated individual solutions to these problems. What we discovered was that the babies could not have had engineers in their genes or their heads with the solutions already figured out. How could a reach program know in advance the energy parameters of the system? The only thing common to the infants' actions was that they got their hands to the toy and that they manipulated the forces involved to do it. Where did their unique solutions come from?

Time-Scale Dynamics and Developmental Process

Although first reaches are novel acts, the processes that support them must, of course, be continuous in time. That is, something that is going on within the baby in his or her environment prior to reaching must allow the infant to generate the first reach. Some of these processes occur over very long time scales; the changes are slow. For example, body proportions change and muscles get stronger. Vision improves, and infants learn to hold their heads upright.

Other processes are occurring on short time scales. In particular, the integrated acts of perceiving and moving occur within seconds and fractions of seconds. Infants move and perceive many times every day for the 3 or 4 months before they reach. As infants look around, as they suckle, or cry, or as they engage the people around them with smiling and cooing, they necessarily cycle through periods of high excitement and periods of relaxation. What is happening in these everyday encounters? As they move, infants must be exploring what it feels like to deliver different levels of energy to their limbs and also what it looks like to have their hands out in front of their faces or clutching their blankets. This is activity on one particular time scale. Changes occur—dynamics—within seconds or even fractions of a second as infants modulate their muscle contractions in each particular context.

These early movements often look to be entirely without form or meaning. But if what neuroscientists tell us about the plasticity of the brain and how it changes is correct, infants are also continually learning something about their perceptual-motor systems and their relations to the world in their repeated, spontaneous activity (see, e.g., Edelman, 1987; Merzenich, Allard, and Jenkins, 1990). That is, what infants sense and what they feel in their ordinary looking and moving are teaching their brains about their bodies and about their worlds. They are in fact *exploring* what range of forces delivered to their muscles get their arms in particular places and then *learning* from their exploration, remembering how certain categories of forces get their hands forward toward something interesting. Thus, the time scale of moving and perceiving becomes part and parcel of the time scale of longer time changes, those of learning, and those we would normally call development. Babies do it themselves; they don't need the additional baby in the head.

When this process is put into the metaphor of dynamics, i.e., that the activity of the system itself changes the ranges of the parameter values, such an account of development may seem unremarkable. But in many contemporary developmental theories change is ascribed to some *deus ex machina* —"the genes," "maturation of the brain," "a shift into a new stage," or "an increase of information-processing capacity." The challenge of a dynamical formulation is to understand how the system can generate its own change, through its own activity, and within its own continuing dynamics, be it the springlike attractors of the limbs or the neural dynamics of the brain. I now report an experimental simulation of a system changing itself through exploration and selection of leg-spring parameters.

Activating a Mobile: Exploration and Selection in a Novel Task

One way to confirm a dynamical view of development is to try to simulate the processes of exploration and discovery in the laboratory. The notion is to create a *microgenesis* experiment. The term *microgenesis* comes from the Soviet psychologist L. S. Vygotsky (1978), who recognized that when a developing system was at a point of transition, it could be coaxed into a more mature phase by a facilitative task structure. In dynamical terms, the experimenter is manipulating putative control parameters to shift the system into a new state. The advantage of such experiments is the ability to trace the real-time changes as an analog to those happening during development. It is like a window on the developmental process, but on a more condensed time scale.

In order to do a microgenesis experiment, one must know the state dynamics of the developing system to identify times of transition. (Systems that are highly stable resist phase shifts when parameter values are changed.) In the experiment I describe here, the states are described by the patterns of coordination of the legs of young infants as they produce spontaneous kicking movements. In previous work (Thelen, 1985), I described the developmental course of bilateral leg coordination. Before 5 months of age, infants in the supine position kick predominantly in two modes, either both legs alternating or a single leg kicking while the other is relatively still. A third pattern, both legs flexing and extending simultaneously, is much less stable and less commonly seen, until about 5 months, when this pattern becomes more prevalent.

One of the tenets of a dynamical approach is that when the attractor states are relatively unstable, the system is free to explore new coordinative modes in response to task demands. Indeed it is this flexibility to discover new solutions that is the source of novel forms. Thus, I asked, if I presented infants with a novel task that made the initially less stable form of coordination more useful, could they could shift their coordination preferences over the course of the experiment?

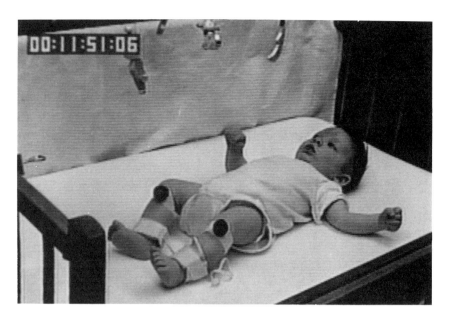

Figure 3.8 Infant in mobile kicking experiment showing elastic leg tether.

To do this, I tested 3-month-old infants in a well-known paradigm, that of *conjugate reinforcement* (Rovee-Collier, 1991). In this procedure, infants' left legs are attached with a ribbon to an overhead mobile. Because their leg kicks are reinforced by the movements and sounds of the attractive mobile, infants learn an increased rate of kicking. To create a task that favored the less stable simultaneous pattern of kicking over the more stable alternating or single-leg form, in some infants I also yoked their ankles together with a soft piece of sewing elastic attached to a foam cuff (Thelen, 1994). The elastic permitted them to kick in single or alternating fashion, but made simultaneous kicking much more effective for vigorous activation of the mobile because full excursions otherwise required stretching the elastic (figure 3.8). Some infants were tested without the tether. I assigned infants to one of four experimental groups, based on whether their legs were yoked together (Y) or free (F) during the three conditions: baseline (4 minutes, no reinforcement, i.e., their leg kicks did not make the mobile jiggle), acquisition (10 minutes, reinforcement; leg kicks activated the mobile), and extinction (2 minutes, no reinforcement: group 1, YYF, group 2, FYF; group 3, FFF, and group 4, YFF). Would the yoked infants, over the course of the experiment, discover the effectiveness of the simultaneous pattern?

To trace the dynamics of the learning process itself, I tracked the excursions of the infants' legs during the 16 minutes of the experiment. Figure 3.8 illustrates what these movements look like. The top panel shows a 30-second segment of the excursions of an infant's leg (the tracked markers were placed on the infants' shins) as he moved in the direction toward and away from his torso during the baseline condition when his kicks were not reinforced

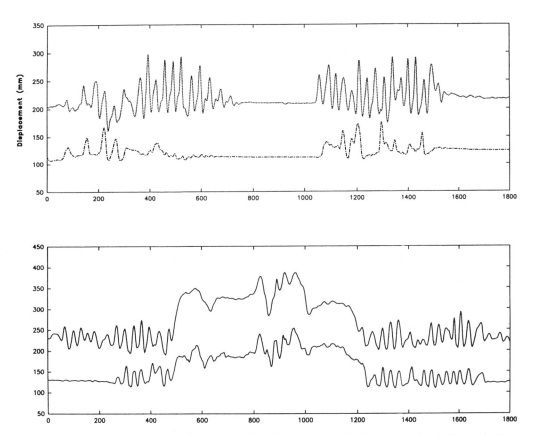

Figure 3.9 Examples from a single infant of leg coordination in the mobile kicking task. (*Top*) Right and left leg excursions in the *x*-direction (toward and away from the torso) during the 30 seconds of the baseline condition. (*Bottom*) Right and left leg excursions in the *x*-direction during 30 seconds of acquisition.

and he had no ankle tether. This baby kicked in a typical fashion, with the right leg kicking quite a lot, and the left leg only occasionally. After several minutes into the acquisition portion of the experiment, where he was activating the mobile and his legs were yoked together, the same infant's coordination patterns changed dramatically, as seen in the bottom panel of figure 3.9. Both legs were moving back and forth nearly perfectly in phase.

All the infants, both those whose legs were yoked and those whose legs were free, increased the overall number of kicks when kicking was reinforced, and they also increased the vigor of their kicks. However, the coordination patterns of two groups diverged during the experiment, as shown in figure 3.10 (Thelen, 1994). This figure reports the percentage of values of a running correlation performed on the leg excursion time series that equaled or exceeded $r = .4.0.$[2] Clearly, the two groups of infants whose legs were yoked during acquisition (YYF and FYF) increased their simultaneous kicking during the acquisition period (A1–A5), whereas those in the free condition (FFF and YFF) decreased their inphase movements. During the extinction phase

Time-Scale Dynamics and the Development of an Embodied Cognition

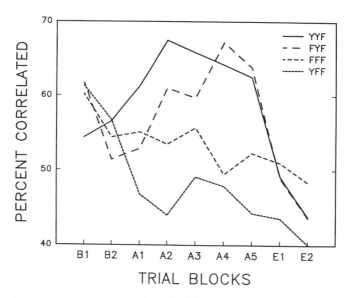

Figure 3.10 Percent of right and left leg excursions correlated at $r = .4$ and above in the four experimental groups. Y, yoked; F, free. Trial blocks are 2 minutes except for extinction when they are 1 minute.

(E1 and E2) when kicks were no longer reinforced and the tether was removed, the yoked infants dramatically resumed the originally favored patterns.

This experiment demonstrated that within the time scale of a few minutes, infants as young as 3 months can shift patterns in response to a novel task. Infants clearly enjoyed making the mobile jiggle with their leg kicks, and they also learned to do this efficiently "on-line." When the task constraint was removed during extinction, there was no longer any need to maintain the novel pattern and they did not.

In dynamical terms, we can envision each leg as having adjustable spring parameters and also there being a modifiable coupling function between the legs. The experiment can be interpreted, therefore, as infants discovering an optimal coupling pattern as well as adjusting the timing and the strength of the energy bursts to the spring, delivering more frequent and stronger pulses. In terms of the dynamical landscape of figure 3.2, the babies have created a new potential well, a newly attractive parameter configuration emerging from their on-line solution to getting the mobile to jiggle in an efficient way.

3.12 FROM ACTION TO COGNITION

Reaching and kicking a mobile are both about learning to adjust limb force dynamics. These studies showed first, that infants generate individual solutions to adjust body forces to do a task and second, that they can select appropriate patterns of coordination from among several within the time scale of acting and learning. What does this mean in terms of changes over longer time scales—development—and, particularly, in terms of my claim that these mundane infant activities support the construct of an embodied cognition?

The critical process here appears to be that of learning *categories*, in this case, that a certain category of force dynamics is appropriate for a certain class of tasks. As Thelen and Smith (1994) discuss at length, perceptual motor category formation is foundational for all cognitive development (see also Edelman, 1987, among others). The ability to recognize that particular perceptual events and actions generalize is what lays the groundwork for being able to make sense of the world. For instance, by watching objects move in space, infants learn that edges that move together define the boundaries of objects, and they come to expect that even novel objects—things they have not seen before—will act as a coherent whole. Likewise, they learn that small, colorful objects 6 in. in front of their bodies mean something that may feel good in the mouth and they acquire and remember a class of muscle parameters for reaching and grasping for all suitable objects in reachable space. Thelen and Smith (1994) use developmental evidence to show the dynamical nature of categories. In particular, that category formation may also be depicted as a landscape of potential wells, where the local acts of perceiving and acting come to form wider basins of attraction that represent more general classes of solutions.

The mobile experiments provide insights into how the *process* of forming higher-level categories from local activities may proceed. Recall that when I tethered infants' legs with elastic, they discovered a force solution, but when the tether was removed, they reverted to different patterns. The appearance and disappearance of the tether is in some ways like what infants encounter in everyday life. Tasks and constraints appear and disappear. Opportunities for action depend on the presence of desired objects, suitable support surfaces, helping social support, and so on. In one way, every particular opportunity is unique—toys are never in the same location or orientation in relation to the infant. But infants commonly encounter similar classes of opportunities, for example, the category "toys able to be reached."

So an important developmental question remains: How do infants generalize from each unique opportunity to act—the here-and-now dynamics—to novel, but similar situations? Then, how do the accumulated classes of solutions themselves influence what we call the qualities of mind?

There are very few experimental studies that span the here-and-now dynamics and the dynamics of developmental time. Some of the most enlightening, in my opinion, use the mobile kicking situation and have been done by Carolyn Rovee-Collier and her colleagues (reviewed in Rovee-Collier, 1991). What Rovee-Collier asked was, once infants learned to kick more in the presence of the mobile, did they remember to do so days or even weeks later, and then, under what conditions do they remember or forget how to match their actions to the task?

Rovee-Collier found that 2- to 3-month-old infants could remember, and if given the mobile the next day or even a week or two later, resumed kicking at the high rate they learned in the original session. (My preliminary evidence is that infants also remember the new pattern of coordination elicited by leg tethering.) Over time, this memory faded, although simply seeing the mobile would reactivate it. Most important is that this action memory was highly specific to the training situation. If Rovee-Collier changed the mobile, or even the designs on the pads that lined the cribs in which infants originally learned the task, infants forgot that kicking a lot makes the mobile move more. The action memory was highly tied to the learning context. However, if Rovee-Collier trained infants on the first day with one mobile or set of crib liners, on the second day with a different set, and on the third day with yet another set, the infants did remember to kick no matter what mobile they were tested with—even a completely novel mobile. Whereas the first learning was highly specific, infants, given different mobiles, generalized from a particular situation to a category of mobiles-to-be-activated-by-kicking. Thus, they tied their bodily actions to a perceptual category such that the sight of the mobile and the learned motor response were united. The common attractor is now "mobileness" in general—depicted in a figure 3.2-type landscape as a broad attractor with several embedded potential wells.

The mobile studies created, of course, highly artificial situations for infants. In normal life, they bang and reach and look and grasp not just one thing, but many different things—toys of many kinds, textures, and weights; people, pets, and in many different places; their crib, the grass, their blanket, and so on. So real life gives abundant opportunity to learn by doing, to discover, and to generalize—that yes, a certain force delivered to my arm will get me any object of a certain size and at a certain distance, but to pick up a Cheerio, I may have to slow down and adjust my fingers. It is indeed this diversity, this variability of experience, that allows more general solutions to emerge.

In both of the examples above, infants solved problems of how to control the forces generated by their limbs and bodies in order to make the world work for them. In each case, the infants must eventually not just meet the situation at hand, but recall and use a category of action solutions that fits what they perceive their task to be. If you think about the developmental tasks of infancy, however, you quickly realize that this cycle of challenge, exploration, discovery, and new challenge within the motor skill domain occupies a large part of the child's waking hours. Although each task is unique, the solutions must be generalized. As each new solution is discovered, that solution opens up new opportunities to learn. It is through these successive generalizations that cognition grows from action and perception (Thelen and Smith, 1994).

3.13 TOWARD A FORCE EMBODIMENT

Indeed, I speculate here (following Johnson, 1987; Lakoff, 1987; Langacker, 1986; Talmy, 1988) that the solutions to force interactions with the world are so pervasive and foundational in infancy and indeed throughout life, that

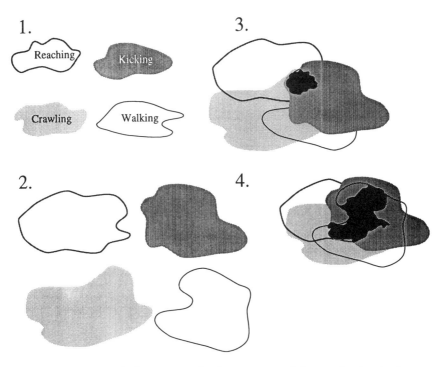

Figure 3.11 Force embodiment pictured as first separate, and then overlapping clouds.

they are carried along, so to speak, as a superordinate category into the very fabric of all cognition and language. Let me illustrate this with a very crude model. Imagine that in some abstract mental space we represent solutions to various force problems infants encounter as four clouds (clouds to indicate their dynamical, nonstructural, processlike character). Initially, as the experiments indicate, the solution space is small and constrained (figure 3.11). The clouds are separate and accessed by constrained situations. Knowing how to kick a mobile does not help with knowing how to adjust forces to stand up. However, as infants gain a wide range of experience, these clouds enlarge—the solutions are generalized and can thus be accessed by a wide variety of situations. Eventually, the solution spaces intersect where the common aspects of each solution overlap. In this case, one superordinate category that may emerge from these specific experiences is a more abstract understanding of force, abstracted from its specific instances by a process identical to how infants learned "mobileness" or "reaching" or not to smash down on a small delicate object. If, as has been suggested, bodily force is a parameter that accompanies very many of our solutions in daily life, the abstraction cloud would become very large indeed. The force cloud would be accessed then not only by perceiving to act but by thinking about acting, by planning to act, and by talking about acting. In this way, thought becomes developmentally constructed. The seamless web of time and process gives bodily foundations to emergent, higher-order abstractions. The root relationships are thus prelinguistic; language is built on connections that exist before language and

Time-Scale Dynamics and the Development of an Embodied Cognition

continue to dominate everyday life. The notion is that we have lived in these intersections so thoroughly that they are embedded and embodied.

Of course, forceful encounters between body and environment are only one way in which we interact with our worlds. Social communication rarely involves direct force, but provides rich information to many of our senses. And social encounters are equally pervasive. We can think of the development of social life also as a series of challenges. The tasks are to figure out what Mom wants and to get her to figure out what you want. Many avenues are explored ("Perhaps lying down, screaming, and kicking my feet will work"). Some are functional, others are not. Over time, however, increasingly general, individualized solutions that involve facial expressions, vocalizations, gestures, postures, and of course language, are selected. As in body actions, the solutions to communication will have many intersections in mental state space. We may thus speculate that our cognition, our very way of thinking, would be equally influenced by the root metaphors of our social exchange and, in particular, by the patterns of social life peculiar to our families and cultures. This has long been the claim of psychologists such as Vygotsky and Luria, and lately Jerome Bruner, that patterns of thought reflect the very societies in which they developed. Perhaps an account such as I have suggested can give "embodiment" to these ideas as well.

NOTES

1. It is important here to clarify the role of goals and intentions. To say that infants are motivated to perform and repeat certain activities, like looking at moving mobiles or reaching for toys, does not require putting an agent back into the baby's head. What is required is that the system come with a few, very general biases, e.g., looking at moving things is better than not looking, having something in the mouth feels good, and so on. With just a minimum of biasing tendencies, the developmental system self-organizes in relation to those tendencies, and indeed creates an additional motivational cascade. For example, the biases "look at moving things and get things in the mouth" are sufficient to provide the motivational basis for reaching, grasping, and exploring. This is not the same as having a little executive in the head programming behavior and its changes. Even the most simple organisms have trophic biases: toward moderate amounts of heat, light, moisture, and so on. Thelen and Smith (1994) discuss further the relation of simple biases and motivation, including its neurophysiological basis.

2. Quantifying patterns of coordination over time is difficult in infants because the phase relations are always changing. To capture these shifting relations, I performed a moving window correlation of the x-displacements of both legs using a 1-second window and a step of 17 ms. I could then determine the frequency bins of each correlation value. Correlations near $+1$ indicated both legs moving toward and away from the body exactly in phase, correlations near -1 resulted from alternating movements, and correlations around 0 meant the movements were unrelated. (See Corbetta and Thelen, 1993, for details.)

REFERENCES

Corbetta, D., and Thelen, E. (1993). Shifting patterns of interlimb coordination in infants' reaching: a case study. In S. P. Swinnen, H. Heuer, J. Massion, et al. (Eds.), *Interlimb coordination: neural, dynamical, and cognitive constraints* (pp. 413–438). New York: Academic Press.

Edelman, G. M. (1987). *Neural Darwinism*. New York: Basic Books.

Gesell, A., and Ames, L. B. (1940). The ontogenetic organization of prone behavior in human infancy. *The Journal of Genetic Psychology, 56*, 247–263.

Johnson, M. (1987). *The body in the mind: the bodily basis of meaning, imagination, and reason*. Chicago: University of Chicago Press.

Lakoff, G. (1987). *Women, fire, and dangerous things: what categories reveal about the mind*. Chicago: University of Chicago Press.

Langacker, R. W. (1986). An introduction to cognitive grammar. *Cognitive Science, 10*, 1–40.

McGraw, M. B. (1940). Neuromuscular development of the human infant as exemplified in the achievement of erect locomotion. *Journal of Pediatrics, 17*, 747–771.

Merzenich, M. M., Allard, T. T., and Jenkins, W. M. (1990). Neural ontogeny of higher brain function: implications of some recent neurophysiological findings. In O. Franzn and P. Westman (Eds.), *Information processing in the somatosensory system* (pp. 293–311). London: Macmillan.

Muchisky, M., Gershkoff-Stowe, L., Cole, E., et al. (In press). The epigenetic landscape revisited: a dynamic interpretation. In C. Rovee-Collier (Ed.), *Advances in infancy research*, Norwood, NJ: Ablex.

Piaget, J. (1952). *The origins of intelligence in children*. New York: International Universities Press.

Rovee-Collier, C. (1991). The "memory system" of prelinguistic infants. *Annals of the New York Academy of Sciences, 608*, 517–536.

Schneider, K., Zernicke, R. F., Ulrich, B. D., et al. (1990). Understanding movement control in infants through the analysis of limb intersegmental dynamics. *Journal of Motor Behavior, 22*, 493–520.

Searle, J. R. (1992). *The rediscovery of the mind*. Cambridge, MA: Bradford Books/MIT Press.

Smith, L. B., and Thelen, E. (Eds.) (1993). *A dynamic systems approach to development: applications*. Cambridge, MA: Bradford Books/MIT Press.

Talmy, L. (1988). Force dynamics in language and cognition. *Cognitive Science, 12*, 49–100.

Thelen, E. (1985). Developmental origins of motor coordination: leg movements in human infants. *Developmental Psychobiology, 18*, 323–333.

Thelen, E. (1989). Self-organization in developmental processes: can systems approaches work? In M. Gunnar and E. Thelen (Eds.), *Systems in Development: The Minnesota Symposia in Child Psychology*, Vol. 22 (pp. 77–117). Hillsdale, NJ: Erlbaum.

Thelen, E. (1994). Three-month old infants can learn task-specific patterns of interlimb coordination. *Psychological Science, 5*, 280–285.

Thelen, E., Corbetta, D., Kamm, K., et al. (1993). The transition to reaching: matching intention and intrinsic dynamics. *Child Development, 64*, 1058–1098.

Thelen, E., and Fisher, D. M. (1982). Newborn stepping: an explanation for a "disappearing" reflex. *Developmental Psychology, 18*, 760–775.

Thelen, E., Fisher, D. M., Ridley-Johnson, R., and Griffin, N. (1982). The effect of body build and arousal on newborn infant stepping. *Developmental Psychology, 15*, 447–453.

Thelen, E., Kelso, J. A. S., and Fogel, A. (1987). Self-organizing systems and infant motor development. *Developmental Review, 7*, 39–65.

Thelen, E., and Smith, L. B. (1994). *A dynamic systems approach to the development of cognition and action*. Cambridge, MA: Bradford Books/MIT Press.

Thelen, E., and Ulrich, B. D. (1991). Hidden skills: A dynamic systems analysis of treadmill stepping during the first year. *Monographs of the Society for Research in Child Development*, Serial No. 223, *56* (1).

Turner, M. (1991). *Reading minds: The study of English in the age of cognitive science*. Princeton, NJ: Princeton University Press.

Varela, F. J., Thompson, E., and Rosch, E. (1993). *The embodied mind: cognitive science and human experience*. Cambridge, MA: MIT Press.

Vygotsky, L. S. (1978). *Mind in society: the development of higher psychological processes*. Cambridge, MA: Harvard University Press.

Guide to Further Reading

Thelen and Smith (1994) contains a full version of a dynamical theory of development, beginning with general principles and then showing how cognition emerges from perception and action. The chapters in Smith and Thelen (1993) give applications of dynamical approaches to the development of movement, perception, infant state, cognition, language, and social interaction. Thelen and Ulrich (1991) is the first developmental study undertaken from a specifically dynamical point of view. A compatible, synthetic view of neuroembryology and brain function can be found in Edelman (1987). The August 1993 issue of the journal *Child Development* (Vol. 64) contains a special section entitled "Developmental Biodynamics: Brain, Body, Behavior Connections" which has many papers relevant to the origins of an embodied cognition. Finally, Savelsbergh (1993) contains a number of papers studying infant development from a dynamical viewpoint, but also provides contrasting perspectives.

Edelman, G. M. (1987). *Neural Darwinism*. New York: Basic Books.

Salvelsbergh, G. J. P. (1993). *The development of coordination in infancy*. Amsterdam: North Holland.

Smith, L. B., and Thelen, E. (Eds.) (1993). *A dynamic systems approach to development: applications*. Cambridge, MA: Bradford Books/MIT Press.

Thelen E., and Lockman, J. J. (Eds.) Developmental biodynamics: Brain, body, behavior connections. *Child Development 64* (special section), 953–1190.

Thelen, E., and Smith, L. B. (1994). *A dynamic systems approach to the development of cognition and action*. Cambridge, MA: Bradford Books/MIT Press.

Thelen, E., and Ulrich, B. D. (1991). Hidden skills: a dynamic systems analysis of treadmill stepping during the first year. *Monographs of the Society for Research in Child Development*, Serial No. 223, *56* (1).

4 Dynamic Representation of Decision-Making

James T. Townsend and Jerome Busemeyer

EDITORS' INTRODUCTION

Those unfamiliar with the dynamical approach often suspect that, while it might be appropriate for low-level or peripheral aspects of cognition, it cannot be used to describe high-level or central aspects. Yet nothing could be more central—more paradigmatically cognitive—than processes of decision-making, the target of Townsend and Busemeyer's work. Their decision field theory (DFT), described in this chapter, is a general dynamical and stochastic framework for modeling decision-making which accounts for data covered by traditional, static-deterministic theories, but whose explanatory capacities go beyond those of traditional theories in a number of respects.

Virtually all quantitative theories of decision-making in psychology, and in cognitive science more generally, are versions of subjective expected utility theory. Many beautiful mathematical theorems have been established that, at the very least, serve as useful guides to optimal choices. Yet, for the great majority of theories and applications to empirical phenomena, there have been no explicit psychological dynamics whatsoever—that is, no attempt to trace out the actual mental processes the subject goes through in reaching a decision. The modus operandi *has simply been to compare two potential choices (i.e., gambles, etc.) and conclude that the decision-maker should choose the one with the higher expected utility. When inevitable "paradoxes" appear, in which human decision-makers do not behave as the theory proclaims, the standard response is to alter the axioms (e.g., change the form of the utility function).*

The DFT framework, by contrast, sets out with the explicit aim of modeling the psychological processes involved in decision-making. In this framework the system begins in a certain preference state with regard to certain choices, and this state evolves over time according to dynamical equations which govern the relationship among factors such as the motivational value of an outcome and the momentary anticipated value of making a particular choice. Importantly, DFT models are able to account for the standard psychological data on the kinds of choices people make, and indeed predict certain data that appear paradoxical from the traditional perspective.

Since key variables in a DFT model evolve over time, the model builds in the capacity to account for temporal features of the deliberation process, such as the way the decision a subject makes depends on deliberation time. Such temporal considerations are inherently out of the reach of traditional models which are either entirely static or specify at best just a bare sequence of steps. The DFT framework thus provides a powerful illustration of the explanatory advantages of adopting a dynamical framework which supposes from the outset that cognitive processes essentially evolve over real time.

4.1 INTRODUCTION

The deliberation may last for weeks or months, occupying at intervals the mind. The motives which yesterday seemed full of urgency and blood and life to-day feel strangely weak and pale and dead. But as little to-day as to-morrow is the question finally resolved. Something tells us that all this is provisional; that the weakened reasons will wax strong again, and the stronger weaken; that equilibrium is unreached; that testing our reasons, not obeying them, is still the order of the day, and that we must wait awhile, patient or impatiently, until our mind is made up "for good and all." This inclining first to one then to another future, both of which we represent as possible, resembles the oscillations to and fro of a material body within the limits of its elasticity. There is inward strain, but no outward rapture. And this condition, plainly enough, is susceptible of indefinite continuance, as well in the physical mass as in the mind. If the elasticity give way, however, if the dam ever do break, and the current burst the crust, vacillation is over and decision is irrevocably there.

—William James, *The Principles of Psychology* (1890/1950, p. 529.).

This deliberation process, so eloquently described by William James more than 100 years ago, seems to be engaged whenever we are confronted with serious decisions such as getting married or divorced, having a child, quitting a job, undergoing elective surgery, or other life-threatening decisions. This process still occurs, but to a lesser extent, with more commonplace decisions such as choosing a car, buying a computer, or planning a vacation. The process is manifested by indecisiveness, vacillation, inconsistency, lengthy deliberation, and distress (Janis and Mann, 1977; Svenson, 1992).

It seems odd that many psychological theories of decision-making fail to mention anything about this deliberation process. Many previous theories of decision-making (e.g., the prospect theory of Kahneman and Tversky, 1979) assume that for any particular situation, individuals assign weights and values to each possible outcome, and the final decision is simply a matter of comparing the summed products of weights and values for each alternative. The entire process is described in a deterministic and static manner. There is no explanation for changes in state of preference over time, and there is no mechanism for deriving the time needed for deliberation. This criticism applies equally well to all static-deterministic theories of risky decision making that have evolved from the basic expected utility formulation (von Neumann and Morgenstern, 1947; Savage, 1954).

We are not claiming that static theories are irrelevant to the understanding of human decision-making. On the contrary, ideas from these theories can be incorporated into the present framework. Instead, we claim that these static theories are seriously incomplete owing to their failure to explain the psycho-

Table 4.1 Decision theory taxonomy

	Static	Dynamical
Deterministic	Expected utility	Affective balance
Probabilistic	Thurstone utility	Decision field theory

Note: Thurstone's utility theory is an example of a more general class called random utility theories (Thurstone, 1959). Affective balance theory was proposed by Grossberg and Gutowski (1987).

logically important dynamical phenomena of human conflict—the evolution of preferences over time during conflict resolution.

The new contribution of decision field theory can be characterized by considering table 4.1, which provides a classification of theories according to two attributes—"deterministic vs. probabilistic," and "static vs. dynamic." *Deterministic* theories postulate a binary preference relation which is either *true or false* for any pair of actions. *Probabilistic* theories postulate a probability function that maps each pair of actions into the closed interval [0,1]. *Static* theories assume that the preference relation (for deterministic models) or the probability function (for probabilistic models) is independent of the length of deliberation time. *Dynamical* theories specify how the preference relation or probability function changes as a function of deliberation time. For the past 45 years, the *deterministic-static* category has dominated research on decision-making under uncertainty. Decision field theory builds on this past work by extending these theories into the *stochastic-dynamical* category.

The purpose of this chapter is to provide a general overview of an alternative framework for understanding decision-making called decision field theory (DFT). Decision field theory provides a dynamical, stochastic description of the *deliberation process* involved in decision-making. It is unique in its capability for deriving *precise* quantitative predictions for (a) the probability of choosing each alternative as a function of deliberation time (Busemeyer and Townsend, 1993), (b) the mean deliberation time needed to make a decision (Busemeyer and Townsend, 1993), (c) the distribution of selling prices, buying prices, and certainty equivalents for gambles (Busemeyer and Goldstein, 1992), and (d) approach-avoidance movement behavior (Townsend and Busemeyer, 1989).

Decision field theory is based on psychological principles drawn from three different areas of psychology. The first is the early learning and motivation theories of approach-avoidance conflict developed by Lewin (1935), Hull (1938), and Miller (1944). The second is the more recent information-processing theories of choice response time (see Townsend and Ashby, 1983; Luce, 1986). The third is research and theory on human decision-making, especially the recent work by Coombs and Avrunin (1988).

The remainder of this chapter is organized as follows. The basic assumptions of DFT are summarized in section 4.2. A brief review of how the theory is applied to choice and selling price preference tasks is presented in section 4.3. Then, in section 4.4, DFT is used to explain two different "paradoxical" empirical findings. The main message of this chapter is the following: often what appears to be "paradoxical" behavior from the viewpoint of static-deterministic theories turns out to be emergent properties of the dynamical-stochastic nature of the human deliberation process.

4.2 GENERAL THEORETICAL STRUCTURE

Figure 4.1 provides an outline of DFT. On the far left are the values of all the potential consequences produced by each course of action. In the figure, six consequences are shown: three rewards or gains, and three punishments or losses. A distinction is made between rewards or attractive consequences, and punishments or aversive consequences. The values of the six consequences can be organized into a 6- × 1-vector **M**, where the first three elements contain the values of the three gains (forming a 3- × 1-subvector

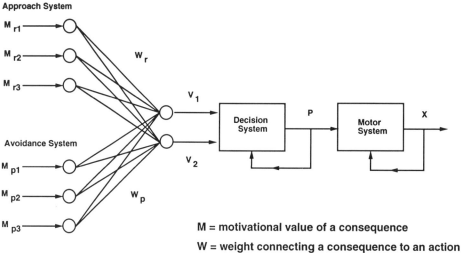

M = motivational value of a consequence

W = weight connecting a consequence to an action

V = valence = momentary anticipated value of an action

P = preference state = tendency to approach–avoid an act

X = output position = actual behavior of decision–maker

Figure 4.1 Diagram of DFT. At the far left are the gains and losses produced by each course of action, denoted *M*. These inputs are then filtered by a set of attention weights that connect each action to each consequence, denoted *W*. These filtered values form the valence or momentary anticipated value of each action, denoted *V*. Valence corresponds to force in a physical system. Then the valence is input to a decision system which temporally integrates the valences to produce a preference state for each action as an output, denoted *P*. Preference state corresponds to velocity in a physical system. Finally, the preference is input to a motor system which temporally integrates the preferences over time to produce the observed action, denoted *X*. The observed action corresponds to the physical position in a physical system.

$\mathbf{M}_r$) and the last three elements contain the values of the three losses (forming another 3- × 1-subvector $\mathbf{M}_p$).

Each course of action has some connection or association with each consequence. The strength of an individual's belief in the connection between each consequence and each action is represented by a weight $\mathbf{W}_{ij}(t)$. In the figure, two acts lead to six possible consequences, producing a total of 12 connection weights. These 12 connection weights can be organized into a 2-×6-weight matrix symbolized as $\mathbf{W}(t) = [\mathbf{W}_r(t)|\mathbf{W}_p(t)]$, where $\mathbf{W}_r(t)$ is the 2-×3-submatrix of weights for the rewards, and $\mathbf{W}_p(t)$ is the 2-×3-submatrix of weights for the punishments.

The connection weights fluctuate over time during deliberation, reflecting changes in the decision-maker's attention to the various consequences produced by each action. For example, at one moment the decision-maker may think about the gains produced by choosing an action, but at a later moment the decision-maker's attention may shift toward the potential losses.

The set of connection weights act like a filter that modifies the impact of the input values of the consequences $\mathbf{M}$. The output of this filtering process is a vector called the valence vector, denoted $\mathbf{V}(t)$. In the figure, $\mathbf{V}(t)$ is a 2-×1-vector because only two actions ($V_1(t)$ and $V_2(t)$) are shown in the figure. Each element of this valence vector represents the momentary anticipated value that would be produced by choosing a particular course of action.

The valence is transformed into action by passing through two different dynamical systems—a decision system and then a motor system. First, valence is the input for a decision system that produces a preference state as output, representing the vector $\mathbf{P}(t)$. In the figure, there are only two actions so that $\mathbf{P}(t)$ has two elements, $P_1(t)$ and $P_2(t)$. Each coordinate of $\mathbf{P}(t)$ represents the temporal integration of the valences generated by a course of action. Thus, each coordinate of $\mathbf{P}(t)$ represents the current estimate of the strength of preference for a course of action.

Finally, the preference state becomes the input for a motor system that produces a response or overt movement as output. The physical position at each time point of the motor mechanism used to execute an action is represented by a vector $\mathbf{X}(t)$.

The basic concepts of DFT shown in figure 4.1 are described in more detail below, beginning with the observable end product (actions) and working backward to the unobservable driving force (valence).

Motor System

In general, the preference state is the input into a motor system that produces a movement as output. If $\mathbf{X}(t)$ is the physical position at time t, and $\mathbf{X}(t + h)$ is the physical position at the next instant in time, then $d\mathbf{X}(t + h)) = \mathbf{X}(t + h) - \mathbf{X}(t)$ is the change in physical position during the small time interval h. The velocity of the movement, denoted $d\mathbf{X}(t + h)/h$, is represented by a difference equation:

$$dX(t + h)/h = R[X(t), P(t + h)].\qquad(1)$$

In other words, the velocity of the movement is a function of the previous position and the current preference state. The physical position $X(t)$ is the integration of the velocity over time. The detailed specification of the response function R depends on the nature of the movement. Later in this chapter, we consider two different types of responses commonly used to measure preference: choice and selling prices.

It is crucial to note that only the motor system changes when different response measures are used for measuring preference. The valence system and the decision system remain invariant. This provides strong leverage for testing the theory; the parameters of the theory may be estimated using one response measure, and then these same parameter values are used to make parameter-free predictions for the remaining response measures. This cross-validation method for testing the model is illustrated later in this chapter.

Decision System

The preference state is driven by the incoming valence associated with each act (see figure 4.1). The valence at time t, denoted $V(t)$, is a point within the preference space that pushes or pulls the preference state at time t. The force of the valence on the preference state is represented by a linear difference equation:

$$dP(t + h)/h = -S \cdot P(t) + C \cdot V(t + h)\qquad(2)$$

In other words, the rate and direction of change in preference is a linear function of the previous preference state and the incoming valence. The preference state $P(t)$ is the integration of these forces over time.

The constant matrix S is called the stability matrix, and it controls the rate of growth of preferences. This is similar to a learning rate parameter in a linear operator learning model (cf. Bush and Mosteller, 1955). For example, if a constant positive valence is applied to one act, then the preference for that act gradually increases from the initial zero state toward the constant value. If the valence is later reset to zero, then preference gradually decays from the previous asymptote toward zero. The rate of growth and decay is determined by the stability matrix S.

The constant matrix C is called the contrast matrix, and it determines how acts are compared to form preferences. To see how this works, assume that there are three acts. If all three acts are evaluated independently, then $C = I$, the identity matrix. In this case, preference for all three actions may increase simultaneously, producing a "race" toward each goal.

Alternatively, one action may be compared to the average of the remaining two

$$C = \begin{array}{ccc} 1 & -1/2 & -1/2 \\ -1/2 & 1 & -1/2 \\ -1/2 & -1/2 & 1 \end{array}.$$

James T. Townsend and Jerome Busemeyer

In the above case, increasing the preference for one alternative corresponds to a decrease in preference for the remaining two alternatives. This would be appropriate if movement toward one goal entailed movement away from other goals.

The linear form of the above difference equation was chosen for four reasons. First, it is the simplest form capable of generating the desired type of behavior. Second, it is mathematically tractable, which allows derivation of interesting empirical tests. Third, it reduces as a special case to a number of previously developed models of decision-making. Fourth, the linear form may be considered a rough approximation to some nonlinear form. Linear approximations have proved to be useful in physics and engineering for analyzing problems within a limited domain. Hopefully, the failures of the linear model will indicate the type of nonlinearity needed to provide a more accurate representation of the dynamics. Townsend and Busemeyer (1989) began a probe of nonlinear dynamics within DFT.

Valence System

Valence is the motivational source of all movement. It is determined by two factors (see figure 4.1): (a) an n- × m-weight matrix, $\mathbf{W}(t)$, representing the strength of connection between each act and consequence, and (b) an m- × l-column vector, $\mathbf{M}(t)$, representing the motivational values of each consequence. *Valence* is defined as the matrix product of the weight matrix and the motivational value vector,

$$\mathbf{V}(t) = \mathbf{W}(t) \cdot \mathbf{M}(t). \tag{3}$$

Each element, $V_i(t)$, is a weighted sum of motivational values.

The n- × m-weight matrix, denoted $\mathbf{W}(t)$, represents the moment-to-moment strength of connection between each act and each consequence. An act-consequence connection refers to the expectation that, under a given set of environmental conditions, an act produces a relevant consequence at some later point in time. The weight $W_{ij}(t)$ connecting act i to consequence j at time t ranges from zero to unity; $0 \leqslant W_{ij}(t) \leqslant 1$; $W_{ij}(t) = 0$ means that the motivational value of consequence j has no influence on act i; $W_{ij}(t) = .5$ means that the motivational value of consequence j is reduced by one half for act i; $W_{ij}(t) = 1$ means that the full force of the motivational value of consequence j is applied to act i. These weights are determined by the product of six factors: attention, learning, relevance, probability, temporal distance, and physical distance.

Attention to an act-consequence connection means that the connection has been retrieved from long-term memory and it is active in short-term memory. Models of memory retrieval (e.g., Raaijmakers and Shiffrin, 1981) may be useful for predicting the effects of attention on decision-making.

Learning refers to changes in the strength of an act-consequence connection based on experience with previous decisions or instruction. Models of learning (e.g., Busemeyer and Myung, 1992) may be used to describe changes in connection strength resulting from experience.

When the weights represent the temporal remoteness of the consequences, then the valence of each act is equivalent to a temporal discounting model (see Stevenson, 1986) *at a specific moment.*

When the weights represent the probabilities of the consequences, then the valence of each act is equivalent to a subjective expected utility model (e.g., Edwards, 1962) *at a specific moment.*

When the weights represent the importance of an attribute or dimension, then the valence of each act is equivalent to a weighted sum of multiattribute values (see von Winterfeldt and Edwards, 1986; Elman, chapter 8) *at a specific moment.* Diederich (in press) has applied DFT to multiattribute, multiple alternative-choice situations.

The effect of physical distance on the weights is referred to as the goal gradient hypothesis (cf., Hull, 1938; Lewin, 1935; Miller, 1944). Sensations associated with the reward or punishment become much more salient as one approaches the goal. For example, a hungry dieter may be able to see and smell food better as he or she approaches it. The fear of a soldier approaching battle rises as the thunder from the guns grows louder.

One final point is that the weights depend on the sign of a consequence. This assumption is based on the principle that avoidance gradients are steeper than approach gradients (Lewin, 1935; Miller, 1944). For example, positive and negative consequences associated with equal delays and probabilities receive different weights.

The motivational value vector, $\mathbf{M}(t)$, represents the decision-maker's overall affective reaction to each of m possible consequences. Here we assume that all desires, feelings, and emotional reactions to consequences can be temporarily mapped onto a single common underlying scale similar to Wundt's hedonic continuum (see Cofer and Appley, 1964). The explicit purpose of this continuum is to compare consequences and make tradeoffs within a single biological system in a manner similar to the way that a monetary continuum is used in economic systems for trading between individuals. This is not to say that feelings and emotions are one-dimensional. On the contrary, motivational value is only a summary of these many dimensions temporarily constructed for the purpose of guiding action.

This is where the internal needs, demands, or motivational states of the decision-maker enter the decision process. Motivational value is derived from the product of two factors: (a) internal demands or drives, and (b) the estimated potential for a consequence to supply or satisfy these demands. The dynamic nature of motivational value now becomes apparent. First, demands often grow over time producing an increase in motivational value. Second, actions yield consequences that satisfy these demands, and reduce motivational value (cf. Atkinson and Birch, 1970). Finally, experience with consequences modifies one's estimate of the potential satisfaction.

The motivational values are positively or negatively signed. Positive values attract a person toward a goal, negative values repel a person away from a goal, and zero represents a neutral point. The sign of the values has an important influence on the dynamic process. For example, avoidance processes induced by two negative acts produce more vacillation than approach processes induced by two positive acts, even when the difference in value between two negatives equals that for two positives. The neutral or reference point can be influenced by context or "framing" (see Helson, 1959; Parducci, 1974; Tversky and Kahneman, 1981).

This concludes our overview of the general theoretical structure. For any given decision task, a specific mathematical model can be constructed from this general framework, and quantitative empirical tests can be derived. In the next section, we outline two different specific models—one for choice tasks and another for selling price tasks. Note that only the motor system changes across these two decision tasks, and the valence and decision systems are assumed to remain invariant across these two measures of preference.

4.3 RESPONSE MODELS FOR CHOICE AND SELLING PRICE TASKS

Binary Choice Response Model

Suppose the decision-maker is asked to choose between two actions by pushing either a left or right response key on a computer. Figure 4.2 gives an outline of the basic ideas of the choice model for this situation. The horizontal axis indicates the deliberation time, and the vertical axis represents the difference in preference states between the right and left actions (positive differences produce a tendency to move toward the right key; negative differences produce a tendency to move toward the left key). The polygonal line is a sample path of the difference in preference states during deliberation, and note that it wanders up and down as the decision-maker considers the various consequences of each action. The flat lines located at the top and bottom of the figure are called the inhibitory thresholds. No movement is emitted until the difference in preference states exceeds or overcomes this inhibitory threshold magnitude. If the upper threshold is exceeded before the lower threshold, then the right key is pushed. The vertical line on the right-hand side of the figure indicates the time required to exceed the threshold and make the decision.

Realistically, the inhibitory threshold would start at some large magnitude at the beginning of deliberation, and gradually weaken or decay toward zero as the deliberation process continued. However, for simplicity, the inhibitory threshold was fixed to a constant value for the predictions computed in the applications described later.

In sum, the first act to exceed the threshold wins the race and determines the choice. The probability of choosing each action is given by the probability that an action will win the race, and the time required to make the decision is determined by the mean time required to exceed the threshold. (See

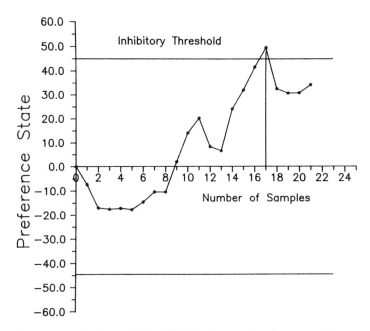

Figure 4.2 Choice model for DFT. The horizontal axis represents time or the number of consequences sampled during deliberation. The vertical axis represents the difference in preference states between two actions. Positive values represent a preference for taking the action located on the right, and negative values represent a preference for taking the action on the left. The horizontal lines parallel to the horizontal time axis represent threshold bounds. The action on the right is taken as soon as the difference in preference exceeds the upper bound, and the action on the left is taken as soon as the difference in preference exceeds the lower bound.

Busemeyer and Townsend, 1992, for the derivation of the mathematical formulas used to compute the choice probabilities and mean response times.)

Indifference Response Model

In some choice tasks, the decision-maker is permitted to express indifference. Consider the case where three options are available: (1) press the left key for one action, (2) press the right key for a second action, or (3) press the middle key for indifference. The binary choice model described above is extended to allow for indifference responses as follows. Each time the difference in preference states crosses zero (the neutral point), there is a probability that the decision-maker will stop and push the indifference response key. The probability of stopping and pushing the indifference key in the neutral state is called the exit probability. (See Busemeyer and Townsend, 1992, for the derivation of the mathematical formulas used to compute the choice probabilities for the indifference response.)

In general, the exit probability would be zero at the beginning of deliberation and gradually increase during deliberation. However, for simplicity, the exit probability was fixed to a constant value for the predictions computed in the applications described later.

Dynamic Matching Model

Suppose a decision-maker owns a risky venture which could yield a win of $500 or a loss of $500 with equal probability. Now the owner considers selling this investment, and the minimum selling price needs to be determined. The minimum selling price is the price at which the decision-maker is indifferent between keeping the risky investment or taking the cash value. This is closely related to finding the cash equivalent of a investment. Below we present an account of how the minimum selling price or cash equivalent is estimated by a dynamical matching process.

According to DFT, the decision-maker proceeds through a series of hypothetical choices between the investment and candidate prices until an indifference response is elicited with a candidate price. The matching process starts by considering a hypothetical choice between the investment and an initial selling price (e.g., the midpoint between the minimum and maximum possible price). If the choice produces a response favoring the selling price, then this initial price is too high, and the price is decreased by a fixed amount, δ. If the choice produces a response favoring the investment, then this initial price is too low, and the price is increased by a fixed amount, δ. In both of the above cases, the matching process is repeated using the newly adjusted price. This matching process continues until the choice between the investment and a candidate price elicits an indifference response, at which point the price currently being considered is selected and reported.

The matching process is illustrated in figure 4.3. The horizontal axis represents candidate prices, with the minimum and maximum points fixed by the minimum and maximum amounts that can be obtained from the investment. The point indicated by the arrow in the figure represents a candidate price currently being considered for the investment. There is a probability u of making a step down, which is determined by the probability of choosing the current price over the investment. There is another probability v of making a step up, which is determined by the probability of choosing the investment over the current price. Finally, there is a probability i of choosing the indifference response, which would terminate the matching process at the current price. (See Busemeyer and Townsend, 1992, for the derivation of the mathematical formulas used to compute the distribution of selling prices for an investment.)

This matching process is not restricted to selling prices or cash equivalents. For example, it can also be used to find probability equivalents. In the latter case, the decision-maker is asked to find a probability value that makes him or her indifferent between a gamble and a fixed cash value. In this case, the matching process is applied to the probability scale, and the decision-maker

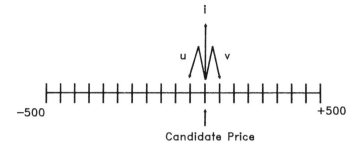

u = Pr[step down] = Pr[prefer candidate price]
v = Pr[step up] = Pr[prefer gamble]
i = Pr[report as final price] = Pr[being indifferent]

Figure 4.3 Dynamic matching model. A candidate price is compared to the gamble that is being evaluated. A choice favoring the price is made with probability *u*, in which case the price is reduced by an increment. A choice favoring the gamble is made with probability *v*, in which case the price is increased by an increment. An indifference response is made with probability *i*, in which case the matching process terminates, and the current price is selected.

performs a sequence of tests of probability values until an indifference response is elicited.

In sum, minimum selling prices, cash equivalents, and probability equivalents are determined by the binary choice and indifference response models discussed previously. Thus, the same parameter values used to compute the predictions for choice probabilities in binary choice tasks can also be used to compute the distribution of prices selected in a selling price task. In the next section, we show how the theory provides a simple explanation for what were previously considered "paradoxical" findings from the view of more traditional static-deterministic derivatives of expected utility theory.

4.4 INCONSISTENCIES AMONG PREFERENCE MEASURES

Static-deterministic decision theories (such as expected utility theory and its variants) generally assume that decision-makers can precisely and reliably determine their minimum selling price. In other words, static-deterministic theories are based on the solvability axiom which states that decision-makers can solve for the unique price such that they are indifferent between keeping an investment or taking the cash value. In fact, empirical research indicates that decision-makers are not very reliable in their estimates of minimum selling prices or cash equivalents. Schoemaker and Hershey (1993) reported a test-retest correlation as low as .50 from management students who were asked to give cash equivalents for simple gambles 1 week apart in time. Although most decision theorists readily acknowledge that selling prices are unreliable, the theoretical implications of this fact have not been thoroughly explored. Below, we show that two different "paradoxical" findings from decision research can be explained as an emergent property of the fundamental stochastic and dynamical nature of preference.

Inconsistencies Between Choice and Selling Price

The two most popular methods for measuring an individual's preference between two actions is the *choice method* and the *minimum selling price method*. According to traditional deterministic-static decision theories, if L and R are two actions, then each action can be assigned a utility, u(L) and u(R) respectively, such that if u(R) > u(L), then action R should be chosen over action L, and the selling price for R should be greater than the selling price for L. In other words, the preference order measured by the choice method should be consistent with the preference order measured by the selling price method.

One "paradoxical" finding in the decision-making literature is that under certain well-known conditions, the preference ordering measured by choice systematically disagrees with the preference ordering measured by selling price (Lichtenstein and Slovic, 1971; Lindman, 1971; see Slovic and Lichtenstein, 1983, for a review). In particular, suppose the decision-maker is asked to consider two gambles called the P-bet and the D-bet. Both gambles are approximately equal in expected value, but the P-bet has a high probability of winning a small amount (e.g., .99 probability of winning $4 or else nothing), and the D-bet has a low probability of winning a large amount (e.g., .33 probability of winning $12 or else nothing). The usual finding is that the P-bet is chosen more frequently over the D-Bet, but the selling price for the D-bet is more frequently larger than the selling price for the P-bet. This finding has even been replicated at a Las Vegas gambling casino using casino players and real money (Lichtenstein and Slovic, 1973)!

Previous theoretical explanations for this type of preference reversal finding have been based on the idea that changing the way preference is measured from choice to selling price changes the parameters that enter the calculation of the utility of each gamble. For example, Tversky, Sattath, and Slovic (1988) hypothesized that individuals assign separate weights to the probability dimension and the value dimension for gambles of the form "win X with probability P." Furthermore, they hypothesize that these weights change depending on whether the individual is asked to make a choice or select a selling price. To account for the preference reversal finding, they assume that more weight is given to probability in the choice task, but more weight is given to the payoff value in the selling price task. Below, we provide an alternative explanation which does not require changes in parameters to account for the inconsistencies between choice and selling price.

It turns out that this "paradoxical" inconsistency in preference ordering between choice and selling prices is an emergent property of the dynamic-stochastic choice and selling price models described above. Figure 4.4 illustrates the predictions computed from the mathematical formulas for the

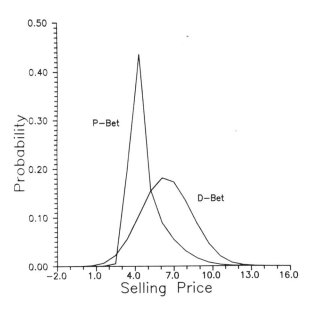

Figure 4.4 Distribution of selling prices predicted by DFT for the P-bet and the D-bet. The horizontal axis represents the various possible prices. The vertical axis represents the relative frequency that a price is selected. Predictions were generated using the exact same parameter values that produced a probability of choosing the P-bet over the D-bet equal to .56.

choice and selling price models (see Busemeyer and Goldstein, 1992, for more details).

First, the parameters of the choice model were selected so that the predictions from the choice model accurately reproduced the observed choice relative frequencies. The figure illustrates an example where the probability of choosing the P-bet over the D-bet was predicted by the choice model to be .56, which is approximately the same as the empirically observed proportions for this particular example choice problem.

Second (and this is the crucial point), these *same exact parameter values* were used to calculate predictions from the selling price model to produce the distributions of minimum selling prices shown in the figure. Note that the predicted distribution of selling prices for the P-bet lies below that for the D-bet, consistent with the observed results. Furthermore, note that the variance of the D-bet distribution is predicted to be larger than that for the P-bet, which is also consistent with known results (e.g., Bostic, Herrnstein, and Luce, 1990). Thus, a systematic reversal in the preference ordering was predicted using the same parameter values for the valence and decision systems and simply changing the motor system.

The precise reason that DFT produces this reversal in preference is an emergent property of the interactions of the dynamic and stochastic components of the model. However, a heuristic explanation might help give the reader some intuition about this mechanism. According to the model, the initial candidate selling price starts near the middle of the price scale. Because of the way the gambles are constructed, the middle of the scale produces an overestimate of the price for each gamble. According to the model, it is easy to discriminate the preference difference between the cash value and the worth of the P-bet because of the low variance of the P-bet. This high level of discriminability causes the initial price to quickly adjust down toward the true indifference point. Also according to the model, it is difficult to discriminate the preference difference between the cash value and the worth of the D-bet because of the high variance of the D-bet. This low level of discriminability causes the initial price to slowly adjust down toward the true indifference point, and the process wanders around and stops far short of a complete adjustment needed to reach the true indifference point.

In sum, DFT provides a simple explanation of the inconsistencies between two measures of preference—choice and selling price—in a coherent manner by using the same model parameter values for both tasks. A stronger test of the theory is provided by using these same parameter values once again to account for an inconsistency in preference found with another two measures of preference, described next.

Inconsistencies Between Certainty and Probability Equivalents

Two methods are commonly used by decision analysts to measure the utility in risky investments: one is called the certainty equivalence method and the other is called the probability equivalence method. Hershey and Schoemaker (1985) proposed a two-stage design for testing the consistency of these two ways of measuring utility. In both stages, a measurement of the utility of a gamble of the form "win $500 with probability P" is obtained. In the first stage, this utility is measured by the certainty equivalence method, and in the second stage it is measured by the probability equivalence method.

In the first stage, the probability of winning is set to $P = .50$, and the decision-maker is asked to find the cash value X that makes him or her indifferent between the cash value (X) and the gamble (win $200 with probability .50). According to most static-deterministic theories, this problem is solved by finding the value of X such that

$$u(X) = w(.50)u(200),$$

where $w(.50)$ is the decision weight assigned to the probability of winning, $u(200)$ is the utility of $200, and $u(X)$ is the utility of the cash value X. For example, suppose the decision-maker is indifferent between the cash value of $X = \$75$ and the gamble "win $200 with probability .50."

In the second stage, utility is measured by a probability equivalence method. This is accomplished by asking the decision-maker to find the probability P such that he or she is indifferent between the cash value X and the gamble "win $200 with probability P" where X is the same cash value obtained from the first-stage task. For example, if $X = \$75$ was selected in the first stage, then the decision-maker is asked to find P such that he or she is indifferent between the cash value of $75 and the gamble "win $200 with probability P." According to most static-deterministic theories, this problem is solved by finding the probability P such that

$$u(X) = w(P)u(200).$$

Obviously, to be consistent across both stages, the decision-maker should choose $P = .50$, the original probability value used to determine X in the first stage. In other words, according to static-deterministic utility theories, the P value selected in the second stage should always be set to $P = .5$, independent of the value of X chosen in the first stage.

According to static-deterministic theories, the variance of the P value selected in the second stage should be zero. In fact, Hershey and Schoemaker (1985) found a considerable amount of variability in the second-stage P value. More important, the variation in the P value was systematically related to the payoff value X selected in the first stage. The observed correlation between the first-stage value of X and the second-stage value of P was $r = .67$. This runs counter to static-deterministic theories which predicted zero correlation between the two stages. These results were later replicated by Schoemaker and Hershey (1992) and Johnson and Shkade (1989).

Table 4.2A provides a summary of the results of the experiments by Hershey and Schoemaker (1985) and Schoemaker and Hershey (1992). This table was constructed as follows. First, the monetary scale was rescaled to match the probability scale (i.e, we replaced X with $X/200$). Then both scales were partitioned into three response categories: $[0, .45)$, $[.45, .55]$, and $(.55, 1.0]$. Each cell of the table indicates the proportion of 300 subjects that made responses within each of the nine categories formed by crossing the three first-stage categories with the three second-stage categories.[1] For example, the middle row indicates the proportion of subjects selecting second-stage values within the interval $[.45, .55]$. According to static-deterministic theories, all of the responses should fall into this interval. Instead, the table shows a strong posi-

Table 4.2 Observed (A) and predicted (B) relative frequencies of probability and certainty equivalents from Hershey and Shoemaker experiments

Second-stage value	First-stage value		
	0.0−.55	.45−.55	.56−1.0
A. Observed relative frequencies for gain conditions			
.56−1.0	.07	.04	.25
.45−.55	.12	.10	.12
0.0−.44	.20	.04	.06
B. Predicted relative frequencies from DFT using the same parameter values as in figure 4.3			
.56−1.0	.08	.07	.27
.45−.55	.08	.06	.06
0.0−.44	.28	.04	.06

Data from Hershey and Shoemaker (1985) and Schoemaker and Hershey (1992).

James T. Townsend and Jerome Busemeyer

tive correlation between the first- and second-stage selections. Note that the largest frequencies occur in the lower-left and upper-right corner cells.

The predictions computed from DFT are shown in table 4.2B. It is important to note that we used the *exact same parameter values* in table 4.2B that were used in figure 4.4. Also note that the model accurately reproduces the positive correlation between first- and second-stage results. Thus, the systemic discrepancies between certainty and probability equivalence methods for measuring utility can be explained without postulating changes in utilities across tasks. Instead, the discrepancies can be explained as the result of the dynamical-stochastic processes required to perform these two tasks.

4.5 CONCLUDING COMMENTS

For the past 50 years, the field of decision-making has been dominated by static-deterministic theories. While these theories have provided a useful first approximation to human decision-making behavior, they fail to describe two very basic facts about human decision-making behavior—the variability and the temporal evolution of preferences. We think it is time to consider a better second-order approximation to human decision-making that captures these two basic properties of human preference. In this chapter, we presented an alternative approach called decision field theory (DFT) which provides a dynamical-stochastic description of decision-making. Furthermore, we showed that what often appears to be "paradoxical" decision behavior from the point of view of static-deterministic theories can be understood as emergent properties of the dynamical-stochastic process that individuals use to perform decision tasks.

NOTE

1. The data in table 4.2A come from experiments by Hershey and Schoemaker (1985) and Schoemaker and Hershey (1992). Each experiment had four conditions: Two conditions employed gambles which produced gains of the form "win $200 with probability P," and the other two conditions employed gambles which produced losses of the form "lose $200 with probability P." Table 4.2 only includes the conditions which employed gains because we used parameter values from previous research on preference reversal that were restricted to gains. The two gain conditions differed according to the task order: the certainty equivalent task in stage 1 followed by the probability equivalent task in stage 2; in the other condition the opposite task order was used. For both task orders, static-deterministic theories predict that all of the subjects should fall into the middle row of table 4.2. We pooled the data across both task orders, and we also pooled across both experiments to produce the results shown in table 4.2.

REFERENCES

Atkinson, J. W., and Birch, D. (1970). *The dynamics of action.* New York: Wiley.

Bostic, R., Herrnstein, R. J., and Luce, R. D. (1990). The effect on the preference-reversal phenomenon of using choice indifference. *Journal of Economic Behavior and Organization, 13,* 193–212.

Busemeyer, J. R., and Goldstein, W. M. (1992). Linking together different measures of preference: a dynamic model of matching derived from decision field theory. *Organizational Behavior and Human Decision Processes, 52*, 370–396.

Busemeyer, J. R., and Myung, I. J. (1992). An adaptive approach to human decision making: learning theory, decision theory, and human performance. *Journal of Experimental Psychology: General, 121*, 177–194.

Busemeyer, J. R., and Townsend, J. T. (1992). Fundamental derivations for decision field theory. *Mathematical Social Sciences, 23*, 255–282.

Busemeyer, J. R., and Townsend, J. T. (1993). Decision field theory: a dynamic-cognitive approach to decision making in an uncertain environment. *Psychological Review 100*, 432–459.

Bush, R. R., and Mosteller, F. (1955). *Stochastic models for learning.* New York: Wiley.

Cofer, C. N., and Appley, M. H. (1964). *Motivation: theory and research.* New York: Wiley.

Coombs, C. H., and Avrunin, G. S. (1988) *The structure of conflict.* Hillsdale, NJ: Erlbaum.

Diederich, A. (in press). A dynamic model for multi-attribute decision problems. *Acta Psychologica.*

Edwards, W. (1962). Subjective probabilities inferred from decisions. *Psychological Review, 69*, 109–135.

Grossberg, S., and Gutowski, W. E. (1987). Neural dynamics of decision making under risk: affective balance and cognitive-emotional interactions. *Psychological Review, 94*, 303–318.

Helson, H. (1959). Adaption level theory. In S. Koch (Ed.), *Psychology: A study of science*, Vol. 1 (pp. 565–621). New York: McGraw-Hill.

Hershey, J. C., and Schoemaker, P. J. H. (1985). Probability versus certainty equivalence: methods in utility measurement: are they equivalent? *Management Science, 31*, 1213–1231.

Hull, C. L. (1938). The goal gradient hypothesis applied to some "field force" problems in the behavior of young children. *Psychological Review, 45*, 271–299.

James, W. (1890/1950). *The principles of psychology*, Vol. 2. New York: Dover.

Janis, I. L., and Mann, L. (1977). *Decision making: a psychological analysis of conflict, choice, and commitment.* New York: Free Press.

Johnson, E. J., and D. A. Schkade (1989). Bias in utility assessments: further evidence and explanations. *Management Science, 35*, 406–424.

Kahneman, D., and Tversky, A. (1979). Prospect theory: an analysis of decision under risk. *Econometrica, 47*, 263–291.

Lewin, K. (1935). *A dynamic theory of personality.* New York: McGraw-Hill.

Lichtenstein, S., and Slovic, P. (1971). Reversals of preference between bids and choices in gambling decisions. *Journal of Experimental Psychology, 89*, 46–55.

Lichtenstein, S., and Slovic, P. (1973). Response-induced reversals of preferences in gambling: an extended replication in Las Vegas. *Journal of Experimental Psychology, 101*, 16–20.

Lindman, H. R. (1971). Inconsistent preferences among gambles. *Journal of Experimental Psychology, 89*, 390–397.

Luce, R. D. (1986). *Response times: their role in inferring elementary mental organization.* New York: Oxford University Press.

Miller, N. E. (1944). Experimental studies of conflict. In J. McV. Hunt (Ed.), *Personality and the behavior disorders*, Vol. 1 (pp. 431–465). New York: Ronald Press.

Parducci, A. (1974). Contextual effects: a range frequency analysis. In E. C. Carterette and M. P. Friedman (Eds.), *Handbook of perception*, Vol. 2. New York: Academic Press.

Raaijmakers, J. G. W., and Shiffrin, R. M. (1981). Search of associative memory. *Psychological Review*, 88, 93–134.

Savage, L. J. (1954). *The foundations of statistics*. New York: Wiley.

Schoemaker, P. J. H., and Hershey, J. C. (1992). Utility measurement: signal, noise, and bias. *Organizational Behavior and Human Decision Processes*, 52, 397–424.

Slovic, P., and Lichtenstein, S. (1983). Preference reversal: a broader perspective. *American Economic Review*, 73, 596–605.

Stevenson, M. K. (1986). A discounting model for decisions with delayed positive and negative outcomes. *Journal of Experimental Psychology: General*, 115, 131–154.

Svenson, O. (1992). Differentiation and consolidation theory of human decision making: a frame of reference for the study of pre- and post-decision processes. *Acta Psychologica*, 80, 143–168.

Thurstone, L. L. (1959). *The measurement of values*. Chicago: University of Chicago Press.

Townsend, J. T., and Ashby, F. G. (1983). *Stochastic modeling of elementary psychological processes*. London: Cambridge University Press.

Townsend, J. T., and Busemeyer, J. R. (1989). Approach-avoidance: return to dynamic decision behavior. In C. Izawa (Ed.), *Current issues in cognitive processes: Tulane Flowerree Symposium on Cognition* Hillsdale, NJ: Erlbaum.

Tversky, A., and Kahneman, D. (1981). The framing of decisions and the psychology of choice. *Science*, 211, 453–458.

Tversky, A., Sattath, S., and Slovic, P. (1988). Contingent weighting in judgment and choice. *Psychological Review*, 95, 371–384.

Von Neumann, J., and Morgenstern, O. (1947). *Theory of games and economic behavior*. Princeton, NJ: Princeton University Press.

Von Winterfeldt, D., and Edwards, W. (1986). *Decision analysis and behavioral research*. New York: Cambridge University Press.

Guide to Further Reading

A recent summary of the traditional static-deterministic approach to decision-making can be found in Kleindorfer, Kunreuther, and Schoemaker (1993). For a review of research on preference reversals for choice and selling price measures of preference, see Slovic and Lichtenstein (1983). A more thorough presentation of the empirical support for DFT can be found in Busemeyer and Townsend (1993). All of the mathematical equations used to calculate the predictions from DFT can be found in Busemeyer and Townsend (1992). An extension of DFT to multiattribute decision problems has been developed by Diederich (in press). An alternative dynamical model of decision-making is described in Grossberg and Gutowski (1987).

Busemeyer, J. R., and Townsend, J. T. (1992). Fundamental derivations in decision field theory. *Mathematical Social Sciences*, 23, 255–282.

Busemeyer, J. R., and Townsend, J. T. (1993). Decision field theory: a dynamic-cognitive approach to decision-making in an uncertain environment. *Psychological Review*, 100, 432–459.

Diederich, A. (in press). A dynamic model for multi-attribute decision problems. *Acta Psychologica*.

Grossberg, S., and Gutowski, W. E. (1987). Neural dynamics of decision making under risk: affective balance and cognitive-emotional interactions. *Psychological Review, 94, 300–318*.

Kleindorfer, P. R., Kunreuther H. C., and Schoemaker, P. J. H. (1993). *Decision sciences: an integrative perspective*. New York: Cambridge University Press.

Slovic, P., and Lichtenstein, S. (1983). Preference reversal: a broader perspective. *American Economic Review, 73, 596–605*.

5 Computational and Dynamical Languages for Autonomous Agents

Randall D. Beer

EDITORS' INTRODUCTION

Most chapters in this book focus on some aspect of specifically human cognition. Randy Beer, by contrast, here takes as his immediate target the behaviors of simple, artificial, insectlike creatures. Yet the issues raised and the insights gained go directly to the heart of what it is to understand human cognition itself.

The latter part of this chapter contains a discussion of detailed modeling. Here Beer studies the behavior of two kinds of creature, one that performs chemotaxis (orienting to a source of chemical stimulation, such as food) and another six-legged walking creature. Both creatures have "brains" that are neural network dynamical systems whose parameters were obtained by an artificial evolutionary process. Beer shows in detail how to deploy the tools and concepts of dynamics in understanding these creatures as dynamical systems comprised of an agent coupled with its environment. This discussion is an elegant case study in how complex behaviors can be understood dynamically, and will be useful to anyone wondering how dynamical approaches might be brought to bear in thinking about aspects of human cognition.

In a wider perspective, Beer's work can be seen as resulting from his stands on two deep theoretical issues; these are discussed in the earlier sections. The first issue is whether most progress is to be made by studying the kind of high-level, "disembodied" cognitive processes on which artificial intelligence (AI) has traditionally focused, or rather, autonomous, embodied agents in active participation with a real environment. The second issue is whether computationalism or dynamics provides the best general framework within which to understand cognitive processes. Beer is especially concerned to emphasize that computationalism—the claim that cognitive systems are internally organized as computational systems—is an empirical *hypothesis that is subject to scientific evaluation and possible refutation.*

Beer clearly sides with the study of autonomous agents and with dynamics as the preferable framework. Now, humans are autonomous agents, but are currently much too complex to be scientifically describable as such in their entirety. For this reason, Beer focuses on simpler artificial systems for which it is possible to develop detailed and rigorous scientific theories. These systems and the understanding they promote constitute steppingstones in the process of understanding how humans negotiate their own, vastly more complex environments.

5.1 INTRODUCTION

Traditionally, work in artificial intelligence (AI) and cognitive science has focused on such disembodied intellectual skills as language and abstract reasoning. However, so-called low-level concerns of embodiment have recently been taking on a growing importance in some areas of research. This shift has been precipitated by the realization that building systems capable of unconstrained interaction with the real world is very difficult and that approaches developed for disembodied systems have not translated well into such situations (Brooks, 1991). Furthermore, many problems that seemed intractable for disembodied systems have turned out to be considerably simplified by active participation in an environment (Agre and Chapman, 1987; Ballard, 1991). Reviews of recent work on embodied systems (or, as I shall call them, *autonomous agents*) can be found in Maes (1990), Meyer and Wilson (1991), and Meyer, Roitblat, and Wilson (1993). Indeed, it may very well be that our capacity for situated action (which we share with all animals) is fundamental to our penchant for language and abstract reasoning (which are evolutionarily recent elaborations). Consequently, work on autonomous agents emphasizes the primacy of actually taking action in the world over the abstract descriptions that we sometimes make of it.

The central problem for any autonomous agent is the generation of the appropriate behavior at the appropriate time as both its internal state and external situation continuously change. One of the most striking features of natural animal behavior is how well-adapted it is to the dynamical and statistical structure of real-world environments. Consider an insect walking, for example (Graham, 1985). On the one hand, walking is a paradigmatic example of a stereotyped behavior, consisting as it does of endless repetition of a seemingly fixed sequence of leg movements. However, insects can walk under a variety of conditions, such as vertically, upside-down, or following the loss of one or two legs, in which the particular forces and movements necessary for each situation are very different. Furthermore, insects can walk over complex terrain, where their gaits must be adjusted on a step-by-step basis. Indeed, there is a very real sense in which the so-called stereotyped behavior of walking is reinvented anew from moment to moment in the interaction between the insect and its environment. This almost paradoxical mixture of stability and flexibility of behavior is central to any agent that must reliably accomplish its goals in the complex, dynamical, and somewhat unpredictable environment of the real world.

What is the proper theoretical framework for the design and analysis of such systems? For the past 40 years, research on intelligent agents has been dominated by a theoretical position that I shall call *computationalism*, the idea that an agent behaves "intelligently" in its environment only insofar as it is able to represent and reason about its own goals and the relevant properties of its environment. In contrast, this chapter explores the idea that the language of dynamical systems may offer a better conceptual framework for autonomous agents. Section 5.2 assesses the relevance of computationalism for autonomous agents. Section 5.3 will then sketch what an alternative dynamical systems perspective on autonomous agents might look like. Finally, some examples of applications of this dynamical framework are presented in section 5.4.

5.2 COMPUTATION IN AUTONOMOUS AGENTS

Computation as a Theoretical Position

How relevant is computationalism to the analysis and design of autonomous agents? Before we can even begin to answer this question, we must first clearly distinguish computation as a theoretical position from the many other uses of the notion of computation, both within cognitive science and in everyday life. This may seem like an unnecessarily long-winded digression, but the word "computation" and its many relatives are actually rather ambiguous terms. For example, "computational neuroscience" is sometimes taken to refer to the construction of computer models of nervous systems and sometimes to the claim that nervous systems themselves are computers, with the intended meaning sometimes switching within a single sentence. In my experience it is all too easy for proponents of computationalism to simply dismiss its critics unless we carefully distinguish between at least the following four notions:

1. Computation as a phenomenon to be explained. Computation is something that people sometimes do. We can ride bicycles, fall in love, build airplanes, and we can compute in the everyday sense of producing a result by consciously following a step-by-step procedure. This phenomenological notion of computation is the sense in which we compute our income tax or the nth digit of π. Indeed, the very word *computer* originally referred not to any mechanical device but to a person performing a tedious mathematical calculation. This ability to deliberately form conceptual representations and manipulate them according to a step-by-step procedure is one of the many human capabilities that any cognitive science must eventually explain.

2. Computation as a mathematical formalism. In an attempt to formalize the above-mentioned ability, a number of logicians (including Gödel, Turing, Church, and Kleene) developed different mathematical models of the intuitive notion of a step-by-step procedure (called an effective procedure or an *algorithm*). These developments can be viewed as the culmination of a centuries-long effort to mechanize human reasoning, dating at least as far back as Leibnitz. For example, a Turing machine, probably the best-known model of computation, is a way of representing all functions over the integers whose values can be calculated by a finite number of primitive mechanical operations. Somewhat surprisingly, the different formalisms all turned out to be equivalent in that they could compute exactly the same set of integer functions (called the computable functions, or the partial recursive functions).

Other fundamental insights that emerged from the development of a formal theory of computation included a realization of the full generality of the notion (any countable set can be coded into the integers and is thus amenable to the formal theory of computation), the discovery that many important questions (such as the famous halting problem) lead to uncomputable functions and are thus undecidable by an algorithm, and the notion of universal machines that can compute any computable function by emulating the behavior of any other machine given a coded description of its behavior.

3. *Computation as a simulation technology.* The mechanizability of computation makes it particularly amenable to material instantiation, and the extreme flexibility of universal machines provides the necessary incentive for doing so. For these reasons, computers, the modern technological manifestation of the ideas of Turing and his contemporaries, have become permanent fixtures in our lives. Especially relevant to the present paper is the use of the computer as a tool for simulation. Computer simulation has been applied to such diverse areas as aircraft design, the greenhouse effect, and the formation of planetary rings. The field of AI was quick to embrace the simulation abilities of computers as a new experimental medium for building and testing theories of cognition.

4. *Computation as a theoretical position.* In cognitive science and AI, not only is computation a cognitive phenomenon to be studied and a technology to be employed but features of the formal theory of computation and computer technology have been elevated to the status of theoretical hypotheses about cognition (Fodor, 1975; Newell and Simon, 1976; Pylyshyn, 1984). Historically, cognition has often been examined through the lens of the most sophisticated technology of the time. Descartes had his water clocks, Freud had his steam engines, and now we have the computer. Taken at face value, there is nothing intrinsically good or bad about this development. Indeed, much of the empirical research in AI and cognitive science can be viewed as a working out of the consequences of these hypotheses.

For our purposes here, the important point is simply that computationalism is a set of theoretical *hypotheses*. The brain is no more obviously a computer than is a thunderstorm, a solar system, or an economy. Furthermore, these hypotheses are logically independent of all of the other notions of computation outlined above. From the mere fact that we can (and sometimes do) compute things, we cannot conclude that computationalism is true any more than we can conclude from the mere fact that stereos produce patterned sound waves that compressed air plays any essential role in their electronic guts. In addition, to question computationalism is certainly not to deny the fact that people can perform computations. Likewise, the formal theory of computation no more demonstrates the validity of computationalism than Riemannian geometry does the validity of general relativity, and a refutation of the latter theory in each case is certainly not an invalidation of the former body of mathematics. Finally, building computer simulations of cognitive systems no more lends support to computationalism than computing planetary orbits supports the hypothesis that planets somehow compute their own orbits. It is entirely possible and even quite fruitful to build computer *models* of noncomputational *theories*. Every other branch of science and engineering does this all the time.

At the risk of belaboring what I hope is by now an obvious distinction, let me briefly mention just one more example. Lenses are an important tool in astronomy. Astronomers rely on lenses to resolve the tiny images of the distant objects that they study. It so happens that the concept of a lens also plays a theoretical role in astronomy in explaining the distortion and multiple images that occur when some massive body lies along the line of sight to a more distant object (a phenomenon called gravitational lensing). Of course, there are many other phenomena that astronomers observe (also with lenses) whose explanation has nothing at all to do with lenses. But despite this dual role of lenses as both a tool and a theoretical construct, astronomers never seem to confuse the object they are looking at and the instrument they are looking with, and neither should we. Computer models contain symbolic structures that represent theoretical entities *to the modeler*, while computationalism claims that agents contain symbolic structures that represent their situation *to themselves* and that play a causal role in generating their behavior. It is this (and only this) notion of computation as a theoretical position that will concern us in the remainder of this section.

The Empirical Claims of Computationalism

Scientific hypotheses are usually valued for their specificity. In order to be a legitimate scientific hypothesis, computationalism must be falsifiable, i.e., it must make empirical predictions that are clear and specific enough to be tested and it must be possible for these predictions to be false. Relativity, for example, made very specific predictions about the bending of light near the sun and the precession of Mercury's orbit which, though at odds with the predictions of Newtonian mechanics, were subsequently verified. While such quantitative predictions are clearly beyond our present capabilities, at the very least it is reasonable to expect computationalism to provide sufficiently specific claims that we could determine whether or not the theory were true of a given agent. If no such determination can be made, then computationalism is too vague to be a theory of anything. If, on the other hand, the predictions are so general that they are automatically true of every physical system, then computationalism is tautological and hence scientifically vacuous.

The basic idea of computationalism is that cognition is a species of computation. The claim is that cognition involves the manipulation of mental symbols in a way entirely analogous to a Turing machine's algorithmic manipulation of strings of symbols, not just when we are "playing computer," but whenever we consciously reason at all. Furthermore, a computational language has come to be applied to processes (such as language comprehension, learning, perception, and motor control) to which we do not have even apparent introspective access and thus for which we have no a priori reason to believe that they are anything like deliberative reasoning, let alone computation. In all of these applications of computationalism, the idea that symbols somehow encode or *represent* information relevant to behavior (e.g., my perception of a car to my left or my belief that apples are red) plays a fundamental theoretical role. Interestingly, this is a significant extension of the formal theory of computation which is, in fact, a purely syntactic theory. However, attempts to interpret the states of an ongoing computation as being *about* something introduce semantic concerns that have come to dominate discussions of computational theories in cognitive science.

Intuitively, the overall shape of computationalism is clear enough. But beyond the somewhat suggestive but vague sense in which at least deliberative reasoning is like computation, just what *are* the falsifiable empirical claims that computationalism is making? What, specifically, am I buying into if I accept this theory and what am I giving up if I reject it? By what series of tests would I determine whether a given agent lent evidence for or against this theory's hypotheses? How would I recognize a representation or a computation if I saw one?

Given its central role in computationalism, let's begin with the question of what constitutes an internal representation. One of the most common intuitions about representations is that they endow an agent with *internal state*. Indeed, the postulation of complex internal states is one of the things that computationalism uses to distinguish itself from behaviorism. Likewise, the debate between proponents and critics of situated agent research has often tacitly assumed the equivalence of internal state and representation, with proponents using criticisms of representation to argue the need for reactive (or state-free) systems and critics using the limitations of state-free systems to argue the need for representation (e.g., Brooks, 1991; Kirsch, 1991). But is the mere possession of internal state a sufficient condition for representation? Obviously not, since all physical systems possess internal state and most computationalists would hesitate in accepting, say, the concentrations of reactants in an industrial fractionation column as representing anything about the company outside. Of course, some of these concentrations may be more or less *correlated* with various aspects of the company, but once again, correlation is a property of the states of physical systems in general and thus does not serve to distinguish a computational system from a merely physical one.

Unfortunately, many commonsense notions of computation suffer from a similar problem. For example, some see the mere presence of a systematic relationship between a system's "inputs" and "outputs" as evidence of its computational nature. On this view, a device that reliably outputs the square root of a given input must be computational because it is "computing" the square root function. But this is once again an empirically vacuous notion of computation because all physical systems exhibit systematic relationships between their various parts (in fact, they must if science's assumption that all natural phenomena are law-governed is correct). Are we to interpret all such systems as *computing* these relationships? Does the fact that planets move in elliptical orbits imply that solar systems are computing these ellipses? Likewise, some view the existence of a computer program that mimics some fragment of human behavior as providing evidence for computationalism (and even go so far as to view such a program as itself a theory). But we can build computer models of many things. If building a computer model of a fluid doesn't make computationalism true of fluids, why should we assume that building a computer model of human behavior makes computationalism true of cognition?

Computationalism as an Organizational Claim

We have seen above that many of the informal intuitions we have about computationalism do not qualify as empirically falsifiable claims because they appear to be true of any physical system. Thus it is perhaps not too surprising that there is currently a great deal of controversy regarding the foundations of computationalism (Smith, 1991; Harnad, 1994). In this section, I argue that, if computationalism can be interpreted as making any empirically falsifiable claims at all, then it is making a claim about the internal organization of a system.

The essence of the picture that computationalism seems to be trying to paint is that of an agent whose causal structure is isomorphic to some computation, i.e., whose physical states and causal laws mirror the functional states and algorithms of a computation. This isomorphism is often referred to as "implementation." Note that this is a claim about a system's internal organization rather than merely its external behavior. But this isomorphism cannot be to just any computation, or we are back to vacuity since, by definition, a computer model of anything is a computation that is isomorphic in some relevant way to that thing. Rather, computational notions must somehow play an essential role in the system's operation. It must be by virtue of this isomorphism, and only by virtue of this isomorphism, that the system behaves the way that it does. For example, a theory of calculator operation is computational because a calculator's internal states have an interpretation as numbers and its causal laws "line up" with the laws of arithmetic. Thus, not only *can* a calculator's internal organization be mapped onto arithmetic computations, but in some sense it *must* be in order to understand its operation as a calculator. At least in principle, this organizational claim is an empirically testable one, because we can presumably always look inside a given system and see if its organization can be interpreted computationally.

As a practical matter, the entire conceptual framework offered by the language of computation seems to work best for systems that, like calculators, wear their computational organization on their sleeves, so to speak, in that, by their very design, they invite a natural computational interpretation. Such systems have a particularly direct relationship between what they do and how they do it, between their competence and performance theories. They

Computational and Dynamical Languages for Autonomous Agents

have reliably identifiable internal configurations of parts that can be usefully interpreted as representing aspects of the domain in which the system operates and reliably identifiable internal components that can be usefully interpreted as algorithmically transforming these representations so as to produce whatever output the system produces from whatever input it receives.

In contrast, the conceptual framework of computation seems to work least well for highly distributed and richly interconnected systems whose parts do not admit of any straightforward functional decomposition into representations and modules which algorithmically manipulate them. This is not to say that a computational explanation of such systems can never be found. However, a computational account of such systems may be much less compelling than for a calculator precisely because the organization that the very terms of the computational language presuppose is nowhere apparent. Here, a computational language may actually mislead us into expecting that representations and algorithms in some form must be lurking in the wings when, in fact, a computational organization is really only one possibility among many. In such cases, it would presumably be better to search for other mathematical languages more suited to characterizing the behavior of highly distributed and richly interconnected systems.

With this organizational claim in mind, let us return to a slightly refined version of the question posed at the beginning of this section: How relevant is the *organizational claim* of computationalism to the analysis and design of autonomous agents? This question can be split into two questions: Can an autonomous agent be organized in a computational fashion? Must an autonomous agent be so organized? It seems obvious that agents *can* be organized in this way, given that AI researchers have had at least some limited success in building such agents, but I can see no a priori reason why an agent *must* be organized in this way. The more interesting questions are probably the following: Are animals organized in this fashion? Should the autonomous agents that we build be so organized?

The functional organization of the neural mechanisms underlying animal behavior is currently very much an open empirical question. It is no exaggeration to say that nervous systems do not in general exhibit any obvious functional decomposition into computational components (except, once again, in the trivial senses in which all physical systems do, namely (1) the outputs of nerve cells are systematically related to their inputs and their internal state, and (2) we can simulate models of nervous systems on a computer). However, there are a few tantalizing examples where a computational language does appear to be a genuinely useful one (Churchland and Sejnowski, 1992). For example, the mammalian visual system seems to be at least partly decomposable into richly interconnected but somewhat distinct functional modules (for a recent review, see Kandel, 1991). Likewise, the vector sum of a population of directionally selective nerve cells in the rhesus monkey appears to represent the subsequent direction of movement of its arm and, when the intended direction changes, the vector sum of this average can be rotate from the old target to the new (Georgopoulos, Lurito, Petric' 1989).

However, many other aspects of nervous systems, such as the neural cir cuitry underlying rhythmic movements, olfaction, and essentially all higher cognitive processes, have so far resisted all attempts to interpret their organization in anything like the terms offered by computationalism. Furthermore, it is worth pointing out that, in order to make a computational language work even in the above-mentioned cases, our notions of representation and computation (already ill-defined) must be significantly extended to include highly distributed and massively parallel analog processes. It is quite possible that such extensions are pushing a language founded on the step-by-step manipulation of discrete symbols by functionally distinct modules past the breaking point. Indeed, given the way in which natural selection operates, it would be somewhat surprising if nervous systems exhibited the almost crystalline structure of a calculator. Thus, while we certainly cannot at this point reject a computational language in our attempts to understand natural agents, there are good reasons to suppose that, at the very least, a significant generalization of it will be required.

Should the autonomous agents that we build be organized in a computational fashion? A significant advantage of this organization is that it leads almost directly to a powerful design methodology: A solution to some complex task is hierarchically composed from many functional modules, each of which solves some simpler subproblem and communicates its solutions to other modules. In addition, systems organized in this way are easy to understand and repair owing to the localization of particular subtasks to individual modules or small collections of modules. However, artificial agents organized along the lines suggested by computationalism have yet to exhibit the versatility and robustness of even the simplest animals, and there is growing evidence that new organizational ideas, perhaps drawn from animals themselves, will be required (Beer, 1990; Maes, 1990; Brooks, 1991; Meyer, Roitblat, and Wilson, 1993). Thus, we have good reason to question the appropriateness of the conceptual framework offered by computationalism for the design of autonomous agents as well, raising once again the need to broaden our organizational horizons.

5.3 A DYNAMICAL SYSTEMS PERSPECTIVE

Given the questions raised above, I believe that, in order to understand the behavior of autonomous agents, we must generalize our organizational notions from computational systems to *dynamical systems* (Beer, 1995). To say that something is a dynamical system is to say only that its future behavior depends on its current state in some principled way, with no additional requirement that this state be interpretable as a representation or that the evolution of this state be interpretable as a computation. Thus, a conceptual framework founded on dynamical systems is potentially applicable to a wider class of systems than is a conceptual framework founded on computation, because the former requires fewer organizational commitments than the latter. A complete review of the modern theory of dynamical systems is clearly beyond the scope of this chapter. However, it is worth pointing out that this theory provides a rich geometric and topological vocabulary for expressing the possible long-term behaviors of a dynamical system and the dependence of those behaviors on parameters (Wiggins, 1990; Hale and Koçak, 1991, Abraham and Shaw, 1992).

While there is a significant body of mathematics on dynamical systems, the mathematical theory of dynamical systems is no more a theory of autonomous agents than is the formal theory of computation. Rather, like computation, dynamical systems theory is best seen as offering a conceptual framework for thinking about complex systems, and a framework that is very different from that offered by computation. Where a computational language suggests that complex but highly structured behavior arises from the step-by-step transformation of discrete symbols by identifiable functional modules, a dynamical language suggests that such behavior can arise as a global property of the continuous interaction of many distributed, cooperative processes. Our task as scientists is to use the language and mathematical tools offered by dynamical systems theory to develop theories of particular phenomena of interest.

A growing number of researchers are finding the language of dynamical systems a fruitful one for understanding neural circuits (Skarda and Freeman, 1987; Rinzel and Ermentrout, 1989; Wang and Rinzel, 1992), the control of movement (Schöner and Kelso, 1988; Turvey, 1990), and even natural language (Elman, 1991; Pollack, 1991) and cognition in general (Smolensky, 1988; Giunti, 1992; van Gelder, 1992; Pollack, 1993). In the remainder of this section, I sketch a view of autonomous agents from the perspective of dynamical systems (Beer, 1995). Some sample applications of this perspective are presented in section 5.4.

Following Ashby (Ashby, 1960), I will model an agent and its environment as two continuous-time dynamical systems $\mathcal{A}$ and $\mathcal{E}$, respectively. Note that the division between an agent and its environment is somewhat arbitrary. For example, it will sometimes be convenient to view an agent's body as part of $\mathcal{A}$ and sometimes as part of $\mathcal{E}$. In general, there are many different ways to partition the world into components whose interactions we wish to understand. Because an agent and its environment are in constant interaction, $\mathcal{A}$ and $\mathcal{E}$ are coupled nonautonomous dynamical systems. This coupling can be represented with a sensory function $\mathbf{S}$ from environmental state variables to agent parameters and a motor function $\mathbf{M}$ from agent state variables to environmental parameters. $\mathbf{S}(\mathbf{x}_{\mathcal{E}})$ corresponds to an agent's sensory inputs, while $\mathbf{M}(\mathbf{x}_{\mathcal{A}})$ corresponds to its motor outputs. Thus, we have the following model of a coupled agent-environment system (figure 5.1):

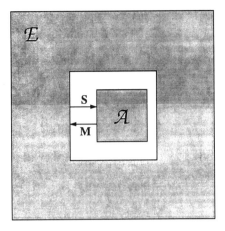

Figure 5.1 An agent and its environment as coupled dynamical systems.

$$\dot{\mathbf{x}}_{\mathscr{A}} = \mathscr{A}(\mathbf{x}_{\mathscr{A}}; \mathbf{S}(\mathbf{x}_{\mathscr{E}}))$$

$$\dot{\mathbf{x}}_{\mathscr{E}} = \mathscr{E}(\mathbf{x}_{\mathscr{E}}; \mathbf{M}(\mathbf{x}_{\mathscr{A}}))$$
(1)

Note that feedback plays a fundamental role in the relationship between an agent and its environment. Any action that an agent takes affects its environment in some way through **M**, which in turn affects the agent itself through the feedback it receives from its environment via **S**. Likewise, the environment's effects on an agent through **S** are fed back through **M** to in turn affect the environment. Thus, each of these two dynamical systems is continuously deforming the flow of the other (perhaps drastically if any coupling parameters cross bifurcation points in the receiving system's parameter space), and therefore influencing its subsequent trajectory. Any agent that is going to reliably accomplish its goals in the face of such environmental perturbations must be organized in such a way that its dynamics can compensate for or even actively exploit the structure of such perturbations.

I have been describing an agent and its environment as two separate nonautonomous dynamical systems which influence one another through sensory and motor maps. This perspective emphasizes the distinction between an agent and its environment in order to discuss the relationships between them. However, an equally legitimate view is that the two coupled nonautonomous systems $\mathscr{A}$ and $\mathscr{E}$ are merely components of a single autonomous dynamical system $\mathscr{U}$ whose state variables are the union of the state variables of $\mathscr{A}$ and $\mathscr{E}$ and whose dynamical laws are given by all of the internal relations (including **S** and **M**) among this larger set of state variables and their derivatives. Any trajectories arising in the interaction between the nonautonomous dynamical systems $\mathscr{A}$ and $\mathscr{E}$ must also be trajectories of the larger autonomous dynamical system $\mathscr{U}$ and, after transients have died out, the observed patterns of interaction between $\mathscr{A}$ and $\mathscr{E}$ must represent an attractor of $\mathscr{U}$. Neither of these perspectives is intrinsically better than the other, and we can switch between them as appropriate.

The coupled system $\mathcal{U}$ provides a dynamical basis for understanding one of the central themes of recent autonomous agent research, namely the idea that an agent's behavior arises not simply from within the agent itself, but rather through its interaction with its environment. Because of the higher dimensionality of its state space, a dynamical system formed by coupling two other systems can generate a richer range of dynamical behavior than could either subsystem in isolation. Since properties of the coupled system cannot in general be attributed to either subsystem individually, an agent's behavior properly resides only in the dynamics of the coupled system $\mathcal{U}$ and not simply in the dynamics of $\mathcal{A}$ or $\mathcal{E}$ alone. This suggests that we must learn to think of an agent as necessarily containing only a latent potential to engage in appropriate patterns of interaction. It is only when coupled with a suitable environment that this potential is actually expressed through the agent's behavior in that environment.

I have repeatedly referred to the "appropriateness" of an agent's behavior, but what makes a given behavior appropriate or inappropriate? For an animal, the appropriateness of behavior is ultimately defined by its survival, its ability to maintain intact the network of biochemical processes that keep it alive. We can think of the integrity of this network of processes as providing a constraint on the admissible trajectories of the animal's behavioral dynamics. On the other hand, the appropriateness of an artificial agent's behavior is often defined in terms of the adequate performance of whatever task it was designed for (e.g., keeping the floor clean, or exploring the surface of Mars), a constraint on the admissible trajectories of the environment. Generally speaking, then, we can define the appropriateness of an agent's behavior in terms of its continued satisfaction of some constraint $\mathbb{C}$ on the trajectories of the coupled agent-environment system $\mathcal{U}$ (figure 5.2). It is sometimes more convenient to express a desired task as a performance measure to be optimized rather than a rigid constraint to be satisfied. In these cases, $\mathbb{C}$ can be thought of as the minimum acceptable level of performance.

5.4 APPLICATIONS

In this section, I present two examples of the application of the dynamical framework sketched above to particular autonomous agent problems. In each case, I show how the problem can be formulated as a constraint on the trajectories of coupled agent and environment dynamics, present examples of agent dynamics which solve the problem, and then show how the operation of this agent dynamics can be understood using the language and tools of dynamical systems theory. In these examples, I focus on the question of how the interactions between an agent's internal control mechanisms (which I interpret as $\mathcal{A}$) and its body (which I interpret as $\mathcal{E}$) give rise to its behavior.

While the dynamical perspective being advocated in this chapter is certainly not limited to neural networks, in all of the examples presented here

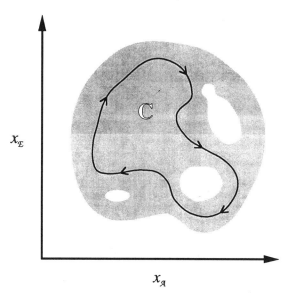

Figure 5.2 An illustration of adaptive fit. This simple example assumes that both the agent and the environment are one-dimensional dynamical systems. The constraint, volume $\mathbb{C}$, is shown in gray. This volume represents the region of the state-space of the coupled agent-environment system corresponding to acceptable performance. Here the coupled agent-environment system is shown exhibiting a limit cycle which satisfies this constraint.

an agent's dynamics is implemented using continuous-time recurrent neural networks with the following general form:

$$\tau_i \dot{y}_i = -y_i + \sum_{j=1}^{N} w_{ji}\sigma(y_j - \theta_j) + I_i(t) \quad i = 1, 2, \ldots, N \tag{2}$$

where τ is the time constant of the neuron, w_{ji} gives the strength of the connection between the jth and the ith neuron, $\sigma(\xi) = (1 + e^{-\xi})^{-1}$ is the standard sigmoidal activation function, θ is a bias term, and $I(t)$ is a possibly time-varying external input to the neuron (i.e., from a sensor). The parameters of these networks (e.g., the time constants, biases, and connection weights) define a space of dynamical systems. Using the public domain genetic algorithm package GAucsd 1.1, this space was searched for networks whose dynamics satisfy a given constraint when coupled to a given environment.

Chemotaxis

Chemotaxis is the problem of orienting to a chemical source such as a patch of food by using local measurements of chemical intensity. In the specific problem considered here, the agent is enclosed in a box containing a single patch of food. The intensity of the food falls off as the inverse square of the distance from the center of the patch. Thus, the agent must cope with a chemical signal that varies five orders of magnitude from the center of the food patch to the corners of the box. Starting from arbitrary locations and

Computational and Dynamical Languages for Autonomous Agents

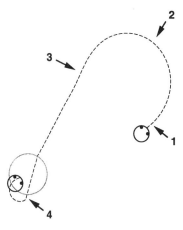

Figure 5.3 Behavior of a typical chemotactic agent. The food patch is shown as a circle circumscribed in gray and the agent's path is shown with a dashed line. The numbers refer to the corresponding plots in figure 5.5.

orientations in the environment, the agent must find and remain in the vicinity of the food patch.

In terms of the framework, I define $\mathscr{E}$ to be the dynamics of the agent's body together with the environment in which it moves. The agent's body is circular, with two chemical sensors placed symmetrically about the center line that can detect the intensity of the chemical signal at their location (figure 5.3). The agent also possesses two effectors placed on opposite sides of its body which can generate translational and rotational forces.

The dynamics of the neural circuit controlling this body is $\mathscr{A}$. For this purpose, a six-neuron, fully interconnected network was employed. The outputs of two of these neurons drive two effectors mentioned above (**M**), while another two neurons receive as inputs the signals from the chemical sensors (**S**). The remaining two neurons are interneurons whose role in the circuit is not prespecified. Owing to the symmetry of the problem, the controller is assumed to be bilaterally symmetric. The chemotaxis controller thus has 3 time constants, 3 biases, and 18 connection weights, forming a 24-dimensional parameter space that was searched using GAucsd 1.1. The performance measure to be minimized was the average distance between the agent and the food patch. Thus, $\mathbb{C}$ can be defined as some minimum acceptable distance from the patch.

A variety of different chemotaxis agents were evolved for this problem (Beer and Gallagher, 1992). By far the most common solution was to move forward while turning toward the side receiving the stronger chemical signal by an amount related to the difference between the stronger and weaker signals. A typical path for one such agent is shown in figure 5.3. Regardless of the agent's initial position and orientation, its path curves toward the food patch. Once there, the agent repeatedly crosses the patch. In a few cases, agents evolved a rather different strategy for chemotaxis. These agents

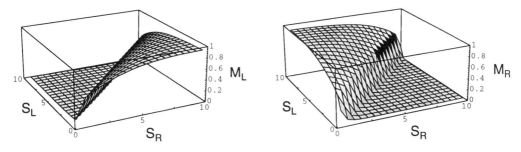

Figure 5.4 Individual motor-space projections of the location of the network's single equilibrium point as a function of the activity of the left and right chemical sensors for the chemotaxis agent shown in figure 5.3.

moved rhythmically from side to side, with the oscillations biased toward the side receiving the stronger chemical signal. Interestingly, once they near the patch, these agents stop oscillating and behave in the more common manner described above. These agents thus switch between distinct behavioral strategies depending on their distance from the patch.

How can we understand the operation of these chemotaxis agents? Recall that these networks are fully interconnected. Perhaps not surprisingly, nontrivial self and feedback connections are a common feature of the evolved controllers. However, these systems can be understood using concepts from dynamical systems theory. In order to illustrate the basic approach, I focus here on the agent shown in figure 5.3. My strategy will be to first examine how the motor space projection $\mathbf{M} = (M_L, M_R)$ of the autonomous dynamics of $\mathscr{A}$ changes as a function of $\mathbf{S} = (S_L, S_R)$ and then to decompose the dynamics of the coupled agent-environment system $\mathscr{U}$ in these terms.

For any constant pair of sensory inputs, this particular controller exhibits a single stable equilibrium point. Motor-space projections of the location of this equilibrium point as a function of S_L and S_R are shown separately for M_L and M_R in figure 5.4. If the sensory inputs were clamped to particular values, then the state of the network would flow toward a fixed point attractor whose corresponding M_L and M_R values are given by these two plots. Of course, owing to the bilateral symmetry of the network, the M_L and M_R equilibrium surfaces are just mirror images of one another about the $S_L = S_R$ diagonal. Note how the location of the M_L and M_R projections of the equilibrium point changes with sensory input. For example, if the chemical signal is stronger on the left side of the body than on the right (i.e., $S_L > S_R$), then the location of the corresponding equilibrium point has an M_R value that is significantly greater than its M_L value. As we shall see in a moment, this property accounts for the turn to the left that would be observed under these conditions.

These surfaces also exhibit several other interesting features. For example, note that the location of the equilibrium point is most sensitive in the neighborhood of the $S_L = S_R$ line, i.e., to small differences between S_L and S_R.

Computational and Dynamical Languages for Autonomous Agents

This is presumably what allows the agent to operate at great distances from the food patch, where the chemical signals (and their differences) are very tiny. However, the surface is relatively insensitive to large differences. The equilibrium surface is also relatively insensitive to the absolute magnitude of the chemical signal since it is almost flat along all lines of constant difference (i.e., lines parallel to the $S_L = S_R$ diagonal), even those near the $S_L = S_R$ diagonal. This relative insensitivity to large signals and large differences is probably what prevents the agent from overreacting near the patch.

These equilibrium surfaces summarize how the autonomous dynamics of the neural controller changes as a function of S_L and S_R. But how can they help us to understand how the agent's observed behavior arises from the interaction between the network dynamics and the dynamics of the body and environment? As the agent moves through its environment, its sensory inputs at any given moment specify a unique location for the network's equilibrium point. Furthermore, if we examine the instantaneous network state at that moment, we will find that it is flowing toward the attractor's current location. Of course, the agent is constantly moving because the two motor neurons activate the body's effectors. Thus, the network's sensory inputs at the next instant, and hence the location of its autonomous attractor, will be slightly different. However, we will still find that the network state is instantaneously flowing toward this new location. Thus, we can picture the agent-environment interaction as one in which the network state is flowing toward a constantly moving equilibrium point, the motion of which depends on the motor outputs of the network itself. However, as was mentioned earlier, the essential feature of this interaction is that when the left chemical input is stronger than the right, the motor-space projection of the equilibrium point lies in a region where the right motor output is stronger than the left (which would cause a turn to the left), and vice versa.

Figure 5.5 illustrates this interaction between the dynamics of the network and the dynamics of the body and environment at several points along the trajectory shown in figure 5.3. At *1*, S_L is slightly greater than S_R, so the motor-space projection of the equilibrium point lies on the M_R side of the diagonal. As the network state flows toward this equilibrium point, the agent begins to turn to the left. At *2*, the network state has essentially reached the attractor. As the turn ends, the equilibrium point moves back to the center line, pulling the system state along behind it. However, owing to a slight overturn at *3*, the attractor actually crosses over to the M_L side of the diagonal, causing a small compensatory turn to the right. Except for another over-compensation when the agent first encounters the patch, both the equilibrium point and the network state then remain on the diagonal (causing the agent to move along a straight line) until the agent leaves the patch at *4*. Because the odor gradient is large so near the patch, S_R is much larger than S_L at this point. This moves the equilibrium point very far onto the M_L side of the diagonal. As the system state follows, the agent makes a sharp turn to the

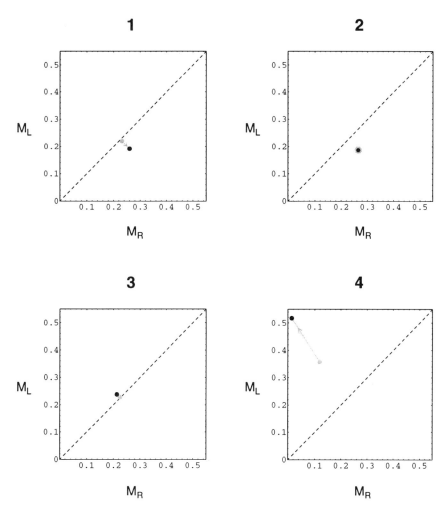

Figure 5.5 Motor-space projections of the network's instantaneous state and trajectory (gray) and the instantaneous location of the attractor (black disk) for the four points indicated in figure 5.3. States above the diagonal ($M_L > M_R$) correspond to right turns, while left turns occur when the state is below the diagonal.

right. Thus we can see how a reciprocal interaction between the effect of the body's chemical sensors on the network's autonomous dynamics and the effect of the network's motor outputs on the body's movement acts to keep the agent oriented toward the patch at all times.

Legged Locomotion

In order for a legged agent to achieve steady forward progress, the relationships among the segments comprising each individual leg and between multiple legs must be properly coordinated. These coordination problems raise some interesting issues for the present framework. In order to explore these issues, a locomotion controller for a six-legged agent was evolved and analyzed (Beer and Gallagher, 1992; Gallagher and Beer, 1993; Beer, 1995). Here I focus on the control of a single leg.

In terms of the framework, single-legged locomotion can be formulated as follows. I once again interpret the dynamics of the agent's body as $\mathscr{E}$. The body has a single leg with a foot that can be either up or down. When the foot is down, any forces generated by the leg serve to move the body (called a *stance phase*). When the foot is up, any forces generated by the leg cause it to swing (called a *swing phase*). The leg is controlled by three effectors: two determine the clockwise and counterclockwise torque about the leg's single joint with the body and the third effector controls the state of the foot. $\mathscr{A}$ corresponds to the dynamics of the neural circuit controlling the leg, for which a five-neuron, fully interconnected network was employed. The outputs of three of these neurons drive the three effectors mentioned above (**M**), while the other two neurons are interneurons whose role in the circuit is not prespecified. In addition, all five neurons received as input a weighted copy of the leg angle (**S**). The leg controller thus had 5 time constants, 5 biases, 25 connection weights, and 5 sensor weights, forming a 40-dimensional parameter space that was searched using GAucsd. Since the goal of locomotion is steady forward progress, the performance measure to be maximized was the total forward distance traveled in a fixed amount of time. The minimum acceptable level of performance ($\mathbb{C}$) can be defined as the constraint that the average velocity of the body be greater than zero.

Leg controllers were evolved under three different conditions. During evolution, sensory feedback was either (1) always available, (2) never available, or (3) available 50% of the time. Successful leg controllers were evolved in all three cases. When sensory feedback was always available during evolution, *reflexive pattern generators* always evolved. The activity of a typical reflexive controller is shown in figure 5.6. Note that, though this is not generally true, the interneurons are not utilized in this particular controller. Reflexive controllers are completely dependent on sensory feedback; if the sensor is later removed, they cease to operate. When sensory feedback was never available during evolution, so-called *central pattern generators* always evolved. Such circuits are capable of intrinsically generating the basic oscillatory motor pattern necessary for walking. Finally, when sensory feedback was available only 50% of the time, *mixed pattern generators* evolved. These controllers can take advantage of sensory feedback when it is available to fine-tune their operation, but, like central pattern generators, they are able to generate a stereotyped walking pattern without any sensory feedback.

In order to illustrate the dynamical analysis of these locomotion controllers, I focus here on analyzing the reflexive controller shown in figure 5.6. I follow the same basic strategy as in the previous section. First, we examine how the phase portrait of the autonomous network dynamics varies as a function of the leg angle. Then, we explore how the interaction between

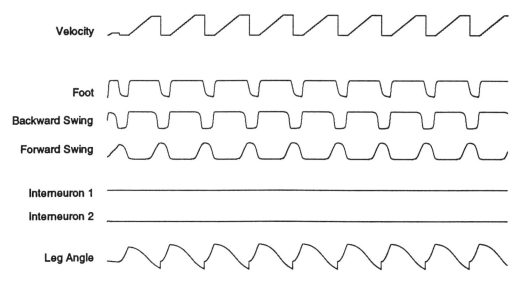

Figure 5.6 Activity of a reflexive pattern generator. Plots of the forward velocity of the body, the output of the foot, backward swing and forward swing motor neurons, the output of the two interneurons, and the leg angle are shown. The velocity ramps up to a maximum value during each stance phase and then drops to zero when the agent lifts its single leg at the beginning of each swing phase and falls.

this autonomous dynamics and the agent's body gives rise to the observed walking behavior.

Projections of the autonomous dynamics of the reflexive controller as a function of leg angle are shown in figure 5.7 for each of the three motor outputs. For our understanding of the operation of this controller, the most important feature of these diagrams to note is that, over most of the range of leg angles, there is a single stable equilibrium point. When the leg is forward, this equilibrium point is located in a region of the state space where the foot and backward swing motor outputs are active and the forward swing motor output is inactive. In contrast, when the leg is backward, the stable equilibrium is located in a region of state space where the forward swing motor output is active and the foot and backward swing motor outputs are inactive.

Between these two extremes, a sequence of bifurcations occur that serve to switch the phase portrait between the two stable equilibrium points. This sequence is perhaps most easily seen in the backward swing diagram. Let us begin with the leg all the way back, where the backward swing projection of the phase portrait exhibits a single stable equilibrium near 0. As the leg swings forward, an additional pair of equilibrium points, one stable and the other unstable, come into existence near 0.9. At slightly more positive angles, this pair increasingly separate and the lower attractor eventually loses stability, bifurcating into another unstable equilibrium point and a stable limit cycle. Note that this limit cycle is not at all appropriate for walking and appears to play no functional role in the network. It is merely an intermediate

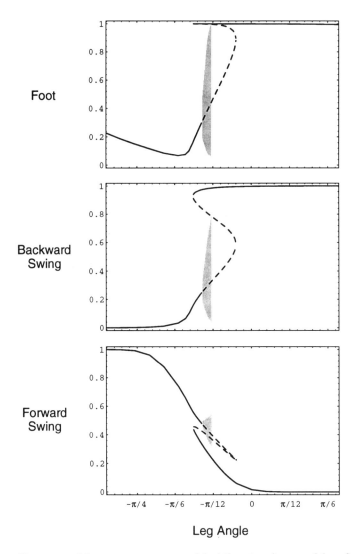

Figure 5.7 Motor-space projections of the bifurcation diagram of the reflexive leg controller shown in figure 5.6 as a function of leg angle. Stable equilibrium points are shown with solid lines, while unstable equilibrium points are shown with dashed lines. Limit cycles are shown in gray. By convention, a leg that is perpendicular to the body has a leg angle of 0. Positive angles correspond to directions toward the front of the body, while negative angles correspond to directions toward the rear. The normal operating range of the leg is $\pm \pi/6$, but the leg often stretches past $-\pi/4$ during stance.

step on the path from one stable equilibrium point to another. At increasingly positive leg angles, this limit cycle grows until it eventually collides with the upper unstable equilibrium point and disappears. Finally, at even more positive angles, the two unstable equilibrium points collide and disappear, leaving a single attractor near 1. Note that this entire sequence of bifurcations takes place in a fairly narrow range of leg angles. This sequence is reversed when the leg swings in the opposite direction.

From these bifurcation diagrams, we can immediately see why this controller does not work when the sensory feedback is removed. Because the autonomous dynamics of this network exhibits only equilibrium points for most leg angles, removing the sensory feedback causes the network state to evolve to the corresponding equilibrium point and then stop. Thus, the normal walking pattern is a property of the coupled agent-environment system $\mathcal{U}$ only and cannot be attributed to either $\mathcal{A}$ or $\mathcal{E}$ alone. In order to understand how the nature of the coupling between $\mathcal{A}$ and $\mathcal{E}$ gives rise to this limit cycle when the sensory feedback is intact, we must follow the interaction between the network and body dynamics through a single swing and stance cycle of the leg, using the above bifurcation diagrams as a guide.

The three-dimensional motor-space projection $\mathbf{M}$ of the limit cycle generated when the controller is coupled to the body is shown at the center of figure 5.8. Surrounding this central plot are smaller plots of the instantaneous autonomous dynamics of the network at different points in the cycle. For each plot, a black disk marks the location of the stable equilibrium point at that instant, while the instantaneous state and trajectory of the network is shown in gray. At any given point in the cycle, the network state moves toward the attractor in whose basin it finds itself. However, since the leg angle is a parameter of the network dynamics that is constantly changing, the phase portrait of the network dynamics (and thus the location of the equilibrium point that is attracting it and the trajectory it is following) is continuously changing as well.

At the start of a stance phase, the network is moving toward an equilibrium point in the back, upper left-hand corner of the motor output space (1). Recall that this region of the state space corresponds to a situation in which the foot is down, the backward swing effector is active, and the forward swing effector is inactive (i.e., a stance phase). At 2, the state has reached this attractor and the leg continues to stance. However, as the leg moves through the region of bifurcations described above, this equilibrium point disappears and the other attractor appears at the front, lower right-hand corner, which the network state now begins to move toward 3. Recall that the region of state space occupied by this attractor corresponds to a situation in which the foot is up, the forward swing effector is active and the backward swing effector is inactive (i.e., a swing phase). As the state nears this attractor at 4, the foot is lifted and the leg begins to swing forward, initiating a swing phase. As the leg swings forward, its angle once again passes through the region of bifurcations (this time in reverse). The first attractor is restored and the network state once again flows toward it (5). As the leg continues to swing (6), the network state crosses the activation threshold for the foot and a new stance phase begins at 1. Thus, we can see how the normal walking pattern arises from a reciprocal interaction between the network dynamics and the body dynamics: when the network state is in the vicinity of each attractor, the body dynamics at that point is such that the other attractor

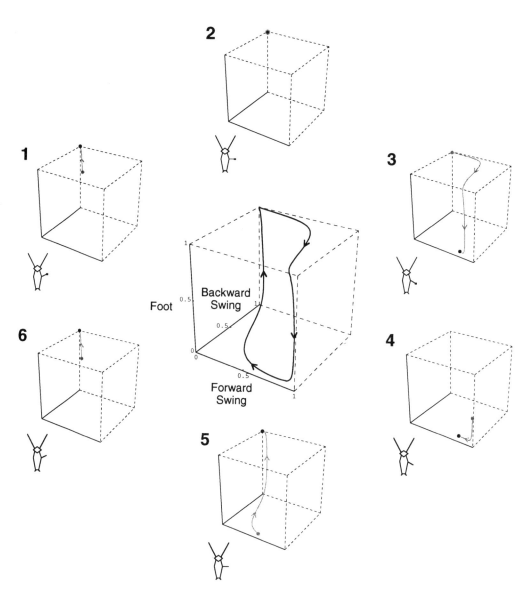

Figure 5.8 Operation of a typical reflexive pattern generator. The output of the foot, backward swing and forward swing motor neurons are plotted. The limit cycle generated when this controller is coupled to the body is shown at center. Surrounding this central plot are plots of the instantaneous autonomous dynamics of the network at different points in the step cycle. In each case, the solid point denotes a stable equilibrium point, the gray point denotes the instantaneous system state, and the gray line shows the trajectory that the system would follow if the leg were to remain fixed at its present angle. As shown by the small pictures of the agent associated with each plot, the top three plots correspond to the beginning (1), middle (2), and end (3) of a stance phase, while the bottom three plots correspond to the beginning (4), middle (5), and end (6) of a swing phase.

appears, causing the network state to be alternately attracted by the two equilibrium points.

Similar analyses have demonstrated that central pattern generators exhibit autonomous limit cycles whose motor space projections are appropriate to make the leg walk, while mixed pattern generators exhibit autonomous limit cycles that are entrained by sensory feedback (Gallagher and Beer, 1993; Beer, 1995). Full six-legged locomotion controllers comprised of six coupled leg controllers were also successfully evolved (Beer and Gallagher, 1992). Here not only did the network have to solve six versions of the single leg control problem but the movements of all six legs had to be properly coordinated so as to continuously maintain static stability. The results of these experiments paralleled those for the single leg case in that reflexive, central, and mixed pattern generators were evolved under analogous conditions. In all cases, the locomotion controllers evolved to generate a tripod gait, in which the front and back legs on each side of the body move in unison with the middle leg on the opposite side. This gait is ubiquitous among fast-walking insects (Graham, 1985).

5.5 CONCLUSION

In this chapter, I have argued that, aside from all of the other roles that the notion of computation plays, it has supplied us with a conceptual framework for thinking about the organization of systems that exhibit complex but highly structured behavior, such as animals in general and human beings in particular. This framework suggests that, like a computer, such systems must operate by the algorithmic manipulation of symbolic representations. A computational language leads us to search for ways to decompose an intelligent agent's machinery into reliably identifiable patterns of elements that can be usefully interpreted as representations and reliably identifiable functional modules that can be usefully interpreted as algorithmically transforming these representations in meaningful ways.

In contrast, I have argued that dynamical systems provide a more appropriate conceptual framework for understanding how the behavior of any agent interacting with the real world can be continuously adjusted to its constantly changing external and internal circumstances. In a dynamical system, complex but highly structured behavior can arise as a global property of the interaction between the system's individual components. In place of discrete symbols and step-by-step manipulations, dynamical systems theory provides a rich geometric and topological language for characterizing the possible long-term behaviors of a complex system and the dependence of those behaviors on parameters.

Using the language of dynamical systems theory, a theoretical framework for autonomous agents research was sketched. In this framework, an agent and its environment are modeled as two coupled dynamical systems whose mutual interaction is jointly responsible for the agent's observed behavior. In general, there need be no clean decomposition of an agent's dynamics into distinct functional modules and no aspect of the agent's state need be interpretable as a representation. The only requirement is that, when coupled to the environment in which it must function, the agent engages in the patterns of behavior necessary to accomplish whatever task it was designed for.

Chemotaxis and walking agents were used to illustrate the framework. In each case, the observed behavior of an agent was understood by first examining how the motor-space projection of its autonomous dynamics changes as a function of its sensory inputs and then using this understanding to explain its behavior when coupled to its environment. In general, such an analysis would need to be carried out for the environment as well. At any given point in the interaction between $\mathscr{A}$ and $\mathscr{E}$, the trajectory of each is determined by its own current state and the geometry of its flow. However, owing to their coupling, the trajectories of each system deform the flow geometry of the other and therefore influence its subsequent evolution.

Two comments on these examples are in order. First, in order to illustrate the basic framework, I have focused on the interaction between an agent's control mechanisms and its body rather than between an agent and its external environment. Nevertheless, these examples clearly support the claim that concepts from dynamical systems theory can be used to understand how behavior arises from the interaction of coupled dynamical systems. Ultimately, we must, of course, examine how the interaction of an agent (itself considered as the interaction of two dynamical systems: control mechanism and body) with a dynamic environment gives rise to its observed behavior. Second, it should be emphasized that, despite the fact that these examples utilized genetic algorithms to evolve continuous-time recurrent neural networks for these behaviors, the general approach is valid for any dynamical system regardless of the nature of its components and the means by which it was created.

The theoretical framework sketched in this paper is at best a beginning. Dynamical systems theory is no more a theory of autonomous agents than is the formal theory of computation. However, it does inspire a very different set of intuitions about an agent's internal organization, and it provides a rather different language for explaining an agent's behavior. Only further empirical work will tell which of these conceptual frameworks will ultimately prove to be more fruitful. Toward this end, dynamical analysis of other chemotaxis and walking agents is ongoing. In addition, this basic approach has been applied to understanding the operation of evolved continuous-time recurrent neural networks that can learn to make short sequences of decisions based on their experience in an environment (Yamauchi and Beer, 1994).

ACKNOWLEDGMENTS

This chapter has benefited from discussions with Phil Agre, Hillel Chiel, Beth Preston, and Tim van Gelder. In addition, both Hillel Chiel and Tim van

Gelder read and commented on an earlier draft of this paper. The simulation experiments reviewed in section 5.4 were carried out in collaboration with John Gallagher. This work was supported by grant N00014-90-J-1545 from the Office of Naval Research. Additional support was provided by the Howard Hughes Medical Institute and the Cleveland Advanced Manufacturing Program through the Center for Automation and Intelligent Systems Research.

REFERENCES

Abraham, R. H., and Shaw, C. D. (1992). *Dynamics—The geometry of behavior*, 2nd ed. Redwood City, CA: Addison-Wesley.

Agre, P. E., and Chapman, D. (1987). Pengi: an implementation of a theory of activity. In *Proceedings of Sixth National Conference on Artificial Intelligence, AAAI-87* (pp. 268–272), Seattle.

Ashby, W. R. (1960). *Design for a brain*, 2nd ed. New York: Wiley.

Ballard, D. H. (1991). Animate vision. *Artificial Intelligence, 48*, 57–86.

Beer, R. D. (1990). *Intelligence as adaptive behavior: an experiment in computational neuroethology.* San Diego, CA: Academic Press.

Beer, R. D. (1995). A dynamical systems perspective on agent-environment interaction. *Artificial Intelligence, 72*, 173–215.

Beer, R. D., and Gallagher, J. C. (1992). Evolving dynamical neural networks for adaptive behavior. *Adaptive Behavior, 1*, 91–122.

Brooks, R. A. (1991). Intelligence without representation. *Artificial Intelligence, 47*, 139–159.

Churchland, P. S., and Sejnowski, T. J. (1992). *The computational brain.* Cambridge, MA: MIT Press.

Elman, J. L. (1991). Distributed representations, simple recurrent networks and grammatical structure. *Machine Learning, 7*, 195–225.

Fodor, J. A. (1975). *The language of thought.* Cambridge, MA: Harvard University Press.

Gallagher, J. C., and Beer, R. D. (1993). A qualitative dynamical analysis of evolved locomotion controllers. In J.-A. Meyer, H. Roitblat, and S. Wilson (Eds.), *From animals to animats 2: Proceedings of the Second International Conference on the Simulation of Adaptive Behavior.* Cambridge, MA: MIT Press.

Georgopoulos, A. P., Lurito, J. T., Petrides, M. et al. (1989). Mental rotation of the neuronal population vector. *Science, 243*, 234–236.

Giunti, M. (1992). *Computers, dynamical systems, phenomena and the mind.* Ph.D. thesis, Indiana University, Bloomington.

Graham, D. (1985). Pattern and control of walking in insects. *Advances in Insect Physiology, 18*, 31–140.

Hale, J. K., and Koçak, H. (1991). *Dynamics and bifurcations.* New York: Springer-Verlag.

Harnad, S. (Ed.). (1994). What is computation? *Minds and Machines.* 4(4).

Kandel, E. R. (1991). Perception of motion, depth and form. In E. R. Kandel, J. H. Schwartz, and T. M. Jessell (Eds.), *Principles of neural science.* New York: Elsevier.

Kirsch, D. (1991). Today the earwig, tomorrow man? *Artificial Intelligence, 47*, 161–184.

Maes, P. (Ed.) (1990). *Designing autonomous agents.* Cambridge, MA: MIT Press.

Meyer, J.-A., Roitblat, H., and Wilson, S. W. (Eds.) (1993). *From animals to animats 2: Proceedings of the Second International Conference on Simulation of Adaptive Behavior.* Cambridge, MA: MIT Press.

Meyer, J.-A., and Wilson, S. W. (Eds.) (1991). *From animals to animats: Proceedings of the First International Conference on Simulation of Adaptive Behavior.* Cambridge, MA: MIT Press.

Newell, A., and Simon, H. A. (1976). Computer science as empirical inquiry: symbols and search. *Communications of the ACM, 19,* 113–126.

Pollack, J. B. (1991). The induction of dynamical recognizers. *Machine Learning, 7,* 227–252.

Pollack, J. (1993). On wings of knowledge: a review of Allen Newell's *Unified theories of cognition. Artificial Intelligence 59,* 355–369.

Pylyshyn, Z. W. (1984). *Computation and cognition.* Cambridge, MA: MIT Press.

Rinzel, J., and Ermentrout, G. B. (1989). Analysis of neural excitability and oscillations. In C. Koch and I. Segev (Eds.), *Methods in neuronal modeling.* Cambridge, MA: MIT Press.

Schöner, G., and Kelso, J. A. S. (1988). Dynamic pattern generation in behavioral and neural systems. *Science, 239,* 1513–1520.

Skarda, C. A., and Freeman, W. J. (1987). How brains make chaos in order to make sense of the world. *Behavioral Brain Sciences, 10,* 161–195.

Smith, B. C. (1991). The owl and the electric encyclopedia. *Artificial Intelligence, 47,* 251–288.

Smolensky, P. (1988). On the proper treatment of connectionism. *Behavioral Brain Sciences, 11,* 1–74.

Turvey, M. T. (1990). Coordination. *American Psychologist, 45,* 938–953.

Van Gelder, T. (1992). *What might cognition be if not computation?* (Technical report no. 75.) Bloomington: Indiana University, Department of Cognitive Science.

Wang, X.-J., and Rinzel, J. (1992). Alternating and synchronous rhythms in reciprocally inhibitory model neurons. *Neural Computation, 4,* 84–97.

Wiggins, S. (1990). *Introduction to applied nonlinear dynamical systems and chaos.* New York: Springer Verlag.

Yamauchi, B., and Beer, R. D. (1994). Sequential behavior and learning in evolved dynamical neural networks. *Adaptive Behavior, 2,* 219–246.

Guide to Further Reading

Currently, the best overviews of work in the fast-growing field of autonomous agents can be found in the collections edited by Maes (1990) and the proceedings of the first two *Simulation of Adaptive Behavior* conferences (Meyer and Wilson, 1991; Meyer, Roitblat, and Wilson, 1993). The latter provide a good snapshot of current work in this area. The journal *Adaptive Behavior*, published by MIT Press, is an ongoing source of new work in this area. Goldberg's book (Goldberg, 1989) provides an excellent general introduction to genetic algorithms. For another example of the use of evolutionary algorithms to design neural controllers for autonomous agents, see Cliff, Harvey, and Husbands (1993). A popular introduction to the general perspective on agents advocated in this chapter can be found in Maturana and Varela (1987). Further details of the particular framework sketched here can be found in Beer (1995).

Beer, R. D. (1995). A dynamical systems perspective on agent-environment interaction. *Artificial Intelligence, 72,* 173–215.

Cliff, D., Harvey, I., and Husbands, P. (1993). Explorations in evolutionary robotics. *Adaptive Behavior 2*, 73–110.

Goldberg, D. E. (1989). *Genetic algorithms in search, optimization and machine learning*. Reading, MA: Addison-Wesley.

Maes, P. (Ed.) (1990). *Designing autonomous agents*. Cambridge, MA: MIT Press.

Maturana, H. R., and Varela, F. J. (1987). *The tree of knowledge*. Boston: Shambhala.

Meyer, J.-A., Roitblat, H., and Wilson, S. W. (Eds.) (1993). *From animals to animats 2: Proceedings of the Second International Conference on Simulation of Adaptive Behavior*. Cambridge, MA: MIT Press.

Meyer, J.-A., and Wilson, S. W. (Eds.) (1991). *From animals to animats: Proceedings of the First International Conference on Simulation of Adaptive Behavior*. Cambridge, MA: MIT Press.

6 Dynamics and Coordinate Systems in Skilled Sensorimotor Activity

Elliot L. Saltzman

EDITORS' INTRODUCTION

A lay-up by a professional basketball player is a spectacular example of bodily coordination involving literally thousands of cooperating components. Yet numerous kinds of everyday performance are just as magical: a mouse licking fur on its belly, a child speaking her first words, or even simply walking across uneven ground. How are such actions possible? How are all the elements involved controlled so as to participate in the overall action in just the right way?

Traditional computational cognitive science has had very little to say about this kind of problem. That approach inherits Descartes' sharp distinction between mind and body, in the form of a rigid separation between cognition and mere bodily motions. Cognition, the proper domain of cognitive science, is regarded as inner, abstract, representational, and rather difficult to study. Bodily motions are external, concrete, mechanistic, and relatively simple; the study of movement is thought to be someone else's problem entirely. Consequently, for most computational cognitive scientists, the nature of sensorimotor coordination—and hence the interaction of the cognitive system with its world—is simply shelved. Further, when the issue does come to be addressed, computationalists face the difficult problem of interfacing the cognitive system with the body, and in particular getting the symbols, which are the output of the cognitive system, to drive complex movements of real flesh and bone in real time.

In this chapter, Saltzman describes coordination from a dynamical perspective. He begins from the assumption that coordinated movements, such as the regular swinging of two limbs, or the pronunciation of a word, are naturally flowing behaviors of dynamical systems. But how, in any given case, is the dynamical system best described? What are the relevant variables and equations, and how are they tied together into complex systems?

Investigating these questions, Saltzman draws some surprising conclusions. For example, it is natural to suppose that the relevant variables in coordinated movement conceived as a dynamical system would correspond to concrete bodily features such as muscle states and joint angles, and that these features would influence one another by direct physical links. Yet Saltzman shows how patterns of coordination are in fact best captured by dynamical models that operate in a much more abstract, high-level "task-space," and that the links between different components of a system must be characterized in informational terms.

In the second half of the chapter, the task-space analysis of coordination is described in some detail for one particularly common and yet subtle form of movement, namely the coordination of lips, jaw, tongue, etc. in speaking. Speech involves constricting the throat and mouth in various ways, and so the abstract task space in this case is defined over constriction types. Underlying these constrictions types, of course, are movements of the particular articulators (lips, etc.) involved in speaking; the dynamics in the task space governs the coordination of these lower-level articulators into specific speech gestures such as the closing of the two lips. In speaking whole words and sentences, multiple gestures must be combined in close succession, with the effect that the detailed movements of the articulators in one gesture shape those of their neighbors; in other words, the specific movements of articulators are heavily context-dependent. Saltzman describes how a dynamical model of speech coordination can smoothly accommodate such phenomena.

This work has a number of wider implications for cognitive science. First, sensorimotor coordination is a much more abstract, medium-independent business than is often assumed. Second, a dynamical account of coordinated movement virtually mandates adoption of a compatible dynamical account of more "central" aspects of cognition, such as assembly of the "gestural score" that drives the speech gestures themselves. Thus, a dynamical perspective on coordinated movement not only reduces the conceptual distance between cognition on the one hand and mere bodily movement on the other, it forces reconceptualization of the nature of the inner cognitive processes themselves in dynamical terms. It thus turns out that cognition is not best thought of as something fundamentally distinct from movements of the body; rather, bodily coordination (and thereby interaction with the world) is really part of cognition itself.

6.1   INTRODUCTION

Skilled sensorimotor activities entail the creation of complex *kinematic* patterns by actors using their limbs and speech articulators. Examples of kinematic patterns include trajectories over time of a reaching hand's position, velocity, or acceleration variables, the spatial shape of the path taken by a handheld pen during handwriting, or the relative timing of the speech articulators to produce the phonemes /p/, /e/, and /n/ in the word "pen." The term *dynamics* is used to refer to the vector field of forces that underlies and gives rise to an action's observable kinematic patterns. In this chapter, a dynamical account of skilled activity is reviewed in which skilled behavior is characterized as much as possible as that of a relatively autonomous, self-organizing dynamical system. In such systems, task-appropriate kinematics are viewed as emerging from the system's underlying dynamical organization (Beek, 1989; Saltzman and Munhall, 1989; Schöner and Kelso, 1988; Turvey, 1990). Thus, the emphasis in the present account is on a dynamical description, rather than a kinematic one, of sensorimotor skills. For example, an extreme and admittedly exaggerated "straw man" counterhypothesis is that of a central executive or homunculus that produces a given movement pattern with reference to an internal kinematic template of the form, tracing out the form provided by the template, and using the articulators as a physiological and biomechanical pantograph to produce a larger version of the pattern in the external world.

An adequate account of skilled sensorimotor behaviors must also address the multiplicity of coordinate systems or state spaces, and the mappings or transformations that exist among them, that appear to be useful in describing such behaviors. For example, a reaching movement can be described simultaneously in terms of patterns of muscle activations, joint angle changes, spatial motions of the hand, etc., and in terms of the ways these patterns relate to one another. This chapter focuses on the roles of both dynamics and coordinate systems in skilled sensorimotor activities. Evidence is reviewed in this chapter supporting the claim that the dynamics of sensorimotor control and coordination are defined in highly abstract coordinate systems called *task spaces* that are distinct from, yet related to, the relatively concrete physiological and biomechanical details of the peripheral musculoskeletal apparatus. It is further hypothesized that such spaces are the media through which actions are coupled perceptually to task-relevant surfaces, objects, and events in the actor's environment.

The chapter is divided into roughly two parts. The first is focused on concepts of dynamics as they have been applied to understanding the performance of single or dual sensorimotor tasks, where each task is defined in a one-to-one manner with a single articulatory degree of freedom. For example, a single task could be defined as the oscillation of a hand about the wrist joint or of the forearm about the elbow joint; a dual task could be defined as the simultaneous oscillations of both the right and left hand, or of the elbow and hand of a given arm. The second part of the chapter is focused on how the notions of dynamics and coordinate systems can be combined or synthesized to account for the performance of single or multiple tasks, where each task is defined over an entire effector system with many articulatory degrees of freedom. For example, in the production of speech the task of bringing the lips together to create a bilabial closure for /p/ is accomplished using the upper lip, lower lip, and jaw as articulatory degrees of freedom.

6.2 DYNAMICS

Why place so much emphasis on the dynamics of sensorimotor coordination and control? A dynamical account of the generation of movement patterns is to be preferred over other accounts, in particular the notion of internal kinematic templates, because dynamics gives a unified and parsimonious account of (at least) four signature properties of such patterns:

1. *Spatiotemporal form.* A movement's spatiotemporal form can be described both qualitatively and quantitatively. For example, qualitatively different hand motions are displayed in situations where the hand moves discretely to

a target position and then stops, and where the hand moves in a continuous, rhythmic fashion between two targets. Quantitative differences are reflected in the durations and extents of various discrete motions, and in the frequencies and amplitudes of the rhythmic motions.

2. *Stability.* A movement's form can remain stable in the face of unforeseen perturbations to the state of the system encountered during movement performances.

3. *Scaling.* Lawful warping of a movement's form can occur with parametric changes along performance dimensions such as motion rate and extent.

4. *Invariance and variability.* A dynamical framework allows one to characterize in a rigorous manner a common intuition concerning skilled actions in general. This intuition is that there is a subtle underlying invariance of control despite an obvious surface variability in performance.

In order to illustrate these points, the behavior of several simple classes of dynamical systems are reviewed (Abraham and Shaw, 1982; Baker and Gollub, 1990; Thompson and Stewart, 1986; see also Norton, chapter 2). Mathematical models based on these systems have been used to provide accounts and to simulate the performance of simple tasks in the laboratory. In such models, the qualitative aspects of a system's dynamics are mapped onto the functional characteristics of the performed tasks. For example, discrete positioning tasks can be modeled as being governed globally by *point attractor* or *fixed point* dynamics. Such dynamical systems move from initial states in a given neighborhood, or *attractor basin*, of an attracting point to the point itself in a time-asymptotic manner. Similarly, sustained oscillatory tasks can be modeled using *periodic attractor* or *limit cycle* dynamics. Such dynamics move systems from initial states in the attractor basin of an attracting cycle to the cycle itself in a time-asymptotic manner (see examples 8 and 9 in Norton, chapter 2, for representative equations of motion and sets of state trajectories for fixed-point and limit-cycle systems, respectively). The performance of simultaneous rhythms by different effectors can be modeled as the behavior of a system of *coupled* limit-cycle oscillators, in which the motion equation of each oscillator includes a coupling term(s) that represents the influence of the other oscillator's ongoing state. For example, the coupling term in oscillator-i's equation of motion might be a simple linear function, $a_{ij}x_j$, of the position of oscillator-j, where x_j is the ongoing position of oscillator-j and a_{ij} is a constant coefficient that maps this position into a coupling influence on oscillator-i. In what follows, the discussion is focused initially on single degree-of-freedom oscillatory tasks, and then moves to comparable, dual degree-of-freedom tasks.

Single Degree-of-Freedom Rhythms

In a typical single degree-of-freedom rhythmic task, a subject is asked to produce a sustained oscillatory movement about a single articulatory degree of freedom, e.g., of the hand or a handheld pendulum about the wrist joint. Usually, the rhythm is performed at either a self-selected "comfortable" frequency or at a frequency specified externally by a metronome; in both cases, the amplitudes of the performed oscillations are self-selected according to comfort criteria. Such movements can be characterized as limit-cycle oscillations, in that they exhibit characteristic frequencies and amplitudes (Kugler and Turvey, 1987) that are stable to externally imposed perturbations (Kay, Saltzman, and Kelso, 1991; Scholz and Kelso, 1989). For example, after such rhythms are subjected to brief mechanical perturbations, they return spontaneously to their original preperturbation frequencies and amplitudes. Additionally, limit-cycle models capture the spontaneous covariation or scaling behavior that is observed among the task's kinematic observables. For example, at a given movement frequency there is a highly linear relationship between a cycle's motion amplitude and its peak velocity, such that cycles with larger amplitudes generally display greater peak velocities. Such a relationship is inherent in the dynamics of near-sinusoidal limit-cycle oscillations. Further, across a series of different metronome-specified frequencies, the mean cycle amplitude decreases systematically as cycle frequency increases (Kay, Kelso, Saltzman, et al., 1987). Such scaling is a natural consequence of the structure of the limit cycle's *escapement*, a nonlinear damping mechanism that is responsible for offsetting frictional losses and for governing energy flows through the system in a manner that creates and sustains the limit cycle's rhythm.

Dual Degree-of-Freedom Rhythms

These tasks consist simply of two single degree-of-freedom tasks performed simultaneously, e.g., rhythmic motions of the right and left index fingers, usually at a common self-selected or metronome-specified frequency and with self-selected amplitudes. Additionally, subjects are requested typically to perform the task with a given relative phasing between the component rhythms (Kelso, 1984; Rosenblum and Turvey, 1988; Sternad, Turvey, and Schmidt, 1992; Turvey and Carello, chapter 13). For example, for bimanual pendulum oscillations performed at a common frequency in the right and left parasagittal planes (see figure 13.7, Turvey and Carello, chapter 13), an *inphase* relationship is defined by same-direction movements of the components, i.e., front-back movements of the right pendulum synchronous with front-back movements of the left pendulum; similarly, an *antiphase* relationship is defined by simultaneous, opposite-direction movements of the components. Models of such tasks begin by specifying each component unit as a separate limit-cycle oscillator, with a 1:1 frequency ratio defined between the pair of oscillators. If this were all there was to the matter, one could create arbitrary phase relations between the component limit cycles, simply by starting the components with an initial phase difference equal to the desired phase difference. This is an inadequate description of dual rhythmic performances, however, since the behavioral data demonstrate that it is only possible to easily perform $1:1$ rhythms that are close to inphase or antiphase; intermediate phase differences are not impossible, but they require a good deal of practice and usually remain more variable than the inphase and antiphase pair.

What makes the inphase and antiphase patterns so easy to perform, and the others so difficult? What is the source of this natural cooperativity? It turns out that these are the same questions that arise when one considers the phenomenon of *entrainment* between limit-cycle oscillators. This phenomenon was observed by the 17th century Dutch physicist Christiaan Huygens, who noticed that the pendulum swings of clocks placed on the same wall tended to become synchronized with one another after a period of time. This phenomenon can be modeled dynamically by assuming that each clock is its own limit-cycle oscillator, and that the clocks are coupled to one another because of weak vibrations transmitted through the wall. Such coupling causes the motions of the clocks to mutually perturb one another's ongoing rhythms, and to settle into a cooperative state of entrainment. These observations suggest that the appropriate theory for understanding the performance of multiple task rhythms is that of coupled limit-cycle oscillators. In this theory, when two limit cycles are coupled bidirectionally to one another, the system's behavior is usually attracted to one of two *modal* states. In each modal state, the components oscillate at a common mode-specific frequency, and with a characteristic amplitude ratio and relative phase. Most important for the present discussion, if the component oscillators are roughly identical and the coupling strengths are roughly the same in both directions, then the two modes are characterized by relative phases close to inphase and antiphase, respectively. It is possible, however, that the frequencies and amplitudes observed in the modal states can be different from those observed when the components oscillate independently of one another.

Thus, we are led to view the inphase and antiphase coordinative patterns in $1:1$ dual oscillatory tasks as the attractive modal states of a system of coupled limit-cycle components. Note that the coupling that creates this modal cooperativity is involuntary and obligatory, in the sense that these modal states are hard to avoid even if the task is to perform with a relative phasing in between those of the naturally easy modes. Such intermediate states are possible to perform, but require much practice and remain more variable than the modal states. What is the structure of the intercomponent coupling? What is the source or medium through which this coupling is defined?

Coupling Structure   Coupling structure refers to the mathematical structure of the coupling functions that map the ongoing states of a given oscillator into perturbing influences on another. It turns out that many types of coupling will create stable modes with relative phases close to inphase and antiphase. For example, even the simple linear positional coupling mentioned earlier, $a_{ij}x_j$, will work, where x_j is the ongoing position of oscillator-j and a_{ij}

is a constant coefficient that maps this position into a perturbation of oscilla-tor-i's motion.

In addition to entrainment, however, human rhythmic tasks display *phase transition* behaviors that place additional constraints on the choice of coupling functions. In an experimental paradigm pioneered by Kelso (Kelso, 1984; Scholz and Kelso, 1989), subjects begin an experimental trial by oscillating two limb segments at the same frequency in an antiphase pattern, and then increase the frequency of oscillation over the course of the trial. Under such conditions, the antiphase coordination abruptly shifts to an inphase coordina-tion when the oscillation frequency passes a certain critical value. A compara-ble shift is not seen, however, when subjects begin with an inphase pattern; under these conditions, the inphase coordination is maintained as frequency increases. The abrupt phase transition from antiphase to inphase patterns when frequency is increased can be characterized mathematically as a *bifurca-tion* phenomenon in the underlying dynamical system. In dynamical models of such phenomena the coupling functions are required typically to be non-linear (Haken, Kelso, and Bunz, 1985; Schöner, Haken, and Kelso, 1986). To summarize briefly, entrainment can be created by limit cycles coupled bidirec-tionally in many ways, but entrainment with bifurcations require typically nonlinear coupling structures.

Coupling Medium What is the source of interoscillator coupling during the performance of simultaneous rhythmic tasks? What are the coordinates along which such coupling is defined? One possibility is that the coupling medium is mechanical in nature, as in the case of Huygens' pendulum clocks, since it is known that biomechanical *reactive coupling* exists among the seg-ments of effector systems during motor skill performances (Bernstein, 1967/1984; Hollerbach, 1982; Saltzman, 1979; Schneider, Zernicke, Schmidt, et al., 1989). Such coupling is defined in segmental or joint-space coordinate sys-tems. A second possibility is that the coupling is neuroanatomical, as in the case of the crosstalk or overflow between neural regions controlling homolo-gous muscle groups that has been hypothesized to underlie mirroring errors in bimanual sequencing tasks such as typing or key-pressing (MacKay and Soderberg, 1971), or associated mirror movements in certain clinical popu-lations (Woods and Teuber, 1978). Such coupling is defined in muscle-based coordinate systems.

An experiment by Schmidt, Carello, and Turvey (1990) indicated that matters might not be so straightforward. In this experiment, subjects per-formed rhythmic motions at their knee joints, but the major innovation of the paradigm was to have the set of two rhythms defined across subjects rather than within subjects. Thus, one subject would perform rhythmic oscillations at one knee joint while watching a nearby partner do the same (see figure 13.9, Turvey and Carello, chapter 13). There were two types of task. In one type, the partners were asked to oscillate their respective legs at a mutually comfortable common frequency either inphase or antiphase with one another, and to increase or decrease the oscillation frequency by self-selected amounts in response to a signal supplied by the experimenter; in the second type of task, a metronome was used to specify both the frequencies and time schedule of frequency scaling. Surprisingly, all the details of entrainment and bifurcation phenomena were observed in this between-person experiment as had been observed previously in the within-person experiments. Clearly, joint-space (biomechanical) and muscle-space (neural) coordinates were not the media of interoscillator coupling in this experiment. Rather, the coupling must have been due to visual *information* that was specific to the observed oscillatory states of the pendulums themselves. The same point has received further support in subsequent studies in which similar behaviors are displayed by subjects who oscillate an index finger either on or off the beat provided auditorily by a metronome (Kelso, Delcolle, and Schöner, 1990), or who oscillate a forearm inphase or antiphase with the visible motion of a cursor on a cathode-ray tube (CRT) screen (van Riel, Beek, and van Wieringen, 1991). All these studies underscore the conclusion that the coupling medium is an abstract one, and that coupling functions are defined by perceptual information that is specific to the tasks being performed.

Coordinative Dynamics   Just as the coupling medium is not defined in simple anatomical or biomechanical terms, several lines of evidence support the hypothesis that the limit-cycle dynamics themselves are also not specified in this manner. That is, the degrees of freedom or state variables along which the oscillatory dynamics are specified, and that experience the effects of interoscillator coupling, are not defined in simple anatomical or biomechanical coordinates. Even tasks that, at first glance, might appear to be specified at the level of so-called articulatory joint rotational degrees of freedom have been found to be more appropriately characterized in terms of the orientations of body segments in body-spatial or environment-spatial coordinate systems. For example, Baldissera, Cavallari, and Civaschi (1982) studied the performance of simultaneous 1:1 oscillations about the ipsilateral wrist and ankle joints in the parasagittal plane. Foot motion consisted of alternating downward (plantar) and upward (dorsal) motion. Hand motion consisted of alternating flexion and extension. The relationship between anatomical and spatial hand motions was manipulated across conditions by instructing subjects to keep the forearm either palm down (pronated) or palm up (supinated). Thus, anatomical flexion or extension at the wrist caused the hand to rotate spatially downward or upward during the pronation condition, but spatially upward or downward during supination. It was found that the easiest and most stably performed combinations of hand and foot movements were those in which the hand and foot motions were in the same spatial direction, regardless of the relative phasing between upper and lower limb muscle groups. Thus, the easiest and most natural patterns were those in which hand and foot motions were spatially inphase. It was more difficult to perform the spatially antiphase combinations, and occasional spontaneous transitions were observed from the spatially antiphase patterns to the spatially inphase patterns. Related findings on combinations of upper and lower limb rhythmic tasks were more recently reported by Baldissera, Cavallari, Marini, et al. (1991) and by Kelso and Jeka (1992).[1]

Thus, the dynamical systems for coordination and control of sensorimotor tasks, and the medium through which these systems are coupled, cannot be described in simple biomechanical or neuroanatomical terms. Rather, they are defined in abstract, spatial, and informational terms. This point becomes even clearer when one examines the performance of tasks that are more realistic and complex than the relatively artificial and simple tasks that have been reviewed above.

Speech Production

Consider the production of speech and what is entailed during the speech gesture of raising the tongue tip toward the roof of the mouth to create and release a constriction for the phoneme /z/, using the tongue tip, tongue body, and jaw in a synergistic manner to attain the phonetic goal. Such systems show a remarkable flexibility in reaching such task goals, and can compensate adaptively for disturbances or perturbations encountered by one part of the system by spontaneously readjusting the activity of other parts of the system in order to still achieve these goals. An elegant demonstration of this ability was provided in an experiment by Kelso, Tuller, Vatikiotis-Bateson, et al. (1984; see also Abbs and Gracco, 1983; Folkins and Abbs, 1975; Shaiman, 1989). In this experiment, subjects were asked to produce the syllables /bæb/ or /bæz/ in the carrier phrase "It's a _____ again," while recording (among other observables) the kinematics of upper lip, lower lip, and jaw motion, as well as the electromyographic activity of the tongue-raising genioglossus muscle. During the experiment, the subjects' jaws were unexpectedly and unpredictably perturbed downward as they were moving into the final /b/ closure for /bæb/ or the final /z/ constriction for /bæz/. It was found that when the target was /b/, for which lip but not tongue activity is crucial, there was remote compensation in the upper lip relative to unperturbed control trials, but normal tongue activity (figure 6.1A); when the target was /z/, for which tongue but not lip activity is crucial, remote compensation occurred in the tongue but not the upper lip (figure 6.1B). Furthermore, the compensation was relatively immediate in that it took approximately 20 to 30 ms from the onset of the downward jaw perturbation to the onset of the remote compensatory activity. The speed of this response implies that there is some sort of automatic "reflexive" organization established among the articulators with a relatively fast loop time. However, the gestural specificity implies that the mapping from perturbing inputs to compensatory outputs is not hard-wired. Rather, these data imply the existence of a task- or gesture-specific, selective pattern of coupling among the component articulators that is specific to the utterance or phoneme produced.

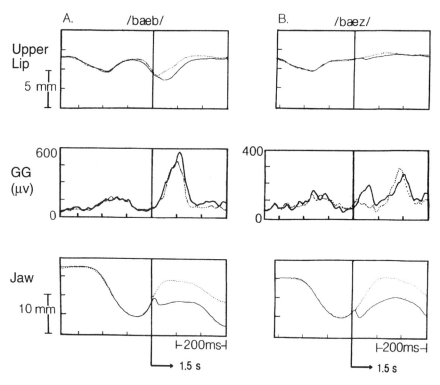

Figure 6.1 Experimental trajectory data for the unperturbed (dotted lines) and perturbed (solid lines) utterances /bæb/ (A) and /bæz/ (B). (*Top row*) Upper lip position. (*Middle row*) Genioglossus muscle activity. (*Bottom row*) Jaw position. Panels in each column are aligned with reference to the perturbation onset (solid vertical lines). Perturbation duration was 1.5 seconds. (Adapted from Kelso, J. A. S., Tuller, B., Vatikiotis-Bateson, E., et al., 1984).

What kind of dynamical system can display this sort of flexibility? Clearly, it cannot be a system in which task goals are defined independently at the level of the individual articulators. For example, if one were to model a bilabial closing gesture by giving each articulatory component (upper lip, lower lip, and jaw) point-attractor dynamics and its own target position, then the system would attain a canonical closure in unperturbed simulations. However, the system would fail in simulations in which perturbing forces were added to one of the articulators during the closing gesture. For example, if a simulated braking force were added to the jaw that prevented it from reaching its target, then the overall closure goal would not be met even though the remaining articulators were able to attain their own individual targets.

Appropriately flexible system behavior can be obtained, however, if the task-specific dynamics are defined in coordinates more abstract than those defined by the articulatory degrees of freedom. Recall that, in earlier discussions of coupled limit-cycle dynamics, the term *modal state* was used to characterize the cooperative states that emerged from the dynamics of the coupled system components. Modal patterns defined the systems' preferred

Elliot L. Saltzman

or natural set of behaviors. The problem at hand, therefore, is to understand how to create modal behaviors that are tailored to the demands of tasks encountered in the real world. This can be accomplished if one can design task-specific coupling functions among a set of articulatory components that serve to create an appropriate set of task-specific system modes. The remainder of this chapter is devoted to describing one approach to the design of task-specific dynamical systems, called *task dynamics*, that has been used with some success to model the dynamics of speech production. This modeling work has been performed in cooperation with several colleagues at Haskins Laboratories (New Haven, Conn.) as part of an ongoing project focused on the development of a gesturally based, computational model of linguistic structures (Browman and Goldstein, 1986, 1991, and chapter 7; Fowler and Saltzman, 1993; Kelso, Saltzman, and Tuller, 1986a,b; Kelso, Vatikiotis-Bateson, Saltzman, et al., 1985; Saltzman, 1986, 1991; Saltzman and Kelso, 1987; Saltzman and Munhall, 1989). For recent reviews, related work, and critiques, see also de Jong (1991), Edwards, Beckman, and Fletcher (1991), Hawkins (1992), Jordan and Rosenbaum (1989), Mattingly (1990), Perkell (1991), and Vatikiotis-Bateson (1988).

6.3 TASK DYNAMICS

The discussion of task dynamics for speech production is divided into two parts. The first focuses on the dynamics of interarticulatory coordination within single speech gestures, e.g., the coordination of lips and jaw to produce a bilabial closure. The second part focuses on the dynamics of intergestural coordination, with special attention being paid to periods of *coproduction* when the blended influences of several temporally overlapping gestures are evident in the ongoing articulatory and acoustic patterns of speech (Bell-Berti and Harris, 1981; Fowler, 1980; Fowler and Saltzman, 1993; Harris, 1984; Keating, 1985; Kent and Minifie, 1977; Öhman, 1966, 1967; Perkell, 1969; Sussman, MacNeilage, and Hanson, 1973). For example, in a vowel-consonant-vowel (VCV) sequence, much evidence supports the hypothesis that the period of control for the medial consonant is superimposed onto underlying periods of control for the flanking vowels. Since vowel production involves (mainly) the tongue body and jaw, and most consonants involve the jaw as well, then during periods of coproduction the influences of the overlapping gestures must be blended at the level of the shared articulators.

Interarticulatory Coordination: Single Speech Gestures

In the task-dynamical model, coordinative dynamics are posited at an abstract level of system description, and give rise to appropriately gesture-specific and contextually variable patterns at the level of articulatory motions. Since one of the major tasks for speech is to create and release constrictions in different local regions of the vocal tract, the abstract dynamics are defined in coordi-

Tract variables		Model articulators
LP	lip protrusion	upper & lower lips
LA	lip aperture	upper & lower lips, jaw
TDCL	tongue dorsum constrict location	tongue body, jaw
TDCD	tongue dorsum constrict degree	tongue body, jaw
LTH	lower tooth height	jaw
TTCL	tongue tip constrict location	tongue tip, body, jaw
TTCD	tongue tip constrict degree	tongue tip, body, jaw
VEL	velic aperture	velum
GLO	glottal aperture	glottis

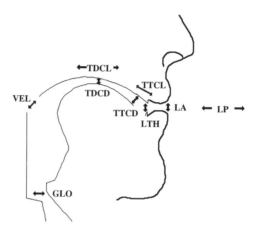

Figure 6.2 (*Top*) Table showing the relationship between tract variables and model articulators. (*Bottom*) Schematic midsagittal vocal tract outline, with tract-variable degrees of freedom indicated by arrows. (From Saltzman, E., 1991.)

nates that represent the configurations of different constriction types, e.g., the bilabial constrictions used in producing /b/, /p/, or /m/, the alveolar constrictions used in producing /d/, /t/, or /n/, etc. Typically, each constriction type is associated with a pair of so-called *tract-variable* coordinates, one that refers to the location of the constriction along the longitudinal axis of the vocal tract, and one that refers to the degree of constriction measured perpendicularly to the longitudinal axis in the midsagittal plane. For example, bilabial constrictions are defined according to the tract variables of lip aperture and lip protrusion (see figure 6.2). Lip aperture defines the degree of bilabial constriction, and is defined by the vertical distance between the upper and lower lips; lip protrusion defines the location of bilabial constriction, and is defined by the horizontal distance between the (yoked) upper and lower lips and the upper and lower front teeth, respectively. Constrictions are restricted to two dimensions for practical purposes, owing to the fact that the simulations use the articulatory geometry represented in the Haskins Laboratories software articulatory synthesizer (Rubin, Baer, and Mermelstein, 1981). This synthesizer is defined according to a midsagittal representation of the vocal tract, and converts a given articulatory configuration in this plane, first to a sagittal vocal tract outline, then to a three-dimensional tube shape, and finally, with the addition of appropriate voice source information, to an acoustic waveform. As a working hypothesis, the tract-variable gestures in the model have been assigned the point-attractor dynamics of damped, second-order systems, analogous to those of damped mass-spring systems. Each gesture is assigned its own set of dynamic parameters: target or rest position, natural frequency, and damping factor. Gestures are active over discrete time intervals, e.g., over discrete periods of bilabial closing or opening, laryngeal abduction or adduction, tongue-tip raising or lowering, etc.

Just as each constriction type is associated with a set of tract variables, each tract variable is associated with a set of *model articulator* coordinates that constitutes an articulatory subset for the tract variable. The model articulators are defined according to the articulatory degrees of freedom of the Haskins software synthesizer. Figure 6.2 shows the relation between tract-variable and model articulator coordinates (see also figure 7.2 in Browman and Goldstein, chapter 7). The model articulators are controlled by transforming the tract-variable dynamical system into model articulator coordinates. This coordinate transformation creates a set of gesture-specific and articulatory posture-specific coupling functions among the articulators. These functions create a dynamical system at the articulatory level whose modal, cooperative behaviors allow them to flexibly and autonomously attain speech-relevant goals. In other words, the tract-variable coordinates define a set of gestural modes for the model articulators (see also Coker, 1976, for a related treatment of vocal tract modes).

Significantly, articulatory movement trajectories unfold as implicit consequences of the tract-variable dynamics without reference to explicit trajectory plans or templates. Additionally, the model displays gesture-specific patterns of remote compensation to simulated mechanical perturbations delivered to the model articulators (figure 6.3) that mirror the compensatory effects reported in the experimental literature (see figure 6.1). In particular, simulations were performed of perturbed and unperturbed bilabial closing gestures (Saltzman, 1986; Kelso, et al., 1986a,b). When the simulated jaw was "frozen" in place during the closing gesture, the system achieved the same final degree of bilabial closure in both the perturbed and unperturbed cases, although with different final articulatory configurations. Furthermore, the lips compensated spontaneously and immediately to the jaw perturbation, in the sense that neither replanning or reparameterization was required in order to compensate. Rather, compensation was brought about through the automatic and rapid redistribution of activity over the entire articulatory subset in a gesture-specific manner. The interarticulatory processes of control and coordination were exactly the same during both perturbed and unperturbed simulated gestures (see Kelso, et al., 1986a,b; and Saltzman, 1986, for the mathematical details underlying these simulations).

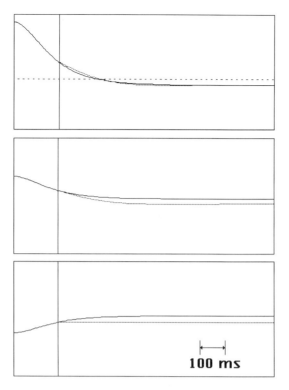

Figure 6.3 Simulated tract-variable and articulatory trajectories for unperturbed (solid lines) and perturbed (dotted lines) bilabial closing gestures. (*Top*) Lip aperture. (*Middle*) Upper lip. (*Bottom*) Jaw. Panels are aligned with reference to the perturbation onset (solid vertical lines). Dashed horizontal line in top panel denotes zero lip aperture, with negative aperture signifying lip compression. (Adapted from Kelso, J. A. S., Saltzman, E. L., and Tuller, B., 1986.)

Intergestural Coordination, Activation, Blending

How might gestures be combined to simulate speech sequences? In order to model the spatiotemporal orchestration of gestures evident in even the simplest utterances, a third coordinate system composed of gestural *activation* coordinates was defined. Each gesture in the model's repertoire is assigned its own activation coordinate, in addition to its set of tract variables and model articulators. A given gesture's ongoing activation value defines the strength with which the gesture "attempts" to shape vocal tract movements at any given point in time according to its own phonetic goals (e.g., its tract-variable target and natural frequency parameters). Thus, in its current formulation the task-dynamical model of speech production is composed of two functionally distinct but interacting levels (see figure 6.4). The *intergestural coordination* level is defined according to the set of gestural activation coordinates, and the *interarticulatory coordination* level is defined according to both model articulatory and tract-variable coordinates. The architectural relationships among these coordinates are shown in figure 6.5.

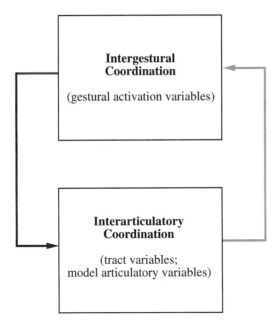

Figure 6.4 Schematic illustration of the two-level dynamical model for speech production, with associated coordinate systems indicated. The darker arrow from the intergestural to the interarticulator level denotes the feedforward flow of gestural activation. The lighter arrow indicates feedback of ongoing tract-variable and model articulatory state information to the intergestural level. (From Saltzman, E. L., and Munhall, K. G., 1989.)

In current simulations, the gestural activation trajectories are defined for simplicity's sake as step functions of time, normalized from zero to one. Thus, outside a gesture's temporal interval of activation (i.e., when activation is zero), the gesture is inactive or "off" and has no influence on vocal tract activity. During its activation interval, when its activation value is one, the gesture is "on" and has maximal effect on the vocal tract. Viewed from this perspective, the problem of coordination among the gestures participating in a given utterance, e.g., for tongue-dorsum and bilabial gestures in a vowel-bilabial-vowel sequence, becomes that of specifying patterns of relative timing and cohesion among activation intervals for those gestures (see Saltzman and Munhall, 1989, for further details of the manner in which gestural activations influence vocal tract movements). Currently, intergestural relative timing patterns are specified by *gestural scores* that are generated explicitly either "by hand," or according to a linguistic gestural model that embodies the rules of Browman and Goldstein's *articulatory phonology* (Browman and Goldstein, 1986, 1991, and chapter 7). The manner in which gestural scores represent the relative timing patterns for an utterance's set of tract-variable gestures is shown in figure 6.6 for the word "pub."

Using these methods, the task-dynamical model has been shown to reproduce many of the coproduction and intergestural blending effects found in the speech production literature. In the model, coproduction effects are

ACTIVATION

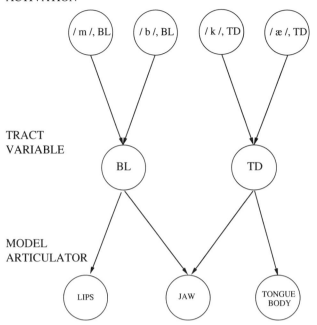

Figure 6.5 Example of the "anatomical" relationships defined among model articulatory, tract-variable, and activation coordinate systems. BL and TD denote tract variables associated with bilabial and tongue-dorsum constrictions, respectively. Gestures at the activation level are labeled in terms of both linguistic identity (e.g., /k/) and tract-variable affiliation (e.g., TD). (From Saltzman, E., 1991.)

generated as the articulatory and acoustic consequences of temporal overlap in gestural activations; blending occurs when there is spatial overlap of the gestures involved, i.e., when the gestures share model articulators in common. Blending would occur, for example, during coproduction of vowel (tongue and jaw) and bilabial (lips and jaw) gestures at the shared jaw articulator. The magnitude of coproduction effects is a function of the degree of spatial overlap of the gestures involved, i.e., the degree to which articulators are shared across gestures. Minimal interference occurs as long as the spatial overlap is incomplete. This is the case when gestures are defined along distinct sets of tract variables, and the gestures share none, or some, but not all articulators in common (see figure 6.2). In this situation, the coproduced gestures can each attain their individual phonetic goals. Figure 6.7A illustrates the behavior of the model for two VCV sequences in which symmetrical flanking vowels, /i/ and /æ/, vary across sequences, the medial consonant is the alveolar /d/ in both sequences, and the time courses of vowel and consonant activations are identical in both sequences. Vowels are produced using the tract variables of tongue-dorsum constriction location and degree, and the associated jaw and tongue-body model articulators; the alveolar is produced using the tract variables of tongue-tip constriction location and degree, and

/pʌb/

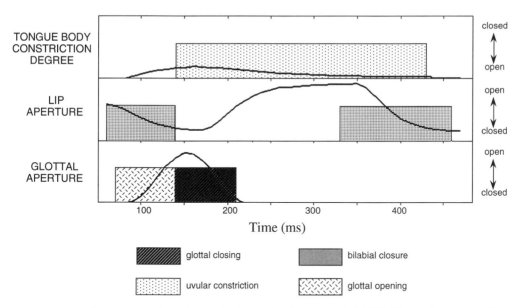

Figure 6.6 Gestural score for the simulated sequence /pʌb/. Filled boxes denote intervals of gestural activation. Box heights are either 0 (no activation) or 1 (full activation). The waveform lines denote tract-variable trajectories produced during the simulation. (From Saltzman, E. L., and Munhall, K. G., 1989a)

the associated jaw, tongue-body, and tongue-tip articulators. Thus, the vowel and consonant gestures share some but not all articulators in common. In this case, the alveolar's tongue-tip constriction goals are met identically in both sequences, although contextual differences in articulatory positions are evident, and are related to corresponding differences in the identities of the flanking vowels (for comparison, see the simulated tract shapes of isolated, steady-state productions of the vowels /i/ and /æ/, shown in figure 6.7C).

However, when coproduced gestures use the same sets of tract variables, all articulators are shared in common, and there is the potential for mutual interference in attaining competing phonetic goals. Figure 6.7B illustrates the behavior of the model for two VCV sequences that are identical to those shown in figure 6.7A, except that the medial consonant is the velar /g/. In this situation, consonant and vowels are produced using the same tongue-dorsum tract variables and the same jaw and tongue-body model articulators. During periods of coproduction the gestures compete for control of tongue-dorsum motion, resulting in contextual variation even in the attainment of the constriction target for /g/. The velar's place of constriction is altered by the identity of the flanking vowels, although the degree of constriction is not. Importantly, the simulations displayed in figure 6.7A and B mirror the patterns observed experimentally during actual VCV production (Öhman, 1967).

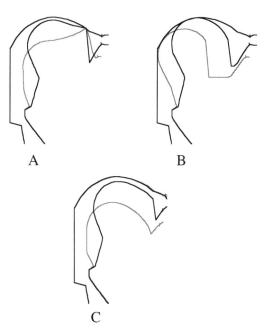

Figure 6.7 Simulated vocal tract shapes. (*A*) First contact of tongue tip and upper tract wall during symmetric vowel-alveolar-vowel sequences. (*B*) First contact of tongue-dorsum and upper tract wall during symmetric vowel-velar-vowel sequences. (*C*) Corresponding steady-state vowel productions. (Dark lines denote /i/ tokens; light lines denote /æ/ tokens.) (From Saltzman, E., 1991.)

Additionally, such processes of within-tract variable blending are consistent with data on experimentally induced vowel production errors (Laver, 1980), in which blended vowel forms were produced that were intermediate between canonical forms.

Future Directions

In its current state, the task-dynamical model offers a useful and promising account of movement patterns observed during unperturbed and mechanically perturbed speech sequences, and during periods of coproduction. Significantly, explicit trajectory planning is not required, and the model functions in exactly the same way during simulations of unperturbed, mechanically perturbed, and coproduced speech gestures. Additionally, the model provides a way to reconcile much of the apparent conflict between observations of surface articulatory and acoustic variability on the one hand, and the hypothesized existence of underlying, invariant linguistic units on the other hand. Invariant units are specified in the form of context-independent sets of gestural parameters (e.g., tract-variable targets), and are associated with corresponding subsets of activation, tract-variable, and articulatory coordinates. Variability emerges in the tract-variable and articulatory movement patterns, as a result of both the utterance-specific temporal interleaving of gestural activations provided by the gestural scores, and the accompanying dynamics of intergestural blending during coproduction.

One of the main drawbacks of the model from a dynamical perspective is that there are no dynamics intrinsic to the level of intergestural coordination that are comparable to the dynamics intrinsic to the interarticulatory level. The patterning of gestural activation trajectories is specified explicitly either "by hand" or by the rules embodied in the linguistic gestural model of Browman and Goldstein. Once a gestural score is specified, it remains fixed throughout a given simulation, defining a unidirectional, rigidly feedforward flow of control from the intergestural to interarticulatory levels of the model. The gestural score acts, in essence, like the punched paper roll that drives the keys of a player piano. Experimental data suggest, however, that the situation is not this simple. For example, transient mechanical perturbations delivered to the speech articulators during repetitive speech sequences (Saltzman, 1992; Saltzman, Kay, Rubin, et al., 1991), or to the limbs during unimanual rhythmic tasks (Kay, 1986; Kay et al., 1991), can alter the underlying timing structure of the ongoing sequence and induce systematic shifts in the timing of subsequent movement elements. These data imply that activation patterns are not rigidly specified over a given sequence. Rather, such results suggest that activation trajectories evolve fluidly and flexibly over the course of an ongoing sequence governed by an intrinsic intergestural dynamics, and that this intergestural dynamical system functions as a sequence-specific timer or clock that is bidirectionally coupled to the interarticulatory level.

Work is currently in progress (with colleagues John Hogden, Simon Levy, and Philip Rubin) to incorporate the dynamics of connectionist networks (Bailly, Laboissière, and Schwartz, 1991; Grossberg, 1986; Jordan, 1986, 1990, in press; Kawato, 1989) at the intergestural level of the model, in order to shape activation trajectories intrinsically and to allow for adaptive on-line interactions with the interarticulatory level. In particular, we have adopted the recurrent, sequential network architecture of Jordan (1986, 1990, in press). Each output node of the network represents a corresponding gestural activation coordinate. The values of these output nodes range continuously from zero to one, allowing each gesture's influence over the vocal tract to wax and wane in a smoothly graded fashion. Additionally, the ongoing tract-variable state will be fed back into the sequential net, providing an informational basis for the modulation of activation timing patterns by simulated perturbations delivered to the model articulatory or tract-variable coordinates. Thus, rather than being explicitly and rigidly determined prior to the onset of the simulated utterance, the activation patterns will evolve during the utterance as implicit consequences of the dynamics of the entire multilevel (intergestural and interarticulatory) system.

6.4 SUMMARY AND CONCLUSIONS

The dynamical approach described in this chapter provides a powerful set of empirical and theoretical tools for investigating and understanding the coordination and control of skilled sensorimotor activities, ranging from simple one-joint rhythms to the complex patterns of speech production. The approach offers a unified and rigorous account of a movement's spatio-temporal form, stability of form, lawful warpings of form induced by scaling performance parameters, and the intuitive relation between underlying invariance and surface variability. Evidence was reviewed supporting the hypothesis that dynamical systems governing skilled sensorimotor behaviors are defined in abstract, low-dimensional task spaces that serve to create modal or cooperative patterns of activity in the generally higher-dimensional articulatory periphery. In this regard, the single and dual degree-of-freedom limb rhythms, considered in section 6.1, can be viewed as tasks with relatively simple mappings between their respective task (or modal) coordinates and articulatory coordinates. Such tasks are rare in everyday life, however. Most real-world activites (e.g., speech production, or the coordination of reaching and grasping for object retrieval and manipulation) involve tasks defined over effector systems with multiple articulatory degrees of freedom, and for which the mappings between task and articulatory coordinates are more complex.

The abstract nature of these coordinative dynamics was highlighted by the demonstration (Schmidt, et al., 1990) that entrainment between two limit-cycle rhythms can occur when the component rhythms are performed by different actors that are linked by visual information. These data suggest that the intent to coordinate one's actions with events in the external environment serves to create a linkage through which perceptual information, specific to the dynamics of these events, flows into the component task spaces that control these actions. The result is a coupled, abstract, modal dynamical system that seamlessly spans actor and environment. It is tempting to speculate that this perspective applies quite generally across the spectrum of biological behaviors.

ACKNOWLEDGMENTS

This work was supported by grants from the following sources: NIH Grant DC-00121 (Dynamics of Speech Articulation) and NSF Grant BNS-88-20099 (Phonetic Structure Using Articulatory Dynamics) to Haskins Laboratories. I am grateful to Claudia Carello, Philip Rubin, and Michael Turvey for helpful comments on earlier versions of this chapter.

NOTES

1. Similar results on rhythms produced at the elbow and wrist joints of the same arm were presented by Kelso, Buchanan, and Wallace (1991), when the forearm was either pronated or supinated across experimental conditions. Again, the easiest combinations to perform were those in which the motions of the hand and forearm were spatially inphase, regardless of the relative anatomical phasing between hand and forearm muscle groups. Furthermore, in trials involving experimentally demanded increases or decreases of coupled oscillation frequency, phase transitions were observed from the spatially antiphase to spatially inphase patterns in both pronation and supination conditions. Relatedly, MacKenzie and Patla (1983) induced

phase transitions in bimanual finger rhythms by increasing cycling frequency within trials, and showed that the transitions were affected systematically by the relative orientation of the fingers' spatial planes of motion.

The primacy of abstract spatial coordinates over anatomical or biomechanical coordinates has also been demonstrated for discrete targeting tasks. For example, Soechting (1982) reported evidence from a pointing task involving the elbow joint, suggesting that the controlled variable for this task is not anatomical joint angle per se, but rather the orientation angle of the forearm in body-referenced or environment-referenced coordinates.

REFERENCES

Abbs, J. H., and Gracco, V. L. (1983). Sensorimotor actions in the control of multimovement speech gestures. *Trends in Neuroscience, 6,* 393–395.

Abraham, R., and Shaw, C. (1982). *Dynamics—the geometry of behavior. Part 1: periodic behavior.* Santa Cruz, CA: Aerial Press.

Bailly, G., Laboissière, R., and Schwartz, J. L. (1991). Formant trajectories as audible gestures: an alternative for speech synthesis. *Journal of Phonetics, 19,* 9–23.

Baker, G. L., and Gollub, J. P. (1990). *Chaotic dynamics: an introduction.* New York: Cambridge University Press.

Baldissera, F., Cavallari, P., and Civaschi, P. (1982). Preferential coupling between voluntary movements of ipsilateral limbs. *Neuroscience Letters, 34,* 95–100.

Baldissera, F., Cavallari, P., Marini, G., et al. (1991). Differential control of in-phase and anti-phase coupling of rhythmic movements of ipsilateral hand and foot. *Experimental Brain Research, 83,* 375–380.

Beek, P. J. (1989). Timing and phase-locking in cascade juggling. *Ecological Psychology, 1,* 55–96.

Bell-Berti, F., and Harris, K. S. (1981). A temporal model of speech production. *Phonetica, 38,* 9–20.

Bernstein, N. A. (1967/1984). *The coordination and regulation of movements.* London: Pergamon Press. Reprinted in H. T. A. Whiting (Ed.) (1984), *Human motor actions: Bernstein reassessed.* New York: North-Holland.

Browman, C., and Goldstein, L. (1986). Towards an articulatory phonology. In C. Ewan and J. Anderson (Eds.), *Phonology yearbook 3* (pp. 219–252). Cambridge, England: Cambridge University Press.

Browman, C. P., and Goldstein, L. (1991). Tiers in articulatory phonology, with some implications for casual speech. In J. Kingston and M. E. Beckman (Eds.), *Papers in laboratory phonology: I. Between the grammar and the physics of speech* (pp. 341–338). Cambridge, England: Cambridge University Press.

Coker, C. H. (1976). A model of articulatory dynamics and control. *Proceedings of the IEEE, 64,* 452–460.

de Jong, K. (1991). An articulatory study of consonant-induced vowel duration changes in English. *Phonetica, 48,* 1–17.

Edwards, J., Beckman, M. E., and Fletcher, J. (1991). The articulatory kinematics of final lengthening. *Journal of the Acoustical Society of America, 89,* 369–382.

Folkins, J. W., and Abbs, J. H. (1975). Lip and jaw motor control during speech: responses to resistive loading of the jaw. *Journal of Speech and Hearing Research, 18,* 207–220.

Fowler, C. (1980). Coarticulation and theories of extrinsic timing. *Journal of Phonetics, 8,* 113–133.

Fowler, C. A., and Saltzman, E. (1993). Coordination and coarticulation in speech production. *Language and Speech, 36,* 171–195.

Grossberg, S. (1986). The adaptive self-organization of serial order in behavior: speech, language, and motor control. In E. C. Schwab and H. C. Nusbaum (Eds.), *Pattern recognition by humans and machines,* Vol. 1. New York: Academic Press.

Haken, H., Kelso, J. A. S., and Bunz, H. (1985). A theoretical model of phase transitions in human hand movements. *Biological Cybernetics, 51,* 347–356.

Harris, K. S. (1984). Coarticulation as a component of articulatory descriptions. In R. G. Daniloff (Ed.), *Articulation assessment and treatment issues* (pp. 147–167). San Diego: College Hill Press.

Hawkins, S. (1992). An introduction to task dynamics. In G. J. Docherty and D. R. Ladd (Eds.), *Papers in laboratory phonology. II. Gesture, segment, and prosody* (pp. 9–25). Cambridge, England: Cambridge University Press.

Hollerbach, J. M. (1982). Computers, brains, and the control of movement. *Trends in Neurosciences, 5,* 189–192.

Jordan, M. I. (1986). *Serial order in behavior: a parallel distributed processing approach. Technical Report No. 8604.* San Diego: University of California, Institute for Cognitive Science.

Jordan, M. I. (1990). Motor learning and the degrees of freedom problem. In M. Jeannerod (Ed.), *Attention and performance XIII* (pp. 796–836). Hillsdale, NJ: Erlbaum.

Jordan, M. I. (in press). Serial order: A parallel distributed processing approach. In J. L. Elman and D. E. Rumelhart (Eds.), *Advances in connectionist theory: speech.* Hillsdale, NJ: Erlbaum.

Jordan, M. I., and Rosenbaum, D. A. (1989). Action. In M. I. Posner (Ed.), *Foundations of cognitive science* (pp. 727–767). Cambridge, MA: MIT Press.

Kawato, M. (1989). Motor theory of speech perception revisited from a minimum torque-change neural network model. In *Proceedings of the 8th Symposium on Future Electron Devices* (pp. 141–150). October 30–31, Tokyo, Japan.

Kay, B. A. (1986). *Dynamic modeling of rhythmic limb movements: converging on a description of the component oscillators.* Unpublished doctoral dissertation, Department of Psychology, University of Connecticut, Storrs.

Kay, B. A., Kelso, J. A. S., Saltzman, E. L., et al. (1987). Space-time behavior of single and bimanual rhythmical movements: data and limit cycle model. *Journal of Experimental Psychology: Human Perception and Performance, 13,* 178–192.

Kay, B. A., Saltzman, E. L., and Kelso, J. A. S. (1991). Steady-state and perturbed rhythmical movements: a dynamical analysis. *Journal of Experimental Psychology: Human Perception and Performance, 17,* 183–197.

Keating, P. A. (1985). CV phonology, experimental phonetics, and coarticulation. *UCLA Working Papers in Phonetics, 62,* 1–13.

Kelso, J. A. S. (1984). Phase transitions and critical behavior in human bimanual coordination. *American Journal of Physiology: Regulatory, Integrative and Comparative Physiology, 15,* R1000–R1004.

Kelso, J. A. S., Buchanan, J. J., and Wallace, S. A. (1991). Order parameters for the neural organization of single, multijoint limb movement patterns. *Experimental Brain Research, 85,* 432–444.

Kelso, J. A. S., Delcolle, J. D., and Schöner, G. S. (1990). Action-perception as a pattern formation process. In M. Jeannerod (Ed.), *Attention and performance XIII* (pp. 139–169). Hillsdale, NJ: Erlbaum.

Kelso, J. A. S., and Jeka, J. J. (1992). Symmetry breaking dynamics of human multilimb coordination. *Journal of Experimental Psychology: Human Perception and Performance, 18,* 645–668.

Kelso, J. A. S., Saltzman, E. L., and Tuller, B. (1986a). The dynamical perspective on speech production: data and theory. *Journal of Phonetics, 14,* 29–60.

Kelso, J. A. S., Saltzman, E. L., and Tuller, B. (1986b). Intentional contents, communicative context, and task dynamics: a reply to the commentators. *Journal of Phonetics, 14,* 171–196.

Kelso, J. A. S., Tuller, B., Vatikiotis-Bateson, E., et al. (1984). Functionally specific articulatory cooperation following jaw perturbations during speech: evidence for coordinative structures. *Journal of Experimental Psychology: Human Perception and Performance, 10,* 812–832.

Kelso, J. A. S., Vatikiotis-Bateson, E., Saltzman, E. L., et al. (1985). A qualitative dynamic analysis of reiterant speech production: phase portraits, kinematics, and dynamic modeling. *Journal of the Acoustical Society of America, 77,* 266–280.

Kent, R. D., and Minifie, F. D. (1977). Coarticulation in recent speech production models. *Journal of Phonetics, 5,* 115–133.

Kugler, P. N., and Turvey, M. T. (1987). *Information, natural law, and the self-assembly of rhythmic movement.* Hillsdale, NJ: Erlbaum.

Laver, J. (1980). Slips of the tongue as neuromuscular evidence for a model of speech production. In H. W. Dechert and M. Raupach (Eds.), *Temporal variables in speech: studies in honour of Frieda Goldman-Eisler.* The Hague: Mouton.

MacKay, D. G., and Soderberg, G. A. (1971). Homologous intrusions: an analogue of linguistic blends. *Perceptual and Motor Skills, 32,* 645–646.

MacKenzie, C. L., and Patla, A. E. (1983). Breakdown in rapid bimanual finger tapping as a function of orientation and phasing. *Society for Neuroscience Abstracts, 9* (2).

Mattingly, I. (1990). The global character of phonetic gestures. *Journal of Phonetics, 18,* 445–452.

Öhman, S. E. G. (1966). Coarticulation in VCV utterances: spectrographic measurements. *Journal of the Acoustical Society of America, 39,* 151–168.

Öhman, S. E. G. (1967). Numerical model of coarticulation. *Journal of the Acoustical Society of America, 41,* 310–320.

Perkell, J. S. (1969). *Physiology of speech production: results and implications of a quantitative cineradiographic study.* Cambridge, MA: MIT Press.

Perkell, J. S. (1991). Models, theory, and data in speech production. In *Proceedings of the XIIth International Congress of Phonetic Sciences,* Vol. 1. Aix-en-Provence, France: Université de Provence, Service des Publications.

Rosenblum, L. D., and Turvey, M. T. (1988). Maintenance tendency in coordinated rhythmic movements: relative fluctuations and phase. *Neuroscience, 27,* 289–300.

Rubin, P. E., Baer, T., and Mermelstein, P. (1981). An articulatory synthesizer for perceptual research. *Journal of the Acoustical Society of America, 70,* 321–328.

Saltzman, E. L. (1979). Levels of sensorimotor representation. *Journal of Mathematical Psychology, 20,* 91–163.

Saltzman, E. (1986). Task dynamic coordination of the speech articulators: a preliminary model. *Experimental Brain Research, 15,* 129–144.

Saltzman, E. (1991). The task dynamic model in speech production. In H. F. M. Peters, W. Hulstijn, and C. W. Starkweather (Eds.), *Speech motor control and stuttering* (pp. 37–52). Amsterdam: Excerpta Medica.

Saltzman, E. L. (1992). Biomechanical and haptic factors in the temporal patterning of limb and speech activity. *Human Movement Science, 11*, 239–251.

Saltzman, E., Kay, B., Rubin, P., et al. (1991). Dynamics of intergestural timing. In *Perilus XIV* (pp. 47–56). Institute of Linguistics, University of Stockholm, Stockholm.

Saltzman, E. L., and Kelso, J. A. S. (1987). Skilled actions: a task dynamic approach. *Psychological Review, 94*, 84–106.

Saltzman, E. L., and Munhall, K. G. (1989). A dynamical approach to gestural patterning in speech production. *Ecological Psychology, 1*, 333–382.

Schmidt, R. C., Carello, C., and Turvey, M. T. (1990). Phase transitions and critical fluctuations in the visual coordination of rhythmic movements between people. *Journal of Experimental Psychology: Human Perception and Performance, 16*, 227–247.

Schneider, K., Zernicke, R. F., Schmidt, R. A., et al. (1989). Changes in limb dynamics during practice of rapid arm movements. *Journal of Biomechanics, 22*, 805–817.

Scholz, J. P., and Kelso, J. A. S. (1989). A quantitative approach to understanding the formation and change of coordinated movement patterns. *Journal of Motor Behavior, 21*, 122–144.

Schöner, G., Haken, H., and Kelso, J. A. S. (1986). Stochastic theory of phase transitions in human hand movement. *Biological Cybernetics, 53*, 1–11.

Schöner, G., and Kelso, J. A. S. (1988). Dynamic pattern generation in behavioral and neural systems. *Science, 239*, 1513–1520.

Shaiman, S. (1989). Kinematic and electromyographic responses to perturbation of the jaw. *Journal of the Acoustical Society of America, 86*, 78–88.

Soechting, J. F. (1982). Does position sense at the elbow joint reflect a sense of elbow joint angle or one of limb orientation? *Brain Research, 248*, 392–395.

Sternad, D., Turvey, M. T., and Schmidt, R. C. (1992). Average phase difference theory and 1:1 phase entrainment in interlimb coordination. *Biological Cybernetics, 67*, 223–231.

Sussman, H. M., MacNeilage, P. F., and Hanson, R. J. (1973). Labial and mandibular dynamics during the production of bilabial consonants: preliminary observations. *Journal of Speech and Hearing Research, 16*, 397–420.

Thompson, J. M. T., and Stewart, H. B. (1986). *Nonlinear dynamics and chaos: geometrical methods for engineers and scientists.* New York: Wiley.

Turvey, M. T. (1990). Coordination. *American Psychologist, 45*, 938–953.

Van Riel, M.-J., Beek, P. J., and van Wieringen, P. C. W. (1991). Phase transitions in rhythmic arm movements under different stimulus-response configurations. In P. J. Beek, R. J. Bootsma, and P. C. W. van Wieringen (Eds.), *Studies in perception and action* (pp. 234–238). Amsterdam: Rodopi.

Vatikiotis-Bateson, E. (1988). *Lingistic structure and articulatory dynamics.* Ph.D. dissertation, Indiana University, Bloomington (distributed by the Indiana University Linguistics Club, Bloomington).

Woods, B. T., and Teuber, H.-L. (1978). Mirror movements after childhood hemiparesis. *Neurology, 28*, 1152–1158.

Guide to Further Reading

The Russian motor physiologist, N. A. Bernstein (1967/1984) produced a classic body of empirical and theoretical work that anticipated and inspired many of today's developments in movement science. It is still a great read. Turvey (1990) reviews and extends this perspective in a broad overview of issues faced in studying the dynamics of coordination, carrying the reader on a tour from Bernstein to the current state of the art. Readers interested in more detailed accounts of various recent trends in the field should consult Jordan (1990; a connectionist perspective on dynamics and coordinate systems in skilled actions), Saltzman and Munhall (1989; task dynamics and speech production), and Schöner and Kelso (1988; an overview of the "synergetics" approach to self-organizing systems, in the context of sensorimotor behaviors).

Bernstein, N. A. (1967/1984). *The coordination and regulation of movements*. London: Pergamon Press. Reprinted in H. T. A. Whiting, (Ed.) (1984), *Human motor actions: Bernstein reassessed*. New York: North-Holland.

Jordan, M. I. (1990). Motor learning and the degrees of freedom problem. In M. Jeannerod (Ed.), *Attention and performance XIII* (pp. 796–836). Hillsdale, NJ: Erlbaum.

Saltzman, E. L., and Munhall, K. G. (1989). A dynamical approach to gestural patterning in speech production. *Ecological Psychology, 1*, 333–382.

Schöner, G., and Kelso, J. A. S. (1988). Dynamic pattern generation in behavioral and neural systems. *Science, 239*, 1513–1520.

Turvey, M. T. (1990). Coordination. *American Psychologist, 45*, 938–953.

7 Dynamics and Articulatory Phonology

Catherine P. Browman and Louis Goldstein

EDITORS' INTRODUCTION

Linguists studying the sound of utterances distinguish between the strictly physical aspects of speech and its production, on the one hand, and its basic linguistic properties on the other. The difference here can be illustrated by two utterances of Here it is, *one produced by Lurch, the laconic butler from* The Addams Family, *and the other by a child discovering an Easter egg. At the phonetic level—the level of the physical sounds—these differ enormously, but at a higher and more abstract phonological level they consist of the same sound units (known as phonemes) assembled in the same order.*

Developing good theories of phonetics, phonology, and the relation between them are central parts of linguistics, but these efforts are important to cognitive science as well. Somehow we manage to produce utterances—to speak—and how we can do this cries out for explanation. The standard assumption is that the phonological level is basic as far as cognitive processes are concerned; the output of the cognitive system is a phonological specification of what it is one wants to say. Actually speaking involves using one's vocal mechanisms to translate a phonological specification into a stream of sound.

Mainstream computational cognitive science assumes that cognitive processes are a matter of processing symbols inside the head. Consequently, it makes the assumption that phonemes are represented in the mind/brain by symbols of basically the same kind as those used by linguists when they write about phonemes. Thus, linguists represent the phoneme /t/ by means of the symbol [tʰ]; computational cognitive science assumes that when you produce an utterance involving this sound, the cognitive system delivers a similar symbol (though in "mentalese") to the motor system, which drives the vocal apparatus to produce the actual sound. (In more detailed versions, the phonemic symbol is more complex; it is a data structure specifying the presence or absence of more basic features.)

This approach turns out to have some deep problems, grounded in the fact that the symbols of phonology are so different from the actual physical processes that constitute speaking. One problem is figuring out the nature of the relationship between phonological specifications and the resulting sounds that the motor system must somehow implement. Another problem is in the nature of the implementation device itself. How does it translate from the sequence of static symbols, which are output by the cognitive system, into the dynamical processes, which constitute speaking? How does it get from atemporal symbols to real speech, which has an extraordinarily subtle and complex temporal character?

Browman and Goldstein do not solve these problems; rather, they avoid them by offering a fundamentally different picture of phonology and its relationship with the physical processes of speaking. In their approach, known as articulatory phonology, *the fundamental units are not abstract units of sound, represented by mental symbols, but rather basic coordinated* gestures *of the speech system. These gestures are high-level descriptions of a single complex dynamical system whose behaviors, at a lower level, constitute the articulatory processes of sound production. Consequently in articulatory phonology there is no deep incommensurability between the phonological and phonetic levels to be overcome. The basic units of phonology are themselves dynamic events of the same kind (though at a higher level) as the physical processes of speech production.*

In this chapter, Browman and Goldstein give an overview of the articulatory phonology approach, and describe its implementation in a speech production system for English. In this system a high-level gestural score drives a dynamical system which organizes movements of components of the articulatory system (in the manner described by Elliot Saltzman in chapter 6). The specifications of these movements are then fed into a sound synthesizer which produces the physical sound itself. (Note that in this chapter they describe this system as a computational model, but by this they mean simulated on a computer *rather than* a model of computational processes.*)*

This work illustrates a number of general characteristics of the dynamical approach to cognition. For example, it rejects the traditional assumptions that cognitive processes and bodily processes are fundamentally different in kind, and that cognition is "inner" while bodily movement is "outer." Articulatory phonology breaks down the difference in kind by reconceptualizing the basic units of cognition as behaviors of a dynamical system, and so as essentially temporal in nature. By making this move, this dynamical approach overcomes problems of embeddedness that plague standard computational cognitive science.

7.1   INTRODUCTION

Traditionally, the study of human speech and its patterning has been approached in two different ways. One way has been to consider it as mechanical or biomechanical activity (e.g., of articulators or air molecules or cochlear hair cells) that changes continuously in time. The other way has been to consider it as a linguistic (or cognitive) structure consisting of a sequence of elements chosen from a closed inventory. Development of the tools required to describe speech in one or the other of these approaches has proceeded largely in parallel, with one hardly informing the other at all (some notable exceptions are discussed below). As a result, speech has been seen as having two structures, one considered physical, and the other cognitive, where the

Catherine P. Browman and Louis Goldstein

relation between the two structures is generally not an intrinsic part of either description. From this perspective, a complete picture requires "translating" between the intrinsically incommensurate domains (as argued by Fowler, Rubin, Remez, et al. 1980).

The research we have been pursuing (Browman and Goldstein, 1986, 1989, 1990a,b, 1992) ("articulatory phonology") begins with the very different assumption that these apparently different domains are, in fact, the low- and high-dimensional descriptions of a single (complex) system. Crucial to this approach is identification of phonological units with dynamically specified units of articulatory action, called *gestures*. Thus, an utterance is described as an act that can be decomposed into a small number of primitive units (a low-dimensional description), in a particular spatiotemporal configuration. The same description also provides an intrinsic specification of the high-dimensional properties of the act (its various mechanical and biomechanical consequences).

In this chapter, we briefly examine the nature of the low- and high-dimensional descriptions of speech, and contrast the dynamical perspective that unifies these with other approaches in which they are separated as properties of mind and body. We then review some of the basic assumptions and results of developing a specific model incorporating dynamical units, and illustrate how it provides both low- and high-dimensional descriptions.

7.2   DIMENSIONALITY OF DESCRIPTION

Human speech events can be seen as quite complex, in the sense that an individual utterance follows a continuous trajectory through a space defined by a large number of potential degrees of freedom, or dimensions. This is true whether the dimensions are neural, articulatory, acoustic, aerodynamic, auditory, or otherwise describable. The fundamental insight of phonology, however, is that the pronunciation of the words in a given language may differ from (i.e., contrast with) one another in only a restricted number of ways: the number of degrees of freedom actually employed in this contrastive behavior is far fewer than the number that is mechanically available. This insight has taken the form of the hypothesis that words can be decomposed into a small number of primitive units (usually far fewer than a hundred in a given language) which can be combined in different ways to form the large number of words required in human lexicons. Thus, as argued by Kelso, Saltzman, and Tuller (1986), human speech is characterized not only by a high number of potential (microscopic) degrees of freedom but also by a low-dimensional (macroscopic) form. This macroscopic form is usually called the "phonological" form. As suggested below, this collapse of degrees of freedom can possibly be understood as an instance of the kind of self-organization found in other complex systems in nature (Haken, 1977; Kugler and Turvey, 1987; Madore and Freedman, 1987; Schöner and Kelso, 1988; Kauffmann, 1991).

Historically, however, the gross differences between the macroscopic and microscopic scales of description have led researchers to ignore one or the other description, or to assert its irrelevance, and hence to generally separate the cognitive and the physical. Anderson (1974) describes how the development of tools in the 19th and early 20th centuries led to the quantification of more and more details of the speech signal, but "with such increasingly precise description, however, came the realization that much of it was irrelevant to the central tasks of linguistic science" (p. 4). Indeed, the development of many early phonological theories (e.g., those of Saussure, Trubetzkoy, Sapir, Bloomfield) proceeded largely without any substantive investigation of the measurable properties of the speech event at all (although Anderson notes Bloomfield's insistence that the smallest phonological units must ultimately be defined in terms of some measurable properties of the speech signal). In general, what was seen as important about phonological units was their *function*, their ability to distinguish utterances.

A particularly telling insight into this view of the lack of relation between the phonological and physical descriptions can be seen in Hockett's (1955) familiar Easter egg analogy. The structure serving to distinguish utterances (for Hockett, a sequence of letter-sized phonological units called phonemes) was viewed as a row of colored, but unboiled, Easter eggs on a moving belt. The physical structure (for Hockett, the acoustic signal) was imagined to be the result of running the belt through a wringer, effectively smashing the eggs and intermixing them. It is quite striking that, in this analogy, the cognitive structure of the speech event cannot be seen in the gooey mess itself. For Hockett, the only way the hearer can respond to the event is to infer (on the basis of obscured evidence, and knowledge of possible egg sequences) what sequence of eggs might have been responsible for the mess. It is clear that in this view, the relation between cognitive and physical descriptions is neither systematic nor particularly interesting. The descriptions share color as an important attribute, but beyond that there is little relation.

A major approach that did take seriously the goal of unifying the cognitive and physical aspects of speech description was that presented in the *Sound Pattern of English* (Chomsky and Halle, 1968), including the associated work on the development of the theory of distinctive features (Jakobson, Fant, and Halle, 1951) and the quantal relations that underlie them (Stevens, 1972, 1989). In this approach, an utterance is assigned two representations: a "phonological" one, whose goal is to describe how the utterance functions with respect to contrast and patterns of alternation, and a "phonetic" one, whose goal is to account for the grammatically determined physical properties of the utterance. Crucially, however, the relation between the representations is quite constrained: both descriptions employ exactly the same set of dimensions (the features). The phonological representation is coarser in that features may take on only binary values, while the phonetic representation is more fine-grained, with the features having scalar values. However, a principled relation between the binary values and the scales is also provided: Stevens's quantal theory attempts to show how the potential continuum of scalar feature values can be intrinsically partitioned into categorical regions, when the mapping from articulatory dimensions to auditory properties is considered.

Further, the existence of such quantal relations is used to explain why languages employ these particular features in the first place.

Problems raised with this approach to speech description soon led to its abandonment, however. One problem is that its phonetic representations were shown to be inadequate to capture certain systematic physical differences between utterances in different languages (Ladefoged, 1980; Port, 1981; Keating, 1985). The scales used in the phonetic representations are themselves of reduced dimensionality, when compared to a complete physical description of utterances. Chomsky and Halle (1968) hypothesized that such further details could be supplied by universal rules. However, the above authors (also Browman and Goldstein, 1986) argued that this would not work—the same phonetic representation (in the Chomsky and Halle sense) can have different physical properties in different languages. Thus, more of the physical detail (and particularly details having to do with timing) would have to be specified as part of the description of a particular language. Ladefoged's (1980) argument cut even deeper. He argued that there is a system of scales that is useful for characterizing the measurable articulatory and acoustic properties of utterances, but that these scales are very different from the features proposed by Chomsky and Halle.

One response to these failings has been to hypothesize that descriptions of speech should include, in addition to phonological rules of the usual sort, rules that take (cognitive) phonological representations as input and convert them to physical parameterizations of various sorts. These rules have been described as rules of "phonetic implementation" (e.g., Klatt, 1976; Port, 1981; Keating, 1985; Liberman and Pierrehumbert, 1984; Keating, 1990; Pierrehumbert, 1990). Note that in this view the description of speech is divided into two separate domains involving distinct types of representations: the phonological or cognitive structure and the phonetic or physical structure. This explicit partitioning of the speech side of linguistic structure into separate phonetic and phonological components which employ distinct data types that are related to one another only through rules of phonetic implementation (or "interpretation") has stimulated a good deal of research (e.g., Liberman and Pierrehumbert, 1984; Fourakis and Port, 1986; Keating, 1988; Cohn, 1990; Coleman, 1992). However, there is a major price to be paid for drawing such a strict separation: it becomes very easy to view phonetic and phonological (physical and cognitive) structures as essentially independent of one another, with no interaction or mutual constraint. As Clements (1992) describes the problem: "The result is that the relation between the phonological and phonetic components is quite unconstrained. Since there is little resemblance between them, it does not matter very much for the purposes of phonetic interpretation what the form of the phonological input is; virtually any phonological description can serve its purposes equally well" (p. 192). Yet, there is a constrained relation between the cognitive and physical structures of speech, which is what drove the development of feature theory in the first place.

In our view, the relation between the physical and cognitive, i.e., the phonetic and phonological, aspects of speech is inherently constrained by their being simply two levels of description—the microscopic and macroscopic—of the same system. Moreover, we have argued that the relation between microscopic and macroscopic properties of speech is one of *mutual* or *reciprocal* constraint (Browman and Goldstein, 1990b). As we elaborated, the existence of such reciprocity is supported by two different lines of research. One line has attempted to show how the macroscopic properties of contrast and combination of phonological units arise from, or are constrained by, the microscopic, i.e., the detailed properties of speech articulation and the relations between speech articulation, aerodynamics, acoustics, and audition (e.g., Stevens, 1972, 1989; Lindblom, MacNeilage, and Studdert-Kennedy, 1983; Ohala, 1983). A second line has shown that there are constraints running in the opposite direction, such that the (microscopic) detailed articulatory or acoustic properties of particular phonological units are determined, in part, by the macroscopic system of contrast and combination found in a particular language (e.g., Wood, 1982; Ladefoged, 1982; Manuel and Krakow, 1984; Keating, 1990). The apparent existence of this bidirectionality is of considerable interest, because recent studies of the generic properties of complex physical systems have demonstrated that reciprocal constraint between macroscopic and microscopic scales is a hallmark of systems displaying "self-organization" (Kugler and Turvey, 1987; see also discussions by Langton in Lewin, 1992, pp. 12–14, 188–191; and work on the emergent properties of "co-evolving" complex systems: Hogeweg, 1989; Kauffman, 1989; Kauffman and Johnsen, 1991; Packard, 1989).

Such self-organizing systems (hypothesized as underlying such diverse phenomena as the construction of insect nests and evolutionary and ecological dynamics) display the property that the "local" interactions among a large number of microscopic system components can lead to emergent patterns of "global" organization and order. The emergent global organization also places constraints on the components and their local interactions. Thus, self-organization provides a principled linkage between descriptions of different dimensionality of the same system: the high-dimensional description (with many degrees of freedom) of the local interactions and the low-dimensional description (with few degrees of freedom) of the emergent global patterns. From this point of view, then, speech can be viewed as a single complex system (with low-dimensional macroscopic and high-dimensional microscopic properties) rather than as two distinct components.

A different recent attempt to articulate the nature of the constraints holding between the cognitive and physical structures can be found in Pierrehumbert (1990), in which the relation between the structures is argued to be a "semantic" one, parallel to the relation that obtains between concepts and their real-world denotations. In this view, macroscopic structure is constrained by the microscopic properties of speech and by the principles guiding human cognitive category formation. However, the view fails to account for the apparent bidirectionality of the constraints. That is, there is no possibility of constraining the microscopic properties of speech by its macroscopic properties in this view. (For a discussion of possible limitations to a dynamic approach to phonology, see Pierrehumbert and Pierrehumbert, 1990.)

The articulatory phonology that we have been developing (e.g., Browman and Goldstein, 1986, 1989, 1992) attempts to understand phonology (the cognitive) as the low-dimensional macroscopic description of a physical system. In this work, rather than rejecting Chomsky and Halle's constrained relation between the physical and cognitive, as the phonetic implementation approaches have done, we have, if anything, increased the hypothesized tightness of that relation by using the concept of different dimensionality. We have surmised that the problem with the program proposed by Chomsky and Halle was instead in their choice of the elementary units of the system. In particular, we have argued that it is wrong to assume that the elementary units are (1) static, (2) neutral between articulation and acoustics, and (3) arranged in nonoverlapping chunks. Assumptions (1) and (3) have been argued against by Fowler et al. (1980), and (3) has also been rejected by most of the work in "nonlinear" phonology over the past 15 years. Assumption (2) has been, at least partially, rejected in the "active articulator" version of "feature geometry" (Halle, 1982; Sagey, 1986; McCarthy, 1988.)

7.3 GESTURES

Articulatory phonology takes seriously the view that the units of speech production are actions, and therefore that (1) they are dynamic, not static. Further, since articulatory phonology considers phonological functions such as contrast to be low-dimensional, macroscopic descriptions of such actions, the basic units are (2) not neutral between articulation and acoustics, but rather are articulatory in nature. Thus, in articulatory phonology, the basic phonological unit is the *articulatory gesture*, which is defined as a dynamical system specified with a characteristic set of parameter values (see Saltzman, chapter 6). Finally, because the actions are distributed across the various articulator sets of the vocal tract (the lips, tongue, glottis, velum, etc.), an utterance is modeled as an ensemble, or constellation, of a small number of (3) potentially overlapping gestural units.

As is elaborated below, contrast among utterances can be defined in terms of these gestural constellations. Thus, these structures can capture the low-dimensional properties of utterances. In addition, because each gesture is defined as a dynamical system, no rules of implementation are required to characterize the high-dimensional properties of the utterance. A time-varying pattern of articulator motion (and its resulting acoustic consequences) is lawfully entailed by the dynamical systems themselves—they are self-implementing. Moreover, these time-varying patterns automatically display the property of context dependence (which is ubiquitous in the high-dimensional description of speech) even though the gestures are defined in a context-

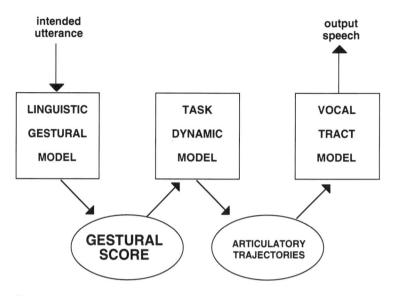

Figure 7.1 Computational system for generating speech using dynamically defined articulatory gestures.

independent fashion. The nature of the articulatory dimensions along which the individual dynamical units are defined allows this context dependence to emerge lawfully.

The articulatory phonology approach has been incorporated into a computational system being developed at Haskins Laboratories (Browman, Goldstein, Kelso, et al., 1984; Saltzman, 1986; Saltzman and Munhall, 1989; Browman and Goldstein, 1990a,c). In this system, illustrated in figure 7.1, utterances are organized ensembles (or *constellations*) of units of articulatory action called *gestures*. Each gesture is modeled as a dynamical system that characterizes the formation (and release) of a local constriction within the vocal tract (the gesture's functional goal or "task"). For example, the word "ban" begins with a gesture whose task is lip closure. The formation of this constriction entails a change in the distance between the upper and lower lips (or *lip aperture*) over time. This change is modeled using a second-order system (a "point attractor," Abraham and Shaw, 1982), specified with particular values for the equilibrium position and stiffness parameters. (Damping is, for the most part, assumed to be critical, so that the system approaches its equilibrium position and doesn't overshoot it.) During the activation interval for this gesture, the equilibrium position for lip aperture is set to the goal value for lip closure; the stiffness setting, combined with the damping, determines the amount of time it will take for the system to get close to the goal of lip closure.

The set of task or *tract* variables currently implemented in the computational model are listed at the top left of figure 7.2, and the sagittal vocal tract shape below illustrates their geometric definitions. This set of tract variables

Catherine P. Browman and Louis Goldstein

	tract variable	articulators involved
LP	lip protrusion	upper & lower lips, jaw
LA	lip aperture	upper & lower lips, jaw
TTCL	tongue tip constrict location	tongue tip, tongue body, jaw
TTCD	tongue tip constrict degree	tongue tip, tongue body, jaw
TBCL	tongue body constrict location	tongue body, jaw
TBCD	tongue body constrict degree	tongue body, jaw
VEL	velic aperture	velum
GLO	glottal aperture	glottis

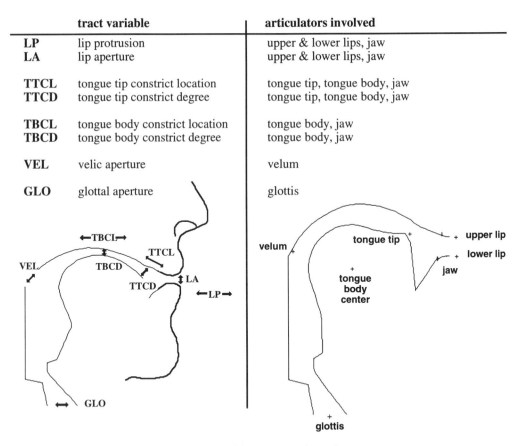

Figure 7.2 Tract variables and their associated articulators.

is hypothesized to be sufficient for characterizing most of the gestures of English (exceptions involve the details of characteristic shaping of constrictions; see Browman and Goldstein, 1989). For oral gestures, two paired tract-variable regimes are specified, one controlling the constriction degree of a particular structure, the other its constriction location (a tract-variable regime consists of a set of values for the dynamic parameters of stiffness, equilibrium position, and damping ratio). Thus, the specification for an oral gesture includes an equilibrium position, or goal, for each of two tract variables, as well as a stiffness (which is currently yoked across the two tract variables). Each functional goal for a gesture is achieved by the coordinated action of a set of articulators, i.e., a coordinative structure (Turvey, 1977; Fowler et al., 1980; Kelso et al., 1986; Saltzman, 1986); the sets of articulators used for each of the tract variables are shown on the top right of figure 7.2, with the articulators indicated on the outline of the vocal tract model below. Note that the same articulators are shared by both of the paired oral tract variables, so that altogether there are five distinct articulator sets, or coordinative structure types, in the system.

In the computational system the articulators are those of a vocal tract model (Rubin, Baer, and Mermelstein, 1981) that can generate speech waveforms from a specification of the positions of individual articulators. When a dynamical system (or pair of them) corresponding to a particular gesture is imposed on the vocal tract, the task-dynamic model (Saltzman, 1986; Saltzman and Kelso, 1987; Saltzman and Munhall, 1989; Saltzman, chapter 6) calculates the time-varying trajectories of the individual articulators constituting that coordinative structure, based on the information about values of the dynamical parameters, and phasing information (see section 7.4), contained in its input. These articulator trajectories are input to the vocal tract model, which then calculates the resulting global vocal tract shape, area function, transfer function, and speech waveform (see figure 7.1).

Defining gestures dynamically can provide a principled link between macroscopic and microscopic properties of speech. To illustrate some of the ways in which this is true, consider the example of lip closure. The values of the dynamical parameters associated with a lip closure gesture are macroscopic properties that define it as a phonological unit and allow it to contrast with other gestures such as the narrowing gesture for [w]. These values are definitional, and remain invariant as long as the gesture is active. At the same time, however, the gesture intrinsically specifies the (microscopic) patterns of continuous change that the lips can exhibit over time. These changes emerge as the lawful consequences of the dynamical system, its parameters, and the initial conditions. Thus, dynamically defined gestures provide a lawful link between macroscopic and microscopic properties.

While tract-variable goals are specified numerically, and in principle could take on any real value, the actual values used to specify the gestures of English in the model cluster in narrow ranges that correspond to contrastive categories: for example, in the case of constriction degree, different ranges are found for gestures that correspond to what are usually referred to as stops, fricatives, and approximants. Thus, paradigmatic comparison (or a density distribution) of the numerical specifications of all English gestures would reveal a macroscopic structure of contrastive categories. The existence of such narrow ranges is predicted by approaches such as the quantal theory (e.g., Stevens, 1989) and the theory of adaptive dispersion (e.g., Lindblom et al., 1983), although the dimensions investigated in those approaches are not identical to the tract-variable dimensions. These approaches can be seen as accounting for how microscopic continua are partitioned into a small number of macroscopic categories.

The physical properties of a given phonological unit vary considerably depending on its context (e.g., Öhman, 1966; Liberman, Cooper, Shankweiler, et al., 1967; Kent and Minifie, 1977). Much of this context dependence emerges lawfully from the use of task dynamics. An example of this kind of context dependence in lip closure gestures can be seen in the fact that the three independent articulators that can contribute to closing the lips (upper lip, lower lip, and jaw) do so to different extents as a function of the vowel

Catherine P. Browman and Louis Goldstein

environment in which the lip closure is produced (Sussman, MacNeilage, and Hanson, 1973; Macchi, 1988). The value of lip aperture achieved, however, remains relatively invariant no matter what the vowel context. In the task-dynamic model, the articulator variation results automatically from the fact that the lip closure gesture is modeled as a coordinative structure that links the movements of the three articulators in achieving the lip closure task. The gesture is specified invariantly in terms of the tract variable of lip aperture, but the closing action is distributed across component articulators in a context-dependent way. For example, in an utterance like [ibi], the lip closure is produced concurrently with the tongue gesture for a high front vowel. This vowel gesture will tend to raise the jaw, and thus less activity of the upper and lower lips will be required to effect the lip closure goal than in an utterance like [aba]. These microscopic variations emerge lawfully from the task-dynamic specification of the gestures, combined with the fact of overlap (Kelso, Saltzman, and Tuller, 1986; Saltzman and Munhall, 1989).

7.4 GESTURAL STRUCTURES

During the act of talking, more than one gesture is activated, sometimes sequentially and sometimes in an overlapping fashion. Recurrent patterns of gestures are considered to be organized into gestural constellations. In the computational model (see figure 7.1), the linguistic gestural model determines the relevant constellations for any arbitrary input utterance, including the *phasing* of the gestures. That is, a constellation of gestures is a set of gestures that are coordinated with one another by means of phasing, where for this purpose (and this purpose only), the dynamical regime for each gesture is treated as if it were a cycle of an undamped system with the same stiffness as the actual regime. In this way, any characteristic point in the motion of the system can be identified with a phase of this virtual cycle. For example, the movement onset of a gesture is at phase 0 degrees, while the achievement of the constriction goal (the point at which the critically damped system gets sufficiently close to the equilibrium position) occurs at phase 240 degrees. Pairs of gestures are coordinated by specifying the phases of the two gestures that are synchronous. For example, two gestures could be phased so that their movement onsets are synchronous (0 degrees phased to 0 degrees), or so that the movement onset of one is phased to the goal achievement of another (0 degrees phased to 240 degrees), etc. Generalizations that characterize some phase relations in the gestural constellations of English words are proposed in Browman and Goldstein (1990c). As is the case for the values of the dynamical parameters, values of the synchronized phases also appear to cluster in narrow ranges, with onset of movement (0 degrees) and achievement of goal (240 degrees) being the most common (Browman and Goldstein, 1990a).

An example of a gestural constellation (for the word "pawn" as pronounced with the back unrounded vowel characteristic of much of the United States) is

'pɑn

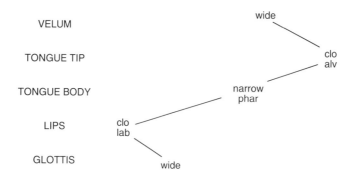

(a)

'pɑn

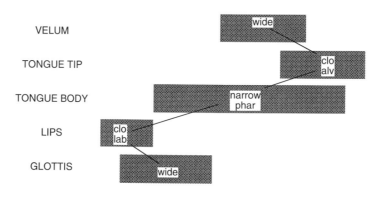

(b)

'pɑn

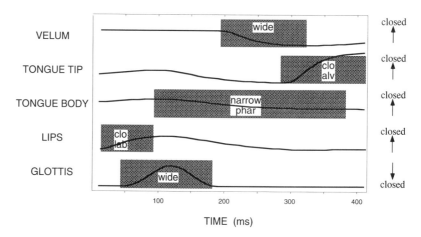

TIME (ms)

(c)

shown in figure 7.3a, which gives an idea of the kind of information contained in the gestural dictionary. Each row, or tier, shows the gestures that control the distinct articulator sets: velum, tongue tip, tongue body, lips, and glottis. The gestures are represented here by descriptors, each of which stands for a numerical equilibrium position value assigned to a tract variable. In the case of the oral gestures, there are two descriptors, one for each of the paired tract variables. For example, for the tongue tip gesture labeled {clo alv}, {clo} stands for −3.5 mm (the negative value indicates compression of the surfaces), and {alv} stands for 56 degrees (where 90 degrees is vertical and would correspond to a midpalatal constriction). The association lines connect gestures that are phased with respect to one another. For example, the tongue tip {clo alv} gesture and the velum {wide} gesture (for nasalization) are phased such that the point indicating 0 degrees—onset of movement—of the tongue tip closure gesture is synchronized with the point indicating 240 degrees—achievement of goal—of the velic gesture.

Each gesture is assumed to be active for a fixed proportion of its virtual cycle (the proportion is different for consonant and vowel gestures). The linguistic gestural model uses this proportion, along with the stiffness of each gesture and the phase relations among the gestures, to calculate a *gestural score* that specifies the temporal activation intervals for each gesture in an utterance. One form of this gestural score for "pawn" is shown in figure 7.3b, with the horizontal extent of each box indicating its activation interval, and the lines between boxes indicating which gesture is phased with respect to which other gesture(s), as before. Note that there is substantial overlap among the gestures. This kind of overlap can result in certain types of context dependence in the articulatory trajectories of the invariantly specified gestures. In addition, overlap can cause the kinds of acoustic variation that have been traditionally described as allophonic variation. For example, in this case, note the substantial overlap between the velic lowering gesture (velum {wide}) and the gesture for the vowel (tongue body {narrow pharyngeal}). This will result in an interval of time during which the velopharyngeal port is open and the vocal tract is in position for the vowel, i.e., a nasalized vowel. Traditionally, the fact of nasalization has been represented by a rule that changes an oral vowel into a nasalized one before a (final) nasal consonant. But viewed in terms of gestural constellations, this nasalization is just the lawful consequence of how the individual gestures are coordinated. The vowel gesture itself has not changed in any way: it has the same specification in this word and in the word "pawed" (which is not nasalized).

Figure 7.3 Various displays from the computational model for "pawn." (*a*) Gestural descriptors and association lines. (*b*) Gestural descriptors and association lines plus activation boxes. (*c*) Gestural descriptors and activation boxes plus generated movements of (*from top to bottom*): velic aperture; vertical position of the tongue tip (with respect to the fixed palate and teeth); vertical position of the tongue body (with respect to the fixed palate and teeth); lip aperture; glottal aperture.

The parameter value specifications and activation intervals from the gestural score are input to the task-dynamical model (see figure 7.1), which calculates the time-varying response of the tract variables and component articulators to the imposition of the dynamical regimes defined by the gestural score. Some of the time-varying responses are shown in figure 7.3c, along with the same boxes indicating the activation intervals for the gestures. Note that the movement curves change over time even when a tract variable is not under the active control of some gesture. Such motion can be seen, for example, in the LIPS panel, after the end of the box for the lip closure gesture. This motion results from one or both of two sources. (1) When an articulator is not part of *any* active gesture, the articulator returns to a neutral position. In the example, the upper lip and lower lip articulators both are returning to a neutral position after the end of the lip closure gesture. (2) One of the articulators linked to the inactive tract variable may also be linked to some active tract variable, and thus cause passive changes in the inactive tract variable. In the example, the jaw is part of the coordinative structure for the tongue-body vowel gesture, as well as part of the coordinative structure for the lip closure gesture. Therefore, even after the lip closure gesture becomes inactive, the jaw is affected by the vowel gesture, and its lowering for the vowel causes the lower lip to also passively lower.

The gestural constellations not only characterize the microscopic properties of the utterances, as discussed above, but systematic differences among the constellations also define the macroscopic property of phonological contrast in a language. Given the nature of gestural constellations, the possible ways in which they may differ from one another is, in fact, quite constrained. In other papers (e.g., Browman and Goldstein, 1986, 1989, 1992) we have begun to show that gestural structures are suitable for characterizing phonological functions such as contrast, and what the relation is between the view of phonological structure implicit in gestural constellations, and that found in other contemporary views of phonology (see also Clements, 1992, for a discussion of these relations). Here we simply give some examples of how the notion of contrast is defined in a system based on gestures, using the schematic gestural scores in figure 7.4.

One way in which constellations may differ is in the presence vs. absence of a gesture. This kind of difference is illustrated by two pairs of subfigures in figure 7.4: (*a*) vs. (*b*) and (*b*) vs. (*d*); (*a*) "pan" differs from (*b*) "ban" in having a glottis {wide} gesture (for voicelessness), while (*b*) "ban" differs from (*d*) "Ann" in having a labial closure gesture (for the initial consonant). Constellations may also differ in the particular tract-variable or articulator set controlled by a gesture within the constellation, as illustrated by (*a*) "pan" vs. (*c*) "tan," which differ in terms of whether it is the lips or tongue tip that performs the initial closure. A further way in which constellations may differ is illustrated by comparing (*e*) "sad" with (*f*) "shad," in which the value of the constriction location tract variable for the initial tongue-tip constriction is the only difference between the two utterances. Finally, two constellations may

Catherine P. Browman and Louis Goldstein

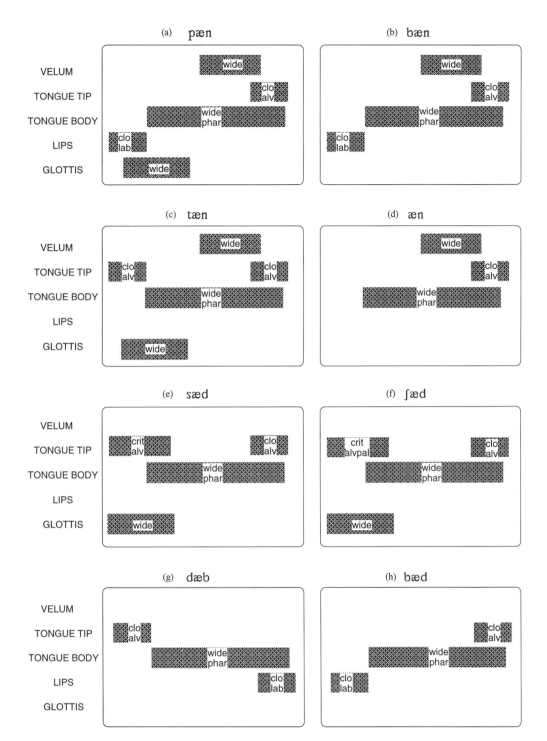

Figure 7.4 Schematic gestural scores exemplifying contrast. (*a*) "pan"; (*b*) "ban"; (*c*) "tan"; (*d*) "Ann"; (*e*) "sad"; (*f*) "shad"; (*g*) "dab"; (*h*) "bad".

contain the same gestures and differ simply in how they are coordinated, as can be seen in (*g*) "dab" vs. (*h*) "bad."

7.5 CONCLUSIONS

This chapter describes an approach to the description of speech in which both the cognitive and physical aspects of speech are captured by viewing speech as a set of actions, or dynamical tasks, that can be described using different dimensionalities: low-dimensional or macroscopic for the cognitive, and high-dimensional or microscopic for the physical. A computational model that instantiates this approach to speech was briefly outlined. It was argued that this approach to speech, which is based on dynamical description, has several advantages over other approaches. First, it captures both the phonological (cognitive) and physical regularities that must be captured in any description of speech. Second, it does so in a way that unifies the two descriptions as descriptions of different dimensionality of a single complex system. The latter attribute means that this approach provides a principled view of the reciprocal constraints that the physical and phonological aspects of speech exhibit.

ACKNOWLEDGMENTS

This work was supported by NSF grant DBS-9112198 and NIH grants HD-01994 and DC-00121 to Haskins Laboratories. We thank Alice Faber and Jeff Shaw for comments on an earlier version.

REFERENCES

Abraham, R. H., and Shaw, C. D. (1982). *Dynamics—the geometry of behavior*. Santa Cruz, CA: Aerial Press.

Anderson, S. R. (1974). *The organization of phonology*. New York: Academic Press.

Browman, C. P., and Goldstein, L. (1986). Towards an articulatory phonology. *Phonology Yearbook, 3*, 219–252.

Browman, C. P., and Goldstein, L. (1989). Articulatory gestures as phonological units. *Phonology, 6*, 201–251.

Browman, C. P., and Goldstein, L. (1990a). Gestural specification using dynamically-defined articulatory structures. *Journal of Phonetics, 18*, 299–320.

Browman, C. P., and Goldstein, L. (1990b). Representation and reality: physical systems and phonological structure. *Journal of Phonetics, 18*, 411–424.

Browman, C. P., and Goldstein, L. (1990c). Tiers in articulatory phonology, with some implications for casual speech. In J. Kingston and M. E. Beckman (Eds.), *Papers in laboratory phonology I: between the grammar and physics of speech* (pp. 341–376). Cambridge: Cambridge University Press.

Browman, C. P., and Goldstein, L. (1992). Articulatory phonology: an overview. *Phonetica, 49*, 155–180.

Browman, C. P., Goldstein, L., Kelso, J. A. S., et al. (1984). Articulatory synthesis from underlying dynamics (abstract). *Journal of the Acoustical Society of America, 75,* S22–S23.

Chomsky, N., and Halle, M. (1968). *The sound pattern of English.* New York: Harper & Row.

Clements, G. N. (1992). Phonological primes: features or gestures?, *Phonetica, 49,* 181–193.

Cohn, A. C. (1990). Phonetic and phonological rules of nasalization. *UCLA Working Papers in Phonetics, 76.*

Coleman, J. (1992). The phonetic interpretation of headed phonological structures containing overlapping constituents. *Phonology, 9,* 1–44.

Fourakis, M., and Port, R. (1986). Stop epenthesis in English. *Journal of Phonetics, 14,* 197–221.

Fowler, C. A., Rubin, P., Remez, R. E., et al. (1980). Implications for speech production of a general theory of action. In B. Butterworth (Ed.), *Language Production.* New York: Academic Press.

Haken, H. (1977). *Synergetics: an introduction.* Heidelberg: Springer Verlag.

Halle, M. (1982). On distinctive features and their articulatory implementation., *Natural Language and Linguistic Theory, 1,* 91–105.

Hockett, C. (1955). *A manual of phonology.* Chicago: University of Chicago.

Hogeweg, P. (1989). MIRROR beyond MIRROR, puddles of LIFE. In C. Langton (Ed.), *Artificial life* (pp. 297–316). New York: Addison-Wesley.

Jakobson, R., Fant, C. G. M., and Halle, M. (1951). *Preliminaries to speech analysis: the distinctive features and their correlates.* Cambridge, MA: MIT Press.

Kauffman, S. (1989). Principles of adaptation in complex systems. In D. Stein (Ed.), *Sciences of complexity* (pp. 619–711). New York: Addison-Wesley.

Kauffman, S. (1991). Antichaos and adaptation. *Scientific American, 265,* 78–84.

Kauffman, S., and Johnsen, S. (1991). Co-evolution to the edge of chaos: coupled fitness landscapes, poised states, and co-evolutionary avalanches. In C. Langton, C. Taylor, J. D. Farmer, et al. (Eds.), *Artificial life II* (pp. 325–369). New York: Addison-Wesley.

Keating, P. A. (1985). CV phonology, experimental phonetics, and coarticulation. *UCLA Working Papers in Phonetics, 62,* 1–13.

Keating, P. A. (1988). Underspecification in phonetics. *Phonology, 5,* 275–292.

Keating, P. A. (1990). Phonetic representations in a generative grammar. *Journal of Phonetics, 18,* 321–334.

Kelso, J. A. S., Saltzman, E. L., and Tuller, B. (1986). The dynamical perspective on speech production: data and theory. *Journal of Phonetics, 14,* 29–59.

Kent, R. D., and Minifie, F. D. (1977). Coarticulation in recent speech production models. *Journal of Phonetics, 5,* 115–133.

Klatt, D. H. (1976). Linguistic uses of segmental duration in English: acoustic and perceptual evidence. *Journal of the Acoustical Society of America, 59,* 1208–1221.

Kugler, P. N., and Turvey, M. T. (1987). Information, natural law, and the self-assembly of rhythmic movement. Hillsdale, NJ: Erlbaum.

Ladefoged, P. (1980). What are linguistic sounds made of? *Language, 56,* 485–502.

Ladefoged, P. (1982). *A course in phonetics,* 2nd ed. New York: Harcourt Brace Jovanovich.

Lewin, R. (1992). *Complexity.* New York: Macmillan.

Liberman, A. M., Cooper, F. S., Shankweiler, D. P., et al. (1967). Perception of the speech code. *Psychological Review, 74*, 431–461.

Liberman, M., and Pierrehumbert, J. (1984). Intonational invariance under changes in pitch range and length. In M. Aronoff, R. T. Oehrle, F. Kelley, et al., (Eds.), *Language sound structure* (pp. 157–233). Cambridge, MA: MIT Press.

Lindblom, B., MacNeilage, P., and Studdert-Kennedy, M. (1983). Self-organizing processes and the explanation of phonological universals. In B. Butterworth, B. Comrie, and O. Dahl (Eds.), *Explanations of linguistic universals* (pp. 181–203). The Hague: Mouton.

Macchi, M. (1988). Labial articulation patterns associated with segmental features and syllable structure in English. *Phonetica, 45*, 109–121.

Madore, B. F., and Freedman, W. L. (1987). Self-organizing structures. *American Scientist, 75*, 252–259.

Manuel, S. Y., and Krakow, R. A. (1984). Universal and language particular aspects of vowel-to-vowel coarticulation. *Haskins Laboratories Status Report on Speech Research, 77/78*, 69–78.

McCarthy, J. J. (1988). Feature geometry and dependency: a review. *Phonetica, 45*, 84–108.

Ohala, J. (1983). The origin of sound patterns in vocal tract constraints. In P. F. MacNeilage (Ed.), *The production of speech* (pp. 189–216). New York: Springer Verlag.

Öhman, S. E. G. (1966). Coarticulation in VCV utterances: spectrographic measurements. *Journal of the Acoustical Society of America, 39*, 151–168.

Packard, N. (1989). Intrinsic adaptation in a simple model for evolution. In C. Langton (Ed.), *Artificial life* (pp. 141–155). New York: Addison-Wesley.

Pierrehumbert, J. (1990). Phonological and phonetic representation. *Journal of Phonetics, 18*, 375–394.

Pierrehumbert, J. B., and Pierrehumbert, R. T. (1990). On attributing grammars to dynamical systems. *Journal of Phonetics, 18*, 465–477.

Port, R. F. (1981). Linguistic timing factors in combination. *Journal of the Acoustical Society of America, 69*, 262–274.

Rubin, P. E., Baer, T., and Mermelstein, P. (1981). An articulatory synthesizer for perceptual research. *Journal of the Acoustical Society of America, 70*, 321–328.

Sagey, E. C. (1986). *The representation of features and relations in non-linear phonology.* Ph.D. Dissertation, Massachusetts Institute of Technology, Cambridge.

Saltzman, E. (1986). Task dynamic coordination of the speech articulators: A preliminary model. In H. Heuer and C. Fromm (Eds.), *Experimental brain research*, Series 15 (pp. 129–144). New York: Springer-Verlag.

Saltzman, E., and Kelso, J. A. S. (1987). Skilled actions: a task dynamic approach. *Psychological Review, 94*, 84–106.

Saltzman, E. L., and Munhall, K. G. (1989). A dynamical approach to gestural patterning in speech production. *Ecological Psychology, 1*, 333–382.

Schöner, G., and Kelso, J. A. S. (1988). Dynamic pattern generation in behavioral and neural systems. *Science, 239*, 1513–1520.

Stevens, K. N. (1972). The quantal nature of speech: evidence from articulatory-acoustic data. In E. E. David and P. B. Denes (Eds.), *Human communication: a unified view* (pp. 51–66). New York: McGraw-Hill.

Stevens, K. N. (1989). On the quantal nature of speech. *Journal of Phonetics, 17*, 3–45.

Sussman, H. M., MacNeilage, P. F., and Hanson, R. J. (1973). Labial and mandibular dynamics during the production of bilabial consonants: preliminary observations, *Journal of Speech and Hearing Research, 16,* 397–420.

Turvey, M. T. (1977). Preliminaries to a theory of action with reference to vision. In R. Shaw and J. Bransford (Eds.), *Perceiving, acting and knowing: toward an ecological psychology.* Hillsdale, NJ: Erlbaum.

Wood, S. (1982). X-ray and model studies of vowel articulation (Vol. 23). Working papers, Lund University, Lund, Sweden.

8 Language as a Dynamical System

Jeffrey L. Elman

EDITORS' INTRODUCTION

One of the most distinctive features of human cognition is linguistic performance, which exhibits unique kinds of complexity. An important argument in favor of the computational approach to cognition has been that only computational machines of a certain kind can exhibit behavior of that complexity. Can the dynamical approach offer an alternative account of this central aspect of cognition?

In this chapter, Jeff Elman confronts this problem head on. He proposes the bold hypothesis that human natural language processing is actually the behavior of a dynamical system, a system quite different than the standard kinds of computational machine traditionally deployed in cognitive science. Demonstrating the truth of this hypothesis requires showing how various aspects of language processing can be successfully modeled using dynamical systems. The particular aspect that Elman focuses on here is the ability to predict the next word in a sentence after being presented with the first n words in a sequence. Success in this task requires both memory for what has already been presented and an understanding of the distinctive complexity of natural language. The model he deploys is a kind of dynamical system that is popular in connectionist work, the SRN (simple recurrent network).

It turns out that it is possible to develop (by training using backpropagation, a connectionist method for determining parameter settings of a dynamical system) networks that exhibit a high degree of success, and whose failings are interestingly reminiscent of difficulties that humans encounter. Perhaps the most important outcome of this work, however, is that it suggests ways to dramatically reconceptualize the basic mechanisms underlying linguistic performance using terms and concepts of dynamics. Thus internal representations of words are not symbols but locations in state space, the lexicon or dictionary is the structure in this space, and processing rules are not symbolic specifications but the dynamics of the system which push the system state in certain directions rather than others.

There are, of course, many aspects of language processing that Elman's models do not even begin to address. At this stage these aspects are interesting open problems for the dynamical approach. In the meantime, it is clear that, contrary to the suspicions of some, dynamics does indeed provide a fruitful framework for the ongoing study of high-level aspects of cognition such as language.

8.1 INTRODUCTION

Despite considerable diversity among theories about how humans process language, there are a number of fundamental assumptions that are shared by most such theories. This consensus extends to the very basic question about what counts as a cognitive process. So although many cognitive scientists are fond of referring to the brain as a "mental organ" (e.g., Chomsky, 1975)—implying a similarity to other organs such as the liver or kidneys—it is also assumed that the brain is an organ with special properties which set it apart. Brains "carry out computation" (it is argued); they "entertain propositions"; and they "support representations." Brains may be organs, but they are very different from the other organs in the body.

Obviously, there are substantial differences between brains and kidneys, just as there are between kidneys and hearts and the skin. It would be silly to minimize these differences. On the other hand, a cautionary note is also in order. The domains over which the various organs operate are quite different, but their common biological substrate is quite similar. The brain is indeed quite remarkable, and does some things which are very similar to human-made symbol processors; but there are also profound differences between the brain and digital symbol processors, and attempts to ignore these on grounds of simplification or abstraction run the risk of fundamentally misunderstanding the nature of neural computation (Churchland and Sejnowski, 1992). In a larger sense, I raise the more general warning that (as Ed Hutchins has suggested) "cognition may not be what we think it is." Among other things, I suggest in this chapter that language (and cognition in general) may be more usefully understood as the behavior of a dynamical system. I believe this is a view which both acknowledges the similarity of the brain to other bodily organs and respects the evolutionary history of the nervous system, while also acknowledging the very remarkable properties possessed by the brain.

In the view I shall outline, representations are not abstract symbols but rather regions of state space. Rules are not operations on symbols but rather embedded in the dynamics of the system, a dynamics which permits movement from certain regions to others while making other transitions difficult. Let me emphasize from the beginning that I am not arguing that language behavior is not rule-governed. Instead, I suggest that the *nature of the rules* may be different from what we have conceived them to be.

The remainder of this chapter is organized as follows. In order to make clear how the dynamical approach (instantiated concretely here as a connectionist network) differs from the standard approach, I begin by summarizing some of the central characteristics of the traditional approach to language processing. I then describe a connectionist model which embodies different operating principles, from the classic approach to symbolic computation. The results of several simulations using that architecture are presented and discussed. Finally, I discuss some of the results which may be yielded by this perspective.

8.2 GRAMMAR AND THE LEXICON: THE TRADITIONAL APPROACH

Language processing is traditionally assumed to involve a *lexicon*, which is the repository of facts concerning individual words, and a set of *rules* which constrain the ways those words can be combined to form sentences. From the point of view of a listener attempting to process spoken language, the initial problem involves taking acoustic input and retrieving the relevant word from the lexicon. This process is often supposed to involve separate stages of *lexical access* (in which contact is made with candidate words based on partial information), and *lexical recognition* (or retrieval, or selection; in which a choice is made on a specific word), although finer-grained distinctions may also be useful (e.g., Tyler and Frauenfelder, 1987). Subsequent to recognition, the retrieved word must be inserted into a data structure that will eventually correspond to a sentence; this procedure is assumed to involve the application of rules.

As described, this scenario may seem simple, straightforward, and not likely to be controversial. But in fact, there is considerable debate about a number of important details. For instance:

Is the lexicon passive or active? In some models, the lexicon is a passive data structure (Forster, 1976). In other models, lexical items are active (Marslen-Wilson, 1980; McClelland and Elman, 1986; Morton, 1979) in the style of Selfridge's "demons" (Selfridge, 1958).

How is the lexicon organized and what are its entry points? In active models, the internal organization of the lexicon is less an issue, because the lexicon is also usually content-addressable, so that there is direct and simultaneous contact between an unknown input and all relevant lexical representations. With passive models, an additional look-up process is required and so the organization of the lexicon becomes more important for efficient and rapid search. The lexicon may be organized along dimensions which reflect phonological, or orthographic, or syntactic properties; or it may be organized along usage parameters, such as frequency (Forster, 1976). Other problems include how to catalog morphologically related elements (e.g., are "telephone" and "telephonic" separate entries? "girl" and "girls"? "ox" and "oxen"?); how to represent words with multiple meanings (the various meanings of "bank" may be different enough to warrant distinct entries, but what about the various meanings of "run," some of which are only subtly different, while others have more distant but still clearly related meanings?); whether the lexicon includes information about argument structure; and so on.

Is recognition all-or-nothing, or graded? In some theories, recognition occurs at the point where a spoken word becomes uniquely distinguished from its competitors (Marslen-Wilson, 1980). In other models, there may be no consistent point where recognition occurs; rather, recognition is a graded process subject to interactions which may hasten or slow down the retrieval of a word in a given context. The recognition point is a strategically controlled threshold (McClelland and Elman, 1986).

How do lexical competitors interact? If the lexicon is active, there is the potential for interactions between lexical competitors. Some models build inhibitory interactions between words (McClelland and Elman, 1986); others have suggested that the empirical evidence rules out word-word inhibitions (Marslen-Wilson, 1980).

How are sentence structures constructed from words? This single question has given rise to a vast and complex literature. The nature of the sentence structures themselves is fiercely debated, reflecting the diversity of current syntactic theories. There is in addition considerable controversy around the sort of information which may play a role in the construction process, or the degree to which at least a first-pass parse is restricted to the purely syntactic information available to it (Frazier and Rayner, 1982; Trueswell, Tanenhaus, and Kello, 1992).

There are thus a considerable number of questions which remain open. Nonetheless, I believe it is accurate to say that there is also considerable consensus regarding certain fundamental principles. I take this consensus to include the following.

1. A commitment to *discrete* and *context-free symbols*. This is more readily obvious in the case of the classic approaches, but many connectionist models utilize localist representations in which entities are discrete and atomic (although graded activations may be used to reflect uncertain hypotheses).

A central feature of all of these forms of representation—localist connectionist as well as symbolic—is that they are *intrinsically context-free*. The symbol for a word, for example, is the same regardless of its usage. This gives such systems great combinatorial power, but it also limits their ability to reflect idiosyncratic or contextually specific behaviors.

This assumption also leads to a distinction between *types* and *tokens* and motivates the need for *variable binding*. Types are the canonical context-free versions of symbols; tokens are the versions that are associated with specific contexts; and binding is the operation that enforces the association (e.g., by means of indices, subscripts, or other diacritics).

2. The view of *rules as operators* and the *lexicon as operands*. Words in most models are conceived of as the objects of processing. Even in models in which lexical entries may be active, once a word is recognized it becomes subject to grammatical rules which build up higher-level structures.

3. The *static nature of representations*. Although the processing of language clearly unfolds over time, the representations that are produced by traditional models typically have a curiously static quality. This is revealed in several ways. For instance, it is assumed that the lexicon preexists as a data structure in much the same way that a dictionary exists independently of its use. Similarly, the higher-level structures created during sentence comprehension are built up through an accretive process, and the successful product of comprehension will be a mental structure in which all the constituent parts (words, categories, relational information) are simultaneously present. (Presumably these become inputs to some subsequent interpretive process which constructs

discourse structures.) That is, although processing models ("performance models") often take seriously the temporal dynamics involved in computing target structures, the target structures themselves are inherited from theories which ignore temporal considerations ("competence models").

4. The *building metaphor*. In the traditional view, the act of constructing mental representations is similar to the act of constructing a physical edifice. Indeed, this is precisely what is claimed in the physical symbol system hypothesis (Newell, 1980). In this view, words and more abstract constituents are like the bricks in a building; rules are the mortar which binds them together. As processing proceeds, the representation grows much as does a building under construction. Successful processing results in a mental edifice that is a complete and consistent structure—again, much like a building.

I take these assumptions to be widely shared among researchers in the field of language processing, although they are rarely stated explicitly. Furthermore, these assumptions have formed the basis for a large body of empirical literature; they have played a role in the framing of the questions that are posed, and later in interpreting the experimental results. Certainly it is incumbent on any theory that is offered as replacement to at least provide the framework for describing the empirical phenomena, as well as improving our understanding of the data.

Why might we be interested in another theory? One reason is that this view of our mental life, which I have just described, that is, a view that relies on discrete, static, passive, and context-free representations, appears to be sharply at variance with what is known about the computational properties of the brain (Churchland and Sejnowski, 1992). It must also be acknowledged that while the theories of language which subscribe to the assumptions listed above do provide a great deal of coverage of data, that coverage is often flawed, internally inconsistent and ad hoc, and highly controversial. So it is not unreasonable to raise the question: Do the shortcomings of the theories arise from assumptions that are basically flawed? Might there be other, better ways of understanding the nature of the mental processes and representations that underlie language? In the next section, I suggest an alternative view of computation, in which language processing is seen as taking place in a dynamical system. The lexicon is viewed as consisting of regions of state space within that system; the grammar consists of the dynamics (attractors and repellers) which constrain movement in that space. As we shall see, this approach entails representations that are highly context-sensitive, continuously varied, and probabilistic (but, of course, 0.0 and 1.0 are also probabilities), and in which the objects of mental representation are better thought of as trajectories through mental space rather than things constructed.

An entry point to describing this approach is the question of how one deals with time and the problem of serial processing. Language, like many other behaviors, unfolds and is processed over time. This simple fact—so simple it seems trivial—turns out to be problematic when explored in detail. Therefore, I turn now to the question of time. I describe a connectionist approach to temporal processing and show how it can be applied to several linguistic phenomena. In the final section I turn to the payoff and attempt to show how this approach leads to useful new views about the lexicon and about grammar.

8.3   THE PROBLEM OF TIME

Time is the medium in which all our behaviors unfold; it is the context within which we understand the world. We recognize *causality* because causes precede effects; we learn that coherent motion over time of points on the retinal array is a good indicator of *objecthood*; and it is difficult to think about phenomena such as *language*, or *goal-directed behavior*, or *planning* without some way of representing time. Time's arrow is such a central feature of our world that it is easy to think that, having acknowledged its pervasive presence, little more needs to be said.

But time has been the stumbling block to many theories. An important issue in models of motor activity, for example, has been the nature of the motor intention. Does the action plan consist of a literal specification of output sequences (probably not), or does it represent serial order in a more abstract manner (probably so, but how?; e.g., Fowler, 1977; Jordan and Rosenbaum, 1988; Kelso, Saltzman, and Tuller, 1986; MacNeilage, 1970). Within the realm of natural language processing, there is considerable controversy about how information accumulates over time and what information is available when (e.g., Altmann and Steedman, 1988; Ferreira and Henderson, 1990; Trueswell, Tanenhaus, and Kello, 1992).

Time has been a challenge for connectionist models as well. Early models, perhaps reflecting the initial emphasis on the parallel aspects of these models, typically adopted a spatial representation of time (e.g., McClelland and Rumelhart, 1981). The basic approach is illustrated in figure 8.1. The temporal order of input events (first to last) is represented by the spatial order (left to right) of the input vector. There are a number of problems with this approach (see Elman, 1990, for discussion). One of the most serious is that the left-to-right spatial ordering has no intrinsic significance at the level of computation which is meaningful for the network. All input dimensions are orthogonal to one another in the input vector space. The human eye tends to see patterns such as 01110000 and 00001110 as having undergone a spatial (or temporal, if we understand these as representing an ordered sequence) translation, because the notation suggests a special relationship may exist between adjacent bits. But this relationship is the result of considerable processing by the human visual system, and is not intrinsic to the vectors themselves. The first element in a vector is not "closer" in any useful sense to the second element than it is to the last element. Most important, it is not available to simple networks of the form shown in figure 8.1. A particularly unfortunate consequence is that there is no basis in such architectures for generalizing what has been learned about spatial or temporal stimuli to novel patterns.

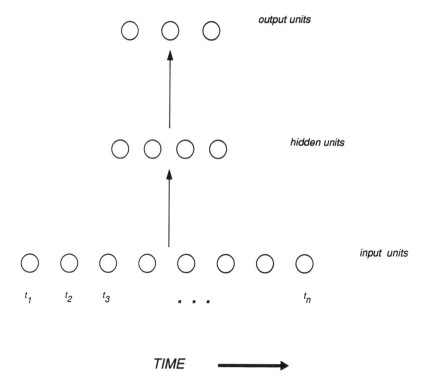

output units

hidden units

input units

t_1 t_2 t_3 $\cdot$ $\cdot$ $\cdot$ t_n

TIME ⟶

Figure 8.1   A feedforward network which represents time through space. Circles represent nodes; arrows between layers indicate full connectivity between nodes in adjacent layers. The network is feedforward because activations at each level depend only on the input received from below. At the conclusion of processing an input, all activations are thus lost. A sequence of inputs can be represented in such an architecture by associating the first node (on the left) with the first element in the sequence, the second node with the second element, and so on.

More recent models have explored what is intuitively a more appropriate idea: let time be represented by the effects it has on processing. If network connections include feedback loops, then this goal is achieved naturally. The state of the network will be some function of the current inputs plus the network's prior state. Various algorithms and architectures have been developed which exploit this insight (e.g., Elman, 1990; Jordan, 1986; Mozer, 1989; Pearlmutter, 1989; Rumelhart, Hinton, and Williams, 1986). Figure 8.2 shows one architecture, the simple recurrent network (SRN) which was used for the studies to be reported here.

In the SRN architecture, at time t hidden units receive external input, and also collateral input from themselves at time $t-1$ (the context units are simply used to implement this delay). The activation function for any given hidden unit h_i is the familiar logistic,

$$f(h_i) = \frac{1}{1 + e^{-net}}$$

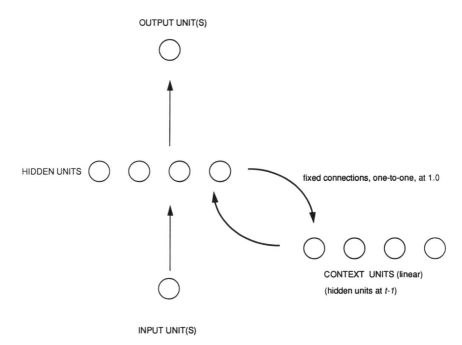

OUTPUT UNIT(S)

HIDDEN UNITS

fixed connections, one-to-one, at 1.0

CONTEXT UNITS (linear)

(hidden units at *t-1*)

INPUT UNIT(S)

Figure 8.2 A simple recurrent network (SRN). Solid lines indicate full connectivity between layers, with weights which are trainable. The dashed line indicates a fixed one-to-one connection between hidden and context layers. The context units are used to save the activations of the hidden units on any time step. Then, on the next time step, the hidden units are activated not only by new input but by the information in the context units—which is just the hidden units' own activations on the prior time step. An input sequence is processed by presenting each element in the sequence one at a time, allowing the network to be activated at each step in time, and then proceeding to the next element. Note that although hidden unit activations may depend on prior inputs, by virtue of prior inputs' effects on the recycled hidden unit—context unit activations, the hidden units do not record the input sequence in any veridical manner. Instead, the task of the network is to learn to encode temporal events in some more abstract manner which allows the network to perform the task at hand.

but where the net input to the unit at time t, $net_i(t)$, is now

$$net_i(t) = \sum_j w_{ij} a_j(t) + b_i + \sum_k w_{ik} h_k(t - 1)$$

That is, the net input on any given tick of the clock t includes not only the weighted sum of inputs and the node's bias but the weighted sum of the hidden unit vector at the prior time step. (Henceforth, when referring to the state space of this system, I shall refer specifically to the k-dimensional space defined by the k hidden units.)

In the typical feedforward network, hidden units develop representations which enable the network to perform the task at hand (Rumelhart et al., 1986). These representations may be highly abstract and are function-based. That is, the similarity structure of the internal representations reflects the demands of the task being learned, rather than the similarity of the inputs' form. When recurrence is added, the hidden units assume an additional function. They now provide the network with memory. But as is true in the feedforward network, the encoding of the temporal history is task-relevant and may be highly abstract; it rarely is the case that the encoding resembles a verbatim tape recording.

One task for which the SRN has proved useful is prediction. There are several reasons why it is attractive to train a network to predict the future. One which arises with supervised learning algorithms such as backpropagation of error is the question of where the teaching information comes from. In many cases, there are plausible rationales which justify the teacher. But the teacher also reflects important theoretical biases which one might sometimes like to avoid (e.g., if one were interested in using the network to generate alternative theories). Since the teacher in the prediction task is simply the time-lagged input, it represents information which is directly observable from the environment and is relatively theory-neutral. Furthermore, there is good reason to believe that anticipating the future plays an important role in learning about the world. Finally, prediction is a powerful tool for learning about temporal structure. Insofar as the order of events may reflect on the past in complex and nonobvious ways, the network will be required to develop relatively abstract encodings of these dependencies in order to generate successful predictions.

The SRN architecture, as well as other forms of recurrent networks, have been used in a variety of applications and has yielded promising results. The SRN's ability to handle temporal sequences makes it a particularly relevant architecture for modeling language behaviors. The deeper question which then arises is whether the solutions found by such recurrent network architectures differ in any substantial ways from more traditional models. And if the solutions are different, are these differences positive or negative?

8.4 RULES AND REPRESENTATIONS: A DYNAMICAL PERSPECTIVE

We begin with the observation that networks such as that in figure 8.2 are dynamical systems. This means that their state at any given point in time is some function which reflects their prior state (see Norton, chapter 2, for a detailed review of the definition and characteristics of dynamical systems). The computational properties of such networks are not yet fully known, but it is clear that they are considerable (Siegelmann and Sontag, 1992). It also seems reasonable that the conceptual notions that are associated with discrete automata theory and symbolic computation may offer less insight into their functioning than the concepts from dynamical systems theory (e.g., Pollack, 1990). How might such networks be applied to problems relevant to language processing, and how might they suggest a different view of the underlying mechanisms of language? One way to approach this is to consider the problem of how the elements of language may be ordered.

Language is a domain in which the ordering of elements is particularly complex. Word order, for instance, reflects the interaction of multiple factors. These include syntactic constraints, semantic and pragmatic goals, discourse considerations, and processing constraints (e.g., verb-particle constructions such as "run up" may be split by a direct object, but not when the noun phrase is long enough to disrupt the processing of the discontinuous verb as a unit). Whether or not one subscribes to the view that these knowledge sources exert their effects autonomously or interactively, there is no question that the final output—the wordstream—reflects their joint interplay.

We know also that the linear order of linguistic elements provides a poor basis for characterizing the regularities that exist within a sentence. A noun may agree in number with a verb which immediately follows it, as in 1(a), or which is separated by an arbitrarily great distance, as in 1(b) (the subscripts "pl" and "sg" refer to plural and singular):

1.   (a)   The **children**$_{pl}$ **like**$_{pl}$ ice cream.
     (b)   The **girl**$_{sg}$ who Emily baby-sits for every other Wednesday while her parents go to night school **likes**$_{sg}$ ice cream.

Such considerations led Miller and Chomsky (1963) to argue that statistically based algorithms are infeasible for language learning, since the number of sentences a listener would need to hear in order to know precisely which of the 15 words which precede *likes* in 1(b) determines the correct number for *likes* would vastly outnumber the data available (in fact, even conservative estimates suggest that more time would be needed than is available in an individual's entire lifetime). On the other hand, recognition that the dependencies respect an underlying hierarchical structure vastly simplifies the problem: subject nouns in English agree in number with their verbs; embedded clauses may intervene but do not participate in the agreement process.

One way to challenge an SRN with a problem which has some relevance to language would therefore be to attempt to train it to predict the successive words in sentences. We know that this is a hard problem which cannot be solved in any general way by simple recourse to linear order. We know also that this is a task which has some psychological validity. Human listeners are able to predict word endings from beginnings; listeners can predict grammaticality from partial sentence input; and sequences of words which violate expectations—i.e., which are unpredictable—result in distinctive electrical activity in the brain. An interesting question is whether a network could be trained to predict successive words. In the following two simulations we shall see how, in the course of solving this task, the network develops novel representations of the lexicon and of grammatical rules.

The Lexicon as Structured State Space

Words may be categorized with respect to many factors. These include such traditional notions as *noun*, *verb*, etc.; the argument structures they are associated with; and semantic features. Many of these characteristics are predictive of a word's syntagmatic properties. But is the reverse true? Can distributional facts be used to infer something about a word's semantic or categorial features? The goal of the first simulation was to see if a network could work backward in just this sense.

A small lexicon of 29 nouns and verbs was used to form simple sentences (see Elman, 1990, for details). Each word was represented as a localist vector in which a single randomly assigned bit was turned on. This input representation insured that there was nothing about the form of the word that was correlated with its properties, and thus that any classifications would have to be discovered by the network based solely on distributional behavior.

A network similar to the one shown in figure 8.2 was trained on a set of 10,000 sentences, with each word presented in sequence to the network and each sentence concatenated to the preceding sentence. The task of the network was to predict the successive word. After each word was input, the output (which was the prediction of the next input) was compared with the actual next word and weights were adjusted by the backpropagation of error-learning algorithm.

At the conclusion of training, the network was tested by comparing its predictions against the corpus. Since the corpus was nondeterministic, it was not reasonable to expect that the network (short of memorizing the sequence) would be able to make exact predictions. Instead, the network predicted the cohort of *potential* word successors in each context. The activation of each cohort turned out to be highly correlated with the conditional probability of each word in that context (the mean cosine of the output vector with the empirically derived probability distribution was 0.916).

This behavior suggests that in order to maximize performance at prediction, the network identifies inputs as belonging to classes of words based on distributional properties and co-occurrence information. These classes were not represented in the overt form of the word, since these were all orthogonal to one another. However, the network is free to learn internal representations at the hidden unit layer which might capture this implicit information.

To test this possibility, the corpus of sentences was run through the network a final time. As each word was input, the hidden unit activation pattern that was produced by the word, plus the context layer, was saved. For each of the 29 words, a mean vector was computed, averaging across all instances of the word in all contexts. These mean vectors were taken to be prototypes, and were subjected to hierarchical clustering. The point of this was to see whether the intervector distances revealed anything about similarity structure of the hidden unit representation space (Euclidean distance was taken as a measure of similarity). The tree in figure 8.3 was then constructed from that hierarchical clustering.

The similarity structure revealed in this tree indicates that the network discovered several major categories of words. The two largest categories correspond to the input vectors, which are verbs and nouns. The verb category

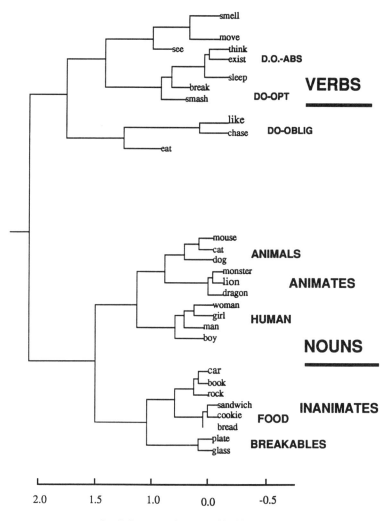

Figure 8.3 Hierarchical clustering diagram of hidden unit activations in the simulation with simple sentences. After training, sentences are passed through the network, and the hidden unit activation pattern for each word is recorded. The clustering diagram indicates the similarity structure among these patterns. This structure, which reflects the grammatical factors that influence word position, is inferred by the network; the patterns which represent the actual inputs are orthogonal and carry none of this information.

is subdivided into those verbs which require a direct object, those which are intransitive, and those for which (in this corpus) a direct object was optional. The noun category is broken into animates and inanimates. The animates contain two classes: human and nonhuman, with nonhumans subdivided into large animals and small animals. The inanimates are divided into breakables, edibles, and miscellaneous.

First, it must be said that the network obviously knows nothing about the real semantic content of these categories. It has simply inferred that such a category structure exists. The structure is inferred because it provides the best basis for accounting for distributional properties. Obviously, a full account of language would require an explanation of how this structure is given content (grounded in the body and in the world). But it is interesting that the evidence for the structure can be inferred so easily on the basis only of form-internal evidence, and this result may encourage caution about just how much information is implicit in the data and how difficult it may be to use this information to construct a framework for conceptual representation.

However, my main point is not to suggest that this is the primary way in which grammatical categories are acquired by children, although I believe that co-occurrence information may indeed play a role in such learning. The primary thing I would like to focus on is what this simulation suggests about the nature of representation in systems of this sort. That is, I would like to consider the representational properties of such networks, apart from the specific conditions which give rise to those representations.

Where is the lexicon in this network? Recall the earlier assumptions: The lexicon is typically conceived of as a passive data structure. Words are objects of processing. They are first subject to acoustic and phonetic analysis, and then their internal representations must be accessed, recognized, and retrieved from permanent storage. Following this, the internal representations have to be inserted into a grammatical structure.

The status of words in a system of the sort described here is very different: Words are not the *objects* of processing as much as they are inputs which *drive* the processor in a more direct manner. As Wiles and Bloesch (1992) suggest, it is more useful to understand inputs to networks of this sort as *operators* rather than as *operands*. Inputs operate on the network's internal state and move it to another position in state space. What the network learns over time is what response it should make to different words, taking context into account. Because words have reliable and systematic effects on behavior, it is not surprising that all instances of a given word should result in states which are tightly clustered, or that grammatically or semantically related words should produce similar effects on the network. We might choose to think of the internal state that the network is in when it processes a word as representing that word (in context), but it is more accurate to think of that state as the *result* of processing the word, rather than as a representation of the word itself.

Note that there is an implicitly hierarchical organization to the regions of state space associated with different words. This organization is achieved through the spatial structure. Conceptual similarity is realized through position in state space. Words that are conceptually distant produce hidden unit activation patterns that are spatially far apart. Higher-level categories correspond to large regions of space; lower-level categories correspond to more restricted subregions. For example, *dragon* is a noun and causes the network to move into the noun region of the state space. It is also [+animate], which is reflected in the subregion of noun space which results. Because large animals typically are described in different terms and do different things than small animals, the general region of space corresponding to *dragon, monster*, and *lion* is distinct from that occupied by *mouse, cat*, and *dog*. The boundaries between these regions may be thought of as hard in some cases (e.g., nouns are very far from verbs) or soft in others (e.g., *sandwich, cookie*, and *bread* are not very far from *car, book*, and *rock*. One even might imagine cases where in certain contexts, tokens of one word might overlap with tokens of another. In such cases, one would say that the system has generated highly similar construals of the different words.

Rules as Attractors

If the lexicon is represented as regions of state space, what about rules? We have already seen that some aspects of grammar are captured in the tokenization of words, but this is a fairly limited sense of grammar. The well-formedness of sentences depends on relationships which are not readily stated in terms of simple linear order. Thus the proper generalization about why the main verb in 1(b) is in the singular is that the main subject is singular, and not that the word 15 words prior was a singular noun. The ability to express such generalizations would seem to require a mechanism for explicitly representing abstract grammatical structure, including constituent relationships (e.g., the notion that some elements are part of others). Notations such as phrase structure trees (among others) provide precisely this capability. It is not obvious how complex grammatical relations might be expressed using distributed representations. Indeed, it has been argued that distributed representations (of the sort exemplified by the hidden unit activation patterns in the previous simulation) cannot have constituent structure in any systematic fashion (Fodor and Pylyshyn, 1988). (As a backup, Fodor and Pylyshyn suggest that if distributed representations *do* have a systematic constituent structure, then they are merely implementations of what they call the "classical" theory, in this case, the language of thought: Fodor, 1976.)

The fact that the grammar of the first simulation was extremely simple made it difficult to explore these issues. Sentences were all declarative and monoclausal. This simulation sheds little light on the grammatical potential of such networks.

A better test would be to train the network to predict words in complex sentences that contain long-distance dependencies. This was done in Elman (1991b) using a strategy similar to the one outlined in the prior simulation, except that sentences had the following characteristics:

1. Nouns and verbs agreed in number. Singular nouns required singular verbs; plural nouns selected plural verbs.

2. Verbs differed with regard to their verb argument structure. Some verbs were transitive, others were intransitive, and others were optionally transitive.

3. Nouns could be modified by relative clauses. Relative clauses could either be object-relatives (the head had the object role in the clause) or subject-

relative (the head was the subject of the clause), and either subject or object nouns could be relativized.

As in the previous simulation, words were represented in localist fashion so that information about neither the grammatical category (noun or verb) nor the number (singular or plural) was contained in the form of the word. The network also only saw positive instances; only grammatical sentences were presented.

The three properties interact in ways designed to make the prediction task difficult. The prediction of number is easy in a sentence such as 2(a), but harder in (2b).

2. (a) The boys$_{pl}$ chase$_{pl}$ the dogs.
    (b) The boys$_{pl}$ who the dog$_{sg}$ chases$_{sg}$ run$_{pl}$ away.

In the first case, the verb follows immediately. In the second case, the first noun agrees with the second verb (*run*) and is plural; the verb which is actually closest to it (*chase*) is in the singular because it agrees with the intervening word (*dog*).

Relative clauses cause similar complications for verb argument structure. In 3(a–c), it is not difficult for the network to learn that *chase* requires a direct object, *see* permits (but does not require) one, and *lives* is intransitive.

3. (a) The cats chase the dog.
    (b) The girls see. The girls see the car.
    (c) The patient lives.

On the other hand, consider:

4. The dog who the cats chase run away.

The direct object of the verb *chase* in the relative clause is *dog*. However, *dog* is also the head of the clause (as well as the subject of the main clause). *Chase* in this grammar is obligatorily transitive, but the network must learn that when it occurs in such structures the object position is left empty (gapped) because the direct object has already been mentioned (filled) as the clause head.

These data illustrate the sorts of phenomena which have been used by linguists to argue for abstract representations with constituent structure (Chomsky, 1975); they have also been used to motivate the claim that language processing requires some form of pushdown store or stack mechanism. They therefore impose a difficult set of demands on a recurrent network.

However, after training a network on such stimuli (Elman, 1991b), it appeared the network was able to make correct predictions (mean cosine between outputs and empirically derived conditional probability distributions: 0.852; a perfect performance would have been 1.0). These predictions honored the grammatical constraints that were present in the training data. The network was able to correctly predict the number of a main sentence verb even in the presence of intervening clauses (which might have the same or conflicting number agreement between nouns and verbs). The network also not only learned about verb argument structure differences but correctly "remembered" when an object-relative head had appeared, so that it would not predict a noun following an embedded transitive verb. Figure 8.4 shows the predictions made by the network during testing with a novel sentence.

How is this behavior achieved? What is the nature of the underlying knowledge possessed by the network which allows it to perform in a way which conforms with the grammar? It is not likely that the network simply memorized the training data, because the network was able to generalize its performance to novel sentences and structures it had never seen before. But just how general was the solution, and just how systematic?

In the previous simulation, hierarchical clustering was used to measure the similarity structure between internal representations of words. This gives us an indirect means of determining the spatial structure of the representation space. It does not let us actually determine what that structure is.[1] So one would like to be able to visualize the internal state space more directly. This is also important because it would allow us to study the ways in which the network's internal state changes over time as it processes a sentence. These trajectories might tell us something about how the grammar is encoded.

One difficulty which arises in trying to visualize movement in the hidden unit activation space over time is that it is an extremely high-dimensional space (70 dimensions, in the current simulation). These representations are distributed, which typically has the consequence that interpretable information cannot be obtained by examining activity of single hidden units. Information is more often encoded along dimensions that are represented across multiple hidden units.

This is not to say, however, that the information is not there, of course, but simply that one needs to discover the proper viewing perspective to get at it. One way of doing this is to carry out a principal components analysis (PCA) over the hidden unit activation vectors. PCA allows us to discover the dimensions along which there is variation in the vectors; it also makes it possible to visualize the vectors in a coordinate system aligned with this variation. This new coordinate system has the effect of giving a somewhat more localized description to the hidden unit activation patterns. Since the dimensions are ordered with respect to amount of variance accounted for, we can now look at the trajectories of the hidden unit patterns along selected dimensions of the state space.[2]

In figures 8.5, 8.6, and 8.7 we see the movement over time through various plans in the hidden unit state space as the trained network processes various test sentences. Figure 8.5 compares the path through state space (along the second principal component, or PCA 2) as the network processes the sentences *boys hear boys* and *boy hears boy*. PCA 2 encodes the number of the main clause subject noun, and the difference in the position along this dimension correlates with whether the subject is singular or plural. Figure 8.6

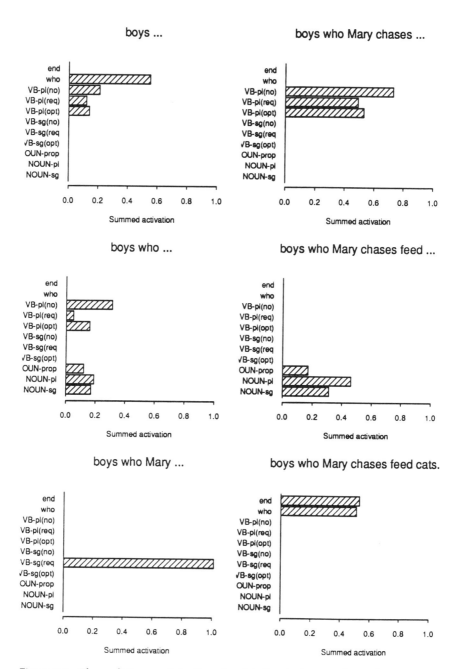

Figure 8.4 The predictions made by the network in the simulation with complex sentences, as the network processes the sentence "boys who Mary chases feed cats." Each panel displays the activations of output units after successive words; outputs are summed across groups for purposes of displaying the data. *V*, verbs; *N*, nouns; *sg*, singular; *pl*, plural; prop, proper nouns; *t*, transitive verbs; *i*, intransitive verbs; *t/i*, optionally transitive verbs.

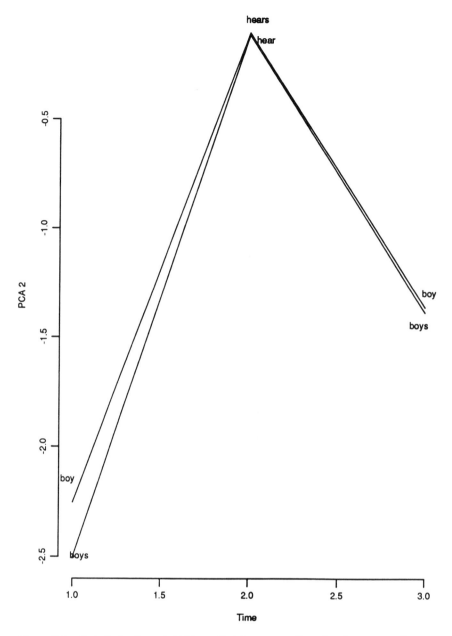

Figure 8.5 Trajectories through hidden unit state space as the network processes the sentences "boy hears boy" and "boys hear boy." The number (singular vs. plural) of the subject is indicated by the position in state space along the second principal component.

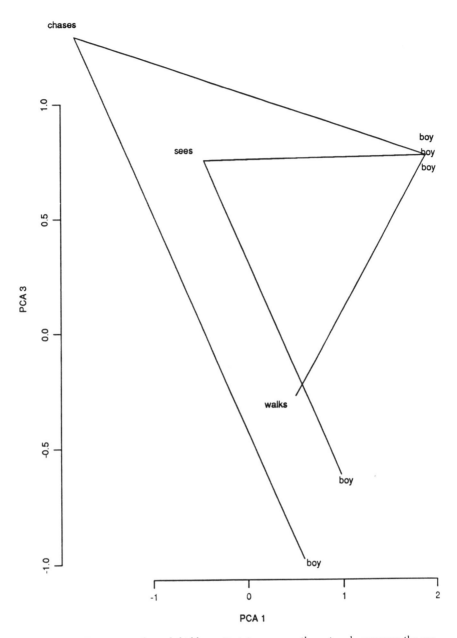

Figure 8.6 Trajectories through hidden unit state space as the network processes the sentences "boy chases boy," "boy sees boy," and "boy walks." Transitivity of the verb is encoded by its position along an axis which cuts across the first and third principal components. PCA, principal components analysis.

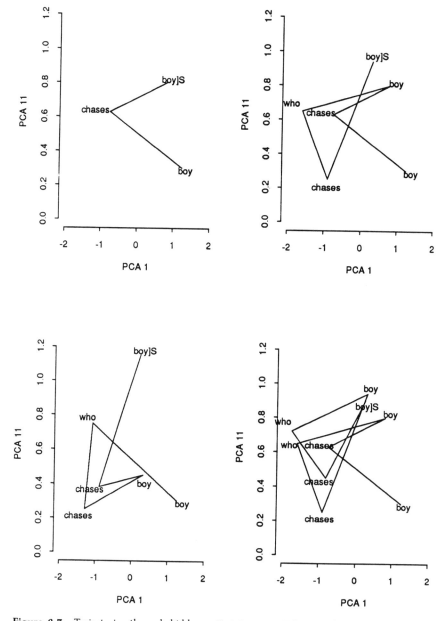

Figure 8.7 Trajectories through hidden unit state space (*PCA* 1 and 11) as the network processes the sentences "boy chases boy," "boy chases boy who chases boy," "boy who chases boy chases boy," and "boy chases boy who chases boy who chases boy" (to assist in reading the plots, the final word of each sentence is terminated with a "]S").

compares trajectories for sentences with verbs which have different argument expectations; *chases* requires a direct object, *sees* permits one, and *walks* precludes one. As can be seen, these differences in argument structure are reflected in a displacement in state space from upper left to lower right. Finally, figure 8.7 illustrates the path through state space for various sentences which differ in degree of embedding. The actual degree of embedding is captured by the displacement in state space of the embedded clauses; sentences with multiple embeddings appear somewhat as spirals.

These trajectories illustrate the general principle at work in this network. The network has learned to represent differences in lexical items as different regions in the hidden unit state space. The sequential dependencies which exist among words in sentences are captured by the movement over time through this space as the network processes successive words in the sentence. These dependencies are actually encoded in the weights which map inputs (i.e., the current state plus new word) to the next state. The weights may be thought of as implementing the grammatical rules which allow well-formed sequences to be processed and to yield valid expectations about successive words. Furthermore, the rules are general. The network weights create attractors in the state space, so that the network is able to respond sensibly to novel inputs, as when unfamiliar words are encountered in familiar contexts.

8.5   DISCUSSION

The image of language processing just outlined does not look very much like the traditional picture we began with. Instead of a dictionary-like lexicon, we have a state space partitioned into various regions. Instead of symbolic rules and phrase structure trees, we have a dynamical system in which grammatical constructions are represented by trajectories through state space. Let me now consider what implications this approach might have for understanding several aspects of language processing.

Beyond Sentences

Although I have focused here on processing of sentences, obviously language processing in real situations typically involves discourse which extends over many sentences. It is not clear, in the traditional scheme, how information represented in sentence structures might be kept available for discourse purposes. The problem is just that on the one hand there are clearly limitations on how much information can be stored, so obviously not everything can be preserved; but on the other hand there are many aspects of sentence-level processing which may be crucially affected by prior sentences. These include not only anaphora, but also such things as argument structure expectations (e.g., the verb *to give* normally requires a direct object and an indirect object, but in certain contexts these need not appear overtly if understood: *Do you plan to give money to the United Way? No, I gave last week.*).

The network's approach to language processing handles such requirements in a natural manner. The network is a system which might be characterized as highly opportunistic. It learns to perform a task, in this case prediction, doing just what it needs to do. Note that in figure 8.5, for example, the information about the number of the subject noun is maintained only until the verb that agrees with the subject has been processed. From that point on, the two sentences are identical. This happens because once the verb is encountered, subject number is no longer relevant to any aspect of the prediction task. (This emphasizes the importance of the task, because presumably tasks other than prediction could easily require that the subject number be maintained for longer.)

This approach to preserving information suggests that such networks would readily adapt to processing multiple sentences in discourse, since there is no particular reanalysis or re-representation of information required at sentence boundaries and no reason why some information cannot be preserved across sentences. Indeed, St. John (1992) and Harris and Elman (1989) have demonstrated that networks of this kind readily adapt to processing paragraphs and short stories. (The emphasis on functionality is reminiscent of suggestions made by Agre and Chapman, 1987, and Brooks, 1989. These authors argue that animals need not perfectly represent everything that is in their environment, nor store it indefinitely. Instead, they need merely be able to process that which is relevant to the task at hand.)

Types and Tokens

Consider the first simulation, and the network's use of state space to represent words. This is directly relevant to the way in which the system addresses the *types/token* problem which arises in symbolic systems.

In symbolic systems, because representations are abstract and context-free, a binding mechanism is required to attach an instantiation of a type to a particular token. In the network, on the other hand, tokens are distinguished from one another by virtue of producing small but potentially discriminable differences in the state space. $John_{23}$, $John_{43}$, and $John_{192}$ (using subscripts to indicate different occurrences of the same lexical item) will be physically different vectors. Their identity as tokens of the same type is captured by the fact that they are all located in a region which may be designated as the *John* space, and which contains no other vectors. Thus, one can speak of this bounded region as corresponding to the lexical type *John*.

The differences in context, however, create differences in the state. Furthermore, these differences are systematic. The clustering tree in figure 8.3 was carried out over the mean vector for each word, averaged across contexts. If the actual hidden unit activation patterns are used, the tree is, of course, quite large since there are hundreds of tokens of each word. Inspection of the tree reveals two important facts. First, all tokens of a type are more similar to one another than to any other type, so the arborization of tokens of *boy* and *dog* do not mix (although, as was pointed out, such overlap is not impossible and may in some circumstances be desirable). Second, there is a substructure to the spatial distribution of tokens which is true of multiple types. Tokens of *boy* used as subject occur more closely to one another than to the tokens of *boy* as object. This is also true of the tokens of *girl*. Moreover, the spatial dimension along which subject-tokens vary from object-tokens is the same for all nouns. Subject-tokens of all nouns are positioned in the same region of this dimension, and object-tokens are positioned in a different region. This means that rather than proliferating an undesirable number of representations, this tokenization of types actually encodes grammatically relevant information. Note that the tokenization process does not involve creation of new syntactic or semantic atoms. It is, instead, a systematic process. The state-space dimensions along which token variation occurs may be interpreted meaningfully. The token's location in state space is thus at least functionally compositional (in the sense described by van Gelder, 1990).

Polysemy and Accommodation

Polysemy refers to the case where a word has multiple senses. Accommodation is used to describe the phenomenon in which word meanings are contextually altered (Langacker, 1987). The network approach to language processing provides an account of both phenomena, and shows how they may be related.

Although there are clear instances where the same phonological form has entirely different meanings (*bank*, for instance), in many cases polysemy is a matter of degree. There may be senses which are different, although metaphorically related, as in 5(a–c):

5. (a) Arturo Barrios runs very fast!
   (b) This clock runs slow.
   (c) My dad runs the grocery store down the block.

In other cases, the differences are far more subtle, though just as real:

6. (a) Frank Shorter runs the marathon faster than I ever will.
   (b) The rabbit runs across the road.
   (c) The young toddler runs to her mother.

In 6(a–c), the construal of *runs* is slightly different, depending on who is doing the running. But just as in 5, the way in which the verb is interpreted depends on context. As Langacker (1987) described the process:

It must be emphasized that syntagmatic combination involves more than the simple addition of components. A composite structure is an integrated system formed by coordinating its components in a specific, often elaborate manner. In fact, it often has properties that go beyond what one might expect from its components alone.... [O]ne component may need to be adjusted in certain details when integrated to form a composite structure; I refer to this as **accommodation**. For example, the meaning of run as applied to humans must be adjusted in certain respects when extended to four legged animals such as horses, dogs, and cats ... in a technical sense, this extension creates a new **semantic variant** of the lexical item. (pp. 76–77)

In figure 8.8 we see that the network's representations of words in context demonstrates just this sort of accommodation. Trajectories are shown for various sentences, all of which contain the main verb *burn*. The representation of the verb varies, depending on the subject noun. The simulations shown here do not exploit the variants of the verb, but it is clear that this is a basic property of such networks.

"Leaky Recursion" and Processing Complex Sentences

The sensitivity to context that is illustrated in figure 8.8 also occurs across levels of organization. The network is able to represent constituent structure (in the form of embedded sentences), but it is also true that the representation of embedded elements may be affected by words at other syntactic levels. This means that the network does not implement a stack or pushdown machine of the classic sort, and would seem not to implement true recursion, in which information at each level of processing is encapsulated and unaffected by information at other levels. Is this good or bad?

If one is designing a programming language, this sort of "leaky" recursion is highly undesirable. It is important that the value of variables local to one call of a procedure not be affected by their value at other levels. True recursion provides this sort of encapsulation of information. I would suggest that the appearance of a similar sort of recursion in natural language is deceptive, however, and that while natural language may require one aspect of what recursion provides (constituent structure and self-embedding), it may not require the sort of informational firewalls between levels of organization.

Indeed, embedded material typically has an elaborative function. Relative clauses, for example, provide information about the head of a noun phrase (which is at a higher level of organization). Adverbial clauses perform a similar function for main clause verbs. In general, then, subordination involves a conceptual dependence between clauses. Thus, it may be important that a language-processing mechanism facilitate rather than impede interactions across levels of information.

There are specific consequences for processing which may be observed in a system of this sort, which only loosely approximates recursion. First, the finite bound on precision means that right-branching sentences such as 7(a) will be processed better than center-embedded sentences such as 7(b):

7. (a)   The woman saw the boy that heard the man that left.
    (b)   The man the boy the woman saw heard left.

It has been known for many years that sentences of the first sort are processed in humans more easily and accurately than sentences of the second kind, and a number of reasons have been suggested (e.g., Miller and Isard,

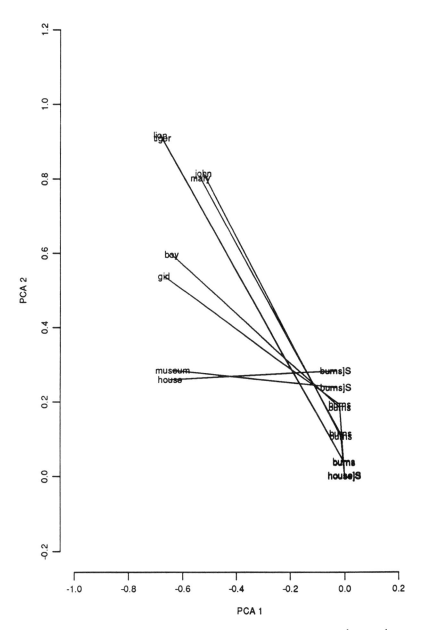

Figure 8.8 Trajectories through hidden unit state space (*PCA* 1 and 2) as the network processes the sentences "{john, mary, lion, tiger, boy, girl} burns house," as well as "{museum, house} burns" (the final word of each sentences is terminated with "]S"). The internal representations of the word "burns" varies slightly as a function of the verb's subject.

1964). In the case of the network, such an asymmetry arises because right-branching structures do not require that information be carried forward over embedded material, whereas in center-embedded sentences information from the matrix sentence must be saved over intervening embedded clauses.

But it is also true that not all center-embedded sentences are equally difficult to comprehend. Intelligibility may be improved in the presence of semantic constraints. Compare the following, in 8 (a and b):

8. (a)   The man the woman the boy saw heard left.
    (b)   The claim the horse he entered in the race at the last minute was a ringer was absolutely false.

In 8(b) the three subject nouns create strong—and different—expectations about possible verbs and objects. This semantic information might be expected to help the hearer more quickly resolve the possible subject-verb-object associations and assist processing (Bever, 1970; King and Just, 1991). The verbs in 8(a), on the other hand, provide no such help. All three nouns might plausibly be the subject of all three verbs.

In a series of simulations, Weckerly and Elman (1992) demonstrated that a simple recurrent network exhibited similar performance characteristics. It was better able to process right-branching structures, compared to center-embedded sentences. And center-embedded sentences that contained strong semantic constraints were processed better compared to center-embedded sentences without such constraints. Essentially, the presence of constraints meant that the internal state vectors generated during processing were more distinct (further apart in state space) and therefore preserved information better than the vectors in sentences in which nouns were more similar.

The Immediate Availability of Lexically Specific Information

One question which has generated considerable controversy concerns the time course of processing, and when certain information may be available and used in the process of sentence processing. One proposal is that there is a first-pass parse during which only category-general syntactic information is available (Frazier and Rayner, 1982). The other major position is that considerably more information, including lexically specific constraints on argument structure, is available and used in processing (Taraban and McClelland, 1990). Trueswell, Tanenhaus, and Kello (1993) present empirical evidence from a variety of experimental paradigms which strongly suggests that listeners are able to use subcategorization information in resolving the syntactic structure of a noun phrase which would otherwise be ambiguous. For example, in 9 (a and b), the verb *forgot* permits both a noun phrase complement and also a sentential complement; at the point in time when *the solution* has been read, either 9(a) or 9(b) is possible.

9. (a)   The student forgot the solution was in the back of the book.
    (b)   The student forgot the solution.

In 10 (a and b), on the other hand, *hope* is strongly biased toward taking a sentential complement.

10. (a) The student hoped the solution was in the back of the book.
     (b) *The student hoped the solution.

Trueswell and his colleagues found that subjects appeared not only to be sensitive to the preferred complement for these verbs but that behavior was significantly correlated with the statistical patterns of usage (determined through corpus analysis). That is, insofar as the actual usage of a verb might be more or less biased in a particular direction, subjects' expectations were more or less consistent with that usage. This is exactly the pattern of behavior that would be expected given the model of processing described here, and we are currently attempting to model these data.

8.6 CONCLUSIONS

Over recent years, there has been considerable work in attempting to understand various aspects of speech and language in terms of dynamical systems. Some of the most elegant and well-developed work has focused on motor control, particularly within the domain of speech (e.g., Fowler, 1980; Kelso et al., 1986). Some of this work makes explicit reference to consequences for theories of phonology (e.g., Browman and Goldstein, 1985; Pierrehumbert and Pierrehumbert, 1990).

More recently, attention has been turned to systems which might operate at so-called higher levels of language processing. One of the principal challenges has been whether or not these dynamical systems can deal in a satisfactory way with the apparently recursive nature of grammatical structure.

I have attempted to show in this chapter that, indeed, networks that possess dynamical characteristics have a number of properties which capture important aspects of language, including their embedded nature. The framework appears to differ from a traditional view of language processors in the way in which it represents lexical and grammatical information. Nonetheless, these networks exhibit behaviors which are highly relevant for language. They are able to induce lexical category structure from statistical regularities in usage; and they are able to represent constituent structure to a certain degree. They are not perfect, but their imperfections strongly resemble those observed in human language users.

Let me close, however, with an obvious caveat. None of the work described here qualifies as a full model of language use. The range of phenomena illustrated is suggestive, but limited. As any linguist will note, there are many, many questions which remain unanswered. The models are also disembodied in a way which makes it difficult to capture any natural semantic relationship with the world. These networks are essentially exclusively language processors and their language use is unconnected with an ecologically plausible activity. Finally, and related to a prior point, the view of language use in these networks is deficient in that it is solely reactive. These networks are input-output devices. Given an input, they produce the output appropriate for that training regime. The networks are thus tightly coupled with the world in a manner which leaves little room for endogenously generated activity. There is no possibility here for either spontaneous speech or for reflective internal language. Put most bluntly, these are networks that do not think!

These same criticisms may be leveled, of course, at many other current and more traditional models of language, so they should not be taken as inherent deficiencies of the approach. Indeed, I suspect that the view of linguistic behavior as deriving from a dynamical system probably allows for greater opportunities for remedying these shortcomings. One exciting approach involves embedding such networks in environments in which their activity is subject to evolutionary pressure, and viewing them as examples of artificial life (e.g., Nolfi, Elman, and Parisi, in press). But in any event, it is obvious that much remains to be done.

NOTES

1. For example, imagine a tree with two major branches, each of which has two subbranches. We can be certain that the items on the major branches occupy different regions of state space. More precisely, they lie along the dimension of major variation in that space. We can say nothing about other dimensions of variation, however. Two subbranches may divide in similar ways. For example, [+human] and [−human] animates may each have branches for [+large] and [−large] elements. But it is impossible to know whether [+large, +human] and [+large, −human] elements differ from their [−large] counterparts in exactly the same way, i.e., by lying along some common axis corresponding to size. Clustering tells us only about distance relationships, not about the organization of space which underlies those relationships.

2. There are limitations to the use of PCA to analyze hidden unit vectors. PCA yields a rotation of the original coordinate system which requires that the new axes be orthogonal. However, it need not be the case that the dimensions of variation in the hidden unit space are orthogonal to one another; this is especially true if the output units that receive the hidden unit vectors as input are nonlinear. It would be preferable to carry out a nonlinear PCA or use some other technique which both relaxed the requirement of orthogonality and took into account the effect of the hidden-to-output nonlinearity.

REFERENCES

Agre, P. E., and Chapman, D. (1987). Pengi: an implementation of a theory of activity. In *Proceedings of the AAAI-87*. Los Altos, CA: Morgan Kaufmann.

Altmann, G. T. M., and Steedman, M. J. (1988). Interaction with context during human sentence processing. *Cognition, 30*, 191–238.

Bever, T. (1970). The cognitive basis for linguistic structure. In J. R. Hayes (Ed.), *Cognition and the development of language*. New York: Wiley.

Brooks, R. A. (1989). A robot that walks: emergent behaviors from a carefully evolved network. *Neural Computation, 1*, 253–262.

Browman, C. P., and Goldstein, L. (1985). Dynamic modeling of phonetic structure. In V. Fromken (Ed.), *Phonetic linguistics*. New York: Academic Press.

Chomsky, N. (1975). *Reflections on language*. New York: Pantheon.

Churchland, P. S., and Sejnowski, T. J. (1992). *The computational brain*. Cambridge, MA: MIT Press.

Elman, J. L. (1990), Finding structure in time. *Cognitive Science, 14*, 179–211.

Elman, J. L. (1991). Distributed representations, simple recurrent networks, and grammatical structure. *Machine Learning, 7*, 195–225.

Ferreira, F., and Henderson, J. M. (1990). The use of verb information in syntactic parsing: a comparison of evidence from eye movements and word-by-word self-paced reading. *Journal of Experimental Psychology: Learning, Memory and Cognition, 16*, 555–568.

Fodor, J. (1976). *The language of thought*. Sussex: Harvester Press.

Fodor, J., and Pylyshyn, Z. (1988). Connectionism and cognitive architecture: a critical analysis. In S. Pinker and J. Mueller (Eds.), *Connections and symbols*. Cambridge, MA: MIT Press.

Forster, K. (1976). Accessing the mental lexicon. In R. J. Wales and E. Walker (Eds.), *New approaches to language mechanisms*. Amsterdam: North-Holland.

Fowler, C. (1977). *Timing and control in speech production*. Bloomington: Indiana University Linguistics Club.

Fowler, C. (1980). Coarticulation and theories of extrinsic timing control. *Journal of Phonetics, 8*, 113–133.

Frazier, L., and Rayner, K. (1982). Making and correcting errors during sentence comprehension: eye movements in the analysis of structurally ambiguous sentences. *Cognitive Psychology, 14*, 178–210.

Harris, C., and Elman, J. L. (1989). Representing variable information with simple recurrent networks. In *Proceedings of the 10th Annual Conference of the Cognitive Science Society*. Hillsdale, NJ: Erlbaum.

Jordan, M. I. (1986). *Serial order: a parallel distributed processing approach*. (Institute for Cognitive Science report 8604.) University of California, San Diego.

Jordan, M. I., and Rosenbaum, D. A. (1988). *Action*. (Technical report 88-26.) Department of Computer Science, University of Massachusetts at Amherst.

Kelso, J. A. S., Saltzman, E., and Tuller, B. (1986). The dynamical theory of speech production: data and theory. *Journal of Phonetics, 14*, 29–60.

King, J., and Just, M. A. (1991). Individual differences in syntactic processing: the role of working memory. *Journal of Memory and Language, 30*, 580–602.

Langacker, R. W. (1987). *Foundations of cognitive grammar: theoretical perspectives*, Vol. 1. Stanford, CA: Stanford University Press.

MacNeilage, P. F. (1970). Motor control of serial ordering of speech. *Psychological Review, 77*, 182–196.

Marslen-Wilson, W. D. (1980). Speech understanding as a psychological process. In J. C. Simon (Ed.), *Spoken language understanding and generation*. Dordrecht, Netherlands: Reidel.

McClelland, J. L., and Elman, J. L. (1986). The TRACE model of speech perception. *Cognitive Psychology, 18*, 1–86.

McClelland, J. L., and Rumelhart, D. E. (1981). An interactive activation model of contexts effects in letter perception: part 1. An account of basic findings. *Psychological Review, 88*, 365–407.

Miller, G. A., and Chomsky, N. (1963). Finitary models of language users. In R. D. Luce, R. R. Bush, and E. Galanter (Eds.), *Handbook of mathematical psychology*, Vol. 2. New York: Wiley.

Miller, G., and Isard, S. (1964). Free recall of self-embedded English sentences. *Information and Control, 7*, 292–303.

Morton, J. (1979). Word recognition. In J. Morton and J. C. Marshall (Eds.), *Psycholinguistics 2: structures and processes*. Cambridge, MA: MIT Press.

Mozer, M. C. (1989). A focused back-propagation algorithm for temporal pattern recognition. *Complex Systems, 3*, 49–81.

Newell, A. (1980). Physical symbol systems. *Cognitive Science, 4*, 135–183.

Nolfi, S., Elman, J. L., and Parisi, D. (in press). Learning and evolution in neural networks. *Adaptive Behavior,*

Pearlmutter, B. A. (1989). Learning state space trajectories in recurrent neural networks. In *Proceedings of the International Joint Conference on Neural Networks* (II-365), Washington, DC.

Pierrehumbert, J. B., and Pierrehumbert, R. T. (1990). On attributing grammars to dynamical systems. *Journal of Phonetics, 18*, 465–477.

Pollack, J. B. (1990). The induction of dynamical recognizers. *Machine Learning, 7*, 227–252.

Rumelhart, D. E., Hinton, G. E., and Williams, R. J. (1986). Learning internal representations by error propagation. In D. E. Rumelhart and J. L. McClelland (Eds.), *Parallel distributed processing: explorations in the microstructure of cognition*, Vol. 1. Cambridge, MA: MIT Press.

Selfridge, O. G. (1958). Pandemonium: a paradigm for learning. *Mechanisation of thought processes: Proceedings of a symposium held at the National Physical Laboratory, November 1958*. London: HMSO.

Siegelmann, H. T., and Sontag, E. D. (1992). *Neural networks with real weights: analog computational complexity*. (Report SYCON-92-05.) Rutgers Center for Systems and Control, Rutgers University, New Brunswick, NJ.

St. John, M. F. (1992). The story gestalt: a model of knowledge-intensive processes in text comprehension. *Cognitive Science, 16*, 271–306.

Taraban, R., and McClelland, J. L. (1990). Constituent attachment and thematic role expectations. *Journal of Memory and Language, 27*, 597–632.

Trueswell, J. C., Tanenhaus, M. K., and Kello, C. (1992). Verb-specific constraints in sentence processing: separating effects of lexical preference from garden-paths. *Journal of Experimental Psychology: Learning, Memory and Cognition*.

Tyler, L. K., and Frauenfelder, U. H. (1987). The process of spoken word recognition: an introduction. In U. H. Frauenfelder, and L. K. Tyler (Eds.), *Spoken word recognition*. Cambridge, MA: MIT Press.

Van Gelder, T. (1990). Compositionality: a connectionist variation on a classical theme. *Cognitive Science, 14*, 355–384.

Weckerly, J., and Elman, J. L. (1992). A PDP approach to processing center-embedded sentences. In *Proceedings of the 14th Annual Conference of the Cognitive Science Society*. Hillsdale, NJ: Erlbaum.

Wiles, J., and Bloesch, A. (1992). Operators and curried functions: training and analysis of simple recurrent networks. In J. E. Moody, S. J. Hanson, and R. P. Lippman (Eds.), *Advances in neural information processing systems 4*. San Mateo, CA: Morgan Kaufmann.

Guide to Further Reading

A good collection of recent work in connectionist models of language may be found in Sharkey (in press). The initial description of simple recurrent networks appears in (Elman, 1990). Additional studies with SRNs are reported in Cleeremans, Servan-Schreiber, and McClelland (1989) and Elman (1991). An important discussion of recurrent networks-based dynamical systems approach to language is found in Pollack (1991).

Cleeremans, A., Servan-Schreiber, D., and McClelland, J. L. (1989). Finite state automata and simple recurrent networks. *Neural Computation, 1,* 372–381.

Elman, J. L. (1990). Finding structure in time. *Cognitive Science, 14,* 179–211.

Elman, J. L. (1991). Distributed representations, simple recurrent networks, and grammatical structure. *Machine Learning, 7,* 195–225.

Pollack, J. B. (1991). The induction of dynamical recognizers. *Machine Learning, 7,* 227–252.

Sharkey, N. (Ed.). (in press). *Connectionist natural language processing: readings from connection science.* Oxford, England: Intellect.

9 Morphodynamics and Attractor Syntax: Constituency in Visual Perception and Cognitive Grammar

Jean Petitot

EDITORS' INTRODUCTION

Language presents some of the most difficult challenges for cognitive science. This is true even for the mainstream computational approach, which supposes that cognitive processes are the manipulation of internal languagelike structures. How might these challenges be confronted from a dynamical perspective?

In this chapter, Jean Petitot tackles an issue which is typically thought to be especially well-suited to a mainstream computational treatment, that of syntactic constituency. *In this ambitious work he combines the foundational ideas of the French mathematician René Thom with Langacker's cognitive grammar and the mathematics of (so-called) computational vision to yield an account that departs radically from standard approaches to syntax. Since this work is very novel for most cognitive scientists, and rather difficult, we provide here an extended introduction which gives a brief overview of the main ideas.*

Language presents at least two kinds of explanatory task. One is the province of linguistics. It is the task of describing and explaining language itself, and in particular the structure (syntax) and meaning (semantics) of sentences, the basic units of language. The other is part of cognitive science: explaining how it is that we are able to use language. What is going on in my head when I hear, understand, or produce a sentence? It has been traditional to suppose that these explanatory tasks are relatively independent. (The famous Chomskyan distinction between competence and performance is an attempt to theoretically underwrite this independence.) From this point of view, syntax and semantics are public phenomena which can be studied without knowing anything about the internal cognitive mechanisms underlying use.

Recently, this traditional view has been challenged by a school of thought known as cognitive grammar, which maintains that understanding the structure of a sentence and its meaning requires focusing on the cognitive processes involved in understanding or producing it. Syntax and semantics thus become branches of a broadened cognitive science. With this transition comes a jump in the level of difficulty, since a cognitive explanation of performance in any given case is far more complex than a formal description of competence.

In this chapter, Petitot adopts the cognitive grammar perspective. His aim is to provide, at the most basic level, a dynamical description of the cognitive processes that constitute thinking the thought corresponding to a given sentence of natural language. Describing these processes is an avenue for understanding the structure and meaning of the sentence itself.

Traditional syntax and semantics associate individual sentences with elements of a set of well-defined abstract entities. Thus traditional syntax might associate a sentence with a particular tree structure, and traditional semantics might associate a sentence with its truth conditions. The association is achieved by pairing the sentence with a symbolic representation of the relevant abstract entity: a tree diagram or parenthesized symbol sequence in the case of syntax, or an expression of a formal language designating truth conditions in the case of semantics. The computational approach to cognition then accounts for language use by basically transferring these symbolic representations into the head. That is, the computational approach hypothesizes that the mental structures underlying my ability to parse and understand a sentence are symbolic representations of much the same kind as are deployed by linguists in describing the structure and meaning of sentences.

Now, the mathematical language of dynamics provides the ability to specify a vast range of abstract dynamical entities, many of which have curiously syntax-like and semantics-like structure. Analogous to the traditional approach, then, a dynamical approach to syntax and semantics associates a sentence of natural language with one of these dynamical entities. However, instead of transferring the symbolic representations *of these abstract entities into the head*, a dynamical approach to cognition hypothesizes that the dynamics of the brain actually instantiates the dynamical entities themselves. That is, when we process a given basic sentence, our brain does not manipulate symbols in the language of dynamics; rather, it realizes the abstract dynamical structures which the theorist uses the mathematical language of dynamics to describe.

What are these dynamical entities? Suppose you have a dynamical system with a certain arrangement of attractors in its state space. This arrangement can be thought of as fixed or "controlled" by the settings of the parameters in the equations that govern the system's dynamics. As these parameters vary, so do the shape and location of the attractors. In many systems, there will be certain critical settings of parameters at which complete qualitative transformations in the arrangement of attractors occur. Particular attractors can, for example, completely disappear, or new ones can emerge. The new arrangement can force a rapid change in the state of the system. These dramatic changes are called bifurcations or catastrophes. More abstractly, we can think of bifurcations in terms of the qualitative arrangement of attractors in a system and the various ways in which these arrangements can be transformed. This way we get a theory of the interactions between entities which are representable by attractors. This theory forms a basis for a theory of constituency.

Catastrophes, as dramatic changes, are particularly salient features of the behavior of a system. A system exhibiting catastrophic behaviors can appear to have a certain kind of structure. Morphodynamics is the general study of how complex structure can emerge in natural systems through dynamical mechanisms of this kind.

Linguistic entities (sentences, meanings) are highly structured, and thus prime candidates for morphodynamical description. From the cognitive grammar perspective, the correct avenue for understanding the structure of these entities is to focus on the corresponding cognitive processes, which must themselves be highly structured. These processes are the behavior of complex dynamical systems—the modules of the brain—and are thus amenable to morphodynamical analysis. In this way, morphodynamics comes to be an appropriate mathematical framework for the study of linguistic structure.

As mentioned, bifurcations are general qualitative shifts in the dynamics (arrangement of attractors) of a system, and the associated rapid changes of state, as changing control parameters pass through critical values. If these critical parameter values are mapped out in the space of control parameter settings for a given system, they form the boundaries and surfaces of complex geometric objects, which can be quite beautiful (butterflies, swallowtails, etc.). Corresponding to each way of crossing one of these boundaries is a particular qualitative transformation in the arrangement of attractors in the system. The basic structure of these transformations can be abstractly diagrammed in line drawings ("actantial graphs").

For classes of very elementary dynamical systems—namely, "gradient descent" systems, in which the only form of behavior is settling into a point attractor—it is possible to classify the various kinds of interactions of attractors. For each of these "elementary" catastrophes, there is just a small set of qualitatively different ways in which boundaries can be crossed; or in other words, a small set of transformations from one qualitative arrangement of attractors to another. Now, let us hypothesize that the behavior of the brain can be described, at some suitably high level, in terms of gradient systems. From this it follows that there is a strictly limited set of ways in which the dynamics of the brain transforms from one qualitative arrangement to another.

In Thom's and Petitot's theory, these transformations are treated as universal cognitive archetypes for relations between semantic roles. Each basic elementary and nuclear sentence of natural language, as the expression of a possible thought, is syntactically structured by one of these cognitive archetypes. The main verb corresponds to the catastrophe transformation as a whole, while the individual terms correspond to the distinct attractors. Since there are a vast number of distinct sentences, many sentences correspond to each cognitive archetype. Differences in the particular semantic content of a sentence falling under a common archetype (i.e., the difference between "John gives the book to Mary" and "Mary sends e-mail to Bob") correspond to differences in the global semantics of the scene (in Fillmore's sense) and in the internal nature of the attractors themselves.

In the limited set of basic catastrophe transformations, there is only a fixed number of positions that attractors can occupy with respect to other attractors (e.g., one being swallowed up by another). A key claim of Petitot's morphodynamical approach to syntax is that these positions correspond to what European linguists call "actants" or "actantial roles" and American linguists often refer to as case roles (Agent, Patient, etc.). Thus the morphodynamical approach can account for the fact that all natural languages appear to draw their cases from a limited set of universal types. Further, the approach provides what Petitot calls a "configurational definition" *of case roles. An Agent is an Agent because of the particular place of the corresponding attractor within a specific catastrophic transformation of attractor arrangements or configurations.*

Thus far, the morphodynamical account seems speculative and remote from real cognitive processes as they have been traditionally understood. One of Petitot's major contributions in this chapter is to demonstrate the cognitive plausibility of the central theoretical constructs of the morphodynamical approach by showing that they can be given an effective computational implementation. This is achieved in two stages. First, the cognitive archetypes corresponding to sentences of natural language are retrieved from the abstract structure of visual scenes by means of what Petitot calls the Localist Hypothesis. According to this key hypothesis of cognitive grammar, spatial relations in visually perceived scenes already form a sufficient basic set of semantic archetypes. The second stage is to show that known processes of computational vision are capable of recovering this syntactic structure of visual scenes. Thus visual perception is capable of providing a repertoire of cognitive processes instantiating precisely the abstract, catastrophe-theoretic structures in terms of which the structure of sentences is understood.

9.1 INTRODUCTION

The development of dynamical models for cognitive processing raises fundamental issues, some of which have already been tackled by connectionist models implementing dynamical systems. One of the most difficult challenges is the following: Can dynamical models be used to adequately model syntactic constituency and constituent structures which, classically, are modeled symbolically? At the linguistic level, one difficulty is to model grammatical relations and semantic roles (in the sense of case grammars) in a purely dynamical way. The problem in a nutshell is this: If terms of sentences are modeled by attractors of some underlying dynamics, what is the dynamical status of a "syntax" relating these attractors? What might an *attractor syntax* be?[1]

The problem is difficult for the following reason. For doing syntax—deep universal and formal syntax and not English or French morphosyntax—we need to make at least the following two distinctions: (1) between two syntactic (categorial) types: things or objects (terms) vs. relations, and (2) between two types of relations: static vs. dynamic (temporal). Now, if we represent terms by activity patterns which are attractors of dynamical systems, how can we incorporate these two differences? It is clear that syntactic relations between attractors cannot be reduced to mere linear superpositions. Indeed, we cannot model entities of *different* syntactic types by attractors of the *same* dynamical type, without taking into account the difference in their grammatical categories. We must model different grammatical categories by mathematical entities of *different* types.

Therefore, static and dynamical relations between terms must be modeled by *dynamical relationships between attractors*. This then is the main problem we must confront: *Under the initial hypothesis that terms can be modeled by attrac-*

tors, can an "attractor syntax" be worked out in the framework of the theory of dynamical systems?

As Domenico Parisi (1991, p. 92) has pointed out, in this sort of dynamical modeling of higher-level capacities such as language, "the most serious problem ... is to free [oneself] from the grip of concepts, definitions of problems, and even description of phenomena, that have been used for decades by symbolic accounts of these capacities."

This problem is essentially theoretical and mathematical. We present here some elements for its solution. Our strategy is the following.

The Concept of "Structure" and Morphodynamics

If we want to model constituency in a purely dynamical way, we must first understand how discrete structures can emerge from continuous substrates in the cognitive realm as in the physical realm. In the physical realm, theories of self-organization have shown that structures are essentially dependent on *critical phenomena*, i.e., on phenomena of symmetry breaking which induce qualitative discontinuities (heterogeneities) in the substrates (Petitot, 1992). Discrete structures emerge via qualitative discontinuities. But a system of qualitative discontinuities in a substrate is called a *morphology* and dynamic theories of morphologies belong to what is called *morphodynamics*. There is therefore a close link between the concept of "structure" and morphodynamics.

Cognitive Processing

To understand constituency dynamically we must also understand how elementary macrostructures can emerge from the underlying (e.g., neural) complex microdynamics in which they are implemented. This link between a complex underlying microlevel and a simple emerging macrolevel is analogous to the link in thermodynamics between statistical physics and basic macroscopic data.

Syntax and Semantics

We will see that in a dynamical constituent structure the difference between the semantic roles and the syntactic relations expressing events of interaction between them corresponds to the difference between attractors and *bifurcations* of attractors. In such a model, semantic roles do not reduce to mere labels which are arbitrarily assigned. Rather, their meaning is *embodied* in the nature of the model. As we shall see, bifurcation theory allows one to work out a *configurational definition* of semantic roles in much the same way as, in the symbolic conception of formal grammars, syntagmatic trees yield a configurational definition of grammatical relations. For us, the problem therefore is not to *symbolically bind* a role label to a filler term, but rather to propose a configurational definition of each role.

The Link with Spatial Cognition

One of our main theses is that syntactic structures linking participant roles in verbal actions are organized by universals and invariants of a topological, geometric, and morphological nature. This thesis is deeply akin to the work of Leonard Talmy, Ronald Langacker, and George Lakoff concerning the central cognitive role of spatial and temporal *Gestalten* or *image schemas*. Actually, we will show how constituent structures can be retrieved from the morphological analysis of perceptual scenes.

The Shift of Mathematical Level

A dynamical approach to cognitive structures, and especially to syntactic constituent structures, upsets the classic conception of formalization because it shifts the level of mathematical modeling. Indeed, in the classic symbolic view, the fact that terms can be linked by relations is taken for granted as a basic elementary fact which deserves no further explanation at all. Consequently, the only interesting structures are not the elementary ones but the sophisticated ones. In the dynamical approach, by contrast, the concept of a relation itself gives rise to tremendously difficult problems. Moreover, even supposing that it can be solved, it would be very difficult to formalize complex structures in this way.

Biochemistry provides a useful analogy. One often symbolizes atoms by points or by small spheres and chemical bonds by lines. Simple molecules such as O_2, H_2O, or even C_6H_6 (benzene) are trivial structures at this representational level. Only very complex structures (e.g., proteins, the DNA double helix, etc.) are nontrivial. But of course, if you aim not only at a mere structural description but also at a physical explanation, you must shift to the quantum level. At this level, the concepts of atoms and chemical bonds give rise to tremendously difficult problems, engaging the basis of quantum mechanics. And at the quantum level, even rather simple molecules such as C_6H_6 are very difficult to manage (try to solve the Schrödinger equation!). Proteins or the DNA double helix are intractable.

It is similar here. Our purpose is to lay the foundations for a dynamical and physical theory of constituency and constituent structures. Modeling in this way even the most elementary structures already requires sophisticated mathematical tools. Complex structures will remain intractable, and require higher levels of description.

Section 9.2 reviews some features of the problem. We emphasize the fact that the main challenge is to achieve a configurational definition of the semantic roles in case grammars. In section 9.3 we explain briefly the precursor idea of an attractor syntax which was already built up by René Thom in the late 1960s and which we presented in 1975 at the "Chomsky-Piaget" Royaumont meeting. At that time, this attractor syntax lacked an effective implementation. The basis for an implementation is now partly available (see section 9.6). In section 9.4 we stress the fact that, to solve the main problem, we need an appropriate linguistic theory. *Cognitive grammars* seem to be most adequate. Using them, it becomes possible to anchor the syntactic constituency problem in that of *perceptual constituency*. In section 9.5 we sketch the algorithms of computational vision—boundary detection, wavelet analysis, diffusion, and spreading activation routines—which we use to analyze perceptual constituency. In section 9.6 we set out the key algorithm of *contour diffusion* and we show how it permits one to scan explicitly some of the image schemas of cognitive grammars and to retrieve the Thomian attractor syntax. This result shows that the theory of dynamical systems is able to work out a model of syntactic constituency.

9.2   THE PROBLEM OF SYNTACTIC CONSTITUENCY AS A CHALLENGE FOR DYNAMICAL MODELING

The Content of the Problem

In what follows we use the gallicisms "actant" and "actantial" to denote the semantic roles of case grammars. Actantiality is a key concept of European linguistic traditions. It is more general than agentivity and concerns all the participants of an action.

Even if one adopts the conception of syntax which is the least symbolic, formalist, and combinatorial, namely that of case grammars and cognitive grammars, one must nevertheless develop a good dynamical account of constituent structures, and in particular of semantic roles. One of the fundamental requirements of a plausible dynamical theory of cognition is therefore to model *actantial relations* dynamically. In particular, we want a *configurational* account of semantic roles, that is, an account in which a semantic role is defined in terms of its geometric relations within a larger dynamical whole.

Of course, within the classic symbolic paradigm, the problem of a configurational definition of actantial relations is easily solved using formal and combinatorial symbolic structures. But this does not entail at all that every configurational definition must be of such a symbolic nature (Petitot, 1991a). It only entails that it is necessary to elaborate a dynamical theory of the geometric wholes within which geometric relations are semantically significant. The main problem of section 9.1 can thus be reformulated as follows: *If the actants A_i of a process are modeled by attractors $\mathscr{A}_i$ a dynamical system, is it possible, within the framework of the mathematical theory of dynamical systems, to elaborate a geometric theory of actantial interactions—i.e., a theory of the verb and its participants?*

In many dynamical models the situation can be greatly simplified if one makes the hypothesis that the dynamics X defining the attractors $\mathscr{A}_i$ admits a global Lyapunov function (see under section 9.3) or, even more simply, that X is a gradient function, $X = -\operatorname{grad} f$. The $\mathscr{A}_i$ are then the minima m_i of the potential function f. The main question can thus be simplified: *If the actants*

A_i of a process are modeled by the minima m_i of a potential function, is it possible, within the framework of the dynamical theory of potential functions, to elaborate a theory of actantial interactions—i.e., a theory of the verb?

The mathematical challenge is therefore to develop a theory of interactions of attractors, what we call an *attractor syntax*. We shall see that bifurcation theory provides tools for solving it.

Note that here we will not be discussing what has come to be known as *the binding problem*.[2] The way by which one can bind a role label with a filler term is certainly a fundamental issue. But the main problem in this chapter is that of the configurational definition which can substitute for role labels. We will see that in such a definition roles are identified with *positions*—places—in configurations of positions. Of course, these places have to be filled by terms (particular attractors; see Contents and Complex Attractors, below).

The Epistemology of the Morphodynamical Paradigm

A dynamical conception of syntactic structures was proposed for the first time by René Thom in the late 1960s and has been developed by the school of morphodynamics. Section 9.3 summarizes its essential content. Before that, we focus very briefly on some epistemological points.

In its most general setting, the term *Morphodynamics* refers to theories whose aim is to explain natural morphologies and iconic, schematic, Gestalt-like aspects of structures, whatever their underlying physical substrate may be, using the mathematical theory of dynamical systems. As it is extensively explained in Thom (1972, 1980a, 1988) and Petitot (1982, 1985a, 1986, 1992), syntactic structures can be treated as Gestalten and morphodynamically modeled.

In my contribution to the 1975 Royaumont debate between Jean Piaget and Noam Chomsky (Petitot, 1979), I explained how morphodynamics could offer an alternative to the Chomskyan symbolic paradigm. The main epistemological points are still valid:

1. The Chomskyan thesis that ignorance of the physical basis of mental structures forces one to restrict syntactic theory to a mere formal description of competence need not be accepted. Even if one does not know the neurophysiological implementation of this competence, one can nevertheless hypothesize that there are *dynamical processes underlying performance* and that the formal structures of competence *emerge* from them.

2. One must therefore carefully distinguish between the *formal description* of symbolic structures on the one hand and their *dynamical explanation* on the other. The correctness of the former does not commit one to a symbolic conception of mental states and processes. As we shall see, in the morphodynamical paradigm the conceptual contents of mental states and their semantic correlates are no longer identified with labels for symbolic ordering. *Their meaning is embodied in the cognitive processing itself.* More precisely, it is identified with the *topology* of the complex attractors of the underlying neural

dynamics, and the mental events are identified with sequences of bifurcations of such attractors. The basic analogy here is with thermodynamics, phases, and phase transitions. Symbolic structures are conceived of as macrostructures emerging from the underlying microneurodynamics.

3. Information processing is therefore thought of not as implemented symbolic processing but as *a dynamical physical process*.

Since those early times, we have strongly emphasized the need for adequate epistemological foundations for the dynamical stance, and developed them extensively in successive works (see, e.g., Petitot 1982, 1985a, 1989d, 1992). One of the most delicate points was that the *naturalization* of syntactic structures—i.e., their interpretation as natural mental phenomena—requires us to model them using the mathematical tools of physical sciences and not those of formal logic. As natural phenomena, linguistic structures (and in particular syntactic structures) must be conceived of as the result of natural processes of self-organization and self-regulation. They are closer to macrophysical (e.g., thermodynamical) or biological structures than to logical ones. There is a fallacy—the formalist fallacy—in concluding that the structures of *natural* languages must be formalized using the symbolic structures of *formal* languages. *The mathematization of performance processes has a priori nothing to do with the formal description of competence rules.* The relationship between linguistic structures and the underlying physics does not reduce to implementation. It is also a process of emergence of macrostructures out of cooperative and collective phenomena on the microlevel.

In the thesis that cooperative, collective, self-organizing phenomena occurring in physical substrates can lead to the emergence of morphodynamical structures, the term *emergence* indicates two apparently opposite things: (1) that these structures are *causally* produced by the underlying physics; and (2) that they are nevertheless to a large extent *independent* of the particular physical properties of the substrate on which the dynamics operate. We will call *dynamical functionalism* the situation in which dynamical structures are to a large extent independent of the particular physical substrate in which they are implemented. Dynamical functionalism is the key to the naturalization of syntactic structures.

9.3 FROM MORPHODYNAMICS TO TOPOLOGICAL SYNTAX: THE WORK OF ZEEMAN AND THOM

As we have already seen, it was at the end of the 1960s and in the early 1970s that morphodynamics settled the basis for a dynamical approach to higher-level cognitive performances such as categorization and syntax. This section reviews the principles, mathematical tools, and results of this work. It is only a crude summary, but although the subject is rather technical, it can help the reader to understand better some key issues of dynamical modeling in cognitive science.

Christopher Zeeman's Initial Move

As far as I know, it was Christopher Zeeman who first introduced the dynamical approach for explaining the links between neurology and psychology. In his seminal 1965 article "Topology of the Brain," he introduced the idea that brain activity can be modeled by dynamical systems (flows) X_w on configuration spaces $M = I^N$ where $I = [0, 1]$ is the range of activity of a neuron, N is the number of neurons of the system under consideration, and the flows X_w depend on control parameters, microparameters such as synaptic ones, and macroparameters such as behavioral or psychological ones. The central idea was to identify mental states with *attractors* of the flows X_w, their content with the topological structure of the attractors, and the flux of consciousness with a "slow" temporal evolution of the X_w. Consequently, the strategy for explaining mental phenomena was to use the mathematical theory of dynamical systems (global analysis), especially theorems concerning the general structure of the attractors and their bifurcations, for drawing empirical conclusions from this dynamical scheme *without knowing explicitly the* X_w.

This strategy was very clearly explained in his 1976 article "Brain Modelling":

What is needed for the brain is a medium-scale theory.... The small-scale theory is neurology: the static structure is described by the histology of neurons and synapses, etc., and the dynamic behavior is concerned with the electrochemical activity of the nerve impulse, etc. Meanwhile the large-scale theory is psychology: the static structure is described by instinct and memory, and the dynamic behavior is concerned with thinking, feeling, observing, experiencing, responding, remembering, deciding, acting, etc. (...) It is difficult to bridge the gap between large and small without some medium-scale link. Of course the static structure of the medium-scale is fairly well understood, and is described by the anatomy of the main organs and main pathways in the brain.... But what is strikingly absent is any well developed theory of the dynamic behavior of the medium-scale....

Question: what type of mathematics therefore should we use to describe the medium-scale dynamic? Answer: the most obvious feature of the brain is its oscillatory nature, and so the most obvious tool to use is differential dynamical systems. In other words for each organ O in the brain we model the states of O by some very high dimensional manifold M and model the activity of O by a dynamic on M (that is a vector field or flow on M). Moreover since the brain contains several hierarchies of strongly connected organs, we should expect to have to use several hierarchies of strongly coupled dynamics. Such a model must necessarily remain implicit because it is much too large to measure, compute, or even describe quantitatively. Nevertheless such models are amenable in one important aspect, namely their discontinuities. (Zeeman, 1977, p. 287).

The fundamental trick was then to use the classification theorem of elementary catastrophes (see Universal Unfoldings and Classification Theorems, below) in the following manner. If mental states are modeled by attractors, then their significant changes during mental processing are modeled by *dis-*

continuities, i.e., by bifurcations. These are empirically given as *catastrophes*. These catastrophes occur at certain points in the control space W of the *relevant* control parameters (the relevance depends, of course, on the nature of the mental phenomena under consideration). We have therefore a dynamics X_w defined on the very high-dimensional manifold $M \times W$ (the direct product of the "internal" manifold M by the "external" control space W). This dynamics X_w is "vertical," i.e., compatible with the fibration (the canonical projection) $\pi: M \times W \to W$. This means that the vector of X_w at a point (x, w) of $M \times W$ has no "horizontal" component parallel to W: it is tangent to the fiber $M \times \{w\}$. In W we observe a set of points K at which discontinuities (catastrophes) occur. Now, if the catastrophes are elementary, then the classification theorem tells us we can generate K *locally* using only elementary models $\chi: \Sigma \to W$, with $\Sigma \subset \mathbb{R}^2 \times W$ (and even $\Sigma \subset \mathbb{R} \times W$). In such a model we consider (figure 9.1):

1. *Potentials* (Lyapunov functions) $f_w(x)$ of two (or even one) real variables which are "parameterized" by $w \in W$.

2. The critical points of the f_w, i.e., the points x where $\mathrm{grad}_x f_w = 0$.

3. The critical subset $\Sigma = \{(x, w) | x = \text{critical point of } f_w(x)\} \subset \mathbb{R}^2 \times W$.

4. The restriction χ to Σ of the canonical projection $\zeta: \mathbb{R}^2 \times W \to W$; the bifurcation set $K \subset W$ is then the *apparent contour* of χ, i.e., the projection of the set of points $x \in \Sigma$ where the tangent map $D_x\chi$ of χ at x is not of maximal rank ($= \dim W$) (i.e., where χ is not a local diffeomorphism between Σ and W).

We get therefore two models which are equivalent with respect to observable discontinuities: one $\mathcal{M}_\pi$ coming from $\pi: M \times W \to W$ and the second $\mathcal{M}_\zeta$ coming from $\zeta: \mathbb{R}^2 \times W \to W$. In the passage from $\mathcal{M}_\pi$ to $\mathcal{M}_\zeta$ we find *a drastic reduction of the dimension* of the internal space (from $\dim M$ to $\dim \mathbb{R}^2 = 2$) which is very similar to that found in thermodynamics when one reduces an enormous number of degrees of freedom using what is called an *order parameter*. This drastic reduction is assimilated by Zeeman (1977, p. 290) to the passage from the dynamical medium scale to the "psychological" large scale.

For example, in the celebrated Zeeman model of the Lorenzian theory of aggression (Zeeman, 1977, pp. 3–8), the conflicting behavioral control factors are "rage" and "fear" and the controlled behaviors are "attack" and "flight." The conflict between simultaneously high values of the two controls induces an instability (bimodality or "double bind") between the two behaviors and explains the "catastrophic" suddenness of the attack or flight. In such a model, the controls "rage" and "fear" are treated as intensive magnitudes measurable by a "degree" on a scale. The behaviors are modeled by attractors of some neural internal dynamics and their "catastrophic" jumps (triggered by critical values of the controls) are modeled by bifurcations of these attractors. The fact that the same bifurcation scheme can be generated by a simple and

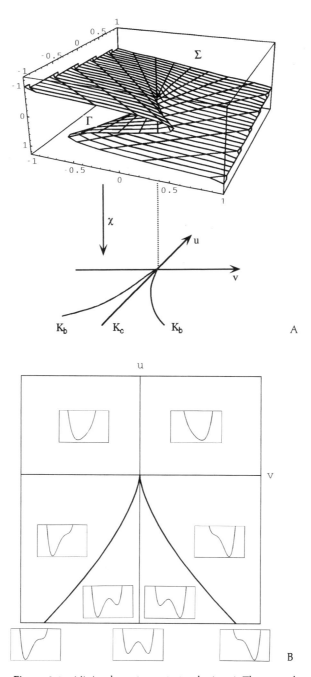

Figure 9.1 (*A*) An elementary catastrophe (cusp). The internal space M is of minimal dimension $= 1$ (coordinate x). The control space W is two-dimensional [coordinates (u, v)]. Every $w \in W$ controls a potential $f_w(x)$ having either one minimum, or two minima separated by a maximum (critical points). The critical surface $\sum$ is the subset of critical points (x, w) of the $f_w(x)$. It is constituted by two stable sheets (the upper one and the lower one) and, between them, an unstable one. The three sheets merge into a single one when $u > 0$. There is a bimodal conflict in the cusp region. χ is the projection of $\sum$ onto the control plane W. The apparent contour of

typical "cusp" catastrophe (where the scales "rage" and "fear" correspond to the diagonal axis $u = -v$ and $u = v$ and the behaviors "attack" and "flight" to the two opposed stable sheets of Σ; see figure 9.1) sets up the desired link between "the observed behavior of aggression [and] the underlying neural mechanism." "Each point of the surface Σ represents an attractor of some huge dynamical system modeling the limbic activity of the brain, and the jumps occur when the stability of an attractor breaks down. The dynamical system remains implicit in the background; the only part that we need to make explicit for experimental prediction is the catastrophe model [of figure 9.1]" (Zeeman, 1977, p. 13).

Moreover, to set up the link with the "psychological" large scale, "We take Σ as an explicit model for the large-scale psychology. We label the various sheets of Σ with psychological words.... For coordinates in $\mathbb{R}^2$ we seek two psychological indices that correlate with the labeled sheets. Then Σ is an explicit quantitative psychological model for testing experimentally" (p. 290). In the "psychological" model $\chi \colon \Sigma \to W$, the generating potentials f_w are Lyapunov functions with no neural interpretation. But, even if a dynamics X_w on M and a potential f_w on $\mathbb{R}^2$ are of a different nature, they generate *isomorphic* qualitative behavior. It is this *nonlinear* diffeomorphism which, according to Zeeman, sets up the *nonquantitative* "connection between the neurological measurements and the psychological measurements" (p. 291).

The General Morphodynamical Model

This rather technical section introduces the mathematical concepts which are the main ingredients of a general morphodynamical model. Our setting will be as general as possible. Let S be a system, e.g., a neural network. We suppose that S satisfies the following hypotheses:

The Internal Dynamics and the Internal States   The first hypothesis is that there exists an internal dynamical mechanism X which defines the *internal states* of S. More precisely:

1. There exists for S—as for every physical system—a configuration space (or a phase space) M which is a differentiable manifold and whose points x represent all the possible instantaneous transient states of S. M is called the *internal space* of S.

2. X is a flow on M, i.e., a system of ordinary differential equations $\dot{x} = X(x)$ with three properties: it is (a) complete (its trajectories are integrable from

---

χ is the projection of the subset of points Γ of Σ at which the direction of projection is tangent to the surface Σ (intuitively, the lines of the fold on the surface of critical points). The catastrophic set K splits into two sorts of components: those (K_b) for which a minimum and the maximum collapse (bifurcations), and those (K_c) for which the two minima compete (conflicts). (B) The shape of the potentials $f_w(x)$ for different places in the control space W.

$t = -\infty$ to $+\infty$); (b) deterministic; and (c) smooth relative to the initial conditions. The smooth vector field X is called the *internal dynamics* of S.

Let Γ_t be the mapping of the manifold M into itself which associates to every point $x \in M$ at time 0 its position at time t. It is easy to show that Γ_t is a *diffeomorphism* of M, i.e., a one-to-one bicontinuous and bidifferentiable mapping. Clearly, $\Gamma_{t'} \circ \Gamma_t = \Gamma_{t+t'}$ and $\Gamma_{(-t)} = (\Gamma_t)^{-1}$. Therefore, $\Gamma \colon \mathbb{R} \to \mathrm{Diff}(M)$ is a morphism of groups from the additive group of $\mathbb{R}$ to the group of diffeomorphisms of M—what is called a *one parameter subgroup of diffeomorphisms of M*. Γ is the *integral* version of the vector field X. It is called its *flow*. The internal states of S are then the (asymptotically stable) *attractors* of X. They must not be confused with the instantaneous transient states $x \in M$.

For further description of attractors, see Norton, (chapter 2.).

The Criterion of Selection of the Actual State   The second hypothesis is that there exists some criterion I (e.g., a physical principle of minimization of energy) which selects from among its possible internal states the *actual* internal state of the system S.

The External Control Space   The third hypothesis is that the system S is *controlled* by control parameters varying in a control space W. W is called the *external space* of S. The internal dynamics X is therefore a dynamics X_w which is parameterized by the external points $w \in W$ and varies smoothly relative to them. In the case of a neural network system, for example, W is the space of the synaptic weights w_{ij} and thresholds T_i. In a neurologically plausible model, many modules are strongly coupled and the external space of each module will in general be the output of some other modules (including the external stimuli in the case of perception). These complex systems are called *dynamical cascades*.

The Field of Dynamics   Let $\mathscr{X}$ be the functional space of the smooth vector fields on the internal space M. $\mathscr{X}$ is the space of the smooth sections of the tangent vector bundle TM of M. The possible dynamical behaviors of S are completely described by the *field of dynamics* $\sigma \colon W \to \mathscr{X}$ which associates X_w to $w \in W$. If another dynamics (an "external" one; see Fast/Slow Dynamics, below) drives the control w, then the controlled internal dynamics X_w drifts and can become unstable.

The Qualitative Discontinuities and the Morphologies   Phenomenologically, the system S manifests itself through *observable and measurable qualities* $q_w^1, \ldots, q_w^n$ which are characteristic of its actual internal state A_w. When the control w varies smoothly in W, X_w and A_w vary smoothly. If A_w subsists as the actual state, then the q_w^i also vary smoothly. But if the actual state A_w bifurcates toward another actual state B_w when w crosses some critical value, then some of the q_w^i must present a *discontinuity*. Thom has called *regular* the points $w \in W$ where locally all the qualities q_w^i vary smoothly and *singular* the points $w \in W$ where locally some of the q_w^i present a qualitative discontinuity. The set R_w of regular points is by definition an open set of W and its complementary set K_W, the set of singular points, is therefore a closed set. By definition, K_W is the *morphology* yielded by the dynamical behavior of the system S.

The Singular Points   The singular points $w \in K_W$ are *critical values* of the control parameters and, in the physical cases, the system S presents for them *a critical behavior*. As far as I know, Thom was the first scientist to stress the point that qualitative discontinuities are phenomenologically dominant, that every qualitative discontinuity is a sort of critical phenomenon, and that a general mathematical theory of morphologies presented by general systems had to be an enlarged theory of critical phenomena.

Structural Stability   The mathematical theory of *structural stability* is needed in order to explain the observable morphologies K_W. Indeed, the critical values $w \in K_W$ are those at which, according to the criterion I (see above), the actual state A_w of S bifurcates toward another actual state B_w. In general, such a bifurcation is forced by the fact that A_w becomes structurally *unstable* when w crosses K_W.

For defining the (deep) concept of structural stability, we need two things:

1. A topology $\mathcal{T}$ on the functional space $\mathcal{X}$. In general, the chosen topology is the *Whitney C^∞-topology* which is the topology of uniform convergence of the vector fields and all their partial derivatives on the compact sets of M, with equality "at infinity" (i.e., outside some compact set).[3]

2. An equivalence relation on $\mathcal{X}$ which allows us to define the notion of "*qualitative type*." In general, if $\mathcal{F} = C^\infty(M, N)$ is the functional space of smooth maps between two manifolds M and N, two elements f and g of $\mathcal{F}$ are called C^∞-equivalent if there exist diffeomorphisms $\varphi \in \mathrm{Diff}(M)$ and $\psi \in \mathrm{Diff}(N)$ s.t. $g = \psi \circ f \circ \varphi^{-1}$, i.e., if f and g are conjugate by two changes of "global coordinates," one in the source space M and the other in the target space N. For the functional space $\mathcal{X}$ of vector fields on M, this definition must be refined.

Now let $X \in \mathcal{X}$ be a vector field on M. Let $\tilde{X}$ be its equivalence class. X is called *structurally stable* if $\tilde{X}$ is (locally) $\mathcal{T}$-open at X, i.e., if there exists a neighborhood $\mathcal{U}$ of X for the topology $\mathcal{T}$ s.t. every $Y \in \mathcal{U}$ is equivalent to X. If X is structurally stable, its qualitative structure "resists" small perturbations.

Categorization   Let $K_{\mathcal{X}}$ be the subset of $\mathcal{X}$ consisting of the structurally *unstable* vector fields. The main fact to be stressed here is that $K_{\mathcal{X}}$ *categorizes* $\mathcal{X}$. The subset $R_{\mathcal{X}}$ of structurally stable vector fields is partitioned into connected components which are identifiable with "species" of vector fields (the structurally stable equivalence classes) and these components are glued together by $K_{\mathcal{X}}$. $K_{\mathcal{X}}$ can therefore be conceived of as a classifying set for the vector fields.

Retrieving the Morphologies $K_{\mathcal{X}}$ is intrinsically and canonically defined. Let $\sigma: W \to \mathcal{X}$ be the field of dynamics describing all the possible behaviors of our system S (see above). The main hypothesis is that the empirically observed morphology K_W can be retrieved (via the criterion I) from the inverse image $K_W' = \sigma^{-1}(K_{\mathcal{X}} \cap \sigma(W))$ of $K_{\mathcal{X}}$ relative to σ. To *explain* the morphologies K_W we need therefore good mathematical theories of structural stability and of the geometry of the bifurcation sets $K_{\mathcal{X}}$. These theories are very complex. In particular, for a general dynamical system there can be an infinite number of attractors, their basins can be inextricably intertwined, and their topology can be infinitely complex ("strange attractors"). On a stable strange attractor the dynamics is at the same time deterministic, structurally stable, and chaotic.

Fast/Slow Dynamics   To explain the temporal evolution of S, we must consider *temporal paths* in the control space W. These paths are in general trajectories of dynamics in W. Such *external* dynamics must be carefully distinguished from the internal ones X_w. For neural networks, some examples of external dynamics are well known: learning dynamics (e.g., the back propagation algorithm), dynamics driving bifurcations (see, e.g., Amit, 1989, on cycles of attractors), cascades of dynamics (see, e.g., Hirsch, 1989). Relative to the internal temporal scale of X_w, which is "fast," the external temporal scale is "slow." We can therefore suppose that the system S is always in an internal nontransient state. Relative to a slow dynamics, a fast one is "instantaneous." It loses its dynamical character and becomes in some sense "static." The "fast/slow" opposition is thus intimately related to the "static/dynamic" opposition pointed out in section 9.1.

As Thom (1984) emphasized, this opposition between fast and slow dynamics is essential for the model:

The main philosophical idea ... is that every phenomenon, every spatio-temporal morphology owes its origin to a qualitative distinction between different acting modes of *time*. Any qualitative distinction in a space W (the substrate) can be attributed to two acting modes of time: a "fast" mode which generates in an internal space "attractors" which specify the local phenomenological *quality* of the substrate; and a "slow" mode acting in the substrate space W itself. (p. 2)

Lyapunov Functions   Let A be an (asymptotically stable) attractor of X and let $B(A)$ be its basin. It can be shown that X is *dispersive* on $B(A) - A$ and that there exists a *Lyapunov function* on $B(A)$. X is called dispersive on N if for every $x, y \in N$, there exist neighborhoods U of x and V of y and $T > 0$ s.t. U and V become asymptotically disconnected, i.e., s.t., for every $t \geqslant T$ and

$t \leqslant -T$, $U \cap \Gamma_t(V) = \varnothing$. X is dispersive on N iff X is trivial on N, i.e., if it is equivalent to a constant field.

A Lyapunov function f on $B(A)$ is a real continuous function $f: B(A) \to \mathbb{R}$ which is strictly > 0 on $B(A) - A$, $\equiv 0$ on A and which decreases strictly along the trajectories of X. It is like a generalized "energy" which is minimized during the evolution of the system. There exist therefore essentially *two* sorts of dynamical behaviors: the *dissipative* ones which minimize a Lyapunov function f and contract the basins $B(A)$ on the attractors A, and the nondissipative (asymptotic) ones which are in general chaotic, ergodic, and conservative relative to an invariant measure (the Ruelle-Bowen-Sinaï measure).

The Reduction to Gradient Systems   We can therefore distinguish in the model the gradient-like dynamics on the basins $B(A) - A$ and the (chaotic) dynamics on the attractor A. As Thom (1984) claimed:

Personally, I think that it is not the too fine notion of attractor which plays the main role, but an equivalence class of attractors which are equivalent because they are encapsulated in the level variety of a Lyapunov function (a quasi-potential), provided that the attractor escape implosions of an exceptional character. According to me, this is the way for finding a mathematically satisfactory definition of the asymptotic stationary regime for a dynamics. (p. 5)

In this perspective we try to approximate a dynamical system by a gradient system and we look for gradient systems which have the same bifurcations (cf. Zeeman's strategy above). This reduction of the bifurcations to those of the Lyapunov functions is identifiable with a change in the level of observation. It is like a "thermodynamical" mean field theory. It is a way from the microlevel to the macrolevel.

Contents and Complex Attractors   In brain modeling, we can suppose, owing to the oscillatory nature of the brain, that the attractors come from the coupling of limit cycles. But it is a well-known fact that quasi-periodic motions on tori (i.e., products of limit cycles) become structurally unstable when the dimension of the tori is sufficiently large. In that case they bifurcate spontaneously toward strange attractors.[4] *The (complex) topology of such a strange brain attractor can be identified with the content of the correlated mental state.* In reducing the attractors to points in a quasi-gradient model *we therefore reduce these mental contents to unanalyzable units.* This reduction is equivalent in the morphodynamical approach to the classic reduction of semantic units to formal symbols. The main difference is that the *relations* between these units *are no longer of a symbolic nature*: they are dynamically generated by an optimization device (minimizing a Lyapunov function).

Critical Points, Jets, and Morse Theory   When the generating dynamics X_w are gradient ones, i.e., when $X_w = -\operatorname{grad} f_w$, with $f_w: M \to \mathbb{R}$ a smooth real function, the theory becomes much simpler. Let $f \in \mathscr{F} = C^\infty(M, \mathbb{R})$ be such a potential on M. One of the deepest achievements of modern differential geometry is to have shown that the *qualitative global structure* of such a geometric entity is essentially encoded in its *local singularities*. Let G_f be the graph of f, i.e., the subset of $M \times \mathbb{R}$ $G_f = \{(x, f(x)) | x \in M\}$ constituted by the values of f over M. Let $a \in M$ be a point of M and $(x_1, \ldots, x_n)$ a system of local coordinates at a. The point a is called a *critical point* of f if the tangent space of G_f at the point $(a, f(a))$ is "horizontal," i.e., parallel to the tangent space of M at a (figure 9.2). The technical condition is that the *Jacobian* of f at a, $J_f(a)$ (i.e., its gradient, or the n-vector of its first partial derivatives $(\partial f / \partial x_1, \ldots, \partial f / \partial x_n)$) is 0 at a. This is an intrinsic geometric property, independent of the chosen coordinate system. Moreover, a is called a *nondegenerate* critical point if it is not the coalescence of several simpler critical points, i.e., if it is as simple as possible, or noncomposite. The technical condition is that the *Hessian* of f at a—i.e., the $n \times n$ symmetric matrix of its second partial derivatives $(\partial^2 f / \partial x_i \partial x_j)$—is of maximal rank $(= n)$ at a. This is also an intrinsic geometric property of a critical point (see figure 9.2).

Nondegenerate critical points are minima, maxima, or (generalized) saddles. Flex points are examples of degenerate critical points. *Generically*, the critical points of a potential are nondegenerate and their values are pairwise different (see Castrigiano and Hayes, 1993, chapter 1).

A potential whose critical points are all nondegenerate with distinct critical values is called an *excellent Morse function*. Excellent Morse functions are generic in $\mathscr{F} = C^\infty(M, \mathbb{R})$: they can approximate *every* potential. Moreover (if M is *compact*) *they are structurally stable*. In fact, one of the main theorems of the theory, *Morse's theorem*, says that, if M is compact, $f \in \mathscr{F}$ is *structurally stable iff it is an excellent Morse function*. Morse's theorem is clearly crucial since it gives a simple geometric characterization of structural stability and therefore of the causes of *instability* (the presence of *degenerate* critical points and *equal* critical values). To find such a characterization for general dynamical systems is one of the most difficult problems of global analysis.

Normal Forms and Residual Singularities Another fundamental theorem of Morse yields a *normal algebraic form* for f near a nondegenerate critical point a: there exists always a local coordinate system at a such that

$$f(x) = f(0) - (x_1^2 + \cdots + x_k^2) + x_{k+1}^2 + \cdots + x_n^2.$$

The number k possesses an intrinsic geometric meaning. It is called the *index* of the critical point a.

Qualitatively, the structure of f near a nondegenerate critical point is completely known. If a is *degenerate*, then another deep theorem, *the residual singularities theorem*, says that if the corank of f at a (corank $= n -$ the rank of the Hessian) is s, then there exists a local coordinate system $(x_1, \ldots, x_{n-s}; y_1, \ldots, y_s)$ s.t. locally $f = H(x) + g(y)$ where $H(x)$ is a nondegenerate quadratic form (the Hessian) and $g(y)$ is a function whose critical point a is *totally degenerate* (with a zero Hessian). This means that we can decompose locally M

Jean Petitot

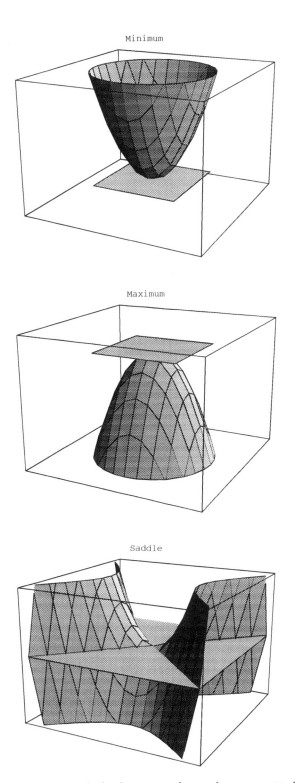

Figure 9.2 The local structure of a nondegenerate critical point a of a potential f. The figure represents the graph G_f of f in a neighborhood of a and the tangent space of G_f at $[a, f(a)]$.

Morphodynamics and Attractor Syntax

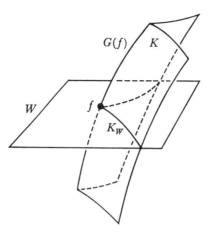

Figure 9.3 The general idea of universal unfolding of a singularity $f \in K$. $G(f) = \tilde{f}$ is the equivalence class (the orbit) of f. It is not locally open at f in $\mathscr{F}$. There exist nontrivial slices $\mathscr{W} \simeq W$ transverse to $\tilde{f}$ at f. K_W is the intersection $K_W = K \cap W$.

into complementary spaces, one in which f is nondegenerate, and another in which f is completely degenerate.

Mather's Theory The problem is therefore to study the local structure of potentials near a totally degenerate critical point. For this, the algebraic tools developed by John Mather are essential. The main result is that if a is a totally degenerate critical point of f and if we *localize* the situation in the neighborhood of a in M and of f in $\mathscr{F}$, then, in "good" cases, the orbit $\tilde{f}$ of f is a subspace of $\mathscr{F}$ admitting supplementary subspaces $\mathscr{W}$ which are all equivalent (figure 9.3). The dimension c of these $\mathscr{W}$ is called the *codimension of f* at a. This leads us to a concept of utmost importance, that of *universal unfolding*.

Universal Unfoldings and Classification Theorems We have seen that when an external control $w \in W$ drives an internal dynamics f_w (or more generally X_w), bifurcations can naturally occur. They occur when $f_w \in K_{\mathscr{F}}$. Now the main fact is that, conversely, *every unstable dynamics naturally generates an entire system of bifurcations*. Insofar as the concept of bifurcation is the key concept allowing us to work out a dynamical theory of constituent structures, we need a clear understanding of this deep fact.

Let f be a totally degenerate singularity of finite codimension. In general, a small perturbation of f will yield a function g which is *less* degenerate than f: small perturbations have a stabilizing effect. But in general there will be *many ways* to stabilize f by small perturbations. The crucial fact is that it is possible to group *all* these possibilities together in one *single* structure: the *universal unfolding* of f.

For instance the two-dimensional family of potentials of figure 9.1 is the universal unfolding $x^4 + ux^2 + vx$ of the codimension 2 singularity x^4 (normal form of a degenerate minimum). Such a degenerate critical point derives from the coalescence of two minima and a maximum and it can therefore "explode" and split into three nondegenerate critical points. Its universal unfolding gathers the semi-stabilized small perturbations possessing only codimension 1 instabilities of type "flex point" or "equality of two critical values," and the completely stabilized small perturbations possessing one simple minima or two simple minima separated by a simple maximum.

The main theorem concerning unfoldings says that *the universal unfoldings of $f = f_0$ are the transversal unfoldings constructed from a basis $h_1, \ldots, h_c$ of $\mathcal{W}$ via the formula*

$$f_w = f + \sum_{i=1}^{i=c} w_i h_i.$$

They are all C^∞-equivalent. It is easy to derive from this theorem *normal algebraic forms* for universal unfoldings. Consider for example the *double cusp* singularity $f(x, y) = x^4 + y^4$. This singularity is already notably complex. It "contains" all the elementary catastrophes. The normal form for the universal unfolding is:

$$f_w = x^4 + y^4 + ax^2y^2 + bx^2y + cxy^2 + dx^2 + exy + fy^2 + gx + hy.$$

In the ten-dimensional space $\mathbb{R}^2_{x=(x,y)} \times \mathbb{R}^8_{w=(a,b,c,d,e,f,g,h)}$ which is the direct product of the internal space and the external space, we consider the subspace $\Sigma = \{(x, w) | x \text{ is a critical point of } f_w\}$. The bifurcation set K_W is the subset of the control values $w \in W$ s.t. f_w presents at least one degenerate critical point. K_W is the apparent contour of the canonical projection $\chi \colon \Sigma \to W$ (see Christopher Zeeman's Initial Move, above). χ is called the *catastrophe map* associated with the unfolding. Its geometry is very complex. K_W *classifies and categorizes* the different qualitative types (of germs) of potentials which can be derived from $f_0 = f$ by small deformations.

The *classification theorems* (Thom, Zeeman, Arnold, etc.) give such explicit algebraic normal forms for the singularities and their universal unfoldings up to codimensions which are not too large (around 12). They constitute one of the most important and beautiful achievements of differential geometry.

Applications of Morphodynamics

Using these results of global analysis, bifurcation theory, and singularity theory, René Thom conceived of a research program leading from physics to cognitive sciences, including linguistics. His main idea was to use these tools to develop a mathematical theory of natural morphologies and natural structures. He showed first that, as far as it concerns the system of connections which "organically" links up parts within a whole in a structurally stable way (see, e.g., Petitot 1986), every structure is reducible to a (self)-organized and (self)-regulated morphology. But, as we have seen, every morphology is itself reducible to a system of qualitative discontinuities emerging from an appropriate underlying substrate.[5] The theoretical problem was therefore to build up dynamical mechanisms which were able to generate, in a structurally stable way, these discontinuities both at the *local* level (what was called by Waddington the theory of "morphogenetic fields" or "chreods") and at the *global* one (aggregation, combination, and integration of chreods).

The classification theorems allowed a revolutionary strategy which can be called *dynamical functionalism* (see The Epistemology of the Morphodynamical Paradigm, above). Instead of first defining the generating dynamics *explicitly* and then deriving from it the observable discontinuities, one first describes the observable discontinuities geometrically and then derives from them a *minimally complex* generating dynamics. This minimal explicit dynamics must be conceived of as a simplification of the real *implicit* generating dynamics. As stressed in Andler, Petitot, and Visetti (1991), this dynamical functionalism is not of a classic (e.g., Fodorian) type. Indeed, classic functionalism entails a strict separation between the cognitive and physical levels, the relation between the two being a matter of mere compilation and implementation. This is no longer the case in an emergentist approach. But dynamical functionalism is nevertheless a "true" functionalism in the sense that classification theorems show that *emergent structures share properties of universality which are to a large extent independent of the specific physical properties of the underlying substrate.*

Such an explanatory paradigm has been extensively developed during the 1970s and the early 1980s. We give now briefly some indications about these precursory trends (see also Petitot, 1989g, h).

Physics: Critical Phenomena   In physics, and particularly in macrophysics, morphodynamics has innumerable applications. They concern the mathematical analysis of the singularities and discontinuities which emerge at the macrolevel from underlying microphysical mechanisms. Here is a very incomplete list: caustics in optics; phase transitions, symmetry breakings, and critical phenomena; elastic buckling; defaults in ordered media; shock waves; singularities of variational problems; dissipative structures; changes of regimes in hydrodynamics, routes toward turbulence; deterministic chaos. In all these exact and quantitative applications, the external space W is in general a true *control* space (e.g., temperature and external magnetic field in the case of spin systems, or synaptic weights and thresholds in the case of neural networks). The main import of these mathematical models is to explain how the observable morphologies which dominate the phenomenological level can emerge from the underlying physics. They heal the breach between physical objectivity and commonsense realism which has been until now a dramatic consequence of the Galilean revolution.[6] In that sense, *morphodynamics can be considered the pure, mathematical way to qualitative physics* (Smith, 1993; Petitot and Smith, 1991). More than 10 years before computational (artificial intelligence) approaches to qualitative physics, morphodynamics has shown that the informationally relevant and salient features of macrophysical processes are constituted by their singularities, their qualitative discontinuities, and their critical behavior.

Cognitive Sciences and Linguistics: Dynamical Syntax and Actantial Graphs One of the most significant achievements of Thom's paradigm concerns cognitive processes such as *perception, action,* and *language.* Here we must distinguish between two trends: a morphodynamical conception of the cognitive processes themselves on the one hand, and a realist and "ontological" conception of perception and language on the other. According to Thom, language is, at its most basic levels, rooted in perception and perception is a cognitive process which builds itself up on the basis of objective morphological structures that are phenomenologically salient. "The geometrico-topological analysis ... allows us to associate with every spatiotemporal process some combinatorial invariants [the singularities] ... which can be reasonably thought of as playing an essential role, according to their fundamental character, in the verbal description of the process. Such is the origin, I think, of the originary schematism which governs the linguistic organization of our vision of the world" (Thom, 1980b, p. 24).

This geometric-topological conception of syntax claimed that there exist syntactic Gestalts constituting a perceptively rooted *iconic protosyntax.* It was a prophetic anticipation of the epistemological turn introduced later in linguistics by cognitive grammars and more precisely by the thesis of perceptive roots of syntactic structures—i.e., precisely, of the *iconicity* of syntax (see section 9.4). If one accepts it, then one soon realizes that in classical linguistic theories there is *a missing link between* language and perception. It concerns an *intermediary* representational level where perceptual scenes are organized by *cognitive organizing Gestalts* and *image schemas* which are *still* of a perceptive nature but *already* of a linguistic nature.

Actually, several new achievements in cognitive linguistics (see, e.g., the works of Talmy, 1978, 1985, 1990; Langacker, 1987, 1991; Lakoff, 1988; Manjali, 1991; and others) have shown that many linguistic structures (conceptual, semantic, and syntactic structures) are organized in essentially the same way as visual Gestalts are. For example, Talmy (1978) has studied many linguistic "imaging systems" which constitute a "grammatically specified structuring [which] appears to be similar, in certain of its characteristics and functions, to the structuring in other cognitive domains, notably that of visual perception" (p. 14).

The general problem is the following. Consider a scene involving *spatiotemporal* events (i.e., a scene which is not only spatiotemporally localized, but also linguistically described by verbs whose semantics is dominantly spatiotemporal). The *iconicity* thesis asserts that there exists a *homology* (though not, of course, an isomorphism) between the structure of the scene as an organized Gestalt and the structure of the sentences which describe it. This thesis is foundational for cognitive grammars, and is now widely accepted. For example, in a forthcoming paper Herbert Simon (1994) develops an analog hypothesis concerning the links between *meanings* and mental *images*. Speaking of *"visualized meanings,"* he claims:

We experience as mental images our encodings of words we have read or of memories we have recovered.... The most common explanation of mental images in cognitive science today, and the one I shall accept here,... is that such images, whether generated from sensations or memories, make use of some of the same neuronal equipment that is used for displaying or representing the images of perceptually recorded scenes.... On this hypothesis, a mental picture formed by retrieving some information from memory or by visualizing the meaning of a spoken or written paragraph is stored in the same brain tissue and acted on by the same mental processes as the picture recorded by the eyes (p. 13).

Such a thesis leads to a new interpretation of the semantic roles founding case grammars (see Fillmore's Challenge and the Localist Hypothesis, below). There is an important part of the content of semantic roles which is of a purely topological and dynamical nature: to be in or out of some place, to move, to enter, to capture, to emit, to receive, to transfer, to control a movement, etc. The central challenge becomes to show how this local semanticism can be retrieved *from perceptual scenes using algorithms which generalize some well-known algorithms of computational vision* (this question is addressed in sections 9.5 and 9.6). It is an essential step in the construction of an artificial cognitive system such as a robot, which can linguistically interpret its perceptual environment.

Now, the problem raised by the iconicity thesis is that the syntactic image-schemas are: (1) abstract and very coarse grained, and (2) in general *virtual* structures constructed from the real components of percepts (think, e.g., of the virtual boundary separating two regions of space occupied by two objects). Thom showed that they can be nevertheless *mathematically modeled* using adequate topological and dynamical tools. We shall return in the following sections to these cognitive models. Here we give only some sketches concerning the topological models of syntax.

We start with a general morphodynamical model of gradient type. Let f be a (germ of a) potential on an internal manifold M. We suppose that f presents at a a singularity of finite codimension. Let (f_w, W, K) be the universal unfolding of f and $\chi: \Sigma \subset M \times W \to W$ the catastrophe map associated with it. In other words, we consider the product $M \times W$ of the internal space M (on which the f_w are defined) by the external space W. We see it as a fibration $\pi: M \times W \to W$ over the external space W, and we consider the "vertical" potentials $f_w(x)$. *We use then the universal unfolding (f_w, W, K) as a geometric generator for events of interaction between attractors.* We introduce *temporal paths* $\gamma = w(t)$ in the external space W and consider that they are driven by *slow* external dynamics. When γ crosses K, events of bifurcation occur. They are events of interaction of critical points. Thom's move is then to interpret the minima of the f_w—the attractors of the internal dynamics—as "actants" (semantic roles), the generating potential f_w as a generator of relations between them,[7] a temporal path $f_{w(t)}$ as a process of transformation of these relations, and the interaction of actants at the crossing of K as a verbal node.

If one interprets the stable local regimes [of the fast internal dynamics] as actants, it becomes possible to give the qualitative appearance of catastrophes a semantic interpretation, expressed in natural language. If ... one introduces time [i.e., a slow external dynamics], [the bifurcations] are interpreted as verbs.... One gets that way what I think to be *the universal structural table* which contains all types of elementary sentences. (Thom, 1980a, p. 188)

In figure 9.4 an example using the cusp catastrophe of figure 9.1 is shown. It corresponds to an event of "capture" of an actant X by an actant Y.

It must be strongly emphasized that in such interactional events, the actants are reduced to pure abstract places—*locations*—which must be filled by "true" participants (even when these participants are concrete places, as in sentences like "John sends an e-mail to Bloomington"). They play for cognitive grammars almost the same function as *symbols* do when one symbolizes a sentence such as "John takes the book" by a symbolic formal expression such as "X R Y." The main difference is that, in the topological-dynamical

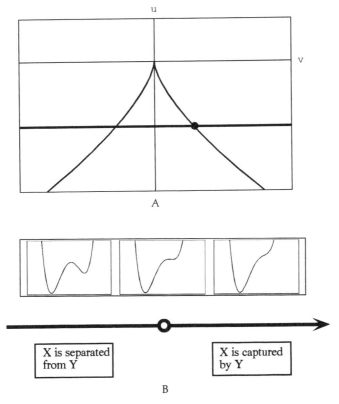

Figure 9.4   A simple example of an actantial interaction derived from a temporal path in a universal unfolding: the "capture" invariant derived from the cusp catastrophe of figure 9.1 *A.* The path γ in the external space. *B* The evolution of the actants ($=$ minima).

paradigm, a basic "local" content (X = "source," Y = "object," etc.) can be retrieved *from the morphology of the event itself*. Such a *configurational* definition of purely local semantic roles is a major consequence of iconicity in syntax. It has no equivalent in the symbolic classical paradigm.

It must also be emphasized that an archetypal dynamical event has *no intrinsic connection* with "objective" outer space-time and can be semantically interpreted in several ways. It is only a dynamical invariant. If, e.g., Y is an agent and X an object it will yield sentences such as "Y catches X," etc. If Y is a place and X an agent or an object, it will yield sentences such as "X enters Y," etc.

To such a dynamical invariant derived from a temporal path in a universal unfolding we can associate a combinatorial structure which is called its *actantial graph*. Such a structure belongs to a sort of *algebraic topology* of syntactic structures. The idea is to reduce the attractors to points (the minima of the generating potentials), and to look at their temporal trajectories (their world lines) and at the nodes (the vertex) where these world lines interact. Actantial graphs are *image schemas* deeply rooted in perception. They are still of an (abstract) perceptual nature but already of a (proto) linguistic nature. They yield *types* of actantial interactions and therefore a *categorization* of the possible interactional *events*.

Let us be a bit more precise. Consider a spatiotemporal scene, e.g., a scene describable by a sentence such as "X gives Z to Y." We split the semanticism of the scene in two completely different parts.

1. The one concerning the purely positional (local) content of "give" as an image schema of "transfer" type. This local content is like a frame, or script, in Shank's sense:

• X, Y, Z are places (locations).
• In the initial state, Z is linked with the "source" X which "emits" it.
• In the final state, Z is linked with the "target" Y which "receives" (or "captures") it.
• Between these two states there is a "movement" of "transfer" type.
• The "movement" is *controlled* by X and this intentional control of the action makes X an agent.

2. The one concerning the semantic lexical content of X, Z, Y, and "give" as a gift action.

After having separated the two types of semanticism, we have to model the local one. For this, we must retrieve the local information *from perceptual data* (in a bottom-up and data-driven manner). We must therefore extract *syntactic invariants* ("syntactic" in the positional sense) from the scenes. This is a very difficult task because the local information is coarser than the topological one. It belongs to an algebraic topology of events of interaction between actants. It is here that the actantial graphs become essential. They belong to the right level of representation. Moreover, they can be explicitly generated by generating potential functions which define dynamically the relations of which they consist. Their main function is to define in a purely configurational manner the local semanticism. Look, e.g., at the "capture graph" of figure 9.5. Its *morphology* and its generating potential *characterize* the local content of the actants (Agent and Object).

Now, we observe that actantial graphs *share all the properties of symbolic structures*. Many combinatorial operations and transformations can be performed on them. Let us take a simple example of type "capture."

The graph "Y captures X" is constructed by *gluing three components*: an event E and two actants X and Y (figure 9.5A).

1. The difference between "Y captures X" and "Y emits X" is schematized by the reversing of the time arrow (figure 9.5B). ("Schematization" of a linguistic procedure denotes here the way in which this procedure is reflected in the actantial graph, which is not a linguistic structure but a geometric one.)

2. That Y is thematized in the formulation "Y captures X" is schematized (figure 9.5C) by the fact that Y and E are first glued together before X is glued to the resulting complex. ("Thematization" consists in focalizing attention on an actant in such a way that it is taken in charge at the grammatical level by the grammatical subject.)

3. The thematization of X (as in the passive variant "X is captured by Y") is schematized by the fact that X and E are first glued together (figure 9.5D).

4. The difference between "Y captures X" and "X captures Y" is schematized by the exchange of the two lines of the graph (figure 9.5E).

A more complete account would introduce (at least) two supplementary elements. First, we must take into account the different ontological categories to which the actants belong. An actant can be, e.g., a localized material thing, a pure locus, or a diffuse field (light, heat, etc.). As a thing, it can be animate or inanimate, etc. Second, we must also take into account what actant possesses the *control* and the *intentionality* of the process (see below).

The theory of actantial graphs shows that it is possible to schematize geometrically the formal transformations characteristic of systematic symbolic structures. Constituency and systematicity are also constitutive properties of geometric representations.

Summary   Let us summarize the main principles of this topological and dynamical conception of syntax and verbal valence:

- We introduce an underlying implicit fast dynamics X_w.

- We use X_w to model the relations between the attractors of X_w; *relations are no longer logical entities but dynamical ones.*

- We use the (complex) *topology* of these attractors in order to model the semantic content of the corresponding actants (semantic roles); we get that way a *geometric* functional semantics.

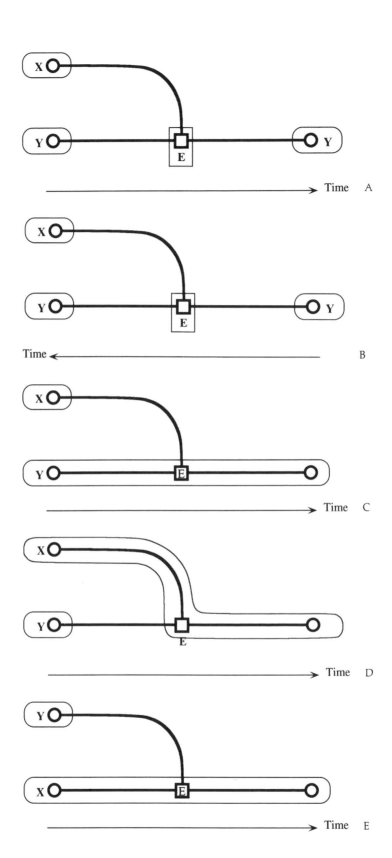

Jean Petitot

- We introduce Lyapunov functions and we reduce the dynamics to the associated quasi-gradient dynamics; such a reduction expresses *the shift of level from semantics to deep iconic structural syntax.*

- We introduce temporal paths in universal unfoldings, i.e., slow dynamics, so as to get actantial processes and actantial interactions.

- We interpret such actantial processes and interactions as verbs.

- We use the classification theorems about universal unfoldings for establishing a universal table of syntactic *archetypes.*

- We associate to the syntactic archetypes actantial graphs which support combinatorial operations analogous to those which operate on symbolic structures.

- We interpret *agentivity* in terms of control dynamics.

It is important to understand that the theory of universal unfoldings is essential if we are to be able to elaborate a correct theory of interactions between attractors. To get interactions we need temporal processes, i.e., temporal deformations f_t of systems f of actantial relations. But these temporal paths "live" in spaces which must be generated by the relations themselves. They must contain potentially the possibility of changes of the relations. The most relevant way to do this is to use the key concept of universal unfolding.

Import and Limits of Thom's Paradigm

Thom's works introduced revolutionary mathematical methods into the linguistic and cognitive science establishment which, at that time, was exclusively dominated by the formalist symbolic paradigm. They gave an extraordinary new impulse to traditions such as Gestalt theory, phenomenology, and structuralism.[8] It was the first time that, in cognitive and linguistic matters, *differential geometry substituted for formal logic* as the main mathematical tool.

But Thom and Zeeman proceeded as mathematicians, not in a "bottom-up" manner, from empirical data first to ad hoc models and then, at the end, to theoretical principles, but rather in a "top-down" manner, from fundamental principles and mathematical structures to empirical data. The advantage of such a strategy was that their perspective was theoretically very well

Figure 9.5 The actantial graph of "capture" and its combinatorial properties. Actantial graphs are a schematic way of diagramming the abstract structure of a bifurcation event in which attractors are interpreted as actants. In this case the upper (curved) line corresponds to the existence over a certain period of an attractor for actant X; the lower (straight) line corresponds to the existence of an attractor for actant Y. The event E is the bifurcation illustrated in figure 9.4. This actantial graph schematizes the structure of one among many dynamic archetypes. This archetype corresponds to a verb and can be semantically interpreted in a variety of ways. (A) The gluing of its three components. (B) The reversing of time. (C) The thematization of Y. (D) The thematization of X. (E) The exchange of the actants.

grounded and mathematically very strong. As Visetti (1990) has stressed, their dynamical functionalism introduced a new level of functional architecture which could operate as a condition of possibility for the inscription of syntactic processes into spatiotemporal mechanisms (the brain dynamics). A plausible functionalism has to be a priori compatible with physics and this is possible only if it is grounded into the geometric-dynamical framework of physics.

But the limits of such a dynamical functionalism, and even its partial failure, were the lack of an effective computational theory to undergird it. Indeed, what can be the *cognitive origin* of the generating dynamics? In the second part of this chapter we address this issue.

On the other hand, more recent models, such as connectionist ones, have proceeded in a rather "bottom-up" manner, elaborating models that are computationally effective, but lack grounding in theoretical principles and mathematical strength. For instance, the key concept of universal unfolding is not used, the stratified geometry of the bifurcation sets K_W in the control spaces of synaptic weights is unknown, the backpropagation algorithms provide external dynamics in the W spaces whose behavior at the crossing of the K_W is not analyzed, the complex topology of strange attractors coming from a coupling between neural oscillators is not used for semantic purposes, nor are their bifurcations used for modeling syntactic structures, etc.

Morphodynamics and Attractor Syntax

We now recall briefly how in *Morphogenèse du Sens* and other works (Petitot 1985a, 1989b, 1989e), Thom's syntactic modeling is linked with some current linguistic trends.

Syntactic Schemes and Deep Iconicity

The first step is to develop a criticism of the Chomskyan formalist symbolic paradigm (see section 9.2). The formal universals, which are not characterizable within the theory of formal grammars, need not necessarily be conceived of as innate. They can be explained by *cognitive* universal structures—as, e.g., archetypal actantial structures, primitive relational morphologies, and syntactic schemes—which are represented by grammatical relations at a higher symbolic level. Insofar as these structures are not symbolic but of a topological and dynamical nature, there exists in syntax a *deep iconicity*. At this level, semantics and syntax are inseparable: syntax is no longer an independent and autonomous linguistic dimension.

Fillmore's Challenge and the Localist Hypothesis

Concerning the general conception of syntactic structures, the perspective is therefore schematic and iconic. The problem is then to define the actantial roles not conceptually, using semantic labels, but configurationally (see section 9.2). It is the only way to resolve the tension between two equally important requirements. On the one hand, if they are really universal, case universals must constitute a very limited set. On the other hand, in order to perform their syntactic discriminative function, they must be sufficiently numerous. A configurational definition of the semantic roles solves the problem because it makes case universals depend on *relational* configurations. It therefore provides an answer to what Fillmore (1977) has called the "truly worrisome criticism of case theory," i.e., the fact that "nobody working within the various versions of grammars with 'cases' has come up with *a principled way* of defining cases, or *principled* procedures for determining how many cases there are" (p. 70, emphasis added). To solve this problem we need a "geometry" of actantial relations. We need actantial *schemes*. We need to be able to define the semantic roles not simply by category labels but configurationally, in terms of positions in geometric structures.

This schematicity of deep actantiality is linked with one of the main hypotheses of linguistic traditions, namely, the *localist hypothesis* (LH). In a nutshell, the thesis is that if we consider spatiotemporal actants, i.e., actants whose identity is reducible to their localization, we can identify the abstract actantial relations with spatiotemporal interactions between them (see The Localist Hypothesis, below).

The Mathematization of Fillmore's Scenes   *Morphogenèse du Sens* (Petitot, 1985a) sketches the link between this dynamical conception of syntactic iconicity and Tesnière's "structural syntax," Fillmore's and Anderson's case grammars, and relational grammars (Johnson, Keenan, Comrie, Perlmutter, and Postal). Regarding case grammar, it gives a Thomian mathematization of the theory of cognitive *scenes* developed by Fillmore (1977) in "The case for case reopened." Fillmore's slogan "meanings are relativized to scenes" leads to a dividing of the verbal semantics between two components: on the one hand, the contextual component of the semantic fields associated with the scenes, and, on the other hand, the pure actantial component of the case frames and of the semantic roles. Such a definition of case values is *conceptual* in the cognitive sense of "conceptual structure": "such descriptions [are] in some sense intuitively relatable to the way people thought about the experiences and events that they [are] able to express in the sentences of their language" (Fillmore, 1977, p. 62). When case grammars are revisited by topological syntax and cognitive grammars, the actants (the semantic roles) are reinterpreted in a localist, topological-dynamical way (see above). The main consequence is that their content is no longer conceived of as a *semantic* one (i.e., as a *meaning*) *but as an iconic-schematic one* (i.e., as an abstract *image*). And, as we have seen, the main problem (which is addressed later in this chapter) is to retrieve from perceptual data this kind of abstract iconic-schematic content.

In this new interpretation a scene Σ consists of the following components:

(a) A *semantic isotopy* (e.g., the "commercial" context in the prototypical scene of buying and selling); its semantics is not reducible to a localist one.

(b) A *global scheme* G of interaction between purely positional actants P_i; these positional actants (source, agent, object, goal, instrumental, etc.) are actantial positions in an *abstract* external space Λ underlying the scene. It must be strongly emphasized that the global actantial graph G is an image schema in the sense of cognitive grammars. It is *not* a linguistic entity but a Gestalt-like one and it defines in a schematic (topological-dynamical) way the local content of case roles.

(c) Specializations of the positional actants P_i into true actants (human beings, objects, forces, etc.) and places.

The scene Σ defines the semantic roles involved both conceptually and semantically [because of (a) and (c)]. But it also defines them *configurationally* [because of (b)]. In general, Σ is spatiotemporally embedded by means of an embedding of its underlying external space Λ in space-time $\mathbb{R}^4$. Through this embedding, the positional actants, which are specialized in places, become true spatiotemporal actants and the positional actants, which are specialized in persons, objects, etc., become concretely localized. Localization is linguistically expressed by adverbial complements.

There are a restricted number of *local archetypal schemes* $\Gamma_1, \ldots, \Gamma_n$ which determine case universals. What Fillmore calls the "orientational or perspectival structuring" of a scene consists in covering the global particular scheme G by gluing together such local archetypes. In general, there will be many different possible coverings. The gluing operators are the *anaphoric* ones.

The choice of an archetype Γ_i is linguistically expressed by the choice of a *verb* (*sell*, *buy*, *pay*, *cost*, etc.). Through its semantics (e.g., its "commercial" meaning), the verb excites the whole scene Σ. But through its valence and case schema it specializes an archetype of type Γ_i. What Fillmore calls the *saliency hierarchy* determines what is the *minimal* part of G which must be covered if we want the sentence chosen to describe the scene to describe it *adequately*. A *case hierarchy* then determines the manner in which the actants of the Γ_i selected for covering G are taken over at the surface level by grammatical relations. The part of G which is not covered by the selected Γ_i can be described by other sentences (using anaphoric gluing) or by adverbs, subordinate sentences, etc. After their grammaticalization, the nuclear sentences coming from the Γ_i covering G become inputs for some transformational cycles. At this stage the approach is akin to classical symbolic conceptions of grammar.

Archetypal Local Schemes, Universal Unfoldings, and Actantial Graphs
We have seen that Thom's deepest innovation in this new emerging field of topological syntax was to generate the archetypal local schemes Γ_i using universal unfoldings. The linguistic specificity of this theoretical move was very precisely pointed out by Wildgen (1982, pp. 264–265):

The structure of the elementary interactions which are derived from paths in the bifurcation space of elementary catastrophes, defines different roles which can be roughly compared to the "schémas actantiels" proposed by Tesnière and to the "case frames" classified by Fillmore. The basic difference between these structures and the semantic archetypes consists:

1. In the *preverbal* character of archetypes. The structures proposed by Tesnière, Fillmore and others are only generalizations of linguistic structures found in natural languages.

2. The foundations of the classification of archetypes in a formalism which is supposed to be basic for many biological systems. It is therefore universal in a very deep sense and it is of interdisciplinary relevance.

3. The semantic archetypes are *irreducible Gestalts*. They are not composed in a single combinatorial way. This fact constitutes a major difference in Thom's theory as against all theories proposed up to now. Some of these have tried to describe field-like structures, but as no tool for consequently doing so was available they all drove away irresistibly attracted by the static-logical paradigm.

The main advantages of such a point of view are the following.

1. Since elementary interactions between local spatiotemporal actants are mathematically characterizable and classifiable, they provide a theoretical means for *deducing* case universals on the basis of prior basic principles.

2. Since the actantial content of case roles is purely local and positional, one avoids the well-known vicious circle of a semantic interpretation of deep structures that plagues classical case grammars.

3. Since the local content of the same case can *change* according to the topological complexity of the relational scheme where it is located, one can understand that way why it is idle to search for a small list of universal case *labels*.

The Localist Hypothesis   Even if it is not very elegant we keep the traditional term *localist* for qualifying this important linguistic hypothesis. Historically, the localist hypothesis goes back to the byzantine grammarians Theodore Gaza and Maxime Planude (Hjelmslev, 1935; Anderson, 1971; Petitot, 1985a). Its key thesis is that cases are grammatical *and* local determinations. Hjelmslev (1935), its leading supporter among modern linguists after the Kantian linguist Wüllner, claims it "recognizes as equivalent the concrete or local and the abstract or grammatical manifestations" of the case dimensions (e.g., direction as in "source ≡ nominative" and "goal ≡ dative") (p. 15). In fact, Hjelmslev strongly emphasized the necessity of substituting a schematic and iconic spatial conception of syntactic relations for a logical and formal one. The idea of a "space grammar" in the Talmyan or Langackerian sense is very akin to Hjelmslev's structuralist perspective, even though his was more of an axiomatic mind than an intuitive one.

For us, the importance of the localist hypothesis is to root the dynamical theory of actantial graphs in a phenomenology of perception. It has become essential in contemporary cognitive linguistics. Let us take as an example Jackendoff's (1983) conception of the "conceptual structure" and of the "projected world" in his *Semantics and Cognition*. Conceptual structure is a cognitive level of mental representation "at which linguistic, sensory and motor information are compatible" (p. 17). The projected world is the phenomenologically experienced sensible world (considered as a cognitive construction). The analysis of the link between the conceptual structure and the projected world leads to "ontological categories." The projected world is constituted of spatiotemporal /things/, /forms/, /places/, /states/, /events/, /paths/, etc. These primitives are represented in the conceptual structure by constituents like [THING], [FORM], [PLACE], [STATE], [EVENT], [PATH], etc., which process also *nonlinguistic*, e.g., *visual*, sensory information. The deep analysis of the verbal semantics then leads Jackendoff to a version of the localist hypothesis inspired by Gruber: "in any semantic field of [EVENTS] and [STATES], the principal event-, state-, path-, and place-functions are a subset of those used for the analysis of spatial location and motion" (p. 188). After Thom and many biologists such as Osgood and Luria, Jackendoff insists in his turn on the evolutionary content of this hypothesis:

The psychological claim behind this methodology is that the mind does not manufacture abstract concepts out of thin air, aether. It adapts machinery that is already available, both in the development of the individual organism and in the evolutionary development of species (p. 189).
All [EVENTS] and [STATES] in conceptual structure are organized according to a very limited set of principles, drawn primarily from the conceptualization of space (p. 209).

But to conceptualize space is to do geometry. We therefore need a geometric mathematization of the localist hypothesis and this is what can be achieved by means of morphodynamics (Petitot, 1989c).

Some Uses of the External Dynamics: Aspectuality, Agentivity, Modality, and "Force Dynamics" The last contributions of morphodynamics we want to point out in the linguistic realm concern the different uses of the *external spaces* (W, K). First, one can interpret *aspectuality*—the temporal structure of the processes—using such devices (Petitot, 1991c). In a nutshell, the idea is the following. Consider a temporal path $\gamma(t)$ (driven by a slow dynamics) in a universal unfolding (f_w, W, K). The stable states fill reversibly open temporal intervals. The processes fill irreversible temporal intervals. The boundaries of such intervals correspond to the beginning and end of the processes. The events correspond to the actantial interaction points where $\gamma(t)$ crosses the bifurcation set K. Aspectuality is grounded in the topological structure of the temporal line intervals. Here, interval models become models for the topology of the embedded paths $\gamma: I \to (W, K)$ (where I is an interval).

Another problem concerns *agentivity*, that is, the manner according to which intentional agents control actions. It is clear that a purely topological (positional) definition of the actantial case roles is not sufficient. To explain, for instance, the difference between Agent, Beneficiary, Patient, Instrument, etc., we need also *causal* relationships between them. But one of the main interests of the morphodynamical models is that the positional syntactic configurations are derived from internal generating dynamics. Agentivity can then be modeled by a *feedback* of the internal dynamics on *external ones*.

Indeed, as far as it is driven by one of the actants, such a feedback expresses precisely that this actant *controls* the action (the evolution in the control space) and is therefore an agent.

There exists a deep connection between agentivity and *modality*. Brandt (1986) has shown, using Talmy's (1985) theory of *Force Dynamics*, that external dynamics in W can be interpreted as *modal dynamics*. In his seminal work "Force Dynamics in Language and Thought," Talmy has shown that modal systems grammatically specify a dynamical conceptual content concerning the notions of force, obstacle, resistance, clamping, overtaking, cooperation, competition, interaction, etc. The associated schemes are agonistic ones which schematize the possible force relations between actants. Talmy's thesis is that this "force dynamics" constitutes "the semantic category that the modal system as a whole is dedicated to express."

It is easy to model such schemes using morphodynamical models. We consider a canonical model (f_w, W, K) and we suppose: (1) that the actants dispose of an *internal energy*, and (2) that each of them can control some external dynamics on W (many external dynamics being therefore in competition). Their internal energy allows actants to jump over potential barriers and their control of external dynamics allows them to act on the dynamical situation of one another (Brandt, 1986; Petitot, 1989f).

9.4 MORPHODYNAMICS AND COGNITIVE GRAMMAR: FROM IMAGE SCHEMAS TO PERCEPTUAL CONSTITUENCY

We now come to the second part of this chapter. The problem here is to achieve *a computationally effective* version of morphodynamical models and, especially, of their generating internal dynamics. It is a difficult problem, and we will only sketch some elements of its full solution. We first use cognitive grammars for justifying a shift from syntactic constituent structures to *Gestalt-like* ones. We then address the problem of an effective computational solution to the problem of perceptual constituency.

The Scanning of Things, Relations, and Processes

We have seen that the dynamical syntax yielded by morphodynamics shares many features with cognitive grammars in the sense of Langacker, Talmy, et al. Let us make this point more explicit. According to Langacker, cognitive grammar is a perceptually rooted "space grammar." It is also a "natural" (as opposed to "formal") grammar. Syntactic structures are conceived of "organically rather than prosthetically" (Langacker, 1987, p. 12). Constituency is not, as in logic, an affair of symbolic combination, but rather, as in biology, an affair of internal self-organization.

1. As Langacker explains at the beginning of volume 2 of his *Foundations* (1991), "a speaker's linguistic knowledge (his internal grammar) is not conceived as an algorithmic constructive device giving (all and only) well-formed

expressions as 'output'" (p. 2). It is rather a set of *cognitive routines* which allow the speaker to schematize and categorize the usage events. Linguistic structures are essentially schematic and figurative. The correlated image schemas are simultaneously iconic *and* abstract structures.

2. It is impossible to separate syntax and semantics. "Grammar (or Syntax) does not constitute an autonomous formal level of representation" (Langacker, 1987, p. 2). Syntax is not an autonomous component but a high-level mode of schematization and categorization. Grammatical relations must therefore be defined not prototypically in terms of categorial labels but schematically as modes of constructing and profiling (i.e., organizing in a Gestalt manner) the complex structure of scenes.

3. At the cognitive level, the most basic processing operation of cognitive grammar is *scanning*, i.e., *a local operation of contrast detection*. Scanning is "an ubiquitous process of comparison and registration of contrast that occurs continuously throughout the various domains of active cognitive functioning" (Langacker, 1987, p. 116). It picks up qualitative discontinuities and builds from them a schematic imagery which is at the same time linguistic *and* perceptual.

4. In cognitive grammar, linguistic units are identified as parts of domains which are themselves based on *basic domains* (space, time, sensible qualities such as color, etc.) endowed with some sort of *geometric* structure. "By definition, basic domains occupy the lowest level in hierarchies of conceptual complexity: they furnish the primitive representational space necessary for the emergence of any specific conception" (Langacker, 1987, p. 149). At the most basic level, concepts are therefore *positions*—"locations"—or *configurations* in some geometric (topological, differentiable, metric, linear) manifold.

Let us recall briefly how Langacker defines *things*, *relations*, and *processes*.

Things   A thing is "a region in some domain" (Langacker, 1987, p. 189). As in Gestalt theory, it is profiled on a ground by means of a boundary. Its scanning is exactly that of a *morphology* (W, K) in the Thomian sense (see section 9.3). A first scanning scans the regular points interior to the domain, another, the exterior regular points, and a third, the singular points of the boundary.

Relations   What is then the profiling of a relation? In a relational profile there exists an asymmetry between a salient figure—called a "trajector"—and the other parts of the profile, which act as "landmarks." According to Langacker (1987), all static relations are reducible to four "basic conceptual relations": identity [A ID B], inclusion [A IN B], separation [A OUT B], and association [A ASSOC B] (figure 9.6). It must be stressed that these relations are positional ones. They are the basic possible spatial relations of co-location. The relation of association deserves particular attention. In a relation of separation [A OUT B], A and B are in some sense independent of one another. They do not constitute a whole individually. On the contrary, in a relation

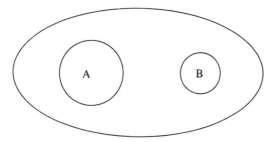

Figure 9.6 A relation of "association" according to Langacker (1987).

of association [A ASSOC B], one of the entities, the "trajector" (e.g., A) is localized relative to the other, the "landmark." As we shall see, this fact is essential.

Processes   Processes describe temporal sequences of profiled relations. Let us consider as an example the Langackerian schematization of a process like [ENTER] (figure 9.7). It is clear in this example that "a process is a relationship scanned sequentially during its evolution through conceived time" (Langacker, 1987, p. 254). If the conceived time is the real time of the process, the scanning is *sequential*. If the different states of the process are conceived "in parallel," then the scanning is "*synchronous*." What we have seen in the discussion of the uses of external dynamics about *aspectuality* is, of course, directly applicable to such temporal profiles.

Summarizing, cognitive grammar leads to the following identifications:

1. Terms (fillers) ≡ *localized domains* in some concrete or abstract space.

2. Relations ≡ *positional* relations between locations.

3. Processes ≡ *temporal deformations* of positional relations.

4. Events ≡ *interactions* between locations.

5. Agentivity ≡ *causal control* of the (inter)actions.

6. Semantic roles ≡ *types* of transformations and controlled interactions (configurational definition).

We see that there is a remarkable convergence with morphodynamical models.

The Main Problem

We take for granted that cognitive grammar is a correct linguistic theory (or at least a plausible one). The problem becomes therefore the following: (1) How are the image schemas of cognitive grammar to be mathematized? (2) What sort of computational devices are able to scan not only regions in domains (static things) but also relations, processes, events, and controls? This problem is not trivial because the positional relations of location and their temporal transformations are global, continuous, Gestalt-like (holistic), and

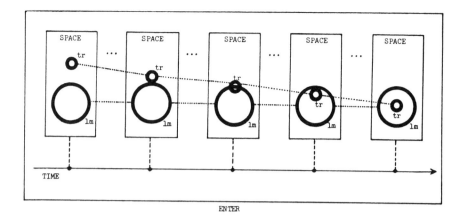

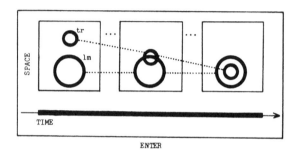

Figure 9.7 The temporal profile of the process [ENTER]. (From Langacker, 1987.)

informationally infinite configurations which nevertheless must be scanned by *local* algorithms using only informationally *finite* devices. We call this *the global Gestalt/local computation dilemma*. How can we find a mathematical escape from it? We address this issue here only in what concerns its *topological* part. We leave aside the feedback of internal to external dynamics.

The Reduction of the Main Problem to Perceptual Constituency

To solve the problem we first reduce it to the perceptual basis of cognitive grammar. We identify positional actants with topologically defined domains in two-dimensional space and we consider configurations $A_1, \ldots, A_n$ of such domains. These configurations can evolve in time. The problem is therefore to scan their relational profiles and their temporal ones.

To achieve this task we make a basic assumption: *we treat configurations as forms*, i.e., as patterns. The problem now becomes: *Are local and finite pattern recognition algorithms able to perform the scanning of relational and temporal profiles*? We recognize here *the central problem of Gestalt theory*: to find a field-theoretical basis for understanding the emergence of the global properties of patterns.

We propose a solution of this main problem in three steps. (1) We first consider some well-known algorithms of computational vision. (2) We then show how some of their generalizations allow us to solve the problem. (3) We show that such a solution is essentially an implementation of the morphodynamical models for syntax.

9.5 CONTOUR DETECTION AND DIFFUSION VISUAL ROUTINES

Our computational problem is now to find, in a principled way, local algorithms which are able to extract in a bottom-up and data-driven manner the global positional information contained in a configuration of domains. To achieve this, we generalize some well-certified algorithms of computational vision. We shall see that there exist devices which can construct from the data *virtual structures* which give rise to a *perceptual-syntactic constituency*.

Boundary Detection and Wavelet Analysis

The first computational vision device we want to introduce is the *wavelet analysis* algorithm. It is well known that the retina performs an important compression of the visual information provided by photoreceptors. The ganglion cells (whose axons are the fibers of the optic nerve) receive through the intermediary bipolar cells (plus the lateral horizontal and amacrine cells forming the plexiform layers) the signal transduced by the photoreceptors. They operate on the signal as filters, by convoluting it with the profile of their receptive field (RF). Now, it is a fundamental fact of neurophysiology that these RFs have a center/periphery antagonist structure: if a ray of light hitting the center of its RF excites/inhibits the cell, then a ray of light hitting its periphery inhibits/excites it. The cells of the first type are called ON-center (and OFF-surround) and the cells of the second type are called OFF-center (and ON-surround). After processing by the RFs of the ganglion cells, the signal is transmitted to the visual cortex with a good retinotopy up to the hypercolumns of the primary visual cortex (striate area) (Buser-Imbert, 1987).

What type of information processing is performed by the layers of retinal ganglion cells? At the end of the 1970s, David Marr (1982) introduced the deep idea of a *multiscale detection of qualitative discontinuities* by means of what he called the *zero-crossing* criterion.

Mathematically, the center/periphery profiles of the RFs approximate *Laplacians of Gaussians*, ΔG (figure 9.8). Now, let $f(x)$ be a smooth function on $\mathbb{R}$ presenting a "discontinuity" at x_0, i.e., a sharp variation. At x_0, the first derivative $f'(x)$ presents a peak (a Dirac distribution δ if x_0 is a true discontinuity) and the second derivative $f''(x)$ presents two peaks (one positive, the other negative) surrounding a zero-crossing (figure 9.9). Let $I(x, y)$ be the input pattern (the pixelized retinal image). The convolution $G * I$ of I by a Gaussian $G(r) = \exp(-r^2/2\pi\sigma^2)$ (where r is the distance to the center of G, and σ is the width of G) corresponds to a *smoothing* of I at a certain scale.

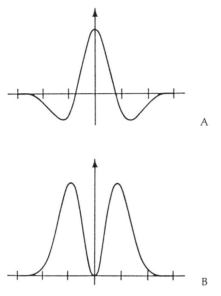

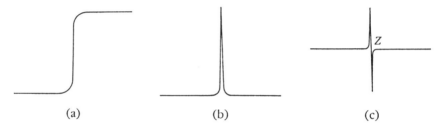

Figure 9.8 *A*. A one-dimensional Laplacian of Gaussian. *B*. Its Fourier transform.

Figure 9.9 A qualitative discontinuity characterized as a zero-crossing. (*a*) The discontinuity of the function *f*. (*b*) The peak of its first derivative *f′*. (*c*) The two peaks and the zero-crossing of its second derivative *f″*. (From Marr, 1982.)

Taking the Laplacian $\Delta(G * I)$ corresponds to taking the second derivative. It extracts locally the zero-crossings of the *G*-smoothed signal $G * I$. But $\Delta(G * I) = \Delta G * I$, with

$$\Delta G = -\frac{1}{\pi\sigma^2}\left(1 - \frac{r^2}{\pi\sigma^2}\right)\exp\left(-\frac{r^2}{2\pi\sigma^2}\right).$$

Hence, the two operations of smoothing and of extracting the zero-crossings at the corresponding scale can be performed using a unique operation: the convolution by an RF profile of the form ΔG (figure 9.10). With its many layers of ganglion cells operating at different scales, the retina can therefore perform a local and multiscale extraction of qualitative discontinuities. In fact, Marr's algorithm was one of the first examples of what is now called a *wavelet analysis*.[9] Wavelet analysis is a sort of Fourier analysis that is spatially localized and multiscale, and that is able to extract the singularities encoded

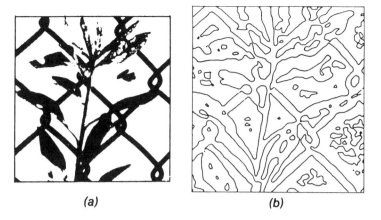

Figure 9.10 The smoothing of an image and the extraction of the qualitative discontinuities at the corresponding scale by means of the zero-crossing criterion. (From Marr, 1982.)

in a signal. As Mallat (1989) emphasized, the wavelet transform can characterize the type of local singularities and detect the signal's sharper variations. With such devices it is possible to compress an image in an intrinsic way, i.e., according to its specific structure.

The main fact we want to stress here regarding Marr's conception and wavelet analysis is that the compression of information, which is an information-processing constraint, appears identical to a morphological analysis, which is a geometric objective fact. The morphological representation of the images, obtained in a bottom-up and data-driven manner by extracting qualitative discontinuities by means of wavelet analysis, provides the basis for more symbolic, higher-level, representations. As Marr (1982) stressed: "the zero crossing provides a natural way of moving from an analogue or continuous representation like the two-dimensional image intensity values $I(x, y)$ to a discrete, symbolic representation" (p. 67).

Diffusion and the Structure of Images

We have just seen that, at the early stages of vision, edge detection is locally processed. At successive levels, global edges are interpreted as boundaries and contours.[10] Indeed, the first general algorithm we want to use for our purpose is *contour detection*.

But we need also a second general algorithm which will allow us to go from the local level to the global one. We need a fieldlike process which produces global emerging structures from local interactions. For this we turn to the multiscale analysis of images proposed by Witkin (1983) and Koenderink (1984) under the name of "scale-space filtering" and "Gaussian blurring."

Let $I(x, y)$ be an image, i.e., a luminance pattern (we adopt here a continuous, not pixelized, approximation). Koenderink's main idea is to embed I in a

Transfer potential

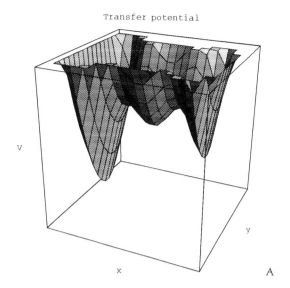

A

Contour Levels

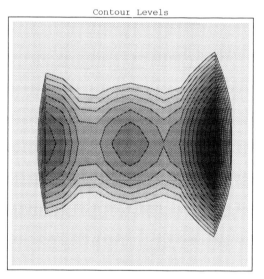

B

C

smooth *family* $F(x, y; s) = I_s(x, y)$ (*s* being a scale $\in [0, 1]$) in such a manner that: (1) $I_0 = I$ (initial condition); (2) I_1 is an undifferentiated blob, an image without any internal structure; and (3) the smooth process of simplification (of dedifferentiation) is as canonical and as straightforward as possible (i.e., an optimal one among all the possibilities).

Let us suppose that one has found such a deformation $I_0 \to I_1$ of I. Then the inverse deformation $I_1 \to I_0$ can be identified with a *morphogenesis* of I, i.e., with a process of progressive and successive differentiations that leads from an initial blob to the full morphology of I.

The constraint (3) can be interpreted as a sort of *causality condition*. One can show that the simplest way to satisfy it is to let the deformation $F = I_s$ be a solution of the *diffusion equation* (heat equation) $\partial_s F = \Delta F$. In fact, Yuille and Poggio (1986) have shown that diffusion according to the heat equation is the simplest way of globally simplifying an image *without introducing new zero-crossings*. Indeed, as was stressed by Hummel and Moniot (1989), this causality constraint on the evolution of the zero-crossings expresses the maximum principle for the heat equation.

Now, it is well known that the kernel of the heat equation is a Gaussian. The family I_s is therefore obtained as the convolution of the initial image I_0 by a family G_s of Gaussians which blur it progressively. This Gaussian blurring is a sort of multiresolution (multiscale) blurring. It leads from a fine-grained initial image to a coarse-grained final one. As Koenderink (1984) claims, "Gaussian blurring is the only sensible way to embed a primal image into a one-parameter family" (p. 365).

Consider the decomposition of the surface $z = I(x, y)$ [the graph of the function $I(x, y)$] into level curves L_z (figure 9.11). If $I(x, y)$ is a smooth function, these level curves are constituted by nested and juxtaposed topological circles and, as is proved in Morse theory (see below), the crossings of the critical points of I as z increases correspond to transformations of the *topological type* of the L_z: when z crosses a minimum/maximum of I a new component appears/vanishes, and when z crosses a saddle point two components fuse into one, or vice versa. When we blur $I(x, y)$ in a Gaussian way, the components of the L_z progressively fuse until one reaches a unique blob whose L_z are concentric topological circles. The fusion process corresponds to a well-defined sequence of bifurcation events: successive vanishings of components through collapse of minima and maxima with saddles. As Koenderink (1984) says, "the image can be described unambiguously as a set of nested and juxtaposed light and dark blobs that vanish in a well defined sequence on progressive blurring" (p. 369). Such a dynamic and morphogenetic analysis of the image yields a *constituent structure* analysis. It can be easily implemented.

Figure 9.11 Examples of level curves of a surface. *A.* A potential occurring in the scenario of transfer of an object between a source and a goal. *B.* Its level curves. *C.* The level curves of a natural image.

Singularity theory (discussed in section 9.3) provides normal algebraic forms for the possible bifurcations occurring in the geometric analysis of I and of the I_s by means of their level curves $L_{s,z}$.[11] These normal forms make use of partial derivatives of the convolutions $I_s = I * G_s$ up to degree 4 only. We have only to generalize Marr's use of the second derivatives of $I * G_s$, and consider layers of cells whose receptive profiles are partial derivative of Gaussians.

9.6 CONTOUR DIFFUSION, SINGULARITY THEORY, AND PERCEPTUAL CONSTITUENCY

The General Strategy for Solving the Main Problem

We suppose first that visual algorithms have already transformed a visual scene into a configuration of domains (blobs profiled on a ground). They are not only algorithms of Marr's or Koenderink's type, but also, e.g., algorithms convexifying the objects. We use then the two algorithms of contour detection and diffusion *as general cognitive ones*. Indeed, they are algorithms which perform the transition from the local level to the global level starting from initial conditions provided by the scanning of qualitative discontinuities. In other words, even if the processing of spatial relations is modular and therefore different from that of shape analysis, we use nevertheless the same sort of algorithms as routines for a bottom-up and data-driven process of relation-pattern recognition and we show that they permit us to solve our main problem (see above).

In general, these algorithms are used in computational vision according to a *coarse-to-fine* strategy. However, for extracting the positional information contained in syntactic image schemas we shall use them according to a *fine-to-coarse* strategy (see Petitot, 1991b, 1993). Let $\mathscr{A} = \{A_1, \ldots, A_n\}$ be a configuration of regions in the plane. Let $B_i = \partial A_i$ be the respective boundaries of the A_i. From them we trigger a process of contour diffusion. This makes them propagate. The main idea is then to focus on the *singularities* of the propagation. They are *local and finitely characterizable* entities which can generically be detected and addressed by *point* processors. Now the key point is that mathematical theorems show that *these critical data characterize the global configurations $\mathscr{A}$*. They provide for them local and finite necessary and sufficient conditions. They permit us therefore to escape the "global Gestalt/local computation" dilemma.

Contour Diffusion and Morse Theory

Contour Diffusion   Let us consider the simplest example, that of Langacker's relation of *association* (see figure 9.6). We start with two domains A_1 and A_2 (with respective boundaries B_1 and B_2) included in a superordinate

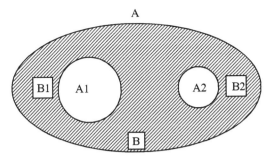

Figure 9.12 A relation of association (A_1, A_2, A).

domain A (with boundary B) (figure 9.12). Initially the distribution of activity $I(x, y)$ is therefore equal to 1 inside A_1 and A_2 and to 0 outside. We trigger a diffusion process I_s, the value of I_s being clamped to 1 inside the A_i (the A_i are identified with constant sources). We consider then the diffusion fronts B^s. There are many ways to define them. For instance, we can consider the level curves L_z of I_s for $z = h_s$, where h_s is some indicator of the separation figure/ ground (profile/base). We can also take the curves where the gradient ΔI_s of I_s has a maximal norm $\|\Delta I_s\|$. We can also modify the diffusion equation (see below). During the diffusion, the virtual contours B^s propagate. For some value of s (that we can normalize to $s = 1$), B^s will play the role of the outer contour B.

The diffusion process permits us to construct a *continuous deformation* (what in differential topology is called a *cobordism*) between the initial boundary $B^0 = B_1 + B_2$ and the final boundary $B^1 = B$. This analysis of the configuration $\mathscr{A} = \{A, A_1, A_2\}$ is of the same type as the analysis of images: we treat configurations as image patterns and we apply the dynamical and morphogenetic analysis of section 9.5.

Now the initial and final contours B^0 and B^1 *are not of the same topological type*. There exists, therefore, a *critical value c* of s for which the diffusion front B^c is critical. B^c makes the transition between the fronts B^s $s < c$, which have two components, and the fronts B^s $s > c$, which have only one component. It presents a saddle-type singularity (figure 9.13). But in Morse theory one can prove the following result: A configuration $\mathscr{A}$ is an association relation iff the contour diffusion process presents only one singularity which is of the saddle type. We have therefore succeeded in solving the main problem in this elementary but fundamental case. In fact, we can generalize the solution to the following construct.

We have considered up to now only the external (outward) contour diffusion. From the initial boundaries B_1 and B_2 we can also trigger an internal (inward) contour diffusion. ("External" and "internal" are used here in their naive sense, and not in their dynamical one.) The critical points of this secondary diffusion are the centers of the initial blobs. If we suppose that these inward propagating contours B^s correspond to decreasing s, we construct

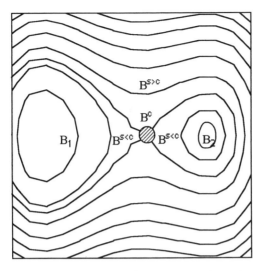

Figure 9.13 A contour diffusion triggered by a relation of association. Observe in the center of the configuration the saddle singularity of the critical diffusion front.

in this way a *potential function* $f_{\mathscr{A}}: \mathbb{R}^2 \to \mathbb{R}$. The B^s are its level curves. The initial boundary $B_1 + B_2 = B^0$ corresponds to a particular level curve $f_{\mathscr{A}} = c_0$ and the outward/inward propagating contours B^s to level curves $f_{\mathscr{A}} = c$ with $c > c_0/c < c_0$. (We can normalize taking $c = s$.) The graph of $f_{\mathscr{A}}$ has the qualitative global shape of a potential pit with A_1 and A_2 as sub-pits. We call $f_{\mathscr{A}}$ the *generating potential* of the configuration $\mathscr{A} = \{A, A_1, A_2\}$ (figure 9.14). In short, the contour diffusion routine applied to a configuration $\mathscr{A}$ constructs a generating potential $f_{\mathscr{A}}$ for $\mathscr{A}$.[12]

The Scanning of Cognitive Grammar's Image Schemas We can now explicitly scan, using only local algorithms, the image schemas of cognitive grammar.

1. For the profiling of the domains, the problem of scanning was already solved (boundary detection).

2. For the profiling of the positional relations, the scanning consists in extracting the singularities of a contour diffusion process and in constructing the generating potential associated with it.

3. Once this main problem is solved, one scans processes in considering temporal deformations of contour diffusion processes and of generating potentials. The contour diffusion processes constitute *fast internal dynamics* and their temporal evolutions *slow external dynamics* in the sense explained in section 9.3 under Fast/Slow Dynamics.

4. The events can then be explicitly scanned as *bifurcation* events happening to the generating potentials. They change the topological type of the potentials and can therefore be identified with actantial *interactions*.

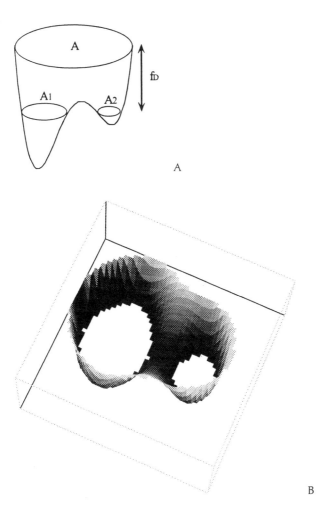

A

B

Figure 9.14 The generating potential of a relation of association. *A*. The complete potential. *B*. A perspective view of its restriction f_D to the domain $A - A_1 \cup A_2$.

Figure 9.15 shows the slow dynamics driving the fast dynamics of contour levels. This yields a dynamical scanning of the "capture" process displayed in figure 9.4, and of Langacker's [ENTER] image schema in figure 9.7. We think that this dynamically grounded scanning of syntactic Gestalten is the most straightforward one. Using a boundary diffusion process, i.e., *a dynamical system defined on the functional space of the intensity patterns* $I(x, y)$, we have explicitly constructed Lyapunov functions f defined on the visual field M. These f are the generating dynamics of the morphodynamical models.[13]

The approach to solving the main problem (see above) described so far relies on one of the best-known equations of diffusion propagation, the heat equation. It is also possible to implement this general strategy using an alternative, the wave equation, $\partial^2 I_s / \partial s^2 = \Delta I_s$. This "optical" approach (what is called the "grassfire" model) has been worked out in detail by Blum (1973) in his pioneering work "Biological Shape in Visual Science." It leads to the

Morphodynamics and Attractor Syntax

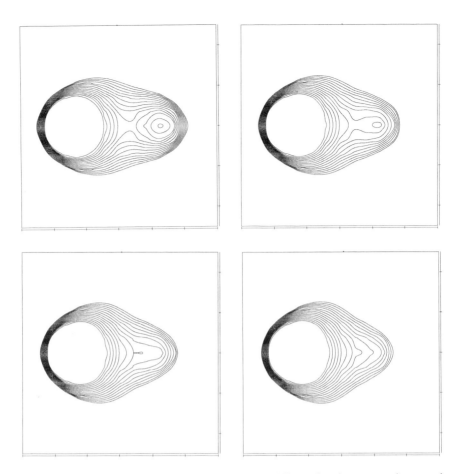

Figure 9.15 The slow dynamics driving the contour diffusion fast dynamics in the case of an event of "capture." The saddle point drifts slowly toward the dominant place and bifurcates.

analysis of the singular locus of the propagation process (what is called the *symmetry axis*, or the *cut locus*, or also the *skeleton* of the shape under consideration). It has been implemented by our student Hugh Bellemare (1991).

9.7   CONCLUSION: TOWARD A COMPUTATIONALLY EFFECTIVE ATTRACTOR SYNTAX

We have shown how the topological basis of an attractor syntax can be implemented. The idea was to represent *relations* by *singularities* of a diffusion-propagation process triggered by the detection of boundaries. With such effective models at hand we can easily construct actantial graphs (see section 9.3) and therefore combinatorial structures that share the combinatorial properties and the systematicity requirements characteristic of symbolic structures. We can also in a second step implement external control dynamics to achieve a causal theory of agentivity.

Regier (1988) has also used a contour diffusion routine for analyzing the cognitive (perceptual and semantic) content of prepositions such as "in," "above," etc. George Lakoff (1988) has generalized his idea to the conjecture that "Ullman-style visual routines[14] ... are sufficient to characterize all known structures in cognitive topology" (p. 304). We believe we have demonstrated the truth of this conjecture for actantial interactions.

In a nutshell, we have shown that by adding to higher levels of computational vision a new module performing contour diffusion and singularity extraction, it is possible to build a bottom-up and data-driven theory of "perceptual" constituency. Relations are encoded in virtual singularities, which organize image schemas, which are themselves linguistically grammaticalized in predicative structures. It will perhaps seem difficult to accept the cognitive relevance of virtual singular structures. Since Gestalt theory, however, it has become a widely confirmed experimental fact that virtual boundaries are essential for perceptual structuring. Moreover, detailed analysis of the relationships between language and perception has shown that many virtual structures are linguistically encoded. We think in particular of Talmy's recent work showing that an astonishing number and variety of schematic and virtual abstract Gestalten are linguistically expressed and play a fundamental role in our conceptualization of the world. These "fictive" lines, surfaces, and motions make the sentences describing scenes and states of affairs not only descriptors of real perceptual contents but true "organizing Gestalts."

We have thus shown that it is possible to work out a dynamical conception of constituent structures using virtual constructs which share the properties of a formal "syntacticity." These geometric constructs do possess an internal structure; moreover, their generating physical mechanisms are "structure-sensitive."

ACKNOWLEDGMENTS

This work has benefited from many discussions with Daniel Andler, Hugh Bellemare, Elie Bienenstock, and Yves Marie Visetti in the context of the DSCC (*Dynamical Systems, Connectionism, and Cognition*) project of the *Centre de Recherche en Épistémologie Appliquée*. It owes much to René Thom's seminal ideas. My joint research with Jean-Pierre Desclés is also essential. It has also taken great advantage of the two Royaumont meetings, *Compositionality in Cognition and Neural Networks*, organized by Daniel Andler, Elie Bienenstock, and Bernard Laks (May 1991 and June 1992), and of two other meetings, *Motivation in Language*, organized by Umberto Eco and Patrizia Violi at the *International Center for Semiotic and Cognitive Studies* in San Marino (December 1990), and *Le Continu en Sémantique linguistique*, organized by Bernard Victorri at the University of Caen (June 1992). It was great to have the opportunity for discussions with Len Talmy, Barry Smith, Ron Langacker, Per Aage Brandt,

Franson Manjali, Paul Smolensky, and George Lakoff. Particular thanks are due to Tim van Gelder and Bob Port for their very constructive suggestions.

NOTES

1. The particular status of dynamical explanations, contrasting with the deductive-nomological ones, has been stressed by van Gelder (1992). The epistemological problems raised by a dynamical interpretation of basic theoretical concepts such as *structure, constituency,* and *syntax* have been analyzed with care by Andler (1990), Bienenstock (1992), and Visetti (1990). They are not exclusively linguistic. They arise also in the realm of perception.

2. We think especially of Smolensky's (1990) *tensor product* and of the idea of *dynamical binding* by means of synchronized oscillatory neural groups developed by Edelman (1987), von der Malsburg, Bienenstock (1986), and Shastri (1990).

3. Dynamical systems and singularities of differentiable maps constitute very technical and difficult topics. For mathematical details, see e.g., Thom (1972); Zeeman (1977); Golubitsky-Guillemin (1973); Arnold, Varchenko, and Goussein-Zade (1985); Chenciner (1980, 1985); Petitot (1992).

4. This property was used by David Ruelle and Floris Takens in the early 1970s for their new theory of turbulence. The idea that the attractors of a general dissipative dynamical system are complex has been deepened by the recognition that these attractors can be *self-organized critical states* characterized by critical exponents and scaling laws. Self-organization provides *emergent structures*. For an introduction to critical phenomena, see Petitot (1992) and its bibliography. For an introduction to the various theories of emergence, see EMG (1992). For self-organized critical states, see Bak et al. (1988) and Zurek (1990).

5. A good example is that of phonological structures in phonetics. Categorical perception of phonemes is a perceptive case of critical phenomena (see Petitot, 1989a).

6. For a discussion of the traditional conflict between physical objectivity and the phenomenal world, see, e.g., Putnam (1987), Smith (1993), Petitot and Smith (1991), and Petitot (1992, chapter 3).

7. It is this dynamical interpretation of relations between entities via a generating potential which is of the utmost technical and philosophical importance. It constitutes the hard core of Thom's "morphodynamical turn."

8. Roman Jakobson, who, as far as I know, was, with Waddington, the first to support the advances of this outstanding mathematical genius outside the domain of hard sciences, said (see Holenstein, 1992) that he acknowledged three "great structuralists": Prince Troubetzkoy, Claude Lévi-Strauss, and René Thom.

9. For an introduction to wavelet analysis, see Meyer (1988, 1989) and Mallat (1989).

10. The neural computations needed for these perceptual tasks implement sophisticated geometric algorithms belonging to theories such as singularity and jet theories (see Petitot, 1990a).

11. In fact, the problem of finding algebraic normal forms for the bifurcations that can occur generically in the level curves of solutions of the heat equation is more complex. As was shown by Damon (1988), the Thom-Mather theory of universal unfoldings must be technically adapted to "scale-space filtering."

12. In fact, the problem of contour diffusion in scale-space analysis is mathematically rather technical. Many aspects of it have been developed only recently. The evolution of contour levels in a contour diffusion process is driven by partial differential equations that are in general

more complex than the simple heat equation (see, e.g., Grayson, 1987; Osher and Sethian, 1988; and Alvarez, Lions, and Morel, 1992).

13. Two completely different levels of "dynamics" must be distinguished here. The generating potentials f and their unfoldings f_w generate constituents and relations in M. But they are themselves produced by dynamical processes which take place on functional spaces.

14. See Ullman (1984).

REFERENCES

Alvarez, L., Lions, P. L., and Morel, J. M., (1992). Image selective smoothing and edge detection by non linear diffusion. *SIAM Journal of Numerical Analysis, 29*, 845–866.

Anderson, J. M. (1971). *The grammar of case, towards a localistic theory.* Cambridge University Press.

Andler, D. (1990). Connexionnisme et cognition: à la recherche des bonnes questions. *Revue de Synthèse, 4*, 1–2, 95–127.

Andler, D., Bienenstock, E., and Laks, B. (Eds.) (1991). *Interdisciplinary Workshop on Compositionality in Cognition and Neural Networks, I.* Abbaye de Royaumont, France.

Andler, D., Bienenstock, E., and Laks, B. (Eds.) (1992). *Interdisciplinary Workshop on Compositionality in Cognition and Neural Networks, II.* Abbaye de Royaumont, France.

Andler, D., Petitot, J., and Visetti, Y.-M. (1991). Dynamical systems, connectionism and linguistics. In D. Andler, E. Bienenstock, and B. Laks (Eds.), *Interdisciplinary Workshop on Compositionality in Cognition and Neural Networks I.* Abbaye de Royaumont, France.

Arnold, V. I., Varchenko, A., and Goussein-Zade, S. (1985). *Singularities of differentiable maps, I.* Boston: Birkhäuser.

Bak, P., Tang, C., and Wiesenfeld, K. (1988). Self-organized criticality. *Physical Review, 38*, 364–374.

Bellemare, H. (1991). *Processus de diffusion en perception visuelle.* (Technical report.) Paris: École des Hautes Études en Sciences Sociales.

Bienenstock, E. (1992). Suggestions for a neurobiological approach to syntax. In D. Andler, E. Bienenstock, and B. Laks (Eds.), *Interdisciplinary Workshop on Compositionality in Cognition and Neural Networks II.* Abbaye de Royaumont, France.

Blum, H. (1973). Biological shape and visual science. *Journal of Theoretical Biology, 38*, 205–287.

Brandt, P-A., (1986). *La charpente modale du sens.* Doctoral thesis. University of Paris III. (John Benjamins, 1992).

Buser, P., and Imbert, M. (1987). *Vision.* Paris: Hermann.

Castrigiano, D. P. L., and Hayes, S. A. (1993). *Catastrophe theory.* Reading, MA: Addison-Wesley.

Chenciner, A. (1980). Singularités des fonctions différentiables. In *Encyclopædia universalis.*

Chenciner, A. (1985). Systèmes dynamiques différentiables. In *Encyclopædia universalis.*

Damon, J. (1988). *Local Morse theory for solutions to the heat equation and Gaussian blurring.* (Technical report.) Chapel Hill: University of North Carolina.

Desclés, J-P. (1990). *Languages applicatifs, Langues naturelles et cognition.* Paris: Hermès.

Edelman, G. M. (1987). *Neural Darwinism. The theory of neuronal group selection.* New York: Basic Books.

EMG, (1992). *Emergence dans les modèles de la cognition.* A. Grumbach and E. Bonabeau (Eds.). Paris: Telecom.

Fillmore, C. (1977). The case for case reopened. In P. Cole and J. M. Saddock (Eds.), *Syntax and Semantics, 8, Grammatical Relations* (pp. 59–81).

Golubitsky, M., and Guillemin, V. (1973). *Stable mappings and their singularities.* New York: Springer Verlag.

Grayson, M. (1987). The heat equation shrinks embedded plane curves to round points. *Journal of Differential Geometry, 26,* 285–314.

Hirsch, M. (1989). Convergent activation dynamics in continuous time networks. *Neural Networks, 2,* 331–349.

Hjelmslev, L. (1935). *La catégorie des cas.* Munich, Wilhelm Fink Verlag [reprinted 1972].

Holenstein, E. (1992). Phenomenological structuralism and cognitive semiotics. In R. Benatti (Ed.), *Scripta Semiotica,* Vol. 1 (pp. 133–158) Peter Lang.

Hummel, R., and Moniot, R. (1989). Reconstruction from zero-crossings in scale space. *IEEE Transactions on Acoustics, Speech and Signal Processing, 37:* 2111–2130.

Jackendoff, R. (1983). *Semantics and cognition.* Cambridge, MA: MIT Press.

Jackendoff, R. (1987). *Consciousness and the computational mind.* Cambridge, MA: MIT Press.

Koenderink, J. J. (1984). The structure of images. *Biological Cybernetics, 50,* 363–370.

Lakoff, G. (1988). A suggestion for a linguistics with connectionist foundations. In *Proceedings of the 1988 Connectionist Models Summer School.* Los Gatos, CA: Morgan Kaufman.

Langacker, R. (1987). *Foundations of cognitive grammar,* Vol. 1. Stanford, CA: Stanford University Press.

Langacker, R. (1991). *Foundations of cognitive grammar,* Vol. 2. Stanford, CA: Stanford University Press.

Mallat, S. G. (1989). Multifrequency channel decomposition of images and wavelet models. IEEE *Transactions on Acoustics, Speech, and Signal Processing, 37,* 2091–2110.

Manjali, F. (1991). *Nuclear semantics.* New-Dehli: Bahri.

Marr, D. (1982). *Vision.* San Francisco: Freeman.

Meyer, Y. (1988). *Ondelettes et opérateurs.* Paris: Hermann.

Meyer, Y. (1989). Ondelettes, filtres miroirs en quadrature et traitement numérique de l'image. *Gazette des Mathématiciens, 40,* 31–42.

Osher, S., and Sethian, J. A. (1988). Fronts propagating with curvature-dependent speed: algorithms based on Hamilton-Jacobi formulations. *Journal of Computational Physics, 79,* 12–49.

Parisi, D. (1991). Emerging compositionality in neural nets. In D. Andler, E. Bienenstock, and B. Laks (Eds.), *Interdisciplinary Workshop on Compositionality in Cognition and Neural Networks I* (pp. 90–98). Abbaye de Royaumont, France.

Petitot, J. (1979). Hypothèse localiste et théorie des catastrophes. In M. Piatelli (Ed.), *Théories du language, théories de l'apprentissage.* Paris: Le Seuil.

Petitot, J. (1982). *Pour un schématisme de la structure.* Doctoral thesis. Paris: École des Hautes Études en Sciences Sociales.

Petitot, J. (1985a). *Morphogenèse du sens.* Paris: Presses Universitaires de France.

Petitot, J. (1985b). *Les catastrophes de la parole.* Paris: Maloine.

Petitot, J. (1986). Structure. In T. Sebeok (Ed.), *Encyclopedic dictionary of semiotics* Vol. 2 (pp. 991–1022). New York: de Gruyter.

Petitot, J. (1989a). Morphodynamics and the categorical perception of phonological units. *Theoretical Linguistics, 15,* 25–71.

Petitot, J. (1989b). On the linguistic import of catastrophe theory. *Semiotica, 74,* 179–209.

Petitot, J. (1989c). Hypothèse localiste, modèles morphodynamiques et théories cognitives: remarques sur une note de 1975. *Semiotica, 77,* 65–119.

Petitot, J. (1989d). Structuralisme et phénoménologie. In J. Petitot (Ed.), *Logos et théorie des catastrophes* (pp. 345–376). Geneva: Editions Patiño.

Petitot, J. (1989e). Catastrophe theory and semio-narrative structures. In P. Perron and F. Collins (Eds.), *Paris school of semiotics* (pp. 177–212). Amsterdam: Benjamins.

Petitot, J. (1989f). Modèles morphodynamiques pour la grammaire cognitive et la sémiotique modale. *RSSI, 9,* 17–51.

Petitot, J. (1989g). Forme. In *Encyclopædia universalis,* Vol. 11 (pp. 712–728).

Petitot, J. (Ed.) (1989h). *Logos et théorie des catastrophes.* Geneva: Editions Patiño.

Petitot, J. (1990a). Le physique, le morphologique, le symbolique. Remarques sur la vision. *Revue de Synthèse, 1-2,* 139–183.

Petitot, J. (Ed.) (1990b). Sciences cognitives: quelques aspects problématiques. Revue de Synthèse, 4, 1–2.

Petitot, J. (1991a). Why connectionism is such a good thing. A criticism of Fodor's and Pylyshyn's criticism of Smolensky. *Philosophica, 47,* 49–79.

Petitot, J. (1991b). Syntaxe topologique et grammaire cognitive. *Langages, 103,* 97–128.

Petitot, J. (1991c). Le schématisme morphodynamique de l'aspectualité. In J. Fontanille (Ed.), *Le discours aspectualisé* (pp. 177–193). Amsterdam: Benjamins.

Petitot, J. (1992). *Physique du sens.* Paris: Editions du CNRS.

Petitot, J. (1993). Natural dynamical models for natural cognitive grammars. In F. Manjali (Ed.), *Language and cognition* (pp. 81–104). New Dehli: Bahri.

Petitot, J., and Smith, B. (1991). New foundations for qualitative physics. In J. E. Tiles, G. J. McKee and G. C. Dean (Eds.), *Evolving knowledge in natural science and artificial intelligence* (pp. 231–249). London: Pitman.

Putnam, H. (1987). *The many faces of realism.* LaSalle: Open Court.

Pylyshyn, Z. (1986). *Computation and cognition.* Cambridge, MA: MIT Press.

Regier, T. (1988). Recognizing image-schemas using programmable networks. In *Proceedings of the 1988 Connectionist Models Summer School.* Los Gatos, CA: Morgan Kaufman.

Shastri, L., and Ajjanagadde, V. (1990). *From simple associations to systematic reasoning: a connectionist representation of rules, variables and dynamic bindings using temporal synchrony.* (Technical Report.) Philadelphia: Computer and Information Science Department, University of Pennsylvania.

Simon, H. (1994). Literary criticism: a cognitive approach. In S. Franchi and G. Güzeldere (Eds.), *Bridging the gap. Stanford Humanities Review, 4, 1,* 1–26.

Smith, B. (1993). The structures of the common-sense world. In A. Pagnini and S. Poggi (Eds.), *Gestalt theory: its origins, foundations and influence.* Florence: Olschky.

Smolensky, P. (1990). Tensor product variable binding and the representation of symbolic structures in connectionist networks. *Artificial Intelligence, 46*, 159–216.

Talmy, L. (1978). The relation of grammar to cognition. In D. Waltz (Ed.), *Proceedings of TINLAP-2*. Urbana: University of Illinois.

Talmy, L. (1985). Force dynamics in language and thought. In *Parasession on Causatives and Agentivity, Chicago Linguistic Society, 21st Regional Meeting*.

Talmy, L. (1990). Fictive motion in language and perception. In *Workshop on motivation in language*. University of San Marino: International Center for Semiotic and Cognitive Studies.

Thom, R. (1972). *Stabilité structurelle et morphogenèse*. New York: Benjamin.

Thom, R. (1980a). *Modèles mathématiques de la morphogenèse*. Paris: Christian Bourgois.

Thom, R. (1980b). Prédication et grammaire universelle. *Fundamenta Scientiæ, 1*, 23–34.

Thom, R. (1984). Classification des sciences et des techniques. In *Apologie du logos*. Paris: Hachette [reprinted 1990].

Thom, R. (1988). *Esquisse d'une sémiophysique*. Paris: InterEditions.

Ullman, S. (1984). Visual routines. *Cognition, 18*, 97–159.

Visetti, Y. M. (1990). Modèles connexionnistes et représentations structurées. In D. Memmi and Y. M. Visetti (Eds.), *Modèles connexionnistes*. *Intellectica, 9-10*, 167–212.

Van Gelder, T., (1992). Connectionism and dynamical explanation, *Proceedings of the Thirteenth Annual Conference of the Cognitive Science Society*, Hillsdale: Ll. Erlbaum.

Von der Malsburg, C., and Bienenstock, E. (1986). Statistical coding and short-term synaptic plasticity: a scheme for knowledge representation in the brain. In E. Bienenstock, F. Fogelman, and G. Weisbuch (Eds.), *Disordered systems and biological organization* (pp. 247–272). Berlin: Springer Verlag.

Wildgen, W. (1982). *Catastrophe theoretic semantics*. Amsterdam: Benjamins.

Witkin, A. (1983). Scale-space filtering. In *Proceedings of the International Joint Conference on Artificial Intelligence* (pp. 1019–1021). Karlsruhe, Germany.

Yuille, A., and Poggio, J. (1986). Scaling theorems for zero-crossings. *IEEE Transactions on Pattern Analysis and Machine Intelligence, 8*, 15–25.

Zeeman, C. (1965). Topology of the brain. In *Mathematics and computer science in biology and medicine*. Medical Research Council.

Zeeman, C. (1976). Brain modelling. In *Structural stability, the theory of catastrophes and applications in the sciences*. *Lecture Notes in Mathematics, 525*, 367–372. Berlin: Springer Verlag. [See also Zeeman, 1977, chapter 8.]

Zeeman, C. (1977). *Catastrophe theory: selected papers 1972–1977*. Redwood City CA: Addison-Wesley.

Zurek, W. H. (Ed.) (1990). *Complexity, entropy and the physics of information*. Redwood City, CA: Addison-Wesley.

Guide to Further Reading

The best pedagogical introduction to catastrophe theory and dynamical modeling in biological and human sciences remains Zeeman (1977). An excellent textbook covering the central mathematical ideas of catastrophe theory is Castrigiano and Hayes (1993). For the deepest aspects of the use of singularity, structural stability, and dynamical systems theories in linguistics (and especially in syntax), the main reference is, of course, Thom (1975); see also Thom (1989). Very good introductions to dynamical modeling in semantics are Wildgen (1982, 1994) and Manjali (1991). Two particularly useful introductions to the mathematical theory of singularities of differentiable maps are Golubitsky and Guillemin (1973) and Arnold, Varchenko and Goussein-Zade (1985). A very complete panorama of cognitive grammar is given in Langacker (1987–1991). Central texts on computational vision include Marr (1982) and Koenderink (1990). For the use of wavelet packet algorithms, see Wickerhauser (1991). Finally, one of the best texts on the dynamical perspective on neural networks is Amit (1989).

Amit, D. (1989). *Modeling brain function.* Cambridge, England: Cambridge University Press.

Arnold, V. I., Varchenko, A., and Goussein-Zade, S. (1985). *Singularities of differentiable maps, I.* Boston, Birkhäuser.

Castrigiano, D. P. L., and Hayes, S. A. (1993). *Catastrophe theory.* Reading, MA: Addison-Wesley.

Golubitsky, M., and Guillemin, V. (1973). *Stable mapping and their singularities.* New York: Springer Verlag.

Koenderink, J. J. (1990). *Solid shape.* Cambridge, MA: MIT Press.

Langacker, R. W. (1987–1991). *Foundations of cognitive grammar,* Vols. 1 and 2. Stanford, CA: Stanford University Press.

Manjali, F. (1991). *Nuclear semantics,* New-Dehli: Bahri.

Marr, D. (1982). *Vision.* San Francisco: Freeman.

Thom, R. (1975). *Structural stability and morphogenesis* (Fowler, D. H., Trans.). Reading, MA: Benjamin.

Thom, R. (1989). *Semiophysics.* Redwood City, CA: Addison-Wesley.

Wickerhauser, M. V. (1991). *Lectures on wavelet packet algorithms.* (Technical report.) St. Louis: Washington University, Department of Mathematics.

Wildgen, W. (1982). *Catastrophe theoretic semantics: an elaboration and extension of René Thom's theory.* Amsterdam: Benjamins.

Wildgen, W. (1994). Process, image and meaning: a realistic model of the meanings of sentences and narrative texts. Amsterdam: Benjamins.

Zeeman, C. (1977). *Catastrophe theory: selected papers 1972–1977.* Redwood City, CA: Addison-Wesley.

10 The Induction of Dynamical Recognizers

Jordan B. Pollack

EDITORS' INTRODUCTION

People possess the quite remarkable ability to easily classify any of a vast number of sentences, including totally novel ones, as grammatically correct or incorrect; moreover, they do this with an extraordinary degree of agreement. How is this possible? This kind of problem led Descartes in the seventeenth century to conclude that people must have a nonmaterial mind in addition to the body, for no mere machine could display such seemingly infinite capacities. In the twentieth-century, scientists assume that cognitive systems are complex physical devices, and hope to uncover the principles of their operation; they must therefore come up with an alternative explanation of the generativity of our linguistic capacities.

A grammar is a recipe, or set of rules, for producing sentences (sequences of symbols) of a language, whether a natural language such as English or a formal language such as predicate calculus or FORTRAN. Grammars can also be used as recipes for recognition, i.e., determining whether a given sequence belongs to the language or not. Grammars come in various levels of sophistication, and describe sentences with corresponding levels of complexity. Moreover, the kind of symbol-manipulating machine that is required to recognize whether a sentence conforms to a given grammar depends on the sophistication of the grammar. Simple machines (such as "finite state automata") can recognize only simple sentences according to simple recipes.

One of the key developments that launched mainstream computational cognitive science was Chomsky's demonstration in 1956 that certain kinds of sentences which occur in natural languages (e.g., sentences containing other embedded sentences) could not plausibly be constructed in accordance with any of the simple rule systems found in what are known as regular grammars. This demonstration had immediate implications for cognitive science. People generally have little trouble determining whether such sentences are well formed or not. Therefore, people cannot be the simplest machines which follow only regular grammars. They must be machines whose power matches the greater complexity of these sentences of natural language.

Reprinted from *Machine Learning, 7,* 227–252, 1991, with permission from Kluwer Academic Publishers.

The only kind of machines that were known to have such a capacity were computational systems more closely related to the very general and powerful Turing machines. Therefore, it seemed, people must be computational systems of this broad kind and cognitive modeling must proceed on this basis.

Now, dynamicists in cognitive science are working on the hypothesis that cognitive systems are not symbol-processing machines of any sort. However, they cannot shirk the problem of explaining people's remarkable linguistic capacities. They must (among other things) show how it is that dynamical systems can recognize sentences with the kind of complexity found in natural languages.

This is the problem Jordan Pollack confronted in this chapter, originally published in 1991. He works within the connectionist paradigm, and is thus investigating the capacities of connectionist dynamical systems with respect to the problem, widely studied in computer science, of learning to recognize the sentences of a given formal language. In his networks, the system bounces around its numerical state space under the influence of successive inputs corresponding to symbols in the sentence to be recognized. A sentence is regarded as successfully recognized if the system ends up in a particular region after exposure to the whole sentence. (Of course, it must not end up in this region for nonsentences!) The way the system bounces around is determined by the settings of the weights between the neural units. These parameters fix the dynamics of the system, i.e., its particular landscape of attractors. The weights are adjusted by a variant of the familiar backpropagation training procedure.

In this chapter, Pollack is led to some remarkable conclusions and fascinating speculations. One conclusion is that noncomputational, dynamical systems can in fact come to recognize nonregular languages. It is thus an open possibility that there are dynamical systems capable of discriminating the complex structures found in natural languages, and hence that we ourselves might be dynamical systems of that kind. Another important conclusion is that there is a new kind of learning, which Pollack terms induction by phase transition. This is when a small variation in the weight parameters is responsible for a dramatic change in the dynamics of the system (i.e., a bifurcation), such that the system is suddenly able to recognize a given language. Pollack concludes by speculating that the Chomskyan computational hierarchy of equivalencies between grammars, languages, and machines is mirrored by a dynamical hierarchy of grammars, languages, and dynamical systems, such that the complexity of the grammar and language corresponds to the manner in which the dynamical landscape of the system is partitioned by the decision region. Pollack is thus sketching some key ingredients of the foundations of a dynamical research program to rival the Chomskyan–computational program in accounting for some of the most challenging aspects of cognition.

10.1 INTRODUCTION

Consider the two categories of binary strings in table 10.1. After brief study, a human or machine learner might decide to characterize the "accept" strings as those containing an odd number of 1's and the "reject" strings as those containing an even number of 1's.

Table 10.1 What is the rule which defines the language?

Accept	Reject
1	0
0 1	0 0
1 0	1 1
1 0 1 1 0	1 0 1
0 0 1	0 1 0 1
1 1 1	1 0 0 0 1
0 1 0 1 1	

The language acquisition problem has been around for a long time. In its narrowest formulation, it is a version of the inductive inference or "theory from data" problem for syntax: Discover a compact mathematical description of string acceptability (which generalizes) from a finite presentation of examples. In its broadest formulation it involves accounting for the psychological and linguistic facts of native language acquisition by human children, or even the acquisition of language itself by *Homo sapiens* through natural selection (Lieberman, 1984; Pinker and Bloom, 1990).

The problem has become specialized across many scientific disciplines, and there is a voluminous literature. Mathematical and computational theorists are concerned with the basic questions and definitions of language learning (Gold, 1967), with understanding the complexity of the problem (Angluin, 1978; Gold, 1978), or with good algorithms (Berwick, 1985; Rivest and Schapire 1987). An excellent survey of this approach to the problem has been written by Angluin and Smith (1983). Linguists are concerned with grammatical frameworks which can adequately explain the basic fact that children acquire their language (Chomsky, 1965; Wexler and Culicover, 1980), while psychologists and psycholinguists are concerned, in detail, with how an acquisition mechanism substantiates and predicts empirically testable phenomena of child language acquisition. (MacWhinney, 1987; Pinker, 1984).

My goals are much more limited than either the best algorithm or the most precise psychological model; in fact I scrupulously avoid any strong claims of algorithmic efficiency, or of neural or psychological plausibility for this initial work. I take as a central research question for connectionism:

How could a neural computational system, with its slowly changing structure, numerical calculations, and iterative processes, ever come to possess linguistic generative capacity, which seems to require dynamic representations, symbolic computation, and recursive processes?

Although a rigorous theory may take some time to develop, the work I report in this paper does address this question. I expose a recurrent higher-order backpropagation network to both positive and negative examples of Boolean strings, and find that although the network does *not* converge on the minimal-description finite state automaton (FSA) for the data (which is NP-Hard), it does induction in a novel and interesting fashion, and searches through a hypothesis space, which, theoretically, is not constrained to machines of finite state.

These results are of import to many related neural models currently under development (e.g., Elman, 1990; Giles, Sun, Chen, et al., 1990; Servan-Schreiber, Cleeremans, and McClelland, 1989), and ultimately relate to the question of how linguistic generative capacity can arise in nature.

Generative capacity is a measure of a formal system's (and thus a natural system's) ability to generate, recognize, or represent languages in the limit, where a language here is defined as an infinite set of finite-length strings composed from a fixed vocabulary. The beautiful results derived from Chomsky's (1956) insights in the earliest years of modern computer science and linguistics research are that certain mechanisms, as well as certain rewrite systems (grammars), are tightly correlated with certain classes of languages. Although we now know of many other language classes, the four main language types—regular, context-free, context-sensitive, and recursive—form an inclusive hierarchy which is precisely matched to a set of computational models.

Furthermore, the existence of certain phenomena of syntactic structure in English, such as center embedding ("the rat the cat the dog chased bit died") or crossed serial dependencies (e.g., the "respectively" construction), which could not be generated by regular or context-free languages, respectively, indicated that the human mind was operating at a higher level of computational behavior.

Thus, the issue of generative capacity is a serious concern for connectionism because since 1956 it has been firmly established that regular languages are inadequate to explain (or at least parsimoniously describe) the syntactic structures of natural languages. To the extent that iterated systems like neural networks are equivalent in their generative capacity to Markov chains and finite-state machines, they should not even be under consideration as appropriate models for natural language.

Of necessity, I make use of the terminology of nonlinear dynamical systems for the remainder of this chapter. This terminology is not (yet) a common language to most computer and cognitive scientists and thus warrants an introduction. The view of neural networks as nonlinear dynamical systems is commonly held by the physicists who have helped to define the modern field of neural networks (Hopfield, 1982; Smolensky, 1986), although complex dynamics have generally been suppressed in favor of more tractable convergence (limit-point) dynamics. But chaotic behavior has shown up repeatedly in studies of neural networks (Derrida and Meir, 1988; Huberman and Hogg, 1987; Kolen and Pollack, 1990; Kurten, 1987; van der Maas, Verschure, and Molenaar, 1990), and a few scientists have begun to explore how this dynamical complexity could be exploited for useful purposes (e.g., Hendin, Horn, and Usher, 1991; Pollack, 1989; Skarda and Freeman, 1987).

In short, a discrete dynamical system is just an iterative computation. Starting in some "initial condition" or state, the next state is computed as a mathematical function of the current state, sometimes involving parameters and/or input or noise from an environment. Rather than studying the *function* of the computations, much of the work in this field has been concerned with explaining universal temporal *behaviors*. Indeed, iterative systems have some interesting properties: Their behavior in the limit reaches either a steady state (limit point), an oscillation (limit cycle), or an aperiodic instability (chaos). In terms of computer programs, these three "regimes" correspond, respectively, to those programs which halt, those which have simple repetitive loops, and those which have more "creative" infinite loops, such as broken self-modifying codes, an area of mechanical behavior which has not been extensively studied. When the state spaces of dynamical systems are plotted, these three regimes have characteristic figures called "attractors": Limit points show up as "point attractors," limit cycles as "periodic attractors," and chaos as "strange attractors," which usually have a "fractal" nature. Small changes in controlling parameters can lead through "phase transitions" to these qualitatively different behavioral regimes; a "bifurcation" is a change in the periodicity of the limit behavior of a system, and the route from steady-state to periodic to aperiodic behavior follows a universal pattern. Finally, one of the characteristics of chaotic systems is that they can be very sensitive to initial conditions, and a slight change in the initial condition can lead to radically different outcomes. Further details can be found in articles and books on the field (e.g., Crutchfield, Fermer, Packard, et al., 1986; Devaney, 1987; Gleick, 1987; Grebogi, Ott, and Yorke, 1987).

10.2 AUTOMATA, RECURRENT NETWORKS, AND DYNAMICAL RECOGNIZERS

I should make it clear from the outset that the problem of inducing *some* recognizer for a finite set of examples is "easy," as there are an infinite number of regular languages which account for a finite sample, and an infinite number of automata for each language. The difficult problem has always been finding the "minimal description," and no solution is asymptotically much better than "learning by enumeration"—brute-force searching of all automata in order of ascending complexity. Another difficult issue is the determination of grammatical class. Because a finite set of examples does not give any clue as to the complexity class of the source language, one apparently must find the most parsimonious regular grammar, context-free grammar, context-sensitive grammar, etc., and compare them. Quite a formidable challenge for a problem solver!

Thus, almost all language acquisition work has been done with an inductive bias of presupposing some grammatical framework as the hypothesis space. Most have attacked the problem of inducing finite-state recognizers for regular languages (e.g., Feldman, 1972; Tomita, 1982).

A finite-state recognizer is a quadruple $\{Q, \Sigma, \delta, F\}$, where Q is a set of states (q_0 denotes the initial state), Σ is a finite input alphabet, δ is a transition

Table 10.2 δ function for parity machine

	Input	
State	0	1
q_0	q_0	q_1
q_1	q_1	q_0

function from $Q \times \Sigma \Rightarrow Q$, and F is a set of final (accepting) states, a subset of Q. A string is accepted by such a device, if, starting from q_0, the sequence of transitions dictated by the tokens in the string ends up in one of the final states.

δ is usually specified as a table, which lists a new state for each state and input. As an example, a machine which accepts Boolean strings of odd parity can be specified as $Q = \{q_0, q_1\}$, $\Sigma = \{0, 1\}$, $F = \{q_1\}$, and δ as shown in table 10.2.

Although such machines are usually described with fully explicit tables or graphs, a transition function can also be specified as a mathematical function of codes for the current state and the input. For example, variable-length parity can be specified as the exclusive-or of the current state and the input, each coded as a single bit. The primary result in the field of neural networks is that under simplified assumptions, networks have the capacity to perform arbitrary logical functions, and thus to act as finite-state controllers (McCulloch and Pitts, 1943; Minsky, 1972). In various configurations, modern multilayer feedforward networks are also able to perform arbitrary Boolean functions (Hornik, Stinchcombe, and White, 1990; Lapedes and Farber, 1988; Lippman, 1987). Thus, when used recurrently, these networks have the capacity to be any finite-state recognizer as well. The states and tokens are assigned binary codes (say, with one bit indicating which states are in F), and the code for the next state is simply computed by a set of Boolean functions of the codes for current state and current input.

But the mathematical models for neural nets are "richer" than Boolean functions, and more like polynomials. What does this mean for automata? In order not to confuse theory and implementation, I will first define a general mathematical object for language recognition as a forced discrete-time continuous-space dynamical system plus a precise initial condition and a decision function. The recurrent neural network architecture presented in the next section is a constrained implementation of this object.

By analogy to a finite-state recognizer, a *dynamical recognizer* is a quadruple $\{Z, \Sigma, \Omega, G\}$, where $Z \subset R^k$ is a "space" of states and $z_k(0)$ is the initial condition. Σ is a finite input alphabet; Ω is the "dynamic," a parameterized set (one for each token) of transformations on the space $\omega_{\sigma_i}: Z \rightarrow Z$; and $G(Z) \rightarrow \{0, 1\}$ is the "decision" function.

Each finite-length string of tokens in Σ^*, $\sigma_1, \sigma_2, \cdots \sigma_n$, has a final state associated with it, computed by applying a precise sequence of transformations to the initial state: $z_k(n) = \omega_{\sigma_n}(\cdots(\omega_{\sigma_2}(\omega_{\sigma_1}(z_k(0)))))$. The language accepted and generated[1] by a dynamical recognizer is the set of strings in Σ^* whose final states pass the decision test.

In the "Mealy machine" formulation (Mealy, 1955), which I use in the model below, the decision function applies to the penultimate state and the final token: $G(z_k(n-1), \sigma_n) \rightarrow \{0, 1\}$. Just as in the case for finite automata, labeling the arcs rather than the nodes can often result in smaller machines.

There are many variants possible, but both Ω and G must be constrained to avoid the vacuous case where some ω or G is as powerful as a Turing machine. For purposes of this chapter, I assume that G is as weak as a conventional neural network decision function, e.g., a hyperplane or a convex region, and that each ω is as weak as a linear or quasi-linear transformation. G could also be a graded function instead of a forced decision, which would lead to a "more-or-less" notion of string acceptability, or it could be a function which returned a more complex categorization or even a *representation*, in which case I would be discussing dynamical *parsers*. Finally, one could generalize from discrete symbols to continuous symbols (MacLennan, 1989; Touretzky and Geva, 1987), or from discrete-time to continuous-time systems (Pearlmutter, 1989; Pineda, 1987).

There are some difficult questions which can be asked immediately about dynamical recognizers. What kind of languages can they recognize and generate? How does this mathematical description compare with various formal grammars on the grounds of parsimony, efficiency of parsing, neural and psychological plausibility, and learnability? I do not yet have the definitive answers to these questions, as this is the first study, but will touch on some of these issues later.

One thing is clear from the outset, that even a linear dynamical recognizer model can function as an arbitrary FSA. The states of the automaton are "embedded" in a finite dimensional space such that a linear transformation can account for the state transitions associated with each token. Consider the case where each of k states is a k-dimensional binary unit vector (a 1-in-k code) Each ω_{σ_i} is simply a permutation matrix which "lists" the state transitions for each token, and the decision function is just a logical mask which selects those states in F. It is perhaps an interesting theoretical question to determine the minimum dimensionality of such a linear "embedding" for an arbitrary regular language.

With the introduction of nonlinearities, more complex grammars can also be accounted for. Consider a one-dimensional system where Z is the unit line, $z_0 = 1$, G tests if $z(n) > .75$, and $\Sigma = \{L, R\}$. If the transformation ω_L is "multiply z by 0.5" and ω_R is "multiply z by 2 modulo 2" [which only applies when $z(i)$ is 0 or 1], then the recognizer accepts the balanced parentheses language. In other words, it is just as mathematically possible to embed an "infinite state machine" in a dynamical recognizer as it is to embed a finite-state machine. I return to these issues in the conclusion.

To begin to address the question of learnability, I now present and elaborate on my earlier work on cascaded networks (Pollack, 1987a), which were used in a recurrent fashion to learn parity and depth-limited parenthesis balancing, and to map between word sequences and propositional representations (Pollack, 1990).

10.3 THE MODEL

A cascaded network is a well-behaved higher-order (sigma-pi) connectionist architecture to which the backpropagation technique of weight adjustment (Rumelhart, Hinton, and Williams, 1986) can be applied. Basically, it consists of two subnetworks in a master-slave relationship: The *function* (slave) network is a standard feedforward network, with or without hidden layers. However, the weights on the function network are dynamically computed by the linear *context* (master) network. A context network has as many outputs as there are weights in the function network. Thus the input to the context network is used to "multiplex" the function computed, a divide-and-conquer heuristic which can make learning easier.

When the outputs of the function network are used as recurrent inputs to the context network, a system can be built which learns to associate specific outputs for variable-length input sequences. A block diagram of a sequential cascaded network is shown in figure 10.1. Because of the multiplicative connections, each input is, in effect, processed by a different function. Given an initial context, $z_k(0)$ (all .5's by default), and a sequence of inputs, $y_j(t)$, $t = 1 \ldots n$, the network computes a sequence of output/state vectors, $z_i(t)$, $t = 1 \ldots n$ by dynamically changing the set of weights, $w_{ij}(t)$. Without hidden units, the forward-pass computation is:

$$w_{ij}(t) = \sum_k w_{ijk} z_k(t - 1)$$

$$z_i(t) = g\left(\sum_j w_{ij}(t) y_j(t)\right)$$

which reduces to:

$$z_i(t) = g\left(\sum_j \sum_k w_{ijk} z_k(t - 1) y_j(t)\right) \tag{1}$$

where $g(v) = 1/1 + e^{-v}$ is the usual sigmoid function used in backpropagation systems.

In previous work, I assumed that a teacher could supply a consistent and generalizable final output for each member of a set of strings, which turned out to be a significant overconstraint. In learning a two-state machine like parity, this did not matter, as the one-bit state fully determines the output. However, for the case of a higher-dimensional system, we may know what the final output of a system should be, but we *don't care* what its final state is.

Jordan (1986) showed how recurrent backpropagation networks could be trained with "don't-care" conditions. If there is no specific target for an output unit during a particular training example, simply consider its error gradient to

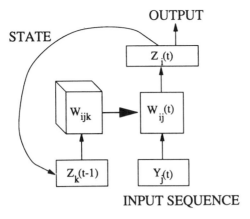

STATE

OUTPUT

$Z_i(t)$

W_{ijk}

$W_{ij}(t)$

$Z_k(t-1)$

$Y_j(t)$

INPUT SEQUENCE

Figure 10.1 A sequential cascaded network. This is a recurrent version of a "higher-order" or "sigma-pi" network in which the outputs of the master net (*left*) are the weights for the slave net (*right*), and the outputs of the slave net are recurrent inputs to the master net.

be 0. This will work, *as long as that same unit receives feedback from other examples.* When the don't-cares line up, the weights to those units will never change. One possible fix, so-called backpropagation through time (Rumelhart et al., 1986), involves a complete unrolling of a recurrent loop and has had only modest success (Mozer, 1988), probably because of conflicts arising from equivalence constraints between interdependent layers. My fix involves a single *backspace*, unrolling the loop only once. For a particular string, this leads to the calculation of only one error term for each weight (and thus no conflict) as follows. After propagating the errors determined on only a subset of the weights from the "acceptance" unit:

$$\frac{\partial E}{\partial w_{aj}(n)} = (z_a(n) - d_a)z_a(n)(1 - z_a(n))y_j(n)$$

$$\frac{\partial E}{\partial w_{ajk}} = \frac{\partial E}{\partial w_{aj}(n)}z_k(n-1)$$

The error on the remainder of the weights $\left(\frac{\partial E}{\partial w_{ijk}}, i \neq a\right)$ is calculated using values from the penultimate time step:

$$\frac{\partial E}{\partial z_k(n-1)} = \sum_a \sum_j \frac{\partial E}{\partial w_{ajk}} \frac{\partial E}{\partial w_{aj}(n)}$$

$$\frac{\partial E}{\partial w_{ij}(n-1)} = \frac{\partial E}{\partial z_i(n-1)}y_j(n-1)$$

$$\frac{\partial E}{\partial w_{ijk}} = \frac{\partial E}{\partial w_{ij}(n-1)}z_k(n-2)$$

The schematic for this mode of backpropagation is shown in figure 10.2, where the gradient calculations for the weights are highlighted. The method

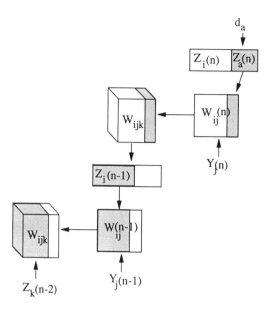

Figure 10.2 The "backspace" trick. Because only one desired output is supplied, only partial information is available for computing error gradients on the weights. The trick, which avoids completely unrolling the loop or carrying along information across an cycles, is to unroll the loop only once. The penultimate configuration of input and outputs is used to calculate gradients that are not directly connected to the known output unit.

applies with small variations whether or not there are hidden units in the function or context network, and whether or not the system is trained with a single "accept" bit for desired output, or a larger pattern (representing a tree structure; see, e.g., Pollack, 1990). The important point is that the gradients connected to a subset of the outputs are calculated directly, but the gradients connected to don't-care recurrent states are calculated one step back in time. The forward and backward calculations are performed over a corpus of variable-length input patterns, and then all the weights are updated. As the overall squared sum of errors approaches 0, the network improves its calculation of final outputs for the set of strings in the training set. At some threshold, e.g., when the network responds with above 0.8 for accept strings, and below 0.2 for reject strings, training is halted. The network now classifies the training set and can be tested on its generalization to a transfer set.

Unfortunately, for language work, the generalization must be infinite.

10.4 INDUCTION AS PHASE TRANSITION

In my original (Pollack, 1987a) studies of learning the simple regular language of odd parity, I expected the network to merely implement "exclusive or" with a feedback link. It turns out that this is not quite enough. Because termination of backpropagation is usually defined as a 20% error (e.g., logical "1" is above 0.8), recurrent use of this logic tends to a limit point. In other

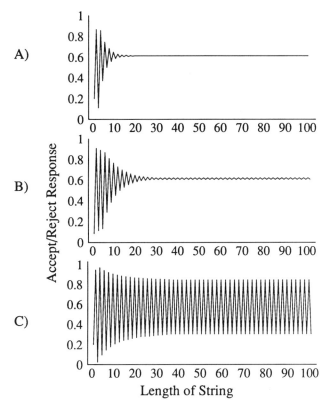

Figure 10.3 Three stages in the adaptation of a network learning parity. *A*) The test cases are separated, but there is a limit point for 1* at about 0.6. *B*) After another epoch, the even and odd sequences are slightly separated. *C*) After a little more training, the oscillating cycle is pronounced.

words, separation of the finite exemplars is no guarantee that the network can recognize sequential parity in the limit. Nevertheless, this is indeed possible as illustrated by the figures below.

A small cascaded network composed of a 1-input 3-output function net (with bias connections, 6 weights for the context net to compute) and a 2-input 6-output context net (with bias connections, 18 weights) was trained on odd parity of a small set of strings up to length 5 (see table 10.1). Of the 3 outputs, 2 were fed back recurrently as state, and the third was used as the accept unit. At each epoch, the weights in the network were saved in a file for subsequent study. After being trained for about 200 epochs, the network tested successfully on much longer strings. But it is important to show that the network is recognizing parity "in the limit."

In order to observe the limit behavior of a recognizer at various stages of adaptation, we can observe its response to either Σ^* or to a very long "characteristic string" (which has the best chance of breaking it). For parity, a good characteristic string is the sequence of 1's, which should cause the most state changes. Figure 10.3 shows three stages in the adaptation of a network for

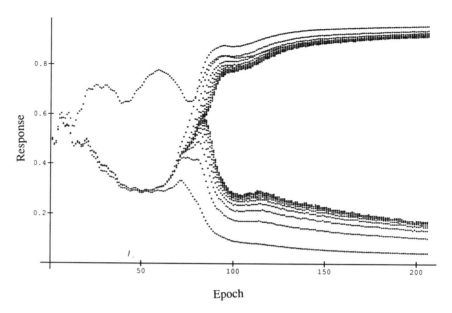

Epoch

Figure 10.4 A bifurcation diagram showing the response of the parity learner to the first 25 characteristic strings over 200 epochs of training. In each column representing an epoch, 25 points, corresponding to 25 different length strings of 1's, are plotted.

parity, by testing the response of three intermediate configurations to the first 100 strings of 1*. In the first figure, despite success at separating the small training set, a single attractor exists in the limit, so that long strings are indistinguishable. After another epoch of training, the even and odd strings are slightly separated, and after still further training, the separation is significant enough to drive a threshold through.

This "phase transition" is shown more completely in figure 10.4. The vertical axis represents, again, the network's accept/reject response to characteristic strings, but the horizontal axis shows the evolution of this response across all 200 epochs. Each vertical column contains 25 (overlapping) dots marking the network's response to the first 25 characteristic strings. Thus, each "horizontal" line in the graph plots the evolution of the network's response to one of the 25 strings. Initially, all strings longer than length 1 are not distinguished. From epoch 60 to epoch 80, the network is improving at separating finite strings. At epoch 84, the network is still failing in the limit, but at epoch 85, the network undergoes a "bifurcation," where a small change in weights transforms the network's limit behavior from limit point to a limit cycle.[2] This phase transition is so "adaptive" to the classification task that the network rapidly exploits it.

I want to stress that this is a new and very interesting form of mechanical induction. Before the phase transition, the machine is in principle *not* capable of performing the serial parity task; after the phase transition it *is*, and this change in abilities is rapidly exploited by adaptive search. This kind of learning dynamic may be related to biological evolution through natural selection as well as to insight problem solving (the "aha" phenomenon). The induction is not "one shot" or instantaneous, but more like "punctuated equilibria" in evolution, where a "preadaptive" capacity enables a population some advantage which then drives very rapid change. Metcalfe and Wiebe (1987) report psychological experiments on insight problems in which human subjects measurably undergo a similar cognitive phase transition, reporting no progress on the problems until the solution appears.

10.5 BENCHMARKING RESULTS

Connectionist and other machine-learning algorithms are, unfortunately, very sensitive to the statistic properties of the set of exemplars which make up the learning environment or data set. When researchers develop their own learning environments, there is a difficult methodological issue bearing on the status of repetitive data set refinement, especially when experimental results concern psychologically measured statistics, or the evolution of the data set is considered too irrelevant to publish. This has correctly led some researchers to include the learning environment as a variable to manipulate (Plunkett and Marchman, 1989). Besides this complicated path, the other methodologically clean choices are to use "real-world" noisy data, to choose data once and never refine it, or to use someone else's published training data. For this experiment, I chose to use someone else's.

Tomita (1982) performed elegant experiments in inducing finite automata from positive and negative exemplars. He used a genetically inspired two-step hill-climbing procedure, which manipulated nine-state automata by randomly adding, deleting, or moving transitions, or inverting the acceptability of a state. Starting with a random machine, the current machine was compared to a mutated machine, and changed only when an improvement was made in the result of a heuristic evaluation function. The first hill-climber used an evaluation function which maximized the difference between the number of positive examples accepted and the number of negative examples accepted. The second hill-climber used an evaluation function which maintained correctness of the examples while minimizing the automaton's description (number of states, then number of transitions). Tomita did not randomly choose his test cases, but instead, chose them consistently with seven regular languages he had in mind (table 10.3). The difficulty of these problems lies not in the languages Tomita had in mind, but in the arbitrary and impoverished data sets he used.

Each training environment was simply defined by two sets of Boolean strings, which are given in table 10.4. For uniformity, I ran all seven cases, as given, on a sequential cascaded network of a 1-input 4-output function network (with bias connections, making 8 weights for the context net to compute) and a 3-input 8-output context network with bias connections. The total of 32 context weights are essentially arranged as a 4- × 2- × 4-array. Only three of the outputs of the function net were fed back to the context

Table 10.3   Training data for seven languages from Tomita (1982)

Set 1 Accept	Set 1 Reject
1	0
1 1	1 0
1 1 1	0 1
1 1 1 1	
1 1 1 1 1	0 1 1
1 1 1 1 1 1	1 1 0
1 1 1 1 1 1 1	1 1 1 1 1 1 1 0
1 1 1 1 1 1 1 1	1 0 1 1 1 1 1 1

Set 2 Accept	Set 2 Reject
1 0	1
1 0 1 0	0
1 0 1 0 1 0	1 1
1 0 1 0 1 0 1 0	0 0
1 0 1 0 1 0 1 0 1 0 1 0	0 1
	1 0 1
	1 0 0
	1 0 0 1 0 1 0
	1 0 1 1 0
	1 1 0 1 0 1 0 1 0

Set 3 Accept	Set 3 Reject
1	1 0
0	1 0 1
0 1	0 1 0
1 1	1 0 1 0
0 0	1 1 1 0
1 0 0	1 0 1 1
1 1 0	1 0 0 0 1
1 1 1	1 1 1 0 1 0
0 0 0	1 0 0 1 0 0 0
1 0 0 1 0 0	1 1 1 1 1 0 0 0
1 1 0 0 0 0 0 1 1 1 0 0 0 0 1	0 1 1 1 0 0 1 1 0 1
1 1 1 1 0 1 1 0 0 0 1 0 0 1 1 1 0 0	1 1 0 1 1 1 0 0 1 1 0

Set 4 Accept	Set 4 Reject
1	0 0 0
0	1 1 0 0 0
1 0	0 0 0 1
0 1	0 0 0 0 0 0 0 0
0 0	1 1 1 1 1 0 0 0 1 1
1 0 0 1 0 0	1 1 0 1 0 1 0 0 0 0 0 1 0 1 1 1
0 0 1 1 1 1 1 1 0 1 0 0	1 0 1 0 0 1 0 0 0 1
0 1 0 0 1 0 0 1 0 0	0 0 0 0
1 1 1 0 0	0 0 0 0 0
0 1 0	

    Jordan B. Pollack

Table 10.3 (cont.)

Set 5 Accept	Set 5 Reject
1 1	0
0 0	1 1 1
1 0 0 1	0 1 1
0 1 0 1	0 0 0 0 0 0 0 0 0
1 0 1 0	1 0 0 0
1 0 0 0 1 1 1 1 0 1	0 1
1 0 0 1 1 0 0 0 0 1 1 1 1 0 1 0	1 0
1 1 1 1 1 1	1 1 1 0 0 1 0 1 0 0
0 0 0 0	0 1 0 1 1 1 1 1 1 1 1 0
	0 0 0 1
	0 1 1

Set 6 Accept	Set 6 Reject
1 0	1
0 1	0
1 1 0 0	1 1
1 0 1 0 1 0	0 0
1 1 1	1 0 1
0 0 0 0 0 0	0 1 1
1 0 1 1 1	1 1 0 0 1
0 1 1 1 1 0 1 1 1 1	1 1 1 1
1 0 0 1 0 0 1 0 0	0 0 0 0 0 0 0 0
	0 1 0 1 1 1
	1 0 1 1 1 1 0 1 1 1 1
	1 0 0 1 0 0 1 0 0 1

Set 7 Accept	Set 7 Reject
1	1 0 1 0
0	0 0 1 1 0 0 1 1 0 0 0
1 0	0 1 0 1 0 1 0 1 0 1
0 1	1 0 1 1 0 1 0
1 1 1 1 1	1 0 1 0 1
0 0 0	0 1 0 1 0 0
0 0 1 1 0 0 1 1	1 0 1 0 0 1
0 1 0 1	1 0 0 1 0 0 1 1 0 1 0 1
0 0 0 0 1 0 0 0 0 1 1 1 1	
0 0 1 0 0	
0 1 1 1 1 1 0 1 1 1 1 1	
0 0	

Table 10.4 Minimal regular languages for the seven training sets

Language #	Description
1	1*
2	(1 0)*
3	No odd zero strings after odd 1 strings
4	No 000's
5	Pairwise, an even sum of 01's and 10's
6	No. of 1's − no. of 0's = 0 mod 3
7	0*1*0*1*

Table 10.5 Performance comparison between Tomita's Hill-climber and Pollack's model (Backprop)

Language	No. Mutations (Hill-Climber)	Avg. Epochs (Backprop)	% Convergent (Backprop)
1	98	54	100
2	134	787	20
3	2052	213	70
4	442	251	100
5	1768	637	80
6	277		0
7	206	595	50

network, while the fourth output unit was used as the accept bit. The standard backpropagation learning rate was set to 0.3 and the momentum to 0.7. All 32 weights were reset to random numbers between ± 0.5 for each run. Training was halted when all accept strings returned output bits above 0.8 and reject strings below 0.2.

Results

Of Tomita's seven cases, all but data sets nos. 2 and 6 converged without a problem in several hundred epochs. Case 2 would not converge, and kept treating negative case 110101010 as correct; I had to modify the training set (by adding reject strings 110 and 11010) in order to overcome this problem. Case 6 took several restarts and thousands of cycles to converge.

In the spirit of the machine-learning community, I recently ran a series of experiments to make these results more empirical. Table 10.5 compares Tomita's stage 1 "number of mutations" to my "average number of epochs." Because backpropagation is sensitive to initial conditions (Kolen and Pollack, 1990), running each problem once does not give a good indication of its difficulty, and running it many times from different random starting weights can result in widely disparate timings. So I ran each problem ten times, up to

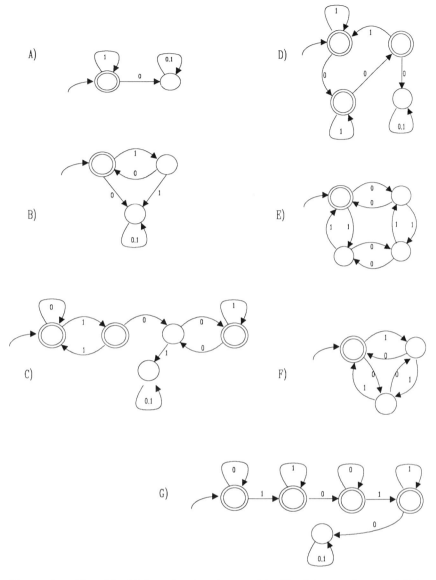

Figure 10.5 The minimal finite-state automata recognizing Tomita's seven data sets. A finite machine consists of a set of states, shown as circles, an initial state, indicated by the lone arrow, and a subset of states called final states, which are indicated by double circles. The transitions from state to state are arrows labeled with tokens from the vocubulary (0 or 1).

1000 epochs, and averaged only those runs which separated the training sets (accepts above 0.6; rejects below 0.4). The column labeled "% Convergent" shows the percent of the ten runs for each problem which separated the accept and reject strings within 1000 cycles. Although it is difficult to compare results between completely different methods, taken together the averaged epochs and the percent convergent numbers give a good idea of the difficulty of the Tomita data sets for my learning architecture.

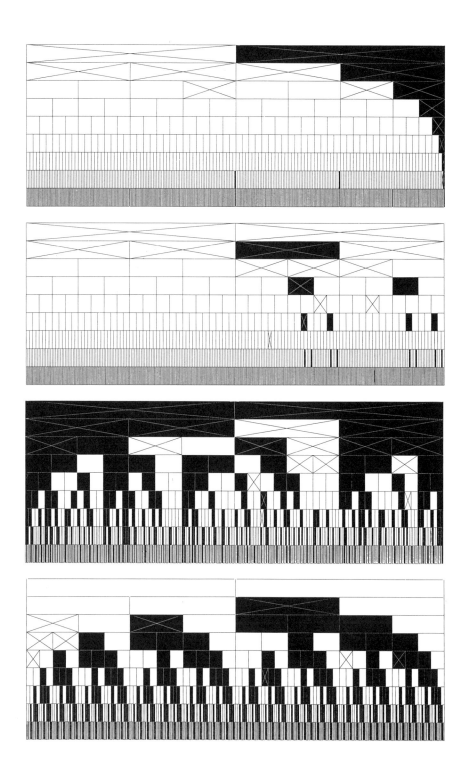

Jordan B. Pollack

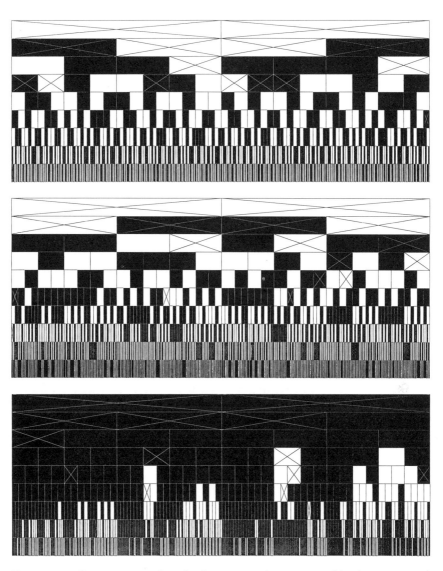

Figure 10.6 Because it is not clear what languages are being generated by the seven trained networks, these figures show the training set (with "X"s) and parts of the languages induced (only for strings of up to nine bits long). Each figure contains nine rows of rectangles, which are colored white for reject and black for accept. The first row is the response to the strings 0 and 1, the second row is the response to the strings 00, 01, 10, and 11, and the third is for 000, 001, and so on. It is engineered so one could locate a network's response to a particular string by moving one's eyes down through a figure.

Analysis

Tomita ran a brute-force enumeration to find the minimal automaton for each language, and verified that his hill-climber was able to find them. These are displayed in figure 10.5. Unfortunately, I ran into some difficulty trying to figure out exactly which FSAs (and regular languages) were being induced by my architecture.

For this reason, in figure 10.6 I present "prefixes" of the languages recognized and generated by the seven first-run networks. Each rectangle assigns a number, 0 (white) or 1 (black), to all Boolean strings up to length 9 (which is the limit of visibility), and thus indicates, in black, the strings that are accepted by the respective network. Starting at the top of each rectangle, each row r contains 2^r subrectangles for all the strings of length r in lexical order, so the subrectangle for each string is sitting right below its prefix. The top-left subrectangle shows a number for the string 0, and the top-right rectangle shows a number for the string 1. Below the subrectangle for 0 are the subrectangles for the strings 00 and 01, and so on. The training sets (see table 10.4) are also indicated in these figures, as inverted "X's" in the subrectangles corresponding to the training strings.

Note that although the figures display some simple recursive patterns, none of the ideal minimal automata were induced by the architecture. Even for the first language 1*, a 0 followed by a long string of 1's would be accepted by the network. My architecture generally has the problem of not inducing "trap" or error states. It can be argued that other FSA-inducing methods get around this problem by presupposing rather than learning the trap states.[3]

If the network is not inducing the smallest consistent FSA, what is it doing? The physical constraint that an implemented network use *finitely specified* weights means that the states and their transitions cannot be arbitrary—there must be some geometric relationship among them.

Based on studies of parity, my initial hypothesis was that a set of clusters would be found, organized in some geometric fashion: i.e., an embedding of a finite-state machine into a finite-dimensional geometry such that each token's transitions would correspond to a simple transformation of space. I wrote a program which examined the state space of these networks by recursively taking each unexplored state and combining it with both 0 and 1 inputs. A state here is a three-dimensional vector, values of the three recurrently used output units. To remove floating-point noise, the program used a parameter ε and only counted states in each ε-cube once. Unfortunately, some of the machines seemed to grow drastically in size as ε was lowered. In particular, figure 10.7 shows the log-log graph of the number of unique states vs. ε for the machine resulting from training environment 7. Using the method of Grassberger and Procaccia (1983) this set was found to have a correlation dimension of 1.4—good evidence that it is "fractal."

Because the states of the benchmark networks are "in a box" (Anderson, Silverstein, Ritz, et al., 1977) of low dimension, we can view these machines

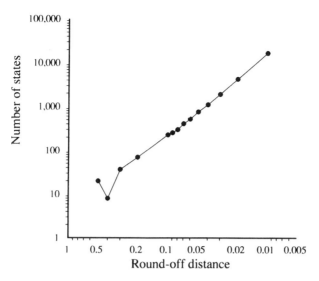

Figure 10.7 The number of states in the seventh machine grew dramatically as ε was lowered.

graphically to gain some understanding of how the state space is being arranged. Each three-dimensional state vector is plotted as a point in the unit cube. Partial graphs of the state spaces for the first-run networks are shown in figure 10.8. States were computed for all Boolean strings up to and including length 10, so each figure contains 2048 points, often overlapping.

The images *A*) and *D*) are what I initially expected, clumps of points which closely map to states of equivalent FSAs. Images *B*) and *E*) have limit "ravines" which can each be considered states as well. However, the state spaces *C*), *F*), and *G*) of the dynamical recognizers for Tomita's cases 3, 6, and 7 are interesting, because, theoretically, they are *infinite* state machines, where the states are not arbitrary or random, requiring an infinite table of transitions, but are constrained in a powerful way by mathematical principle.

In thinking about such a principle, consider systems in which extreme observed complexity emerges from algorithmic simplicity plus computational power. When I first saw some of the state-space graphs (see figure 10.8), they reminded me of Barnsley's iterated function systems (IFS) (Barnsley, 1988), where a compactly coded set of affine transformations is used to *iteratively* construct displays of fractals, previously described *recursively* using line-segment rewrite rules (Mandelbrot, 1982). The calculation is simply the repetitive transformation (and plotting) of a state vector by a sequence of randomly chosen affine transformations. In the infinite limit of this process, fractal "attractors" emerge (e.g., the widely reproduced fern).[4]

By eliminating the sigmoid, commuting the y_j and z_k terms in equation (1):

$$z_i(t) = \sum_k \left(\sum_j w_{ijk} y_j(t) \right) z_k(t-1)$$

and treating the y_j's as an infinite random sequence of binary unit vectors

The Induction of Dynamical Recognizers

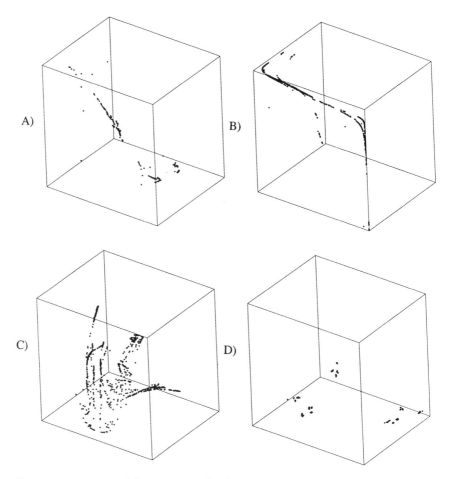

Figure 10.8 Images of the state spaces for the seven training environments. Each network had three output units which could vary between 0 and 1, and so a "state" of the network can be visualized as a point in a three-dimensional cube. Each figure displays 2048 such states, corresponding to all Boolean strings up to length 10.

(1-in-j codes), the forward-pass calculation for my network can be seen as the same process used in an IFS. Thus, my figures of state spaces, which emerge from the projection of Σ^* into Z, are fractal attractors as defined by Barnsley.

10.6   RELATED WORK

The architecture and learning paradigm I used is also being studied by Lee Giles and colleagues, and is closely related to the work of Elman (1990) and Servan-Schreiber et al. (1989) on simple recurrent networks. Both architectures rely on extending Jordan's recurrent networks in a direction which separates visible output states from hidden recurrent states, without making the unstable "backpropagation through time" assumption. Besides our choice of language data to model, the two main differences are that:

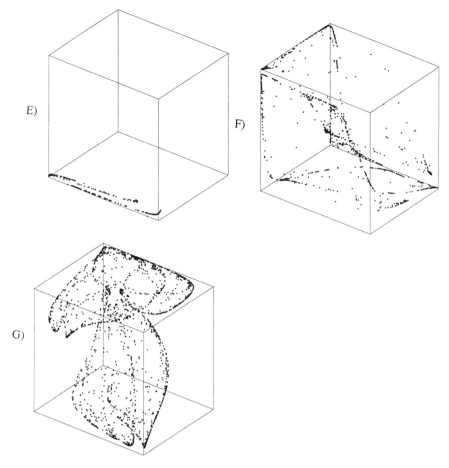

E)

F)

G)

Figure 10.8 (cont.)

1. They use a "predictive" paradigm, where error feedback is provided at every time step in the computation, and I used a "classification" paradigm, feeding back only at the end of the given examples. Certainly, the predictive paradigm is more psychologically plausible as a model of positive-only presentation (cf. Wexler and Culicover, 1980, pp. 63–65), but the Tomita learning environments are much more impoverished. I have no commitment to negative information; all that is required is some desired output which discriminates among the input strings in a generalizable way. Positive vs. negative evidence is merely the simplest way (with one bit) to provide this discrimination.

2. They use a single-layer (first-order) recurrence between states, whereas I use a higher-order (quadratic) recurrence. The multiplicative connections are what enable my model to have "fractal" dynamics equivalent in the limit to an IFS, and it may be that the first-order recurrence, besides being too weak for general Boolean functions (Minsky and Papert, 1988) and thus for arbi-

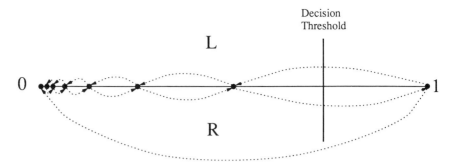

Figure 10.9 A one-dimensional dynamical recognizer for balanced parentheses, which is a context-free language. If an "L" is received, the state is divided by 2, if an "R" is received, the state is multiplied by 2 (modulo 2). This induces a "fractal" state space on the unit line which can be cut at .75 to determine if a string is grammatical.

trary regular languages (such as parity), also results only in simple steady-state or periodic dynamics.

Besides continued analysis, scaling the network up beyond binary symbol alphabets and beyond syntax, immediate follow-up work will involve comparing and contrasting our respective models with the other two possible models, a higher-order network trained on prediction, and a simple recurrent network model trained on classification.

10.7   CONCLUSION

If we take a state-space picture of the one-dimensional dynamical recognizer for parenthesis balancing developed earlier, it looks like figure 10.9. An infinite-state machine is embedded in a finite geometry using "fractal" self-similarity, and the decision function is cutting through this set. The emergence of these fractal attractors is interesting because I believe it bears on the question of how neural-like systems could achieve the power to handle more than regular languages.

Because it is quite clear that human languages are not formal, connectionists can maintain that recursive computational power is not of the "essence of human computation" (Rumelhart and McClelland, 1986, p. 119). However, it is also quite clear that without understanding the issue of generative capacity, connectionists and others working on naturalistic computation can stumble again and again into the trap of making strong claims for their models, easy to attack for not offering an adequate replacement for established theory. (Fodor and Pylyshyn, 1988; Pinker and Prince, 1988). But it is only because of "long-term lack of competition" that descriptive theories involving rules and representations can be defended as explanatory theories. Here is an alternative hypothesis for complex syntactic structure:

The state-space limit of a dynamical recognizer, as $\Sigma^* \rightarrow \Sigma^\infty$, is an attractor, which is cut by a threshold (or similar decision) function. The complexity of the generated *language is regular if the cut falls between disjoint limit points or cycles, context-free if it cuts a "self-similar" (recursive) region, and context-sensitive if it cuts a "chaotic" (pseudorandom) region.*

There is certainly substantial need for work on the theoretical front to more thoroughly formalize and prove or disprove the six main theorems implied by my hypothesis. I do not expect the full range of context-free or context-sensitive systems to be covered by conventional quasi-linear processing constraints, and the question remains wide open as to whether the syntactic systems that can be described by neural dynamical recognizers have any convergence with the needs of natural language systems.

Because information processing provides the "essence" of complex forms of cognition, like language, it is important to understand the relationship between complex emergent behaviors of dynamical systems (including neural systems) and traditional notions of computational complexity, including the Chomsky hierarchy, as well as algorithmic information theory (Chaitin, 1966). The study of this relationship is still in its infancy.

In Pollack (1987b), I constructed a Turing machine out of connectionist parts, and essentially showed that rational values, constants, precise thresholds, and multiplicative connections (all used in the sequential cascaded network architecture) were sufficient primitives for computationally universal recurrent neural networks.

Cellular automata, which we might view as a kind of low-density, synchronous, uniform, digital restriction of neural networks, have been studied as dynamical systems (Wolfram, 1984) and proved to be as powerful as universal Turing machines (e.g., Lindgren and Nordahl, 1990). Furthermore, Moore (1990) has shown that there are simple mathematical models for dynamical systems that are also universal, and it follows directly that determination of the behavior of such dynamical systems in the limit is undecidable and unpredictable, even with precise initial conditions. In stronger terms, the theoretical foundations of computer and information science may be in accord with the lack of predictability in the universe.

Finally, Crutchfield and Young (1989) have studied the computational complexity of dynamical systems reaching the onset of chaos via period-doubling. They have shown that these systems are not regular, but are finitely described by indexed context-free grammars. It may, of course, be just a coincidence that several modern computational linguistic grammatical theories also fall in this class (Joshi, 1985; Joshi, Vijay-Shanker, and Weir, 1989; Pollard, 1984).

In conclusion, I have merely illuminated the possibility of the existence of a naturalistic alternative to explicit recursive rules as a description of the complexity of language. Such a mathematical description would be compact, "parsimonious" in fact, since the infinite-state machine does not require infinite description, but only a finitely described set of weights. It was shown to be feasible to learn this type of description from a finite set of examples using pseudocontinuous hill-climbing parameter adaptation (in other words, backpropagation). However, performance in the limit appears to jump in discrete steps, with inductive phase transitions, which might correspond to psychological "stages" of acquisition. Finally, the languages so described can be recognized and generated efficiently by neural computation systems.

ACKNOWLEDGMENTS

This work has been partially sponsored by the Office of Naval Research under grant N00014-89-J-1200. I thanks the numerous colleagues who have discussed and criticized various aspects of this work or my presentation of it, including: T. Bylander, B. Chandrasekaran, J. Crutchfield, L. Giles, E. Gurari, S. Hanson, R. Kasper, J. Kolen, W. Ogden, T. Patten, R. Port, K. Supowit, P. Smolensky, D. S. Touretzky, and A. Zwicky.

NOTES

1. To turn a recognizer into a generator, simply enumerate the strings in Σ^* and filter out those the recognizer rejects.

2. For the simple low-dimensional dynamical systems usually studied, the "knob" or control parameter for such a bifurcation diagram is a scalar variable; here the control parameter is the entire 32-dimensional vector of weights in the network, and backpropagation turns the knob.

3. Tomita assumed a trap state which did not mutate, and Servan-Schreiber et al. (1989) compared the incoming token to a thresholded set of token predictions, trapping if the token was not predicted.

4. Barnsley's use of the term *attractor* is different from the conventional use of the term given in the introduction, yet is technically correct in that it refers to the "limit" of a iterative process. It can be thought of as what happens when you randomly drop an infinite number of microscopic iron filing "points" onto a piece of paper with a magnetic field lying under it; each point will land "on" the underlying attractor.

REFERENCES

Anderson, J. A., Silverstein, J. W., Ritz, S. A., et al. (1977). Distinctive features, categorical perception, and probability learning: some applications of a neural model. *Psychological Review*, *84*, 413–451.

Angluin, D. (1978). On the complexity of minimum inference of regular sets. *Information and Control*, *39*, 337–350.

Angluin, D. and Smith, C. H. (1983). Inductive inference: theory and methods. *Computing Surveys*, *15*, 237–269.

Barnsley, M. F. (1988). *Fractals everywhere*. San Diego: Academic Press.

Berwick, R. (1985). *The acquisition of syntactic knowledge*. Cambridge, MA: MIT Press.

Chaitin, G. J. (1966). On the length of programs for computing finite binary sequences. *Journal of the AM*, *13*, 547–569.

Chomsky, N. (1956). Three models for the description of language. *IRE Transactions on Information Theory*, *IT-2*, 113–124.

Chomsky, N. (1965). *Aspects of the theory of syntax*. Cambridge, MA: MIT Press.

Crutchfield, J. P., Farmer, J. D., Packard, N, H., et al. (1986). Chaos. *Scientific American, 255*, 46−57.

Crutchfield, J. P., and Young, K. (1989). Computation at the onset of chaos. In W. Zurek (Ed.), *Complexity, entropy and the physics of information*. Reading, MA: Addison-Wesley.

Derrida, B. and Meir, R. (1988). Chaotic behavior of a layered neural network. *Physical Review A, 38*.

Devaney, R. L. (1987). *An introduction to chaotic dynamical systems*. Reading, MA: Addison-Wesley.

Elman, J. L. (1990). Finding structure in time. *Cognitive Science, 14*, 179−212.

Feldman, J. A. (1972). Some decidability results in grammatical inference. *Information and Control, 20*, 244−462.

Fodor, J. and Pylyshyn, A. (1988). Connectionism and cognitive architecture: a critical analysis. *Cognition, 28*, 3−71.

Giles, C. L., Sun, G. Z., Chen, H. H., et al. (1990). Higher order recurrent networks and grammatical inference. In D. S. Touretzky (Ed.), *Advances in neural information processing systems*. Los Gatos, CA: Morgan Kaufman.

Gleick, J. (1987). *Chaos: making a new science*. New York: Viking.

Gold, E. M. (1967). Language identification in the limit. *Information and Control, 10*, 447−474.

Gold, E. M. (1978). Complexity of automaton identification from given data. *Information and Control, 37*, 302−320.

Grassberger, P., and Procaccia, I. (1983). Measuring the strangeness of strange attractors. *Physica D, 9*, 189−208.

Grebogi, C., Ott, E., and Yorke, J. A. (1987). Chaos, strange attractors, and fractal basin boundaries in nonlinear dynamics. *Science, 238*, 632−638.

Hendin, O., Horn, D., and Usher, M. (1991). Chaotic behavior of a neural network with dynamical thresholds. *International Journal of Neural Systems, 1*, 327−335.

Hopfield, J. J. (1982). Neural networks and physical systems with emergent collective computational abilities. *Proceedings of the National Academy of Sciences of the United States of America, 79*, 2554−2558.

Hornik, K., Stinchcombe, M., and White, H. (1990). Multi-layer feedforward networks are universal approximators. *Neural Networks, 3*, 551−560.

Huberman, B. A., and Hogg, T. (1987). Phase transitions in artificial intelligence systems. *Artificial Intelligence, 33*, 155−172.

Joshi, A. K. (1985). Tree adjoining grammars: how much context-sensitivity is required to provide reasonable structural descriptions?. In D. R. Dowty, L. Karttunen and A. M. Zwicky (Eds.), *Natural language parsing*. Cambridge, England: Cambridge University Press.

Joshi, A. K., Vijay-Shanker, K., and Weir, D. J. (1989). Convergence of mildly context-sensitive grammar formalism. In T. Wasow, and P. Sells (Eds.), *The processing of linguistic structure*. Cambridge, MA: MIT Press.

Kolen, J. F., and Pollack, J. B. (1990). Backpropagation is sensitive to initial conditions. *Complex Systems, 4*, 269−280.

Kurten, K. E. (1987). Phase transitions in quasirandom neural networks. In *IEEE First International Conference on Neural Networks*. (II-197-20) San Diego.

Lapedes, A. S., and Farber, R. M. (1988). How neural nets work. In D. Z. Anderson (Ed.), *Neural informational processing systems*. New York: American Institute of Physics.

Lieberman, P. (1984). *The biology and evolution of language*. Cambridge, MA: Harvard University Press.

Lindgren, K., and Nordahl, M. G. (1990). Universal computation in simple one-dimensional cellular automata. *Complex Systems, 4*, 299–318.

Lippman, R. P. (1987). An introduction to computing with neural networks. *IEEE Acoustics Speech and Signal Processing Magazine*, April, pp. 4–22.

MacLennan, B. J. (1989). *Continous computation*. (CS-89-83.) Knoxville: Computer Science Department, University of Tennessee.

MacWhinney, B. (1987). *Mechanisms of language acquisition*. Hillsdale, NJ: Erlbaum.

Mandelbrot, B. (1982). *The fractal geometry of nature*. San Francisco: Freeman.

McCulloch, W. S., and Pitts, W. (1943). A logical calculus of the ideas immanent in nervous activity. *Bulletin of Mathematical Biophysics, 5*, 115–133.

Mealy, G. H. (1955). A method for synthesizing sequential circuits. *Bell System Technical Journal, 43*, 1045–1079.

Metcalfe, J., and Wiebe, D. (1987). Intuition in insight and noninsight problem solving. *Memory and Cognition, 15*, 238–246.

Minsky, M. (1972). *Computation: finite and infinite machines*. Cambridge, MA: MIT Press.

Minsky, M., and Papert, S. (1988). *Perceptrons*. Cambridge, MA: MIT Press.

Moore, C. (1990). Unpredictability and undecidability in dynamical systems. *Physical Review Letters, 62*, 2354–2357.

Mozer, M. (1988). *A focused back-propagation algorithm for temporal pattern recognition*. (CRG-Technical Report-88-3.) University of Toronto.

Pearlmutter, B. A. (1989). Learning state space trajectories in recurrent neural networks. *Neural Computation, 1*, 263–269.

Pineda, F. J. (1987). Generalization of back-propagation to recurrent neural networks. *Physical Review Letters, 59*, 2229–2232.

Pinker, S. (1984). *Language learnability and language development*. Cambridge, MA: Harvard University Press.

Pinker, S., and Bloom, P. (1990). Natural language and natural selection. *Brain and Behavioral Sciences, 12*, 707–784.

Pinker, S., and Prince, A. (1988). On language and connectionism: analysis of a parallel distributed processing model of language inquisition. *Cognition, 28*, 73–193.

Plunkett, K., and Marchman, V. (1989). *Pattern association in a back-propagation network: implications for child language acquisition*. (Technical Report 8902.) San Diego: University of California, San Diego Center for Research in Langauge.

Pollack, J. B. (1987a). Cascaded back propagation on dynamic connectionist networks. In *Proceedings of the 9th Conference of the Cognitive Science Society*, Seattle, pp. 391–404.

Pollack, J. B. (1987b). *On connectionist models of natural language processing*. Ph.D. thesis, Urbana: Computer Science Department, University of Illinois. [Available as MCCS-87-100, Computing Research Laboratory, Las Cruces, NM]

Pollack, J. B. (1989). Implications of recursive distributed representations. In D. S. Touretzky (Ed.), *Advances in neural information processing systems*. Los Gatos, CA: Morgan Kaufman.

Pollack, J. B. (1990). Recursive distributed representation. *Artificial Intelligence, 46,* 77–105.

Pollard, C. (1984). *Generalized context-free grammars, head grammars and natural language.* Doctoral dissertation, Palo Alto, CA: Department of Linguistics, Stanford University.

Rivest, R. L., and Schapire, R. E. (1987). A new approach to unsupervised learning in deterministic environments. In *Proceedings of the 4th International Workshop on Machine Learning,* Irvine, CA pp. 364–475.

Rumelhart, D. E., Hinton, G., and Williams, R. (1986). Learning internal representations through error propagation. In D. E. Rumelhart, J. L. McClelland, and the PDP Research Group (Eds.), *Parallel distributed processing: experiments in the microstructure of cognition,* Vol. 1. Cambridge, MA: MIT Press.

Rumelhart, D. E., and McClelland, J. L. (1986). PDP models and general issues in cognitive science. In D. E. Rumelhart, J. L. McClelland, and the PDP Research Group (Eds.), *Parallel distributed processing: experiments in the microstructure of cognition,* Vol. 1. Cambridge, MA: MIT Press.

Servan-Schreiber, D., Cleeremans, A., and McClelland, J. L. (1989). Encoding sequential structure in simple recurrent networks. In D. S. Touretzky (Ed.), *Advances in neural information processing systems.* Los Gatos, CA: Morgan Kaufman.

Skarda, C. A., and Freeman, W. J. (1987). How brains make chaos to make sense of the world. *Brain and Behavioral Science, 10,* 161–195.

Smolensky, P. (1986). Information processing in dynamical systems: foundations of harmony theory. In D. E. Rumelhart, J. L. McClelland, and the PDP Research Group (Eds.), *Parallel distributed processing: experiments in the microstructure of cognition,* Vol. 1. Cambridge, MA: MIT Press.

Tomita, M. (1982). Dynamic construction of finite-state automata from examples using hill-climbing. In *Proceedings of the 4th Annual Cognitive Science Conference* (pp. 105–108). Ann Arbor, MI.

Touretzky, D. S., and Geva, S. (1987). A distributed connectionist representation for concept structures. In *Proceedings of the Ninth Annual Conference of the Cognitive Science Society* (pp. 155–164), Seattle.

Van der Maas, H., Verschure, P., and Molenaar, P. (1990). A note on chaotic behavior in simple neural networks. *Neural Networks, 3,* 119–122.

Wexler, K., and Culicover, P. W. (1980). *Formal principles of language acquisition.* Cambridge, MA: MIT Press.

Wolfram, S. (1984). Universality and complexity in cellular automata. *Physica D, 10,* 1–35.

Guide to Further Reading and Postscript

In recent years, there has been some further work in the area. Several researchers have focused simply on the task of inducing finite-state machines from data, often using the Tomita data sets or languages as a benchmark (Giles, Miller, Chen, et al., 1992; Watrous and Kuhn, 1992; Angeline, Saunders, and Pollack, 1994; Zeng, Goodman, and Smyth, 1993; Das and Mozer, 1994). In some of this work, the issue of how to prevent the kind of state blurring we observed in this chapter has become a central issue, and techniques ranging from symbolic analysis to clustering states, to using discrete state thresholding, have been developed.

We have studied the issue of where fractal limit sets, such as the "magic mushroom" of figure 10.8G comes from and have found deeper connections between the dynamics of recurrent networks and iterated function systems, which makes dubious the idea of getting a finite information state idea from nonlinear recurrent networks at all (Pollack, 1991; Kolen, 1994a). The fact that there is a deep connection between the dynamics of recurrent networks and fractals led to work using recurrent networks as the basis for mental imagery (Stucki and Pollack, 1992).

Finally, the hypothesis in the conclusion of the chapter, which related the question of where a decision boundary was located in an attractor to what kind of generative complexity such a dynamical recognizer might obtain, has been further developed into the question of whether a dynamical system can even have generative capacity on its own. A simple demonstration suffices to show that in the case of physical systems, complexity implicates the observer who establishes the measurement framework for the sequence of symbols and the boundaries between sentences (Kolen and Pollack, 1994). These questions, which go to the heart of the modern synthesis of cognitive science, are fully explored in John Kolen's Ph.D. dissertation (Kolen, 1994b).

Angeline, P. J., Saunders, G. M., and Pollack, J. B. (1994), An evolutionary algorithm which constructs recurrent neural networks. *IEEE Transactions on Neural Networks, 5,* 54–65.

Das, S., and Mozer, M. (1994) A unified gradient-descent/clustering architecture for finite state machine induction. In J. Cowan, G. Tesauro, and J. Alspector (Eds.), *Advances in neural information processing,* Vol. 6 (pp. 19–26). Los Gatos, CA: Morgan Kaufman.

Giles, L., Miller, C. B., Chen, D., et al. (1992). Learning and extracting finite state automata with second-order recurrent neural networks. *Neural Computation, 4,* 393–405.

Kolen, J. F. (1994a). Fool's gold: extracting finite state machines from recurrent network dynamics. In J. Cowan, G. Tesauro, and J. Alspector (Eds.), *Advances in neural information processing,* Vol. 6 (pp. 501–508). Los Gatos, CA: Morgan Kaufman.

Kolen J. F. (1994b). *Exploring the computational capabilities of recurrent neural networks.* Doctoral dissertation, Department of Computer and Information Science, Ohio State University, Columbus.

Kolen J. F., and Pollack, J. B. (1994). Observer's, paradox: apparent computational complexity in physical systems. *Journal of Experimental and Theoretical Artificial Intelligence,* in press.

Pollack, J. B. (1991). The induction of dynamical recognizers. *Machine Learning, 7,* 227–252.

Stucki, D. S., and J. B. Pollack (1992). Fractal (reconstructive analogue) memory. In *14th Annual Cognitive Science Conference* (pp. 118–123). Los Gatos, CA: Morgan Kaufman.

Watrous, R. L., and Kuhn, G. M. (1992). Induction of finite state languages using second order recurrent networks. *Neural Computation, 4,* 406–414.

Zeng, Z., Goodman, R. M., and Smyth, P. (1993). Learning finite state machines with self-clustering recurrent networks. *Neural Computation, 5,* 976–990.

11 Growth Dynamics in Development

Paul van Geert

EDITORS' INTRODUCTION

Human cognitive capacities are at any time the outcome of an ongoing developmental process, and fully understanding those capacities requires understanding that development. Yet psychologists have found development to be a tangled maze of processes, stages, and interactions. Can basic concepts of dynamics help map this terrain?

Paul van Geert uses the concept of growth as his primary exploratory tool. How much of the diversity and complexity of cognitive development can be subsumed under the relatively simple notion of growth of one or more properties? Growth has the advantage of being mathematically well defined, since its basic properties are captured by a well-known dynamical equation, the so-called logistic growth function. Van Geert's general approach is to isolate aspects of development that can be modeled by one form or another of this logistic equation.

His first move is to demonstrate that real time-series data in a simple example of growth—the early development of a child's lexicon—can be modeled in fine detail. This kind of curve-fitting is, however, just groundwork for investigations into a wide variety of aspects of cognitive development. He describes how the same model can describe qualitatively very different growth patterns, including limit cycles and chaotic fluctuations, and can be extended to complex systems of interactive growth processes which give rise to a wide range of substages, hierarchies, sudden transitions, regressions, and "mountains" in the emergence of particular cognitive capacities.

This work shows that with dynamical tools developmental psychologists can do much more than simply describe the various patterns of emergence in cognitive development; they can reveal how a complex diversity of surface phenomena can be understood as resulting from the operation of simple underlying processes amenable to mathematical description.

11.1 INTRODUCTION

In the physical, cultural, and mental environments of humans there is hardly anything that does not change. These changes do not occur independently, but are interlinked in complex ways. Some of these changes are covered by the term *development*. The notion of development requires that the changes be orderly or follow specific types of paths (van Geert, 1986). One form of development—growth—applies to a wide range of biological, cultural, and psychological phenomena. It can be described by a simple dynamical model which, nevertheless, shows interesting properties.

11.2 PROPERTIES OF THE GROWTH PROCESS

A process is called growth if it is concerned with the increase or decrease (i.e., negative increase) of one or more properties, and if that increase is the effect of a mechanism intrinsic to that process. The growth of cauliflower or of a child's lexicon are both examples. The variable used to indicate the growing property, such as the cauliflower's size, or the number of words in the lexicon, is the growth level, denoted by L. It is trivial that there must be something that can grow (e.g., a cauliflower seed, or at least a minimal lexicon) in order for growth to occur. I call this the minimal structural growth condition, or minimal structural growth level. Although growth is supposed to occur by itself—and not as a consequence of a mere external force adding size to the cauliflower or words to the lexicon—it requires resources to keep the process going. While a cauliflower needs minerals, water, and sunlight, a child's lexicon needs information about possible words in the language, effort, time, parental support, and the like. This is the principle of resource-dependence of a growth process.

Let us dig a little deeper into the nature of the resources necessary for growth in the psychological (cognitive, linguistic, . . .) domain. Several classes of resources can be distinguished. Some of the resources are internal to the person in whom the growth process is taking place. First, in order to learn new words, for example, children must have a capacity to remember. The available mental capacity, which can be measured in various ways, can be thought of as an internal *spatial* resource. Second, in order to learn new words, children must spend *time* at the learning process; this time can be thought of as an internal temporal resource. Third, in order to understand how contexts define the meanings of words, for example, children have to rely on internal *informational* resources, such as knowledge of conceptual categories or event structures. Fourth, children differ in the amount of *motivational* or *energetic* resources they invest—that is, in the effort, interest or motivation put into the learning of new words. Finally, there is a class of internal *material* resources, relating to the bodily outfit of the learner, the presence of correctly working senses, and so on.

A similar set of subclasses can be distinguished that are external to the learner, in the sense that they belong to the accessible environment. Children differ in the *spatial* environments they are allowed to explore, and in the *time* the environment invests in actually helping them to learn new words. External *informational* resources involve aspects such as the "ambient lexicon" (the lexicon actually used in their linguistic environment), as well as explanations given or tasks set by their caregivers. External *energetic* or *motivational* resources concern aspects such as the reinforcement given by the environment following the learning of more new words. Finally, external *material* resources consist of elementary things like food and shelter, as well as the availability of books or television sets.

As far as their relation to the growth process is concerned, resources have two major properties. First, they are limited. Second, resources are interlinked in a dynamical system.

Consider the limited nature of resources. It is a well-established fact, for instance, that the size of human working memory is limited (Miller, 1956). The size of working memory grows during the first stages of development, and puts an upper limit on available logical operations (Case, 1984, 1987). The time that children can invest in a learning task is limited: whatever time is invested in one cognitive endeavour cannot be invested in another one. (There are exceptions for learning processes that are highly correlated or mutually supportive, such as learning words and learning about syntactic categories.) Children have limited knowledge about the world, and the speed and nature of learning words is constrained by what they know. Effort and interest are equally limited: they come and go in cycles of interest alternated by periods of fatigue, boredom, or habituation. Similar stories hold for each and every type of resource. However, within the system of resources, compensatory relations may exist; thus, lack of time can be compensated by effort, or limited natural memory can be extended by the use of external material "memories" such as books or computers.

Second, resources form an interlinked, dynamic structure. Children's knowledge of nonverbal categories, for instance, is an informational resource used in the learning of new words. But the learning of new words may in its turn change the nonverbal conceptual understanding of the child. Consider a different example. The help and support given to a child is not simply a property of the caregiver as such, but is dependent on the growth level of the knowledge to which that help is directed. The properties of the caregiver's language addressed to the child, for instance, depend on children's level of linguistic development, whereas the growth of their linguistic knowledge depends in turn on maternal language (Snow and Ferguson, 1977). There are various logical-cognitive skills and various forms of emotion understanding that are interlinked, in that the cognitive skill codetermines the understanding and management of emotions, while emotions codetermine cognitive discoveries (Fischer, Shave, and Carnochan, 1990; Bloom, 1990). Similar mutual relationships hold for separate knowledge domains and skills in the cognitive domain (Case, 1987).

I have termed the interlinked structure of resources the *cognitive ecosystem*. Each person has his or her own particular cognitive ecosystem consisting of internal as well as external or environmental aspects. I consider the external aspects—such as the help given by caregivers, or the available material resources—as part of the ecosystem of the individual, since each individual has his or her own relationship and modes of access to the subjectively experienced environment (van Geert, 1991, 1993a).

The limited and systemic nature of the available resources leads to another major concept in the model of growth processes. This concept has been developed in ecology and applied to biological growth processes, but it applies equally well to psychological growth, such as the increase of a child's lexicon. It is that of *carrying capacity*, generally denoted by K. It is based on the idea that, since growth is resource-dependent and resources are limited, the final attainable growth level based on those resources must also be limited. Thus, given limitations in their resources, children will evolve toward a state of lexical knowledge that is a reflection of those limited resources. Children who could, on average, rely on more or better resources, such as more or better environmental support, will end up with a lexicon containing more words than children who had less support (all other things being equal). The carrying capacity is a level of equilibrium or stability (other than the zero level), determined by the available resources. Any growth level that is above zero and either above or below the carrying capacity is unstable. The instability can take the form either of further growth toward the equilibrium level, or of oscillations around that level. The latter form of instability will occur when the growth rate is higher than a specific threshold value. The carrying capacity is a one-dimensional notion, in that it corresponds with a stable final level of a particular growth variable (such as the number of words in a child's lexicon). More precisely, it is the one-dimensional correlate of a multidimensional structure, namely, the available resource structure.

Finally, processes that require the exchange of information between biocultural systems (such as parents and their children) are characterized by a certain inertia or slowness. That is, a time lag exists between the starting and the endpoint of some developmental or learning process. For instance, if one changes the teaching conditions in a classroom, it will take some time before the effect on the pupils' learning will become manifest. This inertia or feedback delay is responsible for a certain degree of coarseness or lack of precision in the system.

11.3   THE ITERATIVE GROWTH EQUATION AND ITS APPLICATION TO DATA ON LEXICAL DEVELOPMENT

The simplest possible model for a growth process where the growth level is some delayed function of an earlier state of growth is

$$L_{n+1} = L_n(1 + R_n) \qquad \text{for } L_0 > 0 \tag{1}$$

where L_n is the growth level at point n in a sequence of iterations and R_n is the level of resources at that point. One starts with an initial level L_0, applies the equation to obtain L_1, applies the equation again to obtain L_2, and so on. If the equation is applied to a real sequence of growth levels, e.g., of a child's lexicon, each iterative step corresponds with a real-time interval, known as the feedback delay.

Since growth feeds on limited resources, growth must slow down as more and more of the resources are used. Since the growth level is proportional to the amount of resources consumed, the variable R can be rewritten as a function of a growth parameter r and a decrease variable that gains in magnitude as more and more resources are consumed:

$$R_n = r - a \cdot L_n \qquad (2)$$

It follows then that L reaches an equilibrium at which it no longer increases when

$$r = a \cdot L_n \qquad (3)$$

This equilibrium level has been called the carrying capacity K:

$$K = \frac{r}{a} \qquad (4)$$

Given this equivalence, we can write down an alternative form of the basic growth equation, namely

$$L_{n+1} = L_n \left(1 + r - \frac{r \cdot L_n}{K} \right) \qquad \text{for } L_0 > 0 \qquad (5)$$

Let us see if the model can be applied to an empirically found process of lexical growth in a child.

In a fascinating study of the early language development of her daughter Keren, Dromi (1986) presents a number of growth curves, one of which covers the growth of Keren's lexicon between the ages of 10 and 17 months. It needs to be noted that Keren was a linguistically creative and precocious girl, and that data from other studies reveal a slower growth rate (e.g., Nelson, 1985) in different children. However, the point is not whether the data are characteristic of the whole population of early language learners—they need not be, since there are considerable individual differences in the rate of almost any developmental process—but rather whether the logistic growth model can produce a sequence of growth levels that fit the empirical data.

Dromi's study covers the stage of one-word sentences, i.e., before the onset of true syntax learning. Syntax is an important resource factor in the development of language, since it definitely changes the need for specified words (such as words belonging to different syntactic classes) but also allows for the expression of meaningful contents in the form of word combinations. Let us therefore assume that the one-word stage has a constant carrying capacity, as far as the acquisition of new words is concerned. Since Keren's lexicon consisted of approximately 340 words by the time she started to use multiword sentences, the one-word stage carrying capacity can be set to 340.

Because we have no idea at all as to how long the assumed feedback delay is in the case of early word learning, I shall assume it is just as long as the sampling interval. Dromi sampled the lexical increase every week. Given her sequence of data, we can estimate the growth rate over a 1-week interval by

$$\frac{L_{n+1}/L_{n-1}}{1 - L_n/K} \qquad (6)$$

The value of r will be an average of all successive sampling levels considered. In order to model the data, we write a sequence of iterative equations, based on equation (5). (A simple but adequate method of doing so is to use a spreadsheet, such as Lotus 1-2-3 or Excel, or to write a program in BASIC or C.) The choice of the initial level, L_0, is rather critical. The data sequence as such does not literally present the real initial level. We should always reckon with at least some observation error. Especially at the beginning of word learning, the status of children's vocalizations is unclear. The observation error at the initial sampling points, therefore, might be quite substantial. Are the few recognizable words real words? Do they all contribute to the acquisition of new words? When is the real onset of lexical growth—right at the first sampling moment, or earlier or later? The simplest strategy is of course to set L_0 to the level of the first word sampling. That is, the initial state level is literally the number of words observed at the first sampling, and the growth onset time is believed to be the first sampling week. This is, of course, only a first approximation, and the modeling work should prove whether it is adequate. A good fit between the model and the data is obtained by setting the initial state level (where the computation begins) to two words. As growth onset time I took the fourth week of sampling, where the data show the increase actually begins. The growth rate parameter was estimated as 0.3.

The real growth process is no doubt affected by random perturbations of many different sorts. The effect of such random perturbations can be studied by employing the following equation:

$$L_{n+1} = \left[L_n \left(1 + r - \frac{r \cdot L_n}{K} \right) \right] \cdot (1 + RAND\_L \cdot p) \qquad (7)$$

The equation part between square brackets is the logistic growth equation [equation (5)]. $RAND\_L$ is a random number ranging between -1 and $+1$, and p is a parameter modifying the effect of $RAND\_L$ (e.g., if $p = 0.05$, $RAND\_L$ changes the value of the computed growth rate with a maximum of $\pm 5\%$ of the computed level).

In order to do the preceding simulations I took the sampling interval as feedback delay. If I take a 2-week interval and compute the growth rate for data points separated by 2 weeks, I estimate a growth rate value of 0.71, resulting in an even better fit between data and model (figure 11.1)

On closer inspection, however, Keren's lexical growth curve during the one-word stage seems to consist of two substages. The first is a stage of growth that seems to level off around interval point 5 (week 12), at a growth level of about 50 words. It is immediately succeeded by a second substage of almost explosive growth, leading to the temporary ceiling level of around

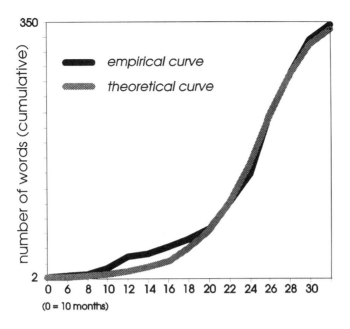

Figure 11.1 Data from Dromi's study on lexical growth (Dromi, 1986) (black line), compared with a simulation based on a simple logistic equation with a feedback delay of 2 weeks (gray line).

340 words. The bend in the growth curve actually corresponds with a change in semantic strategy. First, before week 19 Keren's word meanings and extensions were difficult to predict and seemed rather unsystematic. After week 19, the buildup of meanings was systematic and closely followed the adult meanings (Dromi, 1986). It seems that around week 18 to 19 Keren has established a new and more productive method of word learning which greatly enhances the carrying capacity. In the next section I discuss a model of two connected growers, e.g., the lexicon and a meaning acquisition strategy, and show how the notion of carrying capacity increase follows naturally from the principle of connected growth.

The growth model is not restricted to the Dromi data. Corrigan's data (Corrigan 1983) on lexical development, for instance, can also be modeled quite successfully, although the parameters used differ from the Dromi study (van Geert, 1991). Developmental domains other than just lexical growth show similar growth patterns. The growth of working memory, for instance, follows a trajectory that is easy to model with the simple logistic principle (van Geert, 1994a). Finally, there is a whole variety of cognitive developmental phenomena that develop in the form of a growth spurt highly similar to the trajectory produced by the logistic model (Fischer and Rose, 1993; Fischer and Pipp, 1984).

Besides producing quite realistic growth curves, the logistic growth equation has another theoretical advantage, namely, that it produces qualitatively different growth patterns depending on the size of the growth parameter. It can produce limit cycles as well as chaotic behavior. These patterns do not occur in lexical growth as such, but they can be observed in additional forms of language growth. For example, if one takes the percentage of correct sentences as a criterion for growth in domains such as inflections or the syntax of wh-questions, individual children show a characteristic chaotic fluctuation over a trend of overall increase (see Brown, 1973; Labov and Labov, 1978). The same is true for the fluctuations in the increase in mean length of utterance (Brown, 1973). Chaotic oscillations also apply to lexical growth, if one takes the average growth per time unit as a growth criterion, instead of the cumulative lexicon as I did in the present section (Corrigan, 1983). In our own data, based on samples of Dutch-speaking children between $1\frac{1}{2}$ and $2\frac{1}{2}$ years old, we observed similar oscillatory phenomena (Ruhland and van Geert, 1994; Cats and Ruhland, 1994). One could, of course, object that the oscillations are just observation error or random fluctuations independent of the observed language "signal." Our data—and those of the previously mentioned students of language development, for that matter—are practically error-free, in that they present a reliable account of the actual number of words, utterances, and so forth the child produced during one language-sampling session. If we had come a day later or earlier, we would probably have counted a different number of words or utterances. That difference, however, is not an error, but a sign of the intrinsic variability in children's linguistic production, and that variability is also what our models intend to capture.

As we have seen with the stage of lexical growth preceding the onset of syntax, however, growth models based on a single grower are in general too simple to cover some of the more interesting irregular aspects of the data. Let me now turn to the concept of connecting growers and show how simple systems of growers can display complicated behavior found in a wide variety of data on long-term development.

11.4   THE DYNAMICS OF CONNECTED GROWERS

I have claimed earlier that the resources for growth are limited, and that they form a structure highly reminiscent of an ecological system. It is a well-established empirical fact that different aspects of cognitive development can positively affect one another. The development of general conceptual knowledge about objects, for instance, is closely and positively related to the growth of words and syntactic knowledge (Corrigan, 1983). However, various acquisition and growth processes compete heavily for resources such as memory, effort, and attention. The onset of syntax, for instance, seems to attract a considerable amount of the resources formerly invested only in the learning of new words (Dromi, 1986). It is probably because of this reshuffling of resource investment that the rate of word learning shows a marked drop at the onset of multiword sentences. In the case of Keren's lexical growth, we noted that there seem to be two substages in the one-word stage. These substages appear to be related to the development of a new and powerful strategy for the construction of word meaning. Let us try to model the emergence of these substages by introducing the concept of connected growers.

Assume two cognitive growers exist, namely the lexicon on the one hand, and a meaning acquisition strategy on the other. (Of course there are many more growers, but here we are interested only in the little two-grower system.) The growth level of the meaning strategy is the number of cases in which that strategy is actually employed, relative to an older and developmentally more primitive meaning strategy. Let's call that growth level M. The growth level of the lexicon is the number of words the child knows, L. We don't know what exactly the meaning strategy is in the case of Keren's word learning, but there is evidence that the emergence of that strategy has a positive impact on word learning (Dromi, 1986): the learning of new words is positively dependent on the available meaning extraction strategy. That is, we may assume a support relationship from M to L. M supports the increase of L, and the higher the level of M, the more support it will give to word learning.

However, we may assume that the time, attention, and effort invested in experimenting with new meaning strategies is not available to the learning of new words per se. The more time and effort invested in M, the less remains to be invested in L. Resources such as time, effort, and attention invested are, on average, positively correlated with the increase in M. That is, we may assume that, on average, the more time the child invests in mastering a new meaning strategy, the faster that strategy will grow, all other things being equal (growth occurs in terms of the use of that strategy in comparison with an older strategy). It follows, therefore, that the increase in M is a measure of the average amount of time, effort, attention, and the like invested in M. But any resources invested in M cannot be put to work to the benefit of L (or any other grower, for that matter). Consequently, we may assume a competitive relationship between the growth of L and the growth of M.

The same reasoning holds for the relationship between the growth of the meaning acquisition strategy on the one hand and the growth of the lexicon on the other. The more words children know, the better their chances of finding out about rules of meaning formation. However, resources invested in the learning of new words per se are not available to the learning of better meaning strategies. Put differently, the relationships of support and competition are reciprocal for the two growers L and M.

Given the mutual supportive and competitive relations between M and L, we write the equations for their growth in the following form:

$$L_{n+1} = L_n \cdot \left[1 + r_L - \frac{r_L \cdot L_n}{K_L} - c_L \cdot (M_n - M_{n-1}) + s_L \cdot M_n \right]$$

$$M_{n+1} = M_n \cdot \left[1 + r_M - \frac{r_M \cdot M_n}{K_M} - c_M \cdot (L_n - L_{n-1}) + s_M \cdot L_n \right]$$

(8)

(Note that the first half of each equation is the logistic growth part [coming from equation (5)], whereas the second half specifies the extent to which a grower competes with and is supported by the related grower.)

In this model, the resources consumed to let the competitor grow are a linear function of the amount of growth in the competitor, for instance, a function of $(M_n - M_{n-1})$. It is also possible to think of an alternative, where the attention and effort spent to learn a new skill, principle, or strategy is considerably greater at the earlier states than it is at the later ones. The reasoning behind this assumption is that once the learning task becomes more familiar, less resources will have to be invested to achieve a similar amount of progress. In this alternative version of the model, the competition factors c_L and c_M are multiplied by $(M_n - M_{n-1})/M_n$ and $(L_n - L_{n-1})/L_n$ respectively.

Equation (8) describes a simple model of two coupled growers: each is positively and negatively affected by the other. The carrying capacity of each grower, i.e., the point at which an equilibrium may occur, is now a function of the original K and of the supportive factors. It is easy to show why this is so. Let me denote the sum of supportive and competitive factors by S, and rewrite the first part of equation (8) as follows (for the sake of simplicity, I omit the L-subscripts):

$$L_{n+1} = L_n \cdot \left(1 + r - \frac{r \cdot L_n}{K} + S \right)$$

(9)

L will no longer increase or decrease when

$$r - \frac{r \cdot L_n}{K} + S = 0$$

(10)

i.e., when

$$L_n = \frac{K \cdot (r + S)}{r}$$

(11)

The effect of the supporting factors is that the new carrying capacity level of the grower is a fraction S/r bigger than the original carrying capacity set by the parameter K. This is an interesting conclusion, since the supporting factors are clearly part of the resources on which the grower L feeds.

Connected growers are often related in hierarchical ways. That is, one grower forms a condition for the growth of another one. Structural theories of development, like Piaget's or Fischer's, are clearly hierarchically related. For instance, it requires at least some proficiency with concrete operational thinking in order to develop formal operational thinking skills. The concrete thinking is a prerequisite for the emergence of the formal thinking. In the domain of word learning, there is evidence that the characteristic "naming explosion," i.e., the explosive growth of the lexicon during the one-word period discussed earlier, has a conditional precursor in the form of nonverbal categorization behavior and understanding (Gopnik and Meltzoff, 1992).

The example of the lexicon and the new meaning acquisition strategy is another case in point. It is highly likely that the new meaning strategy develops in reply to new demands on learning words that came about only because the child has developed a minimal lexicon and because the further elaboration of that lexicon requires a better meaning acquisition strategy. Put differently, a certain level of lexical growth is necessary in order for the meaning strategy to emerge or to start growing. The higher the precursor level, the stronger the precursor relationship between L and M. There's a simple way to put this in the form of an equation

$$L_{n+1} = L_n \cdot \left[1 + r_L - \frac{r_L \cdot \mathbf{L}_n}{K_L} - \frac{c_L \cdot (M_n - M_{n-1})}{M_n} + s_L \cdot M_n \right]$$

$$M_{n+1} = M_n + p \cdot M_n \cdot \left[r_M - \frac{r_M \cdot \mathbf{M}_n}{K_M} - \frac{c_M \cdot (L_n - L_{n-1})}{L_n} + s_M \cdot L_n \right] \quad (12)$$

for $p = 0$ if $L_n <$ precursor, and 1 in any other case.

Note that this equation is very similar to equation (8), with the following two exceptions: first, I use the relative increase in either L or M as a competitive factor; second, the variable part of the M-equation is now dependent on a dichotomous variable, p, which is either 0 or 1.

The following values were used with equation (12) to obtain the result in figure 11.2

	Rate	s	c	K	Initial	Precursor
L	0.12	0.2	0.7	1	0.005	—
M	0.1	0.01	0.1	0.7	0.001	0.2

The model used in figure 11.2 has been based on 200 iterative steps. They have been rescaled to fit the 32 steps of the empirical data set.

The principle of hierarchically connected growers applies to a wide variety of developmental phenomena, especially those described by structural theories. Before discussing how long-term, stagewise development can be modeled by using the connected grower principle, a second type of growth model will be introduced.

11.5   GROWTH AND TRANSITIONS

The logistic growth equation produces three types of growth forms, dependent on the size of the growth rate r: (1) growth toward a stable position via an S-shaped path or via an oscillation that dies out, (2) growth toward a cycle of 2, 4, 8, ... states, and (3) growth toward a chaotic, irregular oscillation. Although the canonical growth form is the S-shaped path toward a

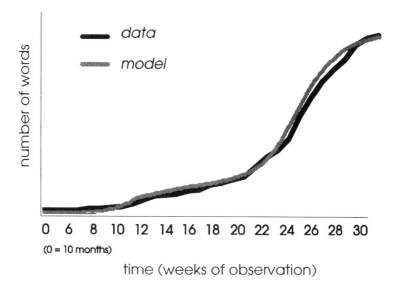

number of words

0   6   8   10 12 14 16 18 20 22 24 26 28 30
(0 = 10 months)

time (weeks of observation)

Figure 11.2 A simulation of the lexical growth data (Dromi, 1986) based on a model of connected growers.

stable state, it is likely that each of the forms generated by the equation actually occurs in different fields of development. What the equation fails to produce, however, is a sudden catastrophic jump from an initial to a final state. Such sudden jumps between states are typical of a variety of natural phenomena, e.g., the transition of liquid into ice (there is no intermediate aggregation state of matter that is partly liquid, partly solid). Sudden jumps also occur in behavior; a well-known example is the dog which, scared by a yelling and gesticulating person, suddenly switches from fear to aggression and attacks. They also occur in development, especially in cognitive development, where they mark a sudden change from one state of knowledge (such as not understanding a principle) to another (understanding the principle). Such sudden jumps in the knowledge state are called transitions. They have been found in early development, and concern sudden changes in infants' social and communicative competencies (van de Rijt-Plooij and Plooij, 1992). They also occur in later development, e.g., in adolescent thinking (Fischer and Pipp, 1984). Finally, sudden jumps are characteristic of problem-solving processes that require planning, such as the Tower of Hanoi problem (Bidell and Fischer, 1993).

A particularly good example of a sudden jump is the development of a grasp of the principle of conservation. A child is presented with two beakers of different shape (e.g., high and narrow vs. low and wide). One of them is filled with a liquid, which is then poured into the other beaker. The child is then asked whether there is as much, more, or less liquid in the present beaker than in the previous one. There exist many test versions of the conservation principle, but they basically boil down to changing the form of a quantity and then asking the child whether the amount has remained the same (has been

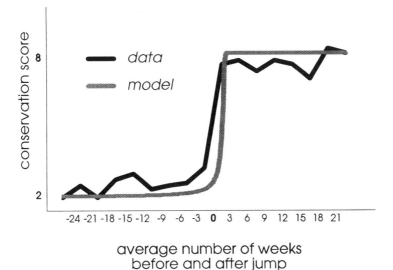

Figure 11.3 Data from van der Maas' (1993) study on conservation growth in individual children (black line) compared with a simulated growth curve, based on the transition version of the logistic growth equation (gray line).

conserved) or has changed. Since Piaget's original studies of the phenomenon (see, e.g., Inhelder and Piaget, 1958) we know that the characteristic developmental path runs as follows. The great majority of children younger than age 5 will say that there is less or more depending on the height of the water column. Their conviction is very strong, and they will stick to it in the face of countersuggestions and social pressure. Children around 5 years old run into an intermediate state, often characterized by rapid switches between the correct answer and the old wrong answer. Such an intermediate state is observed only if the test is administered very regularly, as on a day-to-day basis (van der Maas and Molenaar, 1992; van der Maas, 1993). Then, almost suddenly, a child switches to a correct understanding, and is able to give a wealth of justifications for why the liquid is still the same amount. Figure 11.3 shows data from a longitudinal experiment by Han van der Maas (1993). (Note that the minimal score on the conservation test is 2, since nonconservers were also able to solve two questions.) The maximum score is 8. The standard errors increase dramatically at the extremes of the time series. Since there is always a good deal of chance involved in the conservation score (it amounts to a dichotomous response, allowing for simple trial and error in the answers), the scores fluctuate rather strongly. (The data are compared with a model simulation explained below.)

Data from our longitudinal language samples show similar sudden jump patterns for the use of so-called function words (Ruhland and van Geert, 1994; Cats and Ruhland, 1994). They are words with an explicit syntactic function and are unlikely to occur with a semantic function only. Examples

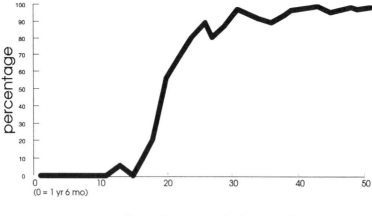

time (weeks of observation)

Figure 11.4 Data from Ruhland's study on the percentage of sentences with verbs in spontaneous language samples of a single child (Ruhland and van Geert, 1994); the child was $1\frac{1}{2}$ years old at the onset of the study.

are determiners, propositions, pronouns, and so forth. The pattern of emergence of such words is comparable to that of conservation, in that it reflects the discovery of some sort of principle, e.g., a grammatical or morphosyntactic rule. Figure 11.4 shows data on the use of verbs (verbs play a major syntactic role in sentences; they are, so to speak, at the heart of the syntactic combinatorial principles that govern the structure of a sentence). The data show the percentage of utterances containing a verb during a 2-hour sampling session.

An equation capable of describing the sudden shift is an alternative form of the logistic growth equation. The standard growth equation is based on the assumption that the growth is more and more inhibited as the growth level approaches the carrying capacity. The so-called braking factor increases with increasing growth level. The transition model adds another assumption, namely that the growth rate r itself is a function of the growth level. The higher that level, the bigger the growth rate. This assumption seems very similar to the original growth equation, since the absolute growth increases as the growth level increases. That is, there is a link between the growth level and the growth effect. In the transition model, however, the growth rate itself is a function of the growth level:

$$L_{n+1} = L_n \cdot \left(1 + F_n - \frac{F_n \cdot L_n}{K}\right) \qquad \text{for } F_n = \frac{r \cdot L_n}{K} \tag{13}$$

By substituting $\dfrac{r \cdot L_n}{K}$ for F_n one obtains the transition form of the growth model

$$L_{n+1} = L_n \cdot \left(1 + \frac{r \cdot L_n}{K} - \frac{r \cdot L_n^2}{K^2}\right) \tag{14}$$

Paul van Geert

Why would the growth rate r be a function of the growth level? Just assume that the growth of a skill like conservation understanding depends critically on children encountering situations in which they receive relevant information about conservation, where information is relevant if it really affects their knowledge state. It could occur in the form of a cognitive conflict, as Piaget would call it, or as a result of testing a hypothesis about the amount of mass after transformation, as information-processing models would claim. The relevant information could be triggered entirely by children themselves, e.g., by asking themselves critical questions about conservation. It could also be triggered by other people, e.g., other children, parents, or kindergarten teachers. But as long as there is only a very minimal understanding of conservation, children are unlikely to find themselves in an informative conservation situation. For instance, if a child believes that pouring a liquid into a different container actually changes the amount, almost any act of pouring liquid is further justification of that belief. Only if the two beakers involved are not very different from one another, but just different enough to notice, could the child be brought to a state of cognitive conflict that would lead to improved understanding. Since we assumed that the growth rate parameter is a function of the information given, and since almost no information is given when conservation understanding is almost zero, there will hardly be any growth. But as soon as it increases, there will be more and more chances for children to experience conservation problems, and the growth rate will increase as the growth level increases. This principle of growth is based on a view shared by many cognitive developmental models. It says that learning and cognitive progress is not just a function of the information and help available, but is also critically dependent on the knowledge one already has.

Figure 11.3 shows the result of applying the transition model to an initial state of 0.04, a carrying capacity level K of 6 and a growth rate of 1, based on 300 iterations of the equation (I then added 2 to each number to account for the minimal score of 2 in the van der Maas, 1993, data). Similar to the logistic model, the transition model produces a whole range of growth forms, dependent on the parameters. Higher initial state values and lower growth rates, for instance, produce curves that are rather similar to the S-shaped curves of the logistic form. High initial states and high growth rates produce jumps at the very start of the growth process. This is what we find in Biddell and Fischer's Tower of Hanoi experiment, with children who are at higher cognitive starting levels at the beginning of the problem-solving task (Biddell and Fischer, 1993). If the growth rate exceeds 1, the resulting curve shows oscillatory growth, limit cycles, and chaos, depending on the magnitude of r.

If cognitive growth depends on children encountering contexts and situations from which they can learn, we should reckon with the fact that such encounters are, to a certain extent, randomly distributed over time. Put differently, a certain probability exists that children will encounter problems that cause cognitive conflict. It is easy to extend the transitory model to one in which growth depends on coincidental factors. In view of the fact that the growth rate in the transition model is a function of the growth level acquired, we can now assume that the probability of running into a learning encounter is a function of the growth level.

A simple way to model this is to generate a random number, $RAND\_T$, with each iterative step and compare this random number with the growth level attained (it is assumed that the variation in the random numbers lies between the minimal and the maximal growth level, that is, between the initial level and K). If the growth level is smaller than $RAND\_T$, nothing happens. If it is bigger, we let L grow one step further. The following equation is the random-driven version of the transitory model:

$$L_{n+1} = L_n \cdot \left(1 + R_{n+1} - \frac{R_{n+1} \cdot L_n}{K} \right) \qquad (15)$$

for $\quad R_{n+1} = 0$ or an arbitrarily small number if $L_n < RAND\_T$

$\quad R_{n+1} = r$ if $L_n \geq RAND\_T$

$\quad K = 1$

This equation yields the same growth patterns as the deterministic version. Thus, with a growth rate r of 1 it will produce the characteristic sudden jump to the maximal level. An interesting difference, though, is that the point where the curve jumps can vary dramatically between different runs (with different random numbers). It is likely that a comparable phenomenon occurs in reality, where it is not so much the form of the transition that differs among children as the time of its occurrence.

11.6 DEVELOPMENTAL STAGES AND CONNECTED GROWTH

The previous dynamic models were used in an attempt to reconstruct empirical curves, but they can also be employed in the building of qualitative models. A good example of such a qualitative model is concerned with the current view on stages in cognitive development.

Piaget's original model of stages assumed that the cognitive system formed a sort of overall structure of tightly interwoven components. The cognitive system was believed to shift as a whole from one stage to the next, for instance, from the preoperational to the concrete operational stage at the age of 5 to 6 years. Several decades of research in a wide variety of cognitive developmental domains have now shown that this picture of overall shifts does not hold. Considerable differences exist between different cognitive domains (such as the social vs. the logical-mathematical) as to when and how they change over time. Although several forms of cognitive change are gradual, or at least not very stagelike, there are a significant number of developments that still follow a stepwise increase, and are thus indicative of (domain-specific) stages (Case, 1987). Stage shifts, for instance, from a representational to an abstract form of thinking in the social domain, take place in the form of typical growth spurts or transitions. These growth spurts are noticeable only if the testing takes place under conditions of support and practice. Standard testing usually reveals a flat monotonic increase which often remains far below the competence level a child would demonstrate if the testing occurred under more "normal," i.e., educationally inspired, testing circumstances (Fischer and Pipp, 1984).

The landscape of overall cognitive development contains more than just stepwise or continuous increase in different cognitive domains. Several authors, for instance, found empirical evidence for transient regressions, i.e., temporary fallbacks in a child's observable competence in specific fields, such as numerical reasoning or face recognition (see, e.g., Strauss, 1982, for an overview; see van de Rijt-Plooij and Plooij, 1992, for comparable data during infancy). Usually the regressions mark the onset of leaps toward higher levels of functioning. This explains why regressions are often seen as the surface effect of restructuring processes in the underlying cognitive rule systems. The hypothesis of restructuring is a posteriori, in the sense that, in order to predict such restructuring one has to know its effect, namely, a leap to a higher level. Finally, the cognitive landscape not only counts steps, levels, and pits but also has "mountains" in the form of competencies, skills, or habits that emerge, grow, and disappear. Each precursor to a later development is an example of such a growth process. Children first develop a "Wh-subject-verb" rule and form sentences such as "Why he is ill?" This rule disappears and is replaced by the correct "Wh-verb-subject" rule. Other examples concern the emergence and later disappearance of major thought forms such as sensorimotor thinking, which is present in a primitive form at birth, grows into "maturity," and then gradually disappears around the age of 2 years.

Fischer and his collaborators have collected data from a variety of different developmental contexts, ranging from emotional development to the understanding of arithmetic operations. They have studied growth and change at different developmental levels. Figure 11.5, for instance, represents the growth of arithmetic understanding measured at two successive developmental levels. The data reveal a characteristic pattern of growth spurts often preceded by a temporary dip in the earlier grower. With the advent of the higher grower whose existence depends on the presence of its predecessor, the predecessor too sets into a new growth spurt. This growth pattern is characteristic of different domains, ranging from reflective judgment to emotional development. The hierarchical growers are believed to be connected by principles of competition and support as described with lexical growth and the growth of a meaning acquisition strategy (Fischer and Rose, 1993).

In summary, the landscape of cognitive growth is a structure consisting of various domains—social, logical, linguistic, and so forth—each consisting of many different subdomains, competencies, or skills. The latter can be considered independent entities that entertain relationships with many other "entities" in the cognitive structure and the environment. The growth patterns are very diverse, ranging from clear stepwise growth to emergence and disappearance. Fischer's model describes 13 developmental levels occurring

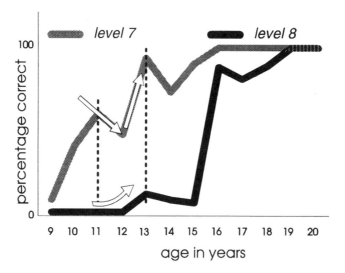

Figure 11.5 Data from Fischer's study on the growth of arithmetic understanding in children and adolescents. The curves represent the average percentage of correct answers on a test for mathematical understanding on developmental levels 7 (single abstractions) and 8 (abstract mappings) respectively (Fischer and Rose, 1993).

between birth and young adulthood. The levels are grouped into "tiers," characterized by a similar structural principle. The tier of abstract thinking, for instance, comprises three levels: (1) the level of single abstractions, emerging around age 11, (2) the level of abstract mappings, around age 15, and (3) the level of abstract systems, emerging around age 19 years. The levels are not considered overall properties of the cognitive system. There is ample evidence that they operate in a domain-specific way, and that different task domains have their own rate of development and time of emergence. Consider, for instance, the adolescent's understanding of arithmetic operations. His abstract understanding of addition, for instance, may have reached the level of abstract mappings, whereas his knowledge of the multiplication operation is still at the lower level of single abstractions.

In our model we confined ourselves to at most 25 different growers (e.g., five domains at five different levels). The basic equation that Fischer and I used is the one described in the section on connected growers [equation (8)]. Let us focus on two domains, called A and N (e.g., the adolescent's understanding of addition and subtraction respectively) and two levels (e.g., single abstractions and its successor, abstract mappings). I represent the growth level of domain A at level 1 by the variable $A_{1(i)}$ the level of A_1 at time i). The equation for $A_{1(i)}$ is copied from equation (8):

$$A_{1(n+1)} = A_{1(n)} \cdot \left[1 + r_{A_1} - \frac{r_{A_1} \cdot A_{1(n)}}{K_{A_1}} \right.$$

$$\left. - c_{A_2} \cdot (A_{2(n)} - A_{2(n-1)}) + s_{A_2} \cdot A_{2(n)} + \cdots \right] \qquad (16)$$

The open space is intended for a second set of competing and supporting factors.

Since the earlier level A_1 is a prerequisite for the emergence of the later level, A_2, I must add a prerequisite or precursor function to the equation for A_2:

$$A_{2(n+1)} = A_{2(n)} + p_{A_2} \cdot A_{2(n)} \cdot \left[1 + r_{A_2} - \frac{r_{A_2} \cdot A_{2(n)}}{K_{A_2}} \right.$$

$$\left. - c_{A_3} \cdot (A_{3(n)} - A_{3(n-1)}) + s_{A_3} \cdot A_{3(n)} + \cdots \right] \qquad (17)$$

for $p_{A_2} = 0$ if $A_{1(n)} < precursor\ value$ and 1 in any other case

(Note that A_2 competes with and is supported by its successor, A_3). From equation (11) we can infer that the introduction of a new, higher level—A_2, for instance—increases the carrying capacity of A_1, resulting in a higher equilibrium level.

What about the relationship between growers at the same level (e.g., single abstractions) but from different domains (e.g., knowledge about the addition and the subtraction operation respectively)? Put differently, how does B_1 (grower B at level 1) contribute to the growth of A_1 (and the other way round)? Fischer and I reasoned that, whereas growers at higher levels contribute to the carrying capacity of growers at lower levels, growers at the same level do not. The emergence of a higher level increases the possibilities, and hence the growth level, of lower growers. Growers at similar levels, e.g., knowledge of addition and of subtraction at the level of single abstractions, support one another's growth, but also compete for limited resources, such as time, effort, and attention. One way to express such a competitive and supportive relationship that does not affect the carrying capacity (or only temporarily affects it) is as follows. Let A_1 and B_1 be different growers (different domains) at the same level (level 1). The contribution of B_1 to the growth of A_1 is specified by the following equation:

$$(s'_{B_1} \cdot B_{1(n)} - c'_{B_1} \cdot (B_{1(n)} - B_{1(n-1)})) \cdot (K_{B_1} - B_{1(n)}) \qquad (18)$$

By multiplying the support and competition factors by $(K_{B_1} - B_{1(n)})$ we limit the effect of those factors to the period in which B_1 actually grows. As soon as B_1 reaches its equilibrium level, K_{B_1}, it no longer affects A_1. That is, B_1 supports and competes with A_1, but alters the carrying capacity of A_1 only for as long as B_1 itself is in the process of growth. Equation (18) is actually a component of equation (16), and should be inserted in place of the dots. All the equations in our model were constructed in accordance with the principles used for equation (16) and its additional component from equation (18). The main goal of our model building work was to simulate the qualitative patterns of stage shifts observed in Fischer's developmental model and data.

Based on the available data in a variety of task domains we defined a developmental stage by the following criteria: A stage is characterized by the

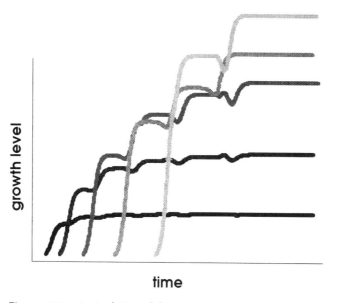

Figure 11.6 A simulation of five connected cognitive growers (principles of cognitive understanding and control on different developmental levels), based on Fischer's model of the growth of cognitive skill (Fischer, 1980).

emergence of growers at a new level. The emergence of a new level is often preceded or accompanied by either a temporary dip or turbulence in the preceding level. An old level profits from the emergence of a new one by increasing its carrying capacity level, i.e., by showing a stepwise growth form. The smaller the developmental distance between an existing grower and a new one, the greater the effect on that existing grower. Finally, a structure of stages and levels settles into an equilibrium state: it does not become unstable or collapse as more growers are added.

The result of our simulations with the dynamical model was a set of simulated growth patterns, consisting of a different number of growers, domains, and levels. Within a broad range of parameter values, the simulations displayed the properties we considered essential for developmental stages. Beyond that range, however, the model tended to become unstable, wildly fluctuating, and it would here eventually collapsed. Figure 11.6 shows the result of one of our simulations with a model of seven levels with two growers each. Further details can be found in van Geert (1994a).

11.7 THE SOCIAL DYNAMICS OF COGNITIVE DEVELOPMENT

In the models discussed so far, the interacting components concerned only "internal" aspects of the cognitive system, such as children's knowledge of numbers or counting skill. A child's cognitive ecosystem, however, does not stop at the boundaries of the brain or the body, but contains all aspects of the environment as well, insofar as that environment is accessible to and understood by the child. It goes without saying that the social environment, and especially caregivers or teachers, are among the most important components of the "external" aspects of a cognitive ecosystem. Caregivers and teachers mediate children's appropriation of sociocultural skills and knowledge. This takes place in the form of a process currently referred to by the term *co-construction* (Valsiner, 1991). Co-construction is a dynamic process of mutual information interchange, in which the activities of a participant change in reaction to the activities of the other. The result is a developmental change in both parties, child and caregiver alike, which is a form of a transactional process (Sameroff and Fiese, 1990; Fogel 1993).

The basic idea behind the dynamic modeling of such processes is that caregivers adapt to the level of competence of children. Ideally, the caregiver or teacher stays ahead of the child, in that, for instance, the help given to children enables them to perform activities that lie at a higher level of competence than would be reached if performed without help. The learning effect of such supported activities is then translated into an increase in the demands made on the caregiver. This bootstrapping process comes to a standstill if child and caregiver reach the educational goal, or if progress is no longer made.

The dynamic models of social interactive learning and co-construction take the form of sets of coupled equations. One equation describes the growth level of a competence under co-construction in children (e.g., their addition competence in a school curriculum); the other specifies the growth level of this competence instantiated in the help or demands given by caregivers or teachers. Basic parameters in these equations are, among others, the growth rate of that competence, and the "adaptation rate" in the second party. The adaptation rate has an optimal value. Sub- or superoptimal values result in lower growth rates. As an example, imagine a parent whose level of linguistic corrections and whose grammatical complexity of language addressed to the child is far ahead of the child's actual level of linguistic competence. A different example would be a teacher who increases the demands too much in response to slight improvement made by a pupil. In those cases, children's ability to match the support or demands will be greatly reduced, and lead to ineffective learning (see, e.g., Nelson, 1973). By varying the caregiver's adaptation rate to the child's increase in performance, it is possible to postulate a simple dynamic interaction model reconstructing the different styles of caregiver-child interaction that have been observed in attachment studies (see van Geert, 1993b for models and discussion of empirical data).

An alternative variant of this model can be used to describe the developmental mechanisms proposed by Vygotsky (1962, 1978), namely, the mechanisms associated with the zone of proximal development (van Geert, 1993b, 1994b). A study of equilibrium planes reveals the interesting nonlinear properties of this model. An equilibrium plane consists of a combination of two control variables, for instance, the control variables "growth rate" and "adaptation rate" (the speed with which one participant adapts to the developmental level of another). A final state corresponds to each combination of values, that is, a final state or level of a sufficiently long dynamic process based on those two values. "Sufficiently long" means long enough to let the system approach its equilibrium level, or long enough to simulate the developmental time that particular process requires in reality. The set of final states forms a kind of mountainous landscape over the plane of control variable values. With the Vygotsky model, the landscape corresponds to an irregularly shaped, domelike structure (highly reminiscent of the mesas one finds in the southwestern United States). This is characteristic of dynamics where small, localized changes in the control variables result in huge differences in equilibrium level. A comparable phenomenon occurs with dynamic processes that behave in accordance with the so-called cusp catastrophe. It is unclear whether or not the Vygotskyan dynamics model belongs to the cusp catastrophe family, that is, whether or not it shows the set of properties characteristic of the cusp (see van der Maas and Molenaar, 1992).

11.8 DYNAMIC GROWTH MODELS AND THE EXPLANATION OF DEVELOPMENT

In what sense do the dynamic growth models described in this chapter *explain* the developmental phenomena? It is easy to object that for almost any set of sufficiently regular developmental data, an equation can be concocted that will describe that set. If that is true, the dynamic growth equations have no specific status compared to any other type of equation and therefore fail in their explanatory goal. Certainly, the models do not explain by offering ultimate causes for the empirical phenomena, for instance, by offering a detailed account of the neural, social, and informational processes that go on during a child's development. Rather, they explain by offering a generalization on the one hand, and a simplification or specification on the other.

The successful application of the models discussed in this chapter lends support to the assumption that many areas of cognitive, emotional, and social development can be subsumed under the general concept of growth. This is more than just the attribution of a word to a class of phenomena, since the dynamical growth model provides an explicit definition of growth cast in terms of mathematical equations. A great advantage of the present model is that it shows that not only smooth S-shaped curves fall under the heading of growth; a multitude of different forms, including seeming irregularities and nonmonotonic increase and decrease, do as well. An additional advantage is that the basic growth models (logistic and transitionary) can be used as simple, uniform building blocks for more complex models.

The dynamical growth model simplifies or specifies the empirically observed phenomena. It reduces sequences of observations to a simple relationship between successive points in time, modified by only a few parameters. This does not imply that this is the ultimate reduction of those phenomena.

What I mean is that there is now reasonable evidence that in spite of their underlying complexity, developmental processes can be viewed as instances of relatively simple growth models. It remains to be explained, of course, what it is in the organization of the brain or of human culture that makes these developmental processes follow their particular growth trajectories. The argument of simplification per se is meaningless, however, if there is no theoretical backing to the simplifying model. For instance, one could use an automated procedure to fit all the curves discussed in this chapter in terms of polynomials. They would provide a significant reduction and simplification of the data series, but they lack any theoretical relationship with a basic mechanism that is assumed to underlie the data.

Finally, the dynamical growth model can act as a source of further empirical and theoretical questions. Singular as well as connected growth equations, for instance, can run into chaos, depending on the value of certain parameters. One could ask whether chaotic fluctuations do indeed occur in some developmental data, and, when they do, whether this is connected with an increase in any significant variable. Moreover, dynamical growth models can be used to make existing, verbal models more explicit. If one tries to build a model of Vygotsky's notion of the zone of proximal development, for instance, it becomes immediately clear that there are a number of crucial theoretical decisions to be made that have not been addressed in the original model (see van Geert, 1994b). The great advantage of transforming an existing model into a set of growth equations is that it offers a procedure for deductively inferring precise hypotheses about developmental pathways which can then be tested against the available data. If no such data are around, the model offers a better and more explicit guideline as to what sort of evidence one should be looking for.

REFERENCES

Bidell, T. R., and Fischer, K. W. (1993). Developmental transitions in children's on-line planning. In M. M. Haith (Ed.), *Development of future oriented processes*. Chicago: University of Chicago Press.

Bloom, L. (1990). Developments in expression: affect and speech. In N. Stein, B. Leventhal and T. Trabasso (Eds.), *Psychological and biological approaches to emotion*. Hillsdale, NJ: Erlbaum.

Brown, R. (1973). *A first language: the early stages*. London: Allen & Unwin.

Case, R. (1984). The process of stage transition: a neo-Piagetian view. In R. J. Sternberg (Ed.), *Mechanisms of cognitive development*. New York: Freeman.

Case, R. (1987). The structure and process of intellectual development. *International Journal of Psychology, 22*, 571–607.

Cats, M., and Ruhland, R. (1994). *Simulatie van vroege taaloutwikkeling [Simulation of early language development]*. The Netherlands: University of Groningen.

Corrigan, R. (1983). The development of representational skills. In K. Fischer (Ed.), *Levels and transitions in children's development*. San Francisco: Jossey-Bass.

Dromi, E. (1986). The one-word period as a stage in language development: quantitative and qualitative accounts. In I. Levin (Ed.), *Stage and structure. Reopening the debate*. Norwood, NJ: Ablex.

Fischer, K. W. (1980). A theory of cognitive development: the control and construction of hierarchies of skills. *Psychological Review, 87*, 477–531.

Fischer, K. W., and Pipp, S. L. (1984). Processes of cognitive development: optimal level and skill acquisition. In R. J. Sternberg (Ed.), *Mechanisms of cognitive development*. New York: Freeman.

Fischer, K. W., and Rose, S. P. (1993). Dynamic development of components in brain and behavior. A framework for theory and research. In G. Dawson and K. Fischer (Eds.), *Human behavior and the developing brain*. New York: Guilford.

Fischer, K. W., Shaver, P. R., and Carnochan, P. (1990). How emotions develop and how they organize development. *Cognition and Emotion, 4*, 81–127.

Fogel, A. (1993). *Developing through relationships*. New York: Harvester Wheatsheaf.

Gopnik, A., and Meltzoff, A. (1992). Categorization and naming: basic level-sorting in eighteen-month-olds and its relation to language. *Child Development, 63*, 1091–1103.

Inhelder, B., and Piaget, J. (1958). *The growth of logical thinking from childhood to adolescence*. New York: Basic Books.

Labov, W., and Labov, T. (1978). Learning the syntax of questions. In R. N. Campbell and P. T. Smith (Eds.), *Recent advances in the psychology of language: language development and mother-child interaction*. London: Plenum.

Miller, G. A. (1956). The magical number seven plus or minus two. Some limits on our capacity for processing information. *Psychological Review, 63*, 81–97.

Nelson, K. (1973). Structure and strategy in learning to talk. *Society for Research in Child Development Monographs, 38*, 149.

Nelson, K. (1985). *Making sense. The acquisition of shared meaning*. New York: Academic Press.

Ruhland, R., and van Geert, P. (1994). *Transitions in early language development*. University of Groningen, Netherlands.

Sameroff, A. J., and Fiese, B. H. (1990). Transactional regulation and early intervention. In S. J. Meisels and J. P. Shonkoff (Eds.), *Handbook of early child intervention*. Cambridge, England: Cambridge University Press.

Snow, C., and Ferguson, C. (1977). *Talking to children. Language input and acquisition*. Cambridge, England: Cambridge University Press.

Strauss, S. (1982). *U-shaped behavioral growth*. New York: Academic Press.

Valsiner, J. Introduction: social co-construction of psychological development from a comparative-cultural perspective. In Valsiner, J. (Ed.), *Child development within culturally structured environments*, Vol. 3: *Comparative-cultural and constructivist perspectives*. Norwood, NJ: Ablex.

Van de Rijt-Plooij, H. H. C., and Plooij, F. X. (1992). Infantile regressions: disorganization and the onset of transition periods. *Journal of Reproductive and Infant Psychology, 10*, 129–149.

Van der Maas, H. L. J., and Molenaar, P. C. M. (1992). A catastrophe-theoretical approach to stagewise cognitive development. *Psychological Review, 99*, 395–417.

Van der Maas, H. (1993). *Catastrophe analysis of stagewise cognitive development. Model, method and applications*. Doctoral dissertation: University of Amsterdam.

Van Geert, P. (1986). The concept of development. In P. van Geert (Ed.), *Theory building in developmental psychology*. Amsterdam: North-Holland.

Van Geert, P. (1991). A dynamic systems model of cognitive and language growth. *Psychological Review, 98*, 3–56.

Van Geert, P. (1993a). A dynamic systems model of cognitive growth: competition and support under limited resource conditions. In E. Thelen and L. Smith (Eds.), *A dynamic systems approach to development: applications*. Cambridge, MA: MIT Press.

Van Geert, P. (1993b). Vygotsky's dynamic systems. *Comenius, 48*, 383–401.

Van Geert, P. (1994a). *Dynamic systems of development: change between complexity and chaos*. New York: Harvester Wheatsheaf.

Van Geert, P. (1994b). Vygotskyan dynamics of development. *Human Development, 37*, 346–365.

Vygotsky, L. S. (1962). *Thought and language*. Cambridge, MA: MIT Press.

Vygotsky, L. S. (1978). *Mind in society*. London: Harvard University Press.

Guide to Further Reading

A very good introduction to the dynamical systems approach in developmental psychology is Gunnar and Thelen's edited volume from the Minnesota Symposia in Child Psychology (Gunnar and Thelen, 1989). Smith and Thelen (1993) present a collection of contributions from various authors. The first part of the volume focuses on the dynamics of motor skill development; the second part extends dynamical systems theory to areas such as perception, emotion, cognition, and language. Thelen and Smith (1994) provide a general, more qualitative account of how dynamic systems thinking can be applied to the development of cognition and action.

My own book (van Geert, 1994) presents an introduction to dynamical systems modeling of developmental growth processes. It discusses the general principles of the approach and provides tutorials on building simple models in spreadsheet formats.

The two volumes by Levine and Fitzgerald (1992) apply dynamical systems theory to psychological processes in general. They focus on general theory, methodological, and statistical aspects and some applications.

Gunnar, M., and Thelen, E. (Eds.) (1989). *Systems and Development. The Minnesota symposia on child psychology*, Vol. 22. Hillsdale, NJ: Erlbaum.

Levine, R. L., and Fitzgerald, H. E. (Eds.) (1992). *Analysis of dynamic psychological systems*, (2 vols.). New York: Plenum.

Smith, L. B., and Thelen, E. (Eds.) (1993). *A dynamic systems approach to development: applications*. Cambridge, MA: Bradford Books/MIT Press.

Thelen, E., and Smith, L. B. (1994). *A dynamic systems approach to the development of cognition and action*. Cambridge, MA: MIT Press.

Van Geert, P. (1994). *Dynamic systems of development. Change between complexity and chaos*. New York: Harvester Wheatsheaf.

12 Naive Time, Temporal Patterns, and Human Audition

Robert F. Port, Fred Cummins, and J. Devin McAuley

EDITORS' INTRODUCTION

Change over time is, in many ways, the raw material of perception. In no modality is this more obvious than in audition. Much if not most of the information that is contained in auditory events like speech is a matter of the way that a signal changes over time. Humans and other animals have remarkable abilities to extract this information from the auditory signal in real time, abilities which far exceed anything available in current technology. A key problem for cognitive scientists is to figure out how natural cognitive systems do it.

In thinking about processes that unfold in time, we are accustomed to applying an objective or absolute measure like the second. A clock marks the passing of seconds, and for a process to happen in time is for the events that make it up to be laid out against this independent yardstick. This way of conceptualizing processes in time is so obvious that it is difficult to see what the alternative might be. Yet Port, Cummins, and McAuley begin this chapter by arguing that this standard approach, which they dub the "naive" view of time, is not particularly useful if our aim is to understand how natural cognitive systems perceive auditory patterns. The use of natural time as a standard in perceptual models typically requires positing a buffer for a raw stimulus trace, in which unit intervals of time are transformed into units of space. The authors argue strongly against the possibility of any such buffer in the auditory system. Furthermore, absolute measurements would not be the most useful basis for recognizing temporal events anyway. Somehow, our auditory systems manage to handle information contained in processes that unfold over time without reliance on buffered sensory traces or on measurements in absolute (millisecond) units.

Port, Cummins, and McAuley argue that temporal information comes in two basic varieties: serial order and durational information. The first is a familiar feature of language: one thing we want to do when hearing what another says is extract from the auditory signal the words or phonemes in the order that they arrive. Most standard computational models for automatic speech recognition, such as hidden Markov models, attempt to obtain this serial order information by abstracting across as much irrelevant durational and rate variation as possible. In the process, however, they typically run into a severe problem of state proliferation in the model. This is because each possible variant must, in effect, be spelled out explicitly in the model. In this chapter the authors present a simple dynamical model for serial order extraction which is able to avoid this difficulty.

For other purposes, nuances of duration are very important. How can a natural cognitive system pick up on the rhythm or period of an auditory signal without prior knowledge of either signal identity or signal rate? In the latter part of their chapter, Port, Cummins, and McAuley present another novel dynamical model, an oscillator which automatically latches onto the period of a stimulus signal, even if this period is irregular or noisy. They propose that the period this oscillator extracts, which is a pattern intrinsic to the signal itself, be used as the standard against which relative duration measurements pertinent to recognizing an input pattern are made. This is practical, since listeners need a standard from somewhere, and the auditory signal to be recognized is always an available source, and it is desirable, because the signal's own period is a more useful measure than the second for patterns like speech, animal gaits, music, and so forth, which can occur at a range of rates.

12.1 INTRODUCTION

This chapter is about time and patterns in time. We are concerned with patterns that can be defined only over time and may have temporal constraints as part of their definition. Although there is a widespread view that time can be treated by nervous systems in the same way it is treated by scientists and engineers, we argue that this approach is naive—that there is no *general* method for representing time in the nervous system, i.e., no single representational mechanism that is applicable to recognition of all temporal patterns. Instead, different patterns are analyzed using different methods of measuring temporal extent. We then present several dynamic mechanisms developed in our laboratory for the recognition of various kinds of patterns in time.

12.2 TIME AND TEMPORAL PATTERNS

Time is one of the slipperiest of concepts to talk about. Everything takes place in time, from the history of the planet to the movements of our body; even our various attempts to talk (or think) about time happen in time. It is often said that the world has "things" and "events." The things endure through time without changing much. Events occupy some amount of it, whether fleeting or glacial. Despite the inexorability and continuity of time, we seem nevertheless to have a contrary intuition that there is a "now," a region in time surrounding the present where things are not changing—where most events stand still for us. This is where the various sciences want to live—where everything can be described now and yet we can have some confidence that the description will hold for the future as well. Of course, the notion of now, as a static description of events, is always understood as assuming some particular time scale, from *seconds* to *years*. We know that

Robert F. Port, Fred Cummins, and J. Devin McAuley

anything static can be seen to involve change if it is looked at over a longer time scale. Conversely, most static things also turn out to have a temporal component when examined on a shorter-than-usual time scale. Thus, solid material objects, color and words, for example, all have temporal structure if looked at either on a very short or very long time scale.

Things that seem intuitively to *happen in time* are events that last longer than a quarter of a second or so. We will call this time scale the "cognitive time scale." It is the time scale over which humans can act; the scale at which events are slow enough that we might grab with our fingers or blink an eye. The timing of events shorter than this often plays a major role in perception, though we are typically not aware of the role of temporal detail in their specification. Thus, if color recognition depends on the frequency of certain waves of energy, color does not thereby become a temporal pattern at the *cognitive* time scale. Typically, we can observe the temporal properties of very short (subcognitive) events only with special technology. Time has certain obvious similarities to physical distance, such as continuity. We talk of events being "near" or "far" in the past or future just as naturally as we use such terms for physical distance. Like physical distance, we can control our own physical activity down to a certain duration: eye blinks and experimental reaction times (around a quarter of a second) are about as fast as we can move. Of course, unlike physical distance, completed events that are now far away can never become near again. Science fiction fantasies like time travel base their intriguing pseudoplausibility on the trick of taking time as if it were *really* reversible—just like positions along a line drawn on the ground: move forward and then move back.

Before discussing these issues any further, it will fix ideas if we specify a few concrete examples of cognitive auditory patterns, the domain we address in this paper. These patterns can be defined only over time and their temporal extent is normally perceived as a time-extended event by humans. These are the kind of auditory events for which we seek plausible recognition mechanisms. Since we are concerned about recognition, it is also critical to clarify what kind of variations in each pattern are irrelevant to pattern identity and what kinds may cause reinterpretation.

1. Consider the sound of a large quadruped locomoting in some gait or other. The trot of a horse sounds quite distinct from a walk or gallop. Since each gait can occur over some range of rates, simply measuring the time periods between footfalls in *milliseconds* will not by itself allow a representation of a gait that will be invariant across different rates. Clearly, the characteristics of trot or gallop must be specified in terms that are relative to the other events in the sound pattern itself.

2. The theme of *The Merry Widow Waltz* is a temporal pattern defined by a particular melody (i.e., by a sequence of tones from the Western musical scale) played with a particular rhythmic pattern that fits in the waltz meter of three beats per measure. This pattern would be "the same tune" even if played in a different key or if played somewhat faster or slower. On the other

hand, if we increased its rate by a factor of 4 or more, or if we severely modified the rhythm (by changing it to a 4/4 meter, for example), we would find that the identity of the tune was destroyed.

3. The spoken word "Indiana" normally has a stress on the [æ] vowel. The word is still the same even when spoken by different voices at a range of speaking rates (up to a factor of about 2 faster or slower). In fact, one could change the stress and say "IN-diana," stretching or compressing various internal portions of the word in time by 15% to 20% and still have it be easily recognizable. Eventually, of course, by such a process one would do severe damage to its linguistic identity for a speaker of English (Tajima, Port, and Dalby, 1993).

4. The spoken sentence "I love you" is also a temporal pattern, although a sentence allows much wider leeway than words or melodies in the actual layout of the events in time. Temporal detail plays a much smaller role in the specification of the structure of a sentence than it does for tunes or spoken words. It seems that they just need to appear in a certain serial order. Still, temporal details are known to affect the parsing listeners construct for ambiguous utterances. Thus, if you read aloud $2(3^2)$, it will be quite different from $(2 * 3)^2$. The difference between them is best described in terms of the location of valleys and peaks in the instantaneous speaking rate, brief decelerations or accelerations that lengthen or shorten speech segments along with any silence. It is not usually a matter of pauses or silent gaps, as it is often described.

It is clear that each of these examples can be defined only over time. Thus a recognition mechanism must collect information over time so that decisions can be delayed long enough to be meaningful. Each of these patterns has a different set of temporal constraints on the essence of the pattern. Still, for all of these examples, the pattern can occur at different rates even though the rate change is of low importance in comparison with the importance of the durational relations internal to each pattern. What kind of mechanism enables humans to recognize such patterns? The view we defend is that nervous systems adopt a variety of ad hoc strategies for describing the temporal structure of patterns.

Living in Time

What is the relevance of time to animals like us? It is critical to differentiate two major uses of the word *time*. First there is history, the Big Pointer, we might say, that persistently moves our lives forward. And then there is time as information about the world. In the latter role, events in time happening now must be related to "similar" events that occurred earlier—either to the individual or to the species. An animal needs to be able to find certain patterns and structure in events that occur in time. To do this requires neural mechanisms for recognizing when an event recurs. Many kinds of clocks, for

Robert F. Port, Fred Cummins, and J. Devin McAuley

example, have been found in animals and plants that track the cycles of the sun, both through the day and through the year. Modern science has developed an absolute time scale for temporal description; a scale that depends on the notion of historical time moving forward incessantly. One question is whether animal nervous systems also have accurate mechanisms of this sort.

Scientific Time   In order to address questions about the physical world over the past few centuries, Western science has developed various mechanical and mathematical tools for measuring and describing time as an absolute variable. Given some form of clock, scientists and other "moderns" can treat time as just another dimension, one that resembles one of the three dimensions of Euclidean space. Instead of meters, we agree on standard units (second, day, year) to provide a basis for absolute measurement. Mathematically, one seldom needs to treat $f(t)$ as different in any way from $f(x)$. We do not hesitate to plot time on the x-axis of a graph displaying temperature, air pressure, velocity, or any other quantity that is measurable over a small Δt. From such displays of waveforms and spectra, we are able to study the properties of many kinds of events: economic cycles, cardiac signals, the motion of physical objects, sound waves, etc. For example, figure 12.1 shows a sound spectrogram of the phrase "mind as motion" spoken by an adult male. Time is one axis and frequency the other. The darkness of stippling shows the amount of energy in rectangular $\Delta f \times \Delta t$ cells of size 300 Hz $\times$ 3 ms. Such displays have become almost second nature to us, and have become integral components of modern thought. Most Americans these days are quite comfortable with stock reports and monthly rainfall graphs. One empirical question that arises for biology and cognitive science is this: *To what extent do the auditory systems of animals employ a display of energy by time in support of the recognition of sound patterns at the cognitive time scale?*

At very short time scales (under a millisecond) measures of time in absolute units like microseconds play a major role in measuring the direction of sound sources using time lags between the two ears (Shamma, 1989). This is, of

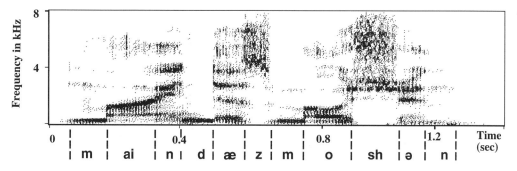

Figure 12.1   A sound spectrogram of the utterance "mind as motion," where the x-axis is time, the y-axis is frequency, and darkness represents intensity. Note that over much of the utterance the regions of greatest intensity are changing continuously.

course, a "subcognitive" phenomenon. But what about at the longer, cognitive time scale; the time scale suitable for recognizing events like words? We propose that in an auditory system for cognitive processing, time is not treated as just another spatial dimension. Spatial axes, like time in a plot of temperature, are reversible. Unlike actual time, one can scan the graph in either direction. If you were using a template to look for a pattern in such a display, you could simply slide the template back and forth until an optimal match were found. But such scannable displays are human artifacts. They are generated by an "assignment clock," some device that moves a sheet of paper past a pen point at a constant rate, or that places equally spaced time samples in a computer buffer, thereby creating a record of "instantaneous" values of the parameter (or, more accurately, values averaged over a short time interval). Since motion across the paper or placement in the buffer is done at a constant rate, distance along the buffer serves as a reliable measure of absolute time.

Scientists use these mechanisms to study the details of events that occurred in the past. Phoneticians, for example, spend plenty of time contemplating spectrograms like figure 12.1. But what about animals (or people) in the field? They have to act immediately. What can they do to analyze and recognize events that only unfold over time? To think clearly about this, we need to first consider the kinds of information that will be of potential use to an animal.

Biological Time   Animals (and humans) use temporal information for at least two general reasons. First, they use timing information to "recognize things," i.e., to relate events in the environment with previous experience of the objects and events. This includes objects like the presence of other animals, spoken words in human language, a banging window shade, the sound of a horse's gait, etc. Each of these "objects" imposes a characteristic structure on sound over time. Patterns that extend in time can often be usefully labeled by a name or by some "cognitive object." That is, temporal events can produce something rather like a "symbol" (van Gelder and Port, 1994). "It's a *waltz*." "She spoke *my name*." "It's *my mother* walking down the hall." A pattern extended in time, then, can cause a stable state to be entered into by the perceptual system, as a kind of recognition state.

The second main reason to use temporal information in sound is to support activity by the body. Ongoing perception directs action. The response of the perceptual system to a familiar auditory pattern will sometimes be to directly adjust the body to the input pattern itself. An animal can simply turn its head to face an important sound, or begin to intercept the object generating a sound, or occasionally to imitate another person's pronunciation of a phrase. Sometimes we even clap hands or dance to sound. So recognition of "things" is only part of the problem. An animal sometimes needs to bind its own real-time behavior to temporal events in stimulation. This frequently requires predicting the timing of future actions of another animal for some period into the future.

These are challenging functions. How can these jobs be fulfilled? And how many of these functions are directly supported by a spatial map of absolute time like figure 12.1?

Naive Time

What we call the "naive view of time" is simply the notion that biological time, i.e., the temporal information used by animals, is based on a representation of absolute time. In the realm of audition, it is manifest in the assumption that a critical early step in auditory processing of cognitive-level information must be to *measure time in absolute terms*. Typically, naive time models assume that humans or animals have access to real historical time. They apparently presume some clock that can measure durations directly in seconds. For auditory perception, the method usually implied is that the brain stores lists of spectrum-time pairs, i.e., a kind of buffer not much different from the sound spectrogram of figure 12.1. Such a display is often described as "short-term auditory memory."

This idea is widespread among psychologists, linguists, and phoneticians, and is probably assumed by most laypeople as well. It is supported by our intuition that we can remember recent sound events rather accurately. In addition, for many people, measurement of time in seconds and hours is the only natural way to think. If one assumes that every event has a location in time,—some angle of the clock at which it occurred—then locations and perhaps even durations in seconds may seem to be almost *intrinsic to the events themselves*, perhaps as intrinsic as the identity of the events that occur at each point in time.

Illustrative Models   What is required for absolute time measurement is what we call an *assignment clock*, a device that moves (changes state) at a constant rate and supplies a unique label to describe each point in time. One also needs a set of descriptors, i.e., a kind of alphabet, for characterizing the set of possible events. Thus, for example, an audio tape recorder uses constantly rolling wheels to lay down values corresponding to the sound pressure over a very short time window on magnetic tape. In the sound spectrogram of figure 12.1, the descriptors are energy levels in a set of frequency bins over some time interval. Time (as long as it is greater than some Δt) is translated into a corresponding unique position.

Psychologists have explored the possibility of such a time-buffer for many years. In the 1960s "visual iconic memory" was discovered—a spatial image of the visual field in which objects are still raw and unidentified (Sperling, 1960). It was a level of visual memory from which a subject can select subportions for verbal description while unattended parts of the image are soon lost. This led to postulation by analogy of a short-term memory for sound (Crowder and Morton, 1969; Massaro, 1972; Baddeley, 1992), one that was sometimes called "echoic memory" (Neisser, 1967). The models actually proposed, however, did not resemble an echo at all. Since a real echo is an event in time, it seems that an echoic memory should be something that *replays* in time, like a tape loop that can be repeatedly scanned. But most theoretical models "cut" the tape loop so it can be examined all at once as an auditory "image."

One model for such a memory might be implemented rather like a postwar radar scope with a phosphorescent screen. These scopes displayed a decaying image of rain clouds or airplanes for a couple of seconds until the radial sweep rescanned that part of the circle and rewrote the image anew. Like the sound spectrogram, of course, this logically requires an assignment clock with its mechanism of constant motion to generate a spatial layout of the input sound spectrum for the past second or so, in order to serve as an auditory memory model. The spectrum just behind the sweeping radius would be the most recent. The sweep wipes out the decaying old information from the buffer. At least that is one way such a model might be implemented. However, without specifying any particular concrete mechanism, many models of auditory pattern recognition (including, e.g., Massaro, 1972, 1987; Klatt, 1980) have proposed a similar kind of short-term auditory memory lasting nearly a second that contains raw spectra straight from the auditory nerve. All meaningful auditory features are to be extracted from this representation. Durational cues, such as voice-onset time, are thus treated exactly the same as spectral cues—measured, apparently, by straightforward examination of the position of various spectral features arrayed along the time axis in short-term auditory memory. Recognition of temporal patterns is thus (naively, we would say) turned into a task that closely resembles recognition of visual patterns.

In the study of phonetics, time has posed recurring theoretical difficulties. Whereas linguistically motivated models of phonetics rely entirely on sequential order (Jakobson, Fant, and Halle, 1952; Stevens and Blumstein, 1978), phoneticians frequently found evidence that timing detail played an important role in speech perception and production (Lehiste, 1970; Klatt, 1976; Port and Dalby, 1982; Port, 1981). In one well-known controversy, Leigh Lisker and Arthur Abramson (1964, 1971) argued that voice-onset time, the time interval between the burst of an aspirated stop to the onset of voicing (as in the word "tin") was an example of a durational feature that was controlled by speakers and also employed by listeners in differentiating "tin" from "din." They claimed that the serial order alone would not properly differentiate these words; only a metrical measure would suffice. Thus, they argued, speech requires better measurement of time than simply the serial order of features (as proposed by Chomsky and Halle, 1968).

Of course, to serve as perceptual information, listeners themselves must somehow be able to utilize actual voice-onset times. Little was said by Lisker

Robert F. Port, Fred Cummins, and J. Devin McAuley

and Abramson (or anyone else) about a practical perceptual mechanism for this. But since phoneticians themselves just measure acoustic durations of speech by applying a ruler to sound spectrograms or from a computer screen, one must conclude that, to the extent that phoneticians consider such measurements relevant at all to the problem of human speech perception, they implicitly suggest that human subjects are also able to extract equivalent measurements. Thus far, however, the evidence for any ability to measure time in milliseconds is strictly circumstantial: it is clear that sometimes people are sensitive to quite small duration changes. But does this imply they measure time in absolute units?

Theories of speech production have also depended on naive time in some cases. Directly analogous to the perceptual models, hypothetical speech production processes are sometimes proposed that include a stage at which there is a list of letterlike phonetic segments paired with appropriate durational specifications. The buffer of these is then read out, from left to right, during actual speech production, and the gesture for each segment is executed so as to last just the specified amount of time. Thus Klatt (1976), followed by Port (1981), proposed specific "temporal implementation rules" that compute how long the phonetic states (i.e., various consonant and vowel segments) are supposed to last given their inherent segment durations and specific features of their context. In order for such numbers to serve as instructions, of course, a "motor executive system" must be assumed that is able to assure that the corresponding gestures do indeed last the correct amount of time. But there are many difficulties with this proposal (Fowler, Rubin, Remez, et al., 1981). To the extent that these are taken to be models of human behavior, they assume that durations in absolute units like milliseconds are intrinsically meaningful and interpretable. In short, temporal implementation rules are instances of naive-time models for motor control. Of course, many other approaches to motor control have avoided this pitfall and are based on dynamical models analogous to what we propose here for perception (Bernstein, 1967; Kelso, Saltzman, and Tuller, 1986; Saltzman and Munhall, 1989; Browman and Goldstein, 1989).

What we are calling the naive view of time, then, amounts to the assumption that time measured in milliseconds (a) is automatically available to a perceiving system and (b) serves as useful information in a system for motor control. Most researchers in both speech and other auditory patterns have focused attention on static problems—perhaps in part to avoid dealing with messy temporal patterns at all. Still there is a longstanding literature of research on specific temporal issues like rhythm production and perception (see, e.g., Fraisse, 1957; Michon and Jackson, 1985), but research on time has generally been treated as a backwater issue, not relevant to the major themes of psychological research. Perhaps in hope of attracting a little attention to the problem, one paper a few years ago bore the title "Time: Our Lost Dimension" (Jones, 1976). With a few notable exceptions (see, e.g., Povel and Essens, 1985; Jones, 1976; Watson and Foyle, 1985; Sorkin, 1987; Warren,

(1993), including a large literature on speech perception, patterns that are distributed in time tend not to be viewed as important theoretical problems for perceptual theory.

Why is there a certain blindness to the unique problems of time in theories of psychology? One reason may be that it is simple to represent sound in a buffer based on absolute time measurements. Also, engineers have had at least some success in handling sound that way. For example, in speech recognition models, a buffer of audio input with discrete time labels (coded as spectral slices) was the basic data structure of the exciting Hearsay-II speech recognition system (Lesser, Fennel, Erman, et al., 1975). Although designed for engineering purposes, Hearsay-II has nevertheless served as a kind of archetypal speech perception theory for a generation of scientists. The model was based on standard structuralist ideas about the organization of a sentence: syntactic structure at the top, then a list of words, then phonemes, allophones, and acoustic cues. So, in order to recognize a sentence of speech, a second or two of audio signal is stored up in a buffer. Then a set of modules analyze various descriptions of the sentence, using phonetic, lexical, prosodic, and grammatical descriptors. These hypotheses are posted onto a "blackboard" with time as its x-axis, as shown in figure 12.2. Hearsay-II interprets the sentence all at once—only after the whole sentence has been presented.

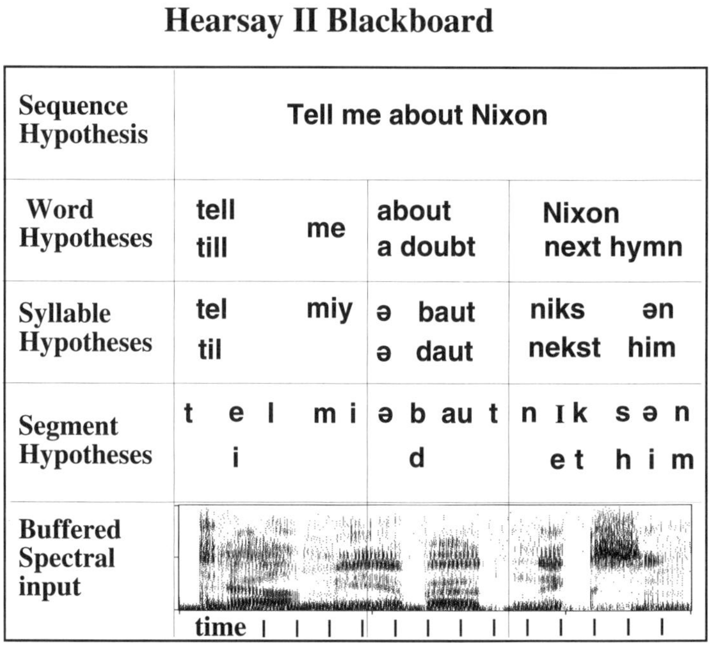

Hearsay II Blackboard

Sequence Hypothesis	Tell me about Nixon			
Word Hypotheses	tell till	me	about a doubt	Nixon next hymn	
Syllable Hypotheses	tel til	miy	ə baut ə daut	niks ən nekst him	
Segment Hypotheses	t e l i	m i	ə b au t d	n ɪ k s ə n e t h i m	
Buffered Spectral input					
	time				

Figure 12.2 The Hearsay-II system stores the raw input in a buffer. Independent demons test hypotheses (such as that a particular phoneme is present in a particular temporal region), while simultaneously other demons look at the posted results of every other demon and create further hypotheses about other possible units (such as syllables). Thus gradually, a roughly simultaneous analysis is achieved for all levels of description for all sections of the utterance.

The behavior of the model over time (if we imagine running it continuously) would thus be to alternately collect data and then process it. One collects "enough" data (however much is needed for the problem at hand) and then crunches it. The structure of this model illustrates the basic form of many naive-time models of speech perception.

Connectionist approaches to speech using classic feedforward networks have had limited success at real speech recognition (Watrous, 1990; Elman and Zipser, 1988). This may reflect the fact that many connectionist models have continued the static tradition of dealing with time. For example, Elman and Zipser (1988) collect a syllable's worth of acoustic input into a buffer. Then the entire pattern is submitted to the neural network for analysis and recognition. Another current model for speech recognition, one that aims for high-quality performance, is the time-delayed neural network (TDNN) (Lang, Waibel, and Hinton, 1990). This model uses precisely controlled time delays to allow at least a syllable-length stretch of speech to be stored in a buffer that contains sampled absolute time as one axis. The recognition of syllable-length patterns takes place only after the whole syllable is present in the buffer. Of course, when researchers are solving practical problems, they should do whatever seems as though it might help. But cognitive perceptual models for speech and music perception, and so on have been copying features of these systems. Unfortunately, to do so is naive.

Problems with Naive Time   There are two critical difficulties with the naive view of time surveyed above: (1) the lack of direct evidence for a temporal buffer and (2) the surprising lack of usefulness of millisecond measurements. If we are to rely on time labels (or physical positions) to record the past, we must depend on a highly accurate assignment clock (e.g., an audio tape recorder, sound spectrograph, digital-to-analog converter, video recorder, etc.). This clock assigns labels to descriptions of the energy layout of events. What evidence supports such a mechanism in humans or other higher animals? Note that our everyday measurement of absolute time is only made possible by various modern technologies that allow us to compare a real-world event with some device whose rate of change is presumed constant: a mechanical pendulum clock, the rotation of the earth, or the oscillation of a cesium atom.

The hypothesis of a spectrographic auditory memory makes at least three strong predictions. First, since the memory must have a limited duration, we should expect very good measurement of time for the duration of the memory, but then a sharp falloff in accuracy and perhaps greater reliance on relative durations for patterns longer than the short-term memory. Second, since it stores time only as absolute values, we should expect that patterns defined by relative durations should be more difficult to learn than ones defined in absolute terms. Similarly, subjects should need to be exposed to rate-varying productions in order to learn to recognize a pattern that is defined only relationally. Third, it should be fairly easy to recognize the absolute time alignment of unrelated events, e.g., "When, during the pronunciation of the word 'Indiana,' did the car door slam?" On any spectrogram of such a complex event, the relative position of the two events is obvious. As far as we can tell, for humans (and presumably other animals), *none* of these expectations holds. Absolute measurements are harder than relative ones for events at most time scales. Generalizing a pattern across a change of rate is easy and natural. Yet we perform very poorly at judging the lineup of unrelated events.[1]

The second major problem with naive-time models is this: time measured in seconds is simply the wrong kind of information for many problems. Listeners to environmental sounds, music, and speech have much less use for absolute time measurements than one might think. Both melodies and words (and many other kinds of auditory patterns as well) retain their identity even when their rate of production is varied. And changes in rate tend to change the durations of all the segments in a pattern uniformly. For example, knowing that some vowel in a word (or a note in a melody) is 150 ms in duration is, by itself, almost useless information regarding its identity and its role in the word (or melody). On the other hand, knowing its duration in relation to the duration of a number of (labeled) neighboring segments is very informative indeed (Port, Reilly, and Maki, 1987). Rather than an absolute time scale, what is much more useful is a scale intrinsic to the signal itself—a scale that will support local comparisons, such as durational ratios (Port and Dalby, 1982). Internal perceptual mechanisms may be able to lock onto some period and measure relative durations as phase angles and even predict future events in the pattern.

Other Ways to Measure Time

We propose that ecological patterns have at least two kinds of time information that are "weaker" than absolute time, but nevertheless very useful: serial order and relative duration.[2] Serial order is a topic with a long and well-developed history. The analysis of strings of symbols is the basis of much of computer science as well as linguistic theory. Relative duration, however, has received much less attention and few mechanisms have been explored for its extraction and description.

We hypothesize that human cognition, like the cognition of other less sophisticated animals, does not have a completely general-purpose store of raw acoustic information that is created in advance of pattern recognition. Instead, recognition, i.e., a labeling process that depends on extensive previous experience, precedes the generation of whatever buffers there may be of events in time. The kind of short-term auditory memory we propose contains labels or "names" for analyzed microevents. Each event contains its own time specification. No abstracted time scale may exist at all. The unfortunate consequence of this state of affairs, is that familiar patterns each have an appropriate temporal representation, but if listeners are presented with a com-

Robert F. Port, Fred Cummins, and J. Devin McAuley

pletely novel pattern (not containing obvious periodicities) or if several familiar patterns overlap in time, listeners have only very weak resources for representation of such complexes (Port, 1990).

Since absolute time representation must be ruled out as a general method, despite clear evidence that animals and people are very sensitive to many temporal structures, what other possibilities are there?

Serial Order   The weakest descriptive scheme for time is just to specify the serial order of events. Such a description is what linguistic models provide: the standard European alphabet, widely used for orthographic writing systems, is a classic tool for linguistic analysis in the slightly modified form of the phonetic alphabet. Words are made up of phonemes, serially ordered like beads on a string but with no durational properties (i.e., the only measure of length is the number of segments). Sentences, in turn, are viewed as nothing but serially ordered words. Our commonsense understanding of how events are ordered due to a relation of cause and effect also leads to expectations of serial order: a sudden squeal of brakes causes us to expect the sound of a collision, thunder follows lightning, and click follows clack in the many whirligigs of modern life. Serial order may be noncausal as well: when one hears a shoe drop on the floor upstairs, one may expect to hear the other one after some unpredictable delay.

Early speech recognition models which grounded measurement in absolute time ran up against a myriad of problems due to the intrinsic variability of speech timing. The most successful of these systems modeled speech as a series of ordered states using techniques like "dynamic time-warping" to get rid of much of the absolute information. Still, mere order, with time measurement achieved by counting segments, will not do the job for many important environmental events. If there is a periodic structure of some sort in the input signal, then an effective auditory system can exploit that regularity both to predict and to describe.

Relative Duration   Relative duration is just the comparison of one duration with another. Like other ratios, it is dimensionless. We may arbitrarily select one unit as a reference unit. If the reference time unit is extremely regular, like the motion of our planet relative to the sun, then relative time approaches equivalence to absolute time. But other, context-sensitive, reference units are also possible—a period detectable from the signal. We can enumerate periods just as well as seconds. Instead of fractions of a second, phase angle can be measured with respect to the reference period. Then if the rate of the input pattern changes slowly, our scale can remain calibrated. The difference between this intrinsic referent and absolute clock time is enormous because for many ecological events, a relative scale of time is much more useful.

The fundamental reason for the value of relative duration measurements is simply that many dynamic events in the environment that are functionally equivalent (i.e., have the same meaning) can occur at a range of rates: characteristic animal or human gaits, musical rhythms, songs, engine noises, the swaying of tree limbs, and, of course, spoken words. If you want to recognize a waltz rhythm, it should not matter much what the rate of the rhythm is in milliseconds per cycle. This property is acknowledged in the standard notation system of Western music which employs a notational variant of phase angle for time measurement: thus, in a 4/4 time signature, a half-note represents the duration of π radians (relative to the "measure"). Indeed, most forms of music around the world are constructed around such periodic, partly rate-invariant hierarchical structures.

But a complex signal may contain subparts, whose duration relative to the signal rate is of importance. For example, it is clear that relative timing, not just serial order and not absolute time, plays a major role in the information for speech timing (Port, Dalby, and O'Dell, 1987; Port, 1981; Port and Dalby, 1982; Lehiste, 1970). A well-known example is the syllable-final voicing distinction in English and other Germanic languages. One of the major cues for the distinction between pairs such as *rabid* and *rapid* or *camber* and *camper* is the relative duration of the vowel to the postvocalic stop consonant or consonants. This is more naturally expressed with reference to the syllable period, rather than the second (Port et al., 1987; Port and Cummins, 1992). A satisfactory account of speech perception requires time measurement that is *more powerful* than just serial order, but clearly must be *less powerful* than absolute time in seconds.

Need for New Approaches

Thus far we have argued that the widespread view of time as somehow naturally assigned in seconds is not usually an appropriate approach to the study of perception of temporal patterns by animals. It presumes neurological mechanisms for which little direct evidence exists, and does not provide the most useful description of information without further arithmetic processing that would throw away the absolute information obtained with such difficulty. As an alternative, one can analyze time with just serial order. This has been attempted many times and seems to be adequate for some aspects of problems like grammatical syntax. However, such an approach leaves many phenomena unaccounted for. For example, what about events that are regularly periodic? Serial order contributes nothing to understanding temporal measurement of this type. It is not sufficient merely to get the notes of *The Merry Widow* in the right order if the note durations vary randomly. And if the note durations are specified symbolically (as in musical notation), how can these be accurately implemented for production or accurately recognized in perception? How do listeners obtain or use this temporal information? What kind of mechanisms can listeners employ to be able to measure all the major classes of temporal information?

Our hypothesis is that listeners employ a bag of temporal tricks. As they gain experience with their auditory environment, they develop a variety of mechanisms for capturing spectrotemporal patterns—the specific ones that occur frequently. To a significant degree these structures are self-organized (Anderson, 1994) and do not require explicit tutoring. Wherever possible, these mechanisms will exploit any periodicity in stimulus patterns. If none can be detected, then serial order may have to suffice—but in any case, temporal structure is learned as part of the patterns themselves, not as an independent abstract dimension. The best way to study these mechanisms in our view, is to simulate them computationally using simple dynamical models and then to compare qualitative properties of performance with human or animal data. The dynamical systems we propose are orders of magnitude simpler than the dynamics of real nervous systems and, consequently, could be plausibly implemented by biological systems. In the following sections, we suggest several general methods for extracting useful temporal information, both with respect to serial order and relative duration.

12.3   MEASUREMENT MECHANISMS

The two methods of serial order and relative duration are closely related to S. S. Stevens's notion of an ordinal scale vs. an interval scale (Stevens, 1951) and, like them, they are conceptual types of measurement. Any actual achievement of such measures in a nervous system may involve a wide range of mechanisms. In this section we review some methods that will allow recognition of both serial order and relative duration. As we shall see, both methods depend on the behavior of internal dynamic models to keep track of time in the perceptual system.

Recognition of Serial Order

Some models that identify the serial order of elements in a temporal sequence were developed by those working on speech recognition in order to overcome the problem of invariance of patterns across changes in the duration of individual components as, for example, due to a change in rate or emphasis. To achieve this, it is useful to factor out as much durational information as possible, focusing on transitions from one element to the next. The first model, the finite-state machine (FSM) has certain strengths. The same ideas appear again in slightly disguised form in the hidden Markov model. We will show how a dynamical system can emulate an FSM that runs in real time and what advantages it possesses in dealing with continuous signals.

Finite-State Machines   The traditional mathematical system that recognizes and classifies sequences of events is called a finite-state machine (see Pollack, chapter 10, for further discussion of these systems). An FSM consists of a set S_i of states, including two privileged kinds of state, S_1, the start state, and S_{accept_i}, a subset of S, containing one or more "accept" states. If the FSM

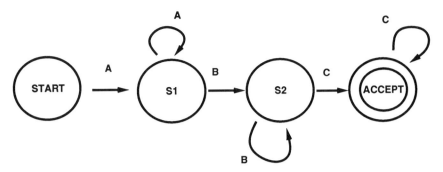

Figure 12.3 A finite-state machine which recognizes the sequence *ABC*. It makes transitions from state to state only when a particular letter is received. Thus only a *B* will allow the transition from *S1* to *S2*. Transitions other than those shown cause the machine to reject the sequence. The final state (with a double circle) is the only "accept" state.

is in an accept state, it has successfully recognized the sequential pattern for which it is specific. Transitions between these states are defined in a transition table, in which entry e_{ij} is the state to which the machine is set when it is already in state S_i and receives the input I_j. Transition is therefore dependent *only* on the state at the previous time step and the current input. The only memory the FSM has for earlier inputs therefore resides in the state of the machine. Figure 12.3 shows a simple FSM which has four states and an input vocabulary of three symbols, *A, B, C*. The transitions that are labeled are the only ones that may appear if the machine is to recognize a sequence. All other possible combinations of input and state lead to an implicit "reject" state, from which there is no return. The illustrated FSM will accept, among others, the sequences *AABBBC* and *ABCCCC*, but will reject *AAABBA* and *AAACCCBBC*.

One of the most successful of the first generation of automatic speech recognizers was Harpy, a system based on a large FSM with some 15,000 states. The Harpy system was the most successful entry in the 1971–1976 speech recognition project sponsored by the Advanced Research Projects Agency of the Department of Defense (Lesser et al., 1975; Klatt, 1977). It contains a hierarchy of nested FSMs plus a search procedure to identify the path through the space of possible input sequences with the least total error. Figure 12.4 shows schematically how these FSMs, here represented as networks or graphs, are layered. Phoneme recognition networks scan the raw acoustic buffer, trying to identify individual phonemes. These in turn serve as input to a lexical-level FSM. One of the principal advantages of a Harpy-like system was the fact that no time normalization was required. Just as in our example FSM above (see figure 12.3), each state has self-recurrent transitions. Thus, if a single element (phoneme, word, etc.) is repeatedly presented (or presented more slowly), the network does not move from its current state. Thus in principle, one could stretch one segment (say, the *a* in *about*) for an indefinite number of time steps and Harpy would still recognize *about*.

Harpy

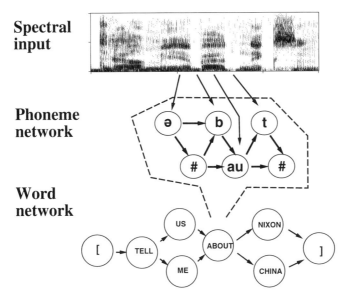

Figure 12.4 A schematic representation of the Harpy system. Hierarchies of finite-state machines scan the acoustic input and recognize units at ever greater scales, from phonemes to words to sentences. Here, a set of phoneme recognizers are fed spectral input. As each in turn recognizes "its" part of the input, it outputs its result to a lexical unit which pieces together words. The order of the spectral slices yields phonemes, the order of the phonemes yields words, and the order of the words yields grammatical (acceptable) sentences.

This contrasts sharply with Hearsay-II, discussed above, since Harpy employs no direct representation of time—merely the order of events. Of course, if such a model is refined to allow recognition of additional variant pronunciations, the size of the transition table for the FSM will increase exponentially. If the signal being studied is not easily reducible to a reasonably small number of states or features, then an FSM model rapidly grows to unmanageable size. This problem of the proliferation of states applies not only to FSMs like Harpy but to any of the more sophisticated Markov models, which are ultimately based on the FSM. We will look briefly at hidden Markov models, which represent the current state of the art in speech recognition, and then show how a simple dynamical model can circumvent this problem of exponential growth in complexity.

Markov Models Finite-state machines are a straightforward way of recognizing sequences and can be used for producing sequences as well. In the example FSM given above, the sequence *ABC* could be presented at any rate (i.e., any number of *A*'s followed by any other number of *B*'s, etc.) and still be recognized by the FSM since it would be guaranteed to reach a goal state. Time has been factored out completely. In dealing with real-world signals,

Naive Time, Temporal Patterns, and Human Audition

however, where the exact sequence of possible states is not known for certain, the model needs more machinery. In many successful models, the FSM is augmented as follows: it is assumed that the unknown signal has been generated by an FSM which outputs a symbol in each state. An attempt can now be made to reconstruct the generating model by a process of inference. In order to do this, probability distributions are obtained for both the outputs associated with each state and with the transitions from one state to the other. The model that is inferred is known as a hidden Markov model. The assumptions of the FSM have been retained, since transitions depend only on the previous state and the current input, but has been augmented by probabilistic transitions between states. It is hidden because the deterministic FSM has been replaced by a best guess, in which the outputs are generated stochastically and cannot be known with certainty. Hidden Markov models are at the base of many contemporary speech and temporal pattern recognition models (e.g., Lee, Rabiner, and Pieraccini, 1992; Lee, 1992). As mentioned above, they too may run into the problem of state proliferation if the underlying signal is not easily reducible to a small number of relatively steady states.

Simple Dynamic Memories In the last few years, several new approaches to speech recognition have emerged within the area of artificial neural networks. Most innovative has been the use of recurrent networks that process a small amount of external input at a time and retain information about the past only in the particular internal activation state of the fully connected units. In the best cases, these networks have outperformed the hidden Markov models, with the advantage of requiring no domain-specific knowledge to be encoded by the programmer (Robinson and Fallside, 1991). They have been applied to a number of problems in speech recognition and appear to hold promise for many kinds of pattern recognition. We present a recurrent network model of our own that is similar in many ways to an FSM recognizer, at least over a limited range of stretching or compression of time. The model nevertheless has some significant advantages that come from having a continuous state space rather than a discrete one.

One of the many tasks which recurrent networks have proved to be good at is the emulation of FMSs (Pollack, 1991; Das, Giles, and Zheng Sun, 1992; Cummins, 1993). They are fed as input the same finite string of symbols as an FSM and the output is trained to reflect the distinction between accepted and rejected sequences. Rather like FSMs, the properly trained network will recognize the same sequence of elements, despite considerable variation in the rate at which they are presented, e.g., *AAAABBCCC* will be recognized as being the same sequence as *ABC*. This "normalization" is perhaps surprising, since, during training, the network may have seen each sequence presented only at a single rate. The generalization across rate changes was obtained "for free." In the remainder of this section, we look more closely at the dynamics of the trained network and see how this "rate normalization" is achieved.

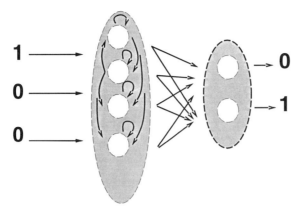

Figure 12.5 Schematic diagram of a recurrent network that accepts (sensory) input on three input lines, processes the input, and outputs a binary tuple. Each unit sums over the input it receives from the input lines and from other units, computes an output value, and passes it on. Because of the recurrent connections, information about previous inputs is retained in the current state of the recurrent units.

A recurrent neural network, like the one shown in figure 12.5, is a processing model comprising several external input lines (from "sensors") feeding to a layer of fully connected processing units. In this system, which we call a simple dynamic memory, each unit collects input from all the external lines and from the other units. At each time step, each unit sums over all its inputs, performs a simple squashing transformation on the sum, and outputs the result. Thus the activation equation is

$$y_i(t + 1) = squash[\alpha y_i(t) + \sum w_{ij}y_j + input + bias] \tag{1}$$

for connections from unit j to i, α is the decay rate, the bias serves as a threshold, and *input* refers to external (sensory) input only. Some units of the network are designated output units and the outputs on these represent the response of the model to the input (see figure 12.5). The input here is the external stimulus fed to some nodes. Because of the recurrent connections, information from previous inputs remains implicit in the state of the recurrent units. Gradient descent training procedures using a teacher signal for just the output nodes is employed (Williams and Zipser, 1989; Anderson and Port, 1990).

We have noted that the memory of a recurrent network arises from the change in internal state after each vector presentation. The dynamics of the trained network can be studied by looking at the trajectories followed by the network in the state space of unit activations. Assume that a network is trained to recognize the sequence *ABC* and distinguish it from, among others, *BAC* and *CAB*. The network signals recognition of *ABC* with an output node which is off (activation = 0) until the last element of *ABC* is seen, at which time it switches on briefly (activation = 1). The state space can be divided into two principal regions, the hyperplanes defined by *outputnode* = 0 and

State space **Sequence recognition**

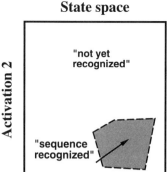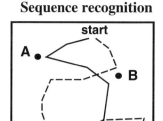

Activation 1

Figure 12.6 *(Left)* The state space, here, for simplicity, illustrated as being two-dimensional, is partitioned into a large *not yet recognized* area and a *sequence recognized* region. When the system trajectory enters the recognition region, it signals sequence identification. *(Right)* For each possible input, *A, B, C*, there is an associated point attractor. As input changes (e.g., from *A* to *B*), the system trajectory is redirected toward the new attractor. Only the trained sequence brings the trajectory through the recognition region (since it was the learning algorithm that located the recognition region in just the right place). The solid line is the trajectory on presentation of *ABC*, and the dashed line is *BAC*.

outputnode = 1, associated with nonrecognition and recognition, respectively. This is illustrated in figure 12.6 (left). If we present the network with a continuous, unchanging input, it rapidly settles into a steady state. Thus a global point attractor can be identified for each of the possible input vectors, including the zero vector (no input). Figure 12.6 (right) illustrates how this system is able to distinguish the sequence *ABC* from all other sequences of *A*'s, *B*'s and *C*'s, such as *BAC*, etc.[3] Assuming that the system is reset to some neutral state between sequences (marked *start*), the trajectory corresponding to the system evolution can be visualized as always starting in the same area of state space. As long as the first element, *A*, is presented, the system gradually approaches a point attractor specific to that input. Once the input changes to *B*, the attractor layout also changes and the system trajectory changes course toward the new attractor. The task of learning to identify a sequence now amounts to insuring that the trajectory passes through the recognition region if and only if the sequence to be identified has been presented. This learning can be based on either tutoring or self-organization, but it must be based on actual experience with the temporal patterns.

We can now illustrate how this general model, the "simple dynamic memory," handles varying rates of presentation. Figure 12.6 (right) shows the system trajectory as jumps in discrete time, since each sequence element is presented for an integral number of clock ticks, *AAABBBCCC*.... The trained network can now be presented with the same sequence, but at a different rate, and it will still successfully distinguish among targets and distractors. This is illustrated in figure 12.7 (right). The two trajectories illustrated are for presen-

Robert F. Port, Fred Cummins, and J. Devin McAuley

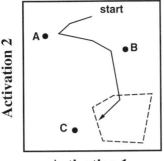 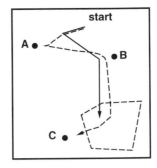

Activation 1

Figure 12.7 (*Left*) System trajectory taken by the network trained on *AABBCC* when the target sequence is presented. (*Right*) Trajectory of the same network when the sequence is presented at novel rates, both faster (*ABC*, solid line) and slower (*AAAAABBBBBCCCCC*, dashed line). The trajectory still passes through the recognition region.

tations of *ABC* (*solid line*) and *AAAAABBBBBCCCCC* (*dashed line*), which, assuming constant sampling of a continuous signal, represent faster and slower presentations of the sequence $A^n B^n C^n$ (for small n). Despite the variation, the underlying dynamics are nearly the same, and the trajectory remains qualitatively unaltered. In each case, the trajectory still passes through the recognition region. Thus, like the FSM, this system intrinsically ignores variations in rate.

There are additional parallels between this model and an FSM. The part of state space we call the recognition region corresponds to an "accept" state, while the individual attractors, together with their vector fields, correspond to individual states. Unlike the FSM approach, the dynamic memory will ultimately break down if patterns are presented too slowly. As the state of the system gets closer to the fixed point of the current input (after the input is repeated many times), it becomes increasingly difficult to differentiate the effects of previous events since there will always be limited precision in activation space. However, this type of solution has its advantages too. In particular, it generalizes to continuously varying input, without growing in complexity. It is therefore more suitable for signals which vary smoothly and are not easily reducible to a small number of discrete states.

In order to show this property imagine an input set of at least two orthogonal vectors, each of which has a distinct point attractor. As input varies continuously from *A* to *B*, the attractor itself may move smoothly from the point associated with *A* to that associated with *B*, as shown in figure 12.8. The continuous nature of the state space allows smooth interpolation between attractor regimes (cf. chapter 5, by Beer, which illustrates a model with this feature). This behavior is without parallel in the perfectly discrete FSM. The induction of such a dynamical system presents a technical problem, as there is no guarantee that the dynamics will always remain as well-behaved

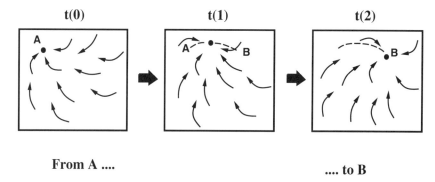

t(0)　　　　　　　t(1)　　　　　　　t(2)

From A ....

.... to B

Figure 12.8 Continuous interpolation between attractor regimes is possible with a dynamic system which emulates a finite-state machine (FSM). Unlike the FSM, the system does not increase in size or complexity as we generalize from a small set of discrete inputs to an unbounded set of continuous inputs.

as observed thus far (see Kolen, 1994). For example, attractors may split in two, producing bifurcation. Or they may be more complicated than simple point attractors and undergo catastrophes. However, recent work in the induction of general FSM-like dynamic systems has been encouraging (see Pollack, chapter 10; Das et al. 1992). With well-behaved dynamics, simple dynamic memory offers the possibility of an FSM-like approach to the recognition of serial order which generalizes to continuous dynamic signals such as speech.

We have shown that serial order is a kind of information about events in time that a simple network can recognize and identify. Although more sophisticated models of serial pattern recognition exist (Grossberg, 1986, 1988; Anderson, 1994), the simple dynamic memory illustrates one method by which problems resulting from variation in rate of presentation can be overcome. The biological correctness of the method described here, it should be noted, has not yet been demonstrated.

Recognition of Relative Time Patterns

The simple dynamic memory model of unstructured fully connected nodes is capable of recognizing a familiar sequence of ordered elements, independent of the rate of presentation. In doing so, it loses (or ignores) absolute time. Many problems, however, depend critically on more powerful measurement of duration than serial order. Simple dynamic memories will not suffice for these patterns. But durations of importance to perception of the environment are frequently relative; i.e., they could be adequately measured with respect to salient intervals within the signal itself. Relative durations are critical for animal gaits, periodic bird and insect sounds, and so forth. In Western music, the basic time unit is the beat. In speech it will be the syllable period for some measurements and perhaps other prosodic units (like the foot or mora) in other languages (Port et al., 1987; Anderson and Port, 1994; Lehiste, 1970).

　　Robert F. Port, Fred Cummins, and J. Devin McAuley

Having such a periodic standard, be it only a slippery and flexible one, can provide a practical means for measuring duration, evaluating rates of change and for entraining activity to an external signal (as in playing music or dancing to it), and for defining rhythmic structure. In order to detect rate and thus calibrate duration, a mechanism which can rapidly entrain to the period of a signal is useful. In fact, it is not too difficult to design such a device as long as a distinctive entraining event can be identified, i.e., an event that defines phase zero. A practical "adaptive oscillator" was developed in our laboratory following earlier work by Carme Torras (Torras, 1985; McAuley, 1994a,b; Large and Kolen, 1994). Once more, this can be achieved with a simple dynamical model. We describe the model in some detail here, because of its importance to our central theme.

First we should distinguish the adaptive oscillator from the more familiar case of a pair of continuously coupled oscillators, in which the phase of each oscillator continuously influences the periodic behavior of the other. The net result is an oscillation frequency for the coupled system that is determined by the coupling strength and the intrinsic oscillation frequencies of each oscillator. As soon as the oscillators become uncoupled, each independent oscillator immediately resumes its intrinsic oscillation frequency.

In contrast, the adaptive oscillator mechanism augments a pair of pulse-coupled oscillators in which only the phase information at each input pulse of one of them is available to influence the oscillation frequency of the other. Based on this phase information, the adaptive mechanism makes a more durable internal change to the intrinsic frequency of the oscillator. Thus, specifically, an input pulse occurring somewhat before the oscillator would spontaneously fire causes two things to occur. First, the oscillator spikes immediately and begins a new cycle. That is, phase is reset to zero. Second, the oscillator makes a small change in its own natural period, so that it more closely resembles the period of the input. In this way, the oscillator will quickly entrain itself so as to fire at the same period as the input signal (or at some integral multiple or fraction). If the input signal ceases, a slowly acting decay process causes it to drift back to its original period. This process of synchronization and decay is based on a gradient descent procedure described in more detail below. It is easy for the model to adapt to tempos that are near its preferred rate, but increasingly difficult to adapt to tempos that are significantly faster or slower. These may result in entrainment to harmonic ratios other than simply $1:1$ or $1:n$. Ratios such as $2:1$ or more exotic ratios like $5:2$ can also be attractor states of the system.

The Adaptive Oscillator Model   The specific adaptive model that we will look at is the adaptive simple harmonic oscillator as described by McAuley (1994a). This model has been applied to psychophysical data on the ability of listeners to discriminate small changes in the rate of isochronous auditory pulses (McAuley, 1994b).

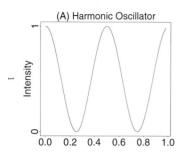 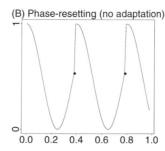 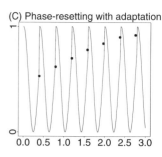

Figure 12.9 (*A*) Two periods of a 2.0-Hz harmonic oscillator. (*B*) Input pulses are now added to the harmonic oscillator every 400 ms, a shorter period than the intrinsic rate. Each input pulse now causes the oscillator to spike and phase-reset to 0. Output values, equal to the activation of the oscillator when it spikes, are marked by the dot at each phase reset. (*C*) Fast-acting synchronization is applied to the oscillator. Note that output values at each phase-reset continue to increase, providing a measure of the degree of entrainment. The output approaches the value of 1 as an attractor.

The preferred period of the oscillator is based on a periodic activation function, which in this case is simply a cosine function, scaled to oscillate between 0 and 1 (figure 12.9A):

$$\phi(t) = \left(1 + \cos\left(\frac{2\pi t}{\Omega(n)}\right)\right)\bigg/ 2 \tag{2}$$

The oscillator period $\Omega(n)$ is initialized to some preferred period: $\Omega(0) = p$. Each time $\phi(t)$ reaches or exceeds a threshold, θ, set to 1, the oscillator generates an output spike. In the absence of external input, this happens at the end of each period (at phase = 0). We now add periodic input (figure 12.9B) to $\phi(t)$, producing a total activity that is the sum of the basic activation function plus the input:

$$a(t) = \phi(t) + i(t) \tag{3}$$

Again, each time the threshold is reached, the oscillator fires, but now it is firing before the end of its period. On firing, we introduce a discontinuity by resetting the phase to 0. Figure 12.9B illustrates the effect of adding the input to the intrinsic activation (the threshold θ is 1.0). Each time input occurs, there is a jump in activation and phase is reset to 0. It is useful to define an output spike function $o(n)$, by letting $o(n) = \phi(t)$ at the point in time when i arrives. This is marked with a dot in figure 12.9B and C.

How does adaptation or entrainment work? If an input happens to arrive exactly in phase with the intrinsic period, it will have no effect, since the oscillator fires then anyway (e.g., at $t = 0.5$ second in figure 12.9A). If it arrives at any other time, however, it will force the oscillator to spike earlier (as shown in figure 12.9B). This phase difference provides information which is used to define a spike-driven gradient-descent procedure which synchronizes or entrains the spontaneous spiking behavior of the oscillator with rhythmic aspects of the input pattern. The result of this adaptation can be

Robert F. Port, Fred Cummins, and J. Devin McAuley

seen in figure 12.9C, where the amount of jump when inputs occur can be seen to decrease as the period of the oscillator comes into line with faster frequency of the input. The synchronization error is defined by squaring the distance in time between input-forced spikes and spontaneous spikes. This is simply the squared difference between the threshold θ and the spontaneous activation $\phi(t)$, scaled by the input:

$$E(n) = 1/2(i(t))(\theta - \phi(t))^2.$$

To minimize the discrepancy between the oscillator's initial spikes and the forced spikes, the oscillator's period $\Omega(n)$ is adapted by a small fraction α that is negatively proportional to the partial derivative of the synchronization error $E(n)$ with respect to $\Omega(n)$:

$$\Omega(n + 1) = \Omega(n) - \alpha \frac{\delta E(n)}{\delta \Omega(n)}.$$

In this way, the oscillator adjusts quickly to the faster or slower frequency of a signal that excites it. One can also arrange for a decay process that will cause the oscillator, once adapted away from its initial frequency, to gradually return to that frequency, as a "preferred frequency." This can be done by including a term in the update rule that pushes the adapted period back toward its preferred period p. This decay should be quite a bit slower than the process of adapting to a periodic input.

Simulations have shown that these oscillators can entrain rapidly (largely within two or three periods of the periodic input). They are very robust to noise and occasional missing inputs since the decay rate is slow compared to the entrainment process. If the input is not perfectly periodic, but varies somewhat in frequency from one period to the next, the oscillator will still closely track the variations and should allow a good guess about the time of the next input.

Measuring Time as Phase Angle   Some useful features of this oscillator model include its behavior in noise and when occasional inputs are absent. If there are irregular or noisy inputs, the oscillator will tend not to be affected. Because the entrainment process takes several oscillator cycles, irregularly spaced inputs tend to cancel out one another's effect, while periodic input will quickly cause the oscillator to approach the input frequency.

If an oscillator has a preferred period that is very different from the input signal, it may also entrain at ratios of, e.g., 2:1 or 3:1. These other ratios allow a single complex pattern to entrain a number of oscillators for different periodic components of the pattern: some at the "measure level" and others at the "beat level," etc. By setting up a number of oscillators with a range of preferred periods, it is possible to use the different entrainment ratios to extract the hierarchical rhythmic structure of the input. Some units will entrain at the most basic level such as the musical beat (or the fundamental frequency of voiced speech), while slower oscillators will pick out larger metrical units such as musical bars (or, hopefully, prosodic units like the syllable or foot). Such a hierarchical structure has been demonstrated in simulations in which a bank of oscillators with a range of preferred periods were exposed to two kinds of rhythmic inputs (McAuley, 1994a). The first was a waltzlike rhythm (*Dah dit-dit, Dah dit-dit*) and the second a two-beat measure (*Dah dit, Dah dit*). In each case, some oscillators in the simulation entrained at the measure level, locking into the strong beats only, while others picked out the individual beats. Those entrained to the beats are therefore measuring events that occur at fixed phase angles with respect to the larger, measure-sized cycle—either thirds or halves of the measure-size unit. Note that modest changes in the rate of the entire hierarchical pattern will not disrupt these relationships. This is a simple example of time measured purely as phase angle, rather like musical notation. The absolute duration of the period is irrelevant to the phase angle time measurements as long as regular periodicity is maintained.

This mechanism entrains rapidly to underlying periodic structures in a signal despite noise, missing beats, and slow variation in rate. Further development of adaptive oscillation should allow the measurement of time as phase angle under a broad range of conditions. All that is required is an unambiguous "start pulse" that must be supplied by a preprocessing system. Measuring relative durations without prior measurement of absolute time is now a possibility. In the case of speech, for instance, we hope it will prove possible eventually to entrain directly to the roughly periodic syllable and foot-sized units in speech. Phonetically relevant vowel durations might then be expressed in relation to these entrained periods rather than in terms of absolute values like milliseconds. By quickly and adaptively identifying and tracking the periodicities intrinsic to the speech signal, useful measurements of duration that are robust under changes in rate of presentation may be possible. Sounds that are merely quasi-periodic abound in nature and are by no means restricted to speech. Anywhere oscillation occurs—after striking, rubbing, blowing, dripping, as well as in animal gaits etc.—the signal may display an underlying period which might be exploited to scale the measurement of its subcomponents or other associated events. Adaptive oscillation offers a plausible mechanism for description of such temporal patterns, both as a model for neural mechanisms in cognition and potentially for engineering purposes as well.

12.4   CONCLUDING DISCUSSION

In this chapter we have highlighted the problem of recognizing auditory patterns in time. We claim that the naive view of time, despite its widespread employment, is not a useful model of any process in human audition. Events do not come with time stamps on them, nor does human audition supply them. It is difficult to imagine how there could be any direct representation of time either using labels marked in seconds or by translating time into physical

Robert F. Port, Fred Cummins, and J. Devin McAuley

distance (for anything beyond extremely short delays). Apparently nothing resembles a sound spectrogram in the auditory system. Thus the exploitation of durations in the acoustic signal is made possible by the use of the serial order of known patterns and by measuring duration relative to some predictable interval—not by measuring absolute time. We have made some first steps toward development of two models of auditory processing in audition that may simulate human performance for periodic patterns and sequences at the cognitive time scale. Both of the general methods described here are formulated as dynamical systems. In both cases, the behavior of these systems over time is exploited to keep track of location within a temporally distributed pattern. And in both cases, predictable features of the stimulus itself provide the yardstick for the measurement of time.

These methods are simple enough that we can imagine them implemented in many ways in the auditory system, but, of course, each method has certain apparent drawbacks. The method of simple dynamic memory for sequence recognition, for example, may offer rate invariance for free, but it requires actually learning an inventory of individual patterns. The system can only represent the serial-order structure of events it is familiar with. In our view, this property in no way disqualifies it as a model of processing in animal auditory systems. After all, most of the sounds we hear are, in fact, very similar to sounds we have heard before. Most animals live in environments in which the same kind of events recur. There may need to be a large inventory of auditory events, but any inventory is still minute compared to the space of possible frequency-by-time auditory patterns. Indeed, it is known that if listeners are presented with very novel yet complex auditory patterns, their ability to compare them or make judgments about their internal structure is astonishingly poor (see, for example, Watson and Foyle, 1985; Espinoza-Varas and Watson, 1986). Only practice with a specific set of novel patterns makes detailed comparison possible if patterns are both complex and completely novel.

In fact, given typical auditory ecosystems, this "drawback" of requiring familiarity with the patterns would have the practical advantage that when several familiar events happen to overlap in time (e.g., a spoken word and the slam of a car door), an auditory system that is able to represent only the learned set of patterns should automatically do "auditory scene analysis" (Bregman, 1990) and parse the complex into its familiar components.[4] Since the serial order of the subcomponents of familiar patterns were learned independently for each pattern, the temporal alignment between the two distinct events will, however, not be well represented. It would be very difficult to say which phonetic segments in the word coincided with the door slam. This accords with our intuition as well as with experimental results (see Port, 1990 for further discussion).

The measurement of relative duration, that is, measurement of a durational ratio between some event and a longer event, is useful for many kinds of sound patterns. Description of duration as an angular sweep of phase within a pattern of known period depends on predicting the duration of the longer event. The adaptive oscillators described here offer a way to do this when the input signal contains salient periodic events that can trigger phase resetting and period adaptation. Adaptive oscillators are quite simple to arrange neurologically, but obviously, to apply this mechanism to very complex auditory structures like speech or music will require (among other things) some highly sophisticated preprocessing in order to supply triggering signals for events of just the right sort. Adaptive oscillation should be a useful mechanism for analysis of many different kinds of environmental events and may be embedded in many places within a general auditory system.

One implication of the employment of adaptive oscillation for handling unfamiliar patterns should be that a pattern of clicks, say, that lack regular periodicity (e.g., with random spacing in time) will be much more difficult to remember or to differentiate one from another, than patterns of periodically spaced clicks. This has been shown to be the case (Sorkin, 1987; Povel and Essens, 1985). More subtly, if subjects listen to a series of several clicks and then try to determine if a second series of clicks has the same rate, performance improves as the number of clicks in each series increases from, say, 2 to 8 (after which there is no further improvement). This follows naturally from the hypothesis that more clicks permit closer adaptation of the perceptual oscillator to the input pattern and thus better discrimination (McAuley, 1994b).

In conclusion, then, it can be seen that the kind of auditory pattern recognition system we envision must be customized for a particular auditory environment. It is a system that organizes itself to construct a large inventory of special-purpose recognition mechanisms appropriate to the inventory of acoustic events that have relevance to the organism. These recognition mechanisms can not simply be part of long-term memory, or part of a system that analyzes the contents of a general-purpose, spatially arrayed short-term memory (like a sound spectrogram). Instead, we propose that these mechanisms themselves provide the first level of auditory memory. On this view, low-level auditory recognition and low-level auditory memory are collapsed into a single system that responds in real time to sound as it occurs. This system does not rely on a universal clock or other representational mechanism for absolute time. It consists, basically, of a bag of dynamical tricks that enable an animal to deal with the dynamically generated sound patterns.

ACKNOWLEDGMENTS

The authors are grateful to Sven Anderson, Kenneth deJong, Michael Gasser, Gary S. Kidd, Catherine Rogers, Tim van Gelder, and Charles Watson for helpful discussion of these matters and for comments on earlier drafts of the manuscript. This work was supported in part by the Office of Naval Research, grant number N00001491-J1261 to R. Port and by the National Institute of Mental Health, grant number MH10667 to J. Devin McAuley.

NOTES

1. There are other difficulties with a "neural spectrogram" model of auditory memory. The main one is, how could it be implemented? The memory could not plausibly be sampled in time, since this should lead to obvious aliasing artifacts for inputs at certain frequencies. Nor could it just be an exponentially decaying trace for independent frequency bands of the spectrum (like the way a piano "records" your voice if you shout at it after lifting the dampers with the pedal). If it worked like this, then later sounds in a given frequency range would tend to be confused with earlier sounds, which does not seem to be the case. Of course, it is undeniable that we *do* have introspective access to recent sound, at least when the sounds are familiar. For these, we probably store some kind of descriptive labels. Evidence for the necessity of learning complex patterns comes from research on patterns that are novel but complex. It is known that subjects cannot make good discriminations of complex patterns that are unfamiliar (Espinoza-Varas and Watson, 1986; Spiegel and Watson, 1981; Port, 1990).

2. By "weaker" and "stronger" measures of time, we refer informally to the set of invariance transformations that are permitted on the scale (Stevens, 1951; Port, 1986), i.e., the transformations that do not disturb the temporal description. For serial order, many complex transformations on the duration of component events are possible without disturbing serial order. For phase angle measurement, only durational transformations that preserve relative duration are allowable. Absolute measurements permit no durational changes at all.

3. These are actually schematic diagrams that illustrate the principles at work. When our simulations (Anderson and Port, 1990; Cummins, 1993) were carried out, the state space was of higher dimension (typically around 12) and the set of targets and distractors was considerably larger (as large as ten each).

4. Of course, the primitive dynamic memory described here can only track one familiar sequence at a time. One would need several distinct simple dynamic memories to track several patterns simultaneously. Presumably animal auditory systems can deal with this for at least several overlapping patterns.

REFERENCES

Anderson, S. (1992). Self-organization of auditory motion detectors. In *Proceedings of the Fourteenth Annual Conference of the Cognitive Science Society* (pp. 684–689). Hillsdale, NJ: Erlbaum.

Anderson, S., and Port, R. (1990). *A network model of auditory pattern recognition.* (Technical report no. 11.) Bloomington: Indiana University Cognitive Science Program.

Anderson, S., and Port, R. (1994). Evidence for syllable structure, stress and juncture from segmental durations. *Journal of Phonetics, 22,* 184–217.

Anderson, S. E. (1994). *A computational model of auditory pattern recognition.* (Technical report no. 112.) Bloomington: Cognitive Science Program, Indiana University.

Baddeley, A. (1992). Working memory. *Science, 255,* 556–559.

Bernstein, N. (1967). *The coordination and regulation of movements.* London: Pergamon.

Bregman, A. S. (1990) *Auditory scene analysis: the perceptual organization of sound.* Cambridge, MA: MIT Press.

Browman, C., and Goldstein, L. (1989). Articulatory gestures as phonological units. *Phonology, 6,* 201–251.

Chomsky, N., and Halle, M. (1968). *The sound pattern of English.* New York: Harper & Row.

Crowder, R., and Morton, J. (1969). Precategorical acoustic storage. *Perception and Psychophysics*, 5, 365–373.

Cummins, F. (1993). Representation of temporal patterns in recurrent neural networks. In *Proceedings of the 15th Annual Conference of the Cognitive Science Society* (pp. 377–382). Hillsdale, NJ: Erlbaum.

Das, S., Giles, C. L., and Zheng Sun, G. (1992). Learning context-free grammars: capabilities and limitations of a recurrent neural network with an external stack memory. In *Proceedings of the 14th Annual Conference of the Cognitive Science Society* (pp. 791–796). Hillsdale, NJ: Erlbaum.

Elman, J., and Zipser, D. (1988). Learning the hidden structure of speech. *Journal of the Acoustical Society of America*, 83, 1615–1626.

Espinoza-Varas, B., and Watson, C. (1986). Temporal discrimination for single components of nonspeech auditory patterns. *Journal of the Acoustical Society of America*, 80, 1685–1694.

Fowler, C., Rubin, P., Remez, R., et al, (1981). Implications for speech production of a general theory of action. In B. Butterworth, (Ed.), *Language production* (pp. 373–420). New York: Academic Press.

Fraisse, P. (1957). *Psychologie du temps*. Paris: Presses Universitaires de France.

Grossberg, S. (1986). The adaptive self-organization of serial order in behavior: speech language, and motor control. In E. Schwab and H. Nusbaum (Eds.), *Pattern recognition by humans and machines: speech perception*. Orlando, FL: Academic Press.

Grossberg, S. (1988). *Neural networks and natural intelligence*. Cambridge, MA: MIT Press.

Jakobson, R., Fant, G., and Halle, M. (1952). *Preliminaries to speech analysis: the distinctive features and their correlates*. Cambridge, MA: MIT Press.

Jones, M. R. (1976). Time, our lost dimension: toward a new theory of perception, attention, and memory. *Psychological Review*, 83, 323–355.

Kelso, J. S., Saltzman, E., and Tuller, B. (1986). The dynamical perspective in speech production: data and theory. *Journal of Phonetics*, 14, 29–59.

Klatt, D. H. (1976). The linguistic uses of segmental duration in English: acoustic and perceptual evidence. *Journal of the Acoustical Society of America*, 59, 1208–1221.

Klatt, D. H. (1977). Review of the ARPA speech understanding project. *Journal of the Acoustical Society of America*, 62, 1345–1366.

Klatt, D. H. (1980). Speech perception: a model of acoustic-phonetic analysis and lexical access. In R. A. Cole (Ed.), *Perception and production of fluent speech*, (pp. 243–288). Hillsdale, NJ: Erlbaum.

Kolen, J. F. (1994). Fool's gold: extracting finite state machines from recurrent network dynamics. In *Advances in Neural Information Processing Systems*, 6, in press.

Lang, K. J., Waibel, A. H., and Hinton, G. E. (1990). A time-delay neural network architecture for isolated word recognition. *Neural Networks*, 3, 23–43.

Large, E. W., and Kolen, J. F. (1994). Resonance and the perception of musical meter. *Connection Science*, in press.

Lee, C. H., Rabiner, L. R., and Pieraccini, R. (1992). Speaker independent continuous speech recognition using continuous density hidden Markov models. In *Speech recognition and understanding. Recent advances, trends and applications* (pp. 135–163). *Proceedings of the NATO Advanced Study Institute, Cetraro, Italy, July 1–13, 1990*, Berlin: Springer Verlag.

Lee, K. (1992). Context-dependent phonetic hidden Markov models for speaker-independent continuous speech recognition. In *Speech recognition and understanding. Recent advances, trends and applications (p. 133). Proceedings of the NATO Advanced Study Institute, Cetraro, Italy, July 1–13, 1990*, Berlin: Springer Verlag.

Lehiste, I. (1970). *Suprasegmentals*. Cambridge, MA: MIT Press.

Lesser, V. R., Fennel, R. D., Erman, L. D., et al. (1975). Organization of the Hearsay-II speech understanding system. *International Conference on Acoustics, Speech, and Signal Processing, 23*, 11–23.

Lisker, L., and Abramson, A. (1964). A cross-language study of voicing in initial stops: acoustical measurements. *Word, 20*, 384–422.

Lisker, L., and Abramson, A. (1971). Distinctive features and laryngeal control. *Language, 44*, 767–785.

Massaro, D. (1972). Preperceptual images, processing time, and perceptual units in auditory perception. *Psychological Review, 79*, 124–145.

Massaro, D. (1987). *Speech perception by ear and eye: a paradigm for psychological inquiry*. Hillsdale, NJ: Erlbaum.

McAuley, J. D. (1994a). Finding metrical structure in time. In Mozer, M. C., Smolensky, P., Touretzky, D. S., et al. *Proceedings of the 1993 Connectionist Models Summer School* (pp. 219–227). Hillsdale, NJ: Erlbaum.

McAuley, J. D. (1994b). Time as phase: A dynamic model of time perception. In *Proceedings of the 16th Annual Meeting of the Cognitive Science Society* (pp. 607–612). Hillsdale, NJ: Erlbaum.

Michon, J. A., and Jackson, J. L. (1985). *Time, mind and behavior*. Berlin: Springer Verlag.

Neisser, U. (1967). *Cognitive psychology*. New York: Appelton-Century-Crofts.

Pollack, J. B. (1991). The induction of dynamical recognizers. *Machine Learning, 7*, 123–148.

Port, R. (1986). Invariance in phonetics. In J. Perkell and D. Klatt (Eds.), *Invariance and variability in speech processes*. Hillsdale, NJ: Erlbaum.

Port, R., and Dalby, J. (1982). C/V ratio as a cue for voicing in English. *Journal of the Acoustical Society of America, 69*, 262–1274.

Port, R., Reilly, W., and Maki, D. (1987). Use of syllable-scale timing to discriminate words. *Journal of the Acoustical Society of America, 83*, 265–273.

Port, R. F. (1981). Linguistic timing factors in combination. *Journal of the Acoustical Society of America, 69*, 262–274.

Port, R. F. (1990). Representation and recognition of temporal patterns. *Connection Science, 2*, 151–176.

Port, R. F., and Cummins, F. (1992). The English voicing contrast as velocity perturbation. In *Proceedings of the Conference on Spoken Language Processing* (pp. 1311–1314). Edmonton, Alberta: University of Alberta.

Port, R. F., Dalby, J., and O'Dell, M. (1987). Evidence for mora timing in Japanese. *Journal of the Acoustical Society of America, 81*, 1574–1585.

Povel, D., and Essens, P. (1985). Perception of temporal patterns. *Music Perception, 2*, 411–440.

Robinson, T., and Fallside, F. (1991). A recurrent error propagation network speech recognition system. *Computer Speech and Language, 5*, 259–274.

Saltzman, E., and Munhall, K. (1989). A dynamical approach to gestural patterning in speech production. *Ecological Psychology, 1,* 333–382.

Shamma, S. A. (1989). Stereausis: binaural processing without neural delays. *Journal of the Acoustical Society of America, 86,* 989–1006.

Sorkin, R. (1987). Temporal factors in the discrimination of tonal sequences. *Journal of the Acoustical Society of America, 82,* 1218–1226.

Sperling, G. (1960). The information available in brief visual presentations. *Psychological Monographs, 74,* 1–29.

Spiegel, M. F., and Watson, C. S. (1981). Factors in the discrimination of tonal patterns. III. Frequency discrimination with components of well-learned patterns. *Journal of the Acoustical Society of America, 69,* 223–230.

Stevens, K. N., and Blumstein, S. E. (1978). Invariant cues for place of articulation in stop consonants. *Journal of the Acoustical Society of America, 64,* 1358–1368.

Stevens, S. S. (1951). Mathematics, measurement and psychophysics. In S. S. Stevens, (Ed.), *Handbook of experimental psychology* (pp. 1–49). New York: Wiley.

Tajima, K., Port, R., and Dalby, J. (1993). Influence of timing on intelligibility of foreign-accented English. *Journal of the Acoustical Society of America, 95,* 3009.

Torras, C. (1985). *Temporal-pattern learning in neural models.* Berlin: Springer-Verlag.

Van Gelder, T. and Port, R. (1994). Beyond symbolic: toward a *kama-sutra* of compositionality. In V. Honavar and L. Uhr (Eds.), *Artificial intelligence and neural networks: steps toward principled integration* (pp. 107–125). New York: Academic Press.

Warren, R. M. (1993). Perception of acoustic sequences: global integration versus temporal resolution. In S. McAdams and E. Bigand (Eds.), *Thinking in sound: the cognitive psychology of human audition,* (pp. 37–68). Oxford University Press, Oxford.

Watrous, R. L. (1990). Phoneme discrimination using connectionist networks. *Journal of the Acoustical Society of America, 87,* 1753–1772.

Watson, C., and Foyle, D. (1985). Central factors in the discrimination and identification of complex sounds. *Journal of the Acoustical Society of America, 78,* 375–380.

Williams, R., and Zipser, D. (1989). A learning algorithm for continually running fully recurrent neural networks. *Neural Computation, 1,* 270–280.

Guide to Further Reading

The problem of timing in speech was considered in Port (1986, 1990). Both papers were partially inspired by the classic work on timing in behavior by Lashley (1951) and on measurement scales by S. S. Stevens (1951). Dealing with time in connectionist networks has been addressed in a simple way by Elman (1990) and in Lippman's review (1989) of neural networks for speech recognition. Many of the basic phenomena of speech timing, especially in English, were reviewed in Klatt (1976). One important recent model of sequence recognition in neural networks is Sven Anderson's thesis (1994).

Anderson, S. (1994). *A computational model of auditory pattern recognition.* (Technical report no. 112). Bloomington: Indiana University Cognitive Science Program.

Elman, J. (1990). Finding structure in time. *Cognitive Science 14,* 179–211.

Klatt, D. H. (1976). Linguistic uses of segmental duration in English: acoustic and perceptual evidence. *Journal of Acoustical Society of America, 59,* 1208–1221.

Lashley, K. (1951). The problem of serial order in behavior. In L. Jeffress (Ed.), *Cerebral mechanisms in behavior* (pp. 112–136). New York: Wiley.

Lippman, R. (1989). Review of neural networks for speech recognition. *Neural Computation 1*, 1–38.

Port, R. (1986). Invariance in phonetics. In J. Perkell and D. Klatt (Eds.), *Invariance and variability in speech processes 1* (pp. 540–558). Hillsdale, NJ: Erlbaum.

Port, R. (1990). Representation and recognition of temporal patterns. *Connection Science 2*, 151–176.

Stevens, S. S. (1951). Mathematics, measurement and psychophysics. In Stevens, S. S. (Ed.), *Handbook of experimental psychology* (pp. 1–49). New York: Wiley.

13 Some Dynamical Themes in Perception and Action

M. T. Turvey and Claudia Carello

EDITORS' INTRODUCTION

The dynamical approach to cognition has turned out to be deeply compatible (though by no means identical) with Gibsonian or ecological psychology. In particular, the dynamical thesis, that natural cognitive performances only arise in the context of a wider system which spans the nervous system, body, and environment, recalls the ecological themes, that to understand perception we must first understand what is being perceived, and that to understand action we must first understand the nature of bodily movement. Further, ecological psychologists have found the tools of dynamics to be essential in describing these phenomena.

In this chapter Turvey and Carello provide case studies of the ecological approach to perception and action and demonstrate the critical role of dynamics in these studies. The first study is focused primarily on dynamic touch—the kind of perception involved in grasping and wielding an object such as a hammer. Despite the constantly changing pressures on muscles and tendons, we are able to perceive unchanging features of the situation such as the shape of the object we are wielding. How is this possible? In Turvey and Carello's approach, the wielding of the object is conceptualized as a dynamical system whose states are in constant flux, but whose parameters remain relatively constant; perception of the shape of an object by dynamic touch thus involves locking onto the parameters. Their detailed mathematical analysis shows that the relevant invariant property is a tensor (the moment of inertia), and experimental studies demonstrate that perception by dynamic touch is systematically tied to this tensor rather than other possibly relevant quantities.

The second case study is focused on action, and in particular on the phenomenon of coordinated movement. Here the situation is just the reverse: the aim is to produce behavior in time, and so the target of theoretical and experimental investigation is the relation between such behavior and constant or invariant properties which might determine its shape. Similarly, however, the general framework is to understand the produced movement as the behavior of a dynamical system and to see that behavior as dependent on the setting of control parameters. Turvey and Carello describe detailed investigations of various forms of coordination, such as moving two fingers at a certain frequency, or swinging two pendulums, one in each hand. They uncover a range of systematic dependencies of coordinated behaviors on the value of control parameters.

The aim in both the perception and action studies is to uncover the general, simple laws which describe the emergent behaviors of self-organizing systems. Such an approach requires considerable technical sophistication and the patience to develop rigorous descriptions of seemingly simple phenomena; however it promises an understanding of cognitive capacities which is mathematically well-founded and fundamentally continuous with the physical sciences.

13.1 INTRODUCTION

How should the perception and action capabilities of biological systems be understood? The common answers emphasize notions of computation and representation, or notions shaped by the forms of local processing and global adaptive change available to neural-like systems. A less common answer emphasizes the laws and symmetry conditions at nature's ecological scale, the scale at which living things and their surroundings are defined. This latter emphasis characterizes the ecological approach to perception and action pioneered by Gibson (1966, 1979/1986). Within this approach, *dynamics* (referring to the laws of motion and change) and *dynamical systems* (referring to the time evolution of observable quantities according to law) are natural companions to the study of perception and action, and have been explicitly recognized as such for more than a decade (Kugler, Kelso, and Turvey, 1980, 1982). A major concern from the ecological perspective is the "loans of intelligence" (Dennett, 1971) freely taken by more conventional efforts to explain perception and action. It is commonplace to ascribe to the nervous system rich varieties of inference mechanisms, knowledge structures, and the like in order to rationalize the capabilities of organisms to perceive and act. These forms of mediating intelligence are usually ad hoc and rarely, if ever, accompanied by viable hypotheses about how they might originate in a system whose basic functioning seems to call for them at the very start (Carello, Turvey, Kugler, et al., 1984; Michaels and Carello, 1981; Turvey, 1977; Turvey, Shaw, Reed, et al., 1981). The careful extension of nonlinear dynamics and the developing physics of self-organizing systems to perception-action systems, and the application of both orthodox and novel strategies for uncovering the lawful regularities behind such systems, promise explanations that require no trips to the credit union. From the ecological perspective, characteristic perception-action capabilities are what they are by virtue of laws and general principles. Consequently, loans on intelligence should be unnecessary at best and minimal at worst.

The success of a dynamics strategy depends on its methodology. Not every perceptual and movement coordination phenomenon lends itself to the rigorous application of dynamics or to the kinds of investigations that can become sufficiently detailed to reveal fundamental ordering principles. One

M. T. Turvey and Claudia Carello

needs model systems (Haken, 1988). In general, the notion of a model system refers to a carefully contrived simplification of a complex system or process, such that the behavior of specific observables as a function of one or relatively few parameters can be studied in a reproducible fashion. A model system should allow for the development of new concepts whose dynamics can be checked rigorously through further studies of the model system and variants of it (Haken, 1988). These new concepts can then be applied to the complex system of which the model system is a simplification. With respect to perception and action, an important requirement for a model system is that well-established physical concepts are expressed by the system and exploitable in investigations of it. The research to be summarized in this chapter illustrates the strategy of finding and using model systems to reveal the classes of principles formative of perception and action capabilities.

The Phase-Control Space

In a very general and abbreviated form, a dynamical system is represented by

$$\dot{x} = F(x, t; c) \tag{1}$$

where x is a state variable such as displacement, $\dot{x}$ is its time derivative, t is time, and c is a control parameter such as mass or stiffness or imposed frequency. Ordinarily there is more than one state variable and more than one control parameter. It is useful to view equation (1) as describing the motion of a point in an n-dimensional space referred to as the phase space P of the system defined by an ordered set of real numbers. If $n = 2$, and the two variables are displacement x and velocity $\dot{x}$, then the points of the phase space are $(x, \dot{x})$. The phase space P is often viewed in conjunction with the control space C (Jackson, 1989). The system will "run" with c held constant (independent of t). Across dynamical runs, however, c can be varied. As a consequence, for each value of c there will be a different trajectory of points $(x, \dot{x})$ in the phase space—a different phase portrait (Abraham and Shaw, 1982). The phase portraits may differ slightly or markedly with changes in c. When a marked, qualitative difference arises at some value of c, a bifurcation is said to have occurred (figure 13.1).

In this chapter we summarize investigations of human perception and action systems through this phase-control space provided by the conjunction of P and C. With respect to perception, where measures of environmental properties are required, the invariant nature of c during a dynamic run, and the systematic dependency of these measures on C, are the foci of concern. The qualities of P are ancillary, reflecting the particulars of the exploratory activity that reveal the invariants of the dynamics (see below). With respect to action, where states of P must be achieved, the focus is on the specific form of variation in P as a function of C. That variation should reveal, ideally, the low-dimensional dynamical laws formative of coordination patterns.

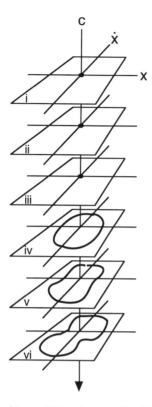

Figure 13.1 An example of the phase-control space. As the control parameter c increases, the trajectories in the phase plane of x and $\dot{x}$ change. In phase planes i through iii, the dynamics are those of a point attractor. In phase planes iv through vi, the dynamics are those of a limit-cycle attractor. A (Hopf) bifurcation occurs at a value of c between iii and iv. Beyond the bifurcation, increases in c are accompanied by different spatiotemporal patterns corresponding to different versions of the limit-cycle dynamics.

13.2 HAPTIC PERCEPTION AS ATTUNEMENT TO THE PARAMETERS OF A DYNAMICAL SYSTEM

The quantities c in equation (1) express the specific way in which causes of motion and the patterns of motion are coupled. They convey upon a system its specific identity independent of whatever radical changes occur in its states. Here we examine their exploitation by perception as the basis for perceiving persistent environmental properties.

The Nature of Dynamic Touch

A kind of touch that is prominent in everyday manipulatory activity involves the hand in contact with only a part of the manipulated object. Both statically and in motion, the manipulated object affects the tensile states of the muscles and tendons of the hand and arm and thereby the patterning of activity in the ensembles of muscle and tendon receptors. Muscle and tendon

M. T. Turvey and Claudia Carello

deformations (induced by the forces and torques engendered by holding and manipulating) characterize the haptic subsystem of dynamic touch, more so than deformations of the skin and changes in joint angles (Gibson, 1966). Dynamic touching, therefore, is the kind of touching that occurs when a utensil (e.g., a fork), a tool (e.g., a hammer), or a small object (e.g., a book), is grasped and lifted, turned, carried, and so on. It contrasts with cutaneous touch (e.g., an object resting on the skin) and haptic touch (e.g., the hands enveloping an object and sweeping thoroughly and freely over its surfaces), the two haptic subsystems (Gibson, 1966) that have been the subject of most experimental inquiry (e.g., Katz, 1925/1989). With respect to manipulatory activity and locomotion guided by a handheld implement (e.g., Burton, 1992) dynamic touch, rather than the cutaneous and haptic versions, plays the most significant role.

In sum, whenever an object is grasped and wielded, or grasped and wielded in probing other objects, dynamic touch is implied. Wielding and probing, as characteristic forms of dynamic touching, are dynamical systems; they are describable by equation (1). Patently, in wielding and probing, the forces (torques, impulses) and the motions vary with time. Providing an invariant coupling between those time-dependent forces and motions, however, are the parameters of wielding and probing. Ordinarily, the goals of perception by dynamic touch are persistent environmental properties and persistent body-environment relations—such as implement length, aperture size, position of grasp. These persistent environmental properties and body-environment relations are linked most intimately to the persistent rather than the transient aspects of the dynamics, that is, to the parameters. Accordingly, the strategy for understanding dynamic touch seems to be as follows: (a) define the dynamical system, (b) identify the parameters that couple the (muscular and other) forces impressed on the system to the system's states, (c) determine, for the given property of handheld object or adjacent surface layout, the parameter(s) that constrains fully the perception, and (d) provide a reasoned basis for the relation between the pertinent parameter(s) and the perception (Carello, Fitzpatrick, and Turvey, 1992; Solomon, 1988).

The Inertia Tensor as the Parameter of Wielding Dynamics

To rotate and twist any rigid object in three-dimensional space about a fixed point O requires time-varying torques N_i (vector components N_x, N_y, N_z) producing time-varying motions with angular velocity ω_j (vector components, $\omega_x, \omega_y, \omega_z$) and angular acceleration $\dot{\omega}_j$ (vector components, $\dot{\omega}_x, \dot{\omega}_y, \dot{\omega}_z$). The inconstant motions are coupled to the inconstant torques through an invariant structured array defined about O, viz., the object's different resistances to rotational acceleration in different directions. This array arises from the fact that a turning force about a given axis, for example, N_x, resolves into a force tangent to the rotational motion and a force normal or radial to the rotational motion. There are, in consequence, two resistances: an inertia force opposing the tangential component of N_x and an inertia force opposing the radial component of N_x. The moment of the former is the moment of inertia about the x-axis, and the moment of the latter is the centrifugal moment or product of inertia about an axis perpendicular to the xy plane formed by the given axis x and a coplanar axis y orthogonal to it. It follows that, for any arbitrary coordinate system $Oxyz$, the parameter I_{ij} representing the rigid body's resistance to rotational acceleration about O consists of three numbers quantifying the moments of inertia I_{xx}, I_{yy}, I_{zz}, and six quantifying the products of inertia, $I_{xy}, I_{xz}, I_{yx}, I_{yz}, I_{zx}, I_{zy}$. Because $I_{xy} = I_{yx}$, and so on, the parameter identified as I_{ij} reduces to six independent numbers. I_{ij} is a tensor. It satisfies the transformation law

$$I_{kl}^* = \alpha_{k \cdot i} \alpha_{l \cdot j} I_{ij} \tag{2}$$

where I_{kl}^*, I_{ij} are the tensors in the new (rectangular) and old (rectangular) coordinate systems O^*xyz and $Oxyz$, respectively, and $\alpha_{k \cdot i}$ is the cosine of the angle between the kth axis of O^*xyz and the ith axis of $Oxyz$ (similarly for $\alpha_{l \cdot j}$). [There is a more general transformation law that applies to arbitrary curvilinear coordinate systems which is expressed through relations between the differentials of the variables. For present purposes, equation (2) will suffice.]

The likely prominence of I_{ij} in dynamic touch follows from the fact that when wielding occurs about a fixed point, I_{ij} is a parameter (a constant) that couples the varying torques and varying motions of wielding. (The dynamics of a wielded object held firmly in the hand can always be referred to the rotation "point" in the wrist; the distance of the handheld object to that point is fixed throughout any manner of arm motions involving the wrist, elbow, and shoulder joints singly or in combination [Pagano, Fitzpatrick, and Turvey, 1993].) As a time- and coordinate-independent quantity, I_{ij} is an invariant rendering of the persistent material distribution of the hand-held, wielded object. It can, therefore, be the basis for perceiving the object's unchanging spatial dimensions.

Consonant with the preceding, experiments have shown that the spatial ability of dynamic touch is tied to I_{ij}. In perceiving the lengths of rods or rod segments that are wielded and not seen, the relevant independent quantity is moment of inertia rather than other possibly relevant quantities such as average torque, average kinetic energy, average muscular torsion, mass, center of mass, and center of oscillation (Burton and Turvey, 1990; Solomon and Turvey, 1988; Solomon, Turvey, and Burton, 1989a,b). Moments of inertia also seem to underlie the perception of the shapes of wielded objects hidden from view (Burton, Turvey, and Solomon, 1990). Moments and products of inertia together have been found to affect the perceived orientation, with respect to the hand, of occluded objects consisting of a stem and a branch perpendicular to the stem (Turvey, Burton, Pagano, et al., 1992). It appears that I_{ij} provides the domains for two sets of functions, one consisting of the principal moments of inertia or eigenvalues, which map onto perceived "magnitudes," such as object length (e.g., Fitzpatrick, Carello, and Turvey, 1994;

M. T. Turvey and Claudia Carello

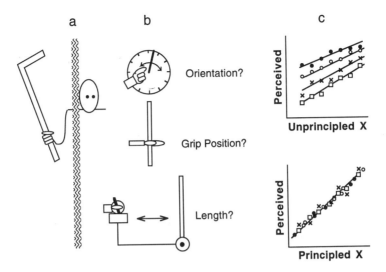

Figure 13.2 (*a*) In a typical haptics experiment objects of different lengths and spatial or material heterogeneity are grasped somewhere along their lengths. (*b*) Perceivers are asked to report a particular property by adjusting an appropriate apparatus that permits some kind of match. As examples, an arrow on a dial is turned to match orientation; the hand is placed along a response rod to indicate grip position; the position of a surface is adjusted to match the felt location of the end of a rod. (*c*) Describing the data with respect to a property not motivated by the dynamics yields a many-to-one function of perception relative to the candidate variable, whereas the principled selection of variables yields a single-valued function.

Pagano and Turvey, 1993; Solomon and Turvey, 1988), shape (Burton et al., 1990), and weight (Amazeen and Turvey, in press), and one consisting of the eigenvectors, which map onto perceived "directions" such as the orientation of an object to the hand (Pagano and Turvey, 1992; Turvey et al., 1992), the location of the hand relative to a wielded object (Pagano, Kinsella-Shaw, Cassidy, et al. 1994), and the orientation of limbs (Pagano and Turvey, in press).

Figure 13.2 illustrates the general form of this research. It gives an appreciation of wielding a firmly grasped object as a model system for approaching the complexity of the haptic perceptual system. The key to the success of this model system is that the fundamental dynamics of this system is known (in contrast to many other alternative experimental settings for investigating the nature of touch) and directly manipulable. To fully appreciate this latter point and the kinds of results hinted at in figure 13.2, we provide further development of the physical character of I_{ij}.

Eigenvectors and Eigenvalues

The actual calculations of the moments and products of inertia comprising I_{ij} are done with respect to a rectangular coordinate system $Oxyz$. Clearly, many triplets of perpendicular axes can be anchored at O. For each choice of $Oxyz$, the components of I_{ij} will differ. There is, however, a single unchanging set of

Some Dynamical Themes in Perception and Action

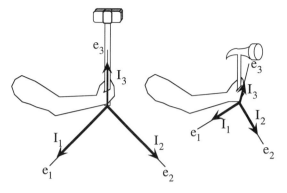

Figure 13.3 The mass distribution of an object being wielded about a point in the wrist is captured by the principle moments of inertia or eigenvalues, $I_1 I_2 I_3$, and the principal directions or eigenvectors, $e_1 e_2 e_3$. The lengths of the arrows indicate resistance to rotation about a particular axis. Owing to the symmetry of the sledge hammer, e_3 is coincident with its handle (*left*). Owing to the symmetry of the claw hammer, the orientation of the eigenvectors is tilted toward the more massive side (*right*).

components independent of $Oxyz$. This invariant form is with respect to the principal axes or eigenvectors of I_{ij}. The eigenvectors e_1, e_2, e_3 are the directions, with respect to O, about which the mass of the object is distributed evenly; they are the symmetry or body axes with respect to the fixed point (figure 13.3). More technically, a vector a is called an eigenvector of I_{ij} with eigenvalue λ, if $I_{ij} \cdot a = \lambda a$, or, equivalently, $(I_{ij} - \lambda 1) \cdot a = 0$, where 1 is the Kronecker delta or unit matrix (a 3×3 matrix with 1s on the diagonal and 0s elsewhere). The condition for the existence of a nontrivial solution is that the determinant (det) of the coefficients vanishes, that is, $\det(I_{ij} - \lambda 1) = 0$. The roots of the cubic equation in λ expressed by the determinant are the eigenvalues, scalar quantities that are invariant over all coordinate systems anchored at O. For a symmetric tensor such as I_{ij}, the three eigenvalues are distinct and the three eigenvectors (given by substituting the λ values into $(I_{ij} - \lambda 1) \cdot a = 0$) are orthogonal. If the eigenvectors are chosen as the axes, then I_{ij} is diagonalized—the eigenvalues I_1, I_2, I_3 are on the diagonal and all other entries are equal to zero (i.e., there are no products of inertia) (Goldstein, 1980).

Armed with the concepts of eigenvectors and eigenvalues, we can now express the equations of motion for wielding an object about a fixed point in the wrist. The equations of motion are Euler's equations (Goldstein, 1980):

$$I_1 \dot{\omega}_1 - \omega_2 \omega_3 (I_2 - I_3) = N_1 \tag{3}$$

$$I_2 \dot{\omega}_2 - \omega_3 \omega_1 (I_3 - I_1) = N_2 \tag{4}$$

$$I_3 \dot{\omega}_3 - \omega_1 \omega_2 (I_1 - I_2) = N_3 \tag{5}$$

Given that any torque N about any arbitrary axis through O is expressed in terms of the above equations, it follows that any act of wielding involves I_{ij} in its entirety. Four experiments by Fitzpatrick et al. were directed at this hypothesis. In all experiments, objects varied in length. Across the experi-

M. T. Turvey and Claudia Carello

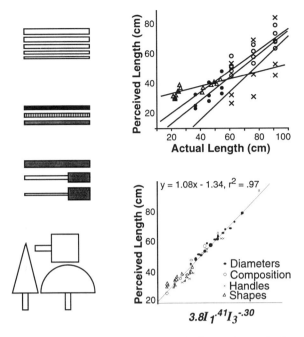

Figure 13.4 (*Left*) Perceivers are asked to indicate the lengths of objects that differ in diameter, material composition, material and spatial homogeneity, or shape. (*Right, top*) Perceived length is a many-valued function of actual length. (*Right, bottom*) Perceived length is a single-valued function of the product of I_1 (with a positive exponent) and I_3 (with a negative exponent).

ments, these variations were accompanied by variations in width, spatial heterogeneity (e.g., a uniform cylinder vs. a small cylinder inserted into a larger cylinder), material heterogeneity (e.g., all wood vs. a wood handle and aluminum shaft), the relation of the tensorial components to mass (e.g., increased mass being accompanied by increases or decreases in I_1), and geometric shape (cubes, hemispheres, cones, etc.). Subjects had no foreknowledge of the variations in object dimensions. Perceived lengths were reported by magnitude production tasks (such as those depicted in figure 13.2b). In each experiment, perceived length was a single-valued function of the product of I_1 and I_3 (the major and minor eigenvalues) raised to a positive and a negative power, respectively (figure 13.4). Another formulation of the results, in terms of alternative tensor invariants that characterize aspects of the ellipsoid of inertia, express perceived length as a power function of the trace (the sum of the three eigenvalues) divided by the cube root of the determinant (the product of the three eigenvalues).

Other Parameters of Dynamic Touching

For many species, patterns of mechanical vibration in the surfaces on which they stand and move are the basis for the perception of objects and events at a distance from them. The desert scorpion (*Paruroctonus mesaensis*) locates burrowing prey within half a meter by the temporal structure and amplitude difference in compressional (horizontal) and Rayleigh (retrograde elliptical) wave fronts transmitted in the sand (Brownell, 1984). The ordinary spider locates prey in its web on the basis of the induced vibrations (Barrows, 1915; Burgess and Witt, 1976). Perceiving on the basis of mechanical waves in a solid medium (such as sand or fiber) requires an effector organ able to maintain contact with the medium and equipped with the means to detect the deformation of its tissues caused by the waves propagated in the medium. The legs of scorpions equipped with slit sensilla and of spiders equipped with lyriform organs satisfy the aforementioned criteria. They are also satisfied by mammalian limbs interpenetrated by mechanoreceptors. This raises the possibility that mammals, like spiders and scorpions, can perceive distal objects on the basis of mechanical waves in a solid medium. Haptic perception's most famous student, David Katz (1925/1989), suspected that this was the case for humans. A model system for investigating this possibility consists of perceiving the distance of an object on a single taut strand vibrated manually. The dynamics are given by the one-dimensional wave equation:

$$\partial^2 u/\partial x^2 = (1/v^2)(\partial^2 u/\partial t^2), \tag{6}$$

where $u = u(x, t)$, a function locating each point x on the string at every instant of time t, and v equals $(T/\mu)^{1/2}$, with T the tension and μ the linear density. The apparatus, referred to as a minimal haptic web, is so designed as to guarantee the application of equation (6). Thus, the model system criterion of taking hold of an unknown feature of biological perception-action capabilities through well-established physical concepts is satisfied. In equation (6), the elastic force $\partial^2 u/\partial x^2$ is coupled to the strand's motions $\partial^2 u/\partial t^2$ by the constant μ/T. A typical task requires subjects to vibrate the strand in order to perceive the distance of an object attached to the strand hidden from the subject's view. Perceived distance is indicated by adjusting the position of a visible marker to match that perceived location. Research has revealed that perceived distance is tied to μ/T and closely approximates actual distance for particular values of μ/T (Kinsella-Shaw and Turvey, 1992).

With respect to perceiving the size of an environmental gap by means of a probe, the dynamical system examined is, simply put, a rotation about a fixed point of a solid cylinder in a horizontal plane contacting two fixed material points at the extremes of its rotary excursion (figure 13.5). Mechanical analysis of the torques, impulse forces, and motions of striking between spatially separate surfaces has revealed a collective dimensionless quantity of this model system

$$\lambda = \sin(\alpha/2) \times [1 - (2a/b) + (ma^2/I_y)] = \sin(\alpha/2) \times \delta. \tag{7}$$

For a given rod, aperture, and distance, this quantity is invariant over muscular forces, resultant impulsive torques, and motions (see Barac-Cikoja and Turvey, 1991, 1993). It is a scalar operator that connects the muscular forces

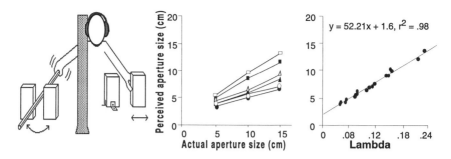

Figure 13.5 (*Left*) The inside edges of an aperture are struck by a rod. (*Middle*) The perceived size of that aperture is modulated by the moment of inertia of the rod (filled vs. open symbols), the distance of the aperture (squares, triangles, circles), and the angle through which the rod moves (affected by aperture size and distance). (*Right*) But all of these variables are captured in Lambda, an invariant that couples the muscular and reactive forces.

imposed on the probe to the reactive forces impressed on the tissues of the body. Haptic perception of aperture size is found to be a single-valued function of λ (which is not to be confused with the eigenvalue notation used above). This collective parameter predicts successfully the interdependent effects of angular displacement, distance of surfaces, and the mechanical properties of the implement. It also predicts the rate at which the resolution of size by dynamic touch declines with b. The upshot is the λ hypothesis of size perception by haptic probing:

$$\textit{Perceived size} \propto \lambda \propto \sin(\alpha/2) \times \delta. \tag{8}$$

Because $I_y = mK_y^2$, where K_y is the radius of gyration,[1] δ can be rewritten as

$$\delta = 1 - (2a/b) + (a^2/K_y^2). \tag{9}$$

Further, because K_y^2/a is the distance p of the center of percussion[2] from O, the expression for δ can be written even more simply as

$$\delta = 1 - (2a/b) + (a/p) \tag{10}$$

What equation (10) brings out is the fact that δ is a configuration of different kinds of distances from O, viz., to the center of mass (a), to the point of contact (b), to the center of percussion (p). Intuitively, these "points" define the constant geometric structure of the probing. During rotational probings about a fixed point O, these distances remain invariant. Collectively, as the single quantity δ, they scale the angle through which the probe moves (more precisely, the component of the contact force associated with a given angular displacement). Experiments have confirmed that perceived size is specific to λ: Perceived size (a) is a single-valued function of λ regardless of the muscles executing, and deformed by, the probing; (b) perceived size equals, underestimates, and overestimates actual size according to $2b/\delta = 1$, $2b/\delta < 1$, and $2b/\delta > 1$, respectively; and (c) perceived size changes with actual size at a rate equal to $(1/2b - a/b^2 + a/2bp)$, the partial derivative of λ with respect to size (Barac-Cikoja and Turvey, 1993).

13.3   DYNAMICS OF INTERLIMB COORDINATION

A dynamical perspective on biological movement systems (e.g., Beek, 1989a; Kugler et al., 1980, 1982; Kugler and Turvey, 1987; Haken and Wunderlin, 1990; Schöner and Kelso, 1988a) leads to the expectation that macroscopic organizations (coordination modes or patterns) can be assembled spontaneously from the many microscopic degrees of freedom when the control parameters c of equation (1) are changed. (Importantly, control parameters themselves are unspecific to the resultant organization.) It also leads to the expectation that amplification of intrinsic nonlinearities, by scaling of c or other means, will form stable and reproducible spectra of coordination modes. And it leads, in addition, to the expectation that movement systems, although they are ordinary physical systems (in the sense of conforming to physical laws and principles), can achieve extraordinary accomplishments through the smart, special-purpose exploitation of the regularities (symmetries) inherent in behavioral tasks. The latter understanding guided the discussion of perceptual subsystems in section 13.2. That discussion can be thought of as focusing on the assembling of task-specific meters. Here the focus is on the assembling of task-specific actuators.

Dynamics of Spontaneous Transitions in Human Interlimb Rhythmic Patterns

As suggested, the central issue to be addressed in this section with respect to equation (1) is how the stabilities of $x(t)$ vary with c. It proves useful to consider an interlimb rhythmic coordination as a dynamical system governed by a smooth potential function $V(\phi; c)$, where ϕ is the phase difference $(\theta_1 - \theta_2)$ between the two oscillators (with θ_i the phase of the individual oscillator) and c is a control parameter that can affect $V(\phi)$ qualitatively. The phase relation ϕ between limbs can be conceptualized as an order parameter (e.g., Haken, 1977, 1983; Haken, Kelso, and Bunz, 1985; Kelso, Schöner, Scholz, et al., 1987) because it is a collective variable that captures the spatiotemporal organization of the component subsystems (here, rhythmic movement units), and changes more slowly than the variables characterizing the states of the component subsystems (e.g., velocity, amplitude). Pursuing the idea of a governing potential function, the equilibria $\phi(c_{critical})$ of an interlimb rhythmic coordination would be defined by $\partial V(\phi; c)/\partial \phi = 0$. Spontaneous changes in coordination patterns can therefore be thought of as occurring when the equilibria are changed (dissolved and created) by changes in c. Even though the dynamic underlying the coordinated behavior is continuous, discontinuities arise. As an equilibrium dissolves, stability is lost and a transition to a new equilibrium results.

The presence of critical points in a smooth dynamic leading to discontinuities is recognizable by a set of criteria that hold regardless of the actual makeup of the system. The criteria are the following: (a) *modality*, meaning

M. T. Turvey and Claudia Carello

that the system has two or more distinct physical states in which it may occur; (b) *inaccessibility*, meaning that the system has an equilibrium state that is unstable (as when a marble rests at the top of an inverted bowl, or a pendulum is vertical with its bob above the axis of rotation—very small perturbations will dislodge them); (c) *sudden jumps*, meaning that a slow change in the control parameter may lead to a relatively rapid change in the order parameter; (c) *hysteresis*, meaning that a sudden jump x_i to x_j and its reciprocal x_j to x_i do not occur at the same values of the control parameter; (d) *critical slowing down*, meaning that subsequent to a perturbation, the time taken by the order parameter to return to its preperturbation value increases as the transition point is approached; (e) *anomalous variance* or *critical fluctuations*, meaning that the variance in the order parameter may become large as the transition point is approached.

A model system for evaluating the above criteria is one in which a person is required to oscillate the two index fingers (or two hands) at the coupled frequency ω_c, where ω_c is varied by a metronome that the person tracks (e.g., Kelso, 1984; Kelso, Scholz, and Schöner, 1986; Scholz, Kelso, and Schöner, 1987). Results show that there are only two steady states: inphase and antiphase. With increasing ω_c, antiphase switches rapidly to inphase. Inphase, however, does not switch to antiphase, and the antiphase-to-inphase transition is not reversed by a reduction in ω_c. Further, ϕ exhibits increases in relaxation time (the time taken to return to its prior value following a brief perturbation) and fluctuations (measured, e.g., by its standard deviation) as the transition point is approached. Importantly, the same basic pattern of results is found when two limbs are connected optically between two people rather than anatomically within a person (Schmidt, Carello, and Turvey, 1990). This fact suggests that the dynamics in question are potentially very general, and that the coupling is best described in informational terms.

The experimentally observed features of the above behavioral transitions have been successfully modeled, and a number of subtle effects have been successfully predicted, by the following order parameter equation expressed in successively enriched forms by Haken et al. (1985), Schöner, Haken, and Kelso (1986), and Kelso, DelColle, and Schöner (1990):

$$\dot{\phi} = \Delta\omega - a\sin(\phi) - 2b\sin(2\phi) + \sqrt{Q}\,\xi_l \tag{11}$$

where $\Delta\omega$ is the uncoupled eigenfrequency difference ($\omega_1 - \omega_2$), a and b are coefficients such that b/a decreases as coupling frequency ω_c increases and coupling strength (stability) decreases, and $\sqrt{Q}\zeta_t$ is a stochastic force. Specifically, the latter is a Gaussian white noise process with characteristics $\langle\zeta_t\rangle = 0$ and $\langle\zeta_t\zeta_{t'}\rangle = \delta(t - t')$, and strength $Q > 0$ (Kelso et al., 1987; Schmidt, Treffner, Shaw, et al., 1992; Schöner et al., 1986). It is assumed that the degrees of freedom (e.g., underlying subsystems) acting as noise on the interlimb or intersegmental coordination operate on a time scale that is considerably faster than the time scale of the order parameter (see Haken, 1983).

Viewing the noise as a random sequence of very brief kicks of equal probability in different directions means that, on the average (represented by the brackets $\langle \ \rangle$), the stochastic force will be zero (Haken, 1977). Forming the product of the stochastic force at time t with the stochastic force at another time t', and taking the average over the times of the kicks and their directions, yields a correlation function equal to the Dirac δ-function (see Haken, 1977, section 6, for details).

Recognizing the contribution of noise is crucial to a general understanding of pattern formation in biological movement systems. Particularly important is the role it plays at the crucial moment of transition, where the system has to perform a critical 'choice.' We can express this idea in a classical model system for the study of physical cooperativities, the Rayleigh-Bénard system. This is a thin layer of liquid trapped between two glass plates, heated gently from below. After a critical thermal point is reached, the water spontaneously self-organizes into a pattern of hexagonal rotating convection cells, resembling a honeycomb. Here, the choice is associated with the appearance of a right-handed or left-handed cell. The macroscopic cells formed at the first instability are composed of approximately 10^{20} atomisms moving coherently: they rotate in a rightward or leftward direction, with adjacent macroscopic cells rotating in opposite directions. The direction of rotation is decided by chance, through the dynamics of fluctuations. In effect, the system explores the dynamical landscape via its fluctuations, testing the different collective motions of the atomisms, and making a few initially unsuccessful attempts at stabilizing. Eventually, a particular fluctuation takes over and becomes stabilized.

As anticipated above, the deterministic part of the order parameter equation, equation (11), is derivable from an underlying smooth potential function

$$V(\phi) = \Delta\omega\phi - a\cos(\phi) - b\cos(2\phi) \tag{12}$$

which provides an "energy landscape" characterized, when $\Delta\omega = 0$, by a global minimum at $\phi = 0$ and local minima at $\phi = \pm\pi$. If $b = 0$, then during a bout of interlimb $1:1$ frequency locking there is only one minimum (0 or π depending on the sign of a); if $a = 0$, then there are three equal minima $(-\pi, 0, +\pi)$. In the superposition of the two cosine functions of equation (12) the minima are distinguished, with stability greatest for $\phi = 0$ (meaning that the potential is least at $\phi = 0$) when $\Delta\omega = 0$, as suggested by the phase-transition experiments summarized briefly above. With respect to the dissolution of the antiphase interlimb pattern in those experiments, this landscape is modulated by ω_c such that at a critical value ($a = 4b$) the local minima are annihilated (see Haken et al., 1985). These features are depicted in figure 13.6.

Pattern Formation as a Competitive-Cooperative Process

Investigating the rhythmic fin movements of *Labrus*, a fish that swims with its longitudinal axis immobile, von Holst (1939/1973) observed two different patterns of phase interactions. Sometimes the fins maintained a fixed phase

M. T. Turvey and Claudia Carello

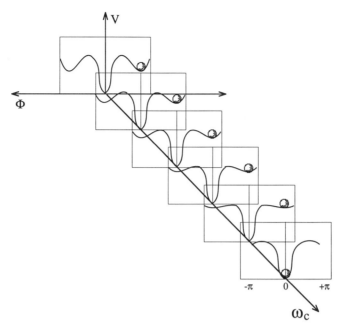

Figure 13.6 The axes represent relative phase ϕ, coupled frequency ω_c, and the potential (V). Figuratively, the lower the potential well, the less potential and, hence, the more stable the coordination. The minimum of the potential function at $\phi = 0$ corresponds to inphase coordination. The local minima at $\phi = \pm\pi$ correspond to antiphase coordination. With an increase in ω_c, the local minima at $\pm\pi$ are annihilated. Behaviorally, this means that a system that had started at a relatively slow ω_c as stable antiphase coordination (represented by the ball settled into the local minimum at $\phi = \pi$) makes an abrupt transition to inphase coordination (represented by the ball falling into the minimum at $\phi = 0$) at some critical ω_c.

relation and oscillated at the same frequency, and sometimes phase and frequency locking were absent. Von Holst referred to the former as *absolute coordination* and to the latter as *relative coordination*. Importantly, an interfin relation that was on the average a strong case of absolute coordination would exhibit brief deviations from strict mode locking and an interfin relation that was on the average a strong case of relative coordination would gravitate temporarily toward such mode locking. These observations suggested to von Holst that in absolute coordination the two fins continued to be in competition (each attempting to proceed at its own pace) and that in relative coordination the two fins continued to be cooperative (each attempting to proceed at the pace of the other). In sum, whatever the average form of the coordination pattern, it was always a distillation of competitive and cooperative processes.

The dynamics expressed by equation (11) comport with von Holst's (1939/1973) far-reaching insights on the forming and sustaining of coordinations among rhythmically moving appendages. For von Holst, an interappendage coordination reflects the *maintenance tendencies* by which individual components continue to do what they prefer to do, identified by $\Delta\omega$, and the *magnet effect* by which individual components are drawn together as a single unit, identified by $-(a \sin \phi + 2b \sin 2\phi)$. In short, equation (11) provides a compact formulation of von Holst's understanding that the phase-interaction patterns ($\dot{\phi}$) of rhythmically moving limbs are selected by the interplay of competitive ($\Delta\omega$) and cooperative ($-a \sin \phi - 2b \sin 2\phi$) processes.

By way of reinforcing and elaborating the observations and intuitions of von Holst, we can examine equation (11) further, particularly with respect to the influences determining the dynamical details of stable and unstable coordination patterns. Equation (11) makes a number of nonobvious predictions about the stationary states of interlimb coordination when the symmetry of the coordination dynamics is broken or lowered. The stationary states can be determined by solving equation (11) numerically for $\dot{\phi} = 0$. Graphically, solutions to equation (11) with $\dot{\phi} = 0$ can be obtained by plotting the right-hand side (excluding the stochastic force) against ϕ for various parameter values. The stationary values are given where $\dot{\phi}$ crosses the ϕ axis. If $d\dot{\phi}/d\phi$ at the zero-crossing is negative, then the point is stable; if $d\dot{\phi}/d\phi$ at the zero-crossing is positive, then the point is unstable. The degree of stability of ϕ_{stable} is given by the magnitude of $|d\dot{\phi}/d\phi|$—the slope of the zero crossing. Numerical analysis reveals that equation (11) makes the following predictions about stable states in interlimb 1:1 frequency locking when b/a is more than the critical value at which the zero crossing near π disappears.

(i) When $\Delta\omega = 0$, ϕ_{stable} equals 0 and π regardless of the magnitude of b/a.

(ii) When $\Delta\omega = 0$, $|d\dot{\phi}/d\phi|$ is greater at $\phi_{stable} = 0$ than at $\phi_{stable} = \pi$.

(iii) When $\Delta\omega \neq 0$, ϕ_{stable} is displaced from 0 and π with different but closely similar degrees of displacement such that the two attractors remain separated by approximately π.

(iv) When $\Delta\omega \neq 0$, $|d\dot{\phi}/d\phi|$ at ϕ_{stable} is smaller the larger the magnitude of $\Delta\omega$.

(v) For a given b/a, the greater the magnitude of $\Delta\omega \neq 0$ the greater are the displacements of the attractors from $\phi = 0$ and $\phi = \pi$. Similarly, for a given $\Delta\omega \neq 0$, the smaller the magnitude of b/a the greater are the displacements of the attractors from $\phi = 0$ and $\phi = \pi$.

(vi) For a fixed b/a, the greater the magnitude of $\Delta\omega \neq 0$ the smaller is $|d\dot{\phi}/d\phi|$ at ϕ_{stable}. Similarly, for $\Delta\omega = 0$ and for a constant $\Delta\omega \neq 0$, the smaller the magnitude of b/a, the smaller is $|d\dot{\phi}/d\phi|$ at ϕ_{stable}.

How might the preceding predictions be evaluated? Von Holst's research suggested four major requirements for studying the dynamics of interlimb rhythmic coordinations, particularly those typifying locomotion. First, the studied movement pattern should be analogous to the locomotory pattern without engendering movement of the body relative to the environment—a fictive or mimed locomotion. Second, the eigenvalues of the individual rhythmic movement units should be manipulable and easily quantified. Third, the

M. T. Turvey and Claudia Carello

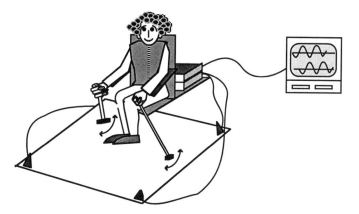

Figure 13.7 In a typical bimanual rhythmic coordination experiment, a person holds a pendulum in each hand and sits with the arms supported so that the pendulums can be swung freely about the wrist joint. Each pendulum has an eigenfrequency (the frequency at which it "prefers" to oscillate) that is determined by its length and mass, as well as the position and size of any attached masses. Eigenfrequencies are manipulated from trial to trial by changing the pendulum configurations. A device attached to the end of each pendulum emits a sonic signal that is picked up by microphones on a floor grid. A sonic digitizer records the three-space motions of the pendulum, and software routines perform the appropriate analyses.

interlimb system should be easily prepared in one of the two basic patterns of inphase and antiphase. And fourth, the focus of measurement and dynamical modeling should be on the interactions of the phase of one oscillator with the phase of the other. A dynamical model satisfying the fourth requirement is given by equations (11) and (12) (see also Rand, Cohen, and Holmes, 1988). A model system satisfying the first three requirements has been developed by Kugler and Turvey (1987) (see also Bingham, Schmidt, Turvey, et al. 1991; Rosenblum and Turvey, 1988; Turvey, Schmidt, Rosenblum, et al., 1988). It is depicted in figure 13.7.

As the within-person case of figure 13.7 shows, a person holds a pendulum in each hand. The pendulums can vary physically in shaft length or the mass of the attached bob, or in both length and mass. Because of these physical magnitudes, a person's comfortable swinging of an individual pendulum about an axis in the wrist (with other joints essentially immobile), parallel to the sagittal plane, will tend to a particular frequency and a particular amplitude (Kugler and Turvey, 1987). Viewing the neuromuscular processes as driving the motion, it is reasonable to assume that the eigenfrequency of a "wrist-pendulum system" is the eigenfrequency of the equivalent simple gravitational pendulum, $\omega = (g/L)^{1/2}$, where L is the simple pendulum length and g is the constant acceleration due to gravity. The quantity L is calculable from the magnitudes of shaft length, added mass, and hand mass, through the standard methods for representing any arbitrary rigid body oscillating about a fixed point as a simple pendulum (den Hartog, 1948; Kugler and Turvey, 1987). For interlimb coordination, if the pendulums held in each hand differ in

Some Dynamical Themes in Perception and Action

physical dimensions (length, mass), then their eigenfrequencies will not correspond. The component rhythmic units will be in frequency competition. With humans as the subjects, the implementation of an inphase or antiphase relation between the rhythmic units is readily achieved by instruction. The effect of a given frequency competition can be evaluated, therefore, for an interlimb coordination "prepared" inphase or antiphase.

In agreement with predictions (i)–(vi), the experiments using the foregoing model system revealed that: (a) when $\Delta\omega = 0$, $\phi_{stable} = 0$ or π over the range of ω_c values tested; (b) when $\Delta\omega \neq 0$ and ω_c is the preferred value or close to it, ϕ_{stable} deviates from 0 and π by nearly equal amounts such that the stable-phase relations remain essentially a distance π apart; (c) $\Delta\omega$ and ω_c contribute multiplicatively to ϕ_{stable} such that the lower the value of ω_c, the more closely ϕ_{stable} approximates 0 or π for any given $\Delta\omega \neq 0$ and, conversely, the higher the value of ω_c, the less closely ϕ_{stable} approximates 0 or π for any given $\Delta\omega \neq 0$ (Schmidt, Beek, Treffner, et al., 1991; Schmidt, Shaw, and Turvey, 1993; Schmidt and Turvey, 1994 Sternad, Turvey, and Schmidt, 1992). Additionally, the experiments found that fluctuations in ϕ_{stable} are greater for a more nearly antiphase than inphase coordination and increase as $\Delta\omega$ deviates from 0 and, therefore, as ϕ_{stable} deviates from 0 or π (Schmidt et al., 1991, 1993; Schmidt and Turvey, 1994), and that these fluctuations are amplified further by increases in ω_c (Schmidt et al., 1993).

As noted above, a potential well can be identified with each of the equilibrium points 0 and π, such that each well has its minimum at its respective equilibrium value with the 0 well more steep-sided than the π well. The cited research demonstrates that the potential wells governing 1:1 interlimb frequency locking are both displaced and rendered more shallow by the interaction of $|\Delta\omega| > 0$ and ω_c. Where the displacement of the potential wells from 0 and π are nearly the same for a given $|\Delta\omega| > 0$ and ω_c, the reduction in the slope of the well is not; the slopes of the wells displaced from 0 become shallower at a faster rate than those displaced from π. With increasing shallowness, the same stochastic force $\sqrt{Q}\zeta_t$ can spawn increasingly larger fluctuations of the order parameter. The character of 1:1 frequency locking expressed through a changing smooth potential function is captured in figure 13.8.

A Common Dynamic for Coordination by the Visual and Haptic Perceptual Systems

Would the relations predicted by equation (11) occur if the two oscillators were not the right and left limbs of a person linked haptically but the right limb of one person and the left limb of another person linked visually? Given that both the haptically based and visually based coordinations exhibit the bistability and bifurcation expected from equation (11), as noted above, it would not be surprising if visual coupling, like haptic coupling, also conformed to the equilibrium predictions of equation (11). All of the quantities

M. T. Turvey and Claudia Carello

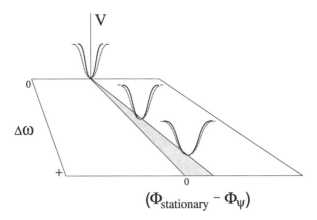

$$(\Phi_{stationary} - \Phi_{\psi})$$

Figure 13.8 The axes represent the difference in the eigenfrequencies of two pendulums $\Delta\omega$, the difference between achieved phase ($\Phi_{stationary}$) and intended phase (Φ_{ψ}), and the potential V. As $\Delta\omega$ increases, $\Phi_{stationary} - \Phi_{\psi}$ increases, i.e., achieved phase differs more and more from intended phase. In addition, the potential well grows increasingly shallow, allowing greater fluctuations. This latter change occurs at a faster rate for inphase (*solid line*) than out-of-phase (*dashed line*) coordination. (For simplicity, the increasing elevation of the potential wells off the $\Delta\omega$ by $\Phi_{stationary} - \Phi_{\psi}$ plane is not depicted.)

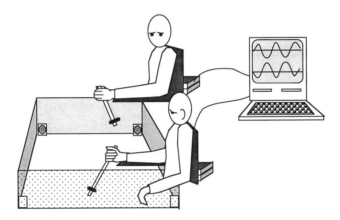

Figure 13.9 The coupled pendulum paradigm can be implemented between two people, with the link achieved visually. In an experiment in which the coupling medium is optic rather than haptic, the right and left hands are supplied by two individuals who look at the movements of each other's pendulum. As in the within-person paradigm, eigenfrequencies are manipulated from trial to trial, and three-space motions are recorded by a sonic digitizer.

in equation (11) can be defined in the procedure depicted in figure 13.9 for a two-person, two-oscillator system in which $1:1$ frequency locking is maintained by the watching of each other's movements. Consequently, the dynamics of equation (11) are as formative, in principle, of the phase interactions between two oscillators in the two-person case as they are of the phase interactions between two oscillators in the one-person case. This expectation has been confirmed (Schmidt and Turvey, 1994). As can be seen from figure

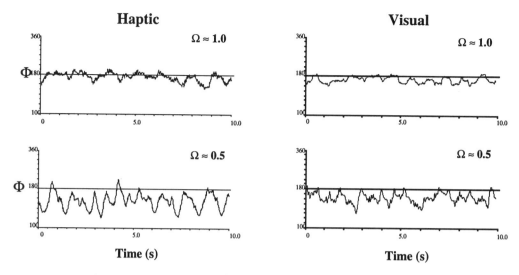

Figure 13.10 Time series of relative phase over 10 seconds of a trial under the intention to perform antiphase coordination. In the top panels, the eigenfrequencies of the two pendulums are the same (hence, their ratio $\Omega = 1.0$) and coordination is maintained successfully around 180 degrees. In the lower panels, the eigenfrequency of one pendulum is twice that of the other (hence, their ratio $\Omega = 0.5$) and achieved phase departs from intended phase, with large fluctuations. These patterns are predicted by the order parameter equation (11) and are obtained equivalently for (*left*) haptic/within-person, and (*right*) visual/between-persons coordination.

13.10, the ϕ time series for visually coupled systems as a function of $\Delta\omega$ mimics that of haptically coupled systems. The important implication is that phase entrainment in biological movement systems might abide by dynamical principles that are indifferent to the physical details of the coupling. This conclusion highlights efforts to develop concepts and methods by which the functional orders characteristic of biological systems might be addressed through very general principles (e.g., Haken, 1977, 1983, 1988; Kugler, and Turvey, 1987; Schöner and Kelso, 1988a; Yates, 1987).

Intentional Constraints on Interlimb Coordination

Interestingly, and perhaps surprisingly, the dynamical perspective can be extended to intentions. The paradigmatic experiment is that of Scholz and Kelso (1990) using a $1:1$ frequency-locking task. They found that the latency to change the order parameter ϕ, on signal, from π (less stable) to 0 (more stable) was less than that to change from 0 to π, and that the difference in latencies was independent of the control parameter ω_c. These findings suggest that intention can actively override certain aspects of the dynamics (the perturbations in ϕ induced by ω_c), but not others (the differential stability associated with 0 and π). The proposed strategy to address such results is to endow intention with dynamics and to make it part of the coordination dynamics as a perturbation so defined that it attracts the order parameter

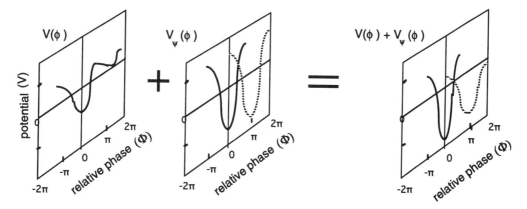

Figure 13.11 (*Left*) The intrinsic dynamic captured by the smooth potential function $V(\phi)$ reflects physical properties of the coordinating units such as the differential stability of $\phi = 0$ and $\phi = \pi$. (*Middle*) The intentional dynamic set up by the intention to coordinate inphase (or antiphase) can also be captured by a potential function $V_\psi(\phi)$, with a minimum at $\phi = 0$ (or $\phi = \pi$). (*Right*) Superposition of the intrinsic dynamic and the intentional dynamic yields a combined dynamic $V(\phi) + V_\psi(\phi)$ that attracts the order parameter (in this case, relative phase) toward the required pattern. For example, the steepness and height of the wells at local minima govern the time taken by someone to switch intentionally from one phase mode to the other. A system positioned at π will attain $\Phi_\psi = 0$ faster than a system positioned at 0 will attain $\Phi_\psi = \pi$. (Adapted from Scholz and Kelso, 1990.)

toward the required pattern (Schöner and Kelso, 1988b). As figure 13.11 shows, the intrinsic differential stability of $\phi = 0$ and $\phi = \pi$ can be visualized as a potential function $V(\phi)$ (roughly, a smooth energy landscape) with a global minimum at 0 and a local minimum at π. The intentions $\phi_\psi = 0$ and $\phi_\psi = \pi$ are similarly captured by a potential function, $V_\psi(\phi)$, with a single (global) minimum (at $\phi = 0$ and $\phi = \pi$, respectively). The summation of the intrinsic and intended dynamics provides the full dynamics $V(\phi) + V_\psi(\phi)$ governing intentional switching time. The switching time is a random variable defined as the time when a coordination first enters a criterion neighborhood of pattern P if it was initially in the neighborhood of pattern Q; intuitively, it is determined by how steeply downhill the process runs to attain the new pattern. In the full dynamics $V(\phi) + V_\psi(\phi)$, $\phi = 0$ is associated with a steeper potential well and thus a system positioned at π will attain $\phi_\psi = 0$ faster than a system positioned at 0 will attain $\phi_\psi = \pi$.

Learning Interlimb Coordinations

There seem to be three essential features of coordination learning, and possibly a fourth. First, coordinations are almost infinitely improvable; there are no asymptotic limits (Crossman, 1959; Fitts, 1964). The power law time dependence that expresses the preceding feature suggests learning is essentially nonlinear. Second, coordination learning is a process of simplification with extraneous aspects dropping out as practice continues (e.g., Jones, 1962). This feature implies an optimizing of subtasks and an increase in pattern stability (Bernstein, 1967). Third, performance variance becomes increasingly affected by constraints unique to the coordination as learning progresses (e.g., Fleischman, 1962). There is an attunement to task invariants, and we may regard the results summarized above with respect to dynamic touch as underscoring this possibility. The contentious fourth feature is that qualitative changes in learning may occur discontinuously (Bryan and Harter, 1899; but see Keller, 1958). It implies (nonlinear) phase transitions in acquiring a coordination. The four features refer to the process of coordination learning. The need to investigate process (the forms of the changes in the coordination pattern in the course of learning) and not just outcome, and the need to use many converging performance measures in doing so, have been frequently emphasized (e.g., Namikas, 1983; Pew, 1974; Starch, 1910). A dynamical approach to coordination learning (e.g., Schöner and Kelso, 1988b) promises to satisfy both needs and to provide the tools by which the four features can be addressed rigorously. The learning of a $1:2$ (left-right with identical pendulums in the two hands) pattern by four subjects over 240 (32-second) trials highlights the preceding claims (Schmidt et al., 1992). Observations included an increase in pattern stability, an evolution to either a harmonic organization of the total power at integer multiples of the base frequency (three subjects) or a $1/f$ distribution (one subject), and a suggestion of discontinuous change. These results are shown in figure 13.12.

Dynamics of Highly Skilled and Novice Jugglers

A dynamics perspective on learning can be carried into more complicated tasks. In an experimental investigation of cascade juggling with number of hands $(H) = 2$, number of objects $(N) = 3$, three juggling speeds, and four skilled jugglers, it was found that the duration T_L of the subtask of carrying the juggled object between catch and throw expressed as a proportion k of the hand-cycle time T_H ranged between .54 and .83 with a mean of .71 (Beek, 1989b). There was a significant effect of hand-cycle time—k was smaller at higher juggling frequencies and thus not strictly invariant. Considerations of space-time constraints and principles of frequency locking suggest 3/4 as the primary ratio and 2/3 and 5/8 as the most accessible options (Beek and Turvey, 1992). Allowing, therefore, for the possible existence of other ratios than $k = 3/4$ in the workspace of cascade juggling, the experimental results have been interpreted in terms of frequency modulation around an underlying mode-locked state of k being 3/4 (Beek, 1989a,b; Beek and Turvey, 1992). Using Denjoy's (1932) method for the decomposition of frequency-modulated waves, Beek (1989b) proposed a measure of the degree of quasi-periodicity evident in an instance of three-object cascade juggling that assumed $k = 3/4$ as the primary value.

The significance of $k = 3/4$ has been underscored in an investigation of the acquisition of three-ball cascade juggling (Beek and van Santvoord, 1992).

M. T. Turvey and Claudia Carello

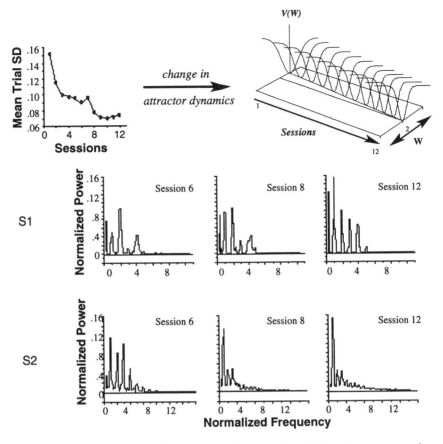

Figure 13.12 Learning a coordination pattern brings about qualitative changes in a number of measures. In 2:1 coordination, a person is required to swing one pendulum twice for every single traverse of the other pendulum while keeping both pendulums moving continuously. (*Top, left*) As a 2:1 coordination is learned over experimental sessions, standard deviations of relative phase decrease. (*Top, right*) This can be understood as changes in the concavity of the attractor underlying 2:1 frequency locking as this coordination becomes more stable. That is, fluctuations are reduced as the potential well becomes steeper. (*Bottom*) During learning, the desired coordination can evolve continuously or it may change discontinuously. Which style is occurring is apparent in the spectral components underlying intracyclic relative coordination. Subject 1 (S1) demonstrates a continuous growth of peaks at integer multiples from Sessions 6–12 that increase the stability of frequency locking. Subject 2 (S2) shows a change from peaks at integer multiples in Session 6 to a 1/f distribution of power a session later. Nonetheless, frequency locking in these two cases is equally stable—i.e., the learning process can differ while leading to the same outcome.

All participants were instructed by the same teacher, who was uninformed of the hypothesis under study. Following the initial three learning sessions, the participants were divided into two groups of equal ability as defined by the mean number of cycles of cascade juggling achievable at this early stage of learning. Seven further sessions with the same instructor then followed. For one group, the learning was conducted with the aid of a computerized metronome that provided auditory signals for the timings of a throw (or catch) by one hand and a throw (or catch) by the other hand. At the outset of a session the metronome beeps corresponded to $k = 3/4$ when the height reached by the balls was 1 m. During the course of a session a participant could alter at will the interbeep interval to more closely match the timings that he or she was employing. For the other group there was no metronome assistance. All participants were filmed at the beginning of the fourth session, during the seventh session, and at the end of the tenth session. Analysis revealed that for both groups of subjects k decreased with practice in the same way: From .77 on the average at session 4, to .76 on the average at session 7, to .74 on the average at session 10 (with between-subjects standard deviations of .05, .05, and .04, respectively). Collectively, the results from all ten sessions of this learning experiment suggest that the initial phase of learning to cascade-juggle involves discovering its real-time requirements (juggling hands and juggled objects must satisfy, on average, a general timing requirement in which the ratio of an object-cycle time to a hand-cycle time equals the ratio of number of objects to number of hands), with the subsequent phase directed at discovering the stability of $k = 3/4$ (Beek and Van Santvoord, 1992). When the results of the learning experiment are coupled with the results from the study of highly skilled jugglers (Beek, 1989b; Beek and Turvey, 1992), a picture of three-object cascade juggling emerges in which fluency is characterized by the ability to operate at k values other than $3/4$. In three-ball cascade juggling, $k = 3/4$ may be the primary fixed point for stable juggling, but the task possesses other sufficiently stable regimes, marked by other k magnitudes, and these are discovered in the course of extended practice.

13.4 SUMMARY AND CONCLUSIONS

Consistent with a strategic approach to perception and action that minimizes (and, for all practical purposes, precludes) mental representations and computations, we have identified some dynamical themes that have been exploited in ecological research in haptic perception and coordinated movement. We consider the general gambit to be a scientifically conservative one. It does not allow the introduction of entities of unconsidered—or unknowable—origin. It pushes for consistency with the natural sciences, not promoting special explanatory concepts for an instance of order and regularity that happens to be associated with human nervous systems. And it has some fairly unambiguous assessments of success that serve as engines of discovery (e.g., the search for single-valued functions). One major purpose of this chapter has been to underscore that the success of such an endeavor lies in the judicious contrivance of model systems, experimental implementations of target complex systems that allow thoroughgoing examinations of the systems' dynamics through the phase-control space.

ACKNOWLEDGMENT

Preparation of this manuscript was supported by National Science Foundation grants BNS 90-11013 and BNS 91-09880.

NOTES

1. The radius of gyration of a rigid body is the distance from the axis of rotation to a point at which a concentrated particle of mass equal to that of the body would have the same moment of inertia as the body.

2. The center of percussion is defined as that point in a rotating rigid body that can be struck without causing an acceleration at the center of rotation. It is the so-called sweet spot in a hitting implement such as a baseball bat or a tennis racket. Importantly, there is no such thing as *the* center of percussion. Its location depends on the location of the center of rotation.

REFERENCES

Abraham, R., and Shaw, C. D. (1982). *Dynamics: The geometry of behavior*, Part 1. *Periodic behavior*. Santa Cruz, CA: Ariel Press.

Amazeen, E., and Turvey, M. T. (in press). Weight perception and the haptic "size-weight illusion" are functions of the inertia tensor. *Journal of Experimental Psychology: Human Perception and Performance*.

Barac-Cikoja, D., and Turvey, M. T. (1991). Perceiving aperture size by striking. *Journal of Experimental Psychology: Human Perception and Performance, 17*, 330–346.

Barac-Cikoja, D., and Turvey, M. T. (1993). Perceiving size at a distance. *Journal of Experimental Psychology: General, 122*, 347–370.

Barrows, W. M. (1915). The reactions of an orb-weaving spider, *Epiera sclopetaria* Cl. to rhythmic vibrations of its web. *Biological Bulletin, 29*, 316–332.

Beek, P. J. (1989a). *Juggling dynamics*. Amsterdam: Free University Press.

Beek, P. J. (1989b). Timing and phase-locking in cascade juggling. *Ecological Psychology, 1*, 55–96.

Beek, P., and Turvey, M. T. (1992). Temporal patterning in cascade juggling. *Journal of Experimental Psychology: Human Perception and Performance, 18*, 934–947.

Beek, P. J., and van Santvoord, A. A. M. (1992). Learning the cascade juggle: a dynamical systems analysis. *Journal of Motor Behavior, 24*, 85–94.

Bernstein, N. A. (1967). *The control and regulation of movements*. London: Pergamon Press.

Bingham, G. P., Schmidt, R. C., Turvey, M. T., et al. (1991). Task dynamics and resource dynamics in the assembly of a coordinated rhythmic activity. *Journal of Experimental Psychology: Human Perception and Performance, 17,* 359–381.

Brownell, P. H. (1984). Prey detection by the sand scorpion. *Scientific American, 251*(6), 86–97.

Bryan, W. L., and Harter, N. (1899). Studies on the telegraphic language: the acquisition of a hierarchy of habits. *Psychological Review, 6,* 345–375.

Burgess, J. W., and Witt, P. N. (1976). Spider webs: design and engineering. *Interdisciplinary Science Reviews, 1,* 322–335.

Burton, G. (1992). Nonvisual judgment of the crossability of path gaps. *Journal of Experimental Psychology: Human Perception and Performance, 18,* 698–713.

Burton G., and Turvey, M. T. (1990). Perceiving the lengths of rods that are held but not wielded. *Ecological Psychology, 2,* 295–324.

Burton G., Turvey M. T., and Solomon, H. Y. (1990). Can shape be perceived by dynamic touch? *Perception and Psychophysics, 5,* 477–487.

Carello, C., Fitzpatrick. P., and Turvey, M. T. (1992). Haptic probing: perceiving the length of a probe and the distance of a surface probed. *Perception and Psychophysics, 51,* 580–598.

Carello, C., Turvey, M. T., Kugler, P. N., et al. (1984). Inadequacies of the computer metaphor. In M. S. Gazzaniga (Ed.), *Handbook of cognitive neuroscience* (pp. 229–248). New York: Plenum.

Crossman, E. R. F. (1959). A theory of acquisition of speed-skill. *Ergonomics, 2,* 153–166.

Den Hartog, J. P. (1948). *Mechanics.* New York: Dover.

Denjoy, A. (1932). Sur les courbes définies par les equations différentielles à la surface du tore [On curves defined by differential equations on a toroidal surface]. *Journal de Mathématique, 4,* 333–375.

Dennett, D. C. (1971). Intentional systems. *Journal of Philosophy, 68,* 87–106.

Fitts, P. M. (1964). Perceptual-motor skill learning. In A. W. Melton (Ed.), *Categories of human learning.* New York: Academic Press.

Fitzpatrick, P., Carello, C., and Turvey, M. T. (1994). Eigenvalues of the inertia tensor and exteroception by the "muscular sense." *Neuroscience, 60,* 551–568.

Fleischman, E. (1962). The description and prediction of perceptual-motor learning. In R. Glaser (Ed.), *Training research and education.* Pittsburgh: University of Pittsburgh Press.

Gibson, J. J. (1966). *The senses considered as perceptual systems.* Boston: Houghton Mifflin.

Gibson, J. J. (1986). *The ecological approach to visual perception.* Hillsdale, NJ: Erlbaum. (Original work published 1979).

Goldstein, H. (1980). *Classical mechanics.* Reading, MA: Addison-Wesley.

Haken, H. (1977). *Synergetics.* Berlin: Springer Verlag.

Haken, H. (1983). *Advanced synergetics.* Berlin: Springer Verlag.

Haken, H. (1988). *Information and self-organization.* Berlin: Springer Verlag.

Haken, H., Kelso, J. A. S., and Bunz, H. (1985). A theoretical model of phase transitions in human hand movements. *Biological Cybernetics, 51,* 347–356.

Haken, H., and Wunderlin, A. (1990). Synergetics and its paradigm of self-organization in biological systems. In H. T. A. Whiting, O. G. Meijer, and P. C. W. van Wieringen (Eds.), *The natural-physical approach to movement control.* Amsterdam: Free University Press.

Jackson, E. A. (1989). *Perspectives of nonlinear dynamics*. Cambridge, England: Cambridge University Press.

Jones, M. B. (1962). Practice as a process of simplification. *Psychological Review, 69,* 274–294.

Katz, D. (1925/1989). *The world of touch*. (Krueger, L., Trans.) Hillsdale, NJ: Erlbaum. (Originally published in 1925.]

Keller, F. S. (1958). The phantom plateau. *Journal of the Experimental Analysis of Behavior, 1,* 1–13.

Kelso, J. A. S. (1984). Phase transitions and critical behavior in human bimanual coordination. *American Journal of Physiology: Regulatory, Integrative and Comparative, 246,* R1000–R1004.

Kelso, J. A. S., DelColle, J. D., and Schöner, G. (1990). Action-perception as a pattern formation process. In M. Jeannerod (Ed.), *Attention and performance XIII* (pp. 139–169). Hillsdale, NJ: Erlbaum.

Kelso, J. A. S., Scholz, J., and Schöner, G. (1986). Nonequilibrium phase transitions in coordinated biological motion: critical fluctuations. *Physics Letters, 118,* 279–284.

Kelso, J. A. S., Schöner, G., Scholz, J. P., et al. (1987). Phase-locked modes, phase transitions, and component oscillators in biological motion. *Physica Scripta, 35,* 79–87.

Kinsella-Shaw, J. M., and Turvey, M. T. (1992). Haptic perception of object distance in a single-strand haptic vibratory web. *Perception and Psychophysics, 52,* 625–638.

Kugler, P. N., Kelso, J. A. S., and Turvey, M. T. (1980). On the concept of coordinative structures as dissipative structures: I. Theoretical lines of convergence. In G. E. Stelmach and J. Requin (Eds.), *Tutorials in motor behavior* (pp. 3–47). Amsterdam: North-Holland.

Kugler, P. N., Kelso, J. A. S., and Turvey, M. T. (1982). On the control and coordination of naturally developing systems. In J. A. S. Kelso and J. E. Clark (Eds.), *The development of movement control and coordination* (pp. 5–78), New York: Wiley.

Kugler, P. N., and Turvey, M. T. (1987). *Information, natural law, and the self-assembly of rhythmic movement*. Hillsdale, NJ: Erlbaum.

Michaels, C. F., and Carello, C. (1981). *Direct perception*. Englewood Cliffs, NJ: Prentice Hall.

Namikas, G. (1983). Vertical processes and motor performance. In R. A. Magill (Ed.), *Memory and control of action*. Amsterdam: North-Holland.

Pagano, C. C., Fitzpatrick, P., and Turvey, M. T. (1993). Tensorial basis to the constancy of perceived extent over variations of dynamic touch. *Perception and Psychophysics, 54,* 43–54.

Pagano, C. C., Kinsella-Shaw, J. M., Cassidy, P., et al. (1994). Role of the inertia tensor in haptically perceiving where an object is grasped. *Journal of Experimental Psychology: Human Perception and Performance, 20,* 276–285.

Pagano, C. C., and Turvey, M. T. (1992). Eigenvectors of the inertia tensor and perceiving the orientation of a hand-held object by dynamic touch. *Perception and Psychophysics, 52,* 617–624.

Pagano C., and Turvey, M. T. (1993). Perceiving by dynamic touch the extents of irregular objects. *Ecological Psychology, 5,* 125–151.

Pagano, C. C., and Turvey, M. T. (in press). The inertia tensor as a basis for the perception of limb orientation. *Journal of Experimental Psychology: Human Perception and Performance.*

Pew, R. W. (1974). Human perceptual-motor performance. In B. H. Kantowitz (Ed.), *Human information processing: tutorials in performance and cognition*. Hillsdale, NJ: Erlbaum.

Rand, R. H., Cohen, A. H., and Holmes, P. J. (1988). Systems of coupled oscillators as models of central pattern generators. In A. H. Cohen, S. Rossignol, and S. Grillner (Eds.), *Neural control of rhythmic movements in vertebrates* (pp. 333–367). New York: Wiley.

Rosenblum, L. D., and Turvey, M. T. (1988). Maintenance tendency in coordinated rhythmic movements: relative fluctuations and phase. *Neuroscience, 27,* 289–300.

Schmidt, R. C., Beek, P. J., Treffner, P., et al. (1991). Dynamical substructure of coordinated rhythmic movements. *Journal of Experimental Psychology: Human Perception and Performance, 17,* 635–651.

Schmidt, R. C., Carello, C., and Turvey, M. T. (1990). Phase transitions and critical fluctuations in the visual coordination of rhythmic movements between people. *Journal of Experimental Psychology: Human Perception and Performance, 16,* 227–247.

Schmidt, R. C., Shaw, B. K., and Turvey, M. T. (1993). Coupling dynamics in interlimb coordination. *Journal of Experimental Psychology: Human Perception and Performance, 19,* 397–415.

Schmidt, R. C., Treffner, P., Shaw, B. K., et al. (1992). Dynamical aspects of learning an interlimb rhythmic movement pattern. *Journal of Motor Behavior, 24,* 67–83.

Schmidt, R. C., and Turvey, M. T. (1994). Phase-entrainment dynamics of visually coupled rhythmic movements. *Biological Cybernetics, 70,* 369–376.

Scholz, J. P., and Kelso, J. A. S. (1990). Intentional switching between patterns of bimanual coordination depends on the intrinsic dynamics of the patterns. *Journal of Motor Behavior, 22,* 98–124.

Scholz, P. J., Kelso, J. A. S., and Schöner, G. (1987). Nonequilibrium phase transitions in coordinated biological motion: critical slowing down and switching time. *Physics Letters A, 123,* 390–394.

Schöner, G., Haken, H., and Kelso, J. A. S. (1986). A stochastic theory of phase transitions in human hand movement. *Biological Cybernetics, 53,* 442–452.

Schöner, G., and Kelso, J. A. S. (1988a). Dynamic pattern generation in behavioral and neural systems. *Science, 239,* 1513–1520.

Schöner, G., and Kelso, J. A. S. (1988b). A dynamic theory of behavioral change. *Journal of Theoretical Biology, 135,* 501–524.

Solomon, H. Y. (1988). Movement-produced invariants in haptic explorations: an example of a self-organizing, information-driven, intentional system. *Human Movement Science, 7,* 201–223.

Solomon, H. Y., and Turvey, M. T. (1988). Haptically perceiving the distances reachable with a hand-held object. *Journal of Experimental Psychology: Human Perception and Performance, 14,* 404–427.

Solomon, H. Y., Turvey, M. T., and Burton, G. (1989a). Perceiving extents of rods by wielding: haptic diagonalization and decomposition of the inertia tensor. *Journal of Experimental Psychology: Human Perception and Performance, 15,* 58–68.

Solomon, H. Y., Turvey, M. T., and Burton, G. (1989b). Gravitational and muscular influences in perceiving length by wielding. *Ecological Psychology, 1,* 265–300.

Starch, D. (1910). A demonstration of the trial and error method of learning. *Psychological Bulletin, 7,* 20–23.

Sternad, D., Turvey, M. T., and Schmidt, R. C. (1992). Average phase difference theory and 1 : 1 phase entrainment in interlimb coordination. *Biological Cybernetics, 67,* 223–231.

Turvey, M. T. (1977). Contrasting orientations to the theory of visual information processing. *Psychological Review, 84,* 67–88.

Turvey, M. T., Burton, G., Pagano, C. C., et al. (1992). Role of the inertia tensor in perceiving object orientation by dynamic touch. *Journal of Experimental Psychology: Human Perception and Performance, 3,* 714–727.

Turvey, M. T., Schmidt, R. C., Rosenblum, L. D., et al. (1988). On the time allometry of coordinated rhythmic movements. *Journal of Theoretical Biology, 130,* 285–325.

Turvey, M. T., Shaw, R. E., Reed, E., et al. (1981). Ecological laws of perceiving and acting: in reply to Fodor and Pylyshyn (1981). *Cognition, 9,* 237–304.

Von Holst, E. (1939/1973). Relative coordination as a phenomenon and as a method of analysis of central nervous system function. In R. Martin (Ed. and Trans.), *The collected papers of Erich von Holst:* Vol. 1. *The behavioral physiology of animal and man.* Coral Gables, FL: University of Miami Press.

Yates, F. E. (Ed.) (1987). *Self-organizing systems: the emergence of order.* New York: Plenum.

Guide to Further Reading

A readable introduction to the ecological approach is provided by Michaels and Carello (1981), while the classic source is Gibson (1979). A detailed treatment of many key philosophical and mathematical issues may be found in Kugler and Turvey (1987). Our standard mechanics source is Goldstein (1980), who does a nice job of laying out tensor algebra and the inertia tensor. Turvey (1990) provides a survey of problems, issues, and strategies in understanding coordinated movement. A similar treatment of haptics may be found in Turvey and Carello (in press); it is also described (with only a light treatment of tensors) in Turvey, Solomon, and Burton (1989). Papers describing ecologically and dynamically oriented studies of perception and action often appear in the journal *Ecological Psychology.*

Gibson, J. J. (1979). *The ecological approach to visual perception.* Boston: Houghton-Mifflin.

Goldstein, H. (1980). *Classical mechanics.* Reading, MA: Addison-Wesley.

Kugler, P. N., and Turvey, M. T. (1987) *Information, natural law, and the self-assembly of rhythmic movement.* Hillsdale NJ: Erlbaum.

Michaels, C. F., and Carello, C. (1981). *Direct perception.* Englewood Cliffs, NJ: Prentice Hall.

Turvey, M. T. (1990). Coordination. *American Psychologist, 45,* 938–953.

Turvey, M. T., and Carello, C. (in press). Dynamic touch. In W. Epstein and S. Rogers (Eds.), *Handbook of perception and cognition, vol. 5: perception of space and notion.* New York: Academic Press.

Turvey, M. T., Solomon, H. Y., and Burton, G. (1989). An ecological analysis of knowing by wielding. *Journal of the Experimental Analysis of Behavior, 52,* 387–407.

14 Dynamics and the Problem of Visual Event Recognition

Geoffrey P. Bingham

EDITOR'S INTRODUCTION

How is visual perception possible? In particular, how is it that what one typically sees is a relatively simple world of objects and behaviors, when what reaches the eyes is a fantastically rich, seemingly chaotic play of stimulation? How does one's visual system manage to reach behind the superficial confusion to the stability and order that are responsible for it?

In this chapter, Geoff Bingham confronts one version of this problem, that of recognition of events. We constantly perceive what is going on around us as meaningful events of certain kinds: a person walking, a ball bouncing, water flowing. Psychologists have established experimentally that people are very good at recognizing the nature of an event from the visual motions the event produces; thus it is easy to see that a flow of light patches against a dark background is produced by a ball bouncing. The event itself is determined by a characteristic dynamics; thus the laws of classical mechanics determine the motion of a bouncing ball. The problem of event recognition is to recover the dynamics of the event from the visual motions, i.e., the kinematics.

One problem in event recognition is that researchers have believed the motions to be ambiguous; the same surface motions might have been produced by many kinds of dynamics. A standard approach to the difficulty of narrowing down the search has been to use the assumption that only rigid objects are involved. Yet, as Bingham points out, events involving rigid objects are just one kind among many that we can distinguish; hence the rigidity assumption is a dead end. Acknowledging this, however, seems to render the problem insoluble. There must be some further kind of structure or information that we rely on in recognizing events.

If we think of the sensory periphery as a kind of boundary between inner and outer, then cognitive scientists can proceed in at least two ways. Traditionally, they focus on what is inside this boundary, on the states and processes that supposedly enable a cognizant agent to piece together an interpretation of the world based on impoverished sensory data. On this approach, the further information that is needed to solve the problem of event recognition must take the form of internally represented background knowledge which is brought to bear in complex computational operations.

An alternative approach is to focus on what is outside *the boundary. Perhaps there is already present in the sensory stimulation information enabling the system to identify the nature of the event. If this is right, the task of the visual system would just be to pick up on that information; the need for internal representations and computations would be minimized. From this perspective, then, an essential prelimi- nary to investigating the internal cognitive mechanisms involved in visual perception is to develop, as Bingham puts it, "a job description for the sensory apparatus."*

In this chapter, Bingham takes this second approach, and argues that the dy- namics of the event is not, in fact, as hopelessly underspecified by the kinematics as might be supposed. Natural events are constrained by natural law, and hence the motions that result reflect certain universally valid circumstances such as the con- stancy of gravitational force and the unidirectionality of time. Further, if one adopts a suitably global perspective (i.e., one that accords with the time scale of the complete event itself), then there exist symmetries in the temporally extended pattern of sen- sory stimulation that further constrain the nature of the event that could have produced it.

Bingham substantiates these points with extended analysis of a particular exam- ple, that of a ball rolling back and forth inside a U*-shaped container. If one visually tracks the movement of individual points on this ball, the result is a myriad of short, disjointed trajectories. The problem is to show that this information, together with further ecologically valid assumptions, uniquely constrains the nature of the event responsible (a ball rolling); or, to put the point another way, that under normal ecological conditions, the mapping from the dynamics of an event to the kinematics of the optic array is unique and reversible. The cognitive task of event identification appears far less daunting if this bold claim can be substantiated.*

14.1 INTRODUCTION

People are able to recognize an indefinite variety of events visually. Motions in events have been shown to provide the information. The question is, What optical information do people use to recognize events, that is, how do mo- tions get into optics? For instance, consider the visual perception of a ball rolling over a surface. This event can be readily recognized even when it appears in a video display in which only small bright irregular patches on the ball are visible in darkness. In analyzing the perception of this event, we must be careful to distinguish between the event and the optics. *In the event itself,* each patch follows a continuous trajectory along a path of particular shape and with a velocity that varies in a particular way along the path. Each patch follows a path of somewhat different shape with a somewhat different veloc- ity pattern and each of these patterns may be shifted somewhat spatially relative to the others along the surface. How are all of these distinct patch trajectories combined to yield the perception of a unitary coherent event? The problem is more difficult than this, however. In the display, the patches blink on and off. They appear and disappear as they roll up over the top of the ball and then around behind the ball. *In the optics,* a patch follows a discontinuous piece of a trajectory. Each trajectory piece has a somewhat different path shape and velocity pattern and each piece is spatially shifted with respect to all of the other pieces across the display. Most important, pieces sampled successively from the trajectory of a single patch in the event itself cannot readily be identified as such. Each sampled piece from a given event trajectory is separated by a relatively large distance from the preceding and following pieces. Neighboring trajectories are arbitrarily close and may be easily confused. The optics consists, therefore, of a very large collection of qualitatively distinct and spatially disparate trajectory pieces. Nevertheless, this extremely complex mess is perceived simply as a single rolling ball. How is this possible? Clearly, the collection of trajectory pieces must be structured and the perceptual system must detect and use that structure.

The difficulty is that events are inherently time extended so that the structure used to identify events must also be time extended. Historically, the trend in analysis of optical structure has been away from structure that is strongly local in space and time toward more global structures. This trend has been largely motivated by the intractability of the problems formulated on the basis of very local structure. The optical array is used to describe the pattern in light projected from all directions to a point of observation. Optical flow is the changing pattern produced when the point of observation moves or when surfaces in the environment around a point of observation move. The optical array was introduced by Gibson (1961) to emphasize spatially extended structure surrounding an observer and to provide a means of capturing optical flow. With the introduction of optical flow, the relevant structure became extended in time beyond instantaneous snapshots. However, the extension in time has only progressed in the majority of extant analyses to a sequence of two or three images obtained over a few milliseconds and yielding an extremely brief sample of optical flow over distances within an infinitesimal neighborhood of a point in the flow field. Because of the strongly local character of these measurements, the results of the analyses have not been stable in the face of perturbations representing noise engendered by the sensory apparatus. An assumption that an event consists of strictly rigid motions has been used in an attempt to make analysis less local. Rigidity of motion means that distances between points in three-dimensional space are preserved so that the motions of a given point constrain those of neighboring points. However, recent investigations have shown that only truly global analysis will resolve these difficulties (Bertero, Poggio and Torre, 1988; Eagleson, 1987; Hildreth and Grzywacz, 1986; Hildreth and Koch, 1987; Jacobson and Wechsler, 1987; Nagel, 1988; Ullman, 1984; Verri and Poggio, 1987, 1989).

A global analysis is advocated in this chapter for a different but related reason. To assume rigid motion is to beg the question of event recognition. Rigid motion is but one of many types of motion that can occur in a wide variety of distinct types of recognizable events. Such motions include, for instance, elastic, plastic, liquid, or ethereal motions, among others. Truly time-extended information is required to enable recognition of these types of events. For instance, imagine trying to distinguish among the following events in which irregular tickets of white paper have been used as patches appearing in otherwise dark displays: patches on the facial skin of a talking person, patches on the surface of vibrating jello, patches on the surface of a trampoline during gymnastic exercises, patches on the surface of water being stirred or splashed by a projectile, patches on a handful of coins being slid across the bottom of a wooden box, patches being blown across a surface like leaves blown across a lawn in autumn, and patches on a collection of Ping-Pong balls dropped on a tile floor. All of these events involve nonrigid motions. All might be distinguished with sufficiently time-extended samples. Each involves different physical constraints on the motions of the patches. Each, accordingly, involves a distinct type of motion. The challenge is to characterize the motions in a way that enables us to begin to formulate the event recognition problem.

For the purpose of providing an initial outline of the problem of event recognition, I will characterize events in terms of *trajectory forms in phase space* (in which velocities are plotted against position).[1] Characterized in this way, *events* appear *as spatiotemporal objects* that can be mapped via perspective projections into an optical phase space of lower dimension. Events then can be distinguished on the basis of qualitative properties.

I begin by reviewing the evidence on event recognition via forms of motion. Next, I consider how mere motions can provide information about the substantial types and properties of events. To anticipate briefly, formulation in terms of the qualitative properties of trajectories allows one to use qualitative dynamics to capture, in a single qualitative characterization, both the substantial properties of events (in terms of dynamics) and the information about them (in terms of kinematics). Geometrically, dynamics corresponds to vector fields in phase space while the kinematics are trajectories in phase space. The forms of dynamic vector fields are identical to the forms of the kinematic trajectories that lie tangent to them and are determined by them. Under this abstract and qualitative way of construing dynamics, kinematics (i.e., motions) and dynamics (i.e., physical properties) are commensurate and kinematics can specify dynamics. Along the way, I describe the relation between the kinematic specification of dynamics and the notion of direct perception.

Next, an example, namely, a ball rolling on a curved surface, is used to illustrate the problems engendered by the projection of event phase-space trajectories into an optical phase space of lower dimension. The question is, What qualitative properties are preserved in the projection to optical flows? Finally, the ultimate difficulty, the degrees-of-freedom problem, is discussed together with methods of qualitative dynamics that can be used to solve it. The degrees of freedom are the separate items that must be measured (or apprehended) and evaluated. The difficulty, as I have already indicated, is that occlusion yields disconnected pieces of trajectories in the optics. When counted, these pieces amount to an excessively large number of potential

Geoffrey P. Bingham

degrees of freedom. The problem of perceptual organization, as formulated by the Gestalt psychologists, must here be confronted. To anticipate, I suggest that a solution can be found in the qualitative properties of event trajectories. Symmetries[2] apparent in the form and layout of trajectory pieces can be used to collapse the pieces together into temporally continuous and spatially coherent forms, reducing the degrees of freedom and revealing information that could be used for recognition.

14.2 THE EVIDENCE FOR EVENT RECOGNITION

Evidence has been amassed over the last 30 to 40 years demonstrating irrefutably that people are able to recognize specific types of events and specific properties of events via detection of particular forms of motion. The majority of the extant research in visual event perception has been focused on scaling problems, that is, the way that magnitudes associated with particular event properties are apprehended. This research has included investigations on the perception of the sizes and distances of objects in free fall (Johansson and Jansson, 1967; Muchisky and Bingham, 1992; Watson, Banks, von Hofsten, et al., 1993); perception of the lengths of swinging pendulums (Pittenger, 1985, 1990); perception of amounts of lifted weight (Runeson and Frykholm, 1981, 1983; Bingham, 1985, 1987b); perception of relative amounts of mass in collisions (Proffitt and Gilden, 1989; Runeson, 1977; Runeson and Vedeler, 1993; Todd and Warren, 1982); perception of the age of growing heads (Mark, Todd, and Shaw, 1981; Pittenger and Shaw, 1975; Shaw, Mark, Jenkins, et al., 1982; Shaw and Pittenger, 1977, 1978; Todd, Mark, Shaw, et al., 1980); perception of the elasticity of bouncing balls (Warren, Kim, and Husney, 1987); and perception of the time of contact of projectiles (Lee, Young, Reddish, et al., 1983; Todd, 1981). All of these scaling studies have implicitly involved the problem of recognition because any property or dimension to be scaled must first be recognized. For instance, to judge pendulum length via the period requires that an observer recognize the freely swinging pendulum event as well as the event property, pendulum length. Successful performance in all of the cited scaling studies has implied that observers have been able to recognize the event properties whose scale values they judged. To this may be added evidence from investigations explicitly on recognition.

The inaugural studies on visual event recognition include those of Duncker, Michotte, Wallach, and Johansson. Duncker (1929/1950) demonstrated the recognition of a rigid rolling wheel via the relative motions of points on the hub and the rim. Michotte (1963) studied the recognition of launching vs. triggering events as the timing along trajectories was varied. Wallach and O'Connell (1953) investigated the recognition of wire frame objects via the so-called kinetic depth effect. Finally, Johannson (1950), in giving event perception research its name, placed it in the context of established problems in perceptual research, namely those of perceptual organization and constancy. Manipulating the motions of points or elements in a two-dimensional display,

Johansson sought properties of relative motions that would result in the perception of a single coherent moving three-dimensional object. In addition, Johansson distinguished between displays that yielded perception of rigid vs. nonrigid objects and inquired as to the conditions yielding the shape constancy of rigid objects (Johansson, 1950, 1964, 1973, 1985). This led to an entire area of research on object recognition called "structure-from-motion" in which the assumption of "rigid motion" has been used in theorems proving that three-dimensional object structure can be derived from sampled optical transformations (Hildreth, 1984; Hildreth and Hollerbach, 1987; Hildreth and Koch, 1987; Longuet-Higgins and Prazdny, 1980; Marr, 1982; Prazdny, 1980; Ullman, 1979).

"Structure-from-motion" research owes as much to Gibson's studies on the visual control of locomotion and flight (e.g., Gibson, 1955, 1958, 1961, 1966; Gibson, Gibson, Smith, et al., 1959) as to Johansson's studies on event perception. The rigid/nonrigid distinction has been used to investigate perspective transformations that occur as a point of observation is moved through the environment. The assumption that the environment should be entirely rigid (and therefore static) yields a reasonable first approximation to optical flows encountered during locomotion (Nayakama and Loomis, 1974). However, the ultimate weakness of this approach is revealed in the context of the more general problem of event recognition. Researchers have claimed that the rigid motion assumption is required for unique interpretation of flow patterns because nonrigid motions allow an indefinite number of interpretations in terms of depth and motions (e.g., Hildreth and Hollerbach, 1987; Nayakama and Loomis, 1974). However, "nonrigid" has been used here incorrectly to mean "arbitrary" motion. Nonrigid motions are not arbitrary, as shown by the number of distinct kinds of "nonrigid" events that are recognizable.

In fact, the majority of studies demonstrating and investigating visual event recognition have involved nonrigid motions (Bingham, Rosenblum, and Schmidt, in press; Cutting, 1982; Fieandt and Gibson, 1959; Jansson and Johansson, 1973; Jansson and Runeson, 1977; Todd, 1982), and in particular those of human actions (Barclay, Cutting, and Kozlowsky, 1978; Cutting, 1978; Cutting and Kozlowsky, 1977; Cutting, Proffitt, and Kozlowsky, 1978; Frykholm, 1983; Johansson, 1973, 1976; Todd, 1983). These studies alone, however, do not reflect the proportion or variety of recognizable events involving different kinds of nonrigid motions. Such motions include varieties of bending, as of a human trunk or elbow, a paper clip or a tree limb buried in snow; types of folding, tearing, and crumpling, as of pieces of paper, the body of a car, or a loaf of fresh Italian bread; varieties of breaking, as of glass, a cookie, a wooden board, or a loaf of stale Italian bread; types of elastic stretching or compressing, as of a hair net, a bouncing ball, a tree branch blowing in the wind, vibrating jello, or a human face forming various expressions; kinds of plastic deformations, as in forming clay figures, kneading bread, making snowballs, or leaving footprints in soil; types of liquid flows involving the pouring, running, bubbling, and splashing of liquids of varying viscosity, as of water, oil, molasses, or thickening gravy cooking on the stove; varieties of flows of gases, as of steam or smoke in air; snow or leaves blown in a breeze, and so on. The great diversity of different types of non-rigid events that might be perceptually identified renders any simple distinction between rigid and nonrigid far too weak and inadequate to address the problem of visual event identification.

The rigidity of objects is a physical property which, like elasticity, plasticity, or fluidity, can generate specific types of motions. The question is whether observers are able to recognize such properties in specific instances and if so, how? More generally, the identification problem is, first, to discover what types of events and event properties observers are able to recognize and, second, to describe the information enabling them to do so. For instance, Bingham et al. (in press) have shown that observers were able to recognize events including free fall and elastic rebound, swinging pendulums, rolling balls, stirred water, objects dropped into water, and tickets of paper blown and falling through air, all from the forms of motion displayed in patch-light video recordings.

The patch-light technique isolates motion as information from static figural properties. Events are filmed so that bright patches of reflective material placed on surfaces in events appear against a dark (structureless) background. When these displays are freeze-framed, they appear as only a random array of irregular patches. When set in motion, the recorded events are typically recognized quite readily.

In the Bingham et al. study, observers' descriptions of the patch-light events reflected the underlying types of dynamics rather than simple kinematic similarities like the presence or absence of rotational motion in the display. Events involving rigid-body dynamics were described as more similar to one another and distinguished from hydrodynamic or aerodynamic events which were similarly grouped. Observers also distinguished the inanimate motion of a falling and bouncing object from the animate motions produced when the same object was moved by hand along the same path, to the same endpoints, and at the same frequency. Motions produced by the biodynamics reflected increases in mechanical energy, while those produced only by rigid-body dynamics reflected strict dissipation of energy. In all cases, recognizably different events were produced by different generative dynamics.

The forms of motion corresponding to each event were sampled from the video recordings and captured in phase-space trajectories. In each case, the trajectory form reflected the dynamics that generated the form. For instance, as shown in figure 14.1, the free fall and bounce produced a parabolic trajectory (characteristic of gravity) with a flat base (corresponding to the impact and elastic rebound) followed by a decelerative parabolic trajectory rising to a height diminished by energy dissipation. In contrast, the object moved by

Free Falling and Bouncing Spring

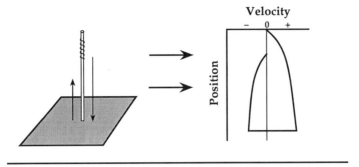

Spring Moved by Hand

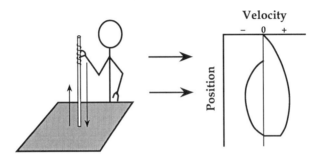

Figure 14.1 (*Top*) The phase trajectory of a free-falling and bouncing spring. (*Bottom*) The phase trajectory of the same spring moved by hand to the same endpoints at the same frequency.

hand produced an elliptical trajectory (characteristic of human limb movement) with a half-flat base (corresponding to inelastic impact and loss of energy), followed by an accelerative elliptical trajectory (which reflected energy increase). These spatiotemporal forms in optical flows provided visual information enabling observers to recognize the corresponding events. Such information is paradigmatic of the understanding of perceptual information developed by Gibson.

14.3 DIRECT PERCEPTION: INFORMATION AND INFORMATIONAL BASES

How can optical patterns have perceptual significance? How can they provide information about objects and events in the surroundings? How can they specify what is happening? Two classic solutions to these questions were rejected by Gibson (Gibson, 1950, 1966, 1979; Reed, 1988; Reed and Jones, 1982). The first, usually attributed to Berkeley, is that optical patterns gain significance by virtue of associations with haptic experience, i.e., touch and kinesthesis. The difficulty with this idea arises with the realization that haptics only functions well in the context of voluntary movements. Objects

Geoffrey P. Bingham

and properties of objects (e.g., surface compliance, surface texture, weight and inertial distribution, shape, etc.) can be identified rapidly and reliably only when an observer is allowed to actively explore and manipulate an object (Gibson, 1962, 1966; Klatzky, Lederman, and Metzger, 1985; Lederman and Klatzky, 1987). Understanding how spatiotemporal patterns of tissue deformation provide information about objects and events (including the perceiver's own activity) is, if anything, a more difficult problem than that encountered in vision. This is, in part, because the problems in understanding the control and coordination of actions are inherited as part of the problem of understanding haptics (although ultimately action is a part of the problem of visual recognition as well) (Bingham, 1988). More to the point, the effective patterns of tissue deformation that impinge on the sensory receptors in haptics are less accessible to measurement and manipulation in experiments. Finally, and most important, it is spatiotemporal patterns of tissue deformation, i.e., change in geometric configurations over time, that provide information in haptics just as in vision (Bingham, Schmidt, and Rosenblum, 1989; Pagano and Turvey, 1993; Solomon, 1988). This realization undercuts any intuition that a solution to problems in vision, if seemingly insoluble, should be found only in haptics.

The second classic solution is that optical patterns have significance by virtue of a similarity relation to that about which they provide information, i.e., that optical patterns are copies of environmental patterns. Gibson also rejected this alternative. Gibson's analysis of optical occlusion is a paradigmatic case (Gibson, 1979; Gibson, Kaplan, Reynolds, et al., 1969). The deletion of optical elements along a boundary specifies one surface becoming hidden by another by virtue of a change in perspective. With progressive deletion, optical elements cease to exist in the optical pattern. However, the significance of this optical flow pattern does not inhere in a similarity relation to what is specified. The optical pattern does not specify surface elements going out of existence in the environment. Why not? Because surfaces do not go out of existence neatly and quietly at an edge, although they do go out of existence in a variety of other ways constrained and determined by natural laws. Surfaces can burn, explode, evaporate, melt, break, and so on. Each of these types of events produces corresponding types of optical transformations that are distinct from progressive deletion along a boundary. Also, each of the former events is irreversible, whereas the hiding of a surface via change in perspective is reversible, yielding accretion of optical elements at a boundary. Thus, Gibson argued that the particular pattern of optical flow can specify an event to which it corresponds by virtue of natural laws that determine the particular form of both the event and the optical flow.

The historical precedents to this understanding take us back at least as far as Hume (1739/1978). He argued that perception only has access to motions, not causes, because optical (or acoustical, etc.) patterns involve space and time, but not mass or force. His skeptical argument was a natural extension of arguments to the effect that perception only has (direct) access to "phenomena" described via only two spatial dimensions and time because the third spatial dimension is absent in optical pattern. Such phenomenalism has been standard fare in the philosophy of perception and widely advocated despite its leading inevitably to the absurdities of solipsism. Rejecting phenomenalism requires that perception have direct access to information specifying substantial properties of the surroundings (Shaw, Turvey, and Mace, 1981; Turvey, Shaw, Mace, et al., 1981).

Hume, writing just after the publication of Newton's *Principia*, resorted to the billiard table to illustrate his understanding. Hume recognized the invariance of the motions that ensue once the cue ball is sent rolling so as to collide with the eight ball. The same motions result each time the balls are positioned and set moving in the same way. Nevertheless, Hume argued that an observer could not obtain epistemological access to the substantial properties of the event because the latter lay beyond the mere motions and only the motions are communicated to the eye via patterns in light. Because of the unique relation between motions and their causes, the two cannot be separated and observers have no means by which to get past the kinematics to reach the dynamics. He argued that the observer has direct access only to patterns of contiguity in space and time.

Two hundred years later, Michotte (1963) performed demonstrations which contradicted Hume's conclusions. The irony is that Michotte used technology that was available to Hume so that Hume might have made the discovery himself. Michotte devised a way to simulate linear collisions in displays that enabled him to perturb the kinematics without concern for underlying dynamics. (See Michotte, 1963, for details. This is now achieved using computer simulations.) When shown Michotte's collision displays, observers recognized them as collisions. In these displays, one simulated object approached a stationary object, contacted it, and stopped moving, while the contacted object instantly carried on the motion. Michotte then inserted a brief delay at the point when the two simulated objects came into contact so that the second object hesitated for fractions of a second before beginning to move. The result was that observers no longer recognized the display as of a collision. The slight perturbation changed the perceptual significance. The implication was that particular kinematic patterns have particular perceptual significance.

The upshot was that Hume's argument should be turned on its head. Indeed, causal constraints on events produce invariant forms of motion given invariant initial conditions. The invariance is a reflection of the underlying determinism which allows motions (and corresponding optical patterns) to be informative. They are informative by virtue of unique correspondence. The correspondence is enforced by natural laws, i.e., by dynamics. Note that not just any kinematic pattern will be perceptually significant. The perturbed kinematics in Michotte's demonstration were rather odd. Forced to describe what they perceived, observers rather creatively described the display as specifying a "triggering" event, as if the first object triggered the release of energy stored in a spring which then sent the second object on its way. However, the instantaneous acceleration of the second object does not look exactly like such a triggering event. Runeson (1977) pointed out that Michotte did not manipulate simulated dynamics to produce his displays and thus the simulations were inaccurate and the displays rather ambiguous.

Todd (1982) inadvertently illustrated this methodological difficulty by manipulating only kinematics while trying to discover the forms of motion specific to bipedal walking and running as recognizable types of locomotor events. Todd began with digitized trajectories from actual walking and running. He then independently manipulated the motions for each of the 7 degrees of freedom in his stick figure legs, mixing and matching motions from the walking and running. The results were always rather ambiguous. Some looked more like running or walking as the case might be, but none were very convincing. Todd concluded that he really did not have a clue as to the essential characteristics of motions identifiable as walking or running and that he was lost in the sea of kinematic possibilities allowed by the 7-degrees-of-freedom system. A better approach would be to start from an understanding of the dynamics of these locomotor events. Walking can be understood as a system of upright and inverted pendulums, whereas running entails a mass-spring dynamic (McMahon, 1984). Investigation should proceed via perturbations performed with respect to these dynamics. For instance, as implied by the pendular dynamics and as shown by Bingham et al. (in press), the orientation of the kinematics in the gravitational field contributes to its perceptual significance. Perturbation of the orientation alters the significance. Likewise, would recognition be stable in the face of perturbation of the gravitational value or the stiffness of the leg or changes that alter the direction of energy flows among the link segments?

Runeson and Frykholm (1983) formulated kinematic specification of dynamics (or KSD) as a principle to be used to guide investigations of perceptual information. They referred to dynamics as an "informational basis," meaning that which enabled kinematic pattern to specify events. In so doing, they made explicit what remained implicit in Gibson's original analysis of occlusion. Gibson was circumspect about the importation of dynamics to the study of perception (Gibson, 1979; Reed, 1988). He emphatically wished to avoid the "error of confusing descriptions with things described" (so named by Dewey and Bentley, 1949). Gibson referred to perceptible properties as "affordances" to keep them well anchored within a functional context in which perception is motivated by action. As such, perceptible properties remain to be discovered and described by perception research. They cannot not be found in a dictionary of physics or in Webster's. Nevertheless, the powerful analytical apparatus of dynamics can be applied to analysis and perturbation of optical information as long as we remain mindful of the fact that types of recognizable events and event properties need not correspond directly to any of the familiar concepts in dynamics (Bingham and Muchisky, 1993a,b; Bingham et al., in press).

An essential aspect of this approach is the realization that unique correspondence between, e.g., optical pattern and events can only be found at certain levels of analysis. The scope must be sufficiently wide to include relevant structure. For instance, no single momentary velocity in a collision is specific to the type of event (anymore than it would be sufficient for a dynamical analysis of the event). Rather, the pattern of variation in velocities over *significant spatial and temporal extents* is required to achieve unique correspondence. This point is central to the current discussion of event recognition and the critique of extant analyses of optical flow. In the "structure from motion" corpus, analysis of optical flow has been restricted to structure captured in brief moments spanning a sampling interval of a few milliseconds, namely, a vector field. Such structure could not be used to identify events because, as shown by Bingham et al. (in press) and related studies, events are only specified by structure in optical flow that emerges over the entire course of an event. The information must be contained in various forms of optical transformation occurring at specific rates corresponding to the rate structure of motions in an event.

The mapping of event motions into optical flows can be described in terms of a relation between kinematic variables. Event velocities at given positions in three-dimensional space project to optical velocities at corresponding positions in the two-dimensional optical array. The question is whether qualitative properties of event trajectories are preserved in the mapping to optical trajectories? The first difficulty is entailed by the projection from three- to two-dimensional space (or if we include velocities associated with each position coordinate, the projection from six- to four-dimensional space). Components of the event kinematics that are radially directed with respect to the point of observation do not map directly into optical flows. Nevertheless, as will be shown, radial components of event kinematics do determine distinguishable components of optical flow that preserve the original forms of the event kinematics.

The final difficulty underlying the problem of event recognition is the degrees-of-freedom problem, that is, the problem of reducing the complex and large number of distinct motions (e.g., of patches) to the simple coherent motion of a single event. The optical phase space mapped from an event will contain an extremely large number of distinct trajectories. Any event consists of a continuous spatial distribution of points, each following a different trajectory. Only portions of the original event kinematics find their way into the optics. During an event, points go out of and come into view as they are occluded by other parts of a moving object or by surrounding objects. This happens not only with a rolling ball but also as limbs appear and disappear behind one another when a person locomotes or when a tree blows in the wind. It occurs as waves on the ocean occlude one another and passing vessels, as cars occlude one another in traffic, or as pedestrians occlude one another on city sidewalks, as a dancer performs pirouettes, as one stirs one's oatmeal, and so on. The result is that most any given trajectory is sliced into myriad disjoint pieces which, together with those from other trajectories, produce a massive collection of nonidentical trajectory pieces. The disjoint character of the pieces from a given trajectory coupled with the simultaneous presence of arbitrarily close pieces from distinct trajectories prevents the simple reconstruction of individual trajectories. Given such a tangled mass of trajectory pieces, how might a single, unitary, and coherent event be apprehended? I will demonstrate how symmetries apparent in the layout of optical trajectories can allow the dimensionality to be reduced so that the underlying form might be apprehended. The suggested bottom line is that the global structure of event trajectories is required to yield a specification of events.

14.4   THE RELATION OF EVENT KINEMATICS TO DYNAMICS: THE KINEMATIC SPECIFICATION OF EVENTS

Rejecting the "Missing-Dimension" Characterization

Originally, the formulation of the kinematic specification of dynamics was inspired by the ability of observers of patch-light displays to apprehend values of dynamic properties such as relative mass or lifted weight (Bingham, 1987b, 1993; Runeson, 1977; Runeson and Frykholm, 1981, 1983; Runeson and Vedeler, 1993; Todd and Warren, 1982). In the context of this scaling problem, kinematic specification of dynamics has been cast as an "inverse dynamics" problem. Inverse dynamics, or the derivation of dynamics from kinematics, has been described, in turn, as a missing-dimension problem (Bingham, 1987b; Runeson and Frykholm, 1983; Warren and Shaw, 1985). Kinematic variables (e.g., position, velocity, acceleration, etc.) are defined using only the length and time dimensions [L, T].[3] For instance, position might be expressed in meters (dimensionally [L]) and velocity in meters per second (dimensionally [L/T]). On the other hand, dynamic variables (e.g., mass, force, stiffness, damping, etc.) also require the mass dimension [M]. So, mass might be expressed in kilograms (dimensionally [M]) and force in kilogram-meters per second squared (dimensionally [ML/T²]). For inverse dynamics, how is the missing mass dimension recovered from kinematics?

For instance, the dynamic equation describing a mass-spring oscillator is $m(d^2x/dt^2) = -kx$, where m is mass, k is stiffness, x is position, and d^2x/dt^2 is acceleration. The terms in this equation involve [M] because each includes a mass-related (i.e., dynamic) parameter, namely m or k, as well as kinematic variables x or d^2x/dt^2. Dimensionally, m and k are [M] and [M/T²] while x and d^2x/dt^2 are [L] and [L/T²], so each term in the equation is dimensionally a force, i.e., [ML/T²]. The dynamic equation determines motions or behaviors described via a kinematic solution equation, in this case $x = A\sin(\omega t + \varphi)$. In this equation, the amplitude, A, and the phase, φ, are kinematic constants that depend only on initial conditions. Thus, they are arbitrary in respect to the dynamics. In contrast, the angular frequency, ω, is determined by the two dynamic parameters, $\omega = (k/m)^{.5}$. In this ratio, the mass dimension cancels out leaving a quantity that is kinematic $(([M/T^2]/[M])^{.5} = [T^{-1}])$, and thus appropriate for the kinematic equation. However, because of this, the kinematics, used as information about the dynamics, can only yield a determination of the ratio of the dynamic parameters, k/m. Determination of unique values of either m or k is not possible. This is a typical instance of the missing-dimension problem of inverse dynamics.

A potentially general solution to this problem is revealed by studying a closely related type of dynamic, that of the simple pendulum. The key to the solution is the observation that a unique value for one parameter would be specified if *identifiable circumstances* constrained the value of the remaining parameter. The dynamic equation for the simple pendulum can be written as $(d^2\phi/dt^2) = (g/l)\sin\phi$, where ϕ is the angular position at the pivot, l is the length of the pendulum, and g is the gravitational acceleration. The situation seems the same as for the mass-spring system because the frequency of motion corresponds to a ratio of parameters, $\omega = (g/l)^{.5}$. However, g is a scaling invariant in the terrestrial sphere. Gravitationally determined trajectories appear as parabolas in phase space. By virtue of this characteristic form, gravitational trajectories can be recognized, in principle. This particular circumstance, or "uniquity condition" (Szücs, 1980), imposes an identifiable scaling constraint so that the frequency of motion (or its inverse, period) specifies the length of the pendulum. Indeed, as shown by Pittenger (1985, 1990), observers are able to evaluate pendulum lengths on the basis of periods of oscillation. Uniquity conditions may provide a general means by which scaling problems are solved (Bingham, 1988). If so, then the particular circumstances that determine a scaling constraint must be identifiable. This is a second way in which scaling would entail recognition.

At this point, the reader might have noted that there was no mass parameter in the pendulum equation. Dimensionally, the equation that I used was kinematic. g is an acceleration $[L/T^2]$ while l is a length $[L]$. However, following the Newtonian procedure of "force balance," the equation would first have been written as $ml^2(d^2\phi/dt^2) = mgl\sin\phi$, where $ml^2 = I$ is the rotational inertia. When the inertia is divided into both sides of the equation, the mass cancels and the terms in the resulting equation have kinematic dimensions only. This trick is not peculiar to the pendulum. For instance, the dynamic equation used to describe the mass-spring oscillator can also be written as $d^2x/dt^2 = -(k/m)x$, which has the dimensions of acceleration $[L/T^2]$. Nor does the elimination of the mass dimension mean that the "dynamics" were eliminated. To the contrary, the dynamics are simply those lawful relations that generate specific forms of behavior given initial (and boundary) conditions.

The fact that this strategy is general and paradigmatic[4] suggests that the "missing-dimension" characterization of the kinematic specification of dynamics is misleading. The problem is not to recover a missing mass dimension so much as to recognize a particular (perhaps scale-specific) type of event generated by a configuration of scaling parameters on kinematic variables.

Ultimately, dynamic equations can always be formulated in a dimensionless form in which no units are associated with any of the terms in the equation. A dimensionless equation is achieved by forming ratios among the elements in an equation so that the associated units cancel, leaving pure numbers (Baker, Westine, and Dodge, 1973; Emori and Schuring, 1977; Szücs, 1980; Thompson and Stewart, 1986). For instance, the equation for a force-driven damped mass-spring oscillator is as follows:

$$m\frac{d^2x}{dt^2} + b\frac{dx}{dt} + kx = F\cos\omega t \qquad (1)$$

Each term in this equation has the dimensions of force, $[ML/T^2]$. So dimensionally, the equation is:

$$[M]\left[\frac{L}{T^2}\right] + \left[\frac{M}{T}\right]\left[\frac{L}{T}\right] + \left[\frac{M}{T^2}\right][L] = \left[\frac{ML}{T^2}\right]\frac{[T]}{[T]}.$$

To write equation (1) in dimensionless form, one can formulate a set of dimensionless numbers (sometimes called pi numbers (Emori and Schuring, 1977)) in terms of ratios and products of the original set of parameters and variables.

$$\pi_1 = \frac{x}{x_0} \stackrel{d}{=} \frac{[L]}{[L]} \qquad \pi_2 = \omega t \stackrel{d}{=} \frac{[T]}{[T]} \qquad \pi_3 = \frac{bt}{m} \stackrel{d}{=} \frac{\left[\frac{M}{T}\right][T]}{[M]}$$

$$\pi_4 = \frac{kt}{b} \stackrel{d}{=} \frac{\left[\frac{M}{T^2}\right][T]}{\left[\frac{M}{T}\right]} \qquad \pi_5 = \frac{mF}{b^2 x_0} \stackrel{d}{=} \frac{[M]\left[\frac{ML}{T^2}\right]}{\left[\frac{M}{T}\right]^2[L]},$$

where x_0 is a reference length, such as the undeformed length of the spring. Next, one can write the original equation in terms of these dimensionless variables as follows:

$$\frac{d^2\pi_1}{d\pi_3{}^2} + \frac{d\pi_1}{d\pi_3} + \frac{\pi_1\pi_4}{\pi_3} = \pi_5\cos\pi_2 \qquad (2)$$

Equations (1) and (2) are analytically equivalent. When the parameters and variables in equation (2) take on values, they are pure numbers with no associated dimensions and the same is true of the solution equation which would be of the form:

$$\pi_1 = f(\pi_2, \pi_3, \pi_4, \pi_5).$$

See Szücs (1980, pp. 275–279) for additional discussion of this example and other techniques for achieving the same results. See also Baker et al. (1973, pp. 22–29). A closely related example can be found in Thompson and Stewart (1986, pp. 292–294) who used forcing frequency and amplitude to scale a forced oscillator system in dimensionless form. In this latter case, if the forcing were treated as a control function, then the behavior of the oscillator would be scaled intrinsically in terms of the controls. In any of these cases, dynamics and kinematics are made dimensionally commensurate because dimensions are removed and no missing-dimension problem exists. Nevertheless, the scaling problem remains because the scale values of dimensionless parameters are still at issue.

Essentially, one tailors an equation to express the dynamics most efficiently by placing an equation in the appropriate dimensionless form so that each dimensionless parameter is directly responsible for a particular aspect of the resulting behavior. Thus, the values of dimensionless parameters determine the specific behavior exhibited by a differential equation, especially in the case of nonlinear dynamics (Hirsch and Smale, 1974; Rosenberg, 1977; Thompson and Stewart, 1986). In principle, the dynamics can be arranged to exhibit scale invariance, that is, a lack of change in the form of behavior despite a change in scale. The dimensionless parameter values and associated behavior can be preserved over scale changes by affecting scale changes in the original dimensional parameters of proportionate degrees determined by the ratios in the dimensionless form of the equations (Mandelbrot, 1983; Schroeder, 1991; Thompson and Stewart, 1986). In the forced mass-spring example, as b, the damping, is changed, one would alter m, the mass, proportionately so as to preserve the value of π_3 and thus maintain the form of the behavior exhibited by the system. Of course, k and F would also have to be altered to preserve the values of π_4 and π_5, respectively.

The problem in the majority of actual events, as known all too well by scale engineers (Baker, Westine, and Dodge, 1973; Emori and Schuring, 1977), is that scale values along various dimensions cannot be arbitrarily varied. The values are associated with specific materials. Some values may occasionally be altered by substituting one material for another; however, a material usually determines, not just one, but a collection of relevant values along different dimensions (Baker, Westine, and Dodge, 1973, pp. 312–322; Emori and Schuring, 1977). So, a scale engineer will typically test a single functional property in a small-scale model that distorts other functionally important properties of the full-scale ship, airplane, or dam. In actual events, all of the ratios in an equation can be preserved over scale changes only in rare instances, and strictly never. The implication is that specific forms of motion are associated with particular types of events occurring at specific scales. This is why the small-scale models used to film disasters (e.g., collapsing dams, bridges, or buildings) in grade B science fiction films are usually quite obvious. Merely filming the small-scale event at high speed and scaling down the time leaves the trajectory forms unchanged and those forms are distorted in the small-scale event.

If the type of event can be recognized via the form of the behavior, then the scaling associated with relevant dynamic parameters might be determined. Generally, only the values of dimensionless parameters might be specified by trajectory forms. However, if recognizable circumstances (e.g., gravity, air resistance) were to constrain the values of dimensional parameters within the dimensionless ratios, then values of other dimensional parameters might also be determined.

I have shown in this section that the kinematic specification of dynamics is not a missing-dimension problem. The missing-dimension characterization is a form of dualism that would render kinematics and dynamics as fundamentally incommensurate aspects of an event. Ultimately, this would make kinematic specification of dynamics or of events impossible (not to mention mechanics itself). Both dynamics and kinematics can be expressed in dimensionless equations. Thus, they are entirely commensurate. Dimensions are relevant, nevertheless, to the formulation of a dynamical model. Dimensions are a necessary part of the bookkeeping required to proceed from law forms and extrinsic measurement procedures to a dynamical model of an event. But it is a mistake to reify such dimensional notation as fundamental ontological types. The so-called fundamental dimensions (i.e., mass, length, and time) are not fundamental. In mechanics, dimensional analysis requires three dimensions, but the particular dimensions vary in different formulations (Duncan, 1953; Ipsen, 1960; Langhaar, 1951; Sedov, 1959). The more productive focus in trying to understand the relation between kinematics and dynamics is on the (abstract) form of events. To anticipate, kinematics corresponds, in this qualitative perspective, to particular trajectory forms, whereas dynamics yields an entire family of trajectories. Kinematics is relatively local, whereas dynamics is relatively global.

Understanding Event Perception via the Qualitative Approach to Dynamics

In the qualitative approach to nonlinear dynamics, both dynamics and kinematics are construed geometrically as alternative, and therefore commensurate, descriptions of common underlying forms (Marmo, Saletan, Simoni, et al., 1985; Thompson and Stewart, 1986). The forms are described in terms of vector fields from the perspective of dynamics, whereas from a kinematic perspective they are described in terms of trajectories. The dynamic vectors are tangent to the kinematic trajectories at all points.

This qualitative characterization is both the more elegant and the more appropriate for two reasons at least.[5] First, a dynamic is determined by the form of the vector field or the trajectories. A dynamic cannot be identified with particular equations used to describe it because many different equations can be used to describe the same dynamic depending on the type of coordinates (Hirsch and Smale, 1974; Marmo et al., 1985). The form of the vector field or the corresponding phase-space trajectories remains the same despite change in coordinates.

Second, a qualitative construal of dynamics is the most natural given our intended application in event perception (Bingham, 1987a; Kugler, 1983). This, given as a reason for a qualitative interpretation, might seem rather circular in this context. However, given the fact that observers do perceive events (i.e., what has sometimes been called an "existence proof"), together with the fact that dynamic factors determine kinematic forms of motion and that kinematics must provide the information allowing events to be recognized, then there must be a commensurate or symmetry relation between kinematics and dynamics. To the extent that dynamic types and perceived types of events correspond, the mapping between kinematics and dynamics must be invertible and by definition there can be no missing-dimension problem. The only possible solution is that provided by the qualitative interpretation.

Events as Dynamics Coupled with Uniquity Conditions

In the linear tradition, dynamics as such is distinguished from specification of the range of potential parameter values and other "uniquity conditions" (Szücs, 1980). The goal in dynamics has been to generalize across events involving different types of objects or materials. Uniquity conditions, namely parameter values as well as initial and boundary conditions, must be specified before solutions to linear dynamics can be derived. These uniquity conditions have been held separate from the dynamic itself because they necessarily restrict the generality of the description. However, the relation between parameter values and dynamics is not so dissociable in nonlinear dynamics because the specific forms of behavior are closely tied to the values of the parameters. With the recognition that dynamics must be identified not with equations, but with forms of behavior, uniquity conditions become an integral part of the dynamics.

Only by tying strongly restricted ranges of parameter values and other uniquity conditions to a given dynamic can we establish a correspondence between perceptually recognizable types of events and dynamics. This means that the formal character of dynamics must be enlarged to incorporate mathematical apparatus that has not been included in the dynamics of the linear tradition. Dynamical systems theory is based on the operations of the calculus which become undefined at discontinuities in trajectories (Hirsch and Smale, 1974; Tufillaro, Abbott, and Reilly, 1992). Some discontinuities are merely effects of the scale of measurement and can be handled by appropriately upgrading the (nonlinear) dynamics at the appropriate scale. For instance, when differential equations have been used to describe the damping of motion in an event involving viscous or kinetic friction, actual cessation of motion has occurred only in infinite time where the trajectory finally asymptotes at zero velocity. In actual events, motion ceases in relatively brief finite time as friction transits from kinetic to static form or as a lubricating substance becomes adhesive at low shear velocities. Nevertheless, improved models could capture such transitions as highly nonlinear forms of damping.

On the other hand, discontinuities are also produced by impacts and contact between object surfaces. These are extremely common in daily events.

The problem in this case is that the relative location of surfaces is contingent, not determinate. Once the contingencies are established, an event does unfold in a determinate fashion that reflects the particular contingencies. Such contingencies are uniquity conditions. To the extent that they are specified in the behavior of a system, they must be included in its dynamics. This entails two modifications in dynamical systems models of actually perceived events (Bingham, 1990). First, piecewise continuous dynamical systems are required and second, some form of Boolean logic will have to be integrated with the calculus of smooth dynamical systems. Boolean logic is a formal means of handling contingencies as conditionals. For instance, modeling the trajectories in a free fall and bouncing event requires a projectile motion dynamic during one position-dependent portion of the trajectory and an extremely stiff mass-spring oscillatory dynamic during another. (For another example, see Thompson and Stewart, 1986, pp. 291–320.) The forms of the trajectories that result are specific both to the nature of the event as a free fall and bounce and to the contingent height of the object above the surface with which it collides (Muchisky and Bingham, 1992). Using Boolean logic, one tests state variables (i.e., positions or velocities) to determine when trajectories have entered regions of the state space that have been assigned different smooth dynamics.

There are two uniquity conditions that are universal in the terrestrial sphere but that are not usually tied to dynamics. One is temporal while the other is spatial. Dynamics is generally isotropic with respect to both time and space. The anisotropy (or irreversibility) of time is a well-recognized problem in the context of linear dynamics (Prigogene, 1980; Prigogene and Stengers, 1984). Nevertheless, for the vast majority of perceptible events, identity is not preserved over time reversal as revealed by Gibson in his study of reversible vs. irreversible events (Gibson and Kaushall, 1973). In such instances, the positive sign on the time variable must be preserved as a uniquity condition. In the terrestrial sphere, dynamics is also spatially anisotropic because gravity contributes as a dynamic scale factor to the form of all perceptible events (including the activity of potential observers). Gravity establishes a definite orientation in the terrestrial domain reflected in the resulting asymmetric forms of events. Objects fall downward and roll down hills to come to rest in valleys. Bingham et al. (in press) found that the perceived significance of many kinematic forms changed when, unknown to observers, the orientation with respect to gravity of event kinematics in displays was changed. Clearly in such cases, both the sign and the value of gravity must be included as uniquity conditions intrinsic to the event dynamics. In general, any factor that contributes to a determination of kinematic forms and the perceived significance of those forms must be included in the dynamics used to model an event.

The final type of uniquity condition that must be included as an inherent part of dynamic event models are initial or boundary conditions. These are values that determine transient states or trajectories. The focus of study in the qualitative approach to nonlinear dynamics is usually on stable trajectories (or attractors).[6] Stable behavior corresponds to phase trajectories that do not change radically in form with small changes in parameter values or in initial conditions. With the appropriate changes in parameters, however, the trajectories will exhibit a bifurcation, that is, a rapid transition to a new stable behavior.

In the study of event perception, the forms of interest must include those of transient trajectories as much as, or more than, those of stable trajectories. All inanimate events are damped and so ultimately cycle down to point attractors. However, once the attractor has been reached, the event is over. The most informative states are the transients yielding optical flow. Examples of such transients would be a branch set oscillating by the wind, a ball that has been dropped and bounces or rolls downhill, a coin that has been dropped and rolls and rattles to a stop, and finally, a swing oscillating until coming to rest after having been abandoned by a child.

The forms of trajectories, transient and stable alike, can be partially classified according to attractor states. But as indicated by the examples, a more specific classification (including perhaps the metric forms of trajectories) will be required in event perception. Exactly what level of scaling (i.e., ratio, interval, ordinal, etc.) will be required to capture the relevant qualitative characteristics of kinematic forms depends both on a theoretical determination of the qualitative properties of event kinematics that are preserved in the mapping to optical flows and on the empirical determination of the detectable qualitative properties of optical flow (e.g., Norman and Todd, 1992).

14.5 MAPPING FROM EVENT KINEMATICS TO OPTICAL FLOWS

If qualitative properties of an event trajectory are to provide information allowing event identification, then those properties must map into optical flows. What are the qualitative properties that map into optical flows? Certain properties are bound to be preserved. For instance, discontinuities corresponding to impacts will map to discontinuities in optical flows. Periodic events will map to periodic optical flows. However, other properties will be lost. For instance, event trajectories exhibiting different conic sections (i.e., an elliptical curve vs. a parabola) are confused in optical flow. Spatial metrics are lost because trajectories are scaled by viewing distance in the mapping to optical flows. This scale transformation induces changes in trajectory shapes because the scaling variable (i.e., distance) is itself a kinematic variable and not a constant. However (assuming an immobile point of observation) the course of values of the scaling variable is phase-locked to the remaining kinematic variables so that *the forms in optical phase space are related to those in event phase space by projective transformations, just as the forms of objects are related to their imaged forms.* The mapping of forms in phase space is essentially the same as the mapping of three-dimensional object forms because the metric structure of the time dimension in events is preserved while the spatial metric is lost in the same way as for objects.

To illustrate the projection of event trajectory forms into patterns of optical flow, I did a simulation of a ball rolling along a U-shaped groove from its release until it nearly stopped moving following appropriate laws of motion. The ball was inelastic, 0.27 m in diameter, and weighed 1 kg. It rolled without slipping along an inelastic U-shaped surface that was 1.0 m high and 2.5 m wide. The event included many aspects typical of rigid-body events, including translation along a constraint surface accomplished via rotations; harmonic motion associated with the gravitational potential; and dissipation associated with air resistance and surface friction. Together, these produce kinematics typical of a damped harmonic oscillator, as shown in figure 14.2. (This can be shown analytically; e.g., see Becker, 1954, pp. 206–207.)

Motion was confined to a vertical X-Y plane. However, the plane of motion did not lie perpendicular to the visual direction,[7] so this case was sufficiently general. The perspective was from directly above the event looking down, so that significant components of motion occurred both parallel and

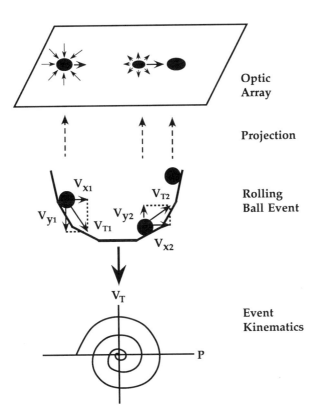

Figure 14.2 The kinematics of the rolling ball event and their projection into optical flow. Event kinematics: A plot of the ball tangential velocity, V_T, against the ball position along the surface yielded a spiral as the ball's oscillation back and forth damped out. Projection to optics: The X component of V_T mapped into a component common to all optical points projected from the ball, represented by a single vector in the projection plane. The Y component of V_T mapped into radial inflow or outflow (i.e., "relative motion") as the ball moved away from or toward the point of observation, respectively.

Dynamics and the Problem of Visual Event Recognition

perpendicular to the visual direction. A rigid-body analysis was employed. Accordingly, translatory and rotational components of motion were separated. Each of these components map respectively into common and relative components in optical flow (see figure 14.2). Johansson (1950, 1973, 1976) has shown that the visual system behaves as if decomposing optical flow into these components. (Subsequently, I discuss the difficulties associated with an inability to assume rigid-body motion.)

Using orthographic projection, as shown in figure 14.2, the tangential velocity of the ball, V_T, maps into the optics via two components, V_X and V_Y. V_X, perpendicular to the visual direction, maps into the optics as a vector common to all points from the ball. V_Y, parallel to the visual direction, maps to a set of vectors organized in a radial inflow or outflow pattern depending on the momentary approach or retreat of the ball, respectively. Thus, the event kinematics map via components into very different aspects of the optical flow.

I simulated the event from the dynamics using numerical methods. The simulated event duration was 12 seconds. A smoothly curved U-shaped surface was approximated via a set of nine contiguous linear segments. Discontinuities that appeared in the resulting trajectories reflected small collisions at transition points between successive segments.

Kinematics of the Center of Mass: Common Translatory Motion

The motion of the center of mass corresponds to translatory motion common to every point in the ball. We reduced the dimensionality of the translatory event kinematics from four dimensions ($X, Y, V_x,$ and V_y) to three by using the tangential velocity, $[V_x^2 + V_y^2]^{.5} = V_T$. These kinematics are depicted in figure 14.3 where the trajectory through a phase space consisting of the X and Y position and the tangential velocity, V_T is plotted together with the X and Y components projected orthographically on the X-Vx and Y-Vy planes respectively. The U-shaped path was also projected on the X-Y plane.

The problem was mapping the forms on the X-Vx and Y-Vy planes into the optics from a perspective at some distance above the event (i.e., in the Y direction). The X-Vx component mapped via a single scaling factor, the viewing distance Y, into a single optical component common to all points from the ball (i.e., divide each by Y). As shown in figure 14.4A, this component carried the essential spiraling damped oscillator form of the original trajectory. However, based on this alone, the event could not be distinguished from horizontal, planar motion produced by an oscillating air hockey puck attached to a spring. The Y-Vy component was essential to completely capture the translatory event structure. This is an important point because in recent reviews research on motion parallel to a projection plane has been reviewed separately from research on perpendicular motion with the corresponding implication that the two components are functionally distinct, the former being used for event perception and the latter for visually guided

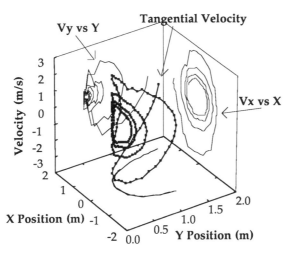

Figure 14.3 The tangential velocity trajectory of the ball plotted against X-Y position, with the corresponding path projected on the X-Y plane. The V_y-Y and V_x-X components were projected onto the respective planes.

activity (Anstis, 1986; Regan, Kaufman, and Lincoln, 1986). Clearly, this cannot be the case.

Next I examined the projection of the Y-V_y component. This did not map directly into a single common component of the optical flow. Using a linear approximation appropriate for the viewing distance, the form on the Y-Vy plane could be mapped, via a single scale factor Y, into optical variables detectable by human observers, namely image size and the rate of expansion (or contraction) of the image. To achieve this mapping, I divided object radius, r, by viewing distance, Y, yielding image size. Taking the derivative of image size, I computed image expansion rate as rVy/Y^2. As shown in figure 14.4B, a plot of rate of expansion vs. image size preserved the form of the Y-Vy phase portrait.[8]

The structure carried into the optics along the Y component was more easily interpreted in a plot of expansion rate vs. X/Y. The latter is the optical correlate of X position. This plot reproduced the form of an X-Vy plot. Trajectories that were successively interspliced in figures 14.3 and 14.4B were unfolded in figure 14.4C, revealing more plainly the trajectory that resulted as the ball rolled up one side of the U, stopped, and rolled down again, reaching zero Vy at the bottom of the U, rolling up the other side of the U to a stop, and so on. The phase-locked relation between the X and V_Y components enabled this plot and reflected the fact that *a perspective on a single three-dimensional form* (a single trajectory in X-Y-V_T phase space) was being described.

To summarize, forms associated with both X and Y components of the center of mass trajectory were mapped successfully into forms associated with detectable optical flow variables. Both components of motion were required to specify the translatory motion of the ball.

Dynamics and the Problem of Visual Event Recognition

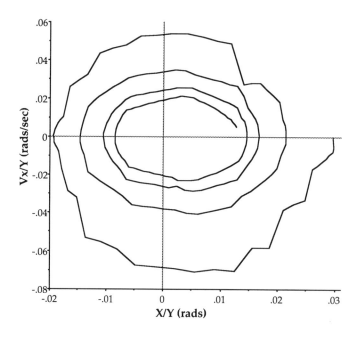

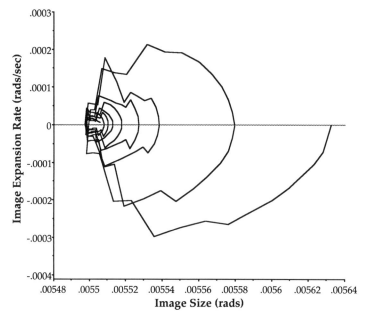

Figure 14.4 (*A*) The V_x-X component mapped into corresponding optical variables via parallel projection. (*B*) The V_y-Y component mapped into corresponding optical variables via parallel projection. (*C*) A plot of V_y vs. X mapped into corresponding optical variables.

Geoffrey P. Bingham

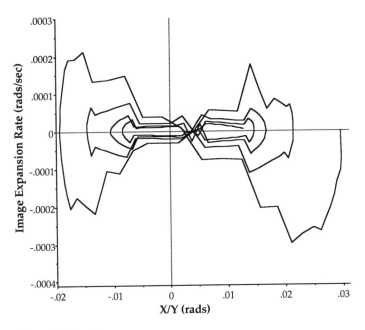

Figure 14.4 (cont.)

Rotational Motion About the Center of Mass

Next, the rotational motion of the ball must be considered. To start simply, the rotational kinematics will be examined within a frame of reference fixed in the ball, ignoring the translatory motion of the ball. In figure 14.5A, the ball is shown side-on, looking along its axis of rotation. Over the course of the event, the angular velocity of the ball about this axis, V_a, varied exactly as did the velocity of the center of mass, V_T. Multiplying V_a by the perpendicular distance, L, from the axis of rotation to the ball surface yielded V_L, the instantaneous linear velocity of corresponding points on the ball surface. This linear velocity vector was of constant magnitude for each point about the axis of rotation within any plane parallel to the plane of motion, as shown in figure 14.5A. Within the plane of motion through the center of the ball, L was equal to the radius of the ball and V_L was equal at each moment to V_T. Moving out of this plane along the ball surface toward the point on the side where the axis of rotation pierced the ball surface, V_L shrank to zero as did L, as shown in figure 14.5B.

As shown in figure 14.5C, when the frame of reference was changed from the (moving) ball to the (fixed) constraint surface, V_T was brought back into consideration and V_L was added to V_T at each point on the ball because V_T was common to all points on the ball. The result was that the ball axis of rotation moved at V_T while the part of the ball in contact with the constraint surface was (momentarily) at rest ($-V_L + V_T = 0$) and the top of the ball opposite this contact point moved at $2V_T$ (because $V_L = V_T$).

Dynamics and the Problem of Visual Event Recognition

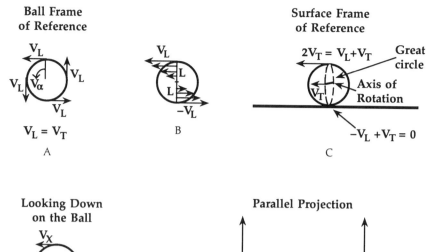

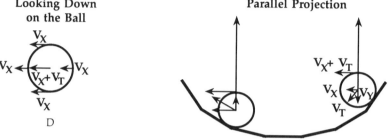

Figure 14.5 (*A*) Ball rotation represented in a frame of reference fixed in the ball. V_T is removed. V_α is the rotational velocity; L is the distance from the axis of rotation to a given point on the ball surface; V_L is the tangential velocity at a point on the ball surface. For points around the midline of the ball, $V_L = V_T$. (*B*) Variation in V_L moving along the ball surface from the midline to the point where the axis of rotation pierces the surface. (*C*) Ball motion represented in a frame of reference fixed in the constraint surface on which it rolls. The axis of rotation translates at V_T. The tangential velocity at the top of the ball is $2V_T$ while at the bottom point in contact with the constraint surface, it is 0. (*D*) Ball motion looking straight down on the ball. At the contour, tangent velocity from rotational motion is pointed directly toward or away from the point of observation and so is lost. Only the V_x component of V_T remains. (*E*) The components for parallel projection into optical flow.

Three points in this kinematic structure are uniquely identifiable. The point on the ball surface pierced by the axis of rotation is identifiable as the center of a vortex of velocities. This point has no rotational component of motion, only the translatory component, V_T.

The points on the top and bottom of the ball are also unique points identifiable as the points of maximum and minimum velocity respectively. These points and the gradient of velocities running between them provide information about the location of the constraint surface relative to the ball. Along a great circle formed by intersecting the ball surface with a plane perpendicular to the direction of V_T and containing the axis of rotation, velocities would follow a gradient from zero at the point of contact with the constraint surface to $2V_T$ at the opposite point. Viewing the event from a distance directly above, the velocity of all points along the contour of the ball's image would be the V_x component of V_T as shown in figure 14.5D, whereas points in

Geoffrey P. Bingham

the interior of the ball's image would follow a gradient up to a velocity of $V_X + V_T$ at the center of the image.

The rate structures associated with the rotational motion of the ball are qualitatively equivalent to those associated with the translatory motion of the center of mass of the ball. Each of the velocities within the gradient along the ball surface project to corresponding X and Y components depending on perspective. These components would follow phase-space trajectories identical in form to those described above for X and Y components of V_T. For instance, viewing the event from a distance directly above, the velocity components at the center of the ball's image would be $V_X + V_T$ and V_Y, respectively, as shown in figure 14.5D and E. The form of the rate structure associated with the $V_X + V_T$ component is qualitatively equivalent to that of the X-V_X plot.

To summarize, qualitative properties of the rate structure of this event mapped successfully into optical flows via both the rotational and translatory components of the ball's motion.

As will be shown subsequently, the spatial gradient of flow vectors associated with the rotational motion provides information about the shape of the ball (Todd and Reichel, 1989; Todd and Akerstrom, 1987). This spatial gradient *in the context of the rate structure* also provides information about the ball's relation to the constraint surface, the surface lying at the momentary point of zero flow. The orientation of the constraint surface, in turn, provides information about the direction of gravity which corresponds to the direction of the constraint surface at moments when V_T reaches its relative maxima along the trajectory. For the ball to roll without slipping, the constraint surface must always lie below the center of mass of the ball. That it does so is specified by the way the projected velocities vary along the constraint surface.

14.5 THE DEGREES-OF-FREEDOM PROBLEM IN VISUAL EVENT PERCEPTION

Nearly all extant analyses of "structure from motion" use the rigidity assumption (e.g., Andersen, 1990; Horn, 1986; Koenderink, 1986; Koenderink and van Doorn, 1975, 1976, 1987; Lee, 1974, 1980; Longuet-Higgins and Prazdny, 1980; Nakayama and Loomis, 1974; Owen, 1990; Rieger, 1983; Rieger and Lawton, 1985; Ullman, 1984; Warren, 1990; Waxman and Ullman, 1985; Zacharias, 1990). The rigidity assumption has been used because it drastically reduces the degrees of freedom in optical flow. Using results from analytical mechanics (Rosenberg, 1977; Whittaker, 1944), the motion of a rigid body can be described in terms of the translation of its center of mass combined with a rotation around that center. Alternatively, translation and rotation relative to the point of observation can be used. In either case, the positional degrees of freedom of the three-dimensional motion are reduced from $3n$ degrees of freedom, where n is the number of distinguishable points in the body, to 6 degrees of freedom, 3 to specify the position of the center of mass and 3 to describe the body's orientation about its center. In mechanics, additional degrees of freedom are required to specify a body's state of motion. The velocities (but only the velocities) corresponding to each of the positional degrees of freedom must also be specified at some time, t_0. When these are specified together with a dynamic, the subsequent motion of the object is determined.

Ultimately, however, the rigidity assumption is untenable because it requires that an observer know in advance what he or she is perceiving to be able to perceive, i.e., a rigid-body event. This is an obvious paradox. Alternatively, the assumption restricts the relevant models to an unrealistically small set of perceivable situations, excluding any sort of nonrigid event. On the other hand, without the rigid-body assumption, the degrees of freedom required to specify the state in an event is $6n$, i.e., 3 positions and 3 velocities for each distinguishable point. Depending on how one distinguishes points on an object surface (with the projection to optics in mind), this number grows indefinitely large fast. Furthermore, the problem projects right into the optics despite both the loss of points via occlusion by opaque surfaces and the reduction to a total of four coordinates for each point in the optical flow (2 positions and 2 corresponding velocities).

The nature and severity of this problem will be conveyed by returning to the rolling ball example. The kinematics of the event were described in spherical coordinates with the origin fixed at an unmoving point of observation located about 2.5 m from the event. The trajectories of a mere 12 points on the surface of the ball were selected for study, 4 points at 90-degree intervals around the ball in each of three planes parallel to the plane of motion, one plane at the center coincident with the plane of motion and one plane to either side at 70% of the distance from the center to the side of the ball. In other respects, the simulation was the same as described earlier, including the duration, which was 12 seconds. The resulting event trajectories were projected into optical flow.

The optical flow trajectories were captured in a three-dimensional optical phase space by using θ and ϕ position coordinates together with the tangential velocity to the optical path or orbit. θ and ϕ are visual angles in a polar projection appropriate for viewing at nearer distances. Only components perpendicular to the visual direction at each point in the event projected into the optics, each scaled by the distance along the visual direction. However, as the ball rolled, each point on its surface successively went out of view as it rolled underneath the ball and then into view as it rolled over the top of the ball. The result was that only discontinuous pieces of trajectories appeared in the optical flow, including only those portions of the trajectories that were not occluded by the ball itself. The optical phase portrait appears in figure 14.6.

If we were able to count only single trajectories associated with each of the 12 points on the ball, then the number of degrees of freedom would be 12×4 coordinates $= 48$. However, as can be seen in figure 14.6, it is not obvious how the various trajectory pieces go together. The trajectories are

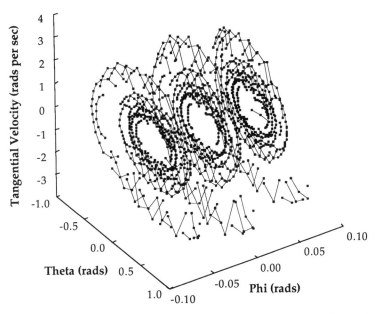

Figure 14.6 An optical phase-space portrait of the ball rolling event. Trajectories correspond to 12 points around the ball surface, 4 around the midline, and 4 around a point to either side of the midline. Tangential optical velocities plotted against two optical (angular) position coordinates, theta and phi. The phi-axis was rescaled relative to the theta-axis to better reveal the structure in the trajectories.

not piecewise continuous. The pieces are separated by significant intervals. Thus, the degrees of freedom in optical phase space had better be enumerated by counting the degrees of freedom associated with each trajectory piece. The 12 points moving over 12 seconds yielded 244 trajectory pieces, each requiring ultimately 4 coordinates which I reduced to 3 using the tangential velocity, with $244 \times 3 = 732$ degrees of freedom resulting! This was from a mere 12 points on the ball. The distinguishable optical texture elements on such a surface could easily yield more than 1000 points resulting in over 45,000 degrees of freedom.

Solving the Degrees-of-Freedom Problem via Symmetries in Optical Phase Space

Recall the description of the rolling ball example with which I began this chapter. The observer is confronted with a random array of moving patches each of which appears, moves a modest distance in the display, and then disappears (perhaps never to be seen again). Despite the apparent complexity and difficulties of this display, observers immediately perceive the display as of a rolling ball. How is this possible? With the denial of the rigid-motion assumption, we arrive at the unmitigated problem of visual event identification. How is the tremendous number of degrees of freedom associated with

Dynamics and the Problem of Visual Event Recognition

the trajectories in optical flow reduced to the relatively few degrees of freedom associated with the coherent and well-formed motions in recognizable events? The effect of occlusion combines with the degrees-of-freedom problem to exacerbate the problem by orders of magnitude. Resort must be made to time-extended samples of optical flow to find enough structure to solve the identification problem. (Time-extended trajectories also yield stability of the optical structure in response to perturbation by noisy measurements.) The strategy will be to find symmetries among the trajectories in the phase plane portrait and to use them effectively to collapse the structure, reducing the degrees of freedom and, at the same time, obtaining coherence and revealing the underlying form.[9]

A glance at figure 14.6 reveals that the phase trajectories contain a number of symmetries (i.e., commonalities of form) that might be used to reduce the degrees of freedom in the optical flow. For instance, the spiral on the phase plane, characteristic of damped oscillatory events, can be seen in common across the three sampled planes of motion, although this form becomes rather lost among the overlapping trajectory pieces past the first cycle. In an earlier section of this chapter, the optical flow from the rolling ball was described using properties such as the contour of the ball's image and the centroid of the image. The advantage in deriving trajectories from these image properties was that the issue of occlusion was avoided, i.e., the resulting trajectories were continuous.

To illustrate this, the flow at 5 points in the ball's image was computed including the centroid as well as the front, back, and opposite side points on the contour relative to the common direction of motion. The resulting optical trajectories were plotted in figure 14.6 where the spiraling forms of the trajectories could be seen much more clearly, as could the symmetries among the trajectories. The continuous trajectories in figure 14.7 certainly represent a reduction in the degrees of freedom from those in figure 14.6.

Note that in a patch-light display there is no closed, continuous contour forming the boundary of the ball's image. There is only a random array of moving patches yielding trajectories, as in figure 14.6. The event is nevertheless identifiable. The question, therefore, is how might we derive the coherent trajectories in figure 14.7 from those in figure 14.6? To solve this question, we need to examine the structure of the trajectories appearing in figure 14.6 more closely. Figure 14.8A shows the trajectories projected from the 4 points around the middle of the ball. The highly structured character of the phase portrait is quite apparent in this figure. Each separate trajectory piece or hoop corresponds to the motion of a single point on the ball as it rises up from the back over the top of the ball and disappears in the front. The variations in θ distances between the ends of each hoop in turn correspond to the variations in image size. The rounded form of the hoops is related to the rotation of the ball. The rounded trajectory form is created as the rotational velocity component is progressively added in and then removed as a point travels from the back over the top to the front of the ball. This first symmetry is common to

Geoffrey P. Bingham

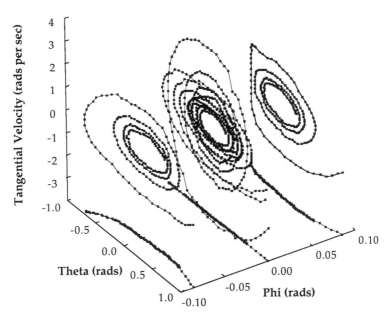

Figure 14.7 An optical phase portrait derived by tracking 4 points on the ball image contour plus the point in the center of the image. The points on the contour were points front and back on the midline and side points farthest from the midline. The paths of motion of these points were projected onto the theta-phi plane.

the trajectories in every plane parallel to the plane of motion and will ultimately allow us to collapse the trajectories in all the planes down to those in one plane, for instance that in figure 14.8A. But first, we should analyze the structure in that plane.

The most important symmetry is the envelope surrounding the train of successive hoops. This provides the means of deriving the trajectories of figure 14.7 from those of figure 14.6. As can be seen in figure 14.8B, where I have plotted one cycle of the motion, the trajectories from figure 14.7 form the boundary on the envelope of trajectory pieces from figure 14.6. The bottom ends of the hoops correspond to the front and back occluding contours of the ball's image. The trajectories of these contour points are implicit, yet apparent in the flow from a mere 4 points. If the trajectories of more points were to be included, the contour trajectories would be more densely specified. The same is true of the image centroid, although in that case it is the apex of successive hoops that is involved.

An alternative and natural coordinate system in which to capture these trajectories is in terms of a phase angle and an energy-related measure of radial distance which I will call "energy." These are polar coordinates on the θ-by-tangential velocity plane (i.e., the plane in figure 14.8A and B) with the origin in the center of the spiral.[10] Thus, these coordinates are intrinsic to the phase portrait. They are determined by landmarks on the trajectories themselves, namely, the points of peak and zero velocity. As implied by the

Dynamics and the Problem of Visual Event Recognition

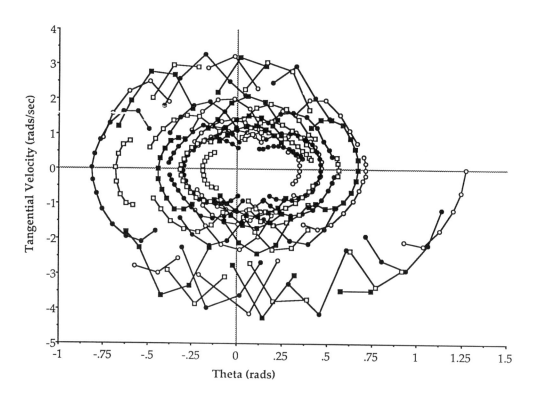

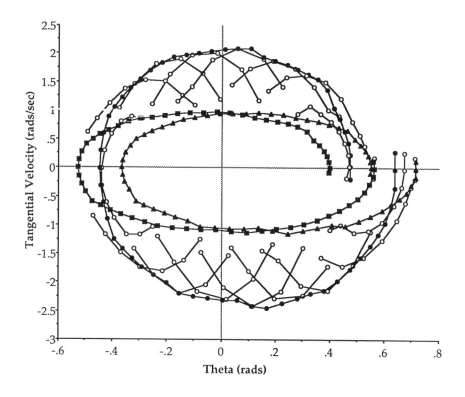

Geoffrey P. Bingham

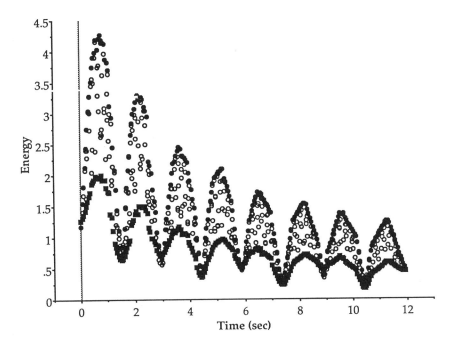

Figure 14.8 (*A*) Trajectories from 4 points around the midline of the ball. The 4 points in turn are represented by open circles, filled circles, open squares, and filled squares, respectively. Note that without these symbols, it would be impossible to determine which trajectory pieces represent a given point in common. (*B*) One cycle from the trajectories in figure 14.6A together (open circles) with midline trajectories from figure 14.5. The contour point on the front of the ball is represented by filled squares; the back of the ball by filled triangles, and the center of the ball image by filled circles. (*C*) The energies for all of the trajectories from figure 14.9A and B plotted against time. Open circles represent the 4 points tracked around the midline of the ball. Filled circles represent the center point of the ball image. Filled squares represent contour points.

coordinate labels, these coordinates also relate directly to the underlying dynamics.

When the trajectories in figure 14.8B were plotted in figure 14.8C as energy vs. time, the manner in which continuous trajectories bounded the envelope of the trajectory pieces could be seen quite clearly.

Returning to figure 14.6, I note that the properties revealed on the center plane obtained as well on the planes to the side. This suggests the solution to the next problem, which was to relate the motions on side planes to those on the center plane. The three sets of trajectories were 1:1 phase-locked. This could be seen by linearly regressing the phase angles (i.e., the first polar coordinate) for corresponding center and side points as "parameterized" by time. This is shown in figure 14.9A. The results were slopes near 1 (= .97 or better), intercepts near 0 ($\pm$.002 or less) and $r^2 = .999$ in all cases. The phase-locked relation between the center and side trajectories meant, given the symmetry of form, that I could collapse the different sets of trajectories

Dynamics and the Problem of Visual Event Recognition

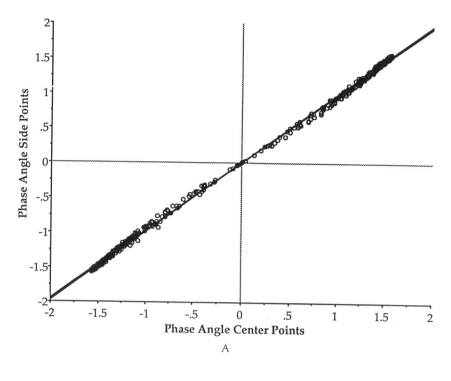

A

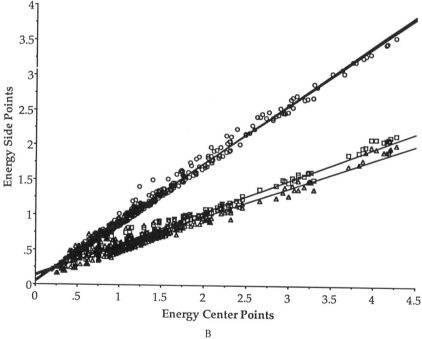

B

Figure 14.9 (*A*) Phase angle of the 4 points tracked about the ball midline linearly regressed on phase angles for the 4 points tracked about a line 70% of the distance from the midline to the side of the ball. (*B*) Energy of the 4 points tracked about the ball midline linearly regressed on the energies for the 8 points tracked about lines 70% of the distance from the midline to the

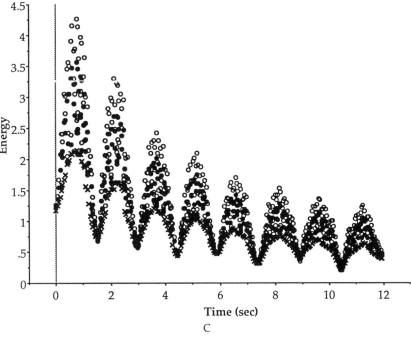

C

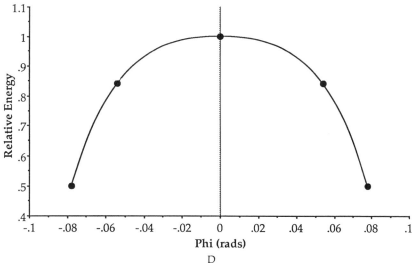

D

side of the ball (open circles); on the energies for the contour points, both front and back (open triangles) and side points (open squares). (C) Energies for the 4 points tracked about the midline (open circles), for the 4 points tracked about a line 70% of the distance to the side (filled circles), and for a contour point on the side (x's). (D) Slopes of the regressions in B plotted against the mean phi position for the corresponding points on the ball and fitted with a polynomial curve.

by normalizing to a common scale, e.g., rescaling by dividing in each case by the peak energy and reducing all trajectories to a common set with a peak energy of 1. These, in turn, could be reduced to trajectories of the same form as the center trajectories appearing in figure 14.7.

Of course, these symmetries of form also serve to make obvious the differences in scale among the sets of trajectories. This is important because the differences in energies (or radial lengths) is also informative. As is apparent in figure 14.7, the sizes of the spirals decrease from those corresponding to the middle of the ball to those at its sides. The relative heights of energies on the center plane, on the plane 70% of the distance to the side contour point, and at the side contour point appear in figure 14.9C plotted against time. The energy of the center points was linearly regressed on that for corresponding side points as parameterized by time, as well as on the energy for points on the contour at the back. The results are shown in figure 14.9B. Center point energy regressed on energy for side points 70% of the way to the outside edge of the ball yielded slopes of .84 with intercepts near 0. When center point energy was regressed on energy for the side point on the contour, the mean slope was .52. When center point energy was regressed on energy for the back point on the contour, the mean slope was .47. These results mean that if I assign 1.0 to the height of the trajectories along the middle of the ball, then the height of the trajectories 70% of the distance toward the sides is .84, while the height of the trajectories on the side contour is .52 (and on the back contour, .47). The relative heights of the middle trajectories, the side point trajectories, and the side contour point trajectories were plotted in figure 14.9D against their (mean) ϕ-coordinate values respectively and fitted with a polynomial curve. There one can see that these relative energies represent the shape of the ball.

Undoubtedly, I could find additional information in the qualitative properties of these trajectories with further analysis. These trajectories are replete with structure that can be discovered via processes sensitive to the symmetries among trajectory forms. Once discovered, the symmetries enable a reduction of the degrees of freedom and a recovery of coherent form which relates directly to the generative dynamics.

14.7 THE NECESSITY OF ANALYZING RATE STRUCTURES IN OPTICAL FLOW FOR EVENT RECOGNITION

Confronting the problems associated with the rate structures in events is not optional in the study of optical flow. By definition, information in optical flow is found in the time evolution of spatially distributed optical structure. One can represent the spatial distribution of the instantaneous values of rate variables as a vector field, but such a snapshot will fail to capture structure specific to given events.

The amount of information contained in the optical phase-space trajectories for the rolling ball should be compared to that contained in the instantaneous optical flow field analyzed in the majority of studies on optical flow.

Orbits corresponding to the middle and side point trajectories were projected on the theta-phi plane in figure 14.7. That these orbits in theta-phi configuration space contain considerably less information is rather apparent. The instantaneous optical flow field would correspond at some arbitrary moment to a set of 2 successive points along each orbit projected on the floor of figure 14.7 and the line drawn between the 2 points in each case. The result would be three very short line segments. This is not quite correct, however. The more appropriate projection would be from points along trajectories in figure 14.6. Also, a more dense set of points would be required than the 12 points represented in figure 14.6. Nevertheless, the character of the event could not be conveyed, no matter how dense the vector field.

Although some information about the shape of the ball can be gleaned from the instantaneous vector field (Koenderink and van Doorn, 1975, 1976, 1978; Waxman and Ullman, 1985) and the assumption of rigidity can often be checked (Longuet-Higgins and Prazdny, 1980), the nature of the event can only be apprehended from the information contained in time-extended trajectories. The spatial distribution in the optical flow corresponding to the rolling ball changed over time in nonarbitrary ways, such that any single sample in time of the spatial distribution could not be representative of the optical structure projected from the event. At endpoints of the trajectories, the ball momentarily stopped moving as it reversed direction and the optical flow field (instantaneously) ceased to exist. Along the trajectory, the point of maximum flow varied in its relative position within the contours of the ball's image. The flow field would not be strictly the same at any two points along the trajectory except at the two endpoints where the flow was null.

Rather than an insufficiency of structure, optical phase portraits contain an overabundance of structure that must be used to reduce the tremendous number of degrees of freedom associated with optical flows. The structure inheres in the forms of trajectory pieces and in symmetries existing across those forms. Of course, the symmetries or similarities of form must be noted to allow their use in reducing the degrees of freedom in optical flows. We have not ventured to describe processes instantiated in the sensory apparatus that would effect the measurements appropriate to uncovering symmetries and forms in optical phase space. Rather, by showing that the relevant properties of trajectories in events map into corresponding properties of optical trajectories and that such properties must be detected to recognize events, I have developed a job description for the sensory apparatus.

ACKNOWLEDGMENTS

This research was supported by National Science Foundation grant BNS-9020590. I express my gratitude to Esther Thelen, James Todd, Dennis Proffitt, and an anonymous reviewer for reading and commenting on an earlier version of this manuscript and acknowledge the assistance of Michael Stassen in deriving and performing the calculations reported in this chapter.

NOTES

1. Phase-space trajectories will not be sufficient for unique characterization of all events, some of which will require an event space, i.e., phase space plus a time axis (Rosenberg, 1977). Do not confuse this event space with an event phase space that is used in contrast to an optical phase space.

2. A symmetry is something that remains the same despite some change in other aspects of a form. For instance, the shape of a circle drawn on paper remains the same when the paper is translated along a table top. See Shaw, McIntyre, and Mace (1974) for a related discussion.

3. Dimensions appear in brackets in uppercase, whereas parameters or variables appear in lowercase.

4. The study of the pendulum was instrumental to the development of dynamics (Dijksterhuis, 1961; Jammer, 1957). Pendular motion was the core event investigated by dynamicists from Galileo, through Huygens (in particular), to Newton, and beyond. In modern nonlinear dynamics, the (force-driven) pendulum remains paradigmatic (Berge, Pomeau, and Vidal, 1984; Tufillaro, Abbott, and Reilly, 1992). In historical perspective, the dynamics of the pendulum is the epitome of dynamics.

5. Historically, it has been more productive to pursue dynamic properties as qualitative, rather than as material entities. The problem in construing dynamics in terms of material entities is the interpretation of forces. The essential nature of forces has been the subject of enduring debate in mechanics (Dijksterhuis, 1961; Jammer, 1957; Mach, 1893/1960). The most widely known phase of the debate involved the reaction to Newton's gravitational theory and "action at a distance." However, Galileo wrote, more than half a century earlier, of how he had elected to abandon attempts to describe the essence of gravitational action in favor of efforts to describe the form of trajectories in events involving gravity (Galileo, 1638/1914). The renowned result was the kinematics of free fall, recognized as among the most profound achievements in science. Newton's dynamics can be interpreted as having succeeded in generalizing Galileo's descriptions, enabling dynamicists to describe, among other things, free-fall trajectories on other planets as well as on earth (Jammer, 1957; Mach, 1893/1960). To this day, our understanding of gravity is couched in terms of geometry and the associated forms of trajectories (Taylor and Wheeler, 1966), although this interpretation remains controversial. The search for gravitational essence continues—e.g., cast as a search for gravity particles. Nevertheless, the historical precedents indicate that a focus on the form of trajectories has been a productive approach.

6. There are different types of stability (see, e.g., Thompson and Stewart, 1986). Structural stability refers to the stability of the form associated with stable trajectories as the dynamic equation is perturbed by adding a new term. A simple dynamic, which is not structurally stable, is the harmonic oscillator. This exhibits elliptical phase trajectories. When an arbitrarily small damping term is added to the equation, the trajectories change to spirals ending in a stable equilibrium state called a point attractor. Attractors are stable states such that all trajectories within a given neighborhood, the "basin of attraction," approach them and once near forever remain so unless perturbed violently enough to be forced from the basin. In the study of qualitative nonlinear dynamics, the forms of interest are the forms of the attractors, i.e., the (long-term) stable trajectories.

7. Releasing motion from the vertical plane would only introduce, in addition, an optical component corresponding to rotation about the visual direction. This has been described using differential operators as a curl (Koenderink and van Doorn, 1975, 1976).

8. Rather than the rate of image expansion and contraction, I also could have used $1/\tau$ or the inverse of tau (Lee, 1980). Computed as Vy/Y, this equals image expansion rate divided by image size. Plotted against image size, this also preserved the form of the Y-Vy plot.

9. Todd (1982) developed a similar approach which he applied instead to the configuration space of paths or orbits. A similar use of symmetries in optics applied within a vector field representation can be found in Lappin (1990).

10. The phase angle is derived as the arctan(tangential velocity/θ) while the length of the radius is [(tangential velocity)^2 + θ^2]$^{.5}$. The latter is related to the mechanical energy which equals the sum of the potential and the kinetic energy. We will call the coordinate "energy," although it is more properly related to the square root of the energy.

REFERENCES

Andersen, G. J. (1990). Segregation of optic flow into object and self-motion components: foundations for a general model. In R. Warren and A. H. Wertheim (Eds.), *Perception and the control of self-motion* (pp. 127–141). Hillsdale, NJ: Erlbaum.

Anstis, S. (1986). Motion perception in the frontal plane: sensory aspects. In K. R. Boff, L. Kaufman, and J. P. Thomas (Eds.), *Handbook of perception and human performance* (pp. 16:1–127). New York: Wiley.

Baker, W. E., Westine, P. S., and Dodge, F. T. (1973). *Similarity methods in engineering dynamics: theory and practice of scale modeling.* Rochelle Park, NJ: Hayden Books.

Barclay, C. D., Cutting, J. E., and Kozlowsky, L. T. (1978). Temporal and spatial factors in gait perception that influence gender recognition. *Perception and Psychophysics, 23,* 145–153.

Becker, R. A. (1954). *Introduction to theoretical mechanics.* New York: McGraw-Hill.

Berge, P., Pomeau, Y., and Vidal, C. (1984). *Order within chaos: toward a deterministic approach to turbulence.* New York: Wiley.

Bertero, M., Poggio, T. A., and Torre, V. (1988). Ill-posed problems in early vision. *Proceedings of the IEEE, 76*(8), 869–889.

Bingham, G. P. (1985). Kinematic form and scaling: further investigations on the visual perception of lifted weight. Doctoral Dissertation, University of Connecticut, Storrs, CT.

Bingham, G. P. (1987a). Dynamical systems and event perception: a working paper, parts I–III. *Perception/Action Review, 2*(1), 4–14.

Bingham, G. P. (1987b). Kinematic form and scaling: further investigations and the visual perception of lifted weight. *Journal of Experimental Psychology: Human Perception and Performance, 13,* 155–177.

Bingham, G. P. (1988). Task-specific devices and the perceptual bottleneck. *Human Movement Sciences, 7,* 225–264.

Bingham, G. P. (1990). Physical constraints on form: investigating visual information for event recognition and the judgment of size [unpublished].

Bingham, G. P. (1993). Scaling judgments of lifted weight: lifter size and the role of the standard. *Ecological Psychology, 5,* 31–64.

Bingham, G. P., and Muchisky, M. M. (1993a). Center of mass perception and inertial frames of reference. *Perception and Psychophysics, 54,* 617–632.

Bingham, G. P., and Muchisky, M. M. (1993b). "Center of mass perception": affordances as dispositions determined by dynamics. In J. M. Flach, P. Hancock, J. Caird, et al. (Eds.) *The ecology of human-machine systems.* Hillsdale, NJ: Erlbaum.

Bingham, G. P., Rosenblum, L. D., and Schmidt, R. C. (in press). Dynamics and the orientation of kinematic forms in visual event recognition. *Journal of Experimental Psychology: Human Perception and Performance*.

Bingham, G. P., Schmidt, R. C., and Rosenblum, L. D. (1989). Hefting for a maximum distance throw: a smart perceptual mechanism. *Journal of Experimental Psychology: Human Perception and Performance, 15*, 507–528.

Cutting, J. E. (1978). Generation of synthetic male and female walkers through manipulation of a biomechanical invariant. *Perception, 7*, 393–405.

Cutting, J. E. (1982). Blowing in the wind: perceived structure of trees and bushes. *Cognition, 12*, 25–44.

Cutting, J. E., and Kozlowsky, L. T. (1977). Recognizing friends by their walk: gait perception without familiarity cues. *Bulletin of the Psychonomic Society, 9*, 333–356.

Cutting, J. E., Proffitt, D. R., and Kozlowsky, L. T. (1978). A biomechanical invariant for gait perception. *Journal of Experimental Psychology: Human Perception and Performance, 4*, 357–372.

Dewey, J., and Bentley, A. F. (1949). *Knowing and the known*. Boston: Beacon.

Dijksterhuis, E. J. (1961). *The mechanization of the world picture*. Princeton, NJ: Princeton University Press.

Duncan, W. J. (1953). *Physical similarity and dimensional analysis*. London: Edward Arnold.

Duncker, K. (1929/1950). Induced motion. In W. D. Ellis (Ed.), *A source book of Gestalt psychology* (pp. 161–172). New York: Humanities Press.

Eagleson, R. (1987). Estimating 3D motion parameters from the changing responses of 2D bandpass spatial frequency filters. In *IEEE Montreal Technologies Conference: Compint '87*, (pp. 102–105). Montreal: IEEE.

Emori, R. I., and Schuring, D. J. (1977). *Scale models in engineering: fundamentals and applications*. New York: Pergamon Press.

Fieandt, K., and Gibson, J. J. (1959). The sensitivity of the eye to two kinds of continuous transformation of shadow pattern. *Journal of Experimental Psychology, 57*, 344–347.

Frykholm, G. (1983). *Action, intention, gender, identity, perceived from body movement*. Uppsala, Sweden: University of Uppsala.

Galileo, G. (1638/1914). *Dialogues concerning two new sciences*. New York: Dover.

Gibson, J. J. (1950). *The perception of the visual world*. Boston: Houghton Mifflin.

Gibson, J. J. (1955). The optical expansion pattern in aerial locomotion. *American Journal of Psychology, 68*, 480–484.

Gibson, J. J. (1958). Visually controlled locomotion and visual orientation in animals. *British Journal of Psychology, 49*, 182–192.

Gibson, J. J. (1961). Ecological optics. *Vision Research, 1*, 253–262.

Gibson, J. J. (1962). Observations on active touch, *Psychological Review, 69*, 477–491.

Gibson, J. J. (1966). *The senses considered as perceptual systems*. Boston: Houghton Mifflin.

Gibson, J. J. (1979). *The ecological approach to visual perception*. Boston: Houghton Mifflin.

Gibson, E. J., Gibson, J. J., Smith, O. W., et al. (1959). Motion parallax as a determinant of perceived depth. *Journal of Experimental Psychology, 58*(1), 40–51.

Gibson, J. J., Kaplan, G., Reynolds, H., et al. (1969). The change from visible to invisible: A study of optical transitions, *Perception and Psychophysics, 5*, 113–116.

Gibson, J. J., and Kaushall, P. (1973). *Reversible and irreversible events* (motion picture). State College, PA: Psychological Cinema Register.

Hildreth, E. C. (1984). The computation of the velocity field. *Proceedings of the Royal Society of London, Series B, 221,* 189–220.

Hildreth, E. C., and Grzywacz, N. M. (1986). The incremental rigidity scheme for recovering structure from motion: position versus velocity based information. In *Proceedings of the IEEE Computer Society Workshop on Motion* (pp. 137–143). IEEE Computer Society.

Hildreth, E. C., and Hollerbach, J. M. (1987). The computational approach to vision and motor control. In F. Plum (ed.), *Handbook of Physiology* Vol. V, section 1. New York: Oxford University Press.

Hildreth, E. C., and Koch, C. (1987). The analysis of visual motion: from computational theory to neuronal mechanisms. *Annual Review of Neuroscience, 10,* 477–533.

Hirsch, M. W., and Smale, S. (1974). *Differential equations, dynamical systems, and linear algebra.* New York: Academic Press.

Horn, B. K. P. (1986). *Robot vision.* Cambridge, MA: MIT Press.

Hume, D. (1739/1978). *A treatise on human nature.* Oxford, England: Oxford University Press.

Ipsen, E. C. (1960). *Units, dimensions and dimensionless numbers.* New York: McGraw-Hill.

Jacobson, L., and Wechsler, H. (1987). Derivation of optical flow using a spatiotemporal-frequency approach. *Computer Vision, Graphics, and Image Processing, 38,* 29–65.

Jammer, M. (1957). *Concepts of force: a study in the foundations of dynamics.* Cambridge, MA: Harvard University Press.

Jansson, G., and Johansson, G. (1973). Visual perception of bending motion. *Perception, 2,* 321–326.

Jansson, G., and Runeson, S. (1977). Perceived bending motions from a quadrangle changing form. *Perception, 6,* 595–600.

Johansson, G. (1950). *Configurations in event perception.* Uppsala, Sweden: Almquist & Wiksell.

Johansson, G. (1964). Perception of motion and changing form. *Scandinavian Journal of Psychology, 5,* 181–208.

Johansson, G. (1973). Visual perception of biological motion and a model for its analysis. *Perception and Psychophysics, 14,* 201–211.

Johansson, G. (1976). Spatio-temporal differentiation and integration in visual motion perception. *Psychological Research, 38,* 379–393.

Johansson, G. (1985). About visual event perception. In W. H. Warren and R. E. Shaw (Eds.), *Persistence and Change: Proceedings of the First International Conference on Event Perception.* Hillsdale, NJ: Erlbaum.

Johansson, G., and Jansson, G. (1967). *The perception of free fall.* Unpublished report, Department of Psychology, University of Uppsala, Uppsala, Sweden.

Klatzky, R., Lederman, S., and Metzger, V. (1985). Identifying objects by touch: an "expert system." *Perception and Psychophysics, 37* 299–302.

Koenderink, J. J. (1986). Optic flow. *Vision Research, 26,* 161–180.

Koenderink, J. J., and van Doorn, A. J. (1975). Invariant properties of the motion parallax field due to the movement of rigid bodies relative to an observer. *Optica Acta, 22*(9), 773–791.

Koenderink, J. J., and van Doorn, A. J. (1976). Local structure of movement parallax of the plane. *Journal of the Optical Society of America, Series A, 66*(7), 717–723.

Koenderink, J. J., and van Doorn, A. J. (1978). How an ambulant observer can construct a model of the environment from the geometrical structure of the visual inflow. In G. Hauske and E. Butenandt (Eds.), *Kybernetik*, (pp. 224–247). Munich: Verlag.

Koenderink, J. J., and van Doorn, A. J. (1987). The structure of the visual field. In W. Güttinger and G. Dangelmayr (Eds.), *The physics of structure formation: theory and simulation* (pp. 68–77). Berlin: Springer-Verlag.

Kugler, P. N. (1983). *A morphological view of information for the self-assembly of rhythmic movement: a study in the similitude of natural law.* Ph.D. dissertation, Department of Psychology, University of Connecticut, Storrs.

Langhaar, H. L. (1951). *Dimensional analysis and the theory of models.* New York: Wiley.

Lappin, J. S. (1990). Perceiving the metric structure of environmental objects from motion, self-motion and stereopsis. In R. Warren and A. H. Wertheim (Eds.), *Perception and the control of self-motion* (pp. 541–579). Hillsdale, NJ: Erlbaum.

Lederman, S., and Klatzky, R. (1987). Hand movements: a window into haptic object recognition. *Cognitive Psychology, 19*, 342–368.

Lee, D. N. (1974). Visual information during locomotion. In R. B. McLeod and H. L. Pick (eds.), *Studies in perception: essays in honor of J. J. Gibson.* Ithaca, NY: Cornell University Press.

Lee, D. N. (1980). The optic flow field: the foundation of vision. *Philosophical Transactions of the Royal Society London. Series B, 290*, 169–179.

Lee, D. N., Young, D. S., Reddish, P. E., et al. (1983). Visual timing in hitting an accelerating ball. *Quarterly Journal of Experimental Psychology, 35A*, 333–346.

Longuet-Higgins, H. C., and Prazdny, K. (1980). The interpretation of a moving retinal image. *Proceedings of the Royal Society London. Series B, 208*, 385–397.

Mach, E. (1893/1960). *The science of mechanics: a critical and historical account of its development.* LaSalle, IL: Open Court.

Mandelbrot, B. B. (1983). *The fractal geometry of nature.* New York: Freeman.

Mark, L., Todd, J. T., and Shaw, R. (1981). The perception of growth: a geometric analysis of how different styles of change are distinguished. *Journal of Experimental Psychology: Human Perception and Performance, 7*, 355–368.

Marmo, G., Saletan, E. J., Simoni, A., et al. (1985). *Dynamical systems: a differential geometric approach to symmetry and reduction.* New York: Wiley.

Marr, D. (1982). *Vision.* San Fransico: Freeman.

McMahon, T. A. (1984). *Muscles, reflexes, and locomotion.* Princeton, NJ: Princeton University Press.

Michotte, A. (1963). *The perception of causality.* London: Methuen.

Muchisky, M. M., and Bingham, G. P. (1992). Perceiving size in events via kinematic form. In J. Kruscke (Ed.), *Proceedings of the 14th Annual Conference of the Cognitive Science Society* (pp. 1002–1007). Hillsdale, NJ: Erlbaum.

Nagel, H.-H. (1988). Image sequences—ten (octal) years—from phenomenology towards a theoretical foundation. *International Journal of Pattern Recognition and Artificial Intelligence, 2*(3), 459–483.

Nakayama, K., and Loomis, J. M. (1974). Optical velocity patterns, velocity sensitive neurons, and space perception: a hypothesis. *Perception, 3*, 63–80.

Norman, J. F. and Todd, J. T. (1992). The visual perception of 3-dimensional form. In G. A. Carpenter and S. Grossberg (Eds.), *Neural networks for vision and image processing*. Cambridge, MA: MIT Press.

Owen, D. H. (1990). Perception and control of changes in self-motion: a functional approach to the study of information and skill. In R. Warren and A. H. Wertheim (Eds.), *Perception and the control of self-motion* (pp. 289–326). Hillsdale, NJ: Erlbaum.

Pagano, C. C., and Turvey, M. T. (1993). Perceiving by dynamic touch the distances reachable with irregular objects. *Ecological Psychology, 5,* 125–151.

Pittenger, J. B. (1985). Estimation of pendulum length from information in motion. *Perception, 14,* 247–256.

Pittenger, J. B. (1990). Detection of violations of the law of pendulum motion: observers' sensitivity to the relation between period and length. *Ecological Psychology, 2*(1), 55–81.

Pittenger, J. B., and Shaw, R. E. (1975). Aging faces as visco-elastic events: implications for a theory of nonrigid shape perception. *Journal of Experimental Psychology: Human Perception and Performance, 1,* 374–382.

Prazdny, K. (1980). Egomotion and relative depth map from optical flow. *Biological Cybernetics, 36,* 87–102.

Prigogine, I. (1980). *From being to becoming: time and complexity in the physical sciences*. San Fransico: Freeman.

Prigogine, I., and Stengers, I. (1984). *Order out of chaos*. Toronto: Bantam Books.

Proffitt, D. R., and Gilden, D. L. (1989). Understanding natural dynamics. *Journal of Experimental Psychology: Human Perception and Performance, 15,* 384–393.

Reed, E., and Jones, R. (1982). *Reasons for realism: selected essays of James J. Gibson*. Hillsdale, NJ: Erlbaum.

Reed, E. S. (1988). *James J. Gibson and the psychology of perception*. New Haven, CT: Yale University Press.

Regan, D. M., Kaufman, L., and Lincoln, J. (1986). Motion in depth and visual acceleration. In K. R. Boff, L. Kaufman, and J. P. Thomas (Eds.), *Handbook of perception and performance: sensory processes and perception* (pp. 19/1–19/46). New York: Wiley.

Rieger, J. H. (1983). Information in optical flows induced by curved paths of observation. *Journal of the Optical Society of America, Series A, 73*(3), 339–344.

Rieger, J. H., and Lawton, D. T. (1985). Processing differential image motion. *Journal of the Optical Society of America, Series A, 2*(2), 354–359.

Rosenberg, R. M. (1977). *Analytical dynamics of discrete systems*. New York: Plenum Press.

Runeson, S. (1977). *On the visual perception of dynamic events*. Uppsala, Sweden: University of Uppsala.

Runeson, S., and Frykholm, G. (1981). Visual perception of lifted weight. *Journal of Experimental Psychology: Human Perception and Performance, 7,* 733–740.

Runeson, S., and Frykholm, G. (1983). Kinematic specification of dynamics as an informational basis for person and action perception: expectations, gender recognition, and deceptive intention. *Journal of Experimental Psychology: General, 112,* 585–615.

Runeson, S., and Vedeler, D. (1993). The indispensability of precollision kinematics in the visual perception of relative mass. *Perception and Psychophysics, 53,* 617–632.

Schroeder, M. (1991). *Fractals, chaos, power laws*. New York: Freeman.

Sedov, L. I. (1959). *Similarity and dimensional methods in mechanics*. New York: Academic Press.

Shaw, R. E., Mark, L. S., Jenkins, H., et al. (1982). A dynamic geometry for predicting growth of gross craniofacial morphology. In *Factors and mechanisms influencing bone growth* (pp. 423–431). New York: Liss.

Shaw, R. E., McIntyre, M., and Mace, W. (1974). The role of symmetry in event perception. In R. MacLeod and H. Pick (Eds.), *Studied in perception: essays in honor of J. J. Gibson* New York: Cornell University Press.

Shaw, R. E., and Pittenger, J. B. (1977). Perceiving the face of change in changing faces: implications for a theory of object perception. In R. E. Shaw and J. Bransford (Eds.), *Perceiving, acting and knowing: toward an ecological psychology* Hillsdale, NJ: Erlbaum.

Shaw, R. E., and Pittenger, J. B. (1978). Perceiving change. In H. L. Pick and E. Saltzman (Eds.), *Modes of perceiving and processing information* (pp. 187–204). New York: Wiley.

Shaw, R. E., Turvey, M. T., and Mace, W. M. (1981). Ecological psychology: the consequence of a commitment to realism. In W. Weimer and D. Palermo (Eds.), *Cognition and the symbolic processes II*. Hillsdale, NJ: Erlbaum.

Solomon, H. Y. (1988). Movement-produced invariants in haptic explorations: an example of a self-organizing, information-driven, intentional system. *Human Movement Science, 7*, 201–224.

Szücs, E. (1980). *Similitude and modelling*. Amsterdam: Elsevier.

Taylor, E. F., and Wheeler, J. A. (1966). *Spacetime physics*. San Fransico: Freeman.

Thompson, J. M. T., and Stewart, H. B. (1986). *Nonlinear dynamics and chaos: geometrical methods for engineers and scientists*. New York: Wiley.

Todd, J. T. (1981). Visual information about moving objects. *Journal of Experimental Psychology: Human Perception and Performance, 7*, 795–810.

Todd, J. T. (1982). Visual information about rigid and non-rigid motion: a geometric analysis. *Journal of Experimental Psychology: Human Perception and Performance, 8*, 238–252.

Todd, J. T. (1983). Perception of gait. *Journal of Experimental Psychology: Human Perception and Performance, 9*, 31–42.

Todd, J. T., and Akerstrom, R. A. (1987). Perception of three-dimensional form from pattern of optical texture. *Journal of Experimental Psychology: Human Perception and Performance, 13*, 242–255.

Todd, J. T., Mark, L. S., Shaw, R. E., et al. (1980). The perception of human growth. *Scientific American, 242*, 106–114.

Todd, J. T., and Reichel, F. D. (1989). Ordinal structure in the visual perception and cognition of smoothly curved surfaces. *Psychological Review, 96*, 643–657.

Todd, J. T., and Warren, W. H. (1982). Visual perception of relative mass in dynamic events. *Perception, 11*, 325–335.

Tufillaro, N. B., Abbott, T., and Reilly, J. (1992). *An experimental approach to nonlinear dynamics and chaos*. Redwood City, CA: Addison-Wesley.

Turvey, M. T., Shaw, R. E., Mace, W. M., et al. (1981). Ecological laws of perceiving and acting: in reply to Fodor and Pylyshyn (1981). *Cognition, 9*, 237–304.

Ullman, S. (1979). *The interpretation of visual motion*. Cambridge, MA: MIT Press.

Ullman, S. (1984). Maximizing rigidity: the incremental recovery of 3-D structure from rigid and nonrigid motion. *Perception, 13*, 255–274.

Verri, A., and Poggio, T. (1987). Against quantitative optical flow. In *First International Conference on Computer Vision* (pp. 171–180). London: IEEE.

Verri, A., and Poggio, T. (1989). Motion field and optical flow: qualitative properties. *IEEE Transactions on Pattern Analysis and Machine Intelligence, 11*(5), 490–498.

Wallach, H., and O'Connell, D. N. (1953). The kinetic depth effect. *Journal of Experimental Psychology, 45,* 205–217.

Warren, R. (1990). Preliminary questions for the study of egomotion. In R. Warren and A. H. Wertheim (Eds.), *Perception and the control of self-motion* (pp. 3–32). Hillsdale, NJ: Erlbaum.

Warren, W. H., Kim, E. E., and Husney, R. (1987). The way the ball bounces: visual and auditory perception of elasticity and control of the bounce pass. *Perception, 16,* 309–336.

Warren, W. H., and Shaw, R. E. (1985). Event and encounters as units for analysis for ecological psychology. In W. H. Warren and R. E. Shaw (Eds.), *Persistence and change* (pp. 1–27). Hillsdale, NJ: Erlbaum.

Watson, J. S., Banks, M. S., von Hofsten, C., et al. (1992). Gravity as a monocular cue for perception of absolute distance and/or size. *Perception, 21,* 69–76.

Waxman, A. M., and Ullman, S. (1985). Surface structure and three-dimensional motion from image flow. *The International Journal of Robotics Research, 4*(3), 72–94.

Whittaker, E. T. A. (1944). *A treatise on the analytical dynamics of particles and rigid bodies.* New York: Dover.

Zacharias, G. L. (1990). An estimation/control model of egomotion. In R. Warren and A. H. Wertheim (Eds.), *Perception and the control of self-motion* (pp. 425–459). Hillsdale, NJ: Erlbaum.

Guide to Further Reading

A good general introduction to event perception is Warren and Shaw (1985). This anthology contains papers by researchers in the various sensory modalities and subspecialities (e.g., development, action, cognition, and language, as well as vision) and includes a review by Johansson. Michotte (1963) is the classic work on the perception of causality. An influential and very enjoyable introduction to scaling is Thompson (1961), while the most useful recent text is Szücs (1980). Schroeder (1991) ranges widely over applications in various sciences, including psychology. For introductory works on ecological psychology, no books are more readable or more worth rereading than Gibson (1966, 1979). Reed (1988) traces Gibson's intellectual development and places his ideas in historical perspective. There are now many works available on nonlinear dynamics. Thompson and Stewart (1986) remains the most readable, yet fairly thorough introduction. Rosenberg (1977) is a good presentation of classical mechanics with a treatment of the various spaces in which events might be represented. Marmo, Saletan, Simoni, et al. (1985) provide the best overview of the strictly qualitative approach to dynamics. This work is rather technically demanding, but still readable. A useful general introduction to the mathematics of form is Lord and Wilson (1986). For a slightly more technical introduction to optical flow than Gibson (1979) or Reed (1988), see Nalwa (1993). For the full dose, see Horn (1986). Norman and Todd (1992) is also a good brief introduction to more advanced topics. Cutting (1986) provides a useful introduction to optics.

Cutting, J. E. (1986). *Perception with an eye for motion.* Cambridge, MA: MIT Press.

Gibson, J. J. (1966). *The senses considered as perceptual systems.* Boston: Houghton Mifflin.

Gibson, J. J. (1979). *The ecological approach to visual perception.* Hillsdale, N.J.: Erlbaum.

Horn, B. K. P. (1986). *Robot vision.* Cambridge, MA: MIT Press.

Lord, E. A., and Wilson, C. B. (1986). *The mathematical description of shape and form*. New York: Wiley.

Marmo, G., Saletan, E. J., Simoni, A., et al. (1985). *Dynamical systems: a differential geometric approach to symmetry and reduction*. New York: Wiley.

Michotte, A. (1963). *The perception of causality*. London: Methuen.

Nalwa, V. S. (1993). *A guided tour of computer vision*. Reading, MA: Addison-Wesley.

Norman, J. F., and Todd, J. T. (1992). The visual perception of 3-dimensional form. In G. A. Carpenter and S. Grossberg (Eds.), *Neural networks for vision and image processing*. Cambridge, MA: MIT Press.

Reed, E. S. (1988). *James J. Gibson and the psychology of perception*. New Haven, CT: Yale University Press.

Rosenberg, R. M. (1977). *Analytical dynamics of discrete systems*. New York: Plenum.

Schroeder, M. (1991). *Fractals, chaos, power laws*. New York: Freeman.

Szücs, E. (1980). *Similitude and modelling*. Amsterdam: Elsevier.

Thompson, D. W. (1961). *On growth and form*. Cambridge, England: Cambridge University Press.

Thompson, J. M. T., and Stewart, H. B. (1986). *Nonlinear dynamics and chaos: geometrical methods for engineers and scientists*. New York: Wiley.

Warren, W. H., and Shaw, R. E. (1985). *Persistence and change*. Hillsdale, NJ: Erlbaum.

15 Neural Dynamics of Motion Perception, Recognition Learning, and Spatial Attention

Stephen Grossberg

EDITORS' INTRODUCTION

Although it has recently been undergoing a surge in popularity, the dynamical approach to cognition is not a new idea. Detailed dynamical modeling has been a continuous feature of the landscape of cognitive science since its inception. There is no better way to demonstrate this than to point to the work of Stephen Grossberg and his colleagues and students at Boston University. Since the 1960s this group has generated neural network dynamical models of a wide range of cognitive processes.

In this chapter, Grossberg describes two models which are both representative of their stream of work and illustrative of the role of interactive dynamics in developing explanations of various aspects of cognition. The first model is the motion-oriented contrast-sensitive (MOC) filter, which is one component of a larger model of the processes by which an animal can visually track the direction of motion of a complex visual object. Here, Grossberg describes how the MOC filter accounts for psychological data on the phenomenon of apparent motion. Suppose you are in a darkened room and two stationary lights flash alternately in front of you: as one goes off, the other goes on. If the rate of alternation and the spatial angle between the lights falls within certain bounds, you will visually experience these flashes as the motion of a single light source. Grossberg argues that this apparent motion effect underlies the ability of animals to detect and track complex moving objects, such as a leopard moving in the jungle. In the MOC model, the successive stimuli create excitation patterns in a specialized map of the visual field. A very broad function, the "G-wave," with a central peak, is fitted over the whole region of the visual field. The location of the central peak of the G-function glides smoothly from one site of excitation to the other. The proposal is that subjects' experience of the light as moving continuously is derived by tracking the location of the peak of the G-function.

The second model is the well-known adaptive resonance theory (ART) model for pattern recognition, including especially visual patterns. One of the most basic and essential aspects of cognition is the ability to recognize some stimulus as belonging to some particular kind or category, even in the face of a cluttered, noisy environment. Recognition is intimately connected with learning, since natural cognitive systems autonomously learn the categories that make recognition possible.

Only in this way could they adapt as well as they do. But Grossberg argues that an effective nervous system must be able to distinguish something novel from the familiar; it must learn when it needs to, yet resist learning when presented with just the same old patterns. The ART model was designed to be able to self-organize and learn to recognize patterns only when something novel is presented. Clever design prevents long-term memory from being corrupted by learning that results from an unusual sequence of inputs.

The ART model is a dynamical model of great generality and power. It takes some effort to understand how it works and even more to evaluate its ability to account for specific sets of experimental data. One prominent and relatively unique feature of Grossberg's style of research is his reliance on mathematical proofs. He and Gail Carpenter and other colleagues have proved many key results about their models. Their research program illustrates two important features of the dynamical approach. The first is that dynamical models are uniquely positioned to bridge the gap between physiological mechanisms and psychological function. As Grossberg points out, the ART model makes contact with neuroscientific findings at many points. In addition, this work clarifies the theoretical inseparability of the cognitive system and its environment. Activity of the cognitive systems has to be understood as shaped by the coevolving activity of the environment; e.g., in the MOC filter the perception of apparent motion is an internal dynamical process unfolding under the influence of highly structured external events.

15.1 MOTION PERCEPTION, RECOGNITION LEARNING, AND WHAT-AND-WHERE ATTENTION

Our brains are designed to control behaviors that are capable of interacting successfully with fluctuating environments whose rules may change unexpectedly through time. They are *self-organizing* systems whereby behaviors may be performed autonomously and adaptively to environmental changes during which no teacher other than the environmental events themselves may be present with correct new answers. This chapter describes two examples of how the brain may achieve autonomous control in a rapidly changing environment. One example concerns motion perception and object tracking. The other concerns recognition learning, categorization, memory search, and recall. Both examples include dynamical processes which may control attention during cognitive information processing. One process suggests how attention may be used to track *where* objects are moving in space. The other process suggests how attention may delimit *what* the defining features of an object may be. These results thus contribute to an analysis of the What cortical stream, which includes area V4 of the visual cortex and temporal cortex, and the Where processing stream, which includes the middle temporal area (MT) of the visual cortex and parietal cortex, which have been the subject of much recent investigation (Desimone and Ungerleider, 1989; Goodale and Milner, 1992; Ungerleider and Mishkin, 1982; Wise and Desimone, 1988).

The Whole is Greater Than the Sum of Its Parts

How can effective models of such complex self-organizing brain processes be derived, given that no one type of behavioral or brain datum can typically characterize its generative neural mechanisms? The several answers to this question each imply that "the whole is greater than the sum of its parts" when interdisciplinary data and modeling constraints are consistently joined. Even the constraint that the model be self-organizing—namely, that it can autonomously and adaptively respond in real time to its intended range of environmental challenges—imposes many constraints on system design that are not obvious from a bottom-up analysis of brain data. Modeling self-organizing perception and recognition learning systems requires that several levels of processing, from the behavioral level through the neural system, circuit, cell, and channel levels, be computationally integrated. This is true because such a system uses internal representations that need to achieve behavioral success despite the inability of individual neurons to discern the behavioral meaning of these representations. How are coding errors corrected, or appropriate adaptations to a changing environment effected, if individual neurons do not know that these errors or changes have even occurred? It is often the case that behavioral success can be computed on the level of networks of neurons. That is why neural network models can clarify how properly designed neurons, when embedded in properly designed neural circuits and systems, can autonomously control behavior in a manner that leads to behavioral success.

For example, it is suggested below how properties of variable-speed object tracking and memory consolidation of recognition categories may emerge from system-wide interactions. The computational linkage of multiple organizational levels also leads to new predictions. In particular, properties of preattentive apparent motion processing are linked below to properties of attentive object tracking. It is also suggested how novelty-sensitive processes within the hippocampal formation may modulate the size, shape, and number of recognition categories that are learned by the inferotemporal cortex (IT).

Granted that the emergent properties that have behavioral meaning are typically not properties of single neurons or other individual neuronal components, we can better understand why behavioral and brain processes are so hard to understand. Whereas correctly designed individual neurons are necessary in such a model, they are not sufficient. A multilevel modeling synthesis is needed in which individual components, their intercellular interactions, and their behaviorally significant emergent properties are all crafted together.

Such a multilevel analysis achieves much of its power by focusing on a natural subset of interdisciplinary data and issues—on a "vertical slice" through the space of phenomena. One never tries to solve "all" the problems at once. In the present instance, these data and issues concern preattentive motion processing, attentive recognition learning, and attentive object tracking. We do not analyze such equally important processes as form and color perception, reinforcement learning, cognitive-emotional interactions, working memory, temporal planning, and adaptive sensorimotor control. On the other hand, larger model systems that integrate aspects of all these processes have been proposed as part of a continuing modeling cycle (Carpenter and Grossberg, 1991; Grossberg, 1982, 1987a,b, 1988; Grossberg and Kuperstein, 1986). This cycle has progressively characterized individual modules, and fitted them together into larger systems. System constraints that are discovered during this fitting process are used, in turn, to further shape the design of individual modules. The puzzle cannot be finished unless each piece is designed to fit.

These modules are designed to be the minimal models that can explain a targeted data base. They are lumped representations of neural processes in which no process is included unless its functional role is required and clearly understood. The insistence upon functional clarity highlights those data that the model should and should not be able to explain, facilitates the discovery of additional neural processes to explain additional data, and clarifies which species-specific variations of the minimal models are workable and which are not. These discoveries have, in the past, led to the progressive unlumping of the models as they embody ever-more-powerful functional competences for explaining ever-more-encompassing data bases.

15.2   MODELING APPARENT MOTION

The Ecological Significance of Apparent Motion

The first model provides a particularly simple example of emergent properties that are due to dynamically interacting network cells. The example seems simple after you see it, but the data properties that led to its discovery are highly paradoxical and have been known and puzzled about for many years.

These data concern phenomena about apparent motion. One might at once complain that apparent motion phenomena are of no ecological interest. To challenge this impression, consider the task of rapidly detecting a leopard leaping from a jungle branch under a sun-dappled forest canopy. Consider how spots on the leopard's coat move as its limbs and muscles surge. Imagine how patterns of light and shade play upon the leopard's coat as it leaps through the air. These luminance and color contours move across the leopard's body in a variety of directions that do not necessarily point in the direction of the leopard's leap. Indeed, the leopard's body generates a scintillating mosaic of moving contours that could easily prevent its detection. Our perceptual processes can actively reorganize such a scintillating mosaic into a coherent object percept with a unitary direction-of-motion. The leopard as a whole then seems to quickly "pop out" from the jungle background and to draw our attention. Such a perceptual process clearly has a high survival value for animals that possess it.

This description of the leaping leopard emphasizes that the process of motion perception is an active one. It is capable of transforming a motion signal that is generated by a luminance contour into a different motion percept. In this sense, our percepts of moving objects are often percepts of apparent motion, albeit an adaptive and useful form of apparent motion. The task of understanding how we see "real" motion thus requires that we also understand "apparent" motion.

The simplest examples of apparent motion were documented in the 1870s, when Exner (1875) provided the first empirical evidence that the visual perception of motion was a distinct perceptual quality, rather than being merely a series of spatially displaced static percepts over time. He did this by placing two sources of electrical sparks close together in space. When the sparks were flashed with an appropriate temporal interval between them, observers reported a compelling percept of continuous motion of a single flash from one location to another, even though neither flash actually moved. At shorter temporal intervals, flashes look simultaneous and stationary. At longer intervals, they look like successive stationary flashes, with no intervening motion percept. When the spatiotemporal parameters of the display are suboptimal, a "figureless" or "objectless" motion called *phi motion* is perceived, wherein a sense of motion without a clearly defined form is perceived. A smooth and continuous motion of a perceptually well-defined form is called *beta motion*, and typically occurs at a larger interstimulus interval, or ISI, between the offset of one flash and the onset of the next flash.

This classic demonstration of apparent motion was followed by a series of remarkable discoveries, particularly by Gestalt psychologists, concerning the properties of motion perception. It was noticed that a decrease in ISI causes the speed of the interpolating motion to increase (Kolers, 1972). A motion percept can also smoothly interpolate flashes separated by different distances, speeding up if necessary to cross a longer distance at a fixed ISI. If a more intense flash follows a less intense flash, the perceived motion can travel backward from the second flash to the first flash. This percept is called *delta motion* (Kolers, 1972; Korte, 1915). *Gamma motion* is the apparent expansion at the onset of a single flash, or its contraction at its offset (Bartley, 1941; Kolers, 1972). A similar expansion-then-contraction may be perceived when a region is suddenly darkened relative to its background, and then restored to the background luminance.

If a white spot on a gray background is followed by a nearby black spot on a gray background, then motion between the spots can occur while the percept changes from white to black at an intermediate position. Likewise, a red spot followed by a green spot on a white background leads to a continuous motion percept combined with a binary switch from red to green along the motion pathway (Kolers and von Grünau, 1975; Squires, 1931; van der Waals and Roelofs, 1930, 1931; Wertheimer, 1912/1961). These results show that the motion mechanism can combine visual stimuli corresponding to different colors, or even opposite directions-of-contrast. Complex tradeoffs between flash luminance, duration, distance, and ISI in the generation of motion percepts were also discovered. For example, the minimum ISI for perceiving motion increases with increasing spatial separation of the inducing flashes. This property is sometimes called Korte's third law (Boring, 1950; Kolers, 1972; Korte, 1915). A similar threshold decrease with distance occurs in the minimum stimulus onset asynchrony, or SOA, which is the difference between the flash-onset times. Interestingly, whereas the minimum ISI decreases with flash duration, the minimum SOA increases with flash duration.

These discoveries raised perplexing issues concerning the nature of the long-range brain interaction that generates a continuous motion percept between two stationary flashes. Why is this long-range interaction not perceived when only a single light is flashed? In particular, why are not outward waves of motion signals induced by a single flash? How does a motion signal get generated from the location of the first flash after the first flash terminates, and only after the second flash turns on? How does the motion signal adapt itself to the variable distances and ISIs of the second flash, by speeding up or slowing down accordingly? In particular, how can the motion signal adapt to the ISI between two flashes even though such adaptation can only begin after the first flash is over? I like to call this the ESP problem. Moreover, what ecologically useful function do these curious properties realize under more normal perceptual conditions?

The figural organization of motion stimuli can also influence motion percepts. The Ternus displays provide a classic example (Ternus, 1926/1950). In frame 1 of a Ternus display, three white elements are placed in a horizontal row on a black background (or conversely). After an ISI, in frame 2 all three elements are shifted to the right so that the two rightward elements in frame 1 are in the same locations as the two leftward elements in frame 2. Depending on the ISI, the observer perceives one of four percepts. At very short ISIs, all four elements appear simultaneously. At long ISIs, observers do not perceive motion at all. At ISIs slightly longer than those yielding simultaneity, the leftmost element in frame 1 appears to jump to the rightmost element in frame 2. This percept is called *element motion*. At somewhat longer ISIs, all three flashes seem to move together between frame 1 and frame 2. This is called *group motion*.

The percept of group motion might suggest that Ternus percepts are due to a cognitive process that groups the flashes into attended objects, and that motion perception occurs only after object perception. Such an explanation is not, however, made easily consistent with the percept of element motion. It has been argued, for example, that at short ISIs, the visual persistence of the brain's response to the two rightmost flashes of frame 1 continues until the two leftmost flashes of frame 2 occur (Braddick, 1980; Braddick and Adlard, 1978; Breitmeyer and Ritter, 1986; Pantle and Petersik, 1980). As a result, nothing changes at these two flash locations when frame 2 occurs, so they do not seem to move. This type of explanation suggests that at least part of the apparent motion percept is determined at early processing stages. It does not,

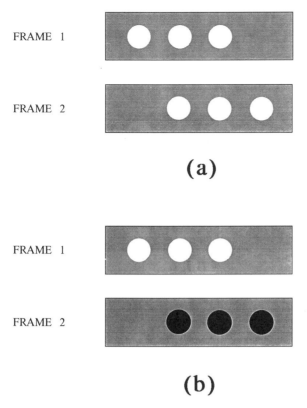

FRAME 1

FRAME 2

(a)

FRAME 1

FRAME 2

(b)

Figure 15.1 The Ternus display. (*a*) Three spots are presented in each frame in such a way that the two leftwardmost spots in frame 2 occupy the same positions as the two rightwardmost spots in frame 1. The two frames are repeatedly cycled with interstimulus intervals (ISIs) inserted between them. At very short ISIs, all dots appear to flicker in place. At longer ISIs the dots at shared positions appear to remain stationary, while apparent motion occurs between the leftwardmost spot in frame 1 and the rightwardmost spot in frame 2 ("element motion"). At still longer ISIs, the three dots appear to move from frame 1 to frame 2 and back as a group ("group motion"). (*b*) When the dots in successive frames have opposite contrast with respect to the frame, only group motion occurs at the ISIs where element motion occurred in (*a*). (From Grossberg and Rudd, 1992.)

however, explain how we see element motion. In particular, why does not the element motion percept collide with the two stationary flash percepts? What kind of perceptual space can carry element motion across, or over, the stationary flashes?

Reverse-contrast Ternus motion also suggests that motion properties may be determined at early processing stages. In this paradigm, three white spots on a gray background in frame 1 are followed by three black spots on a gray background in frame 2 (figure 15.1). At the ISIs where element motion previously occurred, group motion now occurs (Pantle and Picciano, 1976). How does a change of contrast between frame 1 and frame 2 obliterate element motion? Does it do so by altering the effects of visual persistence on frame 2?

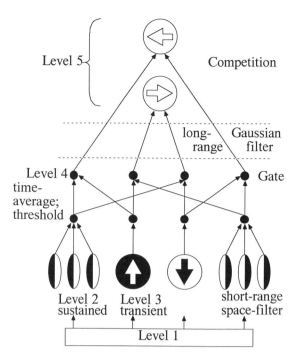

Figure 15.2 The simplest one-dimensional motion-oriented contrast-sensitive (MOC) filter. The input pattern at level 1 is spatially and temporally filtered by sustained response cells at level 2. The sustained cells have oriented receptive fields that are sensitive to the direction of contrast in the image, either dark-to-light or light-to-dark. Level 2 cells play the role of a short-range spatial filter. Spatial and temporal averaging are also carried out by transient response cells at level 3. The transient cells have unoriented receptive fields that are sensitive to the direction of contrast change in the cell input. The arrow pointing upward denotes transient on-cells that are activated by a transition from dark to light. The arrow pointing downward denotes transient off-cells that are activated by a transition from light to dark. Level 4 cells combine sustained and transient cell signals multiplicatively and are thus rendered sensitive to both direction of motion and direction of contrast. Level 5 cells sum across space via a long-range Gaussian spatial filter, and across the two types of level 4 cells. Level 5 cells are thus sensitive to direction of motion but insensitive to direction of contrast. (From Grossberg and Rudd, 1992.)

A unified answer to all of these questions has recently been developed in a neural model of motion segmentation that clarifies the functional significance of many apparent motion percepts (Grossberg, 1991; Grossberg and Mingolla, 1993; Grossberg and Rudd, 1989, 1992). Perhaps the simplest such model is schematized in figure 15.2. It is called a motion-oriented contrast-sensitive filter, or MOC filter. The entire model of motion segmentation consists of multiple copies of the MOC filter, each corresponding to a different range of receptive field sizes, and each inputting to a grouping, or binding, network that is called the motion-oriented cooperative-competitive loop, or MOCC loop. Taken together, these MOC filters and MOCC loops are called the motion boundary contour system, or motion BCS.

The motion BCS is designed to possess the minimal number of processing stages that are capable of tracking an object's direction of motion independent of whether the object's several parts are darker or lighter than the background upon which they are moving. Grossberg and Rudd (1992) showed that each of the MOC filter's processing stages is needed to explain the full corpus of data about beta, gamma, delta, Ternus, and related types of motion. The model's dynamics thereby illustrate how seemingly paradoxical apparent motion data may be explained as emergent properties of ecologically simple design constraints on the tracking of real moving objects.

Variable Speed Apparent Motion

In this chapter, I focus on one key process of the MOC filter; namely, how "large variations in distance are accommodated within a near-constant amount of time" (Kolers, 1972, p. 25). The mechanism that achieves this is posited to exist between levels 4 and 5 in figure 15.2. It is a surprisingly simple mechanism and utilizes components that are generally familiar to psychologists: a Gaussian filter followed by contrast enhancement due to lateral inhibition. Remarkably, in response to temporally successive inputs to the Gaussian filter, a traveling wave can be generated from the first input location to the second input location, and the peak of this wave can be contrast-enhanced by lateral inhibition to generate a focal activation that speeds up or slows down with increases or decreases of distance or ISI, just as in the data.

G-Waves for Long-Range Apparent Motion

How are long-range apparent motion signals generated in such a model? Figure 15.3 schematizes how a flash at level 1 (*a*) leads to a focal activation at level 5 (*c*) after it activates the long-range Gaussian filter that joins level 4 to level 5 (*b*). The broad Gaussian activation of level 5 is sharpened into a focal activation by lateral inhibition, or competition, among the level 5 cells.

Figure 15.4 shows how this input activation looks in time. The input to level 1 (*a*) generates a slowly decaying temporal trace (*b*) that has been called "visual inertia" by Anstis and Ramachandran (1987). When this trace is fed through the Gaussian filter, it generates a spatially distributed input to level 5 that waxes and wanes through time, without spreading across space (*c*). The maximum value of this input does not move. Hence a single flash does not cause a movement across space.

Suppose, however, that two locations both input through the same Gaussian receptive field, and that the activation in response to a flash at the first location is decaying while activation is growing in response to a flash at the second location (figure 15.5). Under these circumstances, the *total* input to level 5 from both flashes is the sum of a temporally waning Gaussian plus a temporally waxing Gaussian, as in figure 15.6. Under appropriate conditions,

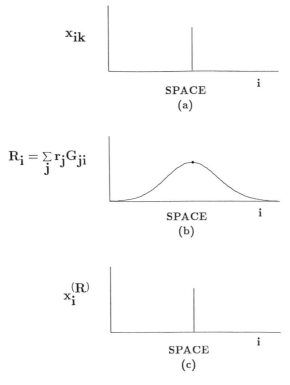

x_{ik}

SPACE i
(a)

$R_i = \sum_j r_j G_{ji}$

SPACE i
(b)

$x_i^{(R)}$

SPACE i
(c)

Figure 15.3 Spatial responses at various levels of the MOC filter to a point input. (*a*) Sustained activity of a level 2 cell. (*b*) Total input pattern to level 5 after convolution with a Gaussian kernel. (*c*) Contrast-enhanced output of level 5 centered at the location of the input maximum. (From Grossberg and Rudd, 1992.)

this sum represents a wave whose maximum travels continuously in time from the location of the first flash to the location of the second flash.

In summary, the time- and space-averaged responses to individual flashes do not change their positions of maximal activation through time. In this sense, nothing moves. When a series of properly timed and spaced flashes is presented, however, the sum of the temporally and spatially averaged responses that they generate can produce a continuously moving peak of activity between the positions of the stroboscopic flashes. This is an emergent property of network dynamics, rather than a property of any cell acting alone.

Motion Speedup and Multiscale Coherence

This Gaussian wave, called a G-wave, was discovered and mathematically analyzed in Grossberg (1977). These results waited 12 years for publication in Grossberg and Rudd (1989) because it took that long to understand how a long-range Gaussian filter fit into a larger theory of motion perception, such as the motion BCS, that also includes a role for transient cells and short-

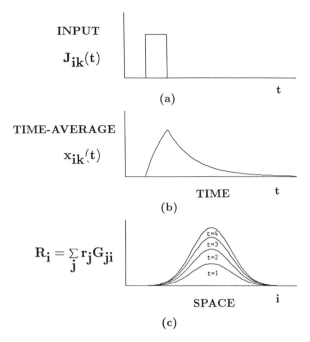

INPUT

$J_{ik}(t)$

(a)

TIME-AVERAGE

$x_{ik}(t)$

TIME   t

(b)

$R_i = \sum_j r_j G_{ji}$

t=4
t=3
t=2
t=1

SPACE   i

(c)

Figure 15.4 Temporal response of the MOC filter to a point input. (*a*) The input is presented at a brief duration at location 1. (*b*) Sustained cell activity at 1 gradually builds after the input onset, then decays after offset. (*c*) Growth of the input pattern to level 5 with transient cell activity held constant. The activity pattern retains a Gaussian shape centered at the location of the input that waxes and wanes through time without spreading across space. (From Grossberg and Rudd, 1992.)

range spatial interactions. A G-wave occurs whenever waxing and waning activation traces interact via a spatial Gaussian kernel under appropriate spatiotemporal conditions. The properties of a G-wave correspond closely to properties of long-range apparent motion, including the remarkable properties whereby an apparent motion percept can speed up when the ISI is decreased at a fixed interflash distance, or when the ISI is held constant and the interflash distance is increased.

The basic mathematical framework for proving these properties is very simple. Let flashes occur at positions $i = 0$ and $i = L$. Suppose that

$$\frac{dx_0}{dt} = -Ax_0 + J_0 \tag{1}$$

defines the activity x_0 and input J_0 at position 0, and

$$\frac{dx_L}{dt} = -Ax_L + J_L, \tag{2}$$

does the same at position L, where $x_0(0) = x_L(0) = 0$. Then

$$x_0(t) = \int_0^t e^{-A(t-v)} J_0(v) \, dv \tag{3}$$

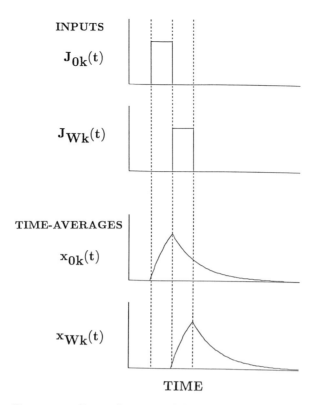

INPUTS

$J_{0k}(t)$

$J_{Wk}(t)$

TIME-AVERAGES

$x_{0k}(t)$

$x_{Wk}(t)$

TIME

Figure 15.5 Temporal response of the sustained cells $x_{ik}(t)$ at level 2 to two brief successive point inputs $I_{ik}(t)$ at locations $i = 0$ and $i = W$. For an appropriately timed display, the decaying response at position 0 overlaps in time the rising response at position W. Parameter k is defined in the full model. (From Grossberg and Rudd, 1992.)

and

$$x_L(t) = \int_0^t e^{-A(t-v)} J_L(v)\, dv. \tag{4}$$

Let the inputs J_0 and J_L switch on to the constant value J at times 0 and $T + I$ for duration T, as in

$$J_0(t) = \begin{cases} J & \text{if } 0 \leqslant t \leqslant T \\ 0 & \text{if } T < t \end{cases} \tag{5}$$

and

$$J_L(t) = \begin{cases} J & \text{if } T + I \leqslant t \leqslant 2T + I \\ 0 & \text{if } 2T + I < t \end{cases} \tag{6}$$

where I is the ISI between the flashes. Then for $T + I \leqslant t \leqslant 2T + I$,

$$x_0(t) = \frac{J}{A}(1 - e^{-AT})e^{-A(t-T)} \tag{7}$$

and

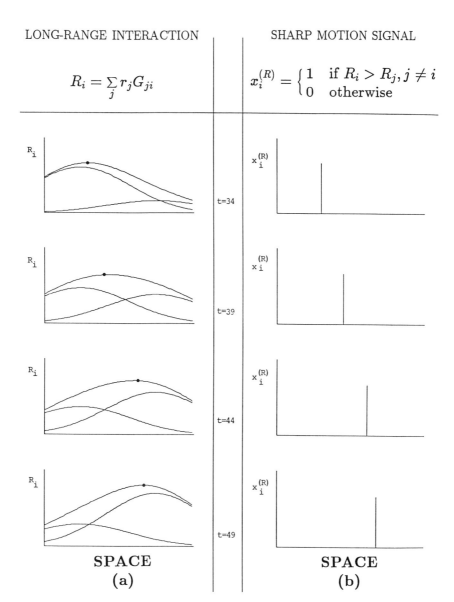

LONG-RANGE INTERACTION

$$R_i = \sum_j r_j G_{ji}$$

SHARP MOTION SIGNAL

$$x_i^{(R)} = \begin{cases} 1 & \text{if } R_i > R_j, j \neq i \\ 0 & \text{otherwise} \end{cases}$$

R_i

R_i

R_i

R_i

$x_i^{(R)}$

$x_i^{(R)}$

$x_i^{(R)}$

$x_i^{(R)}$

t=34

t=39

t=44

t=49

SPACE
(a)

SPACE
(b)

Figure 15.6 Simulated MOC filter response to a two-flash display. Successive rows correspond to increasing times following the frame 1 offset. (*a*) The two lower curves in each row depict the total input R_i at position i of level 5 due to each of the two flashes. The input due to the left flash decreases while the input due to the right flash increases. The summed input due to both flashes is a traveling wave whose maximum value across space moves continuously between the two flash locations. (*b*) Position over time of the contrast-enhanced level 5 response. (From Grossberg and Rudd, 1992.)

$$x_L(t) = \frac{J}{A}(1 - e^{-A(t-T-I)}).$$ (8)

Let $x_0(t)$ and $x_L(t)$ interact via a long-range Gaussian filter

$$G_{ji} = \exp[-(j-i)^2/2K^2]$$ (9)

as in figure 15.2. For simplicity, replace index i by a continuum of cells at positions w in level 5. Then the total input to position w of level 5 is

$$T(w, t) = x_0(t) \exp\left[\frac{-w^2}{2K^2}\right] + x_L(t) \exp\left[\frac{-(w-L)^2}{2K^2}\right].$$ (10)

By equations (7) and (8),

$$T(w, t) = \frac{J}{A}\left[(1 - e^{-AT})e^{-A(t-T)} \exp\left[\frac{w^2}{2K^2}\right]\right.$$

$$\left. + (1 - e^{-A(t-T-I)}) \exp\left[\frac{(w-L)^2}{2K^2}\right]\right].$$ (11)

The main result shows under what combinations of parameters the maximum value of $T(w, t)$ moves continuously from position $w = 0$ toward position $w = L$ through time. It also characterizes the maximum flash separation that can generate a G-wave in response to a Gaussian with size parameter K in equation (9).

Theorem 1 (Apparent Motion) The maximum of $T(w, t)$ moves continuously from position $w = 0$ to position $w = L$ iff

$$L < 2K.$$ (12)

Proof The maximum values of $T(w, t)$ occur only at locations $w = w(t)$ such that

$$\frac{\partial T(w, t)}{\partial w} = 0.$$ (13)

By equation (11), such locations obey the equation

$$\frac{e^{A(t-T)} - e^{AI}}{1 - e^{-AT}} = \frac{w}{L-w} \exp\left[\frac{L(L-2w)}{2K^2}\right].$$ (14)

The function

$$f(t) = \frac{e^{A(t-T)} - e^{AI}}{1 - e^{-AT}}$$ (15)

is an increasing function of t. We want to determine when the positions $w = w(t)$ at which $T(w, t)$ is a maximal increase as a function of t. In order for this to happen, the right-hand side of equation (14), namely function

$$g(w) = \frac{w}{L-w} \exp\left[\frac{L(L-2w)}{2K^2}\right],$$ (16)

must also be an increasing function of w, for all $0 \leqslant w \leqslant L$, since then we can solve for

$$w = g^{-1}(f(t)) \tag{17}$$

as an increasing function of w for all $0 \leqslant w \leqslant L$.

Function $g(w)$ is monotonically increasing if $g'(w) > 0$, which holds iff function

$$h(w) \equiv (L - w)\left[1 - \frac{Lw}{K^2}\right] + w \tag{18}$$

satisfies

$$h(w) > 0. \tag{19}$$

In order for equation (17) to hold for all $0 \leqslant w \leqslant L$, the minimum of $h(w)$ for $0 \leqslant w \leqslant L$ must be positive. The minimum of $h(w)$ occurs at $w = L/2$, and equals

$$h\left(\frac{L}{2}\right) = \frac{L}{2}\left(2 - \frac{L^2}{2K^2}\right). \tag{20}$$

The number $h\left(\frac{L}{2}\right)$ is positive if equation (12) holds.

The next result proves that the apparent motion signal reaches the position $w = L/2$ midway between positions $w = 0$ and $w = L$ at a time $t_{1/2}$ that is independent of L and K. Independence of L illustrates how the wave speeds up to travel over larger interflash distances.

Theorem 2 (Equal Half-Time Property)   The time at which the motion signal reaches position $w = L/2$ is

$$t_{1/2} = T + \frac{1}{A}\ln[e^{AI} + (1 - e^{-AT})]. \tag{21}$$

Proof   By equation (17), we need to compute $t = f^{-1}(g(w))$ when $w = L/2$, namely

$$t_{1/2} = f^{-1}\left(g\left(\frac{L}{2}\right)\right). \tag{22}$$

By equation (16),

$$g\left(\frac{L}{2}\right) = 1. \tag{23}$$

Equation (21) follows immediately from equations (23) and (14).

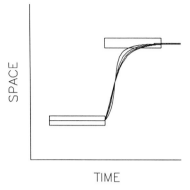

SPACE

TIME

Figure 15.7 Motion paths generated by MOC filters with different Gaussian filter kernel widths K in equation (9). The motion paths are plotted in a space-time diagram wherein each rectangle indicates the spatiotemporal boundaries of one flash in a two-flash display. All the motion paths intersect at a point halfway between the two flash locations. (From Grossberg and Rudd, 1992.)

Remarkably, $t_{1/2}$ in equation (21) also does not depend on the width K of the Gaussian filter, just so long as the filter is wide enough to support a traveling wave. This means that the speedup property, which seems so mysterious in itself, also achieves an ecologically useful property; namely, the ability of multiple spatial scales in the motion perception system to generate G-waves that are all spatially coincident (figure 15.7). Because of this property, a coherent motion percept may be synthesized from data from all the spatial scales that are activated by the stimulus.

Spatial Attention Shifts and Target Tracking by the Where Cortical Stream

Another no less useful ecological property of motion speedup is suggested by the fact that rapidly moving objects may be perceived only intermittently. From this perspective, I suggest that a G-wave may give rise to certain spatial shifts in attention, such as those reported by Ericksen and Murphy (1987), Kwak, Dagenbach, and Egeth (1991), LaBerge and Brown (1989), and Remington and Pierce (1984). For example, if a targeted predator or prey is moving rapidly across a scene, perhaps darting behind protective cover, then an animal may be able to see the target only intermittently. A G-wave can interpolate these temporally discrete views with a continuous motion signal that adapts its speed to the varying speed of the target. Such a continuous motion signal may be used to predict the location and speed of the target, and to command motor responses accordingly. The results of Kwak et al. (1991) and of Remington and Pierce (1984) are of particular interest, since they report a speedup of spatial attention to cover variable distances in equal time.

In those cases where motion mechanisms contribute to spatial attention shifts, it needs to be kept in mind that a spatially continuous motion signal is generated only under certain spatiotemporal conditions, the speed of the motion signal is nonuniform in time (see Grossberg and Rudd, 1992), and spatially discrete jumps in activation may occur in cases where continuous motion is not observed, e.g., if $L > 2K$ in equation (12). These properties may help to disentangle some of the apparently conflicting views about how fast attention shifts and whether it does so continuously or discretely.

In thinking about these possibilities, the reader might wonder how a continuous motion signal could be interpolated behind occluding objects in such a way that it is not seen. Two themes need to be developed to understand how this might happen. First, the theory predicts that a boundary segmentation, whether static or moving, is perceptually invisible within the parvocellular interstripe and magnocellular processing streams of the visual cortex wherein they are predicted to be computed. I like to say that "all boundaries are invisible." Visibility is predicted to be a property of the parallel parvocellular blob cortical stream (figure 15.8). Here boundary segmentations define the domains within which visible properties of brightness, color, and depth fill in surface representations. (See Grossberg and Mingolla, 1993, and Grossberg, Mingolla, and Todorović, 1989, for a discussion of how this is predicted to happen.) In addition, one needs to analyze how a boundary segmentation, whether static or moving, can be completed "behind" an occluding object in such a way that it can influence object recognition without being seen. Examples of such occluded boundary completions are discussed in Grossberg (1994). Bregman (1990, p. 23) has also commented on the possible utility of a motion signal that can interpolate intermittently viewed moving objects. The present theory suggests a dynamical explanation of how this can happen in the brain.

15.3 MODELING RECOGNITION LEARNING AND CATEGORIZATION

Spatial Attention, Featural Attention, and Perceptual Binding in the What and Where Cortical Streams

The hypothesis that a G-wave may give rise to a spatial attention shift is consistent with the fact that the motion perception, or magnocellular, cortical processing stream is part of a larger Where processing stream that includes the cortical region MT as well as the parietal cortex (figure 15.8). The Where processing stream computes the locations of targets with respect to an observer and helps to direct attention and action toward them. In contrast, the form perception, or parvocellular, cortical processing stream is part of a larger What processing stream that includes region V4 as well as the IT (figure 15.8). The What processing stream is used to recognize targets based on prior learning.

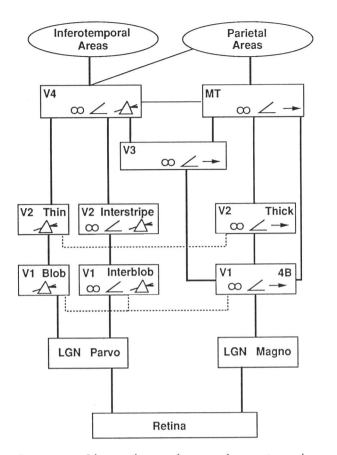

Figure 15.8 Schematic diagram of anatomical connections and neuronal selectivities of early visual areas in the macaque monkey. LGN, lateral geniculate nucleus (parvocellular and magnocellular divisions). Divisions of V1 and V2: Blob, cytochrome oxidase blob regions; interblob = cytochrome oxidase-poor regions surrounding the blobs; 4B, lamina 4B; Thin, thin (narrow) cytochrome oxidase strips; interstripe, cytochrome oxidase-poor regions between the thin and thick stripes; Thick, thick (wide) cytochrome oxidase strips; V3, visual area 3; V4, visual area(s) 4; MT, middle temporal area. Areas V2, V3, V4, MT have connections to other areas not explicitly represented here. Area V3 may also receive projections from V2 interstripes or thin stripes. Heavy lines indicate robust primary connections, and thin lines indicate weaker, more variable connections. Dotted lines represent observed connections that require additional verification. Icons: rainbow, tuned/opponent wavelength selectivity (incidence at least 40%); angle symbol, orientation selectivity (incidence at least 20%); spectacles, binocular disparity selectivity/strong binocular interactions (V2) (incidence at least 20%); pointing arrow direction of motion selectivity (incidence at least 20%). (Adapted from DeYoe and van Essen, 1988.)

The second model of this chapter contributes to the understanding of how humans and other animals can rapidly learn to recognize and categorize objects in their environments under autonomous learning conditions in real time. Here again, attention plays a key role. It does not predict a spatial location of a target. Rather, it amplifies and binds together feature combinations that are used to categorize environmental events into object representations.

Table 15.1 Complementary properties of an ART recognition architecture

Stability	Plasticity
Attention	Orientation
Short-term memory	Long-term memory
Bottom-up	Top-down
Match	Mismatch
Direct access	Memory search
Resonance	Reset
Supraliminal	Subliminal
Specific	Nonspecific
Local features	Global patterns
Attentional gain	Vigilance
Cooperation	Competition
Distributed	Compressed

The Stability-Plasticity Dilemma

An adequate self-organizing recognition system must be capable of *plasticity* in order to rapidly learn about significant new events, yet its memory must also remain *stable* in response to irrelevant or often-repeated events. For example, how do we rapidly learn to recognize new faces without risking the unselective forgetting of our parents' faces? In order to prevent the unselective forgetting of its learned codes by the "blooming, buzzing confusion" of irrelevant experience, a self-organizing recognition system must be sensitive to *novelty*. It needs to be capable of distinguishing between familiar and unfamiliar events, as well as between expected and unexpected events.

A class of neural models, called adaptive resonance theory, or ART, was introduced in 1976 to help understand how this is accomplished (Grossberg, 1976a,b). In ART, dynamical interactions between an attentional subsystem and an orienting subsystem, or novelty detector, self-stabilize learning, without an external teacher, as the network familiarizes itself with an environment by categorizing the information within it in a way that predicts behaviorally successful outcomes (Carpenter and Grossberg, 1991; Grossberg, 1980). ART models combine several types of processes that have been demonstrated in cognitive and neurobiological experiments, but not otherwise synthesized into a model system. Table 15.1 lists some of the cognitive processes that are joined together in a consistent computational format within ART systems. This synthesis illustrates that learning and information-processing mechanisms need to coevolve in order to achieve behaviorally useful properties. It also clarifies how higher-order cognitive processes, such as hypothesis testing of learned top-down expectations. control such apparently lower-order processes as the learning of bottom-up recognition categories. That is why an analysis of *recognition* needs also to be framed as an analysis of *learning*.

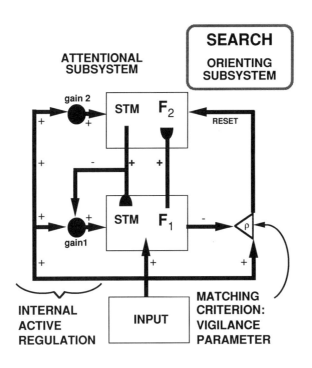

Stephen Grossberg

Competitive Learning and Self-Organizing Feature Maps

All the learning goes on in the attentional subsystem. Its processes include activation of short-term memory (STM) traces, incorporation through learning of momentary STM information into longer-lasting, long-term memory (LTM) traces, and interactions between pathways that carry specific types of information with nonspecific pathways that modulate the specific pathways in several different ways. These interactions between specific STM and LTM processes and nonspecific modulatory processes regulate the stability-plasticity balance during normal learning.

The attentional subsystem undergoes both bottom-up learning and top-down learning between the processing levels denoted by F_1 and F_2 in figure 15.9. Level F_1 contains a network of nodes, or cell populations, each of which represents a particular combination of sensory features. Level F_2 contains a network of nodes that represent recognition codes, or categories, which are selectively activated by the patterns of activation across F_1. Each node in F_1 sends output signals to a subset of nodes in F_2. Each node in F_2 thus receives inputs from many F_1 nodes. The thick symbol from F_1 to F_2 in figure 15.9A represents in a concise way the array of diverging and converging pathways shown in figure 15.9B. Learning takes place at the synapses denoted by semicircular endings in the $F_1 \rightarrow F_2$ pathways. Pathways that end in arrowheads do not undergo learning. This bottom-up learning enables F_2 nodes to become selectively tuned to particular combinations of activation patterns across F_1 by changing their LTM traces. This basic property of recognition learning is mathematically proved below.

Why does not bottom-up learning suffice? An analysis of this problem was carried out in a type of model called a self-organizing feature map, competitive learning, or learned vector quantization that forms part of a larger ART system. Such a bottom-up learning model shows how to combine associative learning and lateral inhibition for purposes of learned categorization. As

Figure 15.9 Interactions between the attentional and orienting subsystems of an adaptive resonance theory (ART) circuit: Level F_1 encodes a distributed representation of an event to be recognized via a short-term memory (STM) activation pattern across a network of feature detectors. Level F_2 encodes the event to be recognized using a more compressed STM representation of the F_1 pattern. Learning of these recognition codes takes place at the long-term memory (LTM) traces within the bottom-up and top-down pathways between levels F_1 and F_2. The top-down pathways can read out learned expectations whose prototypes are matched against bottom-up input patterns at F_1. Mismatches in response to novel events activate the orienting subsystem $\mathscr{A}$ on the right side of the figure, depending on the value of the vigilance parameter ρ. Arousal emitted from $\mathscr{A}$ resets the recognition codes that are active in STM at F_2 and initiates a memory search for a more appropriate recognition code. Output from subsystem $\mathscr{A}$ can also trigger an orienting response. (A) Block diagram of circuit. (From Carpenter and Grossberg, 1990.) (B) Individual pathways of circuit, including the input level F_0 that generates inputs to level F_1. The gain control input to level F_1 helps to instantiate the 2/3 rule (see text). Gain control to level F_2 is needed to instate a category in STM. (From Carpenter, Grossberg, and Reynolds, 1991.)

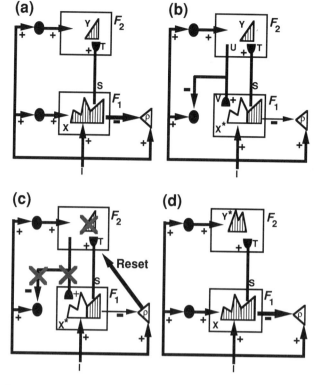

Figure 15.10 ART search for an F_2 recognition code: (*a*) The input pattern **I** generates the specific STM activity pattern **X** at F_1 as it nonspecifically activates the orienting subsystem $\mathscr{A}$. **X** is represented by the hatched pattern across F_1. Pattern **X** both inhibits $\mathscr{A}$ and generates the output pattern **S**. Pattern **S** is transformed by the LTM traces into the input pattern **T**, which activates the STM pattern **Y** across F_2. (*b*) Pattern **Y** generates the top-down output pattern **U** which is transformed into the prototype pattern **V**. If **V** mismatches **I** at F_1, then a new STM activity pattern **X*** is generated at F_1. **X*** is represented by the hatched pattern. Inactive nodes corresponding to **X** are unhatched. The reduction in total STM activity, which occurs when **X** is transformed into **X***, causes a decrease in the total inhibition from F_1 to $\mathscr{A}$. (*c*) If the vigilance criterion fails to be met, $\mathscr{A}$ releases a nonspecific arousal wave to F_2, which resets the STM pattern **Y** at F_2. (*d*) After **Y** is inhibited, its top-down prototype signal is eliminated, and **X** can be reinstated at F_1. Enduring traces of the prior reset lead **X** to activate a different STM pattern **Y*** at F_2. If the top-down prototype due to **Y*** also mismatches **I** at F_1, then the search for an appropriate F_2 code continues until a more appropriate F_2 representation is selected. Then an attentive resonance develops and learning of the attended data is initiated. (From Carpenter and Grossberg, 1990.)

shown in figure 15.10a, an input pattern is normalized and registered as a pattern of activity, or STM, across the feature detectors of level F_1. Each F_1 output signal is multiplied or gated, by the adaptive weight, or LTM trace, in its respective pathway. All these LTM-gated inputs are added up at their target F_2 nodes. Lateral inhibitory, or competitive, interactions across the F_2 nodes contrast-enhance this input pattern. Whereas many F_2 nodes may receive inputs from F_1, lateral inhibition allows a much smaller set of F_2 nodes to store their activation in STM.

Only the F_2 nodes that win the competition and store their activity in STM can influence the learning process. STM activity opens a learning gate at the LTM traces that abut the winning nodes. These LTM traces can then approach, or track, the input signals in their pathways by a process of steepest descent. This learning law is thus often called *gated steepest descent*, or *instar learning*. It was introduced into neural network models in the 1960s (Grossberg, 1969) and is the learning law that was used to introduce ART (Grossberg, 1976a,b). In particular, let x_{1i} denote the STM activity of the ith F_1 node, x_{2j} the STM activity of the jth F_2 node, and z_{ij} the adaptive weight or LTM trace in the bottom-up pathway from node i in F_1 to node j in F_2. Then the rate of change through time of z_{ij}, denoted by $(d/dt)z_{ij}$, obeys an equation of the form

$$\frac{d}{dt}z_{ij} = f(x_{2j})[-z_{ij} + g(x_{1i})], \tag{24}$$

where f and g are non-negative signal functions. Note that if $f(x_{2j}) = 0$, then $(d/dt)z_{ij} = 0$. Thus no learning occurs if the gate $f(x_{2j})$ is closed. This can occur either if no inputs perturb F_1 or if node j loses the competition across F_2. If $f(x_{2j}) > 0$, then z_{ij} increases if $g(x_{1i}) > z_{ij}$ and decreases if $g(x_{1i}) < z_{ij}$.

Such an LTM trace z_{ij} can increase or decrease to track the signal $g(x_{1i})$ in its pathway. It is thus not a Hebbian associative law, which can only increase during a learning episode. Because the adaptive weight z_{ij} can either increase or decrease in size, the same law [equation (24)] can control both long-term potentiation (LTP) and long-term depression (LTD). Equation (24) has been used to model neurophysiological data about hippocampal LTP (Levy, 1985; Levy and Desmond, 1985) and adaptive tuning of cortical feature detectors during the visual critical period (Rauschecker and Singer, 1979; Singer, 1983), lending support to ART predictions that both systems would employ such a learning law (Grossberg, 1976a,b).

Self-organizing feature map models were introduced and characterized computationally in Grossberg (1972, 1976a,b, 1978), Malsburg (1973), and Willshaw and Malsburg (1976). These models were subsequently applied and further developed by many authors (Amari and Takeuchi, 1978; Bienenstock, Cooper, and Munro, 1982; Cohen and Grossberg, 1987; Grossberg, 1982, 1987a,b; Grossberg and Kuperstein, 1986; Kohonen, 1984; Linsker, 1986; Rumelhart and Zipser, 1985). They exhibit many useful properties, especially if not too many input patterns, or clusters of input patterns, perturb level F_1 relative to the number of categorizing nodes in level F_2. It was shown that under these sparse environmental conditions, category learning is stable; the LTM traces track the statistics of the environment, are self-normalizing, and oscillate a minimum number of times (Grossberg, 1976a,b, 1978). In addition, it was observed that the category selection rule tends to minimize error, as in a Bayesian classifier. These are the basic properties that have been used in all subsequent applications.

It was also proved, however, that under arbitrary environmental conditions, learning becomes unstable. If our own learned categorizations exhibited this property, we could forget our parents' faces. Although a gradual switching off of plasticity can partially overcome this problem, such a mechanism cannot work in a recognition learning system whose plasticity needs to be maintained throughout adulthood. This memory instability is due to basic properties of associative learning and lateral inhibition. ART models were introduced to incorporate self-organizing feature maps in such a way as to stabilize their learning in response to an arbitrary stream of input patterns.

Feature Binding and Attentional Focusing

In an ART model (Carpenter and Grossberg, 1987, 1991), learning does not occur as soon as some winning F_2 activities are stored in STM. Instead activation of F_2 nodes may be interpreted as "making a hypothesis" about an input at F_1. When F_2 is activated, it quickly generates an output pattern that is transmitted along the top-down adaptive pathways from F_2 to F_1. These top-down signals are multiplied in their respective pathways by LTM traces at the semicircular synaptic knobs of figure 15.10b. The LTM-gated signals from all the active F_2 nodes are added to generate the total top-down feedback pattern from F_2 to F_1. This pattern plays the role of a learned expectation. Activation of this expectation "tests the hypothesis," or "reads out the prototype," of the active F_2 category. As shown in figure 15.10(b), ART networks are designed to match the "expected prototype" of the category against the bottom-up input pattern, or exemplar, to F_1. Nodes that are activated by this exemplar are suppressed if they do not correspond to large LTM traces in the top-down prototype pattern. The matched F_1 pattern encodes the cluster of input features that are relevant to the hypothesis based on the network's past experience. This resultant activity pattern, called $\mathbf{X}^*$ in figure 15.10b, encodes the pattern of features to which the network starts to "pay attention."

If the expectation is close enough to the input exemplar, then a state of *resonance* develops as the attentional focus takes hold. The pattern $\mathbf{X}^*$ of attended features reactivates the F_2 category $\mathbf{Y}$ which, in turn, reactivates $\mathbf{X}^*$. The network locks into a resonant state through a positive feedback loop that dynamically links, or binds, $\mathbf{X}^*$ with $\mathbf{Y}$. Damasio (1989) has used the term *convergence zones* to describe such a resonant process. The resonance binds spatially distributed features into either a stable equilibrium or a synchronous oscillation (Eckhorn and Schanze, 1991; Grossberg and Somers, 1991, 1992) with properties much like synchronous feature binding in visual cortex (Eckhorn, Bauer, Jordan, et al., 1988; Gray and Singer, 1989; Gray, Konig, Engel, et al., 1989).

In ART, the resonant state, rather than bottom-up activation, drives the learning process. The resonant state persists long enough, at a high enough activity level, to activate the slower learning process; hence the term *adaptive resonance* theory. The resonance process shows how dynamic properties, such as differences in the faster STM rates and slower LTM rates, are exploited by the system as a whole. Fast information processing in STM is altered by previously learned LTM traces, even if the LTM traces do not undergo new learning as a result of the STM patterns that they help to create. When an STM resonance is maintained through a feedback exchange of bottom-up and top-down signals, it lasts long enough for the slower LTM traces to respond to the resonating STM activities and to undergo new learning. In effect, the resonance embodies a global system-wide consensus that the resonating STM patterns are worth learning about.

ART systems learn prototypes, rather than exemplars, because the attended feature vector X^*, rather than the input exemplar itself, is learned. These prototypes may, however, also be used to encode individual exemplars. How the matching process achieves this is described below. If the mismatch between bottom-up and top-down information is too great, then resonance cannot develop. Instead, the F_2 category is quickly reset before erroneous learning can occur, and a bout of hypothesis testing, or memory search, is initiated to discover a better category. This combination of top-down matching, attention focusing, and memory search is what stabilizes ART learning and memory in an arbitrary input environment. The top-down matching process suppresses those features within an exemplar that are not expected and starts to focus attention on the features X^* that are shared by the exemplar and the active prototype. The memory search chooses a new category on a fast time scale, before an exemplar that is too different from the prototype can destabilize its previous learning. How these matching and search operations work will now be summarized.

Phonemic Restoration, Priming, and Consciousness

The ART attentive matching process is realized by combining bottom-up inputs and top-down expectations with a nonspecific arousal process that is called attentional gain control (Carpenter and Grossberg, 1987, 1991). An F_1 node can be fully activated only if two of the three input sources that converge on the node send positive signals to the node at a given time. This constraint is called the 2/3 rule. A bottom-up input pattern turns on the attentional gain control channel in order to instate itself in STM at F_1 (see figure 15.10a). A top-down expectation turns off the attentional gain control channel (see figure 15.10b). As a result, only those input features that are confirmed by the top-down prototype can be attended at F_1 after an F_2 category is selected.

The 2/3 rule enables an ART network to solve the stability-plasticity dilemma. Carpenter and Grossberg (1987) proved that ART learning and memory are stable in arbitrary environments, but become unstable when 2/3 rule matching is eliminated. Thus the matching law that guarantees stable learning also enables the network to pay attention. This type of insight could never be derived without an analysis of the dynamics of autonomous learning in real time.

Matching by the 2/3 rule in the brain is illustrated by experiments on "phonemic restoration" (Repp, 1991; Samuel, 1981a,b; Warren, 1984; Warren and Sherman, 1974). Suppose that a noise spectrum replaces a letter sound, or phonetic segment, in a word heard in an otherwise unambiguous context. Then subjects hear the correct phonetic segment, not the noise, to the extent that the noise spectrum includes the acoustical signal of the phones. If silence replaces the noise, then only silence is heard. Top-down expectations thus amplify expected input features while suppressing unexpected features, but do not create activations not already in the input, just as in the 2/3 rule.

The 2/3 rule for matching also explains paradoxical reaction time and error data from priming experiments during lexical decision and letter gap detection tasks (Grossberg and Stone, 1986; Schvaneveldt and MacDonald, 1981). Although priming is often thought of as a residual effect of previous bottom-up activation, a combination of bottom-up activation and top-down 2/3 rule matching was needed to explain the complete data pattern. This analysis combined bottom-up priming with a type of top-down priming; namely, the top-down activation that prepares a network for an expected event that may or may not occur. The 2/3 rule hereby clarifies why priming, by itself, is subliminal and unconscious, even though it can facilitate supraliminal processing of a subsequent expected event. Only the resonant state can support a conscious event in the model.

These examples illustrate how data from a variety of experimental paradigms can emerge from computational properties that are designed to accomplish quite different functions than the paradigm itself might disclose: in this case, fast and stable recognition learning in response to a rapidly changing environment.

Memory Search, Vigilance, and Category Generalization

The criterion of an acceptable 2/3 rule match is defined by the model parameter ρ that is called *vigilance* (Carpenter and Grossberg, 1987, 1991). The vigilance parameter is computed in the orienting subsystem $\mathscr{A}$. Vigilance weighs how similar an input exemplar $\mathbf{I}$ must be to a top-down prototype $\mathbf{V}$ in order for resonance to occur. It does so by comparing the total amount of inhibition from the attentional focus at F_1 with the total amount of excitation from the input pattern $\mathbf{I}$ (see figure 15.10b). In cases where binary features are processed, the 2/3 rule implies that the attentional focus $\mathbf{X}^*$ equals the intersection $\mathbf{I} \cap \mathbf{V}$ of the bottom-up exemplar $\mathbf{I}$ and the top-down prototype $\mathbf{V}$. Resonance occurs if $\rho|\mathbf{I}| - |\mathbf{X}^*| \leqslant 0$. This inequality says that the F_1 attentional focus X^* inhibits $\mathscr{A}$ more than the input I excites it. If $\mathscr{A}$ is inhibited, then a resonance has time to develop between F_1 and F_2.

Vigilance calibrates how much novelty the system can tolerate before activating $\mathscr{A}$ and searching for a different category. If the top-down expectation and the bottom-up input are too different to satisfy the resonance criterion, then hypothesis testing, or memory search, is triggered, because the inhibition from F_1 to $\mathscr{A}$ is no longer sufficient to prevent the excitation due to I from activating $\mathscr{A}$. Nonspecific arousal from $\mathscr{A}$ to F_2 resets the active category at F_2 and initiates the memory search. Memory search leads to selection of a better category at level F_2 with which to represent the input features at level F_1. During search, the orienting subsystem interacts with the attentional subsystem, as in figure 15.10c and d, to rapidly reset mismatched categories and to select other F_2 representations with which to learn about novel events, without risking unselective forgetting of previous knowledge. Search may select a familiar category if its prototype is similar enough to the input to satisfy the vigilance criterion. The prototype may then be refined by 2/3 rule attentional focusing. If the input is too different from any previously learned prototype, then an uncommitted population of F_2 cells is rapidly selected and learning of a new category is initiated.

Supervised Learning of Many-to-One Maps from Categories to Names

Because vigilance can vary across learning trials, recognition categories capable of encoding widely differing degrees of generalization or abstraction can be learned by a single ART system. Low vigilance ρ leads to broad generalization and abstract prototypes because exemplars I that differ greatly from an active prototype V can satisfy $\rho |I| - |X^*| \leqslant 0$. High vigilance leads to narrow generalization and to prototypes that represent fewer input exemplars, even a single exemplar. Thus a single ART system may be used, say, to recognize abstract categories that encode higher-order invariants of faces and dogs, as well as individual faces and dogs. ART systems hereby provide a new answer to whether the brain learns prototypes or exemplars. Various authors have realized that neither one nor the other alternative is satisfactory, and that a hybrid system is needed (Smith, 1990).

Supervised ART, or ARTMAP systems can perform this hybrid function in a manner that is sensitive to environmental demands (figure 15.11). In an ARTMAP system, predictive errors can be used to trigger searches for new categories. As a result, many categories in one modality (e.g., visual recognition categories) may be learned and associated with each category in another modality (e.g., auditory naming categories), just as there may be many different visual fonts that all have the same name "A." A predictive error in naming increases the vigilance ρ in the visual categorization network just enough to satisfy $\rho |I| - |X^*| > 0$ and thereby to activate $\mathscr{A}$ and initiate a memory search for a better visual category with which to predict the desired name

MANY-TO-ONE MAP

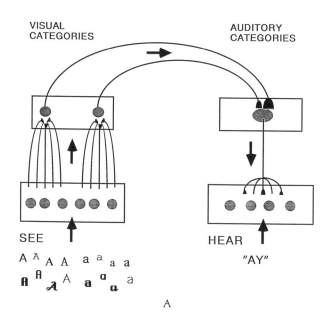

A

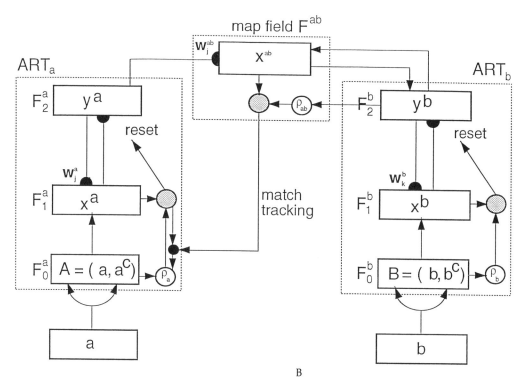

B

Stephen Grossberg

(Carpenter and Grossberg, 1992; Carpenter, Grossberg, and Reynolds, 1991; Carpenter, Grossberg, Markuzon, et al., 1992). Since low vigilance leads to learning of the most general categories, this operation, which is called *match tracking*, sacrifices the minimal amount of visual generalization on each learning trial in order to correct a naming error.

Such a supervised ART system performs extremely well relative to other machine learning, genetic algorithm, and backpropagation networks in benchmark simulations. Objective performance measures show that a fuzzy ARTMAP does much better than these other models on many standard recognition problems. These benchmarks indicate that models of biological learning enjoy major computational advantages over more traditional approaches. These benchmarks are described in detail in Carpenter, Grossberg, and Reynolds (1991) and Carpenter et al. (1992).

Memory Consolidation as an Emergent Property of Network Dynamics

As inputs are practiced over learning trials, the search process eventually converges on stable categories that access the corresponding category directly, without the need for search. The category that is selected is the one whose prototype provides the globally best match to the input pattern at the system's present state of knowledge. In this way, "familiar" patterns can resonate with their category without the need for search, much as Gibson (1979, p. 249) may have intended when he hypothesized that the perceptual system "resonates to the invariant structure or is attuned to it." If both familiar and unfamiliar events are experienced through time, familiar inputs can directly activate their learned categories, even while unfamiliar inputs continue to trigger adaptive memory searches for better categories, until the network's memory capacity is fully utilized (Carpenter and Grossberg, 1987, 1991).

This process whereby search is gradually and automatically disengaged may be interpreted as a form of memory consolidation. This type of memory consolidation is an emergent property of network interactions. It is, once again, a property that can only be understood by studying the network's dynamics. Emergent consolidation does not, however, preclude structural forms of consolidation, since persistent resonance may also be a trigger for other learning-dependent processes, such as transmitter production and protein synthesis, at individual cells.

Figure 15.11 (*A*) Many-to-one learning combines categorization of many exemplars into one category, and labeling of many categories with the same name. (*B*) In an ARTMAP architecture, the ART_a and ART_b networks form recognition categories of the separate streams of input vectors labelled **a** and **b**, as in the case of visual categories and their auditory naming categories. The map field learns an associative map from categories in ART_a to categories in ART_b. When a predicted output in ART_b is mismatched by an input vector **b**, the match tracking process increases the ART_a vigilance value ρ_A until $\rho_A|\mathbf{a}| - |\mathbf{x}^a| > 0$, thereby triggering memory search for a better set of features in **a** with which to build a category that can correctly predict **b**. (From Carpenter and Grossberg, 1992.)

Face Recognition and Inferotemporal Cortex

How do components of the ART model map onto brain mechanisms? To begin with, level F_2 properties may be compared with properties of cell activations in the IT during recognition learning in monkeys. The ability of F_2 nodes to learn categories with different levels of generalization clarifies how some IT cells can exhibit high specificity, such as selectivity to views of particular faces, while other cells respond to broader features of the animal's environment (Desimone, 1991; Desimone and Ungerleider, 1989; Gochin, Miller, Gross, et al., 1991; Harries and Perrett, 1991; Mishkin, 1982; Mishkin and Appenzeller, 1987; Perrett, Mistlin, and Chitty, 1987; Schwartz, Desimone, Albright, et al., 1983; Seibert and Waxman, 1991). In addition, when monkeys are exposed to easy and difficult discriminations, "in the difficult condition the animals adopted a stricter internal criterion for discriminating matching from nonmatching stimuli ... the animals' internal representations of the stimuli were better separated, independent of the criterion used to discriminate them ... [and] increased effort appears to cause enhancement of the responses and sharpened selectivity for attended stimuli" (Spitzer, Desimone, and Moran, 1988, pp. 339–340). These are also properties of model cells in F_2. Prototypes represent a smaller set of exemplars at higher vigilance levels, so a stricter matching criterion is learned. These exemplars match their finer prototypes better than do exemplars that match a coarser prototype. This better match more strongly activates the corresponding F_2 nodes.

Data from IT support the hypothesis that unfamiliar or unexpected stimuli nonspecifically activate level F_2 via the orienting subsystem. According to Desimone (1992), "the fact that the IT cortex has a reduced level of activation for familiar or expected stimuli suggests that a high level of cortical activation may itself serve as a trigger for attentional and orienting systems, causing the subject to orient to the stimulus causing the activation. This link between the mnemonic and attentional systems would 'close the loop' between the two systems, resulting in orienting behavior that is influenced by both current stimuli and prior memories. Such a mechanism has a number of similarities to the adaptive resonance theory" (p. 359). Properties of IT cells during working memory tasks suggest that active reset occurs at the end of each trial (Miller, Li, and Desimone, 1991; Riches, Wilson, and Brown, 1991). Reset of F_2 is also a key ART operation.

These recent neurophysiological data about IT cells during recognition tasks are thus reflected in level F_2 properties. Additional data suggest that the pulvinar may mediate aspects of attentional gain control (Desimone, 1992; Robinson and Peterson, 1992). Data that correlate the IT and pulvinar recordings are needed to critically test this hypothesis. Carpenter and Grossberg (1993) have suggested that the orienting operations whereby vigilance is controlled may take place in the hippocampal formation. They support this hypothesis by showing how a formal lesion of the orienting system in ART creates a set of properties strikingly like symptoms of medial temporal amnesia in human patients with hippocampal lesions. This linkage suggests the prediction that operations which make the novelty-related potentials of the hippocampal formation more sensitive to input changes may trigger the formation of more selective inferotemporal recognition categories. Such a correlation may be sought, for example, when monkeys learn easy and difficult discriminations. The hypothesis also suggests that operations which block hippocampal novelty potentials may lead to the learning of coarser recognition categories, with amnesic symptoms as the limiting case when the hippocampal formation is completely inoperative.

Feature Discovery by Competitive Learning

The above properties of ART systems have been computationally demonstrated and mathematically proved in a series of articles by Gail Carpenter and myself in collaboration with several students. The core articles are brought together in Carpenter and Grossberg (1991). In this chapter, some of the most important mathematical properties of competitive learning and self-organizing feature maps are reviewed. These properties are important both in themselves and as a stepping stone to a mathematical study of ART systems.

Perhaps the simplest competitive learning system is defined by the following equations. Let I_i be the input to the i node in F_1. Let fast competitive interactions within F_1 normalize this input. There are several possible types of normalization. In the simplest type, the normalized activity x_{1i} of the ith node, or cell population, in F_1 satisfies

$$x_{1i} = \theta_i \equiv \frac{I_i}{\sum_k I_k},$$ (25)

so that

$$\sum_i x_{1i} = 1.$$ (26)

Property (1) is called L^1 normalization. In L^p normalization, $\sum_i x_{1i}^p = 1$. The effects of choosing different values of p, notably $p = 2$, were first described in Grossberg (1978). Here we analyze the case $p = 1$, as in the Grossberg (1976a) model that was also used by Rumelhart and Zipser (1985).

The normalized signals θ_i are multiplied by adaptive weights z_{ij} and added to generate the total input

$$S_j = \sum_i \theta_i z_{ij}$$ (27)

to each node j in F_2. A competition between nodes in F_2 rapidly chooses the activity x_{2j} whose total input S_j is maximal for storage in STM, while normalizing the total activity of F_2. Such a network is often said to carry out a winner-take-all (WTA) operation. How a WTA competitive network may be designed was first described in Grossberg (1973). This fast competitive dynamical process may be approximated by the algebraic equation

$$x_{2j} = \begin{cases} 1 & \text{if } S_j > \max(\varepsilon, S_k : k \neq j) \\ 0 & \text{if } S_j \leqslant \max(\varepsilon, S_k : k \neq j) \end{cases}$$ (28)

where ε is a threshold that all inputs must exceed in order to trigger the STM choice and storage process.

Learning in the LTM traces takes place more slowly than the STM processes in equations (25) and (28). Hence learning cannot be approximated by an algebraic equation. Rather, it obeys the instar, or gated steepest descent, differential equation (24). In the present case, this reduces to

$$\frac{d}{dt} z_{ij} = x_{2j}(-z_{ij} + \theta_i).$$ (29)

In order to get a sense of how competitive learning and self-organizing feature maps work, suppose that a single input pattern θ perturbs F_1 through time and activates node $j = J$ in F_2. As a result, the total inputs S_j to F_2 nodes in equation (27) obey the inequalities $S_J > S_k$, $k \neq J$, so $x_{2J} = 1$ and $x_{2k} = 0$, $k \neq J$, by equation (28). By equation (29), only the vector $z_J = (z_{1J}, z_{2J}, \ldots, z_{nJ})$ of LTM traces that abut node J undergo learning, because only $x_{2J} > 0$ in equation (29). During learning, the LTM vector z_J is attracted toward the normalized input vector $\theta = (\theta_1, \theta_2, \ldots, \theta_n)$ as each z_{iJ} is "tuned" by the ith feature activity θ_i. As learning proceeds, the Euclidean length $\|z_J\| = \sqrt{\Sigma_i z_{iJ}^2}$ of the LTM vector is normalized as it approaches the length $\|\theta\| = \sqrt{\Sigma_i \theta_i^{h2}}$ of the input vector, and the total input S_J in equation (27) increases to its maximal possible value.

This result was proved in Grossberg (1976a) and is reviewed below. Its significance is clarified by noting that the total input S_J to node J in equation (27) can be rewritten as

$$S_J = \Sigma_i \theta_i z_{iJ} = \|\theta\| \|z_J\| \cos(\theta, z_J),$$ (30)

because S_J is the dot product, or inner product, of the vectors θ and z_J. Given that $\|z_J\|$ approaches $\|\theta\|$ during learning, equation (30) shows that the maximal S_J, among all S_j, is the one whose $\cos(\theta, z_J)$ is maximal. This quantity corresponds to that vector z_J which is most parallel to θ. In other words, the STM competition [equation (28)] at F_2 chooses the node J whose vector z_J is most parallel to θ, and learning tunes z_J to become even more parallel to θ. In addition, the fact that $\|z_J\|$ approaches $\|\theta\|$ shows that choosing all input vectors so that their length $\|\theta\| = 1$ eliminates the effects of variable input length on the category choice process. Then L^p normalization with $p = 2$ replaces the L^1 normalization in equation (26). This implication of the learning theorem was noted in Grossberg (1978) and used by Kohonen (1984) in his subsequent applications of self-organizing feature maps. Grossberg (1976a) also proved that, when multiple inputs activate F_1, then the LTM weight vectors tend to track the statistics of the input environment. This property was also exploited by Kohonen (1984), among others.

Theorem 3 (Adaptive Tuning of Feature Maps)   Given a pattern θ, suppose that there exists a unique $j = J$ such that

$$S_J(0) > \max\{\varepsilon, S_k(0): k \neq J\}.$$ (31)

Let θ be practiced during a sequence of nonoverlapping intervals $[U_m, V_m]$, $m = 1, 2, \ldots$. Then the angle between $z^{(J)}(t)$ and θ monotonically decreases, the signal $S_J(t)$ is monotonically attracted toward $\|\theta\|^2$, and $\|z^{(J)}\|^2$ oscillates at most once as it pursues $S_J(t)$. In particular, if $\|z^{(J)}(0)\| \leqslant \|\theta\|$, then $S_J(t)$ is monotonically increasing. Except in the trivial case that $S_J(0) = \|\theta\|^2$, the limiting relations

$$\lim_{t \to \infty} \|z^{(J)}(t)\|^2 = \lim_{t \to \infty} S_J(t) = \|\theta\|^2 \tag{32}$$

hold iff

$$\sum_{m=1}^{\infty} (V_m - U_m) = \infty. \tag{33}$$

Proof Consider the case in which

$$\|\theta\|^2 > S_J(0) > \max\{\varepsilon, S_k(0) \colon k \neq J\}. \tag{34}$$

The case in which $S_J(0) \geqslant \|\theta\|^2$ can be treated similarly. First it will be shown that if the inequalities

$$\|\theta\|^2 > S_J(t) > \max\{\varepsilon, S_k(t) \colon k \neq J\} \tag{35}$$

hold at any time $t = T$, then they hold at all future times $t \geqslant T$. By equation (34), $x_{2J}(T) = 1$ and $x_{2k}(T) = 0$, $k \neq J$. Consequently, by equation (29), at any time $t = T$ during a learning interval $[U_m, V_m]$,

$$\frac{d}{dt} z_{iJ}(T) = -z_{iJ}(T) + \theta_i \tag{36}$$

and

$$\frac{d}{dt} z_{ik}(T) = 0 \tag{37}$$

for $k \neq J$ and $i = 1, 2, \ldots, n$. By equations (27) and (35)–(37),

$$\frac{d}{dt} S_J(T) = \sum_i \theta_i \frac{d}{dt} z_{iJ}$$

$$= \sum_i \theta_i (-z_{iJ} + \theta_i) \tag{38}$$

$$= -S_J(T) + \|\theta\|^2.$$

Thus by equation (34), from the first moments of learning onward,

$$\frac{d}{dt} S_J(T) > 0 = \frac{d}{dt} S_k(T), \qquad k \neq J. \tag{39}$$

Since $S_J(t)$ continues to grow while all $S_k(t)$ remain constant, $k \neq J$, the inequality [equation (34)] continues to hold for all $t \geqslant T$ throughout the learning process. Since all $x_{2j} = 0$ whenever no learning occurs, there is no change in any z_{iJ} or S_J during these times. Thus equation (34) holds for all $t \geqslant T$. Moreover, by equation (38), $S_J(t)$ converges monotonically toward $\|\theta\|^2$.

To show that $S_J(t)$ converges to $\|\theta\|^2$ only if equation (33) holds, integrate equation (38) throughout the mth learning interval $[U_m, V_m]$. Then

$$S_J(V_m) = S_J(U_m)e^{-(V_m-U_m)} + \|\theta_J\|^2(1 - e^{-(V_m-U_m)}).\tag{40}$$

Since no learning occurs between time $t = V_m$ and time $t = U_{m+1}$, $S_J(U_{m+1}) = S_J(V_m)$. Using notation $S_{Jm} = S_J(U_m)$ and $W_m = V_m - U_m$ for simplicity, equation (40) may thus be written as

$$S_{J,m+1} = S_{Jm}e^{-W_m} + \|\theta_J\|^2(1 - e^{-W_m}).\tag{41}$$

Equation (41) can be solved recursively by setting $m = 1, 2, \ldots$ in equation (41) to find that

$$S_{J,m+1} = S_{Jm}e^{-\sum_{k=1}^{m}W_k} + \|\theta_J\|^2(1 - e^{-\sum_{k=1}^{m}W_k}),\tag{42}$$

from which it follows that $S_J(t)$ converges to $\|\theta_J\|^2$ only if $\sum_{k=1}^{\infty}W_m = \infty$.

To show that S_J increases toward $\|\theta\|^2$ if

$$\|z^{(J)}(0)\| \leqslant \|\theta\|,\tag{43}$$

we need only to show that $S_J(0) \leqslant \|\theta\|^2$, since then $(d/dt)\, S_J(0) \geqslant 0$ by equation (38). Were

$$S_J(0) > \|\theta\|^2,\tag{44}$$

then by equations (30), (43), and (44),

$$\|\theta\|\,\|z^{(J)}(0)\| \geqslant S_J(0) > \|\theta\|^2 \geqslant \|\theta\|\,\|z^{(J)}(0)\|\tag{45}$$

and thus

$$\|z^{(J)}(0)\| > \|\theta\| \geqslant \|z^{(J)}(0)\|,\tag{46}$$

which is a contradiction.

To show that the learning process normalizes the vector of LTM traces, let us use the notation $N_J = \|z^{(J)}\|^2 = \Sigma_i z_{iJ}^2$. By equation (36),

$$\frac{d}{dt}N_J = 2\sum_i z_{iJ}\frac{d}{dt}z_{iJ}$$

$$= 2\sum_i z_{iJ}(-z_{iJ} + \theta_i)\tag{47}$$

$$= 2(-N_J + S_J).$$

Equations (38) and (47) show that N_J tracks S_J as S_J tracks $\|\theta\|^2$. Consequently the norm $\|z^{(J)}\| = \sqrt{N_J}$ approaches $\|\theta\|$ as learning proceeds. In addition, since S_J monotonically approaches $\|\theta\|^2$, N_J oscillates at most once.

Finally, let us verify that the angle between $Z^{(J)}$ and θ closes monotonically during learning, even while $\|z^{(J)}\|$ is converging to $\|\theta\|$. To do this, the notation $C_J = \cos(z^{(J)}, \theta)$ is convenient. It is sufficient to prove that $C_J(t)$ increases toward 1 as learning proceeds. By equation (30), C_J can be rewritten as

$$C_J = \frac{S_J}{\|\theta\|\sqrt{N_J}}.\tag{48}$$

Differentiating equation (48), we find that

$$\frac{d}{dt}C_J = \frac{N_J^{1/2}\frac{d}{dt}S_J - \frac{1}{2}S_J N_J^{-1/2}\frac{d}{dt}N_J}{\|\theta\|N_J}. \tag{49}$$

Substituting equations (38) and (47) into (49) and canceling the term $N_J S_J$ in two places leads to the equation

$$\frac{d}{dt}C_J = \frac{N_J\|\theta\|^2 - S_J^2}{\|\theta\|N_J^{3/2}}$$

$$= \frac{\|\theta\|}{\sqrt{N_J}}\left(1 - \frac{S_J^2}{\|\theta\|^2 N_J}\right), \tag{50}$$

which by equation (48) is the same as

$$\frac{d}{dt}C_J = \frac{\|\theta\|}{\sqrt{N_J}}(1 - C_J^2) \geqslant 0. \tag{51}$$

Equation (51) shows that C_J increases monotonically toward 1.

15.4   CONCLUDING REMARKS

This chapter has described two models whose explanations of complex data can be understood by analyzing their interactive dynamics in real time. The first model illustrates how classical data about apparent motion can be rationalized in terms of the spatiotemporal dynamics of a long-range Gaussian filter followed by a contrast-enhancing stage of lateral inhibition. The model suggests how paradoxical properties of motion speedup can be linked to the functionally useful property of synthesizing motion data from multiple spatial scales, and to the property of predictively interpolating intermittent motion signals in a way that is capable of continuously tracking a target moving at variable speeds with a focus of spatial attention.

The second model illustrates how a combination of bottom-up adaptive filtering, top-down learned expectations, attentive resonance, and novelty-sensitive memory search can control rapid learning of recognition categories whose shape and coarseness can be matched to complex environmental demands, including culturally imposed demands. The model clarifies how top-down expectations can stabilize the learning process in an arbitrary environment and, in so doing, focus attention upon and coherently bind those prototypal feature clusters that are used in object categorization. Properties such as memory consolidation arise as dynamical properties of network interactions, and data about such varied phenomena as phonemic restoration, priming, and the dynamics of IT were linked to emergent properties of the network model.

These results suggest that basic neural mechanisms, such as contrast-enhancing lateral inhibition, play a role in multiple neural systems, whether to select the peak of a motion wave, as in figure 15.6, or to choose a recognition category, as in equation (28). On the level of the system design itself, the results support the view that two distinct types of attention may modulate visual information processing, one a form of spatial attention that arises in the Where processing stream through the MT and parietal cortex, and the other a form of featural attention that arises within the What processing stream through V4 and temporal cortex (see figure 15.8). How these two types of attention interact during our daily experiences with rapidly changing mixtures of familiar and unfamiliar events remains an important subject for future research.

ACKNOWLEDGMENTS

The author thanks Cynthia E. Bradford and Diana J. Meyers for their valuable assistance in the preparation of the manuscript. Supported in part by ARPA (ONR N00014-92-J-4015), the National Science Foundation (NSF IRI-90-24877), and the Office of Naval Research (ONR N00014-91-J-4100).

REFERENCES

Amari, S.-I., and Takeuchi, A. (1978). Mathematical theory on formation of category detecting nerve cells. *Biological Cybernetics, 29,* 127–136.

Anstis, S., and Ramachandran, V. S. (1987). Visual inertia in apparent motion. *Vision Research, 27,* 755–764.

Bartley, S. H. (1941). *Vision, a study of its basis.* New York: Van Nostrand.

Bienenstock, E. L., Cooper, L. N., and Munro, P. W. (1982). Theory for the development of neuron selectivity: orientation specificity and binocular interaction in visual cortex. *Journal of Neuroscience, 2,* 32–48.

Boring, E. G. (1950). *A history of experimental psychology.* Englewood Cliffs, NJ: Prentice-Hall.

Braddick, O. (1980). Low-level and high-level processes in apparent motion. *Philosophical Transactions of the Royal Society of London. Series B, 290,* 137–151.

Braddick, O., and Adlard, A. (1978). Apparent motion and the motion detector. In J. C. Armington, J. Krauskopf, and B. R. Wooten (Eds.), *Visual psychophysics and psychology.* New York: Academic Press.

Bregman, A. S. (1990). *Auditory scene analysis.* Cambridge, MA: MIT Press.

Breitmeyer, B. G., and Ritter, A. (1986). Visual persistence and the effect of eccentric viewing, element size, and frame duration on bistable stroboscopic motion percepts. *Perception and Psychophysics, 39:*275–280.

Carpenter, G. A., and Grossberg, S. (1987). A massively parallel architecture for a self-organizing neural pattern recognition machine. *Computer Vision, Graphics, and Image Processing, 37,* 54–115.

Carpenter, G. A., and Grossberg, S. (1990). ART 3: hierarchical search using chemical transmitters in self-organizing pattern recognition architectures. *Neural Networks, 3,* 129–152.

Carpenter, G. A., and Grossberg, S. (Eds.) (1991). *Pattern recognition by self-organizing neural networks.* Cambridge, MA: MIT Press.

Carpenter, G. A., and Grossberg, S. (1992). Fuzzy ARTMAP: supervised learning, recognition, and prediction by a self-organizing neural network. *IEEE Communications Magazine, 30,* 38–49.

Carpenter, G. A., and Grossberg, S. (1993). Normal and amnesic learning, recognition, and memory by a neural model of cortico-hippocampal interactions. *Trends in Neurosciences, 16,* 131–137.

Carpenter, G. A., Grossberg, S., Markuzon, N., et al. (1992). Fuzzy ARTMAP: a neural network architecture for incremental supervised learning of analog multidimensional maps. *IEEE Transactions on Neural Networks, 3,* 698–713.

Carpenter, G. A., Grossberg, S., and Reynolds, J. H. (1991). ARTMAP: supervised real-time learning and classification of nonstationary data by a self-organizing neural network. *Neural Networks, 4,* 565–588.

Cohen, M. A., and Grossberg, S. (1987). Masking fields: a massively parallel architecture for learning, recognizing, and predicting multiple groupings of patterned data. *Applied Optics, 26,* 1866–1891.

Damasio, A. R. (1989). The brain binds entities and events by multiregional activation from convergence zones. *Neural Computation, 1,* 123–132.

Desimone, R. (1991). Face-selective cells in the temporal cortex of monkeys. *Journal of Cognitive Neuroscience, 3,* 1–8.

Desimone, R. (1992). Neural circuits for visual attention in the primate brain. In G. A. Carpenter and S. Grossberg (Eds.), *Neural networks for vision and image processing* (pp. 343–364). Cambridge, MA: MIT Press.

Desimone, R., and Ungerleider, L. G. (1989). Neural mechanisms of visual processing in monkeys. In F. Boller and J. Grafman (Eds.), *Handbook of neuropsychology,* Vol. 2. (pp. 267–299). Amsterdam: Elsevier.

DeYoe, E. A., and van Essen, D. C. (1988). Concurrent processing streams in monkey visual cortex. *Trends in Neurosciences, 11,* 219–226.

Eckhorn, R., Bauer, R., Jordan, W., et al. (1988). Coherent oscillations: a mechanism of feature linking in the visual cortex? *Biological Cybernetics, 60,* 121–130.

Eckhorn, R., and Schanze, T. (1991). Possible neural mechanisms of feature linking in the visual system: stimulus-locked and stimulus-induced synchronizations. In A. Babloyantz (Ed.), *Self-organization, emerging properties, and learning.* New York: Plenum.

Eriksen, C. W., and Murphy, T. D. (1987). Movement of attentional focus across the visual field: a critical look at the evidence. *Perception and Psychophysics, 42,* 29–305.

Exner, S. (1875). Ueber das Sehen von Bewegungen und die Theorie des zusammengesetzen Auges. *Sitzungsberichte Akademie Wissenschaft Wien, 72,* 156–190.

Gibson, J. J. (1979). The ecological approach to visual perception. Boston: Houghton Mifflin.

Gochin, P. M., Miller, E. K., Gross, C. G., et al. (1991). Functional interactions among neurons in inferior temporal cortex of the awake macaque. *Experimental Brain Research, 84,* 505–516.

Goodale, M. A., and Milner, A. D. (1992). Separate visual pathways for perception and action. *Trends in Neurosciences, 15,* 20–24.

Gray, C. M., Konig, P., Engel., A. K., et al. (1989). Oscillatory responses in cat visual cortex exhibit inter-columnar synchronization which reflects global stimulus properties. *Nature, 338,* 334–337.

Gray, C. M., and Singer, W. (1989). Stimulus-specific neuronal oscillations in orientation columns of cat visual cortex. *Proceedings of the National Academy of Sciences, 86,* 1698–1702.

Grossberg, S. (1969). On learning and energy-entropy dependence in recurrent and nonrecurrent signed networks. *Journal of Statistical Physics, 1,* 319–350.

Grossberg, S. (1972). Neural expectation: cerebellar and retinal analogs of cells fired by learnable or unlearned pattern classes. *Kybernetik, 10*, 49–57.

Grossberg, S. (1973). Contour enhancement, short term memory, and constancies in reverberating neural networks. *Studies in Applied Mathematics, 52*, 217–257. [Reprinted in Grossberg, S. (1972). *Studies of mind and brain: neural principles of learning, perception, development, cognition, and motor control.* Dordrecht, Netherlands: Kluwer.]

Grossberg, S. (1976a). Adaptive pattern classification and universal recoding, I: Parallel development and coding of neural feature detectors. *Biological Cybernetics, 23*, 121–134.

Grossberg, S. (1976b). Adaptive pattern classification and universal recoding, II: Feedback, expectation, olfaction, and illusions. *Biological Cybernetics, 23*, 187–202.

Grossberg, S. (1977). Apparent motion. Unpublished.

Grossberg, S. (1978). A theory of human memory: self-organization and performance of sensory-motor codes, maps, and plan. In R. Rosen and F. Snell (Eds.), *Progress in theoretical biology,* Vol. 5. New York: Academic Press. [Reprinted in Grossberg, S. (1982). *Studies of mind and brain.* Boston: Reidel.]

Grossberg, S. (1980). How does a brain build a cognitive code? *Psychological Review, 1*, 1–51.

Grossberg, S. (1982). *Studies of mind and brain: Neural principles of learning, perception, development, cognition, and motor control.* Boston: Reidel.

Grossberg, S. (Ed). (1987a). *The adaptive brain, I: Cognition, learning, reinforcement, and rhythm.* Amsterdam: North-Holland.

Grossberg, S. (Ed.) (1987b). *The adaptive brain, II: Vision, speech, language, and motor control.* Amsterdam: North-Holland.

Grossberg, S. (Ed.) (1988). *Neural networks and natural intelligence.* Cambridge, MA: MIT Press.

Grossberg, S. (1991). Why do parallel cortical systems exist for the perception of static form and moving form? *Perception and Psychophysics, 49*, 117–141.

Grossberg, S. (1994). 3-D vision and figure-ground separation by visual cortex. *Perception and Psychophysics, 55*, 48–120.

Grossberg, S., and Kuperstein, M. (1986). *Neural dynamics of adaptive sensory-motor control: ballistic eye movements.* Amsterdam: Elsevier/North-Holland [(1989) expanded edition, Elmsford, NY: Pergamon.]

Grossberg, S., and Mingolla, E. (1993). Neural dynamics of motion perception: direction fields, apertures, and resonant grouping. *Perception and Pyschophysics, 53*, 243–278.

Grossberg, S., Mingolla, E., and Todorović, D. (1989). A neural network architecture for preattentive vision. *IEEE Transactions on Biomedical Engineering, 36*, 65–84.

Grossberg, S., and Rudd, M. (1989). A neural architecture for visual motion perception: group and element apparent motion. *Neural Networks, 2*, 421–450.

Grossberg, S., and Rudd, M. E. (1992). Cortical dynamics of visual motion perception: short-range and long-range apparent motion. *Psychological Review, 99* 78–121.

Grossberg, S., and Somers, D. (1991). Synchronized oscillations during cooperative feature linking in a cortical model of visual perception. *Neural Networks, 4*, 453–466.

Grossberg, S., and Somers, D. (1992). Synchronized oscillations for binding spatially distributed feature codes into coherent spatial patterns. In G. A. Carpenter and S. Grossberg (Eds.), *Neural networks for vision and image processing* (pp. 385–405). Cambridge, MA: MIT Press.

Grossberg, S., and Stone, G. O. (1986). Neural dynamics of word recognition and recall: attentional priming, learning, and resonance. *Psychological Review, 93,* 46—74.

Harries, M. H., and Perrett, D. I. (1991). Visual processing of faces in temporal cortex: physiological evidence for a modular organization and possible anatomical correlates. *Journal of Cognitive Neuroscience, 3,* 9—24.

Kohonen, T. (1984). *Self-organization and associative memory.* New York: Springer Verlag.

Kolers, P. A. (1972). *Aspects of motion perception.* Elmsford, NY: Pergamon.

Kolers, P. A., and von Grünau, M. (1975). Visual construction of color is digital. *Science, 187,* 757—759.

Korte, A. (1915). Kinematoskopische Untersuchungen. *Zeitschrift für Psychologie, 72,* 194—296.

Kwak, H.-W., Dagenbach, D., and Egeth, H. (1991). Further evidence for a time-independent shift of the focus of attention. *Perception and Psychophysics, 49,* 473—480.

LaBerge, D., and Brown, V. (1989). Theory of attentional operations in shape identification. *Psychological Review, 96,* 101—124.

Levy, W. B. (1985). Associative changes at the synapse: LTP in the hippocampus. In W. B. Levy, J. Anderson, and S. Lehmkuhle (Eds.), *Synaptic modification, neuron selectivity, and nervous system organization* (pp. 5—33). Hillsdale, NJ: Erlbaum.

Levy, W. B., and Desmond, N. L. (1985). The rules of elemental synaptic plasticity. In W. B. Levy, J. Anderson, and S. Lehmkuhle (Eds.), *Synaptic modification, neuron selectivity, and nervous system organization* (pp. 105—121). Hillsdale, NJ: Erlbaum.

Linsker, R. (1986). From basic network principles to neural architecture: emergence of spatial-opponent cells. *Proceedings of the National Academy of Sciences, 83,* 8779—8783.

Malsburg, C. von der. (1973). Self-organization of orientation sensitive cells in the striate cortex. *Kybernetik, 14,* 85—100.

Miller, E. K., Li, L., and Desimone, R. (1991). A neural mechanism for working and recognition memory in inferior temporal cortex. *Science, 254,* 1377—1379.

Mishkin, M. (1982). A memory system in the monkey. *Philosophical Transactions of the Royal Society of London. Series B. 298,* 85—95.

Mishkin, M., and Appenzeller, T. (1987). The anatomy of memory. *Scientific American, 256,* 80—89.

Pantle, A. J., and Petersik, J. T. (1980). Effects of spatial parameters on the perceptual organization of a bistable motion display. *Perception and Psychophysics, 27,* 307—312.

Pantle, A., and Picciano, L. (1976). A multistable movement display: evidence for two separate motion systems in human vision. *Science, 193,* 500—502.

Perrett, D. I., Mistlin, A. J., and Chitty, A. J. (1987). Visual cells responsive to faces. *Trends in Neurosciences, 10,* 358—364.

Rauschecker, J. P., and Singer, W. (1979). Changes in the circuitry of the kitten's visual cortex are gated by postsynaptic activity. *Nature, 280,* 58—60.

Remington, R., and Pierce, L. (1984). Moving attention: evidence for time-invariant shifts of visual selective attention. *Perception and Psychophysics, 35,* 393—399.

Repp, B. H. (1991). Perceptual restoration of a "missing" speech sound: auditory induction or illusion? *Haskins Laboratories Status Report on Speech Research, SR-107/108,* 147—170.

Riches, I. P., Wilson, F. A. W., and Brown, M. W. (1991). The effects of visual stimulation and memory on neurons of the hippocampal formation and the neighboring parahippocampal gyrus and inferior temporal cortex of the primate. *Journal of Neuroscience, 11*, 1763–1779.

Robinson, D. L., and Peterson, S. E. (1992). The pulvinar and visual salience. *Trends in Neurosciences, 15*, 127–132.

Rumelhart, D. E., and Zipser, D. (1985). Feature discovery by competitive learning. *Cognitive Science, 9*, 75–112.

Samuel, A. G. (1981a). Phonemic restoration: insights from a new methodology. *Journal of Experimental Psychology: General, 110*, 474–494.

Samuel, A. G. (1981b). The rule of bottom-up confirmation in the phonemic restoration illusion. *Journal of Experimental Psychology: Human Perception and Performance, 7*, 1124–1131.

Schvaneveldt, R. W., and MacDonald, J. E. (1981). Semantic context and the encoding of words: evidence for two modes of stimulus analysis. *Journal of Experimental Psychology: Human Perception and Performance, 7*, 673–687.

Schwartz, E. L., Desimone, R., Albright, T., et al. (1983). Shape recognition and inferior temporal neurons. *Proceedings of the National Academy of Sciences, 80*, 5776–5778.

Seibert, M., and Waxman, A. M. (1991). Learning and recognizing 3D objects from multiple views in a neural system. In H. Wechler (Ed.), *Neural networks for perception*, Vol. 1. New York: Academic Press.

Singer, W. (1983). Neuronal activity as a shaping factor in the self-organization of neuron assemblies. In E. Basar, H. Flohr, H. Haken, et al. (Eds.), *Synergetics of the brain* (pp. 89–101). New York: Springer Verlag.

Smith, E. E. (1990). Categorization. In D. O. Osherson and E. E. Smith (Eds.), *An invitation to cognitive science*, Vol. 3 (pp. 33–53). Cambridge, MA: MIT Press.

Spitzer, H., Desimone, R., and Moran, J. (1988). Increased attention enhances both behavioral and neuronal performance. *Science, 240*, 338–340.

Squires, P. C. (1931). The influence of hue on apparent visual movement. *American Journal of Psychology, 43*, 49–64.

Ternus, J. (1926/1950). Experimentelle Untersuchungen über phänomenale Identität. *Psychologische Forschung, 7*, 81–136. [Abstracted and translated in W. D. Ellis (Ed.) (1950). *A sourcebook of Gestalt psychology*. New York: Humanities Press.

Ungerleider, L. G., and Mishkin, M. (1982). Two cortical visual systems: separation of appearance and location of objects. In D. L. Ingle, M. A. Goodale, and R. J. W. Mansfield (Eds.), *Analysis of visual behavior* (pp. 549–586). Cambridge, MA: MIT Press.

Van der Waals, H. G., and Roelofs, C. O. (1930). Optische Scheinbewegung. *Zeitschrift für Psychologie und Physiologie des Sinnesorgane, 114*, 241–288.

Van der Waals, H. G. and Roelofs, C. O. (1931). Optische Scheinbewegung. *Zeitschrift für Psychologie und Physiologie des Sinnesorgane, 115*, 91–190.

Warren, R. M. (1984). Perceptual restoration of obliterated sounds. *Psychological Bulletin, 96*, 371–383.

Warren, R. M., and Sherman, G. L. (1974). Phonemic restorations based on subsequent context. *Perception and Psychophysics, 16*, 150–156.

Wertheimer, M. (1912/1961). Experimentelle Studien über das Sehen von Bewegung. *Zeitschrift für Psychologie, 61*, 161–265. [Translated in part in T. Shipley (Ed.) (1961), *Classics in psychology*, New York: Philosophical Library.

Willshaw, D. J., and Malsburg, C. von der. (1976). How patterned neural connections can be set up by self-organization. *Proceedings of the Royal Society of London. Series B., 194*, 431–445.

Wise, S. P., and Desimone, R. (1988). Behavioral neurophysiology: insights into seeing and grasping. *Science, 242*, 736–741.

Guide to Further Reading

Three useful reviews of data about motion perception are provided by Kolers (1972), Nakayama (1985), and Cavanagh and Mather (1989). Three volumes that survey psychological data about recognition, categorization, and attention are Davidoff (1991), Harnad (1987), and Humphreys and Bruce (1989). Ungerleider and Mishkin (1982) and Goodale and Milner (1992) discuss data about the What and Where cortical processing streams. Grossberg and Rudd (1992) and Grossberg and Mingolla (1993) develop the neural theory of motion perception that is discussed in this chapter. Carpenter and Grossberg (1991) provide a survey of neural modeling articles about recognition learning, categorization, and attention, with a concentration on self-organizing feature maps and ART systems. The articles in Grossberg (1982, 1987a, 1987b) develop these and related models to analyze a wide range of behavioral and neural data. The journals *Neural Networks, Neural Computation*, and *Biological Cybernetics* regularly publish articles in which neural models are used to explain behavioral and neural data.

Carpenter, G. A., and Grossberg, S. (Eds.) (1991). *Pattern recognition by self-organizing neural networks*. Cambridge, MA: MIT Press.

Cavanagh, P., and Mather, G. (1989). Motion: the long and short of it. *Spatial Vision, 4*, 103–129.

Davidoff, J. B. (1991). *Cognition through color*. Cambridge, MA: MIT Press.

Goodale, M. A., and Milner, A. D. (1992). Separate visual pathways for perception and action. *Trends in Neurosciences, 15*, 20–24.

Grossberg, S. (1982). *Studies of mind and brain*. Boston: Kluwer.

Grossberg, S. (Ed.) (1987a). *The adaptive brain, I: Cognition, learning, reinforcement, and rhythm*. Amsterdam: Elsevier/North-Holland.

Grossberg, S. (Ed.) (1987b). *The adaptive brain, II: Vision, speech, language, and motor control*. Amsterdam: Elsevier/North-Holland.

Grossberg, S., and Mingolla, E. (1993). Neural dynamics of motion perception: direction fields, apertures, and resonant grouping. *Perception and Pyschophysics, 53*, 243–278.

Grossberg, S., and Rudd, M. E. (1992). Cortical dynamics of visual motion perception: short-range and long-range apparent motion. *Psychological Review, 99*, 78–121.

Harnad, S. (Ed.) (1987). *Categorical perception, the groundwork of cognition*. New York: Cambridge University Press.

Humphreys, G. W., and Bruce, V. (1989). *Visual cognition*. Hillsdale, NJ: Erlbaum.

Kolers, P. A. (1972). *Aspects of motion perception*. Elmsford, NY: Pergamon.

Nakayama, K. (1985). Biological image motion processing: a review. *Vision Research, 25*, 625–660.

Ungerleider, L. G., and Mishkin, M. (1982). Two cortical visual systems: separation of appearance and location of objects. In D. L. Ingle, M. A. Goodale, and R. J. W. Mansfield (Eds.), *Analysis of visual behavior* (pp. 549–586). Cambridge, MA: MIT Press.

16 Multiprocess Models Applied to Cognitive and Behavioral Dynamics

Mary Ann Metzger

EDITORS' INTRODUCTION

One feature of human cognition (and probably animal cognition as well) is that when faced with a very difficult problem of prediction, subjects may have to thrash around. Sometimes there may be no very good way to make the necessary predictions and no evidence that strongly justifies one hypothesis over others. Some examples are a football coach predicting the plays about to be called by an opposing coach (run vs. pass, right-end vs. left-end run, etc.), a shopkeeper predicting when he will get robbed, a farmer predicting whether it will rain today (or a month from now). Or, to look at one example, a horseracing fan betting money on a race. It is very difficult to predict who will win a race on the basis of the standard available data. So gamblers develop "systems"—algorithms for combining particular kinds of information to predict the most likely winner—even though none of these algorithms may work particularly well.

In such a situation, one would expect to find several features. First, it will be difficult for an external observer of gambler behavior to know what the algorithm employed by a particular race aficionado will be because each gambler may use a different algorithm. And second, gamblers cannot be presumed to stick to any given method for very long. Thus, in studying such a problem, pooling data across subjects (i.e., across gamblers) would clearly be a mistake. Looking at pooled data is a waste of time since it will probably not represent any of the methods used for picking winners. Similarly, one cannot even assume that each gambler will stick to one method throughout the task. It is likely that each gambler will change his or her method from time to time. Thus, one cannot even pool all the data from a single subject throughout the observation period.

This is the kind of problem addressed by Metzger in this chapter. She seeks to model subject performance in such multiprocess tasks, that is, tasks where a variety of possible strategies are in mutual competition. To do this, she uses a chaotic mathematical function to generate a time series. The function is known to allow only approximate prediction in the best of cases. Subjects are required to predict the next point in the time series. So on each trial they are presented with the current value between 0 and 1 (typically in a computer graphic display) and they try to predict the next output of the system. Hundreds of sequential predictions are recorded for each subject. Then she hypothesizes a set of strategies that subjects might follow in making their prediction, e.g., "the next point is the same as the last point," "guess randomly, paying no attention to the previous value," "remember what happened in a recently observed subsequence similar to this one and make the same prediction," and so on. Then she develops some mathematical methods for estimating which of these models is the most likely one for the subject to be using at this point in the time series. Thus, at each time step the method selects the most likely model for subjects to be using based on the previous few time steps.

A critical feature of this method is that only the most recent few prediction trials play a role in evaluation. This is just what human subjects do when attempting to predict a difficult time series. It is also the most reasonable strategy to follow for a world that is intrinsically chaotic in the long term, although partially predictable in the short run. Apparently humans tend to ignore long-term generalizations in favor of the most recent evidence. Thus, although the modeling style of this chapter differs from most others in this book, the work nevertheless reflects a strongly dynamical interpretation of human behavior.

16.1 MULTIPROCESS MODELS FOR THE DYNAMICS OF COGNITION AND BEHAVIOR

Describing the flow of cognitive and behavioral processes requires a method explicitly adapted to the fact that although the exact form of the underlying processes may be unknown, their nature is known to be dynamical. The goal of the description is not only to obtain a quantitative representation of the flow of thought or behavior but also to use the description to gain insight into the underlying process which might itself require a more abstract representation. If the unknown underlying process is a deterministic dynamical system with true attractors, then the appearance (phenomenology) of the system will consist of a sequence of rapid transients and persistent patterns (stable states). The descriptive method therefore aims at quantifying the flow of stable states of cognition and behavior at the phenomenological level.

The method presented in this chapter should be differentiated from methods specifically addressed to finding the amount and form of organization in a stream of data obtained from observations on a dynamical process. Those methods have been given in chapters throughout this book (see also Atmanspacher and Scheingraber, 1990). They directly address the structure of simple processes that may underlie complex phenomena. Instead of using the direct approach to the search for the underlying process, the method presented here indirectly addresses the problem by focusing on the quantitative description of the process as a sequence of phenomena.

The method describes cognition by means of quantifying the flow of concepts, plans, and strategies inferred from the sequence of behavior of an individual subject in a changing context. Since transients are by definition ephemeral and stable states are persistent, at any instant the system is most likely to be observed in a stable state (attractor). But in a changing environment the system is subjected to both internal and external disturbances that move the system out of its current stable state, giving it the opportunity to enter another stable state. Therefore, the system may be conceived as traveling a path through an sequence of attractors. Correspondingly, the description will express the likelihood that the system is currently in each of its hypothesized attractors, and will characterize the path of the system over time. The method for quantifying the path of the system through its attractors is the method of multiprocess dynamical models.

Multiprocess Dynamical Models

In the method of multiprocess dynamical models, hereinafter called multiprocess models, several models of the process are considered simultaneously. We begin with several different models which represent different modes of behavior of an individual. In the applications to be presented here, all parameters of the models are fixed in advance in the light of theoretical considerations. It is important to note that the primary objective of the method to be illustrated here is not to obtain more precise estimates of the parameters of the models, but rather to place the approximate models into a competition according to the degree to which the accumulating evidence favors each at each instant as the sequence of behavior proceeds over time.

The models are the elements of a set of approximate quantitative descriptions of hypothesized attractors of the system. The models are placed in competition with one another to explain observed sequences of behavior of the system. Even in the absence of knowledge of the true underlying dynamical process, it is possible to devise approximate models of the dynamics within each of its stable states. Since each attractor is associated with a stable state of the system, the models in the set of a multiprocess model are descriptions of the processes associated with each attractor. To be useful each model must be characterized in such a way that it can be applied to the tth observation to generate a prediction, in the sense of giving a probability for each of the possible observations, for the behavior of the system a short time into the future.

Each model in a set can generate a different short-term prediction in a given situation. It is reliance on implications of prediction errors that enables the models to compete for describing an individual dynamical process. That is, every observation of ongoing behavior of the system has a quantitative effect on the conclusion about the adequacy of each model to explain the current state of the system. In turn, the conclusion about the current state of the system provides a context for the interpretation of the next observation of behavior of the system. The quantities that track this relationship are sensitive to the properties of dynamical processes, that is, they do not require the aggregation of observations either within an individual system or across individuals.

In the absence of knowledge of the true underlying process, multiprocess models offer a suitable quantitative alternative to descriptive methods based on statistical techniques for increasing precision of estimates of model parameters via aggregation of sampled observations. Although purely stochastic models based on aggregated observations are not prohibited from competing with other models in the multiprocess model, one of the ways in which multiprocess models are particularly well suited to the description of dynamical processes is that the aggregation of observations on the system is not required. During the progress of an individual system, approximate models are placed in competition with one another to interpret each individual observation.

In this method, improvement in describing the dynamics of a system takes the form of refinements of the models within the multiprocess model. One type of possible refinement is increasing the precision of the model. Another type of refinement is introducing a new model which can be thought of as one which develops out of the coordination of simpler models. When refinements of models have been developed, candidates for more precise or more complex models may be evaluated according to the same principles of competition.

Definitions and Data Requirements

To apply this method the data should consist of a number of observations made on a single individual over conditions and sampling intervals sufficient for the process to exhibit the phenomena of interest to the investigator. The data record should contain observations on both the behavioral variables of interest and on the relevant contextual variables. For the methods given here, only discrete time is used. The data should be recorded either at fixed intervals, i.e., recording behavior observed without intervention; or at event-related intervals, i.e., recording the outcome of a given trial. Whatever the type of recording interval, the method is most useful when, except for transient periods, the system will usually stay within a given attractor for several observation periods.

As approximate representations of attractors in cognitive or behavioral state space, models can be defined at two levels of abstraction. At the phenomenological level the dynamical system can be conceived as traveling a path through a state space whose points are models. At the process level the dynamical system can be conceived as traveling a path through a state space whose points are sets of observable quantities. For the process level, a vector is defined consisting of the observed behavioral and contextual variables. This constitutes the *state vector* of the observed system. When values of its variables have been observed at time t, the state vector contains all of the information necessary to represent the state of the system at time t. The multidimensional space of which the state vector is a point is the *state space* for the observed process. A plot of the sequence of state vectors in which points have been connected in temporal order is the *trajectory* of the process. An *attractor* of the system is a set of limited paths toward which the system tends after a disturbance and in which the state vector tends to remain. For the period of time during which the trajectory remains within a given attractor, it is said to be in the *regime* of the attractor. Within the regime of an attractor the trajectory of the state vector is *low-dimensional* in the sense that the path is organized and limited, not random. A *multiprocess model* is a set of models, each of which approximately defines the dynamics of low-dimensional behavior of the state vector within the regime of a hypothesized attractor. At any time, it is possible to quantify the degree of belief that the system is in any particular regime. To obtain the quantification, the models are placed in an ongoing dynamic competition to describe the process, their respective degrees of success being calculated by repeated applications of *Bayes rule*.

Fundamentals of Bayes Rule

When beliefs about the world can be represented by a set of mutually exclusive hypotheses $A, B, \ldots$, Bayes rule can be used as a normative model which quantifies the degree to which new evidence should change old belief in a rational individual. The degree of an individual's belief in A is given by the probability of A, a quantity that follows the laws of the mathematical theory of probability. Considered jointly with the remaining hypotheses in the set, the effect of the new evidence can be expressed in a formula for calculating the revised (posterior) probability A from its initial (prior) probability and the conditional probability of observation of evidence D.

Equation (1) illustrates a convenient form of Bayes rule, in which the calculations are expressed in terms of ratios. For any two hypotheses A and B, the ratio of their respective probabilities is defined to be the odds favoring A over B. For purposes of defining notation, consider only the quantities in the numerators of equation (1). Let $p(A)$ be the prior probability of A. Let D represent an item of new evidence that has been observed and is to be brought to bear on the degree of belief in A. Let $p(D|A)$, for which read "the conditional probability of D given A," be the probability of observing D if A were true. Similarly, define $p(A|D)$. Let $p(A|D)$, for which read "the posterior probability of A given D," be the probability of A revised by the weight of the evidence of the occurrence of D. Similarly define $p(B)$, $p(D|B)$, and $p(B|D)$. On the condition that none of the quantities in the denominators is zero, equation (1) gives the two-hypothesis formulation of Bayes rule.

$$\frac{p(A|D)}{p(B|D)} = \frac{p(D|A)}{p(D|B)} \times \frac{p(A)}{p(B)} \tag{1}$$

In equation (1) the ratio on the left of the equal sign is known as the posterior odds favoring A over B. The first ratio to the right of the equal sign is the odds favoring the occurrence of D when A is true (compared to when B is true). The second ratio on the right is known as the prior odds favoring A.

Bayes rule is usually derived in the more general form exemplified in equation (2). When hypotheses A, B, and C are not only mutually exclusive but also jointly exhaustive, $p(A|D)$ may be calculated directly according to equation (2), which may obviously be extended to any finite number of hypotheses.

$$p(A|D) = \frac{p(D|A)}{p(D|A)p(A) + p(D|B)p(B) + p(D|C)p(C)} \times p(A) \qquad (2)$$

Although they are obviously different quantities, the ratios with numerator $p(D|A)$ that appear in equations (1) and (2) are both often referred to by the name of Bayes factor or likelihood ratio, with the intended meaning being obvious from the context.

The proof of Bayes rule does not depend in any way on the interpretation of probability as a measure of degree of belief. In the mathematical theory of probability based on enumerating elements in sets, Bayes rule follows directly from the formal definition of conditional probability. Characterizing probability as a measure of degree of belief is, however, a tenet of those who identify themselves as Bayesians. The Bayesian characterization leads directly to an appreciation of qualities obscured when only static sets are considered, the dynamic qualities captured in Bayes rule (see appendix A).

16.2 TECHNIQUES OF APPLICATION OF MULTIPROCESS MODELS

The application of multiprocess models will be divided into two steps. The first step consists of using graphical and analytical methods to identify the attractors of the process. The second step consists of applying Bayes rule to generate a quantitative description of the process for an individual.

Models of attractors will be developed to represent persistent[1] cognitive strategies or behavioral patterns. At each moment, based on recent behavior and context, the method of multiprocess models will yield the subject's current cognitive or behavioral profile, consisting of the respective posterior probabilities of each model in the multiprocess model. The sequence of probabilities of the models is then plotted to give a visual representation of the flow of the process for each individual.

The interpretation of the visual representation of the flow will depend on particulars of the study, illustrated here in two examples, one addressing cognition and the other hyperactivity. Applied to an individual solving a problem, models are stable cognitive states and the graphed result will be a set of concurrent charts of the sequence of strategies, their probabilities, depths, durations, and transitions. Applied to hyperactivity, the models will be normal and abnormal modes of behavior in a certain context and the graphed result will be a set of concurrent charts of the sequence of normal and abnormal modes for an individual child.

Methods for Developing Models of Attractors

Two approaches are illustrated here to assist in identifying hypothetical attractors and in constructing models to represent them. Each approach summarizes the dynamics of the system according to limitations on the paths of the observed state vector. For some systems, attractors can be discerned in a *map*, a graph that plots the value of a variable from the state vector at time $t + 1$ against its value at time t. For others, attractors may be devised by analytical methods of deriving formulas. Whatever the source of the models of the system, every model must eventually be quantified in such a way that it can be used to predict a future value of the state vector from the value of the current state vector and its previous history.

Thus, whether quantitative, qualitative, substantive, statistical, theoretical, descriptive, or mixtures of these, all multiprocess models must have one feature in common to be acceptable: they must assign probabilities to every possible uncertain value of the state vector at least one step ahead in time.

Quantifying the Sequence of Attractors via Bayes Rule

After approximate models have been developed, it is necessary to establish the performance characteristics of each of the models when it is applied during the regime of its attractor. Each model is a representation of the mode of behavior of the system under the regime of a particular attractor. When a given model is applied to generate predictions within the regime from which it was derived, there results a certain distribution of errors of prediction. After the distribution of prediction errors has been estimated for each model, the models can be applied to a value of the state vector at any time in the flow of the process to assign a probability to each of the possible outcomes of the next observation on the system. After the next observation on the system has been obtained, the respective probabilities of the error of prediction for each model can be compared and combined with information about the history of the system. The result of the comparison can then be used to evaluate the degree to which the regime of each model is in force.

For cognition, from observations on a subject solving a problem, a sequence of profiles, consisting at each time t of the respective probabilities of the strategies (models), can be calculated and plotted against time to show the evolution of strategies over the task. Previous mathematical results (West and Harrison, 1989) have shown that, for strategies that persist for even a short time, the method of *model identification by prediction error* will yield results such that the probability of the model that most closely approximates the unknown true model will rapidly approach 1, while the probabilities of all other models in the set converge exponentially to 0. The analysis thereby yields information on cognitive attractors and transients.

Given the data available at time t, the evaluation of the fit of each model is based on the accuracy of its forecast for time $t + 1$. Although the models within the multiprocess model are in competition with one another, it is not necessary to have a step in which one model is judged the best. For application to dynamical systems in which stable states occur, the logic of Bayes rule assures that, when the system is in a stable state, the probability associated with the best approximate model of that state will rapidly approach 1. Thus, if the system has stable states, then, except for transients, the description of the system will represent the path of the system through its stable states.

The mathematical basis for the method of multiprocess models can be illustrated in terms of an example for which each model is a nonstationary Gaussian process, i.e., a normal distribution for which the mean changes over time in a specified way. The notational system used here is adapted from West and Harrison (1989). Consider the sequence of observations on the behavior of the subject $\{f_t\}$ and the set of models $\{M_1, M_2, \ldots, M_p\}$, where for the ith model, f_t is distributed as a Gaussian with a mean, m_{it}, depending on t, and a constant variance, v_i. Define $\mathbf{F}_t = \{f_1, f_2, \ldots, f_t\}$. Represent the unknown true system as M_S. Let $M_i \neq M_S$ for any i, but let one model (M_k) be closer to M_S than the others by the Kullback information measure, J_t, defined by equation (3), in which E represents the expected value. The quantity J_t may be thought of as a number representing the average inadequacy over time of the ith approximate model, compared to the true, unknown system. The measure will be near 0 when the model is close to the true system, and will increase when the model deviates. For a discussion of J_t, see Anderson, Moore, and Hawkes (1978).

$$J_t(M_S, M_i) = E\left[\ln \frac{p(\mathbf{F}_t|M_S)}{p(\mathbf{F}_t|M_i)}\right] \tag{3}$$

To find the probability at time t for each model (posterior probability of the model), apply Bayes rule [equation (4)] at each iteration.

$$p(M_i|\mathbf{F}_t) = \frac{p(f_t|\mathbf{F}_{t-1}, M_i)p(M_i|\mathbf{F}_{t-1})}{\sum_j p(f_t|\mathbf{F}_{t-1}, M_j)p(M_j|\mathbf{F}_{t-1})} \tag{4}$$

Equation (4) is a general statement of relationships given in equation (2). The first factor in the numerator and in each of the terms of the denominator of equation (4) is the probability calculated from the Gaussian density function defined by the corresponding model [equation (5)].

$$p(f_t|\mathbf{F}_{t-1}, M_i) = \exp[-(f_t - m_{it})^2/2v_i]/(2\pi v_i)^{1/2} \tag{5}$$

For Gaussian $\{f_t\}$, for $i \neq k$, $p(M_i|\mathbf{F}_t) \to 0$ exponentially fast with the exponent being determined by J (Anderson, Moore, and Hawkes, 1978). For general models convergence is not limited to Gaussian, or even mathematical models (Pole, West, and Harrison, 1988; West and Harrison, 1989).

The model set need not contain an exact model of the process; the models need only be approximate phenomenological representations of attractors. Further, the set need not be exhaustive; all results are simply conditional upon the particular set of models chosen. The models may be refined, combined, added, or deleted from the set, resulting in a new description of the system. For other treatments of approximate models and mixtures of models, see Fun and Jordan (1992), Golden (1992), Jacobs, Jordan, Nowlan, et al. (1991). For an early application of multiprocess models in psychological research, see Gregson (1980).

Summarizing the method, if the process persists in a given attractor for even a few iterations, this method of analysis will yield results such that, for the model that most closely approximates that attractor, its probability will rapidly approach 1 while the probabilities of all other models in the set converge exponentially to zero. Each model in the set is thereby a potential attractor of the process. Even when the true attractors are only approximately represented by the models, the analysis yields a sequence of attractors and transients, a dynamic profile of the process. In both applied and basic psychology, multiprocess models provide an empirical approach to studying trajectories of dynamical processes for individuals.

Previous Experience with Bayes Rule

Previous practical experience with Bayes rule has not been an unqualified success. In a notable effort to engage Bayes rule in the service of locating deposits of ore for the mining industry, the system Prospector was developed (Duda, 1979). Prospector was not effective enough for practical application, having problems attributed by both the originators and critics to difficulties in establishing precise distributions for the quantities corresponding to those that appear on the right-hand side of equation (4), the prior probabilities and the likelihood ratios (Benchley-Capon, 1990; Cohen, 1985; Buchanan and Duda, 1982). As has been proved mathematically by West and Harrison (1989), although crucial when a single judgment is required in a static situation, exact priors are less important when judgments are accumulated over time in a dynamical situation. On the positive side, Bayes rule has been shown to be a reliable principle of adaptive thought. This has been demonstrated empirically by Anderson (1990). Since the method of multiprocess models is explicitly designed for repeated application of approximate models, rather than precise models, and since the dynamical nature of the application insures that the influence of initial prior probabilities will become negligible, the problems experienced by Prospector are not likely to be of significance for dynamical applications.

16.3   EXAMPLE 1: A STUDY OF JUDGMENT IN A NATURALISTIC TASK

The Strategy of Anchoring

Example 1 explores the behavior of children and adults concerning the utility and development of *anchoring*. Anchoring is a pervasive feature of human judgment, one of the *judgmental heuristics* formulated by Tversky and Kahneman (1974). Anchoring is demonstrated when, having been asked to estimate a numerical quantity, subjects are influenced by a fortuitously present, irrelevant numerical quantity such that their estimate is near the irrelevant quantity.

Anchoring was demonstrated in an example given by Tversky and Kahneman: First an irrelevant quantity x was selected and was represented to the subject to be the result of a random process, spinning a wheel. For one group of subjects the value of x was 10; for a second group x was 65. Subjects were asked to judge whether the percentage of African countries in the United Nations was greater or less than x, then give their best estimate of the true percentage. Median estimates given by the groups were 25 and 45, respectively. That is, their estimates were close to x with no apparent rational justification. Similar phenomena, generally unaffected by incentives offered for correct estimates, have been shown to occur in a wide variety of contexts. Irrelevant numerical quantities or spatial locations substantially influence the estimates given by subjects.

Although anchoring has usually been demonstrated in a static situation in which untrained subjects have been asked to estimate a single quantity, it has also been demonstrated in a dynamical situation in which trained managers were asked to make sequences of judgments and decisions for a complex naturalistic situation involving simulated production plants (Sterman, 1989). Anchoring pervades the judgment even of sophisticated managers.

Although anchoring appears to have no rational justification in a static situation, there is the possibility that anchoring could be useful in a dynamic, naturalistic task. In the example to be presented here, each subject was asked to make a large number of sequential judgments of quantities of a prototypal dynamical system. A model representing the heuristic of anchoring was included in the multiprocess model of the subject's behavior in this dynamic task.

Forecasting as a Naturalistic Dynamic Task

In example 1, a task was devised to permit the study of cognition as a form of adaptation to dynamical features of natural processes. The effort focused in particular on a single idea from dynamical systems: the limitations that apply to forecasting future states of the natural world. For dynamical systems it is in principle not possible accurately to forecast the far future, but it is possible accurately to forecast the near future. Thus emerges the conclusion that the only possible objective of human cognition as related to forecasting natural processes must be to formulate expectancies for the near future. Accordingly, the analysis of example 1 focused on the role of anchoring in forming expectancies for the nearest of near futures, forecasting one step ahead.

Given the implication for dynamical systems that the only reasonable goal for prediction is to predict the near future from the recent past, the question arises whether this seems to be true in practice for naturally occurring processes. From the results of the Makridakis competition (see appendix B), the answer can be taken to be affirmative. Experts competed in an empirical test of 21 mathematical forecasting methods on actual economic time series. The most successful of the statistical forecasting techniques were three simple methods, each a form of anchoring.

Method for Example 1 The data for example 1 were taken from adult subjects, seven University of Maryland Baltimore County students who were fulfilling a course requirement by participating in the study, each of whom was asked to make successive forecasts for a time series, described in Metzger (1991). The time series itself was chosen to have nonlinear dynamical properties that might be representative of natural deterministic chaos, thereby providing a task that would have some features in common with tasks occurring in nature. It was chosen to be in a chaotic regime so that it would be known to be predictable in the short term, but not in the long term. Previous experience revealed that systems in simpler regimes were too easy to forecast. The series was not taken from among the numerous recorded and well-analyzed time series because, although these series can be thought to be naturally occurring, the very fact that they have been selected to be recorded and analyzed can be considered evidence that they can be distinguished from other less well-organized natural processes. The objective series consisted of up to 10,800 successive observations $\{x_t\}$ on the Hénon attractor (Grebogi, Ott, and Yorke, 1987). The successive observations were displayed on a video screen numerically for some subjects, spatially for others. The task was to generate a forecast, f_{t+1}, for the observation x_{t+1} from previous observations $x_t, x_{t-1}, x_{t-2}, \ldots$, where the number of forecasts required ranged from 180 when responses via keyboard typing were required to 600 when responses via mouse movement were required. The experiment yielded a multivariate state-space trajectory of behavior and context variables $\{f_t, x_t\}$, using bracket notation to denote the sequence of all observations on a given subject. The behavioral series $\{f_t\}$ may be treated alone or in conjunction with the objective sequence $\{x_t\}$.

Dynamic Maps Let $\{x_t\}$ be the sequence of observations on the objective attractor, and $\{f_t\}$ be the sequence of forecasts made by the subject. Both $\{x_t\}$ and $\{f_t\}$ are dynamical processes. Therefore, dynamic maps can usefully depict their properties. In addition to plotting f_t against x_t to show *accuracy* (figure 16.1, *top panels*) of the forecast, other graphical displays are useful to

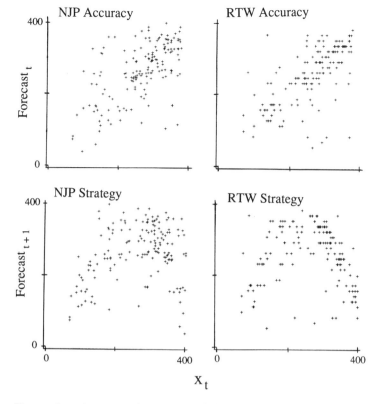

Figure 16.1 Accuracy and strategy graphs for two subjects (NJP who made numerical forecasts and RTW who made spatial forecasts) who had extensive experience, making up to 10,800 observations while forecasting every 60th value of the objective time series. x_t, value of the objective time series at time t. Forecast$_t$, forecast made at time$_{t-1}$ for the value of x_t.

show the dynamic properties of $\{f_t\}$ and its dynamic relationship to $\{x_t\}$. When forecasts are made for consecutive values, plotting f_{t+1} against x_t shows strategy (figures 16.1 and 16.2, *bottom panels*). Plotting x_{t+1} against x_t produces a dynamic map (figure 16.2, *top panels*) of the objective process, showing its attractor. Plotting f_{t+1} against f_t produces a *dynamic map* (figure 16.2, *middle panels*) of the behavioral process, showing its attractors.

Figures 16.1 and 16.2 illustrate the uses of the three types of graphs. Figure 16.1 summarizes the strategies used by two subjects (NJP making numerical forecasts and RTW making spatial forecasts). Both subjects had extensive experience, viewing up to 10,800 observations while forecasting every 60th value of the objective time series. Since they were forecasting every 60th value, rather than consecutive values, anchoring could not be observed in either subject. The errors made by NJP and RTW are summarized in the accuracy graphs (see figure 16.1, *top panels*) and appear as deviations from the diagonal. The accuracy graph, however, does not reveal to what extent NJP and RTW have mastered the shape of the dynamic map of the objective attractor (figure 16.2, *top left*). This information is shown in the strategy

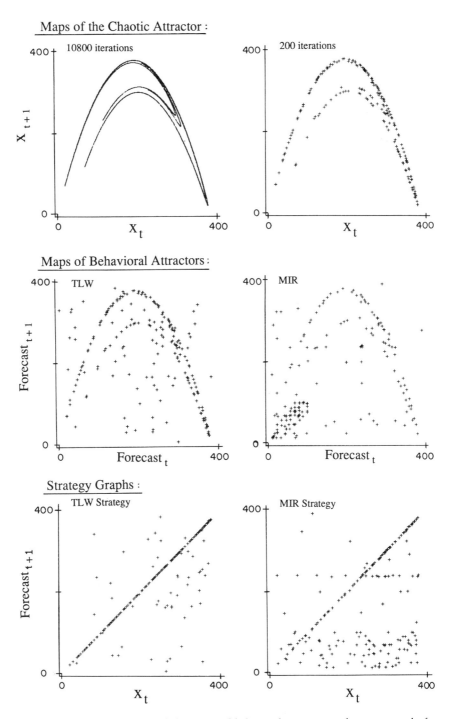

Figure 16.2 Dynamic maps of objective and behavioral attractors, and strategy graphs for subjects making 200 consecutive forecasts. (*Top panels*) Dynamic maps of the chaotic attractor of the objective process. (*Middle panels*) Dynamic maps of the behavioral attractors for two subjects, TLW and MIR. (*Bottom panels*) Strategy graphs for the two subjects.

graphs. Random guessing is represented by unsystematic points on the strategy graphs (see figure 16.1, *bottom panels*). Solution of the problem is represented by points on the strategy graph that are close to the shape of the objective attractor. It can be seen that after forecasting in a manner indistinguishable from random guessing, NJP solved the forecasting problem by mastering the shape of the objective attractor. This occurred after NJP viewed approximately 480 consecutive values. RTW solved it after viewing approximately 240 consecutive values.

In order to study the details of the development of strategies, additional subjects were asked to forecast successive values of the chaotic attractor. Figure 16.2 shows the dynamic maps for two subjects (MIR and TLW, respectively) who had minimal experience, viewing only 200 consecutive numerical values of the objective attractor while making a forecast for each of the 200 values. It can be seen that these subjects used predominantly two types of anchoring. One type of anchoring was seen only occasionally, but can be seen in the dynamic map for MIR seen as an attractor that is essentially a cloud of points concentrated in the box with corners at $(0, 0)$ to $(100, 100)$. This attractor of MIR's behavior was the consequence of MIR repeating the units digit or the tens and units digits of the most recent objective value. The second, more important type of anchoring is indicated in the dynamic maps of the behavioral process for both TLW and MIR. The points on the two maps that are in the shape of the objective attractor are the result of anchoring, i.e., the forecast of the subject was just the most recently observed objective value. That is, $f_{t+1} = x_t$.

The effect of anchoring on the dynamics of the behavioral process is illustrated in figure 16.2. Subjects with minimal experience were generally inaccurate in their forecasts. The median correlation between f_t and x_t or these subjects was $-.08$. All of these subjects had some tendency to anchor their forecast to the most recent observation. This strategy appears on the strategy graphs as points on the diagonal. For the two subjects who had substantial amounts of anchoring, the behavioral attractors in figure 16.2 show that maps of the behavioral process are similar to the map of the objective process. That is, the behavioral attractor resembles the chaotic attractor, though one step out of phase. Therefore, although these subjects had poor accuracy in forecasting the next observation, they had acquired, as a consequence of anchoring, a behavioral analog of the objective process. Although this behavioral analog was a necessary consequence of this type of anchoring, it was not an obvious consequence before the dynamical perspective was taken.

Subjects with more extensive experience forecast more accurately. The median correlation between f_t and x_t for these subjects was .46. Therefore, the map of their behavioral process would also resemble the map of the objective process, but for these subjects the behavioral attractor would be in phase with the objective attractor. Learning to forecast one step ahead for an objective dynamical process may consist of forming a behavioral analog that is one step out of phase with the objective process, which later moves into phase with it. Therefore, anchoring may be understood not only as a judgmental heuristic related to accuracy but also as a method for achieving a behavioral analog of a dynamical process.

Since the simple strategy of anchoring appeared in the dynamic maps of adult subjects, the question arose of how early in development the strategy of anchoring would appear and what would be the developmental course of anchoring and forecasting. Therefore the procedure was adapted and young children were tested. All of the children from the Christian Day Care Center in Baltimore were tested. Ten 3-year-old, sixteen 4-year-old, and twelve 5-year-old children participated.

The task was changed to permit an intermediate number of consecutive forecasts (Metzger and Theisz, 1993). To accomplish this, the spatial display was changed to a graph of points in an evolving time series, x_t plotted against t. As the time series traced a jagged path from left to right across the video screen, the subject was required to use the mouse to indicate his or her forecast for its next vertical position. The mouse pointer was constrained to move only vertically. Using this procedure, it was reasonable to ask college students to make up to 600 forecasts and to ask children 3, 4, and 5 years old to make up to 180 forecasts for the same series. These provided the data streams from which the graphs of sequences of models could be constructed.

Models Describing the Cognitive States   The models of the model set were approximations of the possible strategies, each of which is represented as a Gaussian distribution of possible forecasts with mean determined by context and variance constant. Quantitatively, the five models were expressed as Gaussian distributions of the variable observed at time t, f_t. The ith model has mean m_{it}, and variance v_i and therefore standard deviation $s_i = v_i^{1/2}$. The differences between the models consisted of the method for determining m_{it} and the value of s_i. In any given context, each model makes a prediction of the subject's next forecast. The predictions can then be compared to the subject's behavior and a posterior probability can be calculated for each model by applying equation (4), yielding, at any moment, a current profile of the cognitive state of the subject. The strategies (models) are:

1. *Dynamic forecasting*, defined as correct forecasting:

   $m_{it} = x_t$, $s_i = 100$.

2. *Random guessing*, according to a Gaussian distribution with the same mean and standard deviation as the objective time series:

   $m_{it} = 235$, $s_i = 101$.

3. *Anchoring*, repeating to the most recent observation:

   $m_{it} = x_{t-1}$, $s_i = 100$

4. *Memory for instances*, remembering an instance of a similar pattern:
   $m_{it} = x$ as explained below, $s_i = 100$

5. *Repetition of forecast*, repeating the subject's own most recent forecast:

$$m_{it} = f_{t-1}, s_i = 50$$

Memory for instances (model 4) was included since within the time series similar, but not identical, subsequences appear from time to time interspersed with unique sequences. Whenever a subject's forecast could be approximately characterized as following the closest previously occurring pattern of consecutive observations, model 4 was given some credit as a possible attractor. To determine a value for x, every previous pattern of three consecutive values of the objective time series was compared to the pattern of the three most recent values. The closest pattern from the past was defined to be the one with the least squared distance between corresponding points of the three-point sequence. In the case of ties the most recent occurrence was favored. After the closest pattern was found, the prediction for the subject's next forecast was taken to be the objective value (fourth value) that followed the pattern in the past. A forecast close to that past fourth value would tend to favor model 4.

For each of the models defined above, the value of m_{it} is the prediction from the model of the subject's most likely forecast for time t. The value of s_i is the amount of variability in the forecast expected by the model. A forecast that does not exactly match m_{it} for any of the models can nevertheless be assigned some probability of occurrence by each model, based on the permitted variability. Each model therefore assigns a probability of occurrence to every possible forecast. After the forecast has been registered, these probabilities figure into the continuing competition among models to account for the forecasting behavior of the subjects.

A sequence of calculations applying the method to the models is given in table 16.1. The calculation begins at time $t = 10$ with arbitrary history of forecasts and arbitrary probabilities for each of the j models. The subject's forecast f_t is observed and, based on the probability of that forecast, is calculated for each model [equation (5)]. The respective probabilities of the models are then updated [equation (4)], becoming the initial probabilities for time $t = 11$, after which all steps repeat.

Sequences of Strategies   An example of a sequence of strategies used by an individual subject is displayed in figure 16.3 in two types of graphs, a set of graphs of concurrent time series and a three-dimensional representation of the same data. The three-dimensional graph is intended to convey an impression of a cognitive landscape as it develops over time. Since the set of strategies were exhaustive for the particular analysis, the infrequent strategy of *repetition of forecast* was redundant and therefore not explicitly represented in the graphs. For the graphs of time series (figure 16.3, *top panel*), each subpanel contains p_{it}, the quantity on the left-hand side of the equal sign in equation (4), the posterior probability that the subject is employing the ith strategy at time t.

Table 16.1 Details of the calculations applying the multiprocess model to two consecutive trials

t	History x_{t-1}	History f_{t-1}	i	Prior probability $p(M_i\|F_{t-1})$	Datum f_t	Model mean and SD m_{it}	Model mean and SD s_1	Probability of datum [equation (5)] $p(f_t\|F_{t-1}, M_i)$	Posterior probability [equation (4)] $p(M_i\|F_t)$
...									
10^a	244	15	1	.100	300	351	100	.0350	.114
			2	.100		235	101	.0323	.105
			3	.200		244	100	.0341	.222
			4	.500		355	100	.0344	.559
			5	.100		15	50	.0000[b]	.000
11	351	300	1	.114	200	125	100	.0301	.124
			2	.105		235	101	.0374	.142
			3	.222		351	100	.0128	.103
			4	.559		130	100	.0312	.631
			5	.000		300	50	.0076	.000
...									

[a] The values for the objective series $(\ldots, 244, 351, 125, \ldots)$ and the corresponding forecasts $(\ldots, 15, 300, 200, \ldots)$ were taken from data, but the trial number has been arbitrarily set at 10. In practice, the value of $m_{4,t}$ would have been recalculated on each trial by comparison with all previous sequences. For this example, however, $m_{4,t}$ has been arbitrarily chosen.

[b] For this example, calculations have been rounded. In practice, the values of very small numbers are retained by high-precision calculations.

In the landscape representation (see figure 16.3, *bottom panel*), the vertical axis is $1 - p_{it}$. This quantity was chosen in order that each strategy, when active, would appear as a valley in the landscape, in keeping with the usual conventions of three-dimensional graphical display of attractors. Figure 16.3 shows the cognitive trajectory for one of the 5-year-old children. This child showed a substantial amount of dynamic forecasting early on, which became mixed with both random guessing and memory for instances.

The time-series graphs of p_{it} against t for 18 children are shown in figure 16.4. The graphs in figure 16.4 are arranged in columns of six graphs for each age group. Within each column, the graphs are arranged from top to bottom in order of decreasing amount of dynamic forecasting and then decreasing amount of anchoring. In the age groups, some children exhibited random guessing on almost 100% of the trials with no other strategy. two 3-year-old, two 4-year-old, and no 5-year-old children did so. Except for those children, the graphs in figure 16.4 are representative of the behavior of the children in each age group.

The graphs in figure 16.4 show that children as young as 3 years old had long periods of dynamic forecasting (*bottom subpanels*) and other types of systematic forecasting including anchoring (*upper middle subpanels*) and memory for instances (*top subpanels*). The 4- and 5-year-old children showed substantial amounts of anchoring and some memory for instances.

Strategy Sequences

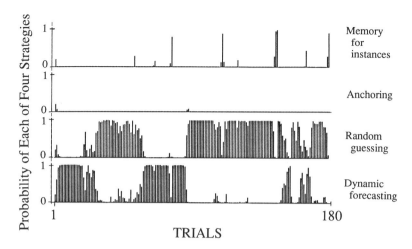

Landscape of Strategies

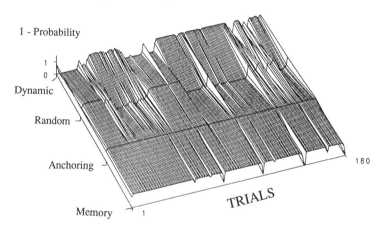

Figure 16.3 Two types of visual displays of the sequence of strategies used by one 5-year-old subject. (*Upper panel*) Concurrent time-series style. (*Lower panel*) Landscape style. The fifth strategy, which is model 5, anchoring to the forecast, is not displayed. Whenever the probabilities of four graphed strategies add up to less than 1, the remaining probability has been attributed to model 5.

One of the seven adult subjects had anchoring as the predominant strategy on about one third of the trials and random guessing elsewhere, the remaining adults had interspersed periods of dynamic forecasting and random guessing.

For comparison with the summary of the results via multiprocess models, the most obvious static measure of performance is the standard error of forecast. For the children aged 3, 4, and 5 years, and the adult subjects, respectively, the average standard error of forecast was 156, 172, 155, and

Strategy Sequences Used By Individual Children

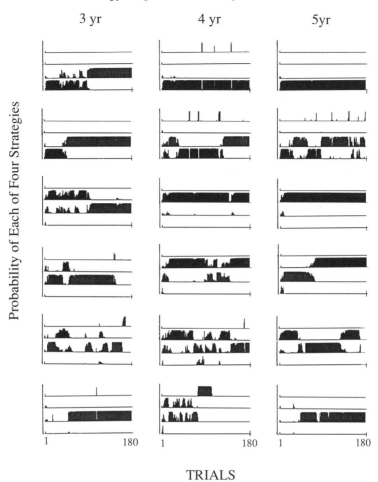

Figure 16.4 Graphs of concurrent time series of probabilities of strategies used by 18 subjects, 3 to 5 years old. The fifth strategy, which is model 5, anchoring to the forecast, is not displayed. Whenever the probabilities of four graphed strategies add up to less than 1, the remaining probability has been attributed to model 5.

101. This summary statistic cannot represent the dynamics of the behavior of the individual subjects.

Conclusion, Forecasting   In this application, analysis via multiprocess models was used to quantify sequences of strategies in individuals. The results showed that the judgmental heuristic of anchoring appeared in the behavior of children as young as 3 years old, giving additional weight to the theory that anchoring is a fundamental adaptation to the dynamical nature of natural processes. A second finding was that young children also exhibited flashes of memory for specific temporal sequences, even in the absence of

Multiprocess Models Applied to Cognitive and Behavioral Dynamics dynamic forecasting, i.e., understanding the process. A third finding was that some very young children exhibit dynamic forecasting. The results, however, leave a problem for future research since they did not shed light on how or whether anchoring leads to correct forecasting via behavioral analog.

16.4   EXAMPLE 2: A STUDY OF RESPONSE TIMES OF HYPERACTIVE CHILDREN

Example 2 illustrates the application of multiprocess models to a behavioral, rather than a cognitive process. Example 2 is a reanalysis of data from a study of 15 children and 3 adults. All of the children had behavior problems. Ten had been diagnosed by standard procedures to have attention-deficit disorder with hyperactivity. I will refer to these children as "hyperactive". Five were diagnosed as not hyperactive. The three adults were normal volunteers. The children were participating in a hospital-based study of the therapeutic and other effects of psychostimulant medication, either dextroamphetamine or piribedil. The subjects and procedures have been described elsewhere (Fisher 1977, 1978).

A fundamental problem of diagnosis and treatment of hyperactivity has been that the only measures of abnormal behavior associated with hyper-activity have been so highly variable that behavioral differences between hyperactivity and nonhyperactivity could be detected only as small but reli-able differences in data aggregated over periods of time for an individual or over a number of similar children in groups. The variability of behavioral measures has affected both diagnosis and treatment of hyperactive children. An individual hyperactive child can behave in a manner similar to a non-hyperactive child much of the time. Therefore, diagnosis has been based predominately on the judgment of an experienced classroom teacher after months of observation of the child in the classroom. In the laboratory, factors such as impulsiveness, activity level, and reaction time can be measured in a few minutes. Several laboratory tests have been shown to detect differences in performance between groups of hyperactive and nonhyperactive children using procedures that last only minutes, but the measures are so variable they can be used only to differentiate between groups of children, not assess the status of individuals. The problems of data aggregation associated with diag-nosis occur also when therapeutic and other effects of various doses of medi-cation must be evaluated for an individual child. The objective of the analysis to be reported here was to find a behavioral test that could evaluate the status of an individual child. That is, a test was sought that was specific and reliable enough to detect the degree of hyperactive behavior in an individual child.

Method for Example 2

Hyperactive children were asked to classify shapes displayed on a computer-managed video screen. The shapes were presented accompanied by three types of distracting visual displays. In individual sessions lasting approximately 30 minutes, the child was instructed to start each trial by pushing the center key of a set of three keys, to observe the resulting display, to find a particular type of information (target dimension, e.g., shape), then to push the correct one of two keys, depending on the value of the target dimension (e.g., square or circle). The content of the display, the selected key, and the time taken to respond (response time) were recorded for each of 240 trials per session for each child, creating the state vectors. The state vector was a combination of behavioral variables (the pattern of response times on the preceding three trials), denoted by b, and contextual variables, x. Omitting the subscript for time, the state vector of eight elements at time t was $\mathbf{x} = (b_1, b_2, b_3, x_4, \ldots, x_8)$.

Models for Example 2

The models used in example 2 were empirically derived, feedforward, artificial neural networks (ANNs). Parameters (connection weights) for each network were determined separately for individual sessions. The ANNs for individual sessions were then subjected to an analysis of similarity of connection weights. This analysis yielded three clusters, each containing similar ANNs. The centroid of the connection weights for each cluster was used to develop an approximate model representing that cluster. There were therefore three models to be used in the multiprocess model describing the process.

Artificial Neural Networks as Models   The purpose of the ANN[2] used in this application was to predict the reaction time (denoted by b to emphasize that it is a behavioral variable) at time $t + 1$ given the three most recent reaction times (denoted, beginning with the most recent, by b_1, b_2, b_3) and five preprogrammed x variables representing context at time $t + 1$, including type of target dimension and the features displayed on the video screen. The ANN supplied predictions about the behavioral variable. For purposes of fitting the ANN, the state vector of eight elements at time t was the input pattern. Thus, the state vector was the θth layer (input) of the ANN, which may be represented as $\mathbf{x} = (b_1, b_2, b_3, x_4, \ldots, x_8)$. The vector $\mathbf{x}$ was mapped sequentially by transformations, first to the hidden layer, which consisted of three elements, then to the output layer, which consisted of one element where the value of the element was the predicted value for reaction time b for time $t + 1$. The ANNs were nonlinear models for predicting response times.

During training, the ANN was adapted, in approximately 240 iterations, to the complete sequence of observed state vectors separately for each session for each child or adult volunteer. Using values of constants for adapting weights as suggested by the authors, the connection weights for the ANNs were determined by an algorithm developed by Scalero and Tepedelenlioglu (1992).

Clusters of ANNs   When fitted to the data from individual subjects, the ANNs yielded connection weights from input to three hidden units and from three hidden units to output. Corresponding connection weights could be directly compared since, when provided with the same initial weights for each subject, the algorithm used yielded the same ordering of the hidden units. The first hidden unit represented primarily temporal features of the three most recent responses. The second and third hidden units represented features of the context. To find groups of ANNs with similar structures, connection weights derived from individual sessions for all subjects were analyzed according to a standard cluster analysis based on Euclidean distance of corresponding connection weights. The cluster analysis revealed three groups of ANNs, each group distinctively associated with aspects of the experiment. For the ANNs within each cluster, corresponding connection weights were averaged, resulting in three models, each named for its generating cluster: the *normalized mode* emulated the behavior of hyperactive children on medication; the *hyperactive mode* emulated the behavior of hyperactive children on placebo; the *normal mode* emulated the behavior of nonhyperactive children and adult controls.

Estimating Error Distributions   The final step in defining the three models that constituted the multiprocess model was to estimate the distribution of prediction errors for each model over all subjects and sessions within its own cluster. This was necessary before the method of multiprocess models could be applied to obtain the quantities needed for the graphical displays. The distribution of errors provided a basis for calculating the quantity on the left-hand side of equation (5).

Sequences of Behavioral Modes

On each trial, the child's behavior was compared to the predictions made by each of the three ANNs and the trajectory through the attractors was determined by applying equation (4). Figure 16.5 contains expanded information for two hyperactive children in sessions on either placebo or medication. Figure 16.5 shows the relationship between the child's recorded behavior, graphed as response time for each trial, and the inferred probabilities of behavioral modes. Comparison of the raw data and the concurrent inferred behavioral modes show that the ANNs are making distinctions that do not arise from any obvious patterns in the raw data. Two sessions are represented for each of two of the children, LM and RN. Each child is shown for one session with placebo and one session with an experimental medication.

The two behavioral modes represented in figure 16.5 correspond to the two models of abnormal behavior, hyperactive mode and normalized mode. Since the three modes of behavior are exhaustive in this analysis, the probability of the normal mode is redundant and so is not graphed. The original ANNs for the sessions depicted in the left-hand panels of figure 16.5 fell

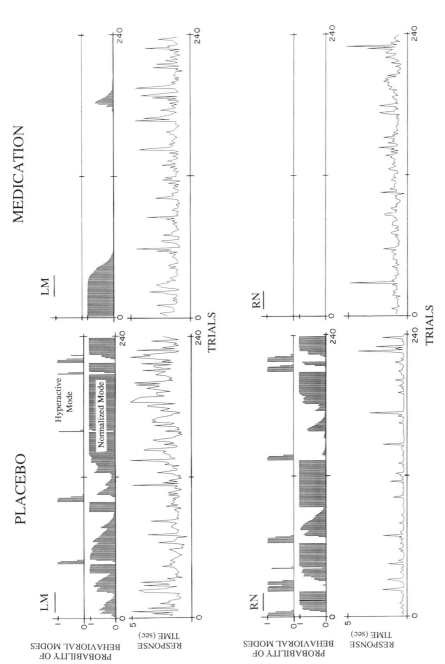

Figure 16.5 Graphs of concurrent time series of probabilities of two abnormal behavioral modes inferred from the time series of response times recorded for individual subjects. For subject LM, the medication was piribedil; for subject RN, dextroamphetamine. The probabilities of the two abnormal modes and the normal mode (not displayed) must add up to 1 at each trial.

into the cluster that determined the model for the hyperactive mode. Although the hyperactive mode was thus derived, it was not the one most often inferred by the analysis. For these two children, the hyperactive mode is distinguished by occurring only in bursts during the placebo sessions and being absent during medication sessions. For the remainder of the time during the placebo sessions, the behavior of the children was most consistent with the normalized mode. The medication sessions depicted in the right-hand panels of figure 16.5 show that during the medication sessions, the behavior of these two children was for the most part closest to the normal mode.

In the results for all children, the hyperactive mode occurred almost exclusively in hyperactive children during a placebo session. Hyperactive children during medication sessions and nonhyperactive children rarely exhibited either of the two abnormal behavioral modes. Figure 16.6 shows the concurrent time-series graphs for the remaining children for whom sessions on both placebo and drug were available. These include two additional sessions for subject LM. Figure 16.6 depicts the general finding for four hyperactive children during placebo and drug sessions. Hyperactive mode occurred only in isolated bursts and only in hyperactive children on placebo. The lone exception to this generalization can be seen in the graph for subject JM in the medication session.

The findings represented in figures 16.5 and 16.6 correspond to clinical observations that a hyperactive child can be identified, but the abnormal behavior of hyperactivity occurs in isolated bursts, embedded in longer periods of unremarkable behavior. The conditions of occurrence and the time course of the hyperactive mode constitute a quantitative confirmation of the clinical impression. In addition, the conditions of occurrence of the normalized mode indicate that there is some additional behavioral abnormality that distinguishes hyperactive from nonhyperactive children, although it distinguishes the two groups less well. The normalized mode was derived as an average of the cluster of hyperactive children on medication. The averaged model (normalized mode) thus derived, however, encompasses enough behavioral abnormalities that, during medication sessions for hyperactive children, it does not often win out in a competition with the model representing the standard behavior of nonhyperactive children and adults (normal mode). This is indicated by the near absence of either abnormal behavioral mode in the panels on the right in figure 16.6.

Conclusion, Hyperactivity

In this application, analysis via multiprocess quantified sequences of behavioral modes in individual hyperactive children. The method overcame problems of data aggregation and supported conclusions about the status of an individual child at a specific time from a behavioral sample taken over a period of 30 minutes. This result suggests it might be possible to develop

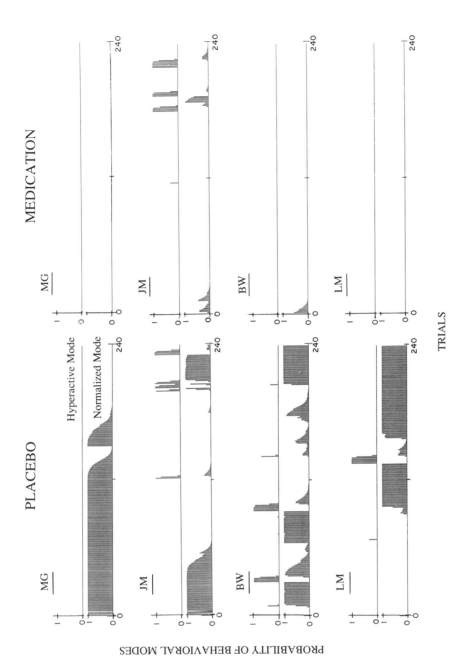

Figure 16.6 Graphs of concurrent time series of probabilities of behavioral modes for four subjects. For subjects MG and BW, the medication was dextroamphetamine; for subjects JM and LM, piribedil. The probabilities of the two abnormal modes and the normal mode (not displayed) must add up to 1 at each trial.

new methods of diagnosing hyperactivity and evaluating the effects of treatment on an individual child.

16.5 DYNAMICAL CONSIDERATIONS RELATED TO BIASES OF JUDGMENT

In addition to the analysis of example 1, which provided a new interpretation of the function of anchoring, the reasoning associated with the dynamical perspective suggests new interpretations for two other pervasive biases of human judgment: *insensitivity to prior probabilities* and *insensitivity to sample size* (Tversky and Kahneman, 1974). The existence of some judgmental biases is puzzling because the biases can lead to gross errors when applied to estimating or forecasting quantities needed for the solution of problems involving static conditions or single observations. As I will now show, when applied cumulatively to problems involving dynamical systems, the biases can be sources of valid conclusions.

Insensitivity to Prior Probability

Insensitivity to prior probabilities is demonstrated when subjects—having been asked to estimate the posterior probability that a hypothesis, e.g., hypothesis A given in equation (1), is true given the initial probability of A and evidence D—estimate the probability $p(A|D)$ according to the probability that D could arise from A, ignoring the prior probability of A. But according to Bayes rule, the prior probability of A should sometimes be extremely influential. Inspection of equation (1) shows that there could be situations when the prior odds have substantial influence on the revised odds. Yet, as demonstrated by Tversky and Kahneman (1974), in many such situations subjects ignore the prior odds. Their judgments of the posterior odds tend to be close to the Bayes factor instead. Their original demonstration, which has since been confirmed in many variations, was made using the following procedure. Adult subjects were shown personality sketches of individuals allegedly sampled at random from a group consisting of 70 engineers and 30 lawyers. The personality sketch was designed to be uninformative.

Dick is a 30-year-old man. He is married with no children. A man of high ability and high motivation, he promises to be quite successful in his field. He is well-liked by his colleagues.

After reading the sketch, subjects were asked to estimate the probability that Dick is an engineer. Subjects judged Dick was equally likely to be an engineer or a lawyer, corresponding to a posterior odds ratio equal to 1. The correct posterior odds are .7/.3, as can be seen by applying equation (1). Let A represent the statement that the sampled individual is an engineer, B that he is a lawyer. Then $p(A) = .7$ and $p(B) = .3$. Thus the prior odds are .7/.3. Let D be the personality sketch. Since the sketch is not any more or less characteristic of an engineer than of a lawyer, $p(D|A) = p(D|B)$ and therefore the Bayes factor equals 1. Therefore, the posterior odds equal the prior odds. Although subjects given no sketch are capable of correctly judging the odds, subjects given the sketch appear to be dominated by the Bayes factor, ignoring prior odds and judging that Dick is equally likely to be an engineer or a lawyer.

It is apparent in the example given above that for a single judgment in a static situation, appreciating the role of prior probabilities is crucial to valid judgment. It is quite a different matter, however, in a dynamic context when judgments are being constantly made and revised based on incoming information. In a dynamic context, the importance of the initially known priors fades rapidly. West and Harrison (1989, p. 451ff.) have shown by mathematical proof that, for stable states of a dynamical system, the influence of the initial prior probabilities rapidly becomes negligible. In other words, initial prior probabilities are virtually irrelevant for forecasting a dynamic sequence with attractors that persist for even a few observations. This justifies insensitivity to prior probabilities in a dynamic world. Therefore, if tracking current states of natural processes is an important function of human judgment, it is reasonable to be insensitive to prior probabilities.

Insensitivity to Sample Size

Insensitivity to sample size (k) is demonstrated when, having been asked to make a judgment based on the means of random samples, subjects fail to appreciate that the variability of the mean is very much less for large random samples (say $k = 1000$) than for small ($k = 10$). As demonstrated by Tversky and Kahneman (1974) and elaborated by Kahneman and Tversky (1982), subjects respond as though the means of samples of any size (greater than about 10) are equally likely to be discrepant from the population mean.[3]

Viewed from the dynamical perspective, however, the possibility of valid forecasting is limited to the nearest of near futures. Therefore precision in estimating means of large samples of past observations has little role in determining the accuracy of forecasting a single event. This was studied for the two nonlinear dynamical systems used in example 1. Moving averages of various size samples were used to forecast one step ahead. The results showed that large samples do not confer an advantage for forecasting a nonlinear dynamical process, and therefore understanding the substantial influence of sample size on the properties of means of large random samples is not relevant to forecasting the next observation in these dynamical processes.

The irrelevance of properties related to large sample size is obvious for nonlinear dynamical processes, but it is also related to the peculiar task of forecasting one step ahead. The restrictions on forecasting into the future do not apply to forecasting for a process consisting of repeated observations from a specified and unchanging distribution. For such a static process, the error in the forecast is independent of how far into the future the forecast is made. Therefore, when forecasting the values of future observations from a fixed distribution, it might seem that, if the mean of the sample is to be used to generate the forecast, then the size of the sample would enter the picture as an important consideration affecting the success of the forecast. Except for very small sample sizes, however, it does not do so. The absolute error of forecast for a single future value is a quantity that depends on the size of the sample, but the expected error of the forecast can never be smaller than the standard deviation of the original distribution. When the size is 1000 or 100, the error of the forecast is 100% of the original standard deviation, but when the size is only 10, the error of the forecast is only 105% of the original standard deviation (shown in appendix C). Therefore, the accuracy of the forecast is essentially unaffected by sample size for sample sizes between 10 and 1000.

For the simple task of forecasting a single observation randomly sampled from a fixed distribution, increasing the sample size above 10 or so confers very little additional accuracy of the forecast. This result is easy to show, but not intuitively obvious since large sample size has a profound effect on the stability of the estimate of the mean. Once it is recognized that large sample size has no appreciable effect on the success of the forecast, it follows that, if it is important in human behavior to forecast single observations one step ahead, then it is reasonable for human judgment to be insensitive to sample size.

16.6 RELATION TO COGNITIVE AND BEHAVIORAL THEORIES

As a method for describing the behavior of individual dynamical systems of unknown structure, the method of multiprocess dynamical models bears a complex relationship to theories of the dynamics of cognition and a more straightforward relationship to theories of the dynamics of behavior.

It is difficult to maintain the distinction between the properties of multiprocess models and the properties of cognition. The method of multiprocess dynamical models is not only a technique for quantifying the phenomenology of dynamical systems of unknown structure, it is, by virtue of that fact, also itself a candidate for the true structure of cognitive processes. That is, if it is the task of cognition to make sense of the natural world, to track and anticipate the phenomenology of individual manifestations of dynamical systems of unknown structure, then it is possible that cognition achieves this end by being itself a multiprocess dynamical model. Therefore, it is understandable that successful theories of cognition have component structures and processes similar to those of multiprocess models.

Features of multiprocess models have appeared in each of four theories that have been proposed as comprehensive theories of cognition or perception. The four theories are *ACT** (Anderson, 1990), *SOAR* (Newell, 1990), *observer mechanics* (Bennett, Hoffman, and Prakash, 1989), and *adaptive resonance theory*

(ART) (Grossberg, 1988). Each of these theories has survived numerous empirical tests. The main feature that distinguishes multiprocess models from the structures of cognition proposed by these four theories is the focus by multiprocess models on the forecast as a central concept in the system and the forecasting error as the source of energy leading to change.

The similarities between multiprocess models and ACT* come in part from the fact that Bayes rule has been put forth as the mechanism of adaptive thought for ACT*. This similarity between ACT* and multiprocess models suggests that there might be a role in ACT* for prediction error as the central feature driving the adaptation of thought. In general, for ACT*, aggregated data has been used both to obtain evidence that Bayes rule is a fundamental mechanism of cognition, and to formulate precise models of problem-solving strategies. In this latter regard ACT* is similar to SOAR, which has also developed precise models of stable states of cognition. Thus, in these two successful theories, the theoretical structures and processes of cognition are similar to structures and processes of multiprocess models.

The theory of observer mechanics is fundamentally different from both ACT* and SOAR, yet also shares features with multiprocess models. In particular, each *observer* is similar to a model; it generates a probability distribution over possible states of the world. One difference is that at each instant an observer yields probability distribution over a set of conclusions, while each of the multiprocess models yields a probability distribution over a set of predictions. Similarly, the energy for the dynamics of observers comes from discrepancies between conclusions of simultaneous observers. Each observer takes account of the conclusions of the other and adjusts its own perspective accordingly. The energy for the dynamics of multiprocess models comes from errors in forecasting. Observers can be conceived as the elements of a state space representing the states visited by thought on its way to drawing a conclusion. Thus, observer mechanics proposes structures of cognition that are similar to the structures of a multiprocess model.

Grossberg's ART model of learning and cognition is based on the properties of specially designed artificial neural networks. An ART-type neural network is designed to interact with the natural environment and to draw conclusions from a sequence of environmental stimulation without the aid of extraenvironmental evaluations of its performance. The energy that supports learning in an ART network comes from discrepancies between experience and expectation. Thus, ART shares this important feature with multiprocess models.

In addition to the major modern theories of cognition, there have been other attempts to quantify the description of problem-solving strategies, rooted in comparative psychology. Strategies (also called hypotheses) have been documented and quantified in rats (Krechevsky, 1932), in nonhuman primates (Harlow, 1959; Levine, 1966; Fisher, 1974), and in children and adults (Zeaman and House, 1963; Metzger, 1986; Trabasso and Bower, 1968). All of the methods for quantifying the strategies in these attempts required aggregated data, hampering the effort to quantify some of the dynamical properties of the process. Nevertheless, these approaches have generally yielded the pervasive finding that subjects change strategies (learn) following errors, rather than following rewards. Thus, these methods postulate structures and processes of cognition that are analogous to structures and processes of multiprocess models.

Successful theories of cognition have characterized cognition as a system that has features in common with multiprocess models. They include theories that postulate that the subject applies ideas, thoughts, and plans to the current situation and that the subject selects among eligible interpretations according to Bayes rule. The application of Bayes rule is inherently a dynamical process, but previous studies have not applied it explicitly to prediction errors. Explicitly taking this step reveals the possibility that an individual may be able to quantify the effects of unique experiences, where the quantity is derived from the discrepancy between expectation and experience. Therefore, it is possible that multiprocess modeling constitutes not only a method for describing cognition but also a candidate for the structure of cognition.

Multiprocess dynamical models can more straightforwardly be related to theories of behavioral dynamics. In particular, multiprocess models can be used to describe the details of the sequence of development of coordinated behavioral supersystems that arise from the combination of separate elementary coordinated systems as they are brought to bear on the demands on an individual in a particular context. This is a characterization of the dynamics of behavioral development as conceived in the theories and supported by the findings of Thelen (see Thelen, 1992, for an overview). In the language of multiprocess models, it is possible to represent both the elementary systems and the supersystem as models. The models could then be put into competition to describe an individual system. The resulting description would be the sequence of appearance of elementary systems and the details of the emergence of their coordination within an individual subject.

16.7 SUMMARY

Human cognition and behavior are dynamical processes adapted to a dynamic world. Explicitly taking the dynamical perspective on both cognition and behavior yields a practical method for describing the course of thoughts and behavior of an individual. The useful contribution of the method of multiprocess models is that it can be used to quantify the description of natural dynamical systems for which the underlying process is only approximately known. Since adapting to and drawing conclusions about natural dynamical processes of unknown structure is a pervasive feature of cognition, the method of multiprocess models is a plausible candidate for a theory of cognition.

ACKNOWLEDGMENT

The research reported here was supported in part by NSF grant BNS-9020357. I thank Keiko Mitsumoto, Michael Theisz, and Amy Easley for assistance throughout these studies. I am grateful for the advice and encouragement I have received from Aleeza Cerf-Beare, Richard Golden, and Peter Killeen.

APPENDIX A

In 1763 Richard Price submitted the essay written by his deceased friend, Thomas Bayes, for publication in the *Philosophical Transactions* of the Royal Society in London (see Deming, 1940). In the foreword to *An Essay towards Solving a Problem in the Doctrine of Chances*, Price showed that the dynamic nature of Bayes Rule was evident from the inception. Price wrote, "Every judicious person will be sensible that the problem now mentioned is by no means merely a curious speculation in the doctrine of chances, but necessary to be solved in order to a sure (*sic*) foundation for all our reasonings concerning past facts, and what is likely to be hereafter."

In 1967, J. R. Gray wrote:

The outcome of a trial of some system is observed to be the event *B*. This event could only happen if the system in which the trial was made was one of the mutually exclusive systems $C_1, C_2, \ldots, C_m$. Prior to making the trial, it was known that the respective initial or *a priori* probabilities of the systems being $C_1, C_2, \ldots, C_m$ were $p(C_1) = p_1, p(C_2) = p_2, \ldots, p(C_m) = p_m$. Once the trial has been performed and found to result in *B* we have additional information and we wish to reassess the respective probabilities of the C_i in the light of this new evidence, i.e., we wish to make a more up-to-date assessment of the probabilities of the C_i and replace the *a priori* probabilities which were based only on information available before the trial with *a posteriori* probabilities based on this information and the additional known fact that *B* occurs.

APPENDIX B

The results of the Makridakis competition (Makridakis, Anderson, Carbone, et al., 1984) are particularly relevant to the understanding of the adequacy of simple approximate models based on recent observations for forecasting natural phenomena. The competition was held among experts, each of whom chose a technical forecasting method and attempted to produce the best forecasts for up to 1001 sets of consecutive observations on actual quantities from macro- and microeconomics. These included quantities from sources in international government and business, such as housing starts in the United States, production of tin in Thailand, and deaths in the United Kingdom. The mean absolute percentage error of forecasting over all methods increased, respectively, from 11% to 21% to 48% as the forecasting horizon increased from 1 to 5 to 18 steps into the future. Thus, the best statistical forecasts far into the future are generally less accurate than near forecasts, affirming that there are severe limitations on long-term forecasting in the natural world.

In competition with sophisticated forecasting methods, three simple forecasting methods were superior overall. These were called *naive 1, simple moving average*, and *simple exponential smoothing*.

For naive 1, the forecast was simply the last observed value, as in equation (B.3.1),

$$f_{t+1} = x_t, \tag{B.3.1}$$

where x_t is the observation at time t and f_t is the forecast at time t. This method generates the next forecast by repeating the most recent observation. In terms of judgmental heuristics, with the anchor defined as the most recent observation, naive 1 is identical to *anchoring*.

For simple moving average the forecast was the average of k previous observations as in equation (B.3.2),

$$f_{t+1} = (x_t + x_{t-1} + x_{t-2} \ldots + x_{t-k+1})/k, \tag{B.3.2}$$

for k a constant determined to be optimal for each time series.

In a reanalysis of the Makridakis data, the moving average method was used to find the accuracy of forecasts as a function of k, ($k = 1, 3, 7, 10, 20, 100$) for the data sets of Makridakis. Since the data sets varied in length, the values of k were limited to those for which a reasonably large number of series could be obtained. The mean absolute percentage error (MAPE) for each forecast was computed for each time series for each applicable value of k. Time series with various known regularities (i.e., nonseasonal, seasonal, and quarterly, and seasonal and monthly) were analyzed separately. The linear regression between MAPE and k was computed. For this analysis, improvement in forecasting accuracy with increasing sample size (k) would appear as a significantly negative regression coefficient. The results showed the opposite effect; regression coefficients for all types of seasonality were near zero but significantly positive. The regression coefficients were .002, .003, and .001 for nonseasonal, quarterly, and monthly, respectively. The results for the regressions were homogeneous and the combined data yielded the following sets of quartiles of MAPE for the 1001 time series for each value of k (in parentheses): 5-9-17 (1), 6-10-18 (3), 7-12-22 (7), 8-13-24 (10),10-15-25 (20), and 15-24-34 (100). Only 191 data sets were sufficiently long to provide data for $k = 100$. At least 875 data sets contributed a MAPE for each $k < 100$. The relationship between k and accuracy indicates that, for these naturally occurring data sets, increasing the sample size of the moving average beyond $k = 1$ confers no advantage to the forecaster.

Using the criterion of smallest MAPE, reanalysis of the Makridakis data showed that the best single value of k, when the same value is applied to all series, is $k = 1$. The simple moving average generates the next forecast by taking the mean of k most recent observations. In terms of judgmental heuristics, for $k > 1$, it does not conform explicitly to a judgmental heuristic, but it involves making predictions by using the means of small nonrandom samples; therefore, it may be helpful in understanding the source of the judgmental bias that applies to random samples, *insensitivity to sample size*. For $k = 1$, this method is identical to anchoring, where the most recent observation serves as the anchor.

For simple exponential smoothings, the forecast for each observation was a linear combination of the most recent forecast and the most recent observation, as in equation (B.3.3),

$$f_{t+1} = f_t + a(x_t - f_t), \qquad (B.3.3)$$

where a is a constant determined by the data. This method generates the next forecast by repeating the most recent forecast adjusted in the direction of the most recent observation. In terms of judgmental heuristics with the anchor defined as the most recent forecast, this method corresponds to the judgmental heuristic of *anchoring and adjustment*.

In summary, over a wide range of actual economic time series, no method was successful at long-term forecasting and simple, approximate methods related to judgmental heuristics were superior to complex methods for short-term forecasting.

APPENDIX C

The mean of the k most recent observations (moving average) of independent observations on a fixed Gaussian distribution is logically the same as the mean of a random sample of size k. Equations (C.1) through (C.5) show that when the mean of a sample of size k is used as the forecast for the next observation randomly drawn from the distribution, setting k greater than about 10 cannot substantially reduce the error of the forecast.

Define s_f to be the error (standard deviation) in the forecast and s_g to be the error (standard deviation) of the Gaussian distribution.

$$s^2{}_f = s^2{}_g + (s^2{}_g)/k \qquad (C.1)$$

$$s^2{}_f = s^2{}_g + (1 + (1/k)) \qquad (C.2)$$

Error in the forecast:

$$s_f = s_g(1 + (1/k))^{1/2} \qquad (C.3)$$

Example for $k = 1000$, the expected error in the forecast is

$$s_f = 1.00 s_g, \qquad (C.4)$$

but for $k = 10$, the expected error is larger by only 5%:

$$s_f = 1.05 s_g \qquad (C.5)$$

NOTES

1. When subjects can be expected to switch among strategies at each instant or two (rapidly), their behavior violates the fundamental idea of a strategy as a persistent behavior pattern. It

may sometimes be useful to go beyond the requirement of persistence and allow the possibility that strategies may change rapidly. In such a case the data may be approached via the method discussed by West and Harrison (1989) under the heading of multiprocess models, class II.

2. General information on ANNs of this type may be found in Jacobs et al. (1991); Jordan and Jacobs (1992); Jordan and Rumelhart (1992); Narendra and Parthasarathy (1990); Metzger and Mitsumoto (1991); and Weigend, Huberman, and Rumelhart (1990).

3. This research into forecasting dynamical systems was inspired by the explication of deterministic chaos. The concept of deterministic chaos and its attendant phenomenology have a profound implication. Even when their processes are fully understood and all relevant variables measured, interesting deterministic systems with nonlinear dynamics cannot be forecast far into the future. Similarly, measurements made in the far past cannot help to forecast the near future. When anyone forms an expectancy for an event, the nonlinear dynamics of natural processes restricts them to making forecasts of the near future from information in the recent past. Therefore, if one uses means of any samples for this purpose, the only useful sample sizes would be small (perhaps around seven or so observations) and nonrandom. This limitation on the possibility of forecasting natural events suggested a new explanation for limitations on human information-processing capacity, namely, that a larger capacity would be of no benefit in forming expectancies for natural events.

REFERENCES

Anderson, D. B. O., Moore, J. B., and Hawkes, R. M. (1978). Model approximations via prediction error identification. *Automatics, 14,* 615–622.

Anderson, J. R. (1990). *The adaptive character of thought.* Hillsdale, NJ: Erlbaum.

Atmanspacher, H., and Scheingraber, H. (Eds.) (1990). *Information dynamics.* New York: Plenum.

Benchley-Capon, T. J. M. (1990). *Knowledge representation: an approach to artificial intelligence.* London: Academic Press.

Bennett, B. M., Hoffman, D. O., and Prakash, C. (1989). *Observer mechanics: a formal theory of perception.* San Diego, CA: Academic Press.

Buchanan, B. G., and Duda, R. O. (1982). *Principles of rule-based expert systems.* (Report No. STAN-CS-82-926.) Stanford, CA: Stanford University.

Cohen, P. R. (1985). *Heuristic reasoning about uncertainty: an artificial intelligence approach.* Boston: Pittman Advanced Publishing Program.

Deming, W. E. (Ed.) (1940). *Facsimiles of two papers by Bayes with commentaries.* Washington DC: The graduate school, Department of Agriculture.

Duda, R. O. (1979). Model design in the Prospector consultant system for mineral exploration. In D. Michie (Ed.), *Expert systems in the microelectronic age.* Cambridge, England: Cambridge University Press.

Fisher, M. A. (1974). Estimating hypothesis strengths. *Behavior Research Methods and Instrumentation, 6,* 309–311.

Fisher, M. A. (1977). Dimensional interaction in hyperactive children: classification of computer-displayed stimuli. *Bulletin of the Psychonomic Society, 10,* 443–446.

Fisher, M. A. (1978). Dextroamphetamine and placebo practice effects on selective attention in hyperactive children. *Journal of Abnormal Child Psychology, 5,* 25–32.

Fun, W., and Jordan, M. I. (1992). *The moving basin: effective action-search in forward models.* (MIT Computational Cognitive Science Technical Report No. 9204.) Cambridge MA.

Golden, R. M. (1992). Making correct statistical inferences using a wrong probability model with applications to story recall data analysis. School of Human Development, University of Texas at Dallas, unpublished.

Gray, J. R. (1967). *Probability*. London: Oliver and Boyd Ltd.

Grebogi, C., Ott, E., and Yorke, J. A. (1987). Chaos, strange attractors, and fractal basin boundaries in nonlinear dynamics. *Science, 238*, 632–638.

Gregson, R. A. M. (1980). Model evaluation via stochastic parameter convergence as on-line system identification. *British Journal of Mathematical and Statistical Psychology, 33*, 17–35.

Grossberg, S. (1988). Nonlinear neural networks: principles, mechanisms, and architectures. *Neural Networks, 1*, 17–61.

Harlow, H. F. (1959). Learning set and error factor theory. In S. Koch (Ed.), *Psychology: a study of a science*, Vol. 2. New York: McGraw-Hill.

Jacobs, R. A., Jordan, M. I., Nowlan, S. J., et al. (1991). Adaptive mixtures of local experts. *Neural Computation, 3*, 79–87.

Jordan, M. I., and Jacobs, R. A. (1992). Hierarchies of adaptive experts. In J. Moody, S. Hanson, and R. Lippmann (Eds.), *Advances in Neural Information Processing Systems*, Vol. 4. San Mateo, CA: Morgan Kaufmann.

Jordan, M. I., and Rumelhart, D. E. (1992). Forward models: supervised learning with distal teacher. *Cognitive Science, 16*, 307–354.

Kahneman, D., and Tversky, A. (1982). Subjective probability: a judgment of representativeness. In D. Kahneman, P. Slovic, and A. Tversky (Eds.), *Judgment under uncertainty: heuristics and biases* (pp. 32–47). New York: Cambridge University Press.

Krechevsky, I. (1932). "Hypotheses" in rats. *Psychological Review, 39*, 516–532.

Levine, M. (1965). Hypothesis behavior. In A. M. Schrier, H. F. Harlow, and F. Stollnitz (Eds.), *Behavior of nonhuman primates*, Vol. 1. New York: Academic Press.

Makridakis, S., Anderson, A., Carbone, R., et al. (Eds.), *The forecasting accuracy of major time series methods*. New York: Wiley.

Metzger, M. A. (1986). Reward context: influence on hypotheses during learning set formation by preschool children. *Psychological Reports, 58*, 879–884.

Metzger, M. A. (1991). Forecasting a chaotic time-series: utility of anchoring, sample size, and prior probabilities in dynamic systems. Presented at the annual meeting of the Society for Mathematical Psychology, Bloomington, IN.

Metzger, M. A., and Mitsumoto, K. (1991). Forecasting multivariate time-series: confidence intervals and comparison of performance on feed-forward neural networks and linear state-space models. In *Proceedings of the International Joint Conference on Neural Networks* (p. II-A-915) Seattle.

Metzger, M. A., and Theisz, M. F. (1994). Forecast: program to obtain forecasts from subjects of successive values of chaotic time-series. *Behavior Research Methods, Instrumentation, and Computers, 26*, 387–394.

Narendra, K. S., and Parthasarathy, K. (1990). Identification and control of dynamical systems using neural networks. *IEEE Transactions on Neural Networks, 1*, 4–27.

Newell, A. (1990). *Unified theories of cognition*. Cambridge, MA: Harvard University Press.

Pole, A., West, M., Harrison, J. (1988). Nonnormal and nonlinear dynamic Bayesian modeling. In J. C. Spall (Ed.), *Bayesian analysis of time series and dynamic model*. New York: Dekker.

Scalero, R. S., and Tepedelenlioglu, N. (1992). A fast new algorithm for training feed-forward neural networks. *IEEE Transactions in Acoustics, Speech, Signal Processing, ASSP-40*, January, *40*, 202–210.

Sterman, J. D. (1989). Deterministic chaos in an experimental economic system. *Journal of Economic Behavior and Organization, 12*, 1–28.

Thelen, E. (1992). Development as a dynamic system. *Current Directions in Psychological Science, 2*, 189–193.

Trabasso, T., and Bower, G. H. (1968). *Attention in learning: theory and research*. New York: Wiley.

Tversky, A., and Kahneman, D. (1974). Judgment under uncertainty: heuristics and biases. *Science*, 185, 1124–1131.

Weigend, A. S., Huberman, B. A., and Rumelhart, D. E. (1990). Predicting the future: a connectionist approach. (Technical Report Stanford-PDP-90-01.) Stanford, CA: Stanford University.

West, M., and Harrison, J. (1989). *Bayesian forecasting and dynamic models*. New York: Springer Verlag.

Zeaman, D., and House, B. (1963). The role of attention in retardate discrimination learning. In N. R. Ellis (Ed.), *Handbook of mental deficiency*, New York: McGraw-Hill.

Guide to Further Reading

Four important books elaborate on modeling dynamical aspects of cognition and behavior. The fundamental techniques of dynamic models are given a useful practical treatment by West and Harrison (1989). The authors include a helpful discussion of the advantages of focusing on prediction error rather than the more abstract pair of errors respectively attributable to process and measurement. In addition, they treat generalizations of the multiprocess models presented in this chapter. Gregson (1992) discusses multiprocess models specifically applied to psychological processes. Anderson (1990) presents an extensive discussion of the role of Baye's rule in cognition. Bennett, Hoffman, and Prakash (1989) introduce an ambitious dynamical model that constitutes a universal theory of perception. In these further readings the authors succeed in making sophisticated models accessible to the general reader.

Anderson, J. R. (1990). *The adaptive character of thought*. Hillsdale, NJ: Erlbaum.

Bennett, B. M., Hoffman, D. O., and Prakash, C. (1989). *Observer mechanics: a formal theory of perception*. San Diego, CA: Academic Press.

Gregson, R. A. M. (1992). *n-Dimensional nonlinear psychophysics*. Hillsdale, NJ: Erlbaum.

West, M., and Harrison, J. (1989). *Bayesian forecasting and dynamic models*. New York: Springer Verlag.

17 The Dynamics of Mind and Body During Clinical Interviews: Research Trends, Potential, and Future Directions

Steven P. Reidbord and Dana J. Redington

EDITORS' INTRODUCTION

It is popular to describe cognitive science as the science of the mind, but the mind is, notoriously, a very difficult thing to have a science of. Cognitive scientists tend to focus on phenomena that lend themselves to repeatable observation and precise modeling, with the result that much of what people ordinarily take to belong to mental life comes to be ignored. Psychiatrists, however, cannot follow this path: the rich, complex interplay of an individual's moods, emotions, and attitudes are exactly what they are required to understand.

The challenge can be divided into two parts: finding a reliable form of observational access to mental life, and an adequate means of describing and predicting what may be observed. Reidbord and Redington proceed on the innovative assumption that dynamics can form a general framework within which these tasks can be carried out. In a clinical setting, they gather fine-grained time-series data of the rate at which a subject's heart is beating, and then use dynamical systems techniques and concepts to analyze how these rates are changing over time. By correlating these changes with developments in the subject's state of mind as observed by more traditional methods, they gain insight into how heart-rate measurements can function as a window onto mental life.

Ideally, it would be possible to develop equations which model the heart-rate data, and thereby indirectly the flow of a subject's mental life itself. At this early stage it is difficult to say whether this goal is likely to be achieved anytime soon. In the meantime, Reidbord and Redington are demonstrating that a dynamical perspective offers a whole new avenue of exploration of mental life. As they put it, "modeling is an iterative procedure which follows observation."

17.1 PSYCHOLOGICAL STATES AND STATE TRANSITIONS

All psychological theory can be understood as attempting to characterize psychological states and state transitions. What is one's state of mind at this moment? How did it reach this state? Where is it going next? One important distinguishing feature of any psychological theory is how it describes a state of interest. Behaviorists describe behavioral states; psychodynamic theorists (e.g., Freudians) describe states of anxiety and defense; other types of therapists define interpersonal or transactional states; cognitive psychologists describe information-bearing internal states. While psychologists of various schools describe mental states differently, all ultimately try to account for the flow from one state to the next.

The word "psychodynamic" points to this directly. It implies systematic motion, an orderly flow in time, of mental processes and phenomena. "Psychodynamics" borrows *dynamics*, a concept native to physics, and applies it to mental life. Historically, this has typically been achieved by likening the dynamics of the mind to those of a better-understood physical system; the dynamics of the physical system stand in as a model of the mental dynamics. The evolution of psychodynamics as an intellectual field is marked by the slowly increasing sophistication of its physical models for the mind. William James (1950) offered a flowing water metaphor. Freud used a hydraulic model to illustrate how basic drives act as though under pressure and seek release by bursting through defenses. Homeostatic models see the mind in a dynamic equilibrium that results from the sum total of forces impinging on the system. Other physical analogs include a simple thermodynamic model that compares mental states to the phases of pure substances, i.e., gas, liquid, and solid (Hilgard, 1980); a more complex thermodynamic approach models mental states and their flow with Belousov-Zhabotinsky chemical reactions that generate a cyclic alteration in the color of a complex solution (Epstein, Kustin, Kepper, et al., 1983; Schore, 1981).

For some decades now digital computers have been popular as physical models of mind. In serial processing models—one instruction or process at a time—the brain is seen as "computer hardware" and mental contents as "software" or "programming" (George, 1973; Weizenbaum, 1976). Recently, computer models have been extended to include parallel processing (Rumelhart, McClelland, and PDP Research Group, 1986). Interestingly, parallel processing computer models share several features of actual nervous systems that are causally related to the dynamics of these systems: nonlinear activation functions for individual processing elements, asynchronous processing by those elements, and summated interactions where ensembles of elements participate in the generation of emergent behavior.

To model a natural process is to simplify it in order to promote understanding. Models are neither "right" nor "wrong," but are more or less useful depending on their ability to account for the natural system's behaviors of interest. The models mentioned above capture some of the general features of psychological dynamics, and may account for observed behavioral data in an inexact way. They are useful to that extent.

For the remainder of this chapter, we will be concerned with the kinds of mental states and processes that are of primary interest to psychiatrists and psychotherapists. As described by Horowitz (1987), a "state of mind" is a complex multidimensional amalgam of thoughts, feelings, memories, and relational stances present in an individual at any given time; such states last from

Steven P. Reidbord and Dana J. Redington

less than 1 second to several minutes. All of a state's features appear to flow in a coordinated or cohesive fashion. This view of mental state is founded in traditional psychodynamics, but also pays homage to what is known empirically about cognition.

Unfortunately, at present the actual dynamics of mental processes in this sense are at best only roughly approximated by the kinds of models mentioned above. In particular, none of those modeling approaches really accounts for the dynamics of short-term mental state changes. Indeed, it is a curious fact that psychodynamic research rarely deals in a serious fashion with the actual dynamics of the psyche. Research tends to study and describe the state, the static or cross-sectional configuration, not the "motion" from state to state, and certainly not the underlying controls that regulate this flow on a moment-to-moment basis. Even theoretical work (i.e., the construction of conceptual models) traditionally neglects the subtlety of this flow. More recent exceptions include neural network models applied to psychodynamics in terms of schematic representation (Stinson and Palmer, 1991), and models based on catastrophe theory that describe the continuous and discontinuous changes associated with psychological states (Callahan and Sashin, 1987; Winquist and Winzenz, 1977). Both of these examples are special cases of a nonlinear dynamical approach, the general features of which are described below. In comparison to the other models reviewed earlier, models of the mind that incorporate nonlinear dynamics may capture more of the subtlety of actual psychodynamics, which, as we argue below, appears to be highly nonlinear. Nonetheless, even models that feature nonlinear dynamics are simplifications. It is the task of the model builder to decide what features of the target system are worth incorporating into the model. In the case of psychological dynamics, this choice is neither obvious nor trivial; it hinges on preliminary data analyses that are usually neglected.

Our work can be seen as a reaction to an unfortunate historical pattern in psychodynamic psychology of putting modeling before data analysis. In our view, a recurrent error in the history of psychodynamic thought has been to liken the dynamics of the mind to simpler physical systems, even before gathering adequate data concerning those dynamics. However, it is more important initially to see what the dynamics *are*, not what they are *like*. Modeling is an iterative process that follows observation. Our studies are founded first in observing the target system. In the early work we describe below, we have developed descriptions of four trajectory types that follow one another in complex patterns over time. These descriptions are not intended as a *model* of psychodynamics in any strict mathematical sense. In our opinion any such model would currently be premature, and destined to prove embarrassing in the long run. In contrast to some of the other kinds of cognitive or behavioral phenomena described elsewhere in this book, "psychodynamic" states of mind are not as yet sufficiently well characterized to permit comparison of human data with the data output of a computerized model. Of course, models will eventually be constructed, but first we need to observe the dynamics we want to model. And the only way truly to know the dynamics of the mind is to study the mind itself as directly as possible using rigorous, high-resolution, data-driven dynamical methods.

17.2   NONLINEAR DYNAMICAL ANALYSES AND CHAOS

To deal more effectively with the complexity of flow from one mental state to the next, there have been fledgling efforts in the recent psychological literature to employ nonlinear dynamical models to describe psychological processes and behavior (e.g., Abraham, 1990). Like earlier physical models, these models treat the mind as a deterministic system with rule-based behavior. Here, however, the focus is on the dynamic complexity of the flow from state to state. Nonlinear systems theory, and the related concept of "chaos" popularized by Gleick's (1987) book of the same name, particularly emphasizes discontinuous behavior in complex systems, and highlights how even fully determined, nonstochastic behavior can appear unpredictable, very complex, and subtle. Use of this paradigm has brought renewed excitement to the modeling of mental dynamics.

Chaos offers a compelling image to laypeople and scientists alike. This term describes systems with certain interesting dynamical properties. Originally applied to physical systems, chaos refers to complex, pseudorandom behavior that follows from well-defined, but usually inapparent, dynamic equations that govern the behavior. Such systems manifest "sensitive dependence on initial conditions": infinitesimal differences in the initial or startup conditions of the system result in marked divergence of behavior. The unfolding dynamics over significant periods of time are unpredictable without absolutely exact knowledge of the initial conditions. Chaotic systems (as well as some nonchaotic nonlinear systems) also exhibit "bifurcations": sudden, discontinuous jumps from one kind of behavior to another. In natural systems, where the initial conditions and the underlying dynamic equations can never be known exactly, these properties account for the pseudorandom behavior seen.

Yet most systems, chaotic or not, operate within a bounded state space. Such systems have dynamic stability; they do not tend to spiral destructively out of control. This is true, for example, of living systems under normal conditions: they maintain sustainable dynamics despite rapid shifts in behavior and environmental circumstances. Given their pseudorandom behavior, it is of particular interest that chaotic systems contain themselves within a bounded universe of behaviors and tend to revisit the same, or very similar, behaviors at different times.

Given the brief characterization above, it is little wonder that nonlinear dynamical modeling, and the concept of chaos in particular, has found its way into psychology. Presumably in large part deterministic, the flow of mental contents seems fundamentally unpredictable on a moment-to-moment basis. There is an apparent sensitive dependence on initial (and ongoing) conditions of experience, internal and external. Furthermore, the mental life of any individual operates over time within a bounded state space, revisiting characteristic states. These characteristic mental states, as inferred by verbal and nonverbal behavior, are how we know an individual's personality. Not only does the nonlinear dynamical approach offer the familiar security of concepts borrowed from physics, the special situation of chaos also treats seriously the well-known inability to account for or predict in detail the flow of human behavior. A chaotic account of mental dynamics seems to strike the right balance between implausible simplicity and implausible randomness.

At this global level, the mind as a chaotic system seems an attractive idea. But this is a far cry from having a useful model of chaotic psychodynamics. While there is nothing wrong with pure theory, the utility of chaos and other dynamical notions awaits more precise characterization of actual mental dynamics. Perhaps these will prove to be chaotic, perhaps not. How may this matter be approached empirically?

This deceptively simple question introduces the knotty problem of measurement in psychology. Dynamical analyses demand precise, valid data, and lots of it. What physical evidence constitutes valid data about the mind? This very basic question underlies all of psychology, cognitive science, and psychiatry. The mind can only be studied scientifically via its objective effects, whether these consist of the subject's verbal report, autonomic outflow, or actual physical behaviors such as gestures and facial expressions. Even neurophysiological imaging, e.g., positron emission tomography (PET) scanning, merely reveals presumed biophysical correlates of mental activity, not the mental activity itself. Attention to these behavioral "signals," their precise resolution and validity, ought to be a central concern for all the behavioral sciences. Yet this pivotal issue, which can make or break a careful study of mental dynamics, is often neglected. A rigorous nonlinear dynamical approach cannot avoid these concerns. If the dynamics of the system are to be studied using mathematically precise tools, the data, too, must be of high precision, valid for the intended analysis, and reliably collected in a timely fashion.

Historically, different methods have been employed to gain access to the mind (Zegans and Victor, 1988). Foremost among these are hypnosis, forced suggestion, and free association. In what arguably marks the inception of modern psychiatry in the first half of the 19th century, Braid refined and applied hypnosis to explore unconscious mental processes. Hypnosis was thought to control the state of the mind, yielding better access and hence better data. In the second half of the 19th century, Bernheim continued to apply hypnosis as a therapeutic tool and later discovered the importance of suggestions given to nonhypnotized patients during the psychotherapy procedure. Here, it was thought that force of will could directly influence patients' mental states. Toward the end of the 19th century, Charcot, through his work with hypnosis and hysteria, began to develop the concept of the unconscious as a storehouse of memories and unprocessed material. His work formed a major foundation of modern psychodynamic theory, but ironically lacked a description of the dynamics themselves.

Around the turn of the century, Freud applied and then abandoned hypnosis in favor of free association (Bonaparte, Freud, and Kris, 1954; Strachey, 1966). To this day, Freud's method of promoting continuous reporting of mental contents provides the best technique for tracking the natural flow of mental states using verbal output alone. Free association was on the right track: it partially accesses the naturally occurring dynamics of the mind. It is designed to allow the mental apparatus to run freely and unhindered, its flow distorted only by the need to provide verbal reporting of subjective experience. In contrast, the usual manipulations of experimental psychology constrain the dynamic flow of mental functioning through strict environmental demands, and in this light seem paradoxically aimed to obscure the innate flow of mental states, and to overlook naturally occurring psychodynamics.

Free association was the breakthrough that led to Freud's psychodynamic model of the mind. Freud realized that coherent narrative reports of mental contents cannot capture the actual flow of mental states; the more one's verbal output resembles a coherent narrative, the less it reflects true subjective experience. Indeed, storytelling during free association is seen as a defense, a less anxiety-provoking alternative to giving genuine voice to the free flow of mental contents. Our research, discussed below, suggests that the flow of mental states during coherent narrative is also less dynamically complex than during free association.

While free association was a groundbreaking development for understanding mental dynamics, it has many shortcomings. The technique relies on what can be expressed verbally, and what is inferred by applying a complex metapsychological theory to this verbal output. When a person truthfully reports his or her mental states, this serves as evidence of the type of state manifest at that time. Verbal report, however, is very weak evidence of internal state. First, conscious subjective experience need not be the entire characterization of mental state. A considerable amount of processing goes on behind the scenes, and the contemporary view is of a highly active cognitive unconscious (Kihlstrom, 1987). And even if a subject's conscious experience alone were of interest, verbal report is still intermittent and incomplete. Language imperfectly translates internal experience into a single serial output channel, limited in its capacity to convey the simultaneous (parallel) processing of the mind, or the multidimensional nature of mental contents. The bandwidth of this signal (its capacity to transmit multiple bits of information simultaneously) seems too narrow to constitute a real-time monitor of subjective experience. Three other issues make matters even worse. First, even an earnest subject is apt to suppress reports of certain unpleasant mental contents. Second, the process of verbal expression itself provides additional feedback which may alter ongoing experience. And finally, language may not provide an adequate symbolic framework for describing certain subtle mental states.

Steven P. Reidbord and Dana J. Redington

The subjective experiences we wish to study may be difficult or impossible to express verbally if there is no easy mapping from mental state to verbal description.

These dilemmas are familiar to practicing psychotherapists, even if they are rarely understood in the above terms. A patient's inner dynamics are presumably continuous or nearly so, but their expression through language is intermittent. Clinicians inevitably employ some form of interpolation. In addition, the clinician accesses additional channels of information. Affect is inferred mainly through nonlexical signals, including facial expression, bodily movements, posture, tears, and tone of voice. These nonverbal behaviors can be very brief, as in momentary facial expressions of anger or sadness (Ekman and Friesen, 1975), and can be viewed as a relatively continuous output channel. In contrast to verbalizations, which reflect cortical output, affect reflects lower-level brain processes. Attending to this lower-level output improves the characterization of psychodynamics by directly providing the evaluator additional data from a different part of the brain. It helps in an important indirect way as well. Much of the powerful subtlety of psychotherapy lies in the feedback loop where the therapist perceives a lower-level brain process (affect) in the patient, and feeds this information back to the patient at a higher level in words (and possibly in other affective signals of his own, as in countertransference). This feedback loop has the effect of improving the higher-level signal, the verbal channel, in its divulging of subsequent mental state changes.

Unfortunately, nonverbal behavior and affective signals also are insufficiently precise to allow rigorous characterization of the nonlinear dynamics of mental functioning. While nonverbal behavior may be more continuous than verbal output, it suffers from nonspecificity and additional difficulties in interpretation. Combinations of verbal and nonverbal information do provide the wide-bandwidth, multidimensional data needed to understand a patient's dynamics. Indeed, this is how therapists eventually come to understand their patients! However, for characterization of transient dynamics, and for rigorous mathematical approaches to nonlinear dynamical analysis, even these multiple data channels lack the requisite precision and information content.

In summary, the psychotherapy situation in general, and free association in particular, are situations optimally suited to observe the natural flow of mental states. Unfortunately, the usual data channels available to the clinician, the verbal and nonverbal behavior of the patient, seem inadequate to convey the dynamics of the psychological system as they occur on a moment-to-moment basis.

17.3 PSYCHOPHYSIOLOGY: OUTPUT CHANNELS TO VIEW MENTAL DYNAMICS

Data consisting of verbal reports and nonverbal behavior do not at the present time allow direct access to transient states of mind that can be analyzed from a dynamical perspective. An alternative approach is to analyze the dynamics of ongoing physiology. This includes central brain function as assessed through electroencephalographic (EEG) activity and peripheral nervous system function as assessed through autonomic measures, e.g., electrocardiographic (ECG) activity. A growing literature supports the suitability of physiological activity for dynamical analyses. Moreover, under the appropriate conditions, such analyses can be applied to psychophysiological methods to shed light on the dynamics of cognition and mental state.

A number of studies reveal that the human nervous system is composed of multiple, yet coupled and interacting, nonlinear systems (Redington, 1993). Scalp EEGs reveal nonlinear cortical processes (Basar, 1990). Deeper brain structures, such as the olfactory tract, exhibit nonlinear dynamics during perception (Freeman, 1975, 1987). The core brain oscillators associated with wakefulness and sleep, also deep within the brain, have been modeled using nonlinear equations (McCarley and Hobson, 1975).

Contemporary research in cardiology (e.g., Goldberger, Rigney, and West, 1990) has found that heart function, and in particular the "interbeat interval," is governed by complex nonlinear dynamics (see Glass and Mackey, 1988, for a discussion and review). The dynamics of the cardiovascular system are largely driven by multiple interconnections with the brain through neural and humoral pathways. These pathways are part of the sympathetic and parasympathetic autonomic nervous system, and form a direct connection between core brain centers and peripheral organs. Thus, under certain circumstances heart function may provide indirect, yet timely and precise access to autonomic nervous system dynamics, and thereby to core brain states.

One important way to characterize the dynamics of the nervous system is to describe the frequency characteristics of its behavior, that is, what components of behavior occur at what frequencies. A spectrum emerges when many types of behavior are considered over a wide span of frequencies. Such a physiological spectrum, constructed on a log scale of frequency, can be arbitrarily bounded by the threshold of human hearing, log 20,000 Hz or 4.3, down to the circadian rhythm, the log reciprocal of the 24 to 26-hour cycle or -4.95. This scale creates a spectral range of approximately -5 to $+5$ which can be used to map a significant portion of physiological processes.

Psychological and behavioral processes can also be added to this spectrum (figure 17.1). Extending along this continuum from higher frequencies to very low frequencies are sensory processes, information processing, transient cognitive and affective states, and finally longer-duration processes such as cycles of interpersonal interaction. This frequency spectrum recapitulates the natural hierarchical integration of information and meaning in the nervous system. Sensory processes are those involved in the translation of physical stimuli such as sound and light into neural signals. Information processing includes the registration of those processes into working and short-term memory. Transient cognitive and affective states, e.g., the display of momentary facial expressions and the orienting-evaluating cycle, extract additional meaning and occur at lower frequencies. Longer-duration processes, such as turn-

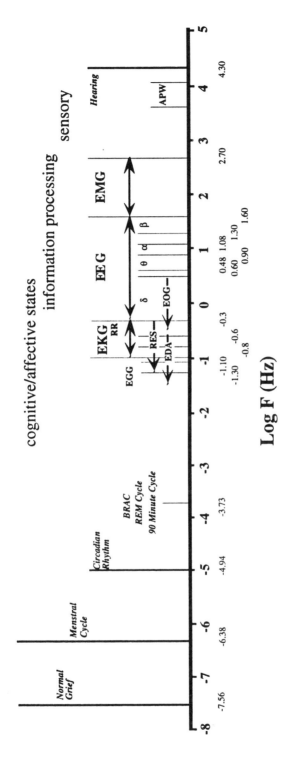

Figure 17.1 The psychophysiological spectrum on a log frequency scale. This serves as a common reference domain for conveniently mapping different mind and body processes. APW, acoustic plane wave; BRAC, basic rest/activity cycle; EDA, electrodermal activity; EEG, electroencephalogram; EKG$_{RR}$, electrocardiogram, R-R interval; EGG, electrogastrogram; EMG, electromyogram; EOG, electro-oculogram; RES, respiration.

taking in discourse, cycles of mood states, and the response to traumatic stressors, contain the most integrated meaning structures.

Different portions of this spectrum can be studied using nonlinear dynamical analysis. The choice of which frequency band to study determines the time resolution and precision of measurement, and also the relevance of the data to naturally observable psychological phenomena. For example, lower-frequency phenomena, such as self-reported mood shifts or interpersonal affiliation, capture important human behavior, but can be studied only with poor temporal resolution and relative imprecision. The moment-by-moment flow of mental states is lost. In contrast, higher-frequency phenomena, such as those found in the study of brain states through EEG, can be studied with high precision and fine temporal resolution, but do not directly capture psychodynamically mediated behavior. An intermediate window would focus on the dynamics of mental states on the order of seconds to a few minutes. This midrange window, while also restricted, spans frequencies of mental processes and phenomena that can be characterized with precise nonlinear dynamical methods, yet also conveys meaning of interest to an integrated cognitive psychology. This is the window we use in our current research.

These preliminary efforts to characterize narrow frequency bands, while an important early step in the application of a novel methodology, overlook the interactions that may lead to emergent psychological phenomena. For example, sudden intrusions into consciousness of past traumatic experiences may be momentary (and thus would be reflected in the higher-frequency region of the spectrum), but also may lead to longer-term mood shifts in a lower-frequency region. In isolation, a model of either the intrusions themselves or the resultant mood shifts neglects the underlying dynamics that link the two. Ideally, a comprehensive model would include behavior across the widest range of the spectrum, so that the system's *global* behavior is reflected in the model.

17.4   CURRENT RESEARCH

We have applied methods of nonlinear analysis to psychophysiological data obtained during psychotherapy interviews. This is an ideal setting in which to observe intrapersonal and interpersonal psychological dynamics, and to monitor the midrange of the psychophysiological spectrum—those processes occurring on the order of seconds to minutes. Psychotherapy interviews serve as a prototype for dyadic interactions. The environment is controlled for extraneous stimuli and there is little physical demand on the participants. While subjects are not literally encouraged to engage in free association, emphasis is placed on spontaneously occurring thoughts, memories, and feelings that may be problematic or stress-inducing for the individual. These interviews are naturalistic and relatively unstructured, so that the normal flow of psychological control and meaning, and its association with physiology, can be observed as closely as possible.

We have described a four-part plan for preliminary application of nonlinear dynamical methods to psychodynamics (Redington and Reidbord, 1992). The four stages involve: (1) initially defining a methodology based on visual inspection of psychophysiological phase spaces, (2) applying the same method to a larger data set to establish clinical correlates, (3) evaluating the same method in a different but complementary data set, and (4) studying nonlinear synchronization between individuals, each treated as a complex psychophysiological system.

The goal of the first study was to develop and present consistent methods of examining patient data (Redington and Reidbord, 1992). To our knowledge, this was the first nonlinear dynamical analysis of psychophysiological data collected in a psychotherapy setting, and, indeed, the first empirically driven nonlinear dynamical analysis looking at short-term "psychodynamic" state changes. As part of a larger study of psychotherapy processes conducted at the University of California, San Francisco, a 33-year-old woman underwent long-term psychodynamic psychotherapy in a research context. All of her sessions were videotaped, and during certain sessions her physiology was monitored by means of small sensors attached to her hands and wrists. Our study consisted of nonlinear dynamical analysis of precise heart-rate data collected during a single 50-minute session, a pivotal hour (no. 211) when the patient announced her decision to stop treatment. Certain characteristic patterns in the heart-rate dynamics were then related in an anecdotal way to interpersonal events observable in the videotape of that session.

We now describe our data analysis; additional details are available in the cited references. Our raw data consisted of ECG output that was monitored by computer and digitally filtered to produce an extremely precise second-by-second measure of the interbeat interval, the reciprocal of which is the instantaneous heart rate. As an initial step, the power spectrum of the data was examined. This is a statistical procedure based on Fourier analysis that reveals periodicities, or recurrent cycles, in time-series data. Highly nonlinear behavior (e.g., chaos), as well as true randomness, show "broad-band noise" (i.e., $1/f$) in the power spectrum; no sharp periodicities are seen. And, indeed, the power spectrum of our heart-rate data had the characteristic broad-band noise of chaos—or randomness.

The next step was to examine the data's autocorrelation. This is a measure of the correlation within the data set between the value at time t and the value at $t + 1$ (and $t + 2$, $t + 3$, etc.). If the heart rate were always exactly the same, there would be a perfect correlation (and perfect predictability) given any single measurement. On the other hand, if the data were truly random, there would be no correlation from one data point to the next. As expected, the actual autocorrelation of the heart-rate data fell somewhere in between. This in itself shows that heart-rate variations are not wholly random.

An additional finding was of particular importance. The autocorrelation for any given data point was fairly high for the point 1 second away, somewhat lower for the point 2 seconds away, and so forth. After about 8 seconds, the autocorrelation was lost in the background noise of the data. In other words, given any heart-rate value in the data set, all predictability for another heart-rate value was lost by 8 seconds later. This relative minimum of autocorrelation at 8 seconds was used as a parameter (referred to by the Greek letter tau, τ) in the next step of the analysis, the construction of a phase portrait.

Our phase-portrait construction relied on methods developed or suggested by others (Takens, 1981). The approach hinges on a mathematical technique called "embedding." This is a way of creating a higher-dimensional variable out of a lower-dimensional one, by using the parameter τ as a lag value. To embed one-dimensional data, like a heart-rate time series, into three dimensions, each three-dimensional data point is created from the instantaneous heart rate at time t (on the x-axis), the heart rate at time $t + \tau$ (on the y-axis), and the rate at time $t + 2\tau$ (on the z-axis). This is repeated for every data point in the original time series. Finally, the transformed data set is plotted in three dimensions.

The rationale for choosing τ at a relative minimum of autocorrelation is that the axes of the resulting space approach orthogonality, at least in a statistical sense. A phase space is Euclidean: each axis drawn at right angles to the others is meant to define another orthogonal dimension of the space. This has sometimes been overlooked in recent literature on "chaos in psychology" (e.g., Sabelli, Carlson-Sabelli, and Javaid, 1990). More pragmatically, orthogonal axes maximize the apparent structure in the phase portrait, and thus the information that can be extracted from it. This is somewhat analogous to rotating the axes of a factor analysis result to maximally separate the observations being factored.

The resulting phase portrait of heart rate, a computer-generated data visualization, was then inspected using graphics software that allows rotation of the scatterplot in three dimensions. In this way, we examined the overall structure of the data for a complete therapy hour, noting that the data filled the phase space in a way that appeared neither random nor simply periodic. This was the first reported phase-space analysis of psychophysiological data derived from a psychotherapy session.

Examining phase portraits that represent a whole therapy hour is analogous to looking at an hour-long videotape compressed into a single photograph. To gain access to the time evolution of states, we also sequentially scanned through the phase portrait, displaying a 30-second moving window of data. This enabled us to observe recurring "trajectories," characteristic types of flow over time. We were able to identify four generic dynamical patterns, or "trajectory types," in heart rate. Briefly, type I were pointlike trajectories; type II appeared as closed loops; type III represented a net shift from one region in the phase space to another; and type IV were random-like wanderings among many states. The first three trajectory types filled relatively less volume in comparison to type IV trajectories. Figure 17.2 shows examples of each of these. To make it easy to visually discriminate and

Steven P. Reidbord and Dana J. Redington

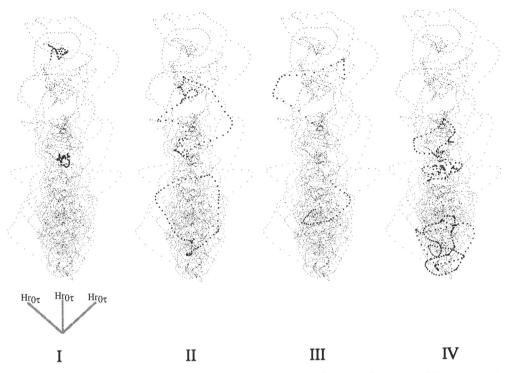

Hr₀τ Hr₀τ Hr₀τ

I   II   III   IV

Figure 17.2 The same phase portrait of a patient's heart-rate data is copied four times. Each copy shows two example trajectories of a particular type as identified by the roman numerals below each plot.

compare trajectory types, four different presentations of the same phase portrait are laid side by side, but with different sets of points highlighted on each. Further, the axes have been rotated and scaled so vertical height in the phase portrait corresponds to increasing heart rate. This is achieved by having the origin of the three axes at the very bottom of the phase-portrait diagram; think of the axes as edges of a cube balanced on one corner which is the origin. Two of the axes (x and z) are thus facing the reader and the third (y) is projecting away. The reader should note that, despite these maneuvers, the necessarily two-dimensional reproduction on paper cannot do justice to the third dimension as seen by rotating a computer image.

As a final step in the first study, we reviewed videotaped excerpts of the session corresponding in time to identifiable heart-rate trajectories. Although this study had no controls and only a single subject-hour of data, we were encouraged by the apparent association of specific heart-rate trajectory types with certain short-term psychological processes and interpersonal events during therapy. For example, during the time the therapist touched on a sensitive issue for this patient, her heart-rate trajectory became dynamically simpler (e.g., type III). Conversely, when the patient was calmly discussing important emotional matters less defensively, her heart-rate trajectory was more complex (i.e., type IV) by visual inspection.

The Dynamics of Mind and Body During Clinical Interviews

It was not possible to establish definitively the presence or absence of chaos in the heart-rate data. Our data are from an actual living system, not a simplified model, and do not orbit around a single, well-behaved, stationary chaotic attractor. The usual means of discerning chaos quantitatively (e.g., calculating the Lyapunov exponent) do not work here. So far, we have not found a way to differentiate true chaos from highly nonlinear, but nonchaotic, behavior of high dimensionality or complexity. It may not be possible with our data. Similarly, bifurcations and other interesting features of complex dynamics can often be characterized with great precision in data that have been generated by specified dynamic equations. Here, in contrast, bifurcations and attractors are inferred from the phase portrait, essentially by means of pattern recognition. We have inferred the presence of bifurcations when there are dramatic shifts in trajectory. Attractors of varying dimensionality are inferred when trajectories revisit characteristic regions in the phase space; this is described in detail in Redington and Reidbord (1992). While we consider it very plausible that such features as bifurcations and true chaos characterize psychodynamics, only weak empirical evidence, and certainly not proof, exists to date.

In a second study (Reidbord and Redington, 1992) we applied the same methodology to another patient's heart-rate data across six therapy sessions. This study further tested the methodology (e.g., the measurement reliability associated with dividing phase portraits into trajectories by visual inspection), and allowed us to collect a larger sample of psychological and behavioral phenomena that might be related to flows in the phase space. We again found the four previously seen trajectory types. In a more systematic fashion, we then reviewed 66 videotaped excerpts from the six sessions, each coinciding with an identified heart-rate trajectory. Our impressions from the first study were reinforced and clarified. Type IV trajectories, those appearing most complex by visual inspection, seemed to coincide with "reposed engagement" in therapy: a fluidity of mental state transitions and relatively lessened defensiveness. The other trajectory types coincided with patient behavior that seemed more anxious or defensive. There were more subtle apparent differences in behavior corresponding with the trajectory types I–III; while in type II, for example, the patient seemed more often to be speaking in a narrative, storytelling tone, and in some cases the type II trajectory corresponded closely in time to a story or anecdote the patient was telling.

Psychophysiological reactivity in *therapists* during psychotherapy has been studied sporadically over the past 50 years. Such changes may relate to "countertransference" (broadly construed, the emotional reactions of the therapist to his or her patient). A third study (Reidbord and Redington, 1993) applied the same methodology to five sessions of a therapist's heart-rate data. The four generic trajectory types were again identified. At this relatively gross level of visual inspection, the obvious differences in the mental processes of patient and therapist were not reflected in differences in the classification of trajectories into four general types, although we did note that the therapist's heart-rate trajectories within each type were more convoluted and complex than the patient's.

To systematically quantify the subjective correlates of these trajectories, a random sample of 56 therapist heart-rate trajectories was selected. Excerpts of the session videotapes corresponding to these sampled trajectories were reviewed by the therapist, who was blind to the selection process. For each excerpt, the therapist completed a written questionnaire that assessed the nature and intensity of his affect, the degree of therapeutic engagement, the balance between exploration and support, and several other important dimensions of psychodynamic psychotherapy. In a statistically significant finding, the therapist reported feeling more empathy *toward* the patient, and less concern *about* the patient, when his heart rate demonstrated the most complex trajectory pattern (type IV). A factor analysis was performed on the therapist's self-reported affects. Interestingly, the first factor, accounting for 37.8% of the variance in the therapist's responses, strongly differentiated empathy from concern, paralleling the observed differences in the incidence of these emotions during type IV trajectories. We speculate that this affective factor, which seems to vary with heart-rate complexity, may be related to the therapist's sense of empathic connection with the patient on a moment-to-moment basis, of "feeling with" instead of "feeling about."

A fourth study in preparation examines the synchronization of two non-linear systems, the patient and therapist, during five psychotherapy sessions. We hope to develop a nonlinear measure of therapeutic interaction based on psychologically mediated patterns of heart-rate interaction between the two participants. This line of investigation may show that nonlinear analyses can document the triggers (perturbations) and effects (bifurcations) of specific interactions and interventions made during interviews. In addition, recent work in the physical sciences has shown that two separate but similar chaotic electrical circuits can quickly synchronize when they share a communication signal (Pecora and Carroll, 1990). We hypothesize that with certain forms of human communication, interpersonal synchronization may occur in an analogous fashion.

In an effort to move to more quantitative nonlinear analysis, we applied a measure of "approximate entropy" developed by Pincus (1991) to heart-rate data obtained from 20 subjects during semistructured interviews. Approximate entropy is a measure that quantifies differences in the complexity of trajectories in the phase portrait at different times. The subjects in these interviews openly discussed three different topics. One topic was relatively neutral in content, another topic was about a current relationship, and the final topic, the most stressful, was about the recent loss of a loved one. Our data show that the three topics differed significantly in nonlinear complexity.

We have also applied nonlinear analyses in other settings. Using both qualitative and quantitative nonlinear analyses, we have done preliminary work on psychophysiological changes during yogic meditation. In one instance, an expert practitioner of yoga was able to alter considerably the complexity of his heart-rate dynamics during various yogic maneuvers (kriyas); this alteration persisted to a lesser degree for a short time afterward (Redington, 1993).

17.5 A FRAMEWORK FOR FUTURE EXPERIMENTS: INTERPERSONAL AND INTRAPERSONAL DYNAMICS

The study of psychophysiological dynamics during individual psychotherapy stands at a methodological crossroads. One road leads to investigations of interpersonal dynamics, the dynamics pertaining to two or more persons interacting. The other road leads to intrapersonal dynamics, the domain known traditionally as "psychodynamics." Clearly, empirical work has hardly begun in either direction. How might these roads be explored using careful scientific methods?

If individuals can be considered complex nonlinear systems, then the study of interpersonal dynamics may benefit from applying careful nonlinear dynamical methods to analyses of two or more persons interacting. As noted above, we are currently investigating the synchrony and dyssynchrony between patient and therapist heart rate during therapy. Additional studies might focus on different kinds of relationships, such as family interactions between parents and children, between spouses or siblings, or in social interactions between individuals of varying degrees of familiarity. The dynamics of such interactions, perhaps gauged through psychophysiological measures, may vary depending on fairly subtle attributes of each participant. Using empirical methods, it may someday be possible to validate notions such as transference and countertransference, which until now have resisted such validation. As mentioned above, an intriguing theoretical impetus for this has recently been offered by experimental physicists, who have found conditions under which two chaotic systems linked by a communication channel may fall into synchrony.

Intrapersonal dynamics, known traditionally as psychodynamics, has long awaited mathematically precise characterization. Several different types of questions may be asked of intrapersonal dynamics; each leads to a different research methodology. One basic question is whether naturally occurring psychophysiological dynamics may differ across clinical subpopulations. This question can perhaps best be addressed by performing studies on larger subject samples. Such studies provide a means of determining what attributes of psychophysiological dynamics are common across different populations and what attributes are limited to particular subgroups. In this context, it may be advantageous to abandon the study of ongoing therapy in favor of studying a wider variety of subjects through semistructured interviews (which may still retain lengthy free-response periods to observe the natural progression of

Steven P. Reidbord and Dana J. Redington

mental states). Additionally, future studies could include free-form interpersonal interactions outside of the clinical context used thus far, or noninteractional situations, such as meditation, which promote a relatively unrestricted flow of mental states. These population studies may identify varieties of nonlinear dynamics specific to important psychopathological conditions, which may then be used for clinical diagnosis.

Another question regarding intrapersonal dynamics concerns experimental manipulations that may alter dynamic flow. This can be addressed by applying a well-known procedure in psychophysiology, stress profiling. Here, the research effort is not to document the spontaneous flow of mental states, but to perturb the system in various ways and monitor the result. This is the psychophysiological variant of quantitatively assessing trajectory divergence in a dynamical system as a result of a specific controlled experimental manipulation or perturbation. Such profiling may include physical stressors such as the cold pressor test, cognitive stressors such as mental arithmetic, and affective stressors such as recall of painful or emotional memories. These are all known to present unique forms of physiological response. Stress profiling could help to define the overall dynamic range of the psychophysiological system and offer baseline data with which to compare naturalistically collected spontaneous activity.

Perhaps the most exciting area of future research is highlighted by a third question: How precisely can subjective experience be linked to spontaneously occurring changes in dynamic flow? Our studies to date have relied on external clinical observations or post hoc ratings by subjects of their experience. Another approach relies on the experimental finding that humans can learn to more clearly describe experiential states following discrimination training. In a discrimination paradigm, subjects are asked to compare and contrast a small set of objectively defined states. For example, two discrimination studies (Gibson, Perry, Redington, et al., 1982; Redington, Perry, Gibson, et al., 1981) demonstrated that subjects could differentiate between electrophysiologically defined states of wakefulness, sleep stage 1, and sleep stage 2. Previous sleep research had found that subjects who were merely asked to describe their state (i.e., awake or asleep) performed at chance levels when queried in the hypnogogic (falling-asleep) period. In contrast, the subjects who participated in these discrimination studies could accurately identify their state at well above chance levels.

This discrimination paradigm may be applied to subtle psychophysiological states once a plausible nonlinear dynamical model of psychodynamics is constructed. Subjects may come to discriminate, and later to recognize, the experience and psychological processes associated with objectively defined states. We hypothesize that careful nonlinear modeling of psychophysiological processes may uncover the assumed, but as yet unmeasured, determinism that drives momentary changes in mental state. In the two sleep studies cited above, as subjects became more practiced in discriminating awake and sleep stages, their verbal reports reflected more distinguishing features of their experience. A similar effect might refine language to better express the dynamics of the mind. Recall that the therapist's feeding back nonverbal affective signals of the patient results in enhanced ability of the patient to describe mental states in words. The analogy to physiology is that feedback of other core brain signals associated with mentation may improve discrimination and hence the ability of the person to describe particular internal states that have important psychodynamic characteristics.

So far, modeling in the nascent field of nonlinear psychodynamics is limited to obviously inadequate models (as in our four heart-rate trajectories), or to analogs in the form of systems with presumably similar dynamics (as in the long history of psychodynamic modeling). Thought-provoking analogs are coming nowadays from the field of nonlinear dynamics itself. For example, the dynamics of olfactory recognition in rabbits (Freeman, 1987, 1991) suggests a basis for nonlinear psychodynamic functioning. Freeman found that the olfactory system evidenced higher complexity in the absence of a previously learned odorant; complexity decreased when an odorant was recognized. The former may represent a state of relative receptivity, while the latter may correspond to a learned condition. As mentioned earlier, the presence of psychological defense seems to lower the dynamic complexity of free association: thoughts and feelings arise in a more constrained, less random-appearing sequence, in contrast to the free, wide-ranging flow that accompanies less defended states. In the psychotherapy setting, various defense patterns serve to avoid new realizations and affects through habitualized behavior. These stereotyped ways of decreasing receptivity to new experiences may constrain the flow of mental states. Conversely, more complex transitions among psychological states may reflect greater receptivity to new experience. An optimal level of receptivity depends on the current demands and goals of the individual.

Nonlinear models of psychodynamics will result from careful observation and analysis of naturally occurring behavior. The usefulness of such models will lie in their explanatory power, and ultimately in the power they offer as tools to recognize and influence psychodynamic states.

17.6 CONCLUSION

Psychology and cognitive science face the difficult task of applying research methods best suited to physical systems to phenomena that are in essence irreproducible and only inferred from observable data. It is time to pay attention to the assumptions and limitations this entails, particularly in our conclusions about mental dynamics. Any theory that purports to model or explain these dynamics must come to grips with issues of reliability and, especially, validity of observations, and only then face the even more challenging matter of characterizing the dynamics of naturally occurring data, replete with error, measurement bias, and an intermittent sampling rate.

The mind is sufficiently complex that understanding the flow of mental phenomena in time requires a data-driven dynamical model, not a model that oversimplifies the dynamics to be explained, or avoids it through unwarranted reductionism. A nonlinear dynamical perspective may offer the conceptual framework, language, and more important, the mathematics, to adequately characterize global human behavior. These may provide a better framework to observe and describe mental activity and behavior. Ultimately, a formal description of psychodynamics, once adequately specified, will not only incorporate concepts central to cognitive psychology but, in turn, form a foundation on which an integrated science of mind will evolve.

REFERENCES

Abraham, F. D. (1990). *A visual introduction to dynamical systems theory for psychology.* Santa Cruz, CA: Aerial Press.

Basar, E. (Ed.). (1990). *Chaos in brain function.* New York: Springer-Verlag.

Bonaparte, M., Freud, A., and Kris, E. (Eds). (1954). *The origins of psychoanalysis, letters to Wilhelm Fliess, drafts and notes: 1887–1902 by Sigmund Freud.* New York: Basic Books.

Callahan, J., and Sashin, J. I. (1987). Models of affect-response and anorexia nervosa. *Annals of the New York Academy Of Sciences, 504,* 241–258.

Ekman, P., and Friesen, W. V. (1975). *Unmasking the face.* Palo Alto, CA: Consulting Psychologists Press.

Epstein, I. R., Kustin, K., Kepper, P. D., et al. (1983). Oscillating chemical reactions. *Scientific American, 248*(3), 112–123.

Freeman, W. J. (1975). *Mass action in the nervous system.* New York: Academic Press.

Freeman, W. J. (1987). Simulation of chaotic EEG patterns with a dynamic of the olfactory system. *Biological Cybernetics, 56,* 139–150.

Freeman, W. J. (1991). The physiology of perception. *Scientific American, 264*(2), 78–85.

George, F. H. (1973). *The brain as a computer.* New York: Pergamon.

Gibson, E., Perry, F., Redington, D., et al. (1982). Discrimination of sleep onset stages: behavioral responses and verbal reports. *Perceptual and Motor Skills, 55,* 1023–1037.

Glass, L., and Mackey, M. C. (1988). *From clocks to chaos: the rhythms of life.* Princeton, NJ: Princeton University Press.

Gleick, J. (1987). *Chaos: making a new science.* New York: Penguin Books.

Goldberger, A. L., Rigney, D. R., and West, B. J. (1990). Chaos and fractals in human physiology. *Scientific American, 262,* no. 2, 43–49.

Hilgard, E. R. (1980). Consciousness in contemporary psychology. *Annual Review of Psychology, 31,* 1–26.

Horowitz, M. J. (1987). *States of mind: configurational analysis of individual psychology, Second edition.* New York: Plenum.

James, W. (1950). *The principles of psychology.* New York: Dover.

Kihlstrom, J. F. (1987). The cognitive unconscious. *Science, 237,* 1445–1452.

McCarley, R. W., and Hobson, J. A. (1975). Neuronal excitability modulation over the sleep cycle: a structural and mathematical model. *Science, 189*, 58–60.

Pecora, L. M., and Carroll, T. L. (1990). Synchronization in chaotic systems. *Physical Review Letters, 64*, 821–824.

Pincus, S. M. (1991). Approximate entropy as a measure of system complexity. *Proceedings of the National Academy of Sciences, 88*:2297–2301.

Redington, D. (1993). Dynamical analyses of end organs as cathodes of core brain states. In B. H. Jansen and M. E. Brandt (Eds.), *Nonlinear dynamical analysis of the EEG.* (pp. 217–230). River Edge, NJ: World Scientific Publishing.

Redington, D., Perry, F., Gibson, E., et al. (1981). Discrimination of early sleep stages: behavioral indicators. *Sleep, 4*, 171–176.

Redington, D., and Reidbord, S. (1992). Chaotic dynamics in autonomic nervous system activity of a patient during a psychotherapy session. *Biological Psychiatry, 31*, 993–1007.

Reidbord, S., and Redington, D. (1992). Psychophysiological processes during insight-oriented therapy: further investigations into nonlinear psychodynamics. *Journal of Nervous and Mental Disease, 180*, 649–657.

Reidbord, S., and Redington, D. (1993). Nonlinear analysis of autonomic responses in a therapist during psychotherapy. *Journal of Nervous and Mental Disease, 181*, 428–435.

Rumelhart, D. E., McClelland, J. L., and PDP Research Group (Eds.) (1986). *Parallel distributed processing: explorations in the microstructure of cognition.* Vol. 2: *Psychological and biological models.* Cambridge, MA: MIT Press.

Sabelli, H. C., Carlson-Sabelli, L. C., and Javaid, J. I. (1990). The thermodynamics of bipolarity: a bifurcation model of bipolar illness and bipolar character and its psychotherapeutic applications. *Psychiatry, 53*, 346–368.

Schore, N. E. (1981). Chemistry and human awareness: natural scientific connections. In R. S. Valle and R. von Eckartsberg (Eds.), *The metaphors of consciousness.* (pp. 437–460). New York: Plenum.

Stinson, C. H., and Palmer, S. E. (1991). Parallel distributed processing models of person schemas and psychopathologies. In M. J. Horowitz (Ed.), *Person schemas and maladaptive interpersonal patterns.* (pp. 339–377). Chicago: University of Chicago Press.

Strachey, J. (1966). *Introductory lectures on psychoanalysis by Sigmund Freud.* New York: Norton.

Takens, F. (1981). Detecting strange attractors in turbulence. In D. A. Rand and L. S. Young (Eds.), *Dynamical systems and turbulence, Warwick, 1980* (pp. 366–381) Berlin: Springer Verlag.

Weizenbaum, J. (1976). *Computer power and human reason.* San Francisco: Freeman.

Winquist, D., and Winzenz, D. (1977). Scientific models and symbolic meanings in altered states of consciousness. *Journal of Drug Issues, 7*, 237–246.

Zegans, L. S., and Victor, B. S. (1988). Conceptual issues in the history of psychiatry. In H. H. Goldman (Ed.), *Review of general psychiatry*, 2nd ed. (pp. 5–19). San Mateo, CA: Appleton & Lange.

Guide to Further Reading

The new discipline of nonlinear psychodynamics is based on published works that apply the science of complexity to physiological processes, and on those that discuss the strengths and weaknesses of applying nonlinear analyses to experimental data. The application of nonlinear methods to psychological processes demands a rigorous empirical foundation; for a further elaboration of this viewpoint, see Redington and Reidbord (1992). Takens (1981) and Grassberger, Schreiber, and Schaffrath (1991) present technical papers on nonlinear time-series analysis using actual, as opposed to simulated, data. Pritchard and Duke (1992) offer a detailed tutorial of nonlinear analysis as applied to electrophysiological data. A comprehensive review of deterministic chaos in physiology may be found in Elbert, Ray, Kowalik, et al., (1993), and a general discussion of the potential impact of chaos theory for the neurosciences may be found in Skarda and Freeman (1990).

Elbert, T., Ray, W. J., Kowalik, Z. J., et al. (1993). Chaos and physiology: deterministic chaos in excitable cell assemblies. *Physiological Reviews, 74,* 1–47.

Grassberger, P., Schreiber, T., and Schaffrath, C. (1991). Nonlinear time sequence analysis. *International Journal of Bifurcation and Chaos in Applied Sciences and Engineering 1,* 521–547.

Pritchard, W. S., and Duke, D. W. (1992). Measuring chaos in the brain: a tutorial review of nonlinear dynamical EEG analysis. *International Journal of Neuroscience, 67,* 636–692.

Redington, D., and Reidbord, S. (1992). Chaotic dynamics in autonomic nervous system activity of a patient during a psychotherapy session. *Biological Psychiatry, 31,* 993–1007.

Skarda, C. A., and Freeman, W. J. (1990). Chaos and the new science of the brain. *Concepts in Neuroscience, 1,* 275–285.

Takens, F. (1981). Detecting strange attractors in turbulence. In D. A. Rand and L. S. Young (Eds.), *Dynamical systems and turbulence, Warwick, 1980* (pp. 366–381). Berlin: Springer Verlag.

18 Dynamical Models of Cognition

Marco Giunti

EDITORS' INTRODUCTION

Dynamics has been employed in various aspects of cognitive science since at least the late 1940s. Until recently, however, this kind of research had received little philosophical attention, especially by comparison with the great deal of effort and care that has been devoted to the articulation and evaluation of the mainstream computational approach. As a result, many foundational questions concerning dynamical models and their relation to more conventional models have remained unaddressed.

In this chapter, Marco Giunti confronts some of the most central foundational questions head-on. First and foremost: What, exactly, is one saying when claiming that a cognitive system is a dynamical system? In answering this question, Giunti is led to address a host of further critical issues, and to formulate and defend the ambitious general empirical hypothesis that all cognitive systems are dynamical systems. *A key insight is that computational systems, as deployed in classical symbolic cognitive science, constitute a specially restricted subclass of dynamical systems. Relaxing these restrictions can therefore lead to noncomputational dynamical models of cognitive processes. (Note that Giunti uses the term* dynamical system *in the broader of the senses discussed in chapter 1, section 1.1.)*

Investigating the philosophical foundations of dynamical research is—like that research itself—an ongoing enterprise. Many more questions remain to be explored. Nevertheless, answers that Giunti provides form an essential part of the general conceptual framework surrounding current research efforts.

18.1 INTRODUCTION

A *cognitive system* is any concrete or real object which has the kind of properties (namely, *cognitive* properties) in which cognitive scientists are typically interested. Note that this definition includes both natural systems such as humans and other animals, and artificial devices such as robots, implementations of artificial intelligence (AI) programs, some neural networks, etc.. Focusing on what all cognitive systems have in common, we can state a very general but nonetheless interesting thesis: *all cognitive systems are dynamical systems*. Section 18.2 explains what this thesis means and why it is (relatively) uncontroversial. It will become clear that this thesis is a basic methodological assumption which underlies practically all current research in cognitive science.

The goal of section 18.3 is to contrast two types of explanations of cognition: computational and dynamical. Computational explanations are characterized by the use of concepts drawn from computability theory, while dynamical explanations employ the conceptual apparatus of dynamical systems theory. Further, I suggest that all explanations of cognition might end up sharing the same dynamical style, for dynamical systems theory may well turn out to be useful in the study of *any* kind of model currently employed in cognitive science. In particular, a dynamical viewpoint might even benefit those explanations of cognition which are based on symbolic models. Computational explanations of cognition, by contrast, can only be based on symbolic models or, more generally, on any other type of computational model. In particular, those explanations of cognition which are based on an important class of connectionist models cannot be computational, for this class of models falls beyond the scope of computability theory. Arguing for this negative conclusion requires a formal explication of the concept of *computational system*.

Finally, section 18.4 explores the possibility that explanations of cognition might be based on a type of dynamical model which cognitive scientists generally have not considered yet. I call a model of this special type a *Galilean* dynamical model of a cognitive system. The main goal of this section is to contrast this proposal with the current modeling practice in cognitive science and to make clear its potential benefits.

18.2 COGNITIVE SYSTEMS AS DYNAMICAL SYSTEMS

This section proposes a methodological interpretation of the thesis that *all cognitive systems are dynamical systems*, and then provides an argument which in fact shows that this thesis underlies all current research on cognition. Before doing this, however, it is crucial to clarify the distinction between *mathematical* and *real* dynamical systems and, second, the relationship which a real dynamical system may bear to a mathematical one.

Real vs. Mathematical Dynamical Systems

A *real* dynamical system is any concrete object which changes over time. A *mathematical* dynamical system, on the other hand, is an abstract mathematical structure which can be used to *describe* the change of a real system as an evolution through a series of *states*. (Thus, only real dynamical systems actually *undergo* change; mathematical dynamical systems are timeless, unchanging entities which can nevertheless be used as models of change in real systems.) If the evolution of the real system is *deterministic*, i.e., if the state at any future time is determined by the state at the present time, then the abstract mathematical structure consists of three elements. The first element is a set T which represents time. T may be either the reals, the rationals, the integers, or the non-negative portions of these structures. Depending on the choice of T, then, time will be represented as continuous, dense, or discrete. The second element is a nonempty set M, which represents all the possible states through which the system can evolve; M is called the *state space* (or sometimes the *phase space*) of the system. The third element is a set of functions $\{g^t\}$ which tells us the state of the system at any instant $t \in T$, provided that we know the initial state.[1] For example, if the initial state is $x \in M$, the state of the system at time t is given by $g^t(x)$, the state at time $w > t$ is given by $g^w(x)$, etc. The functions in the set $\{g^t\}$ must only satisfy two conditions. First, the function g^0 must take each state to itself, for the state at time 0 when the initial state is x obviously is x itself. Second, the composition of any two functions g^t and g^w must be equal to the function g^{t+w}, for the evolution up to time $t + w$ can always be thought as two successive evolutions, the first up to time t, and the second up to time w.

An important subclass of the mathematical dynamical systems is that of all systems with discrete time. Any such system is called a *cascade*. More precisely, a mathematical dynamical system $\langle T\ M\ \{g^t\} \rangle$ is a cascade just in case T is equal to the non-negative integers (or to the integers). To obtain a cascade, we may start from any nonempty set M and any function $g: M \rightarrow M$. We then set T equal to the non-negative integers, and we define the state transitions $\{g^t\}$ as follows: $g^0 =$ the identity function on M and, for any $x \in M$, $g^{t+1}(x) = g(g^t(x))$. In other words, we generate an arbitrary state transition $g^t (t > 0)$ by iterating t times the function g (note that $g^1 = g$).

The distinction between real and mathematical dynamical systems is crucial for understanding the thesis that all cognitive systems are dynamical systems. Before going on, then, let me further illustrate this distinction by means of a classic example. Consider first those concrete objects (falling bodies, spheres on inclined planes, projectiles, etc.) which Galileo studied in the course of his investigations in the field of mechanics. These objects are examples of real dynamical systems. Consider, then, Galileo's laws for the position Y and velocity V of a falling body:

$$Y[y\ v](t) = y + vt + \tfrac{1}{2}ct^2$$

$$V[y\ v](t) = v + ct,$$

where y and v are, respectively, the position and velocity of the falling body at time 0, and c is a constant (the acceleration of gravity). If we identify the state of a falling body with the values of its position and velocity, it is easy to verify that these two laws specify a mathematical dynamical system $G = \langle T\ Y \times V\ \{g^t\} \rangle$, where each state transition g^t is defined by $g^t(y\ v) = \langle Y[y\ v](t)\ V[y\ v](t) \rangle$.

The Instantiation Relation

What is the relation between the mathematical dynamical system G specified by Galileo's laws and a real falling body? We all know that, within certain

Dynamical Models of Cognition

limits of precision, these two laws accurately describe how the position and velocity of a real falling body change in time. Therefore, we may take the mathematical dynamical system G to correctly describe *one aspect* of the change of a real falling body, i.e., its change of position and velocity. However, it is important to note that, if we decided to focus on a different aspect of its change, a different mathematical dynamical system would in general be appropriate. For example, suppose we are interested in how the mass of the body changes. Then, since we may take the mass to be a constant m, we obtain a different mathematical dynamical system $H = \langle T \{m\} \{h^t\}\rangle$, where each state transition h^t is the identity function on the state space $\{m\}$, i.e., $h^t(m) = m$. We may thus claim that the mathematical dynamical system H correctly describes a *different* aspect of the change of a falling body, i.e., its change of mass.

This example thus shows that different mathematical dynamical systems may correctly describe different aspects of the change of the same real dynamical system. Let me now introduce a bit of terminology which will be useful later. I will say that a real dynamical system RDS *instantiates* a mathematical dynamical system MDS just in case MDS correctly describes some aspect of the change of RDS. According to this definition, then, we may take a falling body to instantiate both systems G and H specified above. In general, given a real dynamical system, this system will instantiate *many* mathematical dynamical systems, and each of these systems represents a different aspect of the change of the real system.

All Cognitive Systems Are Dynamical Systems: The Meaning

We are now in the position to see what the distinction between real and mathematical dynamical systems has to do with the interpretation of the thesis that all cognitive systems are dynamical systems. First, if we interpret "dynamical system" as *real* dynamical system, the thesis turns out to be trivial. A real dynamical system is any concrete object which changes in time. But, since *any* concrete object can be said to change in time (in some respect), *anything* is a real dynamical system. Furthermore, a cognitive system is a concrete object of a special type, that is, an object with those kinds of properties usually studied by cognitive scientists. It thus trivially follows that any cognitive system is a real dynamical system. Second, if we instead interpret "dynamical system" as a *mathematical* dynamical system, the thesis affirms an absurdity, for a cognitive system, which is a concrete or real object, is said to be identical to a mathematical dynamical system, which, by definition, is an *abstract* structure.

It thus seems that we face here a serious difficulty: depending on how we interpret the term *dynamical system*, the thesis that all cognitive systems are dynamical systems turns out to be either trivial or absurd. This, however, is a false dilemma, for this thesis is better interpreted in a third way, which gives a definite and nontrivial meaning to it.

When we say that a certain object is a *cognitive* system, we describe this object at a specific level, i.e., the level of its cognitive properties. And when we further say that this object is a *dynamical* system, we are making a *methodological* claim as to how its cognitive properties can be understood. This claim is that they can be understood by studying a mathematical dynamical system which correctly describes some aspect of its change. According to this methodological interpretation, then, a cognitive system is a dynamical system just in case its cognitive properties can be understood or explained by studying a mathematical dynamical system instantiated by it.

Interpreted this way, the thesis that all cognitive systems are dynamical systems thus means that (1) any cognitive system is a *real* dynamical system and (2) this system *instantiates* some *mathematical* dynamical system whose study allows us to understand or explain the *cognitive* properties of the real system.

We have seen above that the first clause of this thesis is trivial. However, the second clause gives us an interesting methodological indication: if we want to understand the cognitive properties of a real system, then we may study an appropriate mathematical dynamical system instantiated by it, that is, a specific mathematical structure which correctly describes some aspect of the change of the real system.

All Cognitive Systems Are Dynamical Systems: The Argument

I have proposed a methodological reading of the thesis that all cognitive systems are dynamical systems. According to this interpretation, the thesis means that *the cognitive properties of an arbitrary cognitive system can be understood or explained by studying a mathematical dynamical system instantiated by it.* How might one argue for this thesis?

First, we need a crucial premise concerning the abstract mathematical *models* currently employed in cognitive science. These models can be basically classified into three different types: (1) symbolic processors, (2) neural networks, and (3) other continuous systems specified by differential or difference equations. Each of these three types corresponds to a different approach to cognition. The *symbolic* or classical approach (Newell and Simon, 1972; Newell, 1980; Pylyshyn, 1984; Johnson-Laird, 1988) employs symbolic processors as models; the *connectionist* approach (Rumelhart and McClelland, 1986b) employs neural networks; and models of the third type are typically proposed by nonconnectionist researchers who nevertheless believe that cognition should be studied by means of *dynamical* methods and concepts. Nonconnectionist researchers favoring a dynamical perspective are active in many fields; for examples, see many of the chapters of this book.

Now, the crucial premise is that *all systems which belong to any of these three types are mathematical dynamical systems*. That a system specified by differential or difference equations is a mathematical dynamical system is obvious, for this concept is expressly designed to describe this class of systems in abstract terms. That a neural network is a mathematical dynamical system is also not difficult to show. A complete state of the system can in fact be identified with the activation levels of all the units in the network, and the set of state transitions is determined by the differential (or difference) equations which specify how each unit is updated. To show that all symbolic processors are mathematical dynamical systems is a bit more complicated. The argumentative strategy I prefer considers first a special class of symbolic processors (such as Turing machines, or monogenic production systems, etc.) and it then shows that the systems of this special type are mathematical dynamical systems. Given the strong similarities between different types of symbolic processors, it is then not difficult to see how the argument given for one type could be modified to fit any other type. Here, I limit myself to show that an arbitrary Turing machine is in fact a mathematical dynamical system.

A Turing machine is an ideal mechanism that evolves in discrete time steps. This mechanism is usually pictured as having three parts. First, a *tape* divided into a countably infinite number of adjacent squares. Each of these squares contains exactly one symbol taken from a finite alphabet $\{a_i\}$.[2] Second, a *head*, which is located on a square of the tape and can perform three different operations: write a symbol on that square, move to the adjacent square to the right, or move to the adjacent square to the left. Third, a *control unit* which, at any time step, is in exactly one of a finite number of internal states $\{q_i\}$. The behavior of the machine is specified by a *set of instructions*, which are conditionals of the form: if the internal state is q_i, and the symbol on the square where the head is located is a_j, write symbol a_k (move one square to the right, move one square to the left) and change internal state to q_l. Each instruction can thus be written as a *quadruple* of one of the three types: $q_i a_j a_k q_l$, $q_i a_j R q_l$, $q_i a_j L q_l$, where R and L stand, respectively, for "move to the right" and "move to the left." The only requirement which the set of quadruples must satisfy is that it be *consistent*, in the sense that this set cannot contain any two conflicting instructions, i.e., two different quadruples which begin with the same state-symbol pair.

Given this standard description of an arbitrary Turing machine, it is now not difficult to see that this ideal mechanism can in fact be identified with a mathematical dynamical system $\langle T \ M \ \{g^t\}\rangle$. Since a Turing machine evolves in discrete time steps, we may take the time set T to be the set of the non-negative integers. Since the future behavior of the machine is determined when the content of the tape, the position of the head, and the internal state are fixed, we may take the state space M to be the set of all triples $\langle$tape content, head position, internal state$\rangle$. And, finally, the set of state transitions $\{g^t\}$ is determined by the set of quadruples of the machine. To see this point, first note that the set of quadruples tells us how the *complete state* of the machine changes after *one* time step. That is, the set of quadruples defines the state transition g^1. We then obtain any other state transition g^t $(t > 1)$ by iterating g^1 t times, and we simply take the state transition g^0 to be the identity function on M. We may thus conclude that any Turing machine is in fact a mathematical dynamical system $\langle T \ M \ \{g^t\}\rangle$ with discrete time, i.e., a cascade. A similar argument can be given for any other type of symbolic processor we may consider, so that we can also conclude that *any* symbolic processor is a mathematical dynamical system.

Having thus established that symbolic processors, neural networks, and continuous systems specified by differential (or difference) equations are three different types of mathematical dynamical systems, we can finally provide an argument for the thesis that all cognitive systems are dynamical systems.

Typical research in cognitive science attempts to produce an explanation of the cognitive properties that belong to a real system, and this explanation is usually obtained by studying a *model* which reproduces, as accurately as possible, some aspect of the change of the real system. This model can be of three types: (1) a symbolic processor, (2) a neural network, or (3) a continuous dynamical system specified by differential (or difference) equations. Any system of these three types is a mathematical dynamical system. Therefore, the explanation of the cognitive properties of a real system is typically obtained by studying a mathematical dynamical system instantiated by it. But, according to the interpretation proposed above, this precisely means that the real system whose cognitive properties are explained by typical research in cognitive science is a dynamical system.

The argument I have just given only shows that any real system which *has been* the object of typical research in cognitive science is a dynamical system. However, the conclusion of this argument also supports the unrestricted version of the thesis. For, unless the cognitive systems that have been considered so far are not representative of all cognitive systems, we may also reasonably conclude that *all* cognitive systems are dynamical systems.

18.3   TWO CONCEPTUAL REPERTOIRES FOR THE EXPLANATION OF COGNITION: COMPUTABILITY THEORY AND DYNAMICAL SYSTEMS THEORY

Section 18.1 first proposed a methodological reading of the thesis that all cognitive systems are dynamical systems, and then gave an argument to support it. According to the proposed interpretation, this thesis means that the cognitive properties of an arbitrary cognitive system can be understood or explained by studying a mathematical dynamical system instantiated by it. If an explanation of the cognitive properties of a real system can be obtained by studying a mathematical dynamical system instantiated by it (i.e., a *model* of the real system), then it is important to pay attention to the *type of theoretical framework* we use when we carry out this study. For the type of *explanation* we construct in general depends on the type of theoretical framework we use in the study of the model. Let me make this point clearer by means of two examples.

According to the symbolic approach, cognition essentially is a matter of the *computations* a system performs in certain situations. But the very idea of a computation belongs to a specific theoretical framework, namely *computability theory*, which is thus presupposed by the explanatory style of this approach. In the last few years, however, both connectionists (e.g., Smolensky, 1988) and nonconnectionist dynamicists (e.g., Skarda and Freeman, 1987; Busemeyer and Townsend, 1993) have been developing a new style of explanation which represents a clear alternative to the computational one. Tim van Gelder (1991, 1992) has called the explanations of this type *dynamical explanations*. One of the key ideas on which this type of explanation is based is that to understand cognition we must first of all understand the *state-space evolution* of a certain system. The point I wish to stress here is that the concept of a state-space evolution (as well as many other concepts employed in dynamical explanations) belongs to dynamical systems theory, which is thus the theoretical framework presupposed by this new explanatory style.

Let me now draw a broad picture of the state of current research in cognitive science. If we look at the *models* employed, i.e., at the *mathematical dynamical systems* actually used in the study of cognition, we can distinguish three different approaches: (1) the symbolic (or classical) approach, which employs symbolic processors; (2) the connectionist approach, which employs neural networks; and, finally, a third approach, let us call it (3) the dynamicists' approach, whose models are neither symbolic nor connectionist, but are nonetheless continuous systems specified by differential (or difference) equations. If, instead, we look at the *explanatory styles*, they can be sorted roughly into (at least) two different types of explanation: *computational* and *dynamical*. These two explanatory styles are characterized by the use of two different sets of concepts, which respectively come from computability theory and dynamical systems theory. More precisely, computational explanations are obtained by studying symbolic models by means of concepts drawn from computability theory, while dynamical explanations are obtained by studying neural networks or models of the third type by means of concepts drawn from dynamical systems theory.

But then, if this is the current situation, two questions arise: (1) Why is it that dynamical explanations are exclusively based on neural networks or models of the third type? Or, to put it in a different way: Why not use dynamical systems theory to study symbolic models too, so that, independently of the type of model employed, all explanations of cognition might end up sharing the same dynamical style? (2) Is it possible to obtain an analogous conclusion for computability theory instead? That is, why not study neural networks and models of the third type by means of concepts drawn from computability theory, thus extending the scope of the computational style of explanation?

Dynamical Systems Theory and the Explanation of Cognition Based on Symbolic Models

With regard to the first question, it is clear that symbolic models can be studied from a dynamical point of view. For these models are special types of mathematical dynamical systems, and the most basic concepts of dynamical systems theory apply to *any* type of mathematical dynamical system. However, there is an important point to keep in mind. Only a *limited part* of the conceptual apparatus of dynamical systems theory applies to symbolic processors. For example, we can think of the *state space* of the processor, and of its *time evolution* as a motion along an *orbit* in this space. We may also classify different types of orbits: *periodic, aperiodic, eventually periodic*. Furthermore, since most symbolic processors have *merging orbits*, also the notions of *attractor* and *basin of attraction* make a clear sense. But not much more. To mention just one example, the whole theory of *chaos* does not seem to apply, in its present form, to symbolic processors. The basic reason is that the usual definitions of chaos presuppose (at least) a topological or metrical structure on the state space of the system. The state space of a symbolic processor, however, typically lacks a natural topology or metric.

Therefore, given that only the most basic part of dynamical systems theory applies to symbolic processors, the real question seems to be the following. If we study a symbolic model of a cognitive system by means of this *restricted dynamical apparatus*, is this sufficient to understand the *cognitive level* of the system? Or, instead, is a *computational perspective* the only way to understand this level?

At the moment, I don't have a definite answer to this question. However, I would like to suggest that, even when symbolic models are concerned, a dynamical viewpoint *might* turn out to be useful for a deeper understanding of the cognitive level. This conjecture is supported by the fact that some problems that are usually treated within the conceptual framework of computability theory can be better solved by applying dynamical concepts.

For example, it is well known that the *halting problem* for the class of *all* Turing machines is undecidable. More precisely, given an arbitrary Turing machine, there is no mechanical procedure to decide whether that machine will stop when started on an arbitrary input. However, it is obvious that the halting problem for certain *specific* machines is decidable. For example, the machine specified by $\{q_0 0 0 q_0 \ q_0 1 1 q_0\}$ immediately stops on any input. The problem which thus arises is to find nontrivial *classes* of Turing machines for which the halting problem is decidable. The interesting result is that *by using dynamical concepts* it is possible to find one such class.

In the first place, we need to think of the halting condition of a Turing machine in dynamical terms. When a Turing machine stops, its tape content, head position, and internal state no longer change. Dynamically, this means that the Turing machine enters a cycle of period 1 in state space. More precisely, there are two possibilities. Either the Turing machine immediately enters the cycle, or it gets to it after one or more steps. In the second case, we say that the Turing machine has an *eventually periodic orbit*.

In the second place, we need the concept of a *logically reversible system*. Intuitively, a mathematical dynamical system $\langle \text{T M} \{g^t\} \rangle$ is logically reversible if, given its state x at an arbitrary time t, we can tell the state of the system at any time $w \leqslant t$. This is formally expressed by the requirement that *any* state transition g^t be *injective*, i.e., for any two different states x and y, $g^t(x) \neq g^t(y)$.

In the third place, we must rely on a theorem of dynamical systems theory: any system $\langle T \, M \, \{g^t\} \rangle$ with eventually periodic orbits has at least one state transition g^t which is not injective (for a proof, see Giunti 1992). In other words, a system with eventually periodic orbits is not logically reversible.

Let us now consider the class of all logically reversible Turing machines. It is then easy to see that the halting problem for this class of machines is decidable. In fact, by the previous theorem, no such machine has eventually periodic orbits. But then, given *any input*, a logically reversible Turing machine either halts immediately or never halts. Therefore, to decide the halting problem for a logically reversible Turing machine, we may just check whether the machine halts on the first step.

The interest of this result is twofold. In the first place, this result gives us a better understanding of the halting problem: we now know that the undecidability of the halting problem is limited to *logically irreversible* Turing machines. In other words, we have discovered an intriguing connection between one of the classic negative results of computability theory and the dynamical concept of logical irreversibility. In the second place, this result is also interesting because it shows that dynamical systems theory can improve the solution of problems which are usually treated by means of the conceptual apparatus of computability theory. Since the explanation of cognition based on symbolic models is one of these problems, this result suggests that a dynamical viewpoint might turn out to be useful in this case too.

Computability Theory and the Explanation of Cognition Based on Neural Networks or Other Continuous Dynamical Models

Thus far, I have argued that a dynamical approach to the study of symbolic models of cognitive systems is possible, and that it might be useful to better understand the cognitive level of these systems. If this conjecture turned out to be true, then all explanations of cognition might end up sharing the same dynamical style, independent of the type of model employed.

I now discuss the analogous question which concerns the computational style of explanation: Is it possible to study neural networks and other continuous dynamical models by means of the conceptual apparatus of computability theory, so that computational explanations of real cognitive systems might no longer be exclusively based on symbolic models?

Computability theory studies a family of abstract mechanisms which are typically used to compute or recognize functions, sets, or numbers. These devices can be divided into two broad categories: automata or machines (e.g., Turing machines, register machines, cellular automata, etc.) and systems of rules for symbol manipulation (e.g., monogenic production systems, monogenic Post canonical systems, tag systems, etc.). I will call any device studied by computability theory a *computational system*. The problem we are concerned with, then, reduces to the following question: Are neural networks and continuous dynamical systems specified by differential (or difference) equations computational systems? If they are, we might be able to extend the computational style of explanation to connectionist models and models of the third type. If they are not, however, this extension is impossible, for these two types of models fall beyond the scope of computability theory.

The strategy I am going to use in order to answer this question consists of two steps. In the first place, I will give an *explication* of the concept of a computational system. That is, I will give a *formal definition* of this concept in such a way that the defined concept (the *explicans*) arguably has the same extension as the intuitive concept (the *explicandum*). Since I have intuitively described a computational system as any system studied by computability theory, this means that I am going to propose (1) a formal definition of a computational system, and (2) an argument in favor of the following claim: all, and only, the systems studied by computability theory are computational systems in the formal sense.

In the second place, I will deduce from the formal definition two sufficient conditions for a system not to be computational, and I will then argue that all continuous systems specified by differential or difference equations and an important class of neural networks satisfy at least one of these conditions. I will thus conclude that, whenever models of the third type or connectionist models that belong to this class are employed, a computational explanation of cognition based on these models is impossible.

A Formal Definition of a Computational System In order to formulate a formal definition of a computational system, let us first of all consider the mechanisms studied by computability theory and ask (1) what type of system they are, and (2) what specific feature distinguishes these mechanisms from other systems of the same type.

As mentioned, computability theory studies many different kinds of abstract systems. A basic property that is shared by all these mechanisms is that they are *mathematical dynamical systems with discrete time*, i.e., *cascades*. I have already shown that this is true of Turing machines, and it is not difficult to give a similar argument for any other type of mechanism which has actually been studied by computability theory. Therefore, on the basis of this evidence, we may reasonably conclude that all computational systems are cascades.

However, computability theory does not study all cascades. The specific feature that distinguishes computational systems from other mathematical dynamical systems with discrete time is that a computational system *can always be described in an effective way*. Intuitively, this means that the constitution and operations of the system are purely mechanical or that the system can always be identified with an idealized machine. However, since we want to arrive at a formal definition of a computational system, we cannot limit ourselves to this intuitive characterization. Rather, we must try to put it in a precise form.

Since I have informally characterized a computational system as a cascade that can be described effectively, let us ask first what a *description* of a cascade is. If we take a structuralist viewpoint, this question has a precise answer. A description (or a representation) of a cascade consists of a second cascade *isomorphic* to it where, by definition, a cascade $S = \langle T \, M \, \{g^t\} \rangle$ is isomorphic to a second cascade $S_1 = \langle T_1 \, M_1 \, \{h^t\} \rangle$ just in case $T = T_1$ and there is a bijection $f: M_1 \rightarrow M$ such that, for any $t \in T$ and any $x \in M_1$, $g^t(f(x)) = f(h^t(x))$.

In the second place, let us ask what an *effective* description of a cascade is. Since I have identified a description of a cascade $S = \langle T \, M \, \{g^t\} \rangle$ with a second cascade $S_1 = \langle T_1 \, M_1 \, \{h^t\} \rangle$ isomorphic to S, an effective description of S will be an *effective cascade* S_1 isomorphic to S. The problem thus reduces to an analysis of the concept of an effective cascade. Now, it is natural to analyze this concept in terms of two conditions: (a) there is an effective procedure for recognizing the states of the system or, in other words, the state space M_1 is a *decidable* set; (b) each state transition function h^t is effective or *computable*. These two conditions can be made precise in several ways which turn out to be equivalent. The one I prefer is by means of the concept of Turing computability. If we choose this approach, we will then require that an effective cascade satisfy: (a') the state space M_1 is a subset of the set P(A) of all finite strings built out of some finite alphabet A, and there is a Turing machine which decides whether an arbitrary finite string is a member of M_1 (b') for any state transition function h^t, there is a Turing machine which computes h^t.

Finally, we are in the position to formally define a computational system. This definition expresses in a precise way the informal characterization of a computational system as a cascade that can be effectively described.

Definition: S is a computational system iff $S = \langle T \, M \, \{g^t\} \rangle$ is a cascade, and there is a second cascade $S_1 = \langle T_1 \, M_1 \, \{h^t\} \rangle$ such that:

1. S is isomorphic to S_1.

2. If P(A) is the set of all finite strings built out of some finite alphabet A, $M_1 \subseteq P(A)$ and there is a Turing machine which decides whether an arbitrary finite string is a member of M_1.

3. For any $t \in T_1$, there is a Turing machine which computes h^t.

This definition is formally correct. However, the question remains whether it is *materially* adequate too. This question will have a positive answer if we can argue that the systems specified by the definition are exactly the systems studied by computability theory. In the first place, we can give an argument a priori. If a cascade satisfies this definition, then computability theory certainly applies to it, for it is always possible to find an effective description of that cascade. Conversely, if a cascade does not satisfy this definition, then there is no effective description of that cascade, so that computability theory cannot apply to it. In the second place, we can also give an argument a posteriori. In fact, it is tedious but not difficult to show that all systems which have been actually studied by computability theory (Turing machines, register machines, monogenic production systems, cellular automata, etc.) satisfy the definition (see Giunti, 1992).

Two Sufficient Conditions for a System Not to Be Computational   The definition allows us to deduce two sufficient conditions for a mathematical dynamical system not to be computational. Namely, a mathematical dynamical system $S = \langle T\ M\ \{g^t\} \rangle$ is not computational if it is continuous in either time or state space or, more precisely, if either (1) its time set T is the set of the (non-negative) real numbers, or (2) its state space M is not denumerable.[3]

An immediate consequence of condition (2) is that *any finite neural network whose units have continuous activation levels is not a computational system.* A complete state of any such network can always be identified with a finite sequence of real numbers and, since each unit has a continuous range of possible activation levels, the set of all possible complete states of this network is not denumerable. Therefore, by condition (2), any finite network with continuous activation levels is not a computational system. (A computational system can, of course, be used to *approximate* the transitions of a network of this type. Nevertheless, if the real numbers involved are not computable, we cannot conclude that this approximation can be carried out to *an arbitrary degree of precision*. This is exactly the same situation that we have when we use computers to approximate the behavior of a physical system. Physical systems are continuous [in both time and state space] so that they can transform infinite amounts of information and, in general, they cannot be described in an effective manner. Computational systems, on the other hand, are limited to a finite amount of information, and they can always be effectively described.) We can reach the same conclusion if we consider a continuous system specified by differential or difference equations. Since these systems are continuous (in time or state space), none of them is computational.[4]

Now, we can finally go back to the question posed on p. 558. Is it possible to produce computational explanations of cognition on the basis of connectionist models or other continuous dynamical models based on differential or difference equations? For this to be possible, computability theory must apply to these two types of models. However, we have just seen that all neural networks with continuous activation levels and all continuous systems specified by differential or difference equations are not computational systems. Therefore, computability theory does not apply to them. We must then conclude that whenever connectionist models with continuous activation levels or other continuous dynamical models specified by differential or difference equations are employed, a computational explanation of cognition based on these models is impossible.

A point of clarification is essential here. Let us approach it by imagining someone objecting to this claim in the following way. A standard digital computer is a physical machine and its operation is based on the storage and interaction of electrical currents. At a relevant microlevel, these electrical activities are continuous and their behaviors are described by differential equations. Yet this is a paradigmatic example of a computational system which is effectively studied using the tools and concepts of computability theory. Therefore it is not impossible to produce computational explanations of continuous systems based on differential equations.

This objection is confused because it fails to keep clear the distinction between real dynamical systems and mathematical dynamical systems that can be used as models of them. Clearly we can have two kinds of mathematical models of a digital computer: one which is a symbolic processor model, and another specified by differential equations. Digital computers are quite special in that they appear to instantiate both mathematical models equally well. The claim for which I have argued here is that it is impossible to base a computational explanation on a continuous dynamical *model* (though it is possible to base dynamical explanations on symbolic models). That is, it is a claim about the relation between conceptual and explanatory frameworks and mathematical models, not between conceptual and explanatory frameworks and real systems. As a matter of empirical fact, it is true that there are many kinds of real dynamical systems for which there are no really good computational explanations based on symbolic models, and it may turn out that cognitive systems belong in this class. However, this can be established only by detailed empirical investigation, not by abstract argument.

18.4   Cognitive Systems and Their Models

Thus far I have identified a *model* of a real system with a mathematical dynamical system *instantiated* by it where, according to the discussion above, the instantiation relation holds just in case a mathematical dynamical system *correctly describes some aspect of the change* of a real system. However, since this clause can in fact be interpreted in different ways, there are different types of instantiation relation. Therefore, we can distinguish different types of models of a real system by looking at the specific type of instantiation relation which holds between the model and the real system. More precisely, the type of instantiation relation depends on three elements: (1) what aspect of the change of a real system the mathematical dynamical system intends to describe; (2) what counts as a description of this aspect, and (3) in what sense this description is correct.

Simulation Models of Cognitive Systems

The three types of models currently employed in cognitive science (symbolic processors, neural networks, and other continuous systems specified by differential or difference equations) are standardly characterized by a special type of instantiation relation, which is based on the fact that these models allow us to *simulate* certain aspects of the behavior of cognitive systems. For this reason, I call a model with this type of instantiation relation a *simulation model of a cognitive system*. The three elements of the instantiation relation proper to this type of model are the following.

First, the aspect of the change of a cognitive system which a simulation model intends to describe is a *cognitive process* involved in the completion of a given task. For example, if the cognitive system is a subject who has been asked to solve a simple logic problem, a simulation model will attempt to describe the *subject's problem-solving process* (see Newell and Simon, 1972). If, instead, the cognitive system is a young child who is learning the past tense of English verbs, a simulation model will attempt to describe the *child's past tense acquisition process* (see Rumelhart and McClelland, 1986a).

Second, a simulation model allows us to produce a *simulation of the cognitive process* it intends to describe, and it is this *simulating process* which counts as a *description* of the real cognitive process. In general, a simulation of a cognitive process is obtained by first implementing the model (usually by means of a computer program), and by then assigning this implemented version of the model a task similar to the one assigned to the cognitive system. In dealing with this task, the implemented model goes through a certain process: this is in fact the *simulating process* which counts as a description of the real cognitive process.

Third, the description of a cognitive process provided by a simulation model is *correct* in the sense that the simulating process is *similar* to the cognitive process in some relevant respect. Which respects are to be considered relevant is usually clear in each specific case.

A classic example of a simulation model is Rumelhart and McClelland's (1986a) *past tense acquisition model*. This neural network is intended to describe the process of past tense acquisition (PTA) in a young child learning English verbs from everyday conversation. Rumelhart and McClelland implemented the model by means of a certain computer program, and they then assigned this implemented version of the model a task which they claim to be similar to the child's task. "Our conception of the nature of this experience is simply that the child learns first about the present and past tenses of the highest frequency verbs; later on, learning occurs for a much larger ensemble of verbs, including a much larger proportion of regular forms" (pp. 240–241). Rumelhart and McClelland divided PTA's task into two parts: first, learning just ten high-frequency verbs, most of which were irregular; and second, learning a greatly expanded repertoire of verbs, most of which were regular. In dealing with this task, PTA went through a certain acquisition process. This is in fact the *simulating process* which counts as a description of the child's PTA process. If the authors were right, the description of this process provided by PTA would be correct, in the sense that the simulating process turns out to be similar to the real acquisition process in many relevant respects.

Galilean Dynamical Models of Cognitive Systems

It is now interesting to ask whether, besides the instantiation relation proper to simulation models, there are other ways in which a cognitive system can instantiate a mathematical dynamical system. To answer this question, however, it is useful to first consider some aspects of the current practice of dynamical modeling. I have in mind here a traditional way of using mathematical dynamical systems to describe the change of real systems. Simple examples of these traditional applications can be found in many elementary books on differential or difference equations, and they cover such different fields as mechanics, electrodynamics, chemistry, population dynamics, engineering, etc.

For the moment, I wish to focus on just one basic aspect of traditional dynamical modeling, namely, the use of *magnitudes* to describe the change of real systems. A magnitude is a property of a real system (or of one of its parts) which, at different times, may assume different values. For example, the position, velocity, acceleration, momentum, and mass of a body are five different magnitudes. Each magnitude is always associated with two mathematical objects. First, the *set of values* which the magnitude can take at different times and, second, its *time evolution function*, that is, a function which tells us the value of the magnitude at an arbitrary instant. Time is a special magnitude, for it is associated with a set of values, but not with a time evolution function.

The set of values of a magnitude usually is the set of the real numbers; however, one may also think of magnitudes whose set of values is the domain of some other mathematical structure (e.g., some magnitudes can only take discrete values, i.e., their set of values is a (subset) of the integers).

In general, the time evolution function of a magnitude is a *parametric function of time*, where the parameters are the *initial values* of the magnitude itself and of other magnitudes. For example, we can take the time evolution function of the position of a falling body to be specified by the Galilean equation

$$Y[yv](t) = y + vt + \tfrac{1}{2}ct^2$$

where t is an arbitrary instant, while y and v are, respectively, the values at time 0 of the position and velocity of the falling body. Since certain magnitudes may be functions of other magnitudes, the time evolution function of a magnitude can often be expressed in a different way. Thus, since velocity is the ratio of momentum and mass, that is $v = p/m = V(p)$, the time evolution function of the position of a falling body can also be expressed by using y and p, i.e.,

$$Y[y\, v](t) = Y[y\, V(p)](t) = y + (p/m)t + \tfrac{1}{2}ct^2 = Y[y\, p](t).$$

To eliminate clutter, I will indicate the time evolution function of magnitude M_i with the symbol $M_i(t)$. The context will then make clear which parameters (besides the initial value x_i of M_i) are used to express this function.

Let me now recall a basic result which links the theory of magnitudes to dynamical systems theory, and is in fact one of the foundations of traditional dynamical modeling. Let us consider n $(n > 0)$ magnitudes $M_1 \ldots M_n$ whose time evolution functions can all be expressed by using their initial values $x_1 \ldots x_n$ as parameters. That is, the time evolution function $M_i(t)$ of magnitude M_i $(1 \leqslant i \leqslant n)$ can be expressed as the parametric function $M_i[x_1 \ldots x_n](t)$. Let us then consider the system

$$P = \langle T \, M_1 \times \ldots \times M_n \, \{g^t\} \rangle$$

where T is the set of values of the magnitude time, each component of the Cartesian product $M_1 \times \ldots \times M_n$ is the set of values of magnitude M_i and, for any $t \in T$,

$$g^t(x_1 \ldots x_n) = \langle M_1[x_1 \ldots x_n](t) \quad \ldots \quad M_n[x_1 \ldots x_n](t) \rangle$$

The system P is called the system *generated* by the magnitudes $M_1 \ldots M_n$. Then, the system P is a mathematical dynamical system just in case the time evolution functions satisfy

(1) $M_i[x_1 \ldots x_n](0) = x_i$, and

(2) $M_i[x_1 \ldots x_n](t + w) = M_i[M_1[x_1 \ldots x_n](t) \quad \ldots \quad M_n[x_1 \ldots x_n](t)](w)$.

Let us now consider all the *magnitudes* proper of a real dynamical system. Among all the sets of n $(n > 0)$ magnitudes of this system, there will be some whose time evolution functions satisfy conditions (1) and (2) above. Each of these sets of magnitudes thus generates a mathematical dynamical system P. I call any mathematical dynamical system P generated by a finite number of magnitudes of a real system a *Galilean dynamical model of the real system*.

It is now quite clear in which specific sense a real system instantiates its Galilean dynamical models. First, the aspect of the change of the real system which a Galilean dynamical model intends to describe is the simultaneous variation in time of those magnitudes $M_1 \ldots M_n$ of the real system that generate the model. Second, the description of this variation is provided by the time evolution functions $M_1(t) \ldots M_n(t)$ of these magnitudes. Third, this description is correct in the (obvious) sense that the value of magnitude M_i at an arbitrary instant t is the value $M_i(t)$ of its time evolution function.

The traditional practice of dynamical modeling is in fact concerned with specifying a mathematical dynamical system, and then justifying the claim that this system is a Galilean dynamical model of a real system. Which dynamical models one tries to specify depends on the *type of properties* of the real system that the study of these models is intended to explain. For example, if we are interested in understanding the *mechanical properties* of a real system, we will try to specify those dynamical models of the real system which are generated by such *mechanical magnitudes* of the system as position, velocity, mass, etc. If we are instead interested in the explanation of the *cognitive properties* of a real system, we will try to specify those dynamical models which are generated by the *cognitive magnitudes* of the system.

Let us now consider a cognitive system. Since any cognitive system is a real dynamical system, it will have a certain class of Galilean dynamical models. These are the *Galilean dynamical models of the cognitive system*. It is then interesting to ask two questions: (1) Are the models employed so far in cognitive science Galilean dynamical models of cognitive systems? (2) If they are not, what would we gain if we instead based the explanation of cognition on Galilean models?

As regards the first question, it is clear that most models employed so far in cognitive science are not Galilean dynamical models of cognitive systems. A Galilean dynamical model is a mathematical dynamical system generated by a finite number of magnitudes of the cognitive system. Therefore, a Galilean model of a cognitive system has a very specific type of interpretation, for each component of the model corresponds to a *magnitude of the cognitive system*. The models currently employed in cognitive science, however, lack this type of interpretation, for their components do not correspond directly to magnitudes of cognitive systems themselves. The correspondence is at best indirect, via the simulation.

Since most models currently employed in cognitive science are not Galilean dynamical models of cognitive systems, it is important to understand what we would gain if we changed this practice, and we instead based the explanation of cognition on Galilean models. The first gain would be a dramatic increase in the strength of the instantiation relation which links our models to the cognitive systems they describe.

We have seen that most models currently employed in cognitive science are simulation models, and that the instantiation relation proper of these models insures, at most, a certain *similarity* between the aspect of change the model intends to describe (a certain cognitive process) and what counts as a description of this aspect (a simulating process). The instantiation relation between a cognitive system and a Galilean dynamical model, instead, is much stronger, for this relation in fact insures an *identity* between the aspect of change the model intends to describe (the simultaneous variation in time of the magnitudes which generate the model) and what counts as a description of this aspect (the time evolution functions of these magnitudes).

Besides this first gain, the use of Galilean dynamical models of cognitive systems may allow us to improve our explanations of cognition. To see this point, we must briefly reconsider how an explanation of cognition is usually obtained. First, we specify a model which allows us to simulate a cognitive process of a real system. Second, we study this simulation model in order to explain certain cognitive properties of the real system. Now, the main problem with this type of explanation is that it is based on a model which is instantiated by the real system in a weak sense. In particular, we have seen that the instantiation relation of a simulation model only insures a *similarity* between a cognitive process and a simulating process. But then, an explanation based on such a model is bound to neglect those elements of the cognitive process which do not have a counterpart in the simulating process. The instantiation relation of a Galilean dynamical model, instead, insures an *identity* between the real process the model intends to describe (the simultaneous variation in time of those magnitudes of the cognitive system which generate the model) and what counts as a description of this process (the time evolution functions of these magnitudes). Therefore if an explanation of cognition were based on a *Galilean dynamical model*, all the elements of the real process could be considered.

A New Possibility for Cognitive Science: Galilean Dynamical Models of Cognition

The use of Galilean dynamical models of cognitive systems stands to yield at least two important benefits. We must now consider how we could in fact proceed to accomplish this goal.

Clearly, this question is not one that can be answered in detail independently of real research which aims at this goal. The current practice of traditional dynamical modeling in other disciplines can, however, give us some useful indications. I mentioned above that traditional dynamical modeling aims at specifying certain Galilean dynamical models of a real system, and that the type of dynamical model of a real system one attempts to specify depends on the type of properties of the system which the study of these models is intended to explain. Since we are interested in explaining the *cognitive* properties of a cognitive system, we should then exclusively consider those Galilean dynamical models of a cognitive system whose study allow us to understand or explain these properties. I call any Galilean dynamical model of this special type a *Galilean dynamical model of cognition*.

The problem we face is thus the following. Suppose that we have specified a mathematical dynamical system MDS $= \langle \text{T M } \{g^t\} \rangle$. Under what conditions can we *justifiably affirm* that this system is a Galilean dynamical model of cognition? By the definition I have just given, the system MDS is a Galilean dynamical model of cognition just in case it satisfies two conditions: (1) The study of this system allows us to devise an explanation of at least some of the *cognitive* properties of a real system RDS, and (2) MDS is a Galilean dynamical model of this real system. Clearly, the justification of the first condition does not present any *special* difficulty. What we must do is in fact produce an explanation of some cognitive property of RDS that is based on the study of MDS. As we saw in section 18.3, we may study MDS by employing different theoretical frameworks, and the type of explanation we produce depends on the theoretical framework we use. If MDS is a *computational* system, we may decide to study it by means of concepts drawn from computability theory. The resulting explanation will thus be a computational one. Otherwise, we may always employ dynamical system theory, and the resulting explanation will thus be a dynamical one.

The problem we face thus reduces to the justification of the claim that MDS is a Galilean dynamical model of RDS. Fortunately, the practice of dynamical modeling allows us to outline a quite standard procedure to deal with this problem. Since the mathematical dynamical system MDS is a Galilean dynamical model of the real system RDS just in case MDS is generated by a finite number of magnitudes of the real system, we must first of all be able to divide the state space M into a finite number of components, and *then associate to each component a magnitude of the real system*. This first step of the justification procedure gives a *conceptual interpretation* to the mathematical dynamical system MDS, for each component of its state space M is now interpreted as the set of values of a magnitude of the real system RDS, and a magnitude is in fact a *property* of the real system which may assume different values at different times.

The conceptual interpretation provided by the first step, however, is not sufficient. To justify the claim that MDS is a Galilean dynamical model of RDS we must also provide MDS with an *empirical* interpretation. The next two steps of the justification procedure take care of this problem. The second step consists in dividing the magnitudes specified in the first step into two groups: (1) those magnitudes which we intend to measure (*observable*) and (2) those which we do not plan to measure (*nonobservable* or *theoretical*). This division of the magnitudes, however, must satisfy two conditions. First, the group of the observable magnitudes must have at least one element and, second, if there are theoretical magnitudes, they must be empirically relevant. More precisely, for any theoretical magnitude, there must be some observable magnitude whose time evolution function depends on it. In fact, if this condition is violated, we can always obtain an empirically equivalent system by simply eliminating all those theoretical components which do not make any difference to the possible evolutions of any observable magnitude.

In the third step, we then complete the empirical interpretation of the mathematical dynamical system MDS by specifying methods or experimental techniques that allow us to measure or detect the values of all the magnitudes of the real system RDS which we have classified *observable* in the previous step.

After we have provided MDS with both a conceptual and an empirical interpretation, we can finally establish under what conditions the claim is justified that MDS is a Galilean dynamical model of RDS. This claim is justified just in case MDS turns out to be an *empirically adequate model* of RDS, that is, if all the measurements of the observable magnitudes of RDS turn out to be consistent with the values deduced from the model.

The Galilean Dynamical Approach to Cognitive Science

I started this chapter by making explicit a basic methodological assumption which underlies all current research in cognitive science, namely, that all cognitive systems are dynamical systems. According to this thesis, the cognitive properties of a cognitive system can be understood or explained by studying a mathematical dynamical system instantiated by it or, i.e., by studying a model of the cognitive system. I then contrasted the computational and the dynamical style of explanation, and argued that the dynamical style does not depend on the type of model employed, while the computational style can only be based on computational models.

Finally, I explored the possibility of basing the explanation of cognition on a type of model which has not been considered yet. This type of model is the class of all the *Galilean* dynamical models of cognitive systems. The methodological assumption underlying this proposal is that, among all Galilean dynamical models of cognitive systems there are some, the Galilean dynamical models of cognition, whose study allow us to understand or explain the cognitive properties of these systems directly. This assumption can thus be interpreted as the basic methodological thesis of a possible research program in cognitive science. Whether we will in fact be able to produce explanations of cognition based on Galilean dynamical models is a question which can only be answered by actually starting a concrete research which explicitly aims at this goal. In this chapter, I have tried to state this goal as clearly as I can, and to show why we should care to pursue it. I see no reason why, *in principle*, this kind of dynamical approach should not turn out to be successful. This, however, does not mean that we will not encounter some serious difficulty along the way. In fact, we can already anticipate some of the problems we will have to solve.

First of all, we will have to radically change our way of looking at cognition. So far, in order to explain cognition, we have been focusing on the cognitive processes involved in the completion of some task, and we have then tried to produce models which *simulate* these processes. If, instead, the explanation of cognition is to be based on Galilean dynamical models, we should not primarily focus on the processes involved in cognition but, rather, on how the values of those magnitudes of a cognitive system that are relevant to cognition vary in time. I call a magnitude of this special type a *cognitive magnitude*.

Now, the two main problems we face are that (1) we will have to *discover* what the cognitive magnitudes are, and (2) we will then have to *invent* appropriate experimental techniques to measure the values of at least some of these magnitudes. If are able to solve these two basic problems, then the way to the actual production of explanations of cognition based on Galilean dynamical models of cognitive systems will be open.

NOTES

1. Each function in $\{g^t\}$ is called a *state transition* (or a *t-advance*) of the system. If T includes all the reals, rationals, or integers, then each positive state transition g^t has the inverse state transition g^{-t} and, for this reason, the dynamical system is said to be *reversible*. If instead, T is limited to the non-negative reals, rationals, or integers, there are no negative state transitions, and the dynamical system is called *irreversible*.

2. The first symbol of the alphabet is usually a special symbol, the *blank*. Only a finite number of squares may contain nonblank symbols. All other squares must contain the blank.

3. A set is denumerable just in case it can be put in a 1:1 correspondence with (a subset of) the non-negative integers. If condition (1) is satisfied, then S is not a cascade, so that, by definition, S is not a computational system. If condition (2) holds, then by condition (1) of the definition, M_1 is not denumerable. But then, M_1 cannot be a subset of the set P(A) of all finite strings built out of some finite alphabet A, for any such subset is denumerable. Therefore, condition (2) of the definition is not satisfied, and S is not a computational system.

4. This conclusion can also be extended to all systems specified by *difference* equations of the form

$$f(t + 1) = g(f(t))$$

where f is a function from the (non-negative) integers to an interval I of the reals and g is a function from I to I. Since the state space of these systems is a real interval I, these systems have a nondenumerable state space. Therefore, by condition (2), they are not computational systems.

REFERENCES

Busemeyer, J. R., and Townsend, J. T. (1993). Decision field theory: a dynamical-cognitive approach to decision making in an uncertain environment. *Psychological Review, 100*, 432–459.

Giunti, M. (1992). *Computers, dynamical systems, phenomena, and the mind*. Doctoral dissertation. Department of History and Philosophy of Science, Indiana University, Bloomington.

Johnson-Laird, P. N. (1988). *The computer and the mind*. Cambridge, MA: Harvard University Press.

Newell, A. (1980). Physical symbol systems. *Cognitive Science, 4*, 135–183.

Newell, A., and Simon, H. A. (1972). *Human problem solving*. Englewood Cliffs, NJ: Prentice-Hall.

Pylyshyn, Z. W. (1984). *Computation and cognition*. Cambridge, MA: MIT Press.

Rumelhart, D. E., and J. L. McClelland (1986a). On learning the past tenses of English verbs. In *Parallel distributed processing*, Vol. 2 (pp. 216–271). Cambridge, MA: MIT Press.

Rumelhart, D. E., and J. L. McClelland, (Eds.) (1986b). *Parallel distributed processing*, 2 vols. Cambridge, MA: MIT Press.

Skarda, C. A., and Freeman, W. J. (1987). Brain makes chaos to make sense of the world. *Behavioral and Brain Sciences, 10*, 116–195.

Smolensky, P. (1988). On the proper treatment of connectionism. *Behavioral and Brain Sciences, 11*, 1–74.

Van Gelder, T. (1991). Connectionism and dynamical explanation. In *Proceedings of the 13th Annual Conference of the Cognitive Science Society* (pp. 499–503). Hillsdale, NJ: Erlbaum.

Van Gelder, T. (1992). The proper treatment of cognition. In *Proceedings of the 14th Annual Conference of the Cognitive Science Society*. Hillsdale, NJ: Erlbaum.

Guide to Further Reading

Most of the issues covered in this chapter, and many others, are explored in considerably more detail in Giunti (1992). The relevance of dynamical systems theory for the study of computational systems is a central theme of Wolfram's work on cellular automata (Wolfram, 1986). The status of computers as dynamical systems and computation in neural systems is discussed in Hopfield (1993). A connectionist-oriented discussion of computational and dynamical models of cognition may be found in Horgan and Tienson (1992; forthcoming). An influential discussion of connectionism as a form of dynamics-based research may be found in Smolensky (1988). An ambitious and provocative work with an interestingly different perspective than presented here is Kampis (1991).

Giunti, M. (1992). *Computers, dynamical, systems, phenomena and the mind.* Ph. D. dissertation, Indiana University, Bloomington.

Hopfield (1993). Neurons, dynamics, and computation. *Physics Today, 47,* 40–46.

Horgan, T., and Tienson, J. (1992). Cognitive systems as dynamical systems. *Topoi, 11,* 27–43.

Horgan, T., and Tienson, J. (forthcoming) A non-classical framework for cognitive science. *Synthese.*

Kampis, G. (1991). *Self-modifying systems in biology and cognitive science.* Oxford, England: Pergamon.

Smolensky, P. (1988). On the proper treatment of connectionism. *Behavioral and Brain Sciences, 11,* 1–74.

Wolfram, S. (1986). *Theory and applications of cellular automata.* Singapore: World Scientific.

Glossary

Attractor   Attractors are the regions of the state space of a dynamical system toward which trajectories tend as time passes. As long as the parameters are unchanged, if the system passes close enough to the attractor, then it will never leave that region.

More technically, A is an attractor if it is a subset of the state space such that (i) the trajectory of any point in A itself lies in A, i.e., A is an invariant set, (ii) all points close enough to A tend closer and closer to A as time progresses, and (iii) A contains no smaller closed subsets with properties (i) and (ii).

If $d(x, A)$ denotes the distance between x and the set A, then condition (ii) can be stated more precisely: there is some number $\delta > 0$ such that if $d(x, A) < \delta$, then

$$\lim_{t \to \infty} d(\phi(t, x), A) = 0$$

in the case of a flow ϕ, or

$$\lim_{t \to \infty} d(f^k(x), A) = 0$$

in the case of a map f.

Basin of attraction   The basin of attraction of an attractor A is the collection of all points of the state space that tend to the attractor in forward time. (This is always an open set.) In the case of $f(x) = x^3 - (3/4)x$ (cf. example 5 in chapter 2), the origin is the only attractor, and its basin of attraction is the interval $(-1/2, 1/2)$.

Bifurcation   A bifurcation is a qualitative change in the dynamics of a system when a certain value of a parameter is reached. In the simplest case, the one from which the term itself is derived (having to do with a fork), a system with one fixed point attractor may, after a small change in a parameter, have two attractors. Further examples include the so-called saddle-node, period doubling, and Hopf bifurcations.

Catastrophe   A catastrophe is a sudden change in the state of a continuous system when the dynamics of the system undergo a bifurcation, i.e., change discontinuously, as some parameter is changed a small amount. An accessible treatment of these ideas may be found in Zeeman, C. (1977). *Catastrophe theory, selected papers 1972–1977*. Redwood City, CA: Addison-Wesley.

Chaos   This refers to a particular kind of dynamics that can occur on an invariant set such as an attractor. Intuitively, chaos happens when the future of a trajectory is computationally unpredictable because small errors in the location of the trajectory lead to exponentially larger errors at later times. A particular dynamical system may or may not be chaotic or have chaotic attractors, but the possibility that chaos may be present (and even persist under perturbations of the system) was unknown to classical scientists.

Technically, Devaney defines a chaotic dynamical system as one which has (i) sensitive dependence on initial conditions, (ii) dense periodic points, and (iii) a dense orbit. Often, simple systems can be chaotic (and therefore have complicated and unpredictable trajectories), while at the same time be "regular" in the sense that they can be completely analyzed and understood.

Closed A closed set is one having the following property: if a sequence of points in the set converges, the limit of that sequence must also lie in the set. For example, the interval $(0, 1)$ is not closed in **R**—since the sequence $\{1/2, 1/3, 1/4, \ldots\}$ converges to 0, a point not in $(0, 1)$—but $[0, 1]$ is.

Coupling Elements of a system are coupled if they influence one another. In a differential equation involving several variables, two of the variables are coupled if changes in the value of one of them influences the behavior of the other. For example, in the simple system $\dot{x} = x$, $\dot{y} = y$, the two variables are uncoupled; in $\dot{x} = x + y$, $\dot{y} = x^2 + y$, the variables are coupled.

Critical point This term is used in several different ways. Usually it refers either to a point at which a vector field is zero (hence a rest point of the flow), or to a point at which some function has a zero derivative.

Cycle A cycle is simply a periodic orbit for a dynamical system. In the case of a flow, this is a closed-loop trajectory traversed repeatedly by the system. In the case of a discrete system, it is the finite orbit of a periodic point.

Derivative A term from calculus referring to the rate of change of a function with respect to one of its variables. Commonly the independent variable is time, in which case the derivative of a function at a given time is the instantaneous rate of change of that function with respect to time. The derivative may not be defined if the function is too "irregular"; if it is defined, we say the function is "differentiable."

Diffeomorphism This is a differentiable mapping of a space to itself with a differentiable inverse. For example, the time-one map of a flow is a diffeomorphism.

Difference equation An equation of the form $x_{t+1} = f(x_t)$, which gives the value of x at the next time step as a function of its current value. Sometimes difference equations also appear in the more elaborate form $x_{t+1} = f(x_t, x_{t-1}, \ldots, t_1)$. See chapter 2 for examples.

Differential equation An equation in which one finds both some function of a variable and one or more of its derivatives. Intuitively, a differential equation relates the rate of change of a variable to the value of that variable and perhaps others. For examples, see chapter 2.

Dynamical system A system whose state changes over time in a way that depends on its current state according to some rule. Mathematically, it can be thought of as a set of possible states (its phase space or state space) plus evolution rules which determine sequences of points in that space (trajectories). In this book, evolution rules are standardly differential equations.

Euclidean space Denoted R^n in dimension n, this is simply the space of all n-tuples of real numbers $(x_1, x_2, \ldots, x_n)$. We think of R^2 as representing the Euclidean plane, and R^3 as representing three-dimensional space. We imagine the geometry of higher-dimensional Euclidean spaces partly by analogy with lower-dimensional ones.

Fixed point This is a point in the state space of a dynamical system which always succeeds itself. Thus it is a resting point or equilibrium of the system. For example, the pendulum of a clock always eventually stops moving, so hanging vertically downward is a fixed point of this system.

Flow This is the complete solution of a differential equation, encompassing all possible initial conditions. It can be thought of as the complete set of all possible trajectories of the system. If F is a vector field on R^n, then the flow ϕ of F is a map $\phi: R \times R^n \to R^n$ such that $\phi(t, x)$ represents the position of a point x of the state space after it has followed the solution trajectory of F for a time t.

Generic behavior This is the behavior of the "average" or "typical" trajectory of a dynamical system. One refers to a generic set A of initial conditions to mean either: (a) A contains all of the state space except for a set of measure zero, or (b) A contains all of the state space except for a countable union of closed nowhere dense sets.

A property is generic in (a) if it occurs with probability one; in (b) if it occurs except on a topologically small set. [One is forced to employ (b) when dealing with state spaces so large that they admit no useful probability measures.]

Gradient system This is a first-order system of differential equations in which the vector field is the gradient of some real-valued function. This function is often called a "potential function," and trajectories are always orthogonal to the surfaces on which the potential function is constant (the equipotential surfaces). Gradient systems are very special—e.g., they can have no periodic trajectories (except fixed points).

Iteration The process of repeatedly applying a diffeomorphism or endomorphism to a space or a point of the space. The sequence of points so obtained is the forward orbit of the initial point.

Invariant set An invariant set is a subset of the state space that contains the whole orbit of each of its points. Often, one restricts attention to a given invariant set, such as an attractor, and considers that to be a dynamical system in its own right.

Kinematics (vs. dynamics) A description of the sequence of states of a system as opposed to a description of the forces (represented as differential equations) that explain that motion.

Linear See Nonlinear.

Lyapunov exponents If an attractor is chaotic, nearby orbits will typically diverge from one another exponentially fast in time. Typically there are certain average exponential rates of divergence associated with each direction in the attractor. If, in a given direction, the distance between orbits is proportional to $e^{\lambda t}$, then λ is called the Lyapunov exponent in that direction. Positive exponents imply divergence, negative mean convergence. In an n-dimensional manifold, there will typically be a collection of n Lyapunov exponents for a given attractor, encoding the rates of divergence and convergence along a set of n linearly independent directions. Thus, for the solenoid in chapter 2, example 15, the exponents are $\log 2$, $\log(1/4)$, $\log(1/4)$, because the solenoid is expanding by a factor of 2 in one direction and contracting by a factor $1/4$ in two other directions.

Manifold A geometric object that has fewer dimensions locally than the parametric space in which it is embedded. Thus the surface of a sphere is a two-dimensional manifold embedded in R^3 since over small regions it has only two dimensions. A one-dimensional manifold is simply a curve on a plane. Manifolds can have any dimension. Generally a manifold is a topological space that is locally homeomorphic to R^n, and is the most common setting for much of geometric dynamical systems theory.

Nonautonomous system This is a system in which the vector field explicitly depends on time, as in

$$\dot{X} = F(X, t).$$

Geometrically, one can think of an autonomous system as representing a time-independent vector field, while a nonautonomous system represents a time-varying one.

The nonautonomous case is treated by declaring the time variable to be a new space variable (increasing at a constant rate), and then studying the resulting autonomous system in one higher spatial dimension. See example 16 in chapter 2.

Nonlinear A linear differential equation is one in which all of the state variables appear only linearly; i.e., not multiplied by one another or raised to a power other than 1. It can be written in the form

$$\dot{X} = AX,$$

where X is a vector in R^n and A is an $n \times n$ matrix depending perhaps on t but not on X. Such linear equations have a simple theory that is completely reducible to linear algebra. A nonlinear equation, then, is one that is not linear. Most nonlinear equations are analytically intractable.

Orbit The orbit of a point x is its trajectory (for a flow), or the sequence $\{f^n(x)\}$ (for a diffeomorphism f).

Order The order of a differential equation (or system of equations) is order of the highest derivative that occurs. Thus an equation that specifies a velocity is a first-order system and one that computes an acceleration is a second-order system.

Parameter   This is a constant in a dynamical system that can be given different values to obtain different systems with varying behaviors. A *control parameter* is a parameter for a physical system which can be manipulated externally, e.g., by an experimenter in the laboratory. For example, the temperature of a chemical dynamical system could be a control parameter in the laboratory. As parameters change, they may move through bifurcation values, where the system undergoes a qualitative change in its behavior.

Period   The time it takes for a trajectory on a periodic cycle to return to its starting point.

Periodic point   This is a point that lies on a periodic cycle, i.e., an orbit that returns to previous values.

Poincaré map   Also called the first-return map, this is a display for a discrete dynamical system that defines a cross-sectional surface (or manifold). The orbit of a point here is defined as the set of successive points of intersection of the trajectory with the cross-sectional surface.

Phase space   A term describing the state space of a system that usually implies that at least one axis is a time derivative, like velocity.

Potential function   See Gradient system.

Qualitative dynamics   The study of long-term general features of a dynamical system without attempting to derive or predict specific numerical values of the variables. For example, knowing the exact position of a planet in space at each moment is quantitative in character; knowing that the planet will (or will not) eventually fall into the sun is qualitative. Frequently, qualitative features, like the long-term stability of a system, are more important to know than the specific state of a system at a given time.

Recurrence   This is a fundamental concept in dynamics, going back to Poincaré. A point x is recurrent if it returns arbitrarily close to itself in the future. The simplest kind of recurrent point is a fixed point or a periodic point. A more interesting example appears, for example, in the irrational rotation of the circle: every point is recurrent, since the orbit of any point x contains points which are arbitrarily close to x (but not equal to x). Recurrence is an essential feature of most interesting systems.

Sensitivity to initial conditions   This is fundamental to the unpredictability found in chaotic systems (see Chaos). It means that a small change in initial condition leads to a large (usually exponentially large) change in the trajectory as time progresses. As a result, tiny computational round-off errors or tiny measurement errors get magnified dramatically with the passage of time, so that later the real and computed trajectories are widely different.

One insight of dynamical systems is that, while such unpredictability for individual trajectories is common, one can still hope to analyze quite fully the behavior of all the trajectories taken together, and therefore understand in detail all the *kinds* of behaviors that occur: Hence the important distinction, when speaking of a chaotic deterministic system, between "unpredictable" and "unfathomable."

Singularity   This multipurpose word is used to identify "special points" in various situations. Often it refers to the zero of a function or its derivative. It can also mean the zero of a vector field (hence a fixed point for the flow), or a point where a function or vector field is undefined or blows up. Context should provide a clue.

Space   Mathematically, a set of points that, taken together, have certain desirable properties, such as the Euclidean space R^n. Spaces in dynamical systems are commonly manifolds or regions in Euclidean space. They serve as domains on which diffeomorphisms or vector fields are defined.

Stability   Stability means that a small change in initial condition leads to only a small change in the trajectory—for all time. Typically one speaks of the stability of a fixed (or periodic) point. A fixed point x in the state space R^n is said to be Lyapunov-stable if, for every $\varepsilon > 0$, there is a $\delta > 0$ such that all points within distance δ of x have trajectories that remain within ε of x.

A fixed point is asymptotically stable if, for some $\varepsilon > 0$, the forward trajectory of every point within distance ε of x tends to x as t tends to infinity.

A final notion is that of *structural stability* of a dynamical system. A dynamical system is structurally stable if every nearby system has qualitatively the same behavior, in all its particulars, as the original system.

State space   This is the space of points whose coordinates completely specify the model system. For a differential equation, it is the space of all possible initial conditions, the choice of which uniquely determines a solution. For example, in the oscillating mass-and-spring system of example 1 of chapter 2, the state space is the space R^2 with coordinates (x, u), where x is the linear distance of the mass from its equilibrium, and u is its velocity.

Stochastic system   In contrast to deterministic dynamical systems coming from fixed differential equations or mappings, one can also imagine a random element entering into the dynamic. Examples include Brownian motion, some models of a gas or liquid, or the result of successive shufflings of a deck of cards. Here one enters into the realm of probability, ergodic theory, and statistical mechanics. This is a very large subject in its own right; we give one reference for further reading: Cornfeld, I. P., Fomin, S. V., and Sinai, Ya. G. (1982). *Ergodic theory*. New York: Springer Verlag.

To mention one illustrative example, consider the random walk along a straight line: Start at the origin, and repeatedly flip a coin. For each head, move one unit to the right; for each tail, one to the left. What is likely to happen in the course of many coin flips? Will you eventually wander off in one direction or the other, never to be seen again, or will you cross and recross the origin infinitely often? How far from the origin are you likely to get after, say, 1×10^6 coin flips? These are representative questions in this setting.

Symbolic dynamics   This is a fundamental technique by which chaotic systems are transformed from their geometric setting into purely symbolic form where certain properties become much easier to analyze.

Topology   Topology is a large field of mathematics concerned with those geometric properties that are independent of distortions that preserve proximity relations (i.e., bending and stretching without tearing). For example, a circle and an ellipse are topologically equivalent, but are inequivalent to a line segment. The topological properties of an object are among its "qualitative" geometric features.

Trajectory   A trajectory is a solution curve of a vector field. It is the path taken by the state of a system through the state space as time progresses.

Vector field   This is a choice of vector based at each point of a state space R^n; it is represented as a function $F: R^n \to R^n$. A vector field is equivalent to a differential equation, and is one way to represent its effect. The value of a vector field at a point is to be interpreted as the velocity vector for a solution trajectory that passes through that point.

Contributors

Randall D. Beer
Department of Computer
Engineering and Science
Case Western Reserve University
Cleveland, Ohio

Geoffrey P. Bingham
Department of Psychology
Indiana University
Bloomington, Indiana

Catherine P. Browman
Haskins Laboratories
New Haven Connecticut

Jerome Busemeyer
Department of Psychology
Purdue University
W. Lafayette, Indiana

Claudia Carello
Department of Psychology
University of Connecticut
Storrs, Connecticut

Fred Cummins
Department of Linguistics
Indiana University
Bloomington, Indiana

Jeffrey L. Elman
Department of Cognitive Science
University of California, San Diego
La Jolla, California

Marco Giunti
Florence, Italy

Louis Goldstein
Department of Linguistics
Yale University
New Haven, Connecticut

Stephen Grossberg
Department of Cognitive and
Neural Systems
Center for Neural Systems
Boston University
Boston, Massachusetts

J. Devin McAuley
Department of Linguistics
Indiana University
Bloomington, Indiana

Mary Ann Metzger
Department of Psychology
University of Maryland
Baltimore, Maryland

Alec Norton
Department of Mathematics
University of Texas
Austin, Texas

Jean Petitot
Centre D'Analyse et de
Mathématique Sociales
École des Hautes Études en
Sciences Sociales
Paris, France

Jordan B. Pollack
Department of Computer and
Information Sciences
The Ohio State University
Columbus, Ohio

Robert F. Port
Department of Linguistics
Indiana University
Bloomington, Indiana

Dana J. Redington
Department of Psychiatry
University of California,
San Francisco
San Francisco, California

Steven P. Reidbord
Department of Psychiatry
University of California,
San Francisco
San Francisco, California

Elliot L. Saltzman
Haskins Laboratories
New Haven, Connecticut

Esther Thelen
Department of Psychology
Indiana University
Bloomington, Indiana

James T. Townsend
Department of Psychology
Indiana University
Bloomington, Indiana

M. T. Turvey
Department of Psychology
University of Connecticut
Storrs, Connecticut

Paul van Geert
Department of Psychology
State University Gröningen
Gröningen, The Netherlands

Timothy van Gelder
Research School of Social Sciences
Australian National University
Department of Philosophy
Indiana University
Bloomington, Indiana

Index

Rigid motion, 405
Rigidity assumption, 429
Robot, 250. *See also* Agent
Roles. *See* Semantic roles
Rovée-Collier, C., 95–96
Rules
  as attractors, 208–215
  linguistic, 196
  of phonetic implementation, 179
  temporal implementation, 347
Rumelhart, D., 24

Saddle-node bifurcation, 57
Saliency hierarchy, 258
Sample size, insensitivity to, 517
Scales of description, macroscopic and
    microscopic, 177–194
Scaling, 152
Schemas, image, 252
Scorpion, prey location by, 382
Script, 252
Searle, J., 70
Selection in a novel task, 91–94
Self-organization, 77, 180, 235
  and emergence of structure, 25–27
  morphological, 247
  in pattern recognition, 353
Self-organizing feature maps, 469–472
Self-organizing systems, 452–453
Self-similarity, 306
Semantic information, 220
Semantic isotopy, 257
Semantic roles, 227–282
  configurational definition of, 231–233
Semantics, 206
  and syntax, 227–282
Sensitivity to initial conditions, 576
Sensorimotor activity, 149–174
Sensory function, 130
Serial order, 350–360
Shank, R., 252
Short-term memory, 469–483
Sigma-pi network, 290–292
Simon, H., 5
Simple recurrent network, 195–226
Simulation of a dynamical model, 21
Simulation models, 562–563
Singularity, 576
Singularity theory, 270–274
Singular points, 240
Sink. *See* Attractor, point
Situated agent research, 126
SOAR, 518–519

Social dynamics, 332–334
Social exchange, 98
Solar system, 2, 45, 46, 126
Solenoid, 64–66
Solvability axiom, 112
Sound Pattern of English, 178
Space, 576
  external, 240
  internal, 239–240
  grammar, 259, 261
Spatial attention, 464–466, 484
Spatiotemporal form, 151
Spectrogram, 343–345
Speech coordination, 149–174
Speech gestures, coproduction of, 163
Speech perception, 347
Speech production, 157–159
Spider, haptics of, 382
Spring constant, 48
SRN. *See* Simple recurrent network
Stability, 46, 58–66, 152, 576. *See also*
    Attractor
  asymptotic, 59
  Lyapunov, 59
  matrix, 106
Stability-plasticity dilemma, 476
Stance phase, 138, 141
State
  internal, 126
  symbolic, 12
State-deterministic theories, 116
State set, 5
State space, 5, 7, 51, 577
  defined, 45
  evolution, 556
State variables, 47
Step disappearance, in newborn, 81
Stochastic system, 577
Storytelling, 532
Structural stability, 241
Structure, grammatical, 208
Structure of real-world environments, 122
Structure from motion, 408, 414, 429
Swing phase, 138, 141
Symbol manipulation, 12
Symbolic dynamics, 577
Symbolic processors, 553
Symbolic representation, 73
Symbols, 9
  context-free, 198
Symmetries in optical phase space, 431–438
Symmetries, 407
Symmetry axis, 274

589   Index